T0185805

A Tester's Guide to .NET Programming

■ ■ ■

Randal Root and
Mary Romero Sweeney

Apress®

A Tester's Guide to .NET Programming

Copyright © 2006 by Randal Root and Mary Romero Sweeney

ISBN-13: 978-1-4842-2014-6

ISBN-10: 1-59059-600-5

Printed and bound in the United States of America 9 8 7 6 5 4 3 2 1

Trademarked names may appear in this book. Rather than use a trademark symbol with every occurrence of a trademarked name, we use the names only in an editorial fashion and to the benefit of the trademark owner, with no intention of infringement of the trademark.

Lead Editor: Jonathan Hassell
Technical Reviewer: Phil Leder
Editorial Board: Steve Anglin, Dan Appleman, Ewan Buckingham, Gary Cornell, Tony Davis, Jason Gilmore, Jonathan Hassell, Chris Mills, Dominic Shakeshaft, Jim Sumser
Project Manager: Beth Christmas
Copy Edit Manager: Nicole LeClerc
Copy Editor: Linda Marousek
Assistant Production Director: Kari Brooks-Copony
Production Editor: Linda Marousek
Compositor: Susan Glinert Stevens
Proofreader: Kim Burton
Indexer: Valerie Perry
Artist: April Milne
Cover Designer: Kurt Krames
Manufacturing Director: Tom Debolski

Distributed to the book trade worldwide by Springer-Verlag New York, Inc., 233 Spring Street, 6th Floor, New York, NY 10013. Phone 1-800-SPRINGER, fax 201-348-4505, e-mail orders-ny@springer-sbm.com, or visit http://www.springeronline.com.

For information on translations, please contact Apress directly at 2560 Ninth Street, Suite 219, Berkeley, CA 94710. Phone 510-549-5930, fax 510-549-5939, e-mail info@apress.com, or visit http://www.apress.com.

The source code for this book is available to readers at http://www.apress.com in the Source Code section.

To my husband and sweetheart, Brian. Thanks for your love and friendship,
without which I'd never get anything done.
—Mary Romero Sweeney

To my wife, Shery, and my children, John, Sasha, and Elaine.
All of you helped me achieve this, and I am forever grateful.
—Randal Root

Contents at a Glance

Contents

■CHAPTER 7   Automation with Console-Based Testware 251

■CHAPTER 8   Introduction to Database Testing 305

Foreword

For many years and through my work as the Chairman and CEO of the International Institute for Software Testing (IIST), I have been trying to find ways to help test professionals gain the technical skills they need in order to test applications that use modern development technologies. I learned about Mary Sweeney's ability to address this need through her first book *Visual Basic for Testers* (Apress, 2001) and, as a result, added her to our faculty. Mary has been a faculty member of IIST for the last two years, teaching testers topics in programming concepts and in testing database applications. Mary's abilities to address technical subjects in software testing are unique and have been additionally proven through her writing of this book. Although I do not normally have the time to write forewords for books, I did not want to pass the opportunity to write the foreword for this book because the topic is an important one to today's test professionals. In fact, this book is long overdue!

I am especially excited about the new opportunities this book will bring to test professionals who really need to master the process of testing .NET applications. The fact is testing a .NET application today can be very difficult in that it can be extremely complex. This complexity makes it highly likely that, in many cases, developers will not have time to test everything in the application. So they will have to rely on professional testers to perform complete testing at all levels. Therefore, this book is a *must read* for every test professional working on a .NET project. Testing .NET applications represents a technical challenge for software developers and test professionals. The methods and techniques presented in this book will certainly help developers, as well as testers, improve the quality of their .NET applications. The hands-on nature of the book makes it easy for test professionals to follow. In my opinion, the authors have done a remarkable job in bringing highly technical concepts to a level that can be easily understood by all test professionals. This did not come as a surprise to me based on what I know about Mary's teaching style. I particularly like the exercises in each chapter. They provide a great learning adjunct to master this very technical subject.

I strongly believe that this book fills a big gap in the knowledge body that test professionals and developers need to master in order to assure the delivery of high quality .NET applications.

Dr. Magdy Hanna, PhD
Chairman and CEO
International Institute for Software Testing
www.iist.org

About the Authors

 **MARY ROMERO SWEENEY** has been developing, using, and testing software systems for over 20 years for companies, including Boeing and Software Test Labs.

She's the author of *Visual Basic for Testers* (Apress, 2001) and a frequent speaker at major software testing conferences. Mary is a college professor and also performs independent consultation and training through her company Sammamish Software (www.sammamishsoftware.com). She has degrees in Mathematics and Computer Science from Seattle University, is an MCP in SQL Server, and is on the board and faculty of the International Institute of Software Testing (IIST).

 **RANDAL ROOT** owns a consulting company, Root Source (www.rootsource4training.com), specializing in technical education. For the last six years, he has provided training at both businesses and schools, including Microsoft and Bellevue Community College. His subjects include Windows, web, and database programming, as well as networking and administration. Randal holds several Microsoft professional certifications including MCSE, MCP+I, MCDBA, and MCAD and has worked in the industry as a network administrator and programmer since the 1980s.

About the Technical Reviewer

 **PHIL R. LEDER** was born November 1, 1979, in Bothell, WA. He is currently a Programmer/Systems Analyst specializing in Client Server Systems at Boeing's Future Combat Systems. He graduated from Central Washington University with a BS in Computer Science.

Acknowledgments

The first person I'd like to thank is my coauthor, Randal Root. His energy and desire to write a book jolted me out of my writing lethargy and inspired me to get to it. As the project progressed, I realized how much nicer it is to have someone along for the ride. So thanks, Randal, for your hard work and friendship.

I must thank those who contributed so much to the writing of this book. Particularly helpful and open to all kinds of questions despite his busy schedule was Tom Arnold, Microsoft's Program Manager for Test Tools on the VSTEST software project (author of the *Visual Test 6 Bible*) of Microsoft. His entire team provided feedback that proved critical, especially in writing Chapter 11 on the Team Test software. Thanks especially to Dominic Hopton for his scintillating presentation—and gamely answering all questions no matter how trivial. Also thanks to Ed Glas, Group Manager for the Web and Load Testing tools in Team Test. He was also very helpful in taking the time to meet with us and answer questions.

Dr. Magdy Hanna and my colleagues at IIST: Thanks for your kind association. And thanks to our clients whose experiences contributed greatly to this book.

Thanks most especially to our hard-working technical reviewer, Phil (Mony) Leder. He put in many long hours above and beyond the call of duty. Good tech reviewers are hard to find because it's largely a thankless task; Randal and I both knew we were lucky to have someone so conscientious and thorough.

Thank you, Apress, for for providing the high-quality staff necessary to put out a book of the caliber I insist upon.

Mary Romero Sweeney

Like Mary, I am especially thankful for my coauthor. Without her assistance and support, I would never have started or finished this book. Thank you Mary!

Although Mary already thanked them, I would personally like to add my thanks to Phil Leder, Beth Christmas, Linda Marousek, and the Apress team. Their professionalism and dedication was inspiring.

Lastly, a special thanks to my brother Bryon Root for his technical advice and support. His knowledge and technical reviews made a huge difference on this project.

Randal Root

Introduction

Today's software testing environment has changed. A common trend we are seeing these days is advertisements for software developers and testers that look virtually the same. Today, companies all seem to require software test professionals with in-depth knowledge of programming languages and with significant database skills. Testers are constantly striving to keep up with the knowledge required to be effective on the complex projects we encounter regularly.

A test engineer is expected to know at least a little about practically everything—from operating systems to networks to databases—in order to find bugs and report them articulately. What we always say to new testers is that this is a great profession for those of us who love to learn continuously. It's like you've never left college—you must study constantly. (Of course, that also makes it a great profession if you like to feel constantly inadequate! Because you can never know enough, can you?) So, this book is for that self-motivated test engineer who is intent on continually upgrading his or her knowledge and now wants to learn more about automated software testing using .NET.

We have also targeted this book toward nonprogramming computer professionals, such as those of you in Networking and IT professions. You are technical, but want to know more about programming in .NET in order to enhance your skills. The additional information about testing will only help to guide you in ways to uncover and deal with problems in systems.

Finally, this book is also for you test leads and managers who want to know what .NET can do for your test project. A not-so-well-kept secret of automated software testing is that the major tools available commercially don't do everything you need them to do, in spite of their advertisements. It's probably unrealistic to expect any tool to be able to fully support the automated testing required for so many diverse applications. This includes the additional new Team Test software added into Visual Studio's Team Edition software (see Chapter 11). This revolutionary new software will be a fabulous resource for mid- to large-size companies, but it is still not going to eliminate the need for testers to become more technically adept.

This is not to say that writing your own tools is always the right answer. However, supplementing automated tools with some scripting done by testers fluent in a traditional language can help a company get more out of its automated testing projects. It is our hope, in these pages, to help you see how you can do just that.

About This Book

This book has a specific, three-fold goal; it will teach the software test engineer the following:

- How to begin to use .NET as a testing tool, including how to create simple testing utilities and the basic mechanics of writing code to test an application

- What to look for in a well-written .NET program

- To understand the software development process and appreciate the efforts of the software developer

These chapters cover beginning to advanced topics in .NET, focusing on areas that can be used for software testing.

What This Book Is Not

Since the focus of this book is software testing with .NET, we will *not* cover all the development features of the Visual Studio development environment. There are many good books for that already.

This is not a software testing fundamentals book either. There are many good books available for that as well (see Appendix C). This book *is* intended to bridge the gap between those two types of books so that you can learn how to write code in .NET to support an automated test project. Even if you do not have a testing background, you should be able to read and understand this book; however, some of the terms and references to testing concepts may be unclear. Appendix C should help you find the information you need.

Who This Book Is For

This book is for software test professionals (usually we just call ourselves *testers*) who want to increase their knowledge of testing in a .NET environment. It is designed to jump-start the tester into using .NET both for automated software testing and for software development of small programs. This book will not cover any software testing basics—the presumption is that all readers are familiar with fundamental testing concepts. Testing experience is helpful, but not required. So, IT and Networking professionals should be able to use the material to help them become more proficient at coding in .NET. Software test managers and leads should also be able to derive some information to help them understand how to interleave .NET into their testing projects. Although other technical professionals should be able to gain some good information, we want to emphasize that this book is primarily targeted toward the test engineer on the test bench striving valiantly to ensure software quality.

Where to Start

We have written this book to support a variety of backgrounds. We'd like to help guide you in where to start.

First, *everyone* should read Appendix A, where you'll find information on downloading the exercise files for this book and help with choosing editions and installation of required software—including setting up your system to run web pages.

Then, if you have

- *No programming experience*: Start at Appendix B for an extensive programming primer, then move to Chapter 1 and proceed through all chapters progressively. Attempt each exercise to gain the most out of each chapter.

- *Programming experience, but no testing experience*: Read Chapter 1 for the testing perspective and then see the Table of Contents section to determine where you should begin, depending on your area of interest. If your programming experience is in another language, you should at least skim the earlier chapters starting with Chapter 2. A quick review of the primer in Appendix B may be useful as well.

- *Programming experience and testing experience:* You can skim earlier chapters as needed, but can probably jump directly into any chapter of interest to see what kinds of things you can do with .NET in a test project. Although the first few chapters are somewhat elementary, topics become increasingly challenging in later chapters.

A Note to Training Organizations and Teachers

A Tester's Guide to .NET Programming is intended to help in classroom instruction on software testing as part of an overall software testing curriculum. This book can be used as the basis for an introductory- to intermediate-level course in automated software testing in either a corporate or an academic setting. A class based on this text, *A Tester's Guide to .NET Programming*, is currently taught by both authors through Sammamish Software. For more information about using the book as the basis for a course, and additional materials for it, contact the authors at `msweeney@sammmamishsoftware.com` or `rroot@rootsource4training.com`.

The Practice Files: Answers to Exercises and Demo Code

Each chapter, beginning with Chapter 2, has exercises. Answers for these exercises, along with additional code demonstrating chapter topics, is available for download from the Source Code section of the Apress website at `www.apress.com`.

We will post additional topics of interest to testers learning and using .NET on the following website: `www.sammamishsoftware.com`. For comments, questions, or to report errata, contact the authors at `msweeney@sammamishsoftware.com` or `rroot@rootsource4training.com`.

■ ■ ■

CHAPTER 1

Automated Software Testing with .NET

Software testing is not a new field but it's growing up in a rather fractured way. Around the country and around the world, you'll find software testing employed in a variety of ways. There is now Agile and Extreme software testing, and various other buzzwords and methodologies to accompany the traditional Black Box testing that is still deeply entrenched in many companies. The emphasis we have had for years on expensive commercial tools to aid our testing efforts has lessened as the demand for their increased capability has become virtually impossible for tool vendors to keep up with. Now many test organizations have turned to producing their own software to help in testing, often using a burgeoning list of open source tools and software.

In 2001, when *Visual Basic for Testers* (Mary Romero Sweeney, Apress, 2001) was published, many test professionals were finding they needed to complement their manual- and tool-automated testing efforts with their own software utilities. In the years since then, we've found that the ability to write code and produce tests and test utilities by writing our own software is even more necessary for the software test community. At every conference and training symposium there are courses and lectures teaching testers more technical topics, including programming, networking, and databases.

We still, and always will, need to get tested software out the door quickly, efficiently, and *profitably*. There are many trade-offs to automating your own software tests; however, if you do it thoughtfully, you can help a test project immensely. If you do it incorrectly, you can slow it down such that you'll run out of budget and fail to accomplish your goals. In this book, we'll explore the use of .NET application software for test projects and show in what ways this specific type of software can support your testing goals.

You will find enough here to get you started on a successful test project using .NET. To begin, you will need some discussion of automated software testing in general. In this chapter, you will look at some of the important management issues involved when starting automated testing, such as guidelines for when and when not to automate testing, what kind of personnel requirements you will need to address, and how to build an automated testing team. You will also look at some ground rules for creating good testing software, and some of the advantages as well as limitations of using two .NET languages, Visual Basic (VB) .NET and C#, for your test projects and utilities.

What a Tester Needs to Know About .NET Coding

Although .NET languages are powerful enough to accomplish some useful testing tasks, you must have knowledgeable testers and programmers to write the code. Unfortunately, there isn't a lot of information out there yet to help test professionals adapt programming for testing purposes. Most of the resources are geared for software developers, not testers.

Using .NET languages for testing requires a shift in perspective. A tester can come out of a standard Visual Basic course still wondering how it could ever be used on a test project. These courses and most books concentrate on the controls to use and the ways to create a great, user-friendly application. A tester doesn't care about that so much—what we want to know is how to quickly develop a utility or get to system information and other testing-related data using code. One of the differences between this book and others is that we won't focus on learning a myriad of cool controls or how to develop a slick front end for an application. While these are great things to learn, there are plenty of other books out there that will teach you this. Instead, we will focus on the things a tester must know to use .NET languages as quickly as possible on a test project:

- How to access intrinsic .NET Framework library functions that return relevant information about the platform, files, registry, operating system, and so on

- How to create a front end with basic controls to view test information and results as soon as possible

- How to access databases quickly and easily

- How to access the Windows Registry to return relevant application information

These topics are just the beginning, of course, but they represent some of the things the testers who have contributed time and code to this book have used to accomplish their testing tasks. We will cover all of these and more in the course of this text.

Why .NET Languages for Testing?

.NET languages are not testing tools; instead, they are programming languages used for software development. Why use Visual Basic or C# for testing—why not use Perl, C, or C++? Scripting languages, as they are popularly called, such as Perl, Python, VBScript, Rexx, and many others, have a large following. Why not use those? Actually, none of those languages were created with testing in mind either. Still, they can be a big benefit on a testing project, especially if they are already installed and you have experienced personnel. We would choose to do much of the testware coding using any of those if we had them readily available, as well as available employees who were at expert level in their use. If .NET languages are already available and there are employees with expertise in them, then they are an excellent choice.

If the development project is itself written in .NET, then it can make sense for the testers to use it in this situation. Although, a common misconception is that if you are testing a .NET application, you will need to use a .NET language for your test automation. That's not true; however, using .NET languages on a Windows platform will provide you with all the power you need to do essentially anything you need to do.

Since .NET languages are not really testing tools, how is it possible to adapt them for use in testing? The .NET Framework libraries have many features that can support the testing process. For example, there are a host of intrinsic functions that can return important information about the test platform and the application under test. .NET's Shell function and SendKeys class can also be used to run an application and manipulate its Graphical User Interface (GUI). The Visual Studio Database Tools allow you to connect to a database and examine its structure and data. You can also get very sophisticated and write essentially anything you want, such as a load testing application. Of course, the trade-off for a more sophisticated programming endeavor is that you will need both the programmers *and* the time.

.NET languages can also be used to test many behind-the-scenes operations of the application. For example, scripts can be written to access the system environmental variables and performance counters. Automated test scripts can verify the correct loading and retrieval of the information from files. The very fact that the .NET languages are powerful development tools makes them promising and capable tools for testing.

Choosing a .NET Language for a Test Project

.NET platforms include a lot of language options. This is because the language implementations are now just a thin layer on top of the .NET Common Language Runtime (CLR). They all compile down into the same Intermediate Language (IL). This makes choosing a language a matter of preference and not a technical decision. You can choose a language based on how easy it is to learn. For beginners, Visual Basic will be a good choice. Alternatively, if you already have done a little work in another language, such as C or Java, you can choose the .NET implementation of those languages: C++ or J#. Also a good choice, in that case, is C#, a new language that is developed specifically for .NET platforms and will be familiar enough to anyone who has programmed in a "swirly brace" language.

It's also true that some testers on the same team can choose to code in VB .NET, while others choose C#, or another language, and still be able to have their software interoperate nicely. We have to confess a little bias towards VB .NET, of course, having written a lot of code in it as well as product literature. A big advantage to using Visual Basic is that it is a popular language because it is easy to learn, and it happens to be the macro language for the widely-used Microsoft Office products and the scripting language for most of the world's ASP web pages. Many other software companies use a form of Basic for their own products. This popularity means there is a wide base of people with a knowledge of Basic, so there should be no shortage of people able to use it or willing to learn it. There is also a proliferation of books and resources available for Visual Basic. Although they may not be written specifically for testing, once you get the hang of it, you will find lots of code available in user's groups and books that you can adapt for testing purposes.

C# has been steadily gaining in popularity since it has some of the ease of VB .NET, as well as a lot of similar programming constructs to languages like Java and Perl. A common misconception about C# is that it is somehow more powerful than VB .NET. However, in the end, both C# and VB .NET are the same.

So, which to choose? How about both? Because they compile down into IL, components written in one language can be used in another. Since both Visual Basic and C# are very popular and simple to learn, we have chosen to include code from both of these languages in the examples in this book. (For reasons of space and time, we will not include J# or C++.)

What Is Automated Software Testing?

Let's take a step back and talk about what automated testing is in general and define some terms. First of all, *automated testing* is any testing that is done using software. In other words, we write code to test other code. Automated testing includes the use of tools written by others since the tools they have written *are* software that tests software. *Automated test scripting* is the process of creating the program code—that is, actually writing the code that will be used to test. *Automated test scripts*, or testware, are the program code used to test the software.

Historically, most testing has been done manually. That is, a tester sits down and runs the application using defined processes to try to find bugs so that they can be fixed prior to releasing the product. Automated software testing goes a step further. Since basic software testing has become more rigorous and more defined, testers have found ways to automate some of the process of testing software by writing software to do it. Of course, many successful testing projects have been completed without ever using automated test scripting. In fact, many applications are still primarily tested manually. There is just no substitute for testing the product in the same way that the user would and there is no substitute for the abilities of an able, experienced tester. So, automated testing will never (and shouldn't) replace manual testing of an application. Used appropriately though, automated testing can significantly enhance the testing process.

Automated testing has received a lot of focus lately due to the ever-increasing complexity and size of software applications that require better and faster ways to test. Rather than replace testers, which might be one of the benefits a manager might expect from automated software testing, automated testing can enhance the testing process with increased capabilities. (In fact, at the start of a new test automation project, often more testers, and more technically astute testers, are required, not less.) There are some tedious and time-consuming, yet important, testing tasks that you may choose not to perform on a project due to time and budget constraints. For example, verifying the transfer of large amounts of files or data from one system to another could be prohibitive if done manually; writing code to do that makes it achievable. There are many benefits to enhancing a testing process with automated test scripting. Here are just a few:

- Performing tedious or repetitive manual-testing tasks, such as platform and application start-up, shutdown, and clean-up routines

- Running tests in batch

- Setting a reference to a COM object or .NET class and testing its interfaces

- Attaching to a database for data verification testing

- Accessing and interrogating the Windows Registry

- Creating testing utilities that support the testing process, such as logging and start-up scripts

Within this book, we will explore all of these uses of automated testing and quite a few more.

Technical vs. Nontechnical Testing

Perhaps it would make sense to think that, as the authors of this book, we would be in favor of all testers being technically adept. After all, both of us are not only testers, but also developers as well. Instead, we think requiring all testers to write code and essentially be programmers in their own right is a mistake. Although it is beneficial and advisable to have some programming-proficient testers on every test team, it should not be required of all testers on the team. This is because, in general, the programmer and the test professional think differently. And they should. The tester who has technical experience as a programmer enhances the project by knowing the kinds of things and situations in which the software developer might be more likely to make mistakes. However, this technical knowledge encourages a person to think analytically and not generally, like a typical user or nontechnical tester would. So the technical tester may miss the errors that nontechnical testers would find, and vice versa. Still, there is no substitute for a professional, knowledgeable, nontechnical test professional with experience; her knowledge and thoroughness cannot be replaced by user-testing only. So you need all three kinds of people: technical testers, nontechnical testers, and user testers.

When to Automate?

Not all testing situations benefit from writing your own test code. In fact, there are many times when it's not a good idea to automate testing. So how do you decide whether and when to automate or not? The decision to automate requires analysis and the definition of boundaries between the automated test plan and the manual test plan. Using a programming language like Visual Basic or C# requires additional careful planning since writing test scripts is essentially software development in its own right and can eat up plenty of time in a schedule.

How do you determine what to test manually and what to test using automated test scripts? While experience is the best judge, there are also some basic questions you can ask yourself prior to embarking on an automated test project. The following three sections will help you determine whether your project is a good candidate for automated testing.

Project and Personnel Issues

Too many times test managers undertake automated testing projects without fully considering the abilities and availability of their personnel. Proper staffing is critical to the success of any project. Here are some important things to consider:

- *What is the scope of the automated testing?* If your goal is to fully automate all tests, then your scope is unrealistic. If you are trying to incorporate automated testing into existing projects or into a new one, then it's best to start with small, manageable goals. For example, you can ask your team to write some simple utilities to support your test project using Visual Basic or C#. This has the added advantage of checking their experience level as well. Not all testers/programmers have the same capabilities!

- *What is the automated testing skill level of your testing personnel?* If automated testing is new to your personnel, then you need to allow time and budget for them to take classes and learn. You will need to add experienced automated testing personnel to your staff *prior* to your first project. The level of experience will determine the level of automation you will be able to undertake. One introductory course in programming will not be enough to enable your testers to undertake a large project. However, they could possibly use some of Visual Studio's tools and wizards to support a test project, and perhaps create and use some simple test utilities.

- *What is the availability of your technically skilled testers?* If you do have technically skilled testers, are they actually available? Many projects start with some experienced members who get pulled off for other projects. This may seem like a no-brainer, but we have seen this situation occur too many times to think it is just an aberration.

Product Issues

Not all applications to be tested are created equal. In general, when you write automated test code yourself, you are working behind the GUI. That is, you are harnessing just pieces of the software. You have to spend some time to determine if this is appropriate for your product. You must do a thorough analysis. The following questions are a short list of things to consider:

- *Is the feature set of the application you are testing relatively stable?* If not, the scripts you write need to change as often as the application changes. You may find yourself spinning your wheels if you start too soon, using up precious budget. Automated testing works best for products that are relatively stable in structure and components.

- *Do you plan to test the UI? Is your product GUI–based?* Some automated testing tools are geared specifically for the GUI. If your project is to test the application's GUI, then certain automated testing tools, commercial or open source, may be a better choice than others. .NET languages can be used for GUI testing to a certain extent, but they require a significant amount of coding to do so. For this reason, in most cases, we would not choose using .NET for extensive GUI–based testing.

- *Does your product have areas where tests are run repetitively, greater than ten times per test?* Any repetitive tasks are candidates for automated testing. Computers perform repetitive tasks well. For example, writing regression tests for high-priority bugs or developing a Build Verification Test (BVT) suite for verification of product robustness after each build are good examples of tests that will be required to be run many times.

- *Will your product need to be compatible with multiple platforms?* Most products need to run on the various versions of Windows: Windows XP, Windows 2K, Windows NT, Windows 95, and Windows 98. There are many other compatibility issues, of course. Automated testing scripts can be written to address some of these compatibility issues.

- *Is your project size and budget large enough to support an automated test piece?* Last but certainly not least, you must consider the additional time and budget required for automated testing. Although automated testing adds a lot to a test project, it can, especially initially, be time-consuming and costly. On a relatively small test project, adding automated test capability may not be worth it.

Note These questions may seem a bit Microsoft-centric. It is true that .NET languages can be a tool for testing mostly Windows-based software systems. There are some exceptions to this, but not many.

Additional Test-Management Issues

Here are a few more management-level questions to ask yourself and your team:

- *Do you have Visual Studio .NET software available to the project?* If not, can you purchase the proper number of licenses and have them in place in time?

Note The .NET Framework can be downloaded and installed for free. With the Framework libraries come compilation tools so that it is possible to write test scripts, i.e., code, in .NET for free. In this book, we focus on using Visual Studio rather than taking this direction because of the simplicity of using the interface. It's a lot more difficult to write the code without Visual Studio .NET unless you're an experienced programmer.

- *Can you insert automated testing without affecting existing testing?* For example, installing Visual Studio .NET and investigating the integration of the test scripting with other tests, such as manual tests or commercial tools, takes time and planning. Can you do this without adversely affecting your total project time and budget?

- *Do you have enough time to analyze requirements as well as code, debug, and maintain test scripts?* Development of automated test scripts is software development and requires all of the same considerations. It's easy to use up time and budget.

- *Who will manage the automated testing for each project and across projects?* An important consideration is to keep and maintain the work done on a project for future use. For example, scripts for logging test results (covered in Chapter 5) can be used in any project. Identify a group or an individual who will be responsible for ensuring that code that can be reused on other projects is maintained for future use.

Managing the testing process is a big topic and an important one. There are many excellent texts available so we won't attempt to compete with them here; check Appendix C of this book for more information on this topic.

Building a Team for Automated Testing

What is the makeup of a good test team? Ideally, automated testing personnel and those members of the team using manual processes should not be kept separate. They can enhance each other's capabilities and they do need to keep in close communication. If you are part of a fairly large company, it is beneficial to have members of the team experienced in different kinds of automated testing: some with applied experience in one or more of the major tools available on the market, and at least a couple of testers who have significant programming experience using Perl, C#, Visual Basic, C/C++, Java, or other languages.

One large company we worked with had a sizeable test group dedicated to automated testing. In this group, they hired personnel experienced in several major tools. On each test project, this team determined which tools, if any, were appropriate for that project, as well as the backgrounds and experience required for the test team. They were integrally involved in the setup for all company test projects and monitored each project as it progressed. This is an ideal way to proceed. The team was able to keep a repository of test plans and code, as well as a detailed history of the projects and their results. They were instrumental in arranging appropriate training in the tools selected for the project, as well. This model worked quite well for this company, although so far it's the only company we have seen do it quite this way. It takes time and money to set up such a model, but it has many benefits in the long run.

If you are a midsize company with a team of ten testers, the makeup of your test team could be something like this:

- Four to five testers experienced in traditional manual-testing processes

- Three testers experienced in automated test tools such as Segue, Mercury, and Rational

- Two to three testers experienced in software development, at least two of whom could be considered advanced programmers

---

Note Testers who develop code for use in testing are increasingly gaining titles of their own. This type of testing specialist is sometimes called an *automator* or *Developer-in-Test*—or a *Software Design Engineer in Test (SDE/T)*, as Microsoft calls them.

Of course, there could and should be some overlap. However, don't make the mistake of having nine manual testers but only one person experienced in software development, test tools, and so on. If there is only one person with experience, that person will end up spending all of his time coaching everyone else and getting nothing done. It's best to avoid depending too much on a single person or, nearly as bad, only two people in a test project.

When it isn't possible to form your ideal team with technical programming professional skills onboard immediately, some teams rely on developers to assist them with writing testware. And, if there's sufficient time, alongside these developers, place your most technical testers and get them some training. Hopefully, this will work, until you can compose the team you need.

Test Scripts Are Software

When test engineers write automated test scripts, they must take the time to define and analyze the requirements. This is when the process of writing the scripts actually begins. This process is necessarily interactive as the testers repeatedly run the scripts, then improve and perfect them to meet the ever-changing testing requirements.

After the scripts are working, they must be updated on a regular basis to ensure they work with new versions of the application being tested. A professional software developer would recognize this process of developing and updating automated test scripts as essentially the same one used to develop software applications. So, the writing of automated test scripts *is* software development. The skills needed to be a good automator are similar to those required of a good software developer. In addition to software development skills, automators must also be skilled at testing. To find out more about how to be a good tester, get Cem Kaner's book, *Testing Computer Software, 2nd Edition* (Wiley, 1999). Another good book is Edward Kit's *Software Testing in the Real World* (Addison-Wesley, 1995). (For publication information and other good books on software testing, see Appendix C of this book.)

It is important to recognize that the same rules for developing good software apply to developing good test scripts. Good planning and design are important, as is allowing sufficient time to develop the code and supporting utilities.

Goals of Good Testing Software

Test scripts, like application code in general, should be

- *Readable*: Using standard naming conventions and constants, and creating project standards for code development make code more readable. If code is readable, it can be more readily understood and modified, which makes it easier to work with and to adapt to future projects.

- *Reusable*: Writing routines that can be reused within the same project (and sometimes modified to work within another project, as well) can save time and duplication of effort. Some possibilities may include logging utilities to document test results, front-end or driver routines to make running test suites easy, or specialized utilities that make working with your test target easier, like start-up and shutdown routines.

- *Maintainable*: Writing code that is easy to update is important. You can account for a changing application in many ways, including the use of constants, library files, the Windows Registry, and initialization files.

- *Portable*: Writing suites that can be easily changed makes them portable. For example, don't directly place file paths into your code. Instead place files within the assembly of your application and use relative paths to reference them, or let the user specify locations by providing options for them to set. (We'll see how to do this as we proceed in the book.)

Of course, these are guidelines to follow within reason. As testers, we are far more likely than developers to write simple testware that ends up being thrown away because it's a one-time, special-purpose situation we are addressing. And there are times that copying and pasting can be a good thing. The most important of the four "able" qualities is the ability of your testware to be readable. Reusability, maintainability, and portability should be considered for testware that is intended to be used many times, such as test utilities, and test drivers, i.e., code, that are used as a front end to run other tests.

Code can be written in many different ways. When we review code written by others, we try to determine its readability and, therefore, the ease with which we can maintain or alter it. When we write code for testing purposes, we will try to levy that same mandate on our own work. We will then reap the same rewards as the developers and, in the process, learn a bit about why they do the things they do. Throughout this text, we will emphasize good programming technique. Even when in a hurry on a test project, it is absolutely true that it is just as easy to write code properly as it is to write it poorly.

In this book, you will explore ways to implement these goals for yourself and for the applications you test.

Limitations of Programming Languages for Testing

Because they are not intended as test tools, programming languages usually do not include many of the bells and whistles that most commercial automated test tools, and some open source test tools, do. For example, in all but the Team and Enterprise level editions, .NET languages have no inherent support for bug reporting or test design and documentation as many testing tools have. In .NET's Enterprise and Team editions, they have attempted to help integrate the software development and software testing process using the new Team Test software. We provide an introduction to that software in Chapter 11. If you want these kinds of things in your .NET testware, your company must purchase the Enterprise level software versions of .NET (or your test team will have to write them). If you decide to write this kind of functionality yourself, you might find you have entered the business of test-tool writing instead of the testing business. That will be a time-consuming effort. So, .NET languages should not be considered a substitute for the major test tools, or manual testing, but simply a powerful adjunct to them and all of your test strategies.

Summary

.NET languages are powerful enough to accomplish any testing task as long as you have testers with the skill and ability to write effective code, and test management capable of administrating it effectively. This book is intended to guide you and your team in your efforts.

CHAPTER 2

■■■

Understanding .NET Testing Choices

In Chapter 1, we discussed the fact that all .NET languages compile into the same Intermediate Language (IL) so that the choice of a language is largely one of preference. If you have already used a form of Basic (such as an earlier version of Microsoft's Visual Basic or VBScript), then you will feel more at home with Visual Basic .NET. That will also be true if you don't have a preference and are just learning how to program.

Note For quick-start programming tutorials on Visual Basic programming and C#, see Appendix B.

You may find yourself more comfortable using another .NET language if you're more familiar with C-like languages, or Java. In that case, C# would be a good option since it's a new language that has some C language constructs and is similar in many ways to Java. In this book, for simplicity's sake, we'll show example code in just two of the .NET languages: VB .NET and C#.

There is more than just one way to use .NET on a test project. There may be times when a quick, short program to uncover the value of a system variable is wanted, or a more complete test utility requiring multiple forms and a nice user interface. In this section, we'll sample the three main kinds of projects you'll use to create most all of your testware: Windows Forms project, Console project, and Web Forms project. We will present all exercises using both C# and VB .NET code; however, we recommend you try all exercises in the chapter in just one language first. Then, if you'd like, go back and attempt them in the other language. More than likely, this route will be less confusing and ensure greater success.

Objectives

By the end of this chapter, you will be able to

- Create, run, and save a simple testware Console application, Windows Forms application, and Web Forms application

- Use the System.IO namespace

- Describe the meaning of the term "namespace"

- Explain the basic differences between a Console application, Windows Forms application, and Web Forms application

- Explain the basic differences between a simple C# and VB .NET application

.NET Namespaces for Testing

One of the most important things that a tester needs to do is to find and return information: information about the application under test as it runs as well as information about the state of the system before, during and after, the application runs. At this point, you are not quite ready to test a specific application, but you can learn about ways to gain important system information. To do that, you will first learn a bit about how to get information by navigating within .NET. The first thing you'll need to understand is how to use .NET namespaces.

.NET uses *namespaces* as an organizing principle for the voluminous amount of routines, classes, and other programming components contained within the .NET Framework libraries. The word "namespace" itself is what can be confusing, but it's really a very simple concept to aid organization. The Framework libraries are voluminous and that's great because it means there are a lot of resources and information available to both the developer and the tester. The libraries are organized sort of like the way a regular public library is organized: into logical sections, i.e., sections for juvenile fiction, adult fiction, history, and the like. These sections make it easy to find logically related topics in the library. You can't touch a section in a public library because it's not a physical thing, it's an idea—a location; it's an organizing principle. That's exactly the way namespaces work in .NET. Namespaces are like the sections of a library and allow code, structures, constants, and other resources that are logically related to be placed together in the library.

Having said this, it might seem logical that there would be one namespace where you'd find all information that you could return about the platform, system, etc., but, in fact, there are many namespaces within the .NET Framework libraries where routines for accessing system information are stored. Why? The libraries are organized into locations where, hopefully, the developers can find them more easily for their purposes. We testers are still able to get to them too, it just wasn't set up with us in mind. It's not necessary to know where everything is and what it's called right away to be useful within a test project. This book will introduce you to some key namespaces for testing. Here are a few of the ones that you'll look at in this book:

- System.IO (covered in this chapter and in Chapter 3)

- System.Data (covered in Chapter 8)

- System.Text.RegularExpressions (covered in Chapter 3)

- Microsoft.Win32 (covered in Chapter 3)

- System.Web (covered in Chapter 10)

- Microsoft.VisualStudio.TestTools (covered in Chapter 11)

- Microsoft.VisualBasic (covered in Chapter 5)

- System.Diagnostics (covered in Chapters 4 and 5)

Working with and understanding .NET namespaces will be very important to your overall testing efforts. Because of that, let's take a few moments here to explore what's available (see Exercise 2-1).

Exercise 2-1: Working with .NET Namespaces

Note These exercises are designed for you to be able to do them in either the Express editions of .NET (download these from the Microsoft website at www.microsoft.com, or see Appendix A) or Visual Studio 2005. Most of the screenshots were captured using the Beta Express editions, so your screens may vary slightly; however, the differences in the versions should be minimal.

1. Launch Visual Studio .NET.

   You'll find some namespaces that contain valuable routines for testing by opening and exploring a very useful window: the Object Browser.

2. On the main menu, select View ➤ Object Browser or locate the following button on the main toolbar (see Figure 2-1):

Figure 2-1. *The Object Browser button*

   Next you'll see the Object Browser window display as a tab (see Figure 2-2).

   The Object Browser is where you can find the objects you have available from the extensive .NET Framework libraries. When you create a project, you get your own namespace for the project. In the next exercise, we're going to use the System.IO namespace to access the Windows file system. So next, we will look into that namespace to see what resources it contains.

3. Type **System.IO** into the Search Box in the Object Browser and click the arrow (or press Enter). The System.IO namespace will appear in the left side of your window.

4. Click on the System.IO namespace and expand it. Within the System.IO namespace, you'll see the File class (we'll define classes in Chapter 3).

   By clicking on the File class, the methods and other components available within it are visible in the pane just to the right (see Figure 2-3).

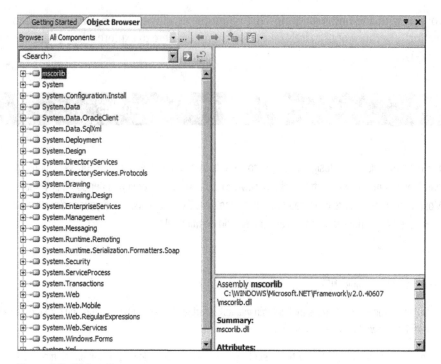

Figure 2-2. *Object Browser*

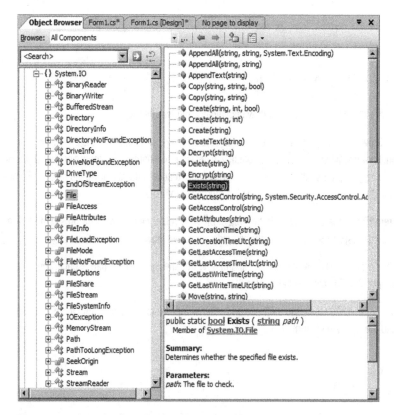

Figure 2-3. *The File class displayed in the Object Browser window*

5. Click the `Exists` method in the right pane. (In the top-right pane of Figure 2-3, the `Exists` method is selected.) Notice that once you have clicked the `Exists` method, it is described in the pane just below it. The pane gives a summary that describes the purpose of the method and the parameters that will be required to run it. This information is given in command syntax, which describes the method independent of the language that uses it. In other words, this pane will look the same whether you access it from within Visual Basic .NET or from within C# or any other .NET language. Let's take some time out from our exercise steps for a moment to examine this command description:

VB .NET

```
Public Shared Function Exists(ByVal path As String) As Boolean
```

C#

```
Public static bool Exists (string path)
```

■**Note** This may look slightly different depending on which edition you're using. It should be close enough to complete the exercise.

What this says is that this is a function called "Exists" that needs an input (or argument) of the string data type. It will return something of type "bool," which is short for "Boolean," and means it will return either true or false. In the parameters description, "path" is described as the "file to check." An example of how to call this routine then would be the following:

VB .NET

```
If File.Exists(c:\myfile.txt) then …
```

C#

```
If (File.Exists(textBox1.text))  …
```

In both of these cases, the `File.Exists` function will determine the existence of a file. In the VB .NET code example, a file is typed directly into the argument of the `Exists` function. The purpose is to determine if that particular file exists or not and the return value will either be yes or no, i.e., true or false. In the C# code example, the value the user types into `textBox1` at runtime will contain the name of a file and then the code will determine if that value represents a valid path and filename or not. You can see that other than a few parentheses, the code is basically doing the same thing. We will be using this function in the next exercise.

6. Take some time to explore the items in the `System.IO` namespace, and also to explore the other namespaces and resources within them. While you explore, it can be very helpful to use the Dynamic Help feature in Visual Studio. To access Visual Studio's Dynamic Help, select Help ➤ Dynamic Help from the main menu. It will bring up a Help window that will change as you move around within the Object Browser. Watch the Dynamic Help window because it will display links that are relevant to the items that you are looking at in the Object Browser. This is a great way to learn more about the available resources in the Object Browser, as well as the features of Visual Studio.

7. Close Visual Studio .NET (select File ➤ Exit from the main menu).

In his first book on .NET, *Moving to VB .NET: Strategies, Concepts, and Code* (Apress 2001), Dan Appleman stated that one of his biggest concerns with .NET is that developers do not take the time to understand the full power of what is available in the .NET libraries. That's my same concern for test professionals—there is so much available. The only effective way to find out what is there is to research, study, and share code. For testing, there will be many namespaces that you'll find useful to testing; those mentioned in this section are just the beginning. Your next step is to write some code to put these resources you've found to work. In the next exercise, you'll use the System.IO namespace you just researched to determine the existence of a file.

Creating a Simple Application for Testing

In this section, you will follow steps to create simple .NET testware that will verify the existence of a file on your system. Why verify a file? This is essentially a way to get started testing, but also could end up being useful in a test situation. Very often, applications we test create files or delete them, and verifying that those files exist when and where they should (and don't exist when they shouldn't) are common testing tasks. A task like this is a good one for test automation because it would likely be a boring and tedious task. You can use a program to do this boring task for you. So let's write one.

First Windows Forms Testware Application

Windows Forms are the most basic way to use .NET. You get a form already created on which you can drag and drop controls and design a simple, yet functional, and efficient application. It's a great way to get something done quickly. (See Exercise 2-2.)

■**Note** For the most basic programming concepts, please review the tutorials in Appendixes A and B.

Exercise 2-2: First Windows Forms Testware Application

1. Launch Visual Studio .NET.

2. Select File ➤ New Project.

3. Select the Windows Application template (see Figure 2-4).

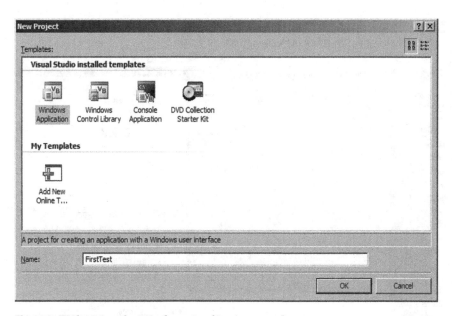

Figure 2-4. *Choosing the Windows Application template*

■**Note** Code samples will always be in both VB .NET and C# code; however, figures, for simplicity, will usually just show the VB .NET dialogs. They are similar to the C# windows so, therefore, will differ only in minor ways. In cases where there are major differences, we will display both; otherwise, consider that the differences between the figures for VB .NET and C# are not appreciable.

---

4. In the Name box, type **FirstTest** and click OK. The next Window you'll see is the Development environment (see Figure 2-5).

   This IDE provides the tools and Windows we need to create our testware, i.e., our testing software.

5. Place two controls, one button control and one textbox control, on the form by dragging them from the toolbox (if you cannot see the Toolbox window, then you can load it by selecting View ➤ Toolbox). Set their Text properties from within the Properties window as shown in Table 2-1 (there is no need to change the names of the objects; i.e., you do not need to change their Name properties for this simple exercise).

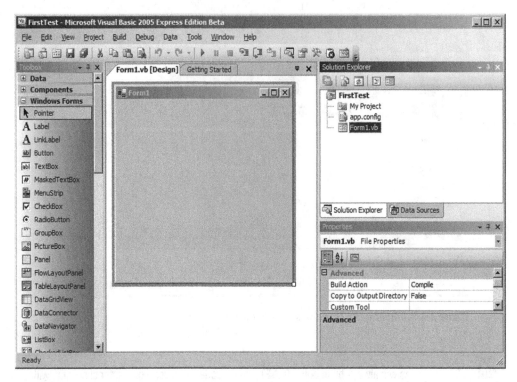

Figure 2-5. *The Visual Basic Integrated Development Environment (IDE)*

TESTER'S TIP: WHEN TO SET AND CHANGE PROPERTIES

In many of these examples, we will not ask you to change the default properties of the textboxes and labels. This makes getting started much easier and allows us to get to the point we are trying to make much quicker, but there is a downside. When you are actually creating your testware applications you should always start by adding your controls to the form. Then, before you start coding, set all the properties you can think of. This is especially true for setting the names of those controls. Changing the names after you have started writing code can be done, but then you will have to go back and change all the references to those controls. We recommend that you always create the form, set the properties, and then write your code to make your project go smoother.

Table 2-1. *Properties to Set*

Object	Property	Value
Button1	Text	File Exists?
Textbox1	Text	(leave this blank)

When you've placed the controls and set their properties, your designer window should look something like Figure 2-6.

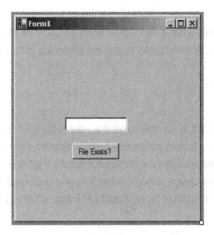

Figure 2-6. *The FirstTest program initial controls layout*

6. Now enter the code for the program by double-clicking the button control in the designer. Double-clicking the button control opens the code window with the code for the button's Click event displayed. Type the code in Listing 2-1 into the button's Click event.

Listing 2-1. *Code Used in the Button's Click Event*

VB .NET

```
If File.Exists(TextBox1.Text) Then
    MessageBox.Show("File Exists: Test passed")
Else
    MessageBox.Show("File doesn't Exist: Test failure")
End If
```

C#

```
if (File.Exists(textBox1.Text))
    MessageBox.Show("File Exists: Test passed");
else
    MessageBox.Show("File doesn't Exist: Test failure");
```

After you've typed this, you will notice you have a little blue squiggly underneath the word "File". This is because we haven't pointed the environment to look in the appropriate spot in the Framework libraries, so it doesn't know anything about how to work with the File class. To point the environment to the right spot, we will need to refer to the System.IO namespace.

7. Access the functions in the System.IO namespace by typing the following line at the top of the code file:

VB .NET

```
Imports System.IO
```

C#

```
using System.IO;
```

■**Note** C# users will need to expand the directives region in the code window. See Listing 2-2 for how your code window will look with all the code entered properly. Don't forget to type in the semicolon at the end of the using directive!

The Imports line (VB .NET) and the using directive (C#) are statements that refer to the System.IO namespace within the .NET Framework libraries. These libraries are available to you without this statement; the statement simply allows you to refer to the resources within this namespace directly. If you don't put these statements at the top, you would have to refer to each resource within the namespace explicitly. For example, you would have to get to the Exists function by typing **System.IO.Exists**, which is just a lot more unnecessary typing.

After you've typed the Imports statement or using directive, the full code in the code window will look like Listing 2-2.

Listing 2-2. *Code Used in Form1*

VB .NET

```
Imports System.IO
Public Class Form1

    Private Sub Button1_Click(ByVal sender As System.Object, _
            ByVal e As System.EventArgs) Handles Button1.Click
        If File.Exists(TextBox1.Text) Then
            MessageBox.Show("File Exists: Test passed")
        Else
            MessageBox.Show("File doesn't Exist: Test failure")
        End If

    End Sub
End Class
```

C#

```
#region using directives

using System;
using System.Collections.Generic;
using System.ComponentModel;
using System.Data;
using System.Drawing;
using System.Windows.Forms;
using System.IO;

#endregion
```

```
namespace FirstTest
{
    partial class Form1 : Form
    {
        public Form1()
        {
            InitializeComponent();
        }

        private void button1_Click(object sender, EventArgs e)
        {

            if (File.Exists(textBox1.Text))
                MessageBox.Show("File Exists: Test passed");
            else
                MessageBox.Show("File doesn't Exist: Test failure");
        }
    }
}
```

8. Now it's time to run and test your new testware. Click the Start button on the toolbar (see Figure 2-7) or select Debug ➤ Start from the main menu.

Figure 2-7. *The Start button*

If you've made any syntax errors, the environment will display a dialog box indicating there are errors. It will ask if you want to continue. If you get this dialog box, click No (in fact, it will always be a good idea to click No if you get build errors) and go back to your code. Compare it to the full code in Listing 2-2 and edit it until it is exactly the same. Try running the program again.

Once your program compiles and runs properly, you'll see the FirstTest dialog. This means you are in Run mode and the IDE will display the name of your program and the word "(Running)" in its caption. Your running program, IDE, and dialog will look similar to Figure 2-8.

9. Type an invalid filename into the Form1 textbox. That should be easy, just make something up—you don't have to type in a valid file path or format because we are testing this program (yes, we are testing our testware!) to see if it fails when it should. By the way, this is called *negative testing*, i.e., testing with invalid values. Once you've typed in an invalid filename (like **slkdjf**), then click the File Exists? button. You should now see a dialog box display the message "File doesn't exist; Test failure." Click OK on this dialog box.

10. Now try *positive testing*, i.e., type a valid path and filename into the textbox. In order to make sure it's valid, you may just want to create a simple Notepad text file somewhere simple, like right in the root directory of your computer. Then type the full path to this file as well as its name into the textbox. Most systems will have the file autoexec.bat at the root level, so try typing this into the textbox: **c:\autoexec.bat**. Your new test utility will tell you whether or not you have that file! Verify that you do, or do not, by checking its location using Windows Explorer.

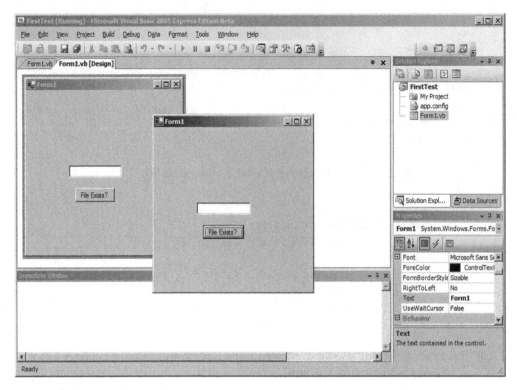

Figure 2-8. *Running the FirstTest program*

11. Close the Form1 dialog box by clicking the Close button in the upper-right corner, or select Debug ➤ Stop Debugging from the main menu. This will take you out of Run mode and put you back into Development mode where you can edit the program and the form, if desired.

12. Save your program by selecting File ➤ Save All from the menu. Your file is saved by default into the My Documents\Visual Studio 2005\Projects folder on your system. This is a very good spot for it, so go ahead and leave it there. You can reopen this file any time by navigating to that location and clicking the FirstTest.sln (Solution) file. Compare your work to the Download Files for this chapter's exercise (see the following Note).

Note Answers to this and all exercises in this book will be located in the DownloadFiles\ChapterX\ folder (substitute the number of the chapter for the letter X in the path). These files are available for download from the Source Code section of the Apress website (www.apress.com). See the Introduction of this book for instructions on where and how to download these files. All answers will be written in both C# and VB .NET code, so you will see separate folders for each within the Exercises folder of each chapter.

TESTER'S TIP: FINDING APPLICATION FILES

Exercise 2-2 created a very simple .NET application with, admittedly, limited usefulness. Although simple, it does have some relevance, however. There are many times when applications you are testing create files, either permanent files or temporary files, as they run. It may be your job, at some point, to determine if the proper files are created and/or deleted as the application runs. The code you just wrote will be useful in that situation. You'll probably want to spiff it up a bit more once you know more .NET, but it is a start. However, the main point of the exercises in this chapter is to get you started and give you an idea of what it will take to work with .NET. As you move into more advanced chapters, you'll create many small testware applications that will show you even more .NET power in testing projects. The testware you create will become more sophisticated and more complex as well, but you'll find that you can write many useful tests and also create powerful test utilities using the muscle of the .NET libraries.

Using Console Applications to Create Testware

You've just learned how to work, in a very basic way, with .NET forms applications. While it is useful to have a form available for your applications, there are often times when a form gets in the way. What if you want to have an application return some information about the system without having to sit there and input and respond to the application? Maybe you'd like to have your testware run overnight and have a report waiting for you when you arrive at the office in the morning. In situations like this, it can be very useful to skip the Windows Forms application template and use a Console application. This section introduces you to using Console applications for creating your testware. It's another useful option for testware creation.

A *Console application* is any program with access to three basic data streams: standard input, standard output, and standard error. As the names suggest, *standard input* represents data going into the program, *standard output* represents data going out, and *standard error* represents a special kind of data out: error messages. Along with its command-line arguments, these data streams represent the runtime context of the Console application. In the upcoming exercise, you'll work with all three of these data streams using the Console class.

Console applications, by the way, were not available in Visual Basic 6.0. The addition of Console applications expands your choices for creating testware. You will not drag and drop controls onto a form, but will instead work in a command-line interface.

It'll be easier to talk about the pros and cons of working with Console applications vs. working with Windows Forms applications once you've written one. So, first you'll create a small Console application (see Exercise 2-3) and then compare the two types of applications, Windows Forms and Console, for use in testing.

Exercise 2-3: First Console Testware Application

1. If necessary, launch Visual Studio .NET.

2. From the main menu, select File ➤ New Project. The New Project dialog box displays. Click the Console application option.

3. Click the OK button. The IDE for a Console application displays (Figure 2-9 shows the IDE for Visual Basic .NET). Notice that there is no toolbox window displayed. You still have the Solution Explorer and Properties windows displayed. Note, also, that there is no Forms Designer window displayed either. This is because there won't be any user interface (i.e., form) to display to the user. You are taken straight to the code window.

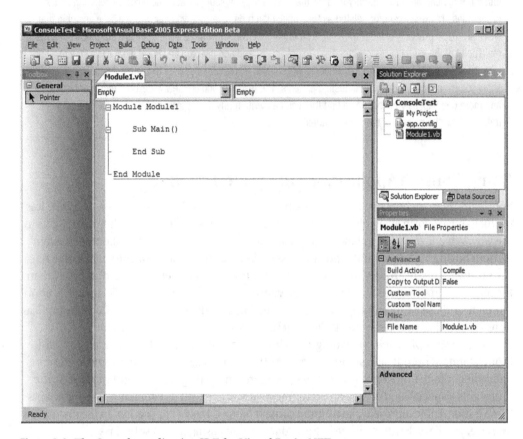

Figure 2-9. *The Console application IDE for Visual Basic .NET*

For C#, the Console application IDE looks similar except the code is different, of course. In C#, the code looks like Listing 2-3. (Note that we've expanded the `using` directives region so you can see it. To do this, click the "+" sign next to that line in your code window.)

Listing 2-3. *Code Used in the C# Console Application Start-Up*

C#

```
#region using directives

using System;
using System.Collections.Generic;
using System.Text;
```

```
#endregion

namespace ConsoleTest
{
    class Program
    {
        static void Main(string[] args)
        {

        }
    }
}
```

For both VB .NET and C#, this is just bare bones code that provides the shell where you'll place your own code.

4. Add the following code to create a Console application to check for the existence of a file.

For VB .NET, first add the following line to the very beginning of the file:

```
Imports System.IO
```

Then add the code in Listing 2-4 between the Sub Main() line and the End Sub lines.

Listing 2-4. *Code to Add for the VB .NET Console Application*

```
Dim strInput As String = ""

Console.WriteLine()
Console.WriteLine("Enter the file to find or enter 'Q' to Quit")
Do Until strInput = "Q"
    strInput = UCase(Console.ReadLine())
    If File.Exists(strInput) Then
        Console.WriteLine("File Exists: Test passed")
    Else
        Console.WriteLine("File doesn't Exist: Test failure")
    End If
    Console.WriteLine("Enter the file to find or enter 'Q' to Quit")
Loop
```

For C#, first add the following line to the using directives region. That is, add it just before the #End Region line:

```
using System.IO;
```

Now modify the code in the window so that it looks like the code in Listing 2-5. (You will be adding ten lines of code between the swirly braces just after the static void Main... line of code.)

Listing 2-5. *Code to Add for the C# Console Application*

```
static void Main(string[] args)
{
Console.WriteLine();
Console.WriteLine("Enter the file to find or enter 'Q' to Quit");
string strInput = "";

while (strInput != "Q") {
    strInput = Console.ReadLine();
    if (File.Exists(strInput))
        Console.WriteLine("File Exists: Test passed");
    else
        Console.WriteLine("File doesn't Exist: Test failure");
    Console.WriteLine("Enter the file to find or enter 'Q' to Quit");
    }
}
```

Once you have typed in the code in Listing 2-4 (VB .NET) or Listing 2-5 (C#), your full code will look like Listing 2-6.

Listing 2-6. *Full Code for the FirstConsoleTest Application*

VB .NET

```
Imports System.IO
Module Module1

    Sub Main()
        Dim strInput As String = ""

        Console.WriteLine()
        Console.WriteLine("Enter the file to find or enter 'Q' to Quit")
        Do Until strInput = "Q"
            strInput = UCase(Console.ReadLine())
            If File.Exists(strInput) Then
                Console.WriteLine("File Exists: Test passed")
            Else
                Console.WriteLine("File doesn't Exist: Test failure")
            End If
            Console.WriteLine("Enter the file to find or enter 'Q' to Quit")
        Loop
    End Sub

End Module
```

C#

```csharp
#region using directives

using System;
using System.Collections.Generic;
using System.Text;
using System.IO;

#endregion

namespace ConsoleTest
{
    class Program
    {
        static void Main(string[] args)
        {
            Console.WriteLine();
            Console.WriteLine("Enter the file to find or enter 'Q' to Quit");
            string strInput = "";

            while (strInput != "Q") {
                strInput = Console.ReadLine();
                if (File.Exists(strInput))
                    Console.WriteLine("File Exists: Test passed");
                else
                    Console.WriteLine("File doesn't Exist: Test failure");
                Console.WriteLine("Enter the file to find or enter 'Q' to Quit");
                }
        }
    }
}
```

This code is similar to the code you wrote for the Windows Forms application in Exercise 2-1. There are two major differences: First, we use the Console class to read and write messages. The Console.ReadLine statement reads from the standard input stream and the Console.WriteLine statement writes to the standard output stream. This just means that these statements read and write to a command window that you'll see once you build and run the program in steps 5 and 6. The second major difference is that you must use a looping structure to allow the user to continue finding files as desired. That's a consequence of the fact that with a Console application, you don't have a nice form to display information to the user as you did in the Windows Forms application.

Remember the Object Browser from Exercise 2-1? We used it to look at the System.IO namespace. Take a look at the Console class in the Object Browser to see what else is available in addition to routines for reading and writing. Figure 2-10 shows the Console class in the Object Browser. Note: The simplest way to display this window is to put your cursor on the word "Console" in the code window, right-click it, and then select Go To Definition from the pop-up menu.

Figure 2-10. *The Console class displayed in the Object Browser window*

As a test professional, you're probably the curious type, so snooping around in here will satisfy your desire to know a little more about what's available to you in a Console application. When you're done with this window you can close it, or you can leave it open and simply click on a different tab to work elsewhere. Now it's time to build and run the application, which you will do in the next couple of steps.

5. This time, let's build the program first before attempting to run it. When you clicked the Start button on the toolbar in the Exercise 2-2, it both built and then ran your program. If problems were encountered, the program stopped and displayed a message box that asked if you wanted to continue or break (see Exercise 2-1, step 10). Instead, if you want to check for problems first, you can build the program separately.

   To do this, select Build ➤ Build Solution from the main menu. If there are any syntax errors, you will see a message displayed in the Error List window just below the code window. You'll want to fix all the errors in the Error List window before attempting to run the code again.

6. Once the code has been built successfully, i.e., there are no messages in the Error List, go ahead and run the program by clicking the Start button. You will see the command window displayed (see Figure 2-11) with the word "Console" in its caption.

7. Click the caption of this window in order to give it the focus and then type a valid filename in response to the statement, "Enter the file to find or enter 'Q' to Quit." Test out your Console application with valid and invalid data similar to what you see in Figure 2-11.

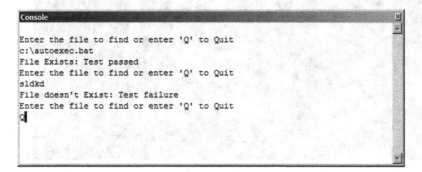

```
Console
Enter the file to find or enter 'Q' to Quit
c:\autoexec.bat
File Exists: Test passed
Enter the file to find or enter 'Q' to Quit
sldkd
File doesn't Exist: Test failure
Enter the file to find or enter 'Q' to Quit
q
```

Figure 2-11. *Running the ConsoleTest application*

8. When you are satisfied that your application runs correctly, enter **Q** to quit.

9. Save your application and compare it, if desired, to the code we have in the Download Files for this chapter. You're still not quite done though. Now you will need to see your Console application the way the end user of this application will see it.

10. Open a command prompt by selecting the Windows Start ➤ Run menu item. Type **cmd** in the Open box (see Figure 2-12).

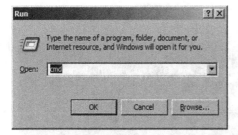

Figure 2-12. *Creating a command prompt from the Windows Start ➤ Run menu item*

A command window similar to Figure 2-13 will appear.

11. Now open Windows Explorer and find the ConsoleTest.exe file in your project's bin folder (your application will have been saved into the following folder by default: My Documents\Visual Studio 2005\Projects\ConsoleTest). Drag this .exe file onto the command window. Now press Enter to run your program (see Figure 2-14).

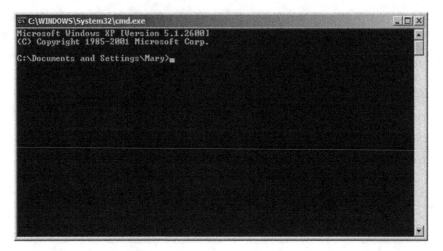

Figure 2-13. *A command prompt window*

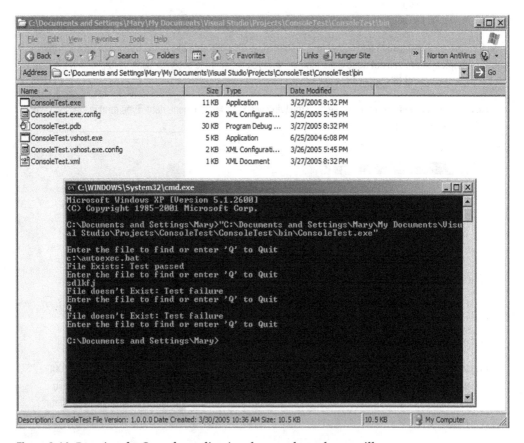

Figure 2-14. *Running the Console application the way the end user will*

What you just did in this step was to test your application in its natural working environment. Using Visual Studio's command window is much more convenient for our purposes, but before you release your testware you should always test it from the actual user's perspective. Of course, when you are writing testware, your "user" will likely be you or another tester. Still, you must test your own code!

Now you've written two simple programs: one in Windows Forms and one using the Console. It took a little more coding and the use of a looping structure and the `Console` class to write the Console application, but the code didn't need a form to run. You did prompt the user for information, but the Console application is actually good for situations where you just want to run a test and perhaps print the results to a file instead of reporting back to the user right away. In the next chapter, you'll see how to write to files—this will make the Console application a more appealing choice.

You still have one more type of application to explore before moving on, and that is a Web Forms application.

Using Web Applications to Create Testware

Now you will get a feel for creating the third kind of application you will work with in this book: a Web Forms application (see Exercise 2-4). Creating Web Forms applications is so much easier to do in ASP.NET than in earlier versions of ASP. You will be able to create a web page in a very similar manner to how you create a Windows Forms application. In fact, for very simple web pages, there's very little difference in the process of creating the application. You will be able to drag and drop controls onto a designer and write code for what happens when the end user interacts with these controls. Of course ASP.NET is very powerful and there are many more things that can be done that will underscore the differences between working with Web Forms applications and Windows Forms as you'll see in Chapter 8. For now, you'll look at the similarities in a simple application.

Exercise 2-4: First Web Testware Application

1. Launch Visual Studio .NET Express Web Developer's Edition or Visual Studio 2005.

2. From the main menu, select the File ➤ New Web Site menu item. (Note: In some versions, you may need to select File ➤ New ➤ Web Site.) The New Web Site dialog box displays. Change the name of the new website in the Location box from

`C:\WebSites\WebSite1`

to

`C:\WebSites\WebTest`

as shown in Figure 2-15. Be sure to select your desired language choice from the Project Types list view on the left side of this dialog box. (In Figure 2-15, the Visual Basic language is highlighted.) Click OK to create the new website accepting the default: ASP.NET Web Site.

Note The website you create is located by default in a folder off your system root in c:\WebSites. In previous editions, ASP.NET web pages were located in the standard location for websites: c:\Inetpub\wwwroot. This new location allows you to create and test a website without having it immediately deployed to the server on which you're working. Please see Appendix A for information on how to set up your computer to run as a web server.

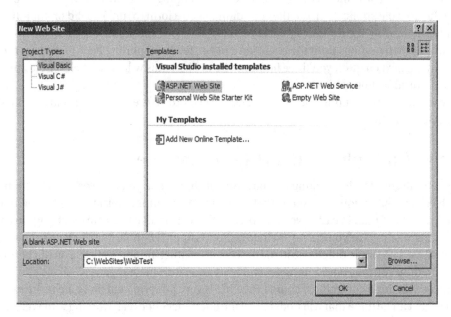

Figure 2-15. *Creating the WebTest application*

After clicking OK in the New Web Site dialog box, you'll see the Web Developer IDE display (see Figure 2-16).

The biggest difference here is that you're not looking at a Designer, you're looking at a source window and the code you see is neither Visual Basic nor C#, it's actually HTML. You're in the web world now! Don't worry though, you can get back to a development environment you're more familiar with by simply clicking the Design link at the bottom-left corner of the Source window. Now you'll be viewing a Designer that is similar, but not exactly like what you have seen when developing a Windows Forms application.

3. Using the toolbox (if you don't see the toolbox, you can always bring it up by selecting View ➤ Toolbox from the main menu), add a textbox control to the web page. To add the control, double-click the textbox control in the Toolbox. Now try to drag the textbox around. Notice that you cannot drag and drop this control wherever you'd like. Your web page is in "flow" mode. The textbox will want to stay in the upper-left corner. That's okay. You'll just leave it there. (To create controls you can move around, select Layout ➤ Insert Layer from the menu and place the control inside the layer box.) Place your cursor right after the textbox, hit the space bar a couple of times, and then type **Tester's Name** right onto the page. The HTML code will be generated for you as you modify this page.

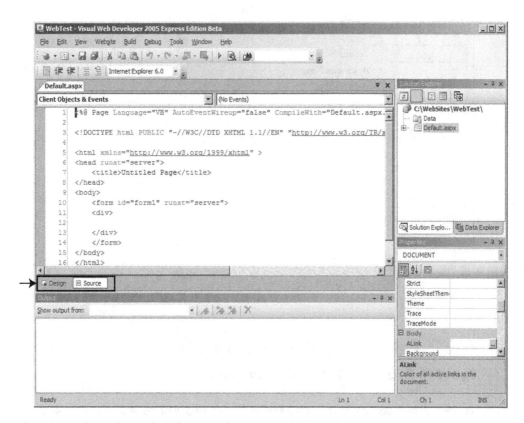

Figure 2-16. *The Web Developer's IDE with Design and Source links highlighted*

4. Using this same process, add four more textboxes, a button control, a label control, and accompanying text to the web page so that it looks similar to Figure 2-17. (To create the spacing shown, press Enter before adding each textbox.) For the button control, you will need to change its text property in the Properties window in order to get its caption to read "Submit Bug". Similarly, for the label control, you will change its text property by erasing it (even after its text property is erased, the label control will still display the value "[Label1]"). Otherwise, note that at this point you still will not change any other properties of the controls since you're trying to make this as simple as possible.

In this Web Forms application, you are not going to search for a file; instead, you are designing a front end for a web-based, bug-tracking application. Writing sophisticated bug-reporting software takes a lot of work, so for this exercise you'll make it easy by simply reporting back information without storing it. In Chapter 3, you'll learn how to store information in a variety of ways. In Chapter 5, you will finish the bug-tracking software once you've learned more about .NET coding.

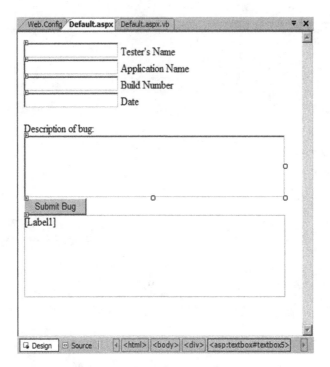

Figure 2-17. *Designing the WebTest application page*

5. Double-click the button control. This will take you to the code window for the Web Forms application. Enter the code in Listing 2-7 into the Button1_Click event.

Listing 2-7. *Code for the Button1_Click Event of the WebTest Application*

VB .NET

```
Label1.Text = "Tester's Name: " + TextBox1.Text + "<br>" + _
              "Application Name: " + TextBox2.Text + "<br>" + _
              "Build Number: " + TextBox3.Text + "<br>" + _
              "Date: " + TextBox4.Text + "<br>" + _
              "Description of bug: " + "<br>" + _
              TextBox5.Text
```

C#

```
Label1.Text = "Tester's Name: " + TextBox1.Text + "<br>" +
              "Application Name: " + TextBox2.Text + "<br>" +
              "Build Number: " + TextBox3.Text + "<br>" +
              "Date: " + TextBox4.Text + "<br>" +
              "Description of bug: " + "<br>" +
              TextBox5.Text;
```

■**Note** The code for Visual Basic displayed in Listing 2-7 uses an underscore character (_) to continue the single assignment of a value into the `label1.text` property to multiple lines. The underscore is the line-continuation character in Visual Basic. A character like this is needed because Visual Basic does not have any other way to tell the compiler when a statement is completed. In C#, the semicolon (;) is used as the statement terminator, so underscores are not needed. You must precede the underscore character by at least one space.

For both C# and VB .NET, the values in the text properties of the controls on the form are loaded into the text property of the label control. You are simply reading the information and reporting it back.

TESTER'S TIP: PROGRAM STUBS

The code in the `Button1_Click` event in your WebTest application simply reports back the information that you have typed into the controls. This is called *stubbing*. Programmers use stubbing to write pieces of software in a top-down fashion. It's a way to break down the complexity of an application and make sure part of it works before proceeding to the rest of the code. Of course when we testers write our testware, we will want to do the same, especially when writing complex tests or test utilities. By stubbing out the code (for example, using a Prompt window or a label control to display the information, rather than actually saving the bug report information into a file or a database), we are simply ensuring that our form works properly. You'll write the rest of the code to save the Bug Report information in Chapter 6. In other words, you have not written any actual functionality into this software, you are merely making sure that the end user can enter information and your code will correctly read and return it. In successive chapters, you will make this code report to a database and out to a file. For now, reporting back using a *stub* will be enough.

By the way, stubs are something that programmers use all the time. Sometimes, as you might imagine, they can forget to finish the code and the stubs remain in place, looking as if the application is really doing something when it's not. This is why a good tester always double-checks database files and other resources to be sure the software really is doing what it says its doing!

The full code for the WebTest application will look like Listing 2-8. Double-check that your code looks like the code in Listing 2-8.

Listing 2-8. *Full Code for the WebTest Application*

VB .NET

```
Partial Class Default_aspx

    Sub Button1_Click(ByVal sender As Object, ByVal e As System.EventArgs)

        Label1.Text = "Tester's Name: " + TextBox1.Text + "<br>" + _
                "Application Name: " + TextBox2.Text + "<br>" + _
                "Build Number: " + TextBox3.Text + "<br>" + _
```

```
            "Date: " + TextBox4.Text + "<br>" + _
            "Description of bug: " + "<br>" + _
            TextBox5.Text

    End Sub

End Class
```

C#

```
using System;
using System.Data;
using System.Configuration;
using System.Web;
using System.Web.Security;
using System.Web.UI;
using System.Web.UI.WebControls;
using System.Web.UI.WebControls.WebParts;
using System.Web.UI.HtmlControls;

public partial class Default_aspx
{
    void Button1_Click(object sender, EventArgs e)
    {
        Label1.Text = "Tester's Name: " + TextBox1.Text + "<br>" +
                "Application Name: " + TextBox2.Text + "<br>" +
                "Build Number: " + TextBox3.Text + "<br>" +
                "Date: " + TextBox4.Text + "<br>" +
                "Description of bug: " + "<br>" +
                TextBox5.Text;
    }
}
```

6. Now test out your new application. With Web Forms, you have a few options. The fastest way to test your new Web Form is to right-click it in the Solution Explorer and select View In Browser, as shown in Figure 2-18.

Note For this to work, your system must have properly been set up to run websites. If you get errors, see Appendix A.

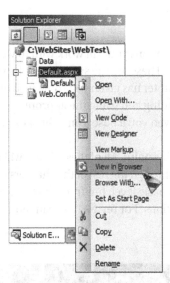

Figure 2-18. *Starting the WebTest application by selecting the View In Browser command*

Notice that your default browser window is launched. You are viewing a web page! You can also bring up this page by clicking the Start button (or the Debug ➤ Start Debugging menu item) on the toolbar, as you have done in the other applications.

Enter a variety of information into the textboxes of your new web page and then click Submit Bug. The information will be displayed in the label control. You can stop the web page by closing the browser. This will take you back to the Web Development IDE.

7. Save your work and close the application. Your web page information is stored in the c:\websites folder; however, the solution file (.sln) for the application is still located in your My Documents\Visual Studio 2005\Projects folder inside the application folder called "WebTest." The answer for this exercise is in the Download Files for this chapter. In order to open the answer, you will launch the Web Developer's Edition and navigate to the folder that contains the answer. You will then select File ➤ Open Web Site from the main menu. (Appendix A contains instructions for opening all exercise answers.) You will complete the Bug Report application in Chapter 6.

One advantage to using web pages for your testware is that you can share it easily with other testers on your team by simply deploying it to a company intranet web server. Bug-reporting software is one example of the kind of software that test teams might want to share. There are many others that you'll see as you progress in your knowledge of .NET. Keep Windows Forms, Console, and Web Forms applications in mind as you consider creating automated tests and utilities.

Summary

In this chapter, we've introduced the three types of applications you will work with to write your testware: Windows Forms, Console, and Web Forms. These are the same types of applications that developers who use .NET will also use. This chapter has given you some insight into software development, including the use of stubs and finding and using the appropriate namespace within the Framework libraries. It has also given you a base from which to start your automated test creation.

You're not expected to be an expert at any of this at this point. All of these things will need practice and more depth, which you will get as you work through the rest of the chapters in this book. You've also walked through the exercises on a very basic level, but from now on we will assume a little more proficiency in creating your applications. For review, you can return to this section and to Appendix B.

Tester's Checklist

☑ Investigate the Object Browser, Help files, and any other resources available for namespaces that will provide important system information and functionality. Good software, including testware, will take full advantage of what's available in the .NET Framework libraries. The challenge is to be able to find out what is there. The best way to do that is through investigation and practice. In this chapter, you learned about the System.IO namespace, which is an area that contains information and routines to access the Windows file system.

☑ Use the Imports statement (VB .NET) or the using directive (C#) to refer to namespaces within the .NET Framework libraries. Either simplifies the code.

☑ Use program stubbing to develop your testware a little at a time. Stubs allow you to simulate the way lower-level code would work so you can ensure the functionality of the code you write a little at a time. The stubs will be filled in later with code that works with the correct functionality.

☑ Always check the application software under test to be sure that it is doing what it says it is doing. Remember that program stubs can accidentally be left in place and can be deceiving because they will report that the application is doing something when it really isn't. For example, an application may report that a file is saved when it is not. A good tester will always double-check the database or files that the application is supposed to create to ensure functionality.

☑ Create all three kinds of .NET applications to become comfortable with the differences and advantages of each. This way, on a testing project, you'll be able to choose the right application type for your needs more quickly when the time comes.

CHAPTER 3

■ ■ ■

The Basics of Storing Test Data

In Chapter 2, you learned about the three different kinds of .NET applications you can choose to write your testware. In each application, you wrote the results of your tests out to either a message box or a label. This kind of test reporting—while quick and simple—isn't very practical for long-term projects. What if you want to run your tests overnight? Also, you will need to provide test result documentation to management and customers, so you'll have to be able to store this data somehow and provide reports. And what about other kinds of data besides test results? For example, say you want to store some settings for your tests to compare from one test run to the next, like the last date they were run or who ran them? So, there are all kinds of data that you'll need to work with on a test project, and controlling and accessing this data is an essential part of your job. Think about it, what does it matter if you find bugs if you can't prove that you did? In fact, some of the most important things you will do on a test project are document, store, and retrieve test data.

In addition to test results reporting, there are a lot of other reasons why you will need to work with data on a test project. The software applications we test also use all kinds of data files for many different reasons, including, for example, to log and store user-specific information, to store error information, and many others. As a tester, you may need to open and access these files to ensure that the system is creating and interfacing with them correctly.

In this chapter, you'll learn how to work with data and files in several different ways. You will learn how to write and read information to and from a text file, a database, and the Windows Registry. While doing so, we'll discuss when and why you might want to use either of these choices. You'll also take a look at working with strings using the intrinsic string functions available in the .NET Framework and also using another language—Regular Expressions.

Objectives

By the end of this chapter, you will be able to

- Discuss the importance of storing test data

- Discuss the kinds of test data you might need to store on a test project

- Write code to open and close a text file

- Write code to read and write values to and from the Windows Registry

- Write code to manipulate strings

- Write code to open and close a database and write to an existing database

Test Results Logging and Project Planning

Setting up the necessary kinds of file access for any kind of project, whether it's a software development project or a test project, can be time consuming. This is an example of the kind of task that can, and should, be done early in the project, even before there is any testable software released to the test organization. Setting up file access for test results reporting in advance can save you time when you get to the more intense phases of the project. Too often, we see testers in the beginning of the project complain that they don't have anything to work on because the first build release is delayed (as usual). Then later, when in the middle of the time-critical phases of a project, those same testers, in addition to running actual tests, are also furiously working on writing and documenting the test results by writing test reports and testware coding, which could have been done earlier. This is poor project planning, and it is exacerbated by the fact that test management and testers don't always think about all the other things they could be doing before the test execution phase begins. One of these things is setting up your test reports and test logging strategies. We'll show you how to do this more specifically in the next few sections, and then we'll revisit the issue in Chapter 5. Since there are a lot of other reasons to work with data files, in addition to reporting test results, we'll also explore more reasons to work with each kind of file (text file, database, and the Windows Registry) and how to do so.

Working with Text Files on a Test Project

Without question, the quickest way to document your tests is to write out information to a simple text file. Opening, closing, reading, and writing text files are very fast operations for a computer to perform. In addition to using these operations to document your tests, you may find you need them to perform other important testing tasks. For example, since software applications often create log files as they run, on several different occasions we have been asked to open up a log file created by the application, search it for a specific error message, and then count the number of times this error occurred. We wrote the code to do this using similar commands to the ones you will learn in the next section. This same code can be modified a bit to search any kind of text file—for example, you might find you need to search the source code behind a web page to find how many links, or graphics, the page contains to verify that the correct number exists.

In Exercise 2-2, you did a short exercise that worked with the System.IO namespace. You will use this same namespace to create files that you can write to and store your test data. You'll need to work with a couple of classes within the IO namespace: the StreamWriter and StreamReader classes. The StreamWriter class contains all of the routines for creating and writing to a file, and the StreamReader class does the same for reading from a file.

Writing to Text Files

Once the System.IO namespace is imported into your code, the three lines in Listing 3-1 will create an object of the StreamWriter class, create a text file for writing, and write a line into that file. A lot of work for just three lines of code!

Listing 3-1. *Writing to a Text File*

VB .NET

```
Dim Writer As StreamWriter
Writer = File.CreateText("TestResults.log")
Writer.WriteLine("Test Results for Test Run XYZ; " & Now)
```

C#

```
StreamWriter Writer;
Writer = File.CreateText("TestResults.log");
Writer.WriteLine("Test Results for Test Run XYZ; " + DateTime.Now);
```

In Exercise 3-1, Part I, you'll take the simple exercise created in Exercise 2-2 and turn it into a more useful test utility by writing the results to a text file.

Exercise 3-1, Part I: Using Text Files to Store Test Data

In this exercise, you'll start with the results of Exercise 2-2. If you didn't do that exercise, you will find the appropriate files in the DownloadFiles\Chapter3\VB\Exercise3-1\FirstTestStartWithThis folder (or replace the VB with C#). You can open the code for this project by double-clicking on the FirstTest.sln file (in Windows Explorer, this file's type will be listed as "Microsoft Visual Studio Solution"). Or, you can start Visual Studio and use the File ➤ Open menu item to open the project by navigating to this same file.

In Part I of this exercise, you will take this project and change it so that the results of the test, pass or fail, are logged into a text file, rather than reported, using a message box. In Exercise 3-1, Part II, you'll add some code to make this project a little more functional.

Part I: Creating and Writing to the Test Results File

1. Locate and then open the FirstTest.sln file. This will open the project into Visual Studio, and the Visual Studio IDE will display.

2. Open the code window and enter the following code at the very beginning of the Button1 Click event:

VB .NET

```
Dim Writer As StreamWriter
Writer = File.CreateText("TestResults.log")
Writer.WriteLine("Test Results for Test Run XYZ; " & Now)
```

C#

```
StreamWriter Writer;
Writer = File.CreateText("TestResults.log");
Writer.WriteLine("Test Results for Test Run XYZ; " + DateTime.Now);
```

> This code declares an object named Writer of the StreamWriter class. Within that class is a method, CreateText, for creating a text file. We gave it the name TestResults.log that will be its physical name on the disk. Within the code, the file will be referred to as Writer, its logical name. The Writer object has a method called WriteLine that you can use to write to the file. What this code will do when the program runs is create a file and give that file both a physical and logical name. Then it will write a line of text into this file. The line written into the file will include the date and time, which is what the Now function will do. (Don't forget, you can put your cursor on this function, right-click it, and find out more about it by reading its description in the Object Browser. You can also look it up in the Help system, too.)

3. Now find the line that brings up the MessageBox:

```
MessageBox.Show("File Exists: Test passed")
```

> Replace this line with the following line of code:

```
Writer.WriteLine("File Exists: Test Passed")
```

Note These lines are the same for both VB .NET and C#, except you will add a semicolon (;) to the end of the line for C#.

---

4. Replace the second MessageBox line (the one that reports test failure) with a similar line to the one in step 3.

5. Add the following lines of code just before the end of the Button1 Click event:

```
Writer.WriteLine("Test Completed for Test Run XYZ; " & DateTime.Now)
Writer.Close()
```

> (These lines of code are the same for both VB .NET and C# as long as you end the C# line with a semicolon, *and* you must also replace the & with a + for C#.)

> These two lines of code will write a closing line into the file and then close the StreamWriter object. Once the object is closed, you can't write to the file again without reopening the StreamWriter.

> The full code for the Button1 Click event should now look like Listing 3-2.

Listing 3-2. *Code Used in the Button's Click Event*

VB .NET

```
Private Sub Button1_Click _
(ByVal sender As System.Object, ByVal e As System.EventArgs) _
            Handles Button1.Click
```

```vbnet
Dim Writer As StreamWriter
Writer = File.CreateText("TestResults.log")
Writer.WriteLine("Test Results for Test Run XYZ; " _
                & DateTime.Now)

If File.Exists(TextBox1.Text) Then
  Writer.WriteLine("File Exists: Test Passed")
Else
  Writer.WriteLine("File Doesn't Exist: Test Failed")
End If

Writer.WriteLine("Test Completed for Test Run XYZ; " & _
DateTime.Now)
Writer.Close()

End Sub
```

C#

```csharp
private void button1_Click(object sender, EventArgs e)
{
  StreamWriter Writer;
  Writer = File.CreateText("TestResults.log");
  Writer.WriteLine("Test Results for Test Run XYZ; " + DateTime.Now);
  if (File.Exists(textBox1.Text))
  {
    Writer.WriteLine("File Exists: Test Passed");
  }
  else
  {
    Writer.WriteLine("File Doesn't Exist: Test Failed");
  }
  Writer.WriteLine("Test Completed for Test Run XYZ; " + DateTime.Now);
  Writer.Close();
}
```

At this point, the major elements of the code are complete. You have created a file for test results, and you have opened, written to, and closed that file. It's not perfect, though, nor very flexible either as you'll see, so you'll upgrade it a bit in Part II of the exercise. First, let's make sure that the code runs correctly and creates and writes to the file as expected.

6. Build and run your program. Try it out with both valid and invalid data as you did in Exercise 2-2. You will notice that this little test utility you've written doesn't give you any feedback about whether the file you've typed in exists or not. The results are reported into the file; so to find out what happened, you'll have to find the file and open it. (Not a very good test utility is it? Be patient, we'll fix it.)

Where is the `testresults.log` file? We gave it a physical name, `testresults.log`, but we did not specify a path for it, so it will be located in the default path for this application, which is in the application's bin folder. If you followed the instructions at the start of this exercise and used the DownloadFiles\Chapter3\VB\Exercise3-1\FirstTest\ (or replace the VB with C#) application, then you can open that folder and find the bin directory within it, then the Debug directory within that. The `testresults.log` file will be there. So the full location will be DownloadFiles\Chapter3\VB\Exercise3-1\FirstTest\bin\ Debug (or replace the VB with C#). However, hold off—there's an easier way to find it, and you'll do that in the next two steps.

7. Locate the Solution Explorer window in the .NET IDE. Note that it has three buttons in its toolbar. Click the middle button to "Show All Files." Your Solution Explorer window will look like Figure 3-1.

Figure 3-1. *Showing all files in the Solution Explorer window*

8. Expand the bin folder in the Solution Explorer window (using C#, you will also have to expand the Debug folder). Inside this window, you will see the `testresults.log` file listed. Double-click it to open the `testresults.log` file as a tab in the .NET IDE.

The contents will look similar to the following:

```
Test Results for Test Run XYZ; 4/23/2005 7:07:24 PM
File Doesn't Exist: Test Failed
Test Completed for Test Run XYZ; 4/23/2005 7:07:42 PM
```

No matter how many different files you searched for when you ran this utility, this is all that will display. This is because the code creates the text file each time the button is clicked, so it wipes out any results except those results for the last click. There are some other issues with this code as well. For example, it doesn't even say which file it failed to find! We'll fix all of this in Part II of this exercise. You can find the answer for Part I of this exercise in the Download Files folder.

Expanding the File Existence Utility

In Exercise 3-1, Part I, you learned how to use the `StreamWriter` and `StreamReader` to create and write to a text file. The program you wrote was a good beginning for learning the bare-minimum code you need to write to a file. However, as a test utility, it will need some work to make it truly useful. Adding logic to determine when to append to the file versus rewriting the whole file (and also, of course, reading and reporting in a nicer format) will make this utility, and others you might write, easier to work with. Generally, you shouldn't try to create sophisticated user interfaces on test projects because, frankly, there isn't time and it's often not necessary; however, with a little effort, you can make your testware more functional and friendly.

In Exercise 3-1, Part II, you will add code to make a more useful utility out of this little program. You'll add code that will either create or append to the test results file, depending on whether it's the first time the button is clicked or not. You'll also add code to open and read information from the test results file. Then you'll customize this testware a bit by adding some code and modifying properties so that it's easier to use.

Exercise 3-1, Part II: Creating the File Existence Test Utility

Here you'll make the utility for verifying file existence more useful by adding additional code to access files from the System.IO namespace. Start with the code you wrote in Part I (or use the answer to the Part I exercise located within the Download Files folder for this chapter).

1. First, you'll update the interface for this utility. While you're at it, you will also change some other form properties, such as creating an Accept button for the form. (The AcceptButton property is found in the Misc. section in the form's Property window. Note: An Accept button is the default button on the form, so when you press Enter, it will be the same as clicking this button).

   Add a label control and a button control to the form anywhere that you like. Set their properties, and the form's text and AcceptButton properties, according to Table 3-1.

Table 3-1. *Properties to Set for the Form and the Added Button and Label Control*

Object	Property	Value
Form	Text	File Existence Utility
Form	AcceptButton	Button1
Label1	Text	(leave this blank)*
Button2	Text	Show Results

* *When you blank out the Label1 property, the control seems to disappear—don't worry, it's still there!*

   Both the Button2 and Label1 controls will be used to give us feedback. In the label control, we'll write code to display the results of the most recent test for a file's existence. The code in the new button will be used to retrieve our logged test results.

2. Return to the code window and locate the following line in the button1_Click function:

VB .NET

```
Dim Writer as StreamWriter
```

C#

```
StreamWriter Writer;
```

   Add the following code just below the declaration of the Writer variable:

VB .NET

```
Static iCount As Int16 = 1
Dim strCount As String
```

C#

```
string strCount;
Int16 iCount = 1;
```

In the VB .NET code, the first declaration (Static iCount As Int16 = 1) is a Static variable, and that means that it will retain its value the entire time the application runs. (Note: C# does not have Static variables, so in order to make the value of this variable persist between clicks of the button, we will elevate its scope to the class level later on in step 4.) In step 3, we will use the iCount variable as a counter to number the lines in the testresults.log file output. Having a line number in each of your output lines will be handy for discussing specific lines in the file, and will make these lines easier to find and refer to.

You will also use this iCount variable (in step 2) as a switch to determine whether you have already created the file or not within your code. Knowing this will allow you to either create the file brand new or open it for appending once you've already created it, which you will do in the next step.

3. Locate the following lines of code:

```
Writer = File.CreateText("TestResults.log")
Writer.WriteLine("Test Results for Test Run XYZ; " & DateTime.Now)
```

and replace them with the following branching statement:

VB .NET

```
If iCount = 1 Then
    Writer = File.CreateText("TestResults.log")
    Writer.WriteLine("Test Results for Test Run XYZ; " & DateTime.Now)
Else
    Writer = File.AppendText("TestResults.log")
End If

strCount = Convert.ToString(iCount)
```

C#

```
if (iCount == 1)
{
    Writer = File.CreateText("TestResults.log");
    Writer.WriteLine("Test Results for Test Run XYZ; " + DateTime.Now);
}
else
{
    Writer = File.AppendText("TestResults.log");
}
strCount = Convert.ToString(iCount);
```

This If statement will ensure that you get all your test results no matter how many files you check, because it creates a new file the first time and simply appends to the existing file for every additional file you check for.

The last line of code loads the value of your iCount variable into the strCount variable, thereby converting this value into a string. You do this so that you can load the value into a textbox later on in your code without getting a conversion error.

4. Next, you will add code to load the label control. To do this, locate the following code:

VB .NET

```
If File.Exists(TextBox1.Text) Then
  Writer.WriteLine("File Exists: Test Passed")
Else
  Writer.WriteLine("File Doesn't Exist: Test Failed")
End If
```

C#

```
if (File.Exists(textBox1.Text))
{
  Writer.WriteLine("File Exists: Test Passed");
 }
else
{
  Writer.WriteLine("File Doesn't Exist: Test Failed");
}
```

You're going to modify this code to improve the line of code that is written to the file, and to add code to set the value of the label control. Modify this code so that it looks like the code in Listing 3-3.

Listing 3-3. *Modified Code for Checking for File Existence*

VB .NET

```
If File.Exists(TextBox1.Text) Then
  Writer.WriteLine(strCount & " File " & TextBox1.Text & " Exists: Test Passed")
  Label1.Text = "File " & TextBox1.Text & " Exists: Test Passed"
Else
  Writer.WriteLine(strCount & " File " & TextBox1.Text & _
    " doesn't exist: Test Failed")
  Label1.Text = "File " & TextBox1.Text & _
    " doesn't exist: Test Failed"
End If
iCount += 1
```

C#

```
if (File.Exists(textBox1.Text))
{
  Writer.WriteLine(strCount + " File " + textBox1.Text + " Exists:Test Passed");
  label1.Text = "File " + textBox1.Text + " Exists: Test Passed";
}
else
{
  Writer.WriteLine(strCount + " File " + textBox1.Text +
   " doesn't exist: Test Failed");
  label1.Text = "File " + textBox1.Text +
    " doesn't exist: Test Failed";
}
iCount += 1;
```

The first line of this branching statement hasn't changed, but most of the rest of it has. The code still writes to the test results file, but it now includes a line number for each entry that is made into the results file. The code also displays the name of the file whose existence is checked—what a great idea, huh? We've added a line to load the label control with the results, as well. We snuck one additional line in there also, and that is to increment the value of iCount so that each time the button is clicked, iCount will have an incremented value.

5. Locate the following line(s) again and move them outside of the button1 Click event so that it has class level scope:

VB .NET

```
Dim Writer as StreamWriter
```

C#

```
StreamWriter Writer;
Int16 iCount = 1;
```

Extending the scope of this variable (in the case of C#, these *two* variables) to the class level means that it can be used within the button1 Click event and also within any other routine inside this form. You will create another event for the form in the next step, and you will need to access the Writer object from there, so elevating the scope of this variable is necessary.

6. You have one last line to deal with—the line that reports that tests are completed. The way things are working now, the code will end up adding this line into the test results file every time you check a file for existence; i.e., every time the File Exists button is clicked. Really, this line only needs to execute once at the end of the test session. Let's move this line of code so that it only executes once at the end of the test run. First, you need to create the code for the FormClosed event, and then you'll move the line of code there.

To create the code for the FormClosed event, return to the form's Designer window and take a look at the Properties sheet. In the Properties drop-down menu, select the form to view the form's properties. See the lightning bolt at the top of the Properties window (see Figure 3-2)? Click that and then double-click the empty space next to the FormClosed event.

Figure 3-2. *Using the Properties window to get the code shell for the FormClosed event*

This will take you back to the code window and place the shell of the FormClosed event into the code window as well.

Note For VB6 programmers, you can still get the shell for the FormClosed event by clicking the object and procedure drop downs in the VB .NET code window. However, the method we use in step 5 is consistent for both VB .NET and C#.

---

7. Locate the following line:

VB .NET

```
Writer.WriteLine("Test Completed for Test Run XYZ; " & DateTime.Now)
```

C#

```
Writer.WriteLine("Test Completed for Test Run XYZ; " + DateTime.Now);
```

Cut and paste it into the Form1 closed event. Add two more lines of code to this event to open and close the file. The code for this event will look like this:

VB .NET

```
Writer = File.AppendText("Testresults.log")
Writer.WriteLine("Test Completed for Test Run XYZ; " & DateTime.Now)
Writer.Close()
```

C#

```
Writer = File.AppendText("Testresults.log");
Writer.WriteLine("Test Completed for Test Run XYZ; " + DateTime.Now);
Writer.Close();
```

Almost done. To finish the utility, you do have one more thing to do: add the code for the second button. You'll do that in the next step.

8. To add the code for the second button, you can stay in the code window and select button2 from the Objects drop-down list, just as you did for the Form1 closed event. Then select the Click event from the Methods drop-down list.

Add the following code into the button2 Click event (for C#, add a semicolon at the end):

```
System.Diagnostics.Process.Start("Notepad.exe","TestResults.log")
```

Okay, this is cheating. You're not actually reading the file, but instead enlisting the Notepad utility and the Process class within the System.Diagnostics namespace to give you a quick and simple way to open the test results file. Why don't you open the file for reading? This one line of code is simpler and provides a way to start another process within your code. You may find other reasons to use the Process.Start method, for example, to start an application to test. The ability to start multiple process threads running simultaneously is a powerful .NET feature, but you have to be careful—too many running processes can suck up available memory quickly.

Another question to answer is "Why you don't just continue to look at your test results file from within the Visual Studio IDE?" Of course, you could continue to do that, but at some point you will want to distribute your test utilities to others, and you don't want to require users of your utilities to run them from within Visual Studio. This method will allow the user of your application to look at the test results file even after you've deployed it.

The full code will look like Listing 3-4.

Listing 3-4. *Full Code for the File Existence Utility*

VB .NET

```
Imports System.IO

Public Class Form1
    Private Writer As StreamWriter

Private Sub Button1_Click(ByVal sender As System.Object, _
  ByVal e As System.EventArgs) Handles Button1.Click
```

```vbnet
    Static iCount As Int16 = 1
    Dim strCount As String

    If iCount = 1 Then
      Writer = File.CreateText("TestResults.log")
      Writer.WriteLine("Test Results for Test Run XYZ; " & _
        DateTime.Now)
    Else
      Writer = File.AppendText("TestResults.log")
    End If

    strCount = Convert.ToString(iCount)
    If File.Exists(TextBox1.Text) Then
      Writer.WriteLine(strCount & " File " & _
      TextBox1.Text & " Exists: Test Passed")
      Label1.Text = "File " & TextBox1.Text & _
        " Exists: Test Passed"
    Else
      Writer.WriteLine(strCount & " File " & TextBox1.Text & _
        " doesn't exist: Test Failed")
      Label1.Text = "File " & TextBox1.Text & _
        " doesn't exist: Test Failed"
    End If

    iCount += 1
    Writer.Close()

End Sub


Private Sub Form1_FormClosed(ByVal sender As Object, _
  ByVal e As System.Windows.Forms.FormClosedEventArgs) _
  Handles Me.FormClosed
  Writer = File.AppendText("Testresults.log")
  Writer.WriteLine("Test Completed for Test Run XYZ; " & _
  DateTime.Now)
  Writer.Close()
End Sub

Private Sub Button2_Click(ByVal sender As System.Object, _
    ByVal e As System.EventArgs) Handles Button2.Click
  System.Diagnostics.Process.Start("Notepad.exe","TestResults.log")
End Sub

End Class
```

C#

```csharp
#region using directives

using System;
using System.Collections.Generic;
using System.ComponentModel;
using System.Data;
using System.Drawing;
using System.Windows.Forms;
using System.IO;
#endregion

namespace FirstTest
{
  partial class Form1 : Form
  {

    public Form1()
    {
      InitializeComponent();
    }

    StreamWriter Writer;
    Int16 iCount = 1;

    private void button1_Click(object sender, EventArgs e)
    {
      string strCount;
      if (iCount == 1)
      {
        Writer = File.CreateText("TestResults.log");
        Writer.WriteLine("Test Results for Test Run XYZ; "
          + DateTime.Now);
      }
       else
      {
        Writer = File.AppendText("TestResults.log");
      }
        strCount = Convert.ToString(iCount);
        if (File.Exists(textBox1.Text))
        {
        Writer.WriteLine(strCount + " File " + textBox1.Text
          + " Exists: Test Passed");
        label1.Text = "File " + textBox1.Text
          + " Exists: Test Passed";
      }
        else
```

```
    {
      Writer.WriteLine(strCount + " File " + textBox1.Text
        + " doesn't exist: Test Failed");
      label1.Text = "File " + textBox1.Text
        + " doesn't exist: Test Failed";
    }
    iCount += 1;
    Writer.Close();
  }

  private void button2_Click(object sender, EventArgs e)
  {
  System.Diagnostics.Process.Start("Notepad.exe","TestResults.log");

  }

  private void Form1_FormClosed(object sender,
    FormClosedEventArgs e)
  {
    Writer = File.AppendText("Testresults.log");
    Writer.WriteLine("Test Completed for Test Run XYZ; " +
    DateTime.Now);
    Writer.Close();
  }

  }
}
```

9. Build, run, test, debug, and save your new utility. Now you can view the output by clicking the Show Results button (see Figure 3-3).

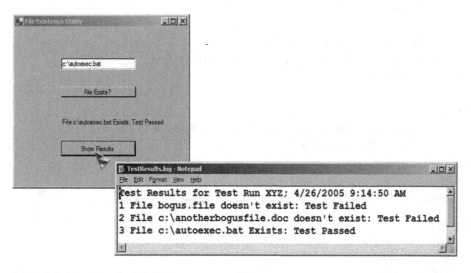

Figure 3-3. *Running the File Existence test utility*

In this exercise, you saw how to create testware that automates the task of checking for a file's existence. The File Existence utility could be even more useful with some upgrades. For example, the System.IO namespace also contains many other useful file access routines, such as methods for copying and moving files, and to find directories. The code could be changed to allow the users to specify the location of the test results file. You could add another textbox to the form to do this and use a variable to refer to the test results file location that they select. These upgrades will be left as an exercise for you to try on your own.

One important thing that you didn't learn how to do in the last two exercises is to read from text files (because you were directed to use the Notepad as your text file reader). Although it was handy here, Notepad won't work for every testing task, and there will definitely be times when you will need to read from a file. In the next section, you'll learn how to open text files for reading.

Reading from Text Files

There are many reasons to read from text files on a test project. It's actually a pretty common chore. Opening a log file and searching for instances of the number of errors found or opening a web page and searching for all the bitmaps or Hrefs it contains, for example, are not infrequent tasks on a test project. (An *Href* in the source code of an HTML document defines a link to another page.) These tasks all require the code to open a text file and read from it; the code will be similar for all of these tasks.

To read from a text file, you'll continue to work with resources from within the System.IO namespace, in this case, the StreamReader object. Consider the code in Listing 3-5.

Listing 3-5. *VB .NET Code for the Text Read Utility*

VB .NET

```vbnet
Dim strFile As String
Dim MyPos As Integer = 1
Dim iCount As Int16 = 0

' Open the stream and read it back.
Dim reader As StreamReader = File.OpenText(txtFile.Text)
strFile = reader.ReadToEnd()

Do
    MyPos = strFile.IndexOf(txtFindString.Text, MyPos + 1)
    If MyPos > 0 Then iCount += 1
Loop Until (MyPos = -1)

lblResult.Text = "Number of times found: iCount = " & iCount
```

C#

```csharp
string strFile;
int MyPos = 1;
Int16 iCount = 0;
```

```
StreamReader reader = File.OpenText(txtFile.Text);
strFile = reader.ReadToEnd();
 do
{
  MyPos = strFile.IndexOf(txtFindString.Text, MyPos + 1);
  if (MyPos > 0)
  {
     iCount += 1;
   }
} while (!(MyPos == -1));
lblResult.Text = "Number of times found: iCount = " + iCount;
```

This code will open a text file for reading, read it all into a String variable, and then search the contents for the value loaded into the text property of a textbox control. So you will be able to use this code to search for anything: an error message, number, bitmap extension, or whatever you need.

Let's examine the code in Listing 3-5 more closely. The code refers to some controls on the form. There are two textboxes (txtFile and txtFindString) and a label control (lblResult) on the form. The user will place the contents of the file to be searched and the string they want to search for, respectively, in these two textboxes. The first three lines of Listing 3-5 declare a string called strFile that will hold the contents of the file; a variable called Pos that will be used to determine the position of the search value; and a variable called iCount that will be used to count how many times the search value is found. Then the StreamReader object is declared:

VB .NET

```
Dim reader As StreamReader = File.OpenText(txtFile.Text)
```

C#

```
StreamReader reader = File.OpenText(txtFile.Text);
```

Here we have immediately initialized this reader object to link to the file entered into the txtFile textbox on the form. In Exercise 3-1 (Parts I and II), you used two lines of code to do a similar declaration for a variable of the StreamWriter class, but it's just as easy to do it in one line. The following line uses the ReadToEnd method of the reader object to read every bit of the text file into a single string:

```
strFile = reader.ReadToEnd()
(Note: for C# you will add a semicolon at the end)
```

A String variable can contain a lot of data, up to two billion unicode characters, so it's going to be big enough for most every log file you'll want to read. The next grouping of code is the loop structure:

VB .NET

```
Do
  MyPos = strFile.IndexOf(txtFindString.Text, MyPos + 1)
  If MyPos > 0 Then iCount += 1
Loop Until (MyPos = -1)
```

C#

```
do
{
  MyPos = strFile.IndexOf(txtFindString.Text, MyPos + 1);
  if (MyPos > 0)
  {
     iCount += 1;
  }
} while (!(MyPos == -1));
```

This do loop uses the IndexOf method. It's a great little method of the String class that will find an instance of one string within another and, if found, return the number of the position of the search string.

```
MyPos = strFile.IndexOf(txtFindString.Text, MyPos + 1)
(Note: for C# you will add a semicolon at the end)
```

The IndexOf function is just one of many String functions provided by the .NET Framework libraries. This method has two arguments. In our code, the first argument is the string that we want to find. It takes a numeric value for which character position to start reading the string. For example, if this argument takes a 1, then it will start reading at the first character. The code uses Pos + 1 as the value for this argument. If you notice, Pos starts out equal to zero, so adding one to it the first time through the loop means the code will start reading at the beginning of the string.

If the IndexOf function finds the text it is searching for within the strFile variable, it will return an integer value in the strPos variable specifying the starting position of where it was found. Then the next time through the loop the code uses the new value of Pos but adds 1 to it so that we don't end up finding the same occurrence of the value over and over. When IndexOf doesn't find any more occurrences of the string, it will return –1, and the code exits the loop. So, we loop until the Pos value becomes –1. (A value of –1 means "false" when it is returned from a method.) Finally, the last line of this utility reports the value of iCount (number of times found) into the lblResult label on the form.

TESTER'S TIP: STRING FUNCTIONS

There is an excellent chance that, no matter how long your career as a test professional develops nor how limited your programming experience, you will eventually work with strings. This is true for developers, as well. There are so many times that data ends up stored in a text format and you end up having to parse a string. So, it's a good idea to get familiar with all the String functions available in the .NET Framework. You can get to them quickly by simply placing your cursor on the IndexOf function in the code window and pressing F1. This will bring up a Help window with information on how to use IndexOf. Click the See Also link and it will take you to more information about strings. Or, you can just search directly in Help under "String Manipulation."

A copy of this utility is located within the Chapter 3 Exercises folder of the Download Files. You can try it out by creating a file in Notepad. Load the Notepad file with a lot of text information, such as the Gettysburg Address, and insert the word "error" somewhere within it several times. Then run the TextReadUtility and type the full pathname to your Notepad file and the word "error" in the second textbox.

While it's imperative to get very familiar with string manipulation functions in any programming language, the .NET Framework contains another namespace that can be extremely useful in working with strings for those who have to do it a lot. This namespace contains resources for using Regular Expressions. You'll learn a little about how to use these in the next section.

Using Regular Expressions to Read from a File

Any discussion of working with strings should include Regular Expressions. Regular Expressions are a powerful way of manipulating text. When you use Regular Expressions, you are actually using another language that has been designed and optimized to work with character data. If you know you will be doing extensive work with strings, it will be worth your while to learn this language. (Yes, Regular Expressions really is a language of its own. It's totally contained within the Framework libraries so it's a "language within a language," which you can call from any of the .NET programming languages, like VB .NET and C#). It can save you lots of time.

Regular Expressions have their own set of classes and other resources within the .NET Framework libraries. While the code in Listing 3-5 is short, simple, and very useful, consider the code in Listing 3-6 that uses Regular Expressions to do a similar task.

Listing 3-6. *Code to Search For and Count Hrefs Using Regular Expressions*

VB .NET

```
Private Sub Button1_Click(ByVal sender As System.Object, _
ByVal e As System.EventArgs) Handles Button1.Click
  Dim r As Regex
  Dim m As Match
  Dim i As Integer

  r = New Regex("href\s*=\s*(?:""(?<1>[^""]*)""|(?<1>\S+))", _
    RegexOptions.IgnoreCase Or RegexOptions.Compiled)

  m = r.Match(TextBox1.Text)
  While m.Success
    i += 1
    ListBox1.Items.Add("Found Href " & m.Value  & " at " & _
          .Index.ToString())
    m = m.NextMatch()
  End While
  label1.text = (i & " Total Href's found")
End Sub
```

C#

```csharp
private void button1_Click(object sender, EventArgs e)
{
  Regex r;
  Match m;
  int i;
  i = 0;
  r = new Regex("href\\s*=\\s*(?:\"(?<1>[^\"]*)\"|(?<1>\\S+))",
                RegexOptions.IgnoreCase | RegexOptions.Compiled);
  m = r.Match(textBox1.Text);
  while (m.Success)
  {
    i += 1;
    listBox1.Items.Add("Found Href " + m.Value +
      " at " + m.Index.ToString());
    m = m.NextMatch();
  }
  label1.Text = (i + " Total Href's found");
}
```

Let's examine this code in detail. First of all, assume that the namespace System.Text. RegularExpressions has been imported at the top of the code (with the Imports statement in VB .NET or the using directive in C#). This namespace is needed so that we can use the Regex and Match classes from within this library. Now, consider the following line:

```
r = New Regex("href\s*=\s*(?:""(?<1>[^""]*)""|(?<1>\S+))", _
    RegexOptions.IgnoreCase Or RegexOptions.Compiled);
```

It looks pretty strange, doesn't it? The variable r has been defined as an object of the Regex class. In this line of code, it is assigned what looks like a bunch of junk, but it's actually a regular expression that defines the format for a web page's Href. We could've found the Hrefs using the previous code from Listing 3-4; however, this code, although more obscure if you aren't familiar with Regular Expressions, does an even better job because it ensures that the Href it finds is in the correct format for an Href. The next line of code compares this format to what is typed into the text property of TextBox1 on the form:

```
m = r.Match(textBox1.Text);
```

The loop structure in the code performs the task of counting how many Hrefs are found using the variable i as the counter variable:

```csharp
while (m.Success)
{
  i += 1;
  listBox1.Items.Add("Found Href " + m.Value + " at "
    + m.Index.ToString());
  m = m.NextMatch();
}
```

Finally, the code reports the results into a label control. If you spend some more time learning about Regular Expressions, you'll learn how to create format strings (like the one used here for Hrefs) for many common search items, for example, e-mail addresses or picture file formats. Additionally, you can use them in your testware to format input into your own applications, which is their intended use!

To learn more about Regular Expressions, there is an excellent book by Dan Appleman available for download. Check Appendix C of this book for specific details.

Working with the Windows Registry on a Test Project

The Windows Registry is a place where you can find a lot of important data about an application and the platform on which it's running—such as data that the application stores when it installs and often even while it's running. Applications frequently store important information such as user options, file locations, license and version information, and, sometimes, even passwords (bad idea) in the Windows Registry. Additionally, the Windows Registry can be a good place to set certain values for your tests, like the date of your last test run and other relevant settings.

Another reason why the Windows Registry is a good place for testers to know about is because the system stores important operating system information here. As you are aware, it is important to know about the test platform (i.e., the system on which you are running your tests). For example, depending on what your test requirements are, you may need to document what drivers are installed, how many CD-ROM drives or printers are installed, and the manufacturers of these devices since this information may have an impact on the frequency and type of defects on the software you are testing. Of course, this all just depends on what you are looking for and what kind of software you are working with. In your test career, you will very likely find that you will need to know about installed hardware devices and drivers—the Windows Registry is the place where you will find this information.

Windows Registry Basics

The Windows Registry is actually a hierarchical database consisting of top-level keys called *hives*. (Named so because of their structural resemblance to beehives. You can really just think of these as folders since they work the same way, essentially, in that they are hierarchical containers.) These Windows Registry hives are composed of keys, subkeys, and value entries. The keys and subkeys are denoted by folder icons and work essentially the same as the folders you see in the Windows Explorer in that they contain other subkeys and values. The first four hives are the following:

- HKEY_CLASSES_ROOT

- HKEY_CURRENT_USER

- HKEY_LOCAL_MACHINE

- HKEY_USERS

These four keys are always considered open. (*HKEY*, by the way, stands for Hive Key, so we can refer to these as hives or keys interchangeably.) An open key means that applications may add their own keys and data to these main hives. To see this structure, you can take a look at the Windows Registry by using the RegEdit utility provided with every Windows operating system.

To launch the RegEdit utility, click the Start button on your Windows start bar and then click Run. Type **regedit** into the Run dialog and click OK. The Windows RegEdit utility displays, as shown in Figure 3-4.

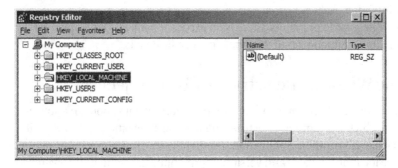

Figure 3-4. *The Windows RegEdit utility*

If you double-click on one of the hives in the RegEdit utility, you will see that it will expand to include keys for all kinds of useful information and also a bunch of things that, at least at first, probably won't make a lot of sense. However, the information stored here is very relevant to the innumerable software applications and hardware installed on your computer. Checking values using the Registry Editor is very useful in itself, but it can be cumbersome and tedious to check it manually. It's good to know that you can easily write code to do so automatically, as you'll see in the next section.

Accessing the Windows Registry Programmatically

Luckily, the Windows Registry is very simple to access in .NET compared to what you had to do in VB6 or C++. With those languages, you used to have to make a call to the Windows Application Programmer's Interface (API), and the code was long and usually fairly complex. In .NET, the calls to the Windows Registry have been simplified because all of the routines and resources needed to access it are now located within the .NET Framework libraries in the Microsoft.Win32 namespace. You can make your code even simpler by adding this namespace to your code files using the Imports statement (VB .NET) or the using directive (C#). Once that is done, the few lines of code in Listing 3-7 are all that you will need to retrieve a value from a Windows Registry key.

Listing 3-7. *Retrieving a Value from the Windows Registry*

VB .NET

```
Dim line As String
Dim strMyKey As String = "control panel\international\"
Dim aKey As RegistryKey
aKey = Registry.CurrentUser.OpenSubKey(strMyKey)
Console.WriteLine("Value of the international key setting is: " + _
            aKey.GetValue("sCountry"))
Console.WriteLine("Press any key to quit")
line = Console.ReadLine
```

C#

```
string line;  /* dummy line for reading the response */
string strMyKey = "control panel\\international\\";
RegistryKey aKey;
aKey = Registry.CurrentUser.OpenSubKey(strMyKey);
Console.WriteLine("Value of the international key setting is: " +
            aKey.GetValue("sCountry"));
Console.WriteLine("Press any key to quit");
line = Console.ReadLine();
```

This code retrieves the Country setting from the registry subkey HKEY\Current User\ control panel\international. To use this code to retrieve any Windows Registry setting, all you need to do is change the key specification in the OpenSubKey() method to identify the one that you want to retrieve. In this case, you use a Console application; however, of course, the Registry can be accessed with any type of .NET application.

In general, testers will usually end up reading Registry entries more often than actually writing to the Registry. However, occasionally, you may want to use the Registry yourself on test projects to store options or settings for your testware. Luckily, writing to the Registry is also pretty easy. Listing 3-8 shows how to create your own test project subkey and write values. Again, this code presumes that the Microsoft.Win32 namespace has been added with Imports or using.

IMPORTS AND USING STATEMENTS: WHAT DO THEY DO?

The Imports (VB .NET) and using (C#) statements are merely statements that point the code to the correct location in the .NET Framework libraries. The Imports statement is misleading because it implies that code is being brought in, but it's really not. It's already there since you have the .NET Framework libraries available to you. In fact, it just keeps you from having to type the full location of an item from the libraries in your code. For example, it's cumbersome to have to type the following line:

```
Dim TestProject as System.Microsoft.Win32.RegistryKey
```

when you could just use the Imports or using statement at the top and then type

```
Dim TestProject as RegistryKey
```

Of course, this makes the most sense when you use many different items from that library. It simply saves a lot of typing!

Listing 3-8. *Creating a Subkey and Writing Registry Values*

VB .NET

```
Dim TestProject As RegistryKey = _
            Registry.CurrentUser.CreateSubKey("TestProject2005")
TestProject.SetValue("Test Date", DateTime.Now)
```

```
TestProject.SetValue("Level", "Priority 2")
TestProject.SetValue("ID", 123)
TestProject.Close()
```

C#

```
RegistryKey TestProject =
                Registry.CurrentUser.CreateSubKey("TestProject2005");
TestProject.SetValue("Test Date", DateTime.Now);
TestProject.SetValue("Level", "Priority 2");
TestProject.SetValue("ID", 123);
TestProject.Close();
```

The first line of this code creates an object of the RegistryKey class, called TestProject, and then sets its value to TestProject2005. This will create a subkey under the CurrentUser key. The next three lines create three registry settings by providing the name of the setting and its initial value. These are just examples of the kind of data that you might want to store in the Registry. Notice that it's not a large volume of test result information, but simply values that let the system "remember" values and options between test runs. Finally, the last line of code closes the key.

In Exercise 3-2, you'll combine the code to create and read Windows Registry settings into a utility.

Exercise 3-2: Using the Console to Create a Windows Registry Utility

In this exercise, you'll work with a template to finish a utility that's partially created for you. You'll have an opportunity to work with some of the classes and methods available to you in the Microsoft.Win32 namespace for working with the Windows Registry.

Caution This exercise creates a utility that will modify the Windows Registry. To avoid corrupting the Registry, do not attempt to delete any keys other than the ones created in this exercise. Corrupting your Windows Registry may compromise the functionality of some of your applications. Proceed with caution!

Caution This code does not contain any error handling. Be careful to enter values exactly as described, including case sensitivity! You will see detail on how error handling can be added to testware in Chapter 4.

---

1. Locate the Chapter 3 Exercises folder and open the Exercise 3-2 folder. Within this folder, you'll find a folder named RegistryUtilityTemplate. Double-click on this folder and then double-click on the solution file (.sln) to open the template project. Continue with the steps in this exercise to finish this project.

2. Examine the existing code and try to determine what it is doing without changing anything. You will see how the current code works in these next few steps, and then you'll add functionality in following steps.

3. Test the existing working code by pressing F5 or clicking the Start button on the main menu. (Be careful not to select the option to delete any Registry keys at this point!) The menu appears in a Console window (see Figure 3-5).

```
Console                                                                      ▣
Enter 1 to Create a new key                                                  ▲
Enter 2 to add a setting to a key
Enter 3 to delete a key
Enter 4 to delete a setting
Enter 5 to retrieve a setting value
Enter 6 to report all subkeys under a key
Enter 9 to quit
1
Enter 1 to Create a new key
Enter 2 to add a setting to a key
Enter 3 to delete a key
Enter 4 to delete a setting
Enter 5 to retrieve a setting value
Enter 6 to report all subkeys under a key                                    ▼
```

Figure 3-5. *Running existing code from the RegistryUtilityTemplate application*

If you enter the number 3 or 6 in response to the menu and then press Enter, nothing will happen and the same menu will print again. (Figure 3-5 shows what happens when you type in the number 1.) This is because these options are not coded yet. Go ahead and try entering these two numbers. Before we write more, let's try adding and retrieving a Registry value.

4. Enter the number **1** and press Enter. You are prompted to enter the name of a key. Enter **Testkey** and press Enter. This will create a new subkey under the Current_User registry key. (To verify this, you can open the RegEdit utility. To remind yourself how to do this, see the "Windows Registry Basics" section in this chapter.) The menu displays again. Next, you will add a setting to your new key.

5. Enter the number 2 in response to the menu and press Enter. You are now prompted to "Enter the key." Enter the key you just created, **Testkey**, and press Enter. You are now prompted to enter the setting. Enter **TestDate** and press Enter once again. Finally, you are prompted to enter the value. Enter today's date in any format you like and press Enter. Now you have added a setting under the Testkey registry key. To verify this, once again you can look it up in the RegEdit utility (you may have to refresh to see the new addition), but you will also see it by retrieving it with your own utility in the next step.

6. Enter 5 in response to the menu in order to retrieve a setting. You will be prompted to "Enter the key" again. Enter **Testkey** and press Enter. Now you are prompted to enter the setting name, so enter TestDate and press Enter. The application will print a line similar to the following (depending on the date and format you entered):

Value of HKEY_CURRENT_USER\Testkey\TestDate is: 1/1/2006

7. Now you can use the menu item for deleting a setting for the entry you have just added yourself. (Be careful not to delete any other settings in the Registry!) In response to the menu, select 4 to delete a setting. In response to the prompt to enter the key, type **Testkey** and press Enter. Then enter **TestDate** for the setting. You will be asked if you really mean to delete this value. If you're sure you typed the correct registry key and setting (i.e., the ones you just created in this exercise), then go ahead and enter **YES**. You will be advised that the setting has been deleted. Verify this by looking in the RegEdit utility. (You have deleted the setting but the key is still there. You'll write the code to delete the key in following steps.)

8. Exit the utility by selecting **9** from the menu choices. Next, you will add some lines of code to finish the utility by completing the code for menu options 3 and 6.

9. Open the code window for Module 1 and locate the following comment:

```
Enter code here for menu option 3
```

After this statement, enter the following code:

VB .NET

```
Dim strKey, strAns As String
Console.WriteLine("Enter the key under HKEY_CURRENT_USER to delete")
strKey = Console.ReadLine()
Console.WriteLine("Do you really mean to delete: " & strKey & _
            " and its settings?")
strAns = Console.ReadLine()
If strAns.ToUpper = "YES" Or strAns.ToUpper = "Y" Then
    Registry.CurrentUser.DeleteSubKeyTree(strKey)
    Console.WriteLine("Key " & strKey & " deleted")
Else
    Console.WriteLine("No deletion performed")
End If
```

C#

```
string strKey;
string strAns;
Console.WriteLine("Enter the key under HKEY_CURRENT_USER to delete");
strKey = Console.ReadLine();
Console.WriteLine("Do you really mean to delete: " + strKey +
            " and its settings?");
strAns = Console.ReadLine();
strAns = strAns.ToUpper();
if (strAns == "YES" | strAns == "Y")
{
    Registry.CurrentUser.DeleteSubKeyTree(strKey);
    Console.WriteLine("Key " + strKey + " deleted");
}
else
{
    Console.WriteLine("No deletion performed");
}
```

This first line of this code creates two String variables (for C#, it's the first two lines). The first variable, strKey, will be used to hold the value of the key you want to delete. The second variable, strAns, will be used to verify if the user really does want to delete the key. Once verified, the following line of code does all the real work:

```
Registry.CurrentUser.DeleteSubKeyTree(strKey)
```

This line of code will delete an entire registry key plus all subkeys and settings underneath it. It's a powerful command, that's why we've written code to ask the user to verify that the correct key has been selected. Note, however, that this code never verifies that the key actually exists, so if you type in a key that doesn't exist, you will get a runtime error exception. This won't hurt your Registry or your system if the key truly does not exist. Error handling will be covered in Chapter 4.

10. Test this new code by executing the program and selecting menu option 3. Be sure to enter **Testkey** as the key to delete! Verify that the key has been deleted by looking for it in RegEdit.

11. Finally, you'll add the code to list all subkeys underneath a registry key. This code can be very useful for determining installed printers and other devices. Stop the program and return to the code window. Locate the following comment in the code for Module 1:

```
Enter code here for menu option 6
```

After this line, enter the following code:

VB .NET

```
Dim strKey As String
Dim cHive As Char
Console.WriteLine("Select the hive you want to start with: ")
Console.WriteLine( _
    "Enter 'L' for HKEY_LOCAL_MACHINE or 'C' for HKEY_CURRENT_USER")
cHive = Console.ReadLine()
Console.WriteLine("Enter the key")
strKey = Console.ReadLine()
If UCase(cHive) = "L" Then
    TestProject = Registry.LocalMachine.OpenSubKey(strKey)
    Console.WriteLine("HKEY_LOCAL_MACHINE selected")
Else
    TestProject = Registry.CurrentUser.OpenSubKey(strKey)
    Console.WriteLine("HKEY_CURRENT_USER selected")
End If
For Each subKeyName As String In TestProject.GetSubKeyNames()
    Console.WriteLine(subKeyName)
Next
TestProject.Close()
```

C#

```
string strKey;
string strHive;
Console.WriteLine("Select the hive you want to start with: ");
Console.WriteLine(
    "Enter 'L' for HKEY_LOCAL_MACHINE or 'C' for HKEY_CURRENT_USER");
strHive = Console.ReadLine();
Console.WriteLine("Enter the key");
strKey = Console.ReadLine();
if (strHive == "L" | strHive == "l")
{
```

```
    TestProject = Registry.LocalMachine.OpenSubKey(strKey);
    Console.WriteLine("HKEY_LOCAL_MACHINE selected");
 }
else
{
    TestProject = Registry.CurrentUser.OpenSubKey(strKey);
    Console.WriteLine("HKEY_CURRENT_USER selected");
}
foreach (string subKeyName in TestProject.GetSubKeyNames())
{
    Console.WriteLine(subKeyName);
}
TestProject.Close();
```

The first few lines after the declarations prompt the user to determine which hive in the Registry the user wants to work with. For simplicity, we limit it to two important keys: HKEY_LOCAL_MACHINE and HKEY_CURRENT_USER. However, you could add the code to include the other hives as well.

In this code, all the real work is being done using a function, GetSubKeyNames, that returns an array of strings. This array of strings contains all of the subkeys under the given key. The code uses a loop structure to iterate through all of these SubKey names and then prints them to the Console.

12. Test this new option by executing the code again. Choose menu item 6 and press **L** when prompted. You're going to go into the HKEY_LOCAL_MACHINE hive to retrieve the names of the installed printers. When prompted to enter the key, enter the following string *on one line*:

```
SYSTEM\CurrentControlSet\Hardware Profiles
\Current\System\CurrentControlSet\Control\Print\Printers
```

Figure 3-6 shows the session.

```
Console                                                                                    ⊠
Enter 1 to Create a new key                                                                ▲
Enter 2 to add a setting to a key
Enter 3 to delete a key
Enter 4 to delete a setting
Enter 5 to retrieve a setting value
Enter 6 to report all subkeys under a key
Enter 9 to quit
6
Select the hive you want to start with:
Enter 'L' for HKEY_LOCAL_MACHINE or 'C' for HKEY_CURRENT_USER
l
Enter the key
SYSTEM\CurrentControlSet\Hardware Profiles\Current\System\CurrentControlSet\Control\Print\Printers
HKEY_LOCAL_MACHINE selected
EPSON Stylus C42 Series
hp officejet 5500 series                                                                   ▼
```

Figure 3-6. *Running existing code from the RegistryUtilityTemplate application*

The printers installed on your machine will be listed. As you can see in Figure 3-6, we have an Epson Stylus and an HP officejet installed on our machine.

13. Save your work. The full code for the Registry utility is shown in Listing 3-9. You can also find the answer to this exercise in the Chapter 3 Download Files folder, inside the Demo Code folder. Within the Demo Code folder, the solution is in the folder titled RegistryUtility.

Listing 3-9. *Full Code for the Registry Utility*

VB .NET

```vbnet
Imports Microsoft.Win32
Module Module1

Sub Main()

  Dim iEntry As Byte
' Create a subkey named TestProject under HKEY_CURRENT_USER.
  Do While iEntry <> 9
    Console.WriteLine("Enter 1 to Create a new key")
    Console.WriteLine("Enter 2 to add a setting to a key")
    Console.WriteLine("Enter 3 to delete a key")
    Console.WriteLine("Enter 4 to delete a setting")
    Console.WriteLine("Enter 5 to retrieve a setting value")
    Console.WriteLine("Enter 6 to report all subkeys under a key")
    Console.WriteLine("Enter 9 to quit")
    iEntry = Console.ReadLine()
    Dim TestProject As RegistryKey
    Select Case iEntry
      Case 1
        Dim strNewKey As String
        Console.WriteLine("Enter Name of Subkey to create.")
        Console.WriteLine _
          ("(This will create a key under HKEY_CURRENT_USER)")
        strNewKey = Console.ReadLine()
        TestProject = Registry.CurrentUser.CreateSubKey(strNewKey)
      Case 2
        Dim strKey, strSetting, strValue As String
        Console.WriteLine("Enter the key")
        strKey = Console.ReadLine()
        TestProject = Registry.CurrentUser.OpenSubKey(strKey, True)
        Console.WriteLine("Enter the setting")
        strSetting = Console.ReadLine()
        Console.WriteLine("Enter the value")
        strValue = Console.ReadLine
        TestProject.SetValue(strSetting, strValue)
      Case 3
        Dim strKey, strAns As String
        Console.WriteLine _
          ("Enter the key under HKEY_CURRENT_USER to delete")
        strKey = Console.ReadLine()
        Console.WriteLine("Do you really mean to delete: " & _
          strKey & " and all settings within this key?")
        strAns = Console.ReadLine()
        If strAns.ToUpper = "YES" Or strAns.ToUpper = "Y" Then
```

```vb
        Registry.CurrentUser.DeleteSubKeyTree(strKey)
        Console.WriteLine("Key " & strKey & " deleted")
      Else
        Console.WriteLine("No deletion performed")
      End If
    Case 4
      Dim strKey, strSetting, strAns As String
      Console.WriteLine("Enter the key")
      strKey = Console.ReadLine()
      TestProject = Registry.CurrentUser.OpenSubKey(strKey, True)
      Console.WriteLine("Enter the setting")
      strSetting = Console.ReadLine()
      Console.WriteLine("Do you really mean to delete: " & _
        strKey & "\" & strSetting & "?")
      strAns = Console.ReadLine()
      If strAns.ToUpper = "YES" Or strAns.ToUpper = "Y" Then
        TestProject.DeleteValue(strSetting)
        Console.WriteLine("Key setting " & _
            strKey & "\" & strSetting & " deleted")
     Else
        Console.WriteLine("No deletion performed; key closed")
        TestProject.Close()
      End If
    Case 5
      Dim strKey, strSetting As String
      Console.WriteLine("Enter the key")
      strKey = Console.ReadLine()
      TestProject = Registry.CurrentUser.OpenSubKey(strKey)
      Console.WriteLine("Enter the setting")
      strSetting = Console.ReadLine()
      Console.WriteLine("Value of " & TestProject.ToString & "\" & _
          strSetting & " is: " & _
            TestProject.GetValue(strSetting).ToString)
    Case 6
      Dim strKey As String
      Dim cHive As Char
      Console.WriteLine("Select the hive you want to start with: ")
      Console.WriteLine _
  ("Enter 'L' for HKEY_LOCAL_MACHINE or 'C' for HKEY_CURRENT_USER")
      cHive = Console.ReadLine()
      Console.WriteLine("Enter the key")
      strKey = Console.ReadLine()
```

```
            If UCase(cHive) = "L" Then
              TestProject = Registry.LocalMachine.OpenSubKey(strKey)
              Console.WriteLine("HKEY_LOCAL_MACHINE selected")
            Else
              TestProject = Registry.CurrentUser.OpenSubKey(strKey)
              Console.WriteLine("HKEY_CURRENT_USER selected")
            End If
            For Each subKeyName As String In TestProject.GetSubKeyNames()
              Console.WriteLine(subKeyName)
            Next
            TestProject.Close()

        Case 9
          Console.WriteLine("Good bye!")
        Case Else
          Console.WriteLine _
            ("Invalid Entry; please enter 1-5 (or 9 to quit)")
      End Select
    Loop
```

C#

```
#region using directives

using System;
using System.Collections.Generic;
using System.Text;
using Microsoft.Win32;

#endregion

namespace RegistryUtility
{
  class Program
  {
    static void Main(string[] args)
    {
      byte iEntry = 0;
      while (iEntry != 9)
      {
        Console.WriteLine();
        Console.WriteLine("Enter 1 to Create a new key");
        Console.WriteLine("Enter 2 to add a setting to a key");
        Console.WriteLine("Enter 3 to delete a key");
        Console.WriteLine("Enter 4 to delete a setting");
        Console.WriteLine("Enter 5 to retrieve a setting value");
        Console.WriteLine(
          "Enter 6 to report all subkeys under a key");
```

```csharp
      Console.WriteLine("Enter 9 to quit");
      iEntry = Convert.ToByte(Console.ReadLine());

      RegistryKey TestProject;
      if (iEntry == 1)
      {
        string strNewKey;
        Console.WriteLine(
          "Enter Name of Subkey to create.");
        Console.WriteLine(
         "(This will create a key under HKEY_CURRENT_USER)");
        strNewKey = Console.ReadLine();
        TestProject = Registry.CurrentUser.CreateSubKey(strNewKey);
      }
      else if (iEntry == 2)
      {
        string strKey;
        string strSetting;
        string strValue;
        Console.WriteLine("Enter the key");
        strKey = Console.ReadLine();
        TestProject = Registry.CurrentUser.OpenSubKey(strKey, true);
        Console.WriteLine("Enter the setting");
        strSetting = Console.ReadLine();
        Console.WriteLine("Enter the value");
        strValue = Console.ReadLine();
        TestProject.SetValue(strSetting, strValue);
      }
      else if (iEntry == 3)
      {
        string strKey;
        string strAns;
        Console.WriteLine(
          "Enter the key under HKEY_CURRENT_USER to delete");
        strKey = Console.ReadLine();
        Console.WriteLine("Do you really mean to delete: " +
          strKey + " and its settings?");
        strAns = Console.ReadLine();
        strAns = strAns.ToUpper();
        if (strAns == "YES" | strAns == "Y")
        {
          Registry.CurrentUser.DeleteSubKeyTree(strKey);
          Console.WriteLine("Key " + strKey + " deleted");
        }
```

```csharp
      else
      {
        Console.WriteLine("No deletion performed");
      }
  }
  else if (iEntry == 4)
  {
    string strKey;
    string strSetting;
    string strAns;
    Console.WriteLine("Enter the key");
    strKey = Console.ReadLine();
    TestProject = Registry.CurrentUser.OpenSubKey(strKey, true);
    Console.WriteLine("Enter the setting");
    strSetting = Console.ReadLine();
    Console.WriteLine("Do you really mean to delete: " +
                                  strKey + "\\" + strSetting + "?");
    strAns = Console.ReadLine();
    strAns = strAns.ToUpper();

    if (strAns == "Y" | strAns == "YES")
    {
      TestProject.DeleteValue(strSetting);
      Console.WriteLine("Key setting " + strKey +
        "\\" + strSetting + " deleted");
    }
    else
    {
      Console.WriteLine("No deletion performed; key closed");
      TestProject.Close();
    }
  }
  else if (iEntry == 5)
  {
    string strKey;
    string strSetting;
    Console.WriteLine("Enter the key");
    strKey = Console.ReadLine();
    TestProject = Registry.CurrentUser.OpenSubKey(strKey);
    Console.WriteLine("Enter the setting");
    strSetting = Console.ReadLine();
    Console.WriteLine("Value of " +
        strKey + "\\" + strSetting + " is: " );
    Console.WriteLine(
    Convert.ToString(TestProject.GetValue(strSetting)));
  }
```

```
            else if (iEntry == 6)
            {
              string strKey;
              string strHive;
              Console.WriteLine(
                "Select the hive you want to start with: ");
              Console.WriteLine(
              "Enter 'L' for HKEY_LOCAL_MACHINE or 'C' for HKEY_CURRENT_USER");
              strHive = Console.ReadLine();
              Console.WriteLine("Enter the key");
              strKey = Console.ReadLine();
              if (strHive == "L" | strHive == "l")
              {
                TestProject = Registry.LocalMachine.OpenSubKey(strKey);
                Console.WriteLine("HKEY_LOCAL_MACHINE selected");
              }
              else
              {
                TestProject = Registry.CurrentUser.OpenSubKey(strKey);
                Console.WriteLine("HKEY_CURRENT_USER selected");
              }
              foreach (string subKeyName in TestProject.GetSubKeyNames())
              {
                Console.WriteLine(subKeyName);
              }
              TestProject.Close();
            }
            else if (iEntry == 9)
            {
              Console.WriteLine("Good bye!");
            }
            else
            {
              Console.WriteLine(
                "Invalid Entry; please enter 1-5 (or 9 to quit)");
            }
        }
      }
    }
}
```

In the exercise, you saw how to read and write to the Windows Registry. This Registry utility can be improved not only with error handling, but also with additional routines provided for working with the Registry, such as retrieving settings underneath a key. The basic structure is all there, though, so you can add to and customize this utility to be useful for your own purposes.

Working with Database Files on a Test Project

Now you've seen two different ways to store test information: writing to text files and the Registry. Let's take stock so far. As we mentioned earlier, the Registry is not really a good place to store test results, but it's good for storing test options and other settings. A text file can store test results and anything else you want, so it's a good option to use for many things. There may be times when you'll want more structure in your test results files. By default, there isn't any structure to a text file, like a specific number of fields, unless you write a lot of code to impose this structure yourself. If you need structure, you may want to consider using a database for your test results.

Databases can be an excellent way of storing test result information in a structured format. They also provide a way to store data that is flexible. Databases are a more sophisticated way to store data than simply using text files. The trade-off is that the opening, closing, reading, and writing are a bit more complex than working with text files. The payoff is big though! You will get the power of a professional Database Management System (DBMS) to organize and store your test data. This can be very beneficial for use in a long-term or large test project, not only because it's easier to manage, but also because it's easier to create and store reports using a database. For small projects, the trade-off may not be worth it because DBMSs can be expensive and they take up a lot of room. However, if you can use an inexpensive database program, like Microsoft Access, or the application you're testing is already using a database, then this can make it a viable option for any size test project.

There are a lot of other reasons that may lead you to work with databases on a test project. For one, DBMSs are the way most data is stored in any significant application. DBMSs include Microsoft's SQL Server, IBM's DB2, Oracle's Oracle database, Sybase's SQL Server, and a host of others. If you work on a project that uses a DBMS, and it's pretty hard these days to find one that doesn't, then you may end up needing to test the application's interface to this database. So learning the principals of how an application opens and connects to a database can be very important. Important enough that we go into much greater detail on this subject in Chapter 8.

Still, in this section, we'll streamline our work with databases to focus solely on opening, writing test results into, and then closing a database file. To keep things simple, we'll use Microsoft Access, but the code we use will apply to most any database.

Database Access Basics

To work with a database, you will need access to another important namespace within the .NET Framework libraries: the System.Data namespace. The classes and methods found in this namespace provide the means to connect to any ODBC (Open Database Connectivity)–compatible database (see the "ODBC and OLE DB" sidebar), which includes pretty much any database you'd need or want to work with. The .NET Framework provides resources for data access in the ADO.NET library. To write to a Microsoft Access database, you'll need only two classes from the ADO.NET library: the Connection class and the Command class. The Connection class will provide methods for connecting to and opening the database. The Command class will provide you with an object to use for sending SQL (Structured Query Language) commands to the database [see the "SQL (Structured Query Language)" sidebar].

ODBC AND OLE DB

The official definition of ODBC from the MSDN (Microsoft Developer's Network) Library is

A standard set of programming language interface routines used to connect to a variety of data sources.

Before ODBC, programmers had to use data access languages specific to each database in order to write code to access them. If you were accessing data in just a single database, then that was fine, but with the need to access many different kinds of data in many different kinds of data stores—such as spreadsheets, or flat files, as well as data stored in larger systems such as Oracle, SQL Server, Informix, and DB2 databases—it became very complex to try to write code to effectively access them all in a single software application. Why not come up with a standard way to open, access, and close a database? So, ODBC was born and this library of routines was created. ODBC basically revolutionized and, more importantly, standardized the ability to access multiple kinds of data. The companies that make databases, such as Oracle and Microsoft, provide "drivers" or code modules that access their software in a predefined, standard way. This makes life easier for the programmer writing code to manipulate data.

OLE DB happens to be an additional standardized programming language interface. It's a similar notion to ODBC. OLE DB goes further than ODBC to allow access to even non–Windows databases, such as Unix data stores and legacy databases. Any database that is ODBC–compliant, and most all of them are, can also be accessed using OLE DB; thus, when we import the OLE DB namespace from the .NET Framework, we are able to work with ODBC databases. We will revisit this when we tackle database testing in Chapter 8.

SQL (STRUCTURED QUERY LANGUAGE)

SQL is the ANSI (American National Standards Institute) standard language for retrieving and manipulating data in a relational database. Unlike VB .NET and C#, SQL is not a full programming language. ANSI SQL deals with data access only, including commands to create, retrieve, update, and delete rows of data in data tables. If you will be working with databases on a test project in any capacity, you would be well advised to establish a good base of knowledge in this important language. If you are not sure whether you will be working with databases much in your testing career, keep in mind that virtually all software applications use and store data in some type of database. In Chapter 8, we will present some SQL statements that are practical for testing purposes. However, you will want to increase your knowledge with further training. One good link where you can find free online training is `www.sqlcourse.com`.

As usual, you'll first take a look at the minimum commands needed to do a simple task, in this case, writing a line of code into an existing database. For this example, presume that you already have a Microsoft Access database called `TestResultsDB.mdb` with a table for holding test results named `TestResults`. The code in Listing 3-10 shows the code to write one row into the `TestResults` table.

■Note To try the examples in this section, you will need to have Microsoft Access installed.

Listing 3-10. *Writing Test Results to a Microsoft Access Database*

VB .NET

```
'Make sure to add Imports System.Data.OleDb at the top of the code page
Dim cn As New OleDbConnection _
    ("Provider=Microsoft.jet.oledb.4.0;Data Source=TestResultsDB.mdb")
Dim iRet As Integer
cn.Open()
Dim cmd As New OleDbCommand( _
  "Insert into TestResults (TestID, TestDate, Reqmt, Tester, Result) " & _
  "Values (3, '01-Jan-2006', 'Test Reqmt ABC', 'M. Sweeney', 1)", cn)
iRet = cmd.ExecuteNonQuery
cn.Close()
```

C#

```
//Make sure to add using System.Data.OleDb at the top of the code page
OleDbConnection cn = new OleDbConnection(
  "Provider=Microsoft.jet.oledb.4.0;Data Source=TestResultsDB.mdb");
int iRet;
cn.Open();
OleDbCommand cmd = new OleDbCommand(
  "Insert into TestResults (TestID, TestDate, Reqmt, Tester, Result) " +
  "Values (3, '01-Jan-2006', 'Test Reqmt ABC', 'M. Sweeney', 1)", cn);
iRet = cmd.ExecuteNonQuery();
cn.Close();
```

Let's examine this code. The first line imports or uses the System.Data.OleDb namespace. This OleDb namespace contains code for ODBC database access, and the System.Data.SQLClient namespace contains resources for accessing Microsoft's SQL Server database. Since you want to use Microsoft Access, you must use the general library, which is located in the System.Data.OleDb namespace. The next line creates a Connection object and points it to the TestResultsDB.mdb database. (The TestResultsDB database is a sample Access database that we've created for this book and have included in the code for this chapter. You will use it in Exercise 3-3.) In this example, the database resides in the bin folder of the application; otherwise, you could need a full pathname to the database location.

After the integer variable declaration, the following command actually opens the connection:

```
cn.Open();
```

Once the database is opened successfully, the next few lines of Listing 3-10, repeated here, comprise a single statement that will create a Command object and set it up so that when the Command object is executed, it will send a SQL Insert statement to the TestResults table within the database:

VB .NET

```
Dim cmd As New OleDbCommand( _
   "Insert into TestResults (TestID, TestDate, Reqmt, Tester, Result) " & _
   "Values (3, '01-Jan-2006', 'Test Reqmt ABC', 'M. Sweeney', 1)", cn)
```

C#

```
OleDbCommand cmd = new OleDbCommand(
   "Insert into TestResults (TestID, TestDate, Reqmt, Tester, Result) " +
   "Values (3, '01-Jan-2006', 'Test Reqmt ABC', 'M. Sweeney', 1)", cn);
```

Finally, in the last line of Listing 3-10, repeated here, the ExecuteNonQuery() method of the Command object is called to actually execute the command against the database:

VB .NET

```
iRet = cmd.ExecuteNonQuery
```

C#

```
iRet = cmd.ExecuteNonQuery;
```

Now that you know the basics of creating and using the Connection and Command objects, you're ready to start exploring how to incorporate database access into your automated tests.

Reporting Test Results to a Database

The SQL Insert statement used in Listing 3-10 inserts into a specially created table called TestResults. The TestResults table in the TestResultsDB database has a number of fields useful for reporting test information. You can modify this table within Microsoft Access, to add or remove columns, as desired (note that you will need to have Microsoft Access installed to make changes).

Table 3-2 lists the fields in the TestResults table with explanations for their intended use.

Table 3-2. *Fields in the TestResults Table (TestResultsDB Sample Database)*

Field	Data Type	Explanation
TestID	Integer	A unique number so that every test result can be identified individually.
TestDate	Date	Date this entry is added.
Reqmt	Text	Requirements identifier so this test result can be traced back to test requirements.
Tester	Text	Name of the tester running the test that entered this record.

Table 3-2. *Fields in the TestResults Table (TestResultsDB Sample Database) (Continued)*

Field	Data Type	Explanation
TestNumber	Integer	This number represents the test run. Many test IDs could be linked to one TestNumber.
BuildNumber	Integer	This number represents the particular build of the software release.
Result	Boolean	Pass or Fail of this test. "0" will be stored if the test fails and "1" if the test passes.
Comments	Text	Any additional comments desired for this particular test result.

Notice that in the code in Listing 3-10, our Insert statement inserts into only five columns of the table: TestID, TestDate, Reqmt, Tester, and Result. It may not be necessary to use every column every time, but you should be consistent across all tests.

Note The code in Listing 3-10 is contained in the Chapter 3 Exercise folder. This demo application is called DatabaseAccess.

Listing 3-10 shows inserting a single record into the table with values that are literally typed into the statement (this is sometimes referred to as *hard coded*). Of course, it will be more useful to create a routine where you can customize the Insert statement so that you can fill in whatever values are needed as you go. The code in Listing 3-11 shows a subroutine that you can create and call that has parameters for the columns in the TestResults table.

Listing 3-11. *A Subroutine for Customizing TestResults Values*

VB .NET

```
Sub TestLog(ByVal tid As Integer, ByVal testdate As Date, _
    ByVal reqmt As String, _
    ByVal Tester As String, ByVal result As Boolean)
  Dim cnTestResults As New OleDbConnection( _
    "Provider=Microsoft.jet.oledb.4.0;Data Source=TestResultsDB.mdb")
  Dim iRet As Integer
  cnTestResults.Open()
  Dim cmd As New OleDbCommand( _
    "Insert into TestResults (TestID, TestDate, Reqmt, Tester, Result)  Values (" & _
            tid & ", '" & testdate & "', '" & reqmt & "', '" & _
            Tester & "', " & result & ")", cnTestResults)
  iRet = cmd.ExecuteNonQuery
  cnTestResults.Close()
End Sub
```

C#

```
void TestLog(int tid, System.DateTime testdate,
    string reqmt, string Tester, bool result)
{
  OleDbConnection cnTestResults = new OleDbConnection(
    "Provider=Microsoft.jet.oledb.4.0;Data Source=TestResultsDB.mdb");
  int iRet;
  cnTestResults.Open();
  OleDbCommand cmd = new OleDbCommand(
  "Insert into TestResults (TestID, TestDate, Reqmt, Tester, Result) Values (" +
              tid + ", '" + testdate + "', '" +
              reqmt + "', '" + Tester + "', " + result + ")", cnTestResults);
  iRet = cmd.ExecuteNonQuery();
  cnTestResults.Close();
}
```

This is the first time you've created your own subroutine in this book. Subroutines provide a way to reuse code, rather than retype, or copy and paste, the same statements over and over. You can type it in once and then call it multiple times.

Notice that the methods to create, open, and close the connection are contained within this subroutine. That means that each time you write a test result, you'll be opening and closing the connection, which creates extra IO. It also means that if the system breaks while you're running your test, you'll have less chance of a corrupted test results file since you'll have closed it immediately after writing to it. The Insert statement in this code has been modified to include the parameters that will be provided for the subroutine by catenating the values into the command. Although this makes the command look a little more obscure, when the code executes this Insert statement, it will be essentially the same as the one you used in Listing 3-10. It's just customized so that it's able to insert any values you choose when you call the routine. You'll put this routine to good use in the next exercise.

Exercise 3-3 shows you how to open a Microsoft Access database, execute and test a stored query (called a View in database terminology) in the database, and then store test results in a database table with a subroutine.

Exercise 3-3: Writing Test Results to a Database

In this exercise, you'll perform some simple database-focused testing using a Microsoft Access database. You'll be testing a query on the database to ensure that it's returning the correct number of rows. This is similar to a project we participated in where the object of the tests was to ensure the proper functioning of critical queries. Some of these tests include ensuring correct rowcount. You'll simulate that here in this exercise.

■**Note** It's not necessary to have Microsoft Access installed to accomplish this exercise.

1. Launch Visual Studio .NET and open the DatabaseTest1Template solution from within the Chapter3\ VB\Exercise3-3\DatabaseTest1Template folder (or replace the VB with C#).

   This template does not have any prewritten code, but does contain the Microsoft Access database, TestResultsDB.mdb, that you will access for this exercise. To see this database file, open the Solution Explorer window and select the All Files button. If you have Microsoft Access installed, you can double-click on this file and Microsoft Access will launch and you can view the two tables, Customers and TestResults, within this database. (Note that although it's *not* necessary for you to have Microsoft Access installed to perform this exercise, it *is* required if you want to open the database and view it by double-clicking it. You do not need to view it.)

2. Add a button control to the form in any location you like. Change the form properties and button properties according to Table 3-3.

Table 3-3. *Properties to Set for the Form and the Button on the DatabaseTest1 Project*

Object	Property	Value
Button1	Text	Run Test
Form	Text	Database1 Test bed
Form	AcceptButton	Button1
Form	Name	frmTestBed

3. Now open the code window for the form by right-clicking on the form in the Windows Designer. Import the System.Data.OleDb namespace into the code by typing the following line at the top of your code window (in the usual location):

VB .NET

```
Imports System.Data.OleDb
```

C#

```
using System.Data.OleDb;
```

If you get a squiggly line underneath VB .NET's Imports statement, this means you will have to set a reference to this library in your code. At this writing, the VB .NET Beta Express edition does not reference the System.Data library while the C# Beta Express does, and so do all languages within Visual Studio 2005. So do the following *ONLY* if you get the squiggly line or have problems getting to this library:

   a. Select Project ➤ Add Reference from the main menu. The Add Reference dialog box will display.

   b. In the .NET tab, scroll down in the Components list box until you find the System.Data line. Click this line to select it.

   c. Click OK to dismiss the dialog box. You have now set a reference to the correct library.

4. Now type in the code in Listing 3-11 to create a new subroutine. To make sure you type it in the correct spot, place it in the same location as can be seen in Listing 3-12.

Listing 3-12. *Creating a TestLog Subroutine*

VB .NET

```
Public Class frmTestBed

  Sub TestLog(ByVal tid As Integer, _
    ByVal testdate As Date, ByVal reqmt As String, _
    ByVal Tester As String, ByVal result As Boolean)
    Dim cnTestResults As New OleDbConnection( _
    "Provider=Microsoft.jet.oledb.4.0;Data Source=TestResultsDB.mdb")
    Dim iRet As Integer
    cnTestResults.Open()
    Dim cmd As New OleDbCommand( _
    "Insert into TestResults (TestID, TestDate, Reqmt, Tester, Result) " & _
      "Values ("  & tid & ", '" & testdate & "', '" & _
        reqmt & "', '" & Tester & "', " & result & ")", _
      cnTestResults)
    iRet = cmd.ExecuteNonQuery
    cnTestResults.Close()
  End Sub

End Class
```

C#

```
namespace DatabaseTest1
{
  partial class frmTestBed : Form
  {
    void TestLog(int tid, System.DateTime testdate,
     string reqmt, string Tester, bool result)
    {
      OleDbConnection cnTestResults =
          new OleDbConnection(
          "Provider=Microsoft.jet.oledb.4.0;Data Source=TestResultsDB.mdb");
DatabaseTest1;
      int iRet;
      cnTestResults.Open();
      OleDbCommand cmd = new OleDbCommand(
          "Insert into TestResults (TestID, TestDate, Reqmt, Tester, Result) " +
          "Values (" + tid + ", '" + testdate + "', '" + reqmt + "', '" +
          Tester + "', " + result + ")", cnTestResults);
      iRet = cmd.ExecuteNonQuery();
      cnTestResults.Close();
    }
```

```
  public frmTestBed()
  {
   InitializeComponent();
  }
 }
}
```

At this point, you can build your project to check your syntax, but of course, nothing will happen if you run the program and click the button because you need to include a call to this subroutine in order for it to execute. You'll do that in step 5 by adding code to the button's Click event.

5. Return to the Designer window and double-click on the button control to add an event handler for the button's Click event. Add the following code to the button's Click event:

VB .NET

```
Dim cn As New OleDbConnection( _
      "Provider=Microsoft.jet.oledb.4.0;Data Source=TestResultsDB.mdb")
Dim iRet1, iret2 As Integer
cn.Open()
Dim cmd As New OleDbCommand("select count(*) from contactList", cn)
iRet1 = cmd.ExecuteScalar
cmd.CommandText = "select count(*) from customers"
iret2 = cmd.ExecuteScalar
```

C#

```
OleDbConnection cn = new OleDbConnection(
     "Provider=Microsoft.jet.oledb.4.0;Data Source=TestResultsDB.mdb");
int iRet1;
int iret2;
cn.Open();
OleDbCommand cmd = new OleDbCommand(
   "select count(*) from contactList", cn);
iRet1 = Convert.ToInt16(cmd.ExecuteScalar());
cmd.CommandText = "select count(*) from customers";
iret2 = Convert.ToInt16(cmd.ExecuteScalar());
```

The first code statement creates the Connection object that you'll use to send statements to the database. Notice that it's a separate connection from the one you use in the subroutine to log the test results. It is possible to have many connections to the same database and connections to other databases open at the same time. While you could accomplish this whole thing with one connection, it keeps things easier to manage and clearer to have two in this case. This is a strategy that is up to you as the coder though. Fewer connections may sometimes be optimal.

The next line of code declares two integer variables, and the next line opens the connection. After that, the following two lines, shown again here, create and execute a SQL statement that will be sent to the database. Don't retype these lines, we just want you to focus on them:

VB .NET

```
Dim cmd As New OleDbCommand("select count(*) from contactList", cn)
iRet1 = cmd.ExecuteScalar
```

C#

```
OleDbCommand cmd = new OleDbCommand("select count(*) from contactList", cn);
iRet1 = Convert.ToInt16(cmd.ExecuteScalar());
```

This particular SQL statement "select count(*) from contactList" will execute the database view called "ContactList" and return how many rows are returned by that query. Note that ContactList is not a table in the database, but Access allows you to return the rows in a query this way. Then, the next line of code calls the ExecuteScalar method of the Command object. It is this statement that actually runs the query against the database. The return value of this function will give you the number of rows returned by the ContactList query. (Note that in the C# example, you have to convert it to an integer using the Convert object.) Finally, the last two lines of code in this segment do the same for the customers table and return its number of rows.

The intent of this code is to count the rows returned from the query and rows in the table. In the next code segment, you'll compare these values to see if they're the same. Let's say that the expected result is that they *will* be the same; i.e., that the query and the table will have the same rowcount. This means the test will pass if they are the same and fail if they are not.

6. Add the following code just under the code from step 5:

VB .NET

```
If iRet1 = iret2 Then
  TestLog(100, DateTime.Now, "XYZ122", "Sweeney, M.", True)
  MessageBox.Show("Test pass reported to database")
Else
  TestLog(100, DateTime.Now, "XYZ122", "Sweeney, M.", False)
  MessageBox.Show("Test failure reported to database")
End If
cn.Close()
```

C#

```
if (iRet1 == iret2)
{
  TestLog(100, DateTime.Now, "XYZ122", "Sweeney, M.", true);
  MessageBox.Show("Test pass reported to database");
}
else
{
  TestLog(100, DateTime.Now, "XYZ122", "Sweeney, M.", false);
  MessageBox.Show("Test failure reported to database");
}
cn.Close();
```

Since `iRet1` returns the number of rows returned from the query and `iret2` returns the number of rows that are in the table, the code compares these two values to see if they are the same. Next, the code calls the `TestLog` subroutine, which will report the test results, pass or fail, to the `TestResults` table in the database. Then, just to make the application a little more user-friendly, we also return the pass/fail information back to the user in a `MessageBox`.

In the last line of this code segment, you close the connection using the `Close` method of the `Connection` object.

The full code for the finished exercise should look like Listing 3-13.

Listing 3-13. *Full Code for Exercise 3-3*

VB .NET

```
Imports System.Data.OleDb
Public Class frmTestBed

  Sub TestLog(ByVal tid As Integer, ByVal testdate As Date, _
      ByVal reqmt As String, _
      ByVal Tester As String, ByVal result As Boolean)
    Dim cnTestResults As New OleDbConnection( _
      "Provider=Microsoft.jet.oledb.4.0;Data Source=TestResultsDB.mdb")
    Dim iRet As Integer
    cnTestResults.Open()
    Dim cmd As New OleDbCommand( _
        "Insert into TestResults (TestID, TestDate, Reqmt, Tester, Result) " _
        "Values (" & tid & ", '" & testdate & "', '" & reqmt & _
        "', '" & Tester & "', " & result & ")", cnTestResults)
    iRet = cmd.ExecuteNonQuery
    cnTestResults.Close()
End Sub


Private Sub Button1_Click(ByVal sender As System.Object, _
    ByVal e As System.EventArgs) Handles Button1.Click
  Dim cn As New OleDbConnection( _
    "Provider=Microsoft.jet.oledb.4.0;Data Source=TestResultsDB.mdb")
  Dim iRet1, iret2 As Integer
  cn.Open()
  Dim cmd As New OleDbCommand("select count(*) from contactList", cn)
  iRet1 = cmd.ExecuteScalar
  cmd.CommandText = "select count(*) from customers"
  iret2 = cmd.ExecuteScalar

  If iRet1 = iret2 Then
    TestLog(100, Now, "XYZ122", "Sweeney, M.", True)
    MessageBox.Show("Test pass reported to database")
```

```
    Else
      TestLog(100, Now, "XYZ122", "Sweeney, M.", False)
      MessageBox.Show("Test failure reported to database")
    End If
    cn.Close()
End Sub

End Class
```

C#

```
#region using directives

using System;
using System.Collections.Generic;
using System.ComponentModel;
using System.Data;
using System.Drawing;
using System.Windows.Forms;
using System.Data.OleDb;

#endregion

namespace DatabaseTest1
{
partial class frmTestBed : Form
{
  void TestLog(int tid, System.DateTime testdate,
      string reqmt, string Tester, bool result)
  {
    OleDbConnection cnTestResults = new OleDbConnection(
      "Provider=Microsoft.jet.oledb.4.0;Data Source=TestResultsDB.mdb");
    int iRet;
    cnTestResults.Open();
    OleDbCommand cmd = new OleDbCommand( _
      "Insert into TestResults (TestID, TestDate, Reqmt, Tester, Result) " +
      "Values (" + tid + ", '" + testdate + "', '" + reqmt +
           "', '" + Tester + "', " + result + ")", cnTestResults);
    iRet = cmd.ExecuteNonQuery();
    cnTestResults.Close();
  }
  public frmTestBed()
  {
    InitializeComponent();
  }
  private void button1_Click(object sender, EventArgs e)
  {
    OleDbConnection cn = new OleDbConnection(
```

```
      "Provider=Microsoft.jet.oledb.4.0;Data Source=TestResultsDB.mdb");
int iRet1;
int iret2;
cn.Open();
OleDbCommand cmd = new OleDbCommand(
      "select count(*) from contactList", cn);
iRet1 = Convert.ToInt16(cmd.ExecuteScalar());
cmd.CommandText = "select count(*) from customers";
iret2 = Convert.ToInt16(cmd.ExecuteScalar());
if (iRet1 == iret2)
{
  TestLog(100, DateTime.Now, "XYZ122", "Sweeney, M.", true);
  MessageBox.Show("Test pass reported to database");
}
else
{
  TestLog(100, DateTime.Now, "XYZ122", "Sweeney, M.", false);
  MessageBox.Show("Test failure reported to database");
}
cn.Close();

  }
    }
}
```

This exercise showed how to open, write to, and close a database. If you try to execute the same code twice, you will get an error unless you change the value of the TestID column from 100 to something else. The TestID must be a unique value. To improve this code, you can change the value of TestID to be a variable value that you increment each time the routine is called. Also, this code could be greatly improved by adding error trapping and handling, which we'll cover in Chapter 4.

Summary

In this chapter, you looked at three different ways to store test data: text files, the Windows Registry, and a Microsoft Access database. When you compare these options for working with data, you can conclude that on a test project you should do the following:

- Use text files for quick reporting of unformatted test results. This is a situation where you simply want to know "Did the test pass or fail?".

- Use the Windows Registry to read and write options and settings for your own tests, but not to store test results.

- Use a database to store test results that need to be structured and formalized into more sophisticated reports.

Along the way, you found that there are other reasons to work with all three of these data storage options on our test projects:

- Text files can often be produced by the application under test, and you may need to open them and read the contents to determine the application's ability to correctly manipulate these files.

- The Windows Registry stores a lot of useful system information that you may need to investigate.

- Databases store a lot of application data, and, at some point, you will very likely need to test the application's ability to correctly interface with its database component.

You also had an opportunity to write code to work with strings, both the intrinsic String functions from the String class and also Regular Expressions, a language good for more sophisticated string handling.

Now that you're armed with the information to work with data files, you're ready to engage in more extensive testing projects in .NET. First, one more important task you'll need to address is error and exception handling in .NET—for both your own testware and the applications you test. Chapter 4 will take you there.

Tester's Checklist

On a test project,

☑ Use the Windows Registry to set options and settings for your automated test runs.

☑ Use text files for reporting test results quickly.

☑ Use database files for reporting test information that requires structure.

On the application you are testing,

☑ All data into and out of the application should be investigated and verified.

☑ Check the application's effects on the Registry.

☑ Check the application's effects on the file system and investigate the files with which it interfaces.

☑ Check the application's interface with any and all databases (see Chapter 8 for more information).

CHAPTER 4

■ ■ ■

An Overview of .NET Error Handling

Programs today are becoming more complex than ever. These include the ones you are asked to test and the test utilities you will soon write. As your knowledge progresses, you will find that better tools are required to help write these complex applications. One important tool is a good debugger.

While Microsoft has included debuggers with all previous versions of Visual Studio, each version seems to get better and better. In this chapter, you will look at how to use the Visual Studio .NET (VS .NET) Debugger to help you write and test your programs.

Note The process for error handling is significantly changed from Visual Basic 6.0 to Visual Basic .NET. The new error handling capabilities in .NET bring it inline with modern programming languages. The old OnError-GoTo method that was used in Visual Basic 6.0 is still available for backward compatibility; however, it's not recommended.

Objectives

By the end of this chapter, you will be able to

- Define the difference between syntax, runtime, and logic errors

- Explain how to use and modify breakpoints

- Explain how to use the debugging windows

- Explain how Try-Catch blocks work

- Explain what the Exception class is

- Create code to Throw Exception errors

- Use Debug and Trace to get debugging information

Syntax, Runtime, and Logic Errors

Errors that occur in a program are often called *exceptions*. Exceptions can be broken down into three basic categories: syntax, runtime, and logic errors. The syntax exceptions are the most commonly created and easiest to fix of these three. Let's take a quick look at some things you need to know about syntax errors before you look at the other two.

Working with Syntax Errors

Syntax exceptions are the errors you make when you type in a keyword incorrectly or you forget to use a symbol (like a parenthesis):

```
MessageBox.Show TextBox1.Text 'Wrong
MessageBox.Show = TextBox1.Text 'Wrong
MessageBox.Show (TextBox1.Text) 'Right
```

These can be easily fixed if you know the correct way they should have been typed. However, if you're not sure about what the code should look like, they can be a real pain. VS .NET lets you know when you have made a syntax error by underlining the code causing the error. It also gives you information about the error when you hover over it with your mouse cursor. In addition, Visual Studio 2005 now includes an Error List window (errors were shown in the Task List window before this). You can open this new window by going to the menu at the top of Visual Studio and choosing View ➤ Error List. Although having your errors pointed out is helpful, sometimes the error messages you receive are not—unless you already know some of the terms used by Microsoft's developers.

For example, here is a simple error message that is easy to understand. The errors shown in Figure 4-1 indicate that a parenthesis is missing. It also tells you that the statement has not been ended yet.

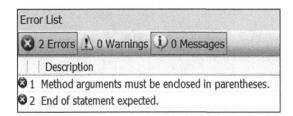

Figure 4-1. *A simple error message*

Fixing this exception is just a matter of adding the missing parenthesis to complete the statement, at which time both of these errors will disappear from the Error List. Now let's look at a more cryptic error message, as shown in Figure 4-2.

This message makes sense if you already know what an "overloaded method" is, but it is much less helpful if you don't have a clue, or you cannot quite remember what that means. In those cases, you need to translate the message into individual terms to see if you can figure out what it is trying to tell you.

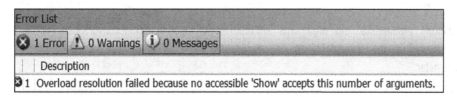

Figure 4-2. *A more complex error*

Starting with the first term "overloaded," an *overloaded method* is where you create two or more methods (*method* is a generic term for a function or subroutine) with the exact same name, but each has its own unique set of parameters. You can think of this as having just one method of that name, but with multiple versions of the way it works. Here is an example:

VB .NET

```
Public Function RunTest() As String
 'Put some code here to do something
End Function
Public Function RunTest(ByVal Parm1 As String) As String
 'Put some code here to do something
 'this time using Parameter 1
End Function
```

C#

```
public string RunTest()
  {
    //Put some code here to do something
  }

public string RunTest(string Parm1)
  {
    //Put some code here to do something
    //this time using Parameter 1
  }
```

In this code, the RunTest() function now has two versions of itself: one that has no parameters and the other with one parameter. This is commonly referred to in *object-oriented programming* (OOP) terms as "overloading the method" (we will take a closer look at these terms later in the book, specifically in Chapter 6). In .NET, Microsoft uses this same design choice in many places. For example, when you start typing out **MessageBox.Show**(), a ToolTip pops up in the code window and explains that there are 21 versions, or overloads, of the Show() method and what parameters they use (see Figure 4-3).

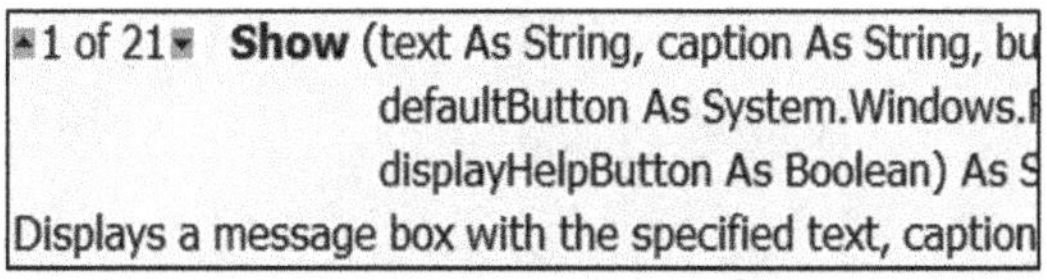

```
▲1 of 21▼  Show (text As String, caption As String, bu
                 defaultButton As System.Windows.
                 displayHelpButton As Boolean) As S
Displays a message box with the specified text, caption
```

Figure 4-3. *ToolTip showing 21 versions of MessageBox.Show()*

■**Note** The terms "parameters" and "arguments" are often interchanged in normal conversation. For the sake of clarity, we will use the formal definition of an *argument* as being the actual value passed into the method's *parameter*.

Whenever you create a method with parameters, you need to pass in arguments to use them. So, in order to call the version of RunTest() with one parameter, you would write code like this:

VB .NET

```
RunTest(5)
'Or maybe like this:
Dim x as int16 = 5
RunTest(x)
```

C#

```
RunTest(5);
//Or maybe like this:
int16 x = 5;
RunTest(x);
```

In the first sample, the 5 is the argument that will be passed into the Parm1 parameter defined earlier. In the second example, x is used as the argument it and would be passed into Parm1. In either case, they are the values that we wish to pass over to a method for processing. Now look at that error in the Error List window again (see Figure 4-2); Table 4-1 breaks it down for you.

Table 4-1. *A Translation of the Error Message*

Term	Translation
Overload	Many versions of the function.
resolution failed	Could not find a matching one.
because no accessible	There may be a hidden one, but you cannot get to that version from here.
'Show'	The name of the method.
accepts this number of arguments.	The number of arguments it thinks you are trying to pass into the method.

As you can see, errors like these can be tricky to read if you are not familiar with the terms used, but can make perfect sense if you know the basic concepts of OOP. As we said, you will look at these concepts in more detail in Chapter 6.

Working with Runtime Errors

Runtime errors are the ones that happen as the program, well, runs. When the code was typed out, and then later compiled, everything looked fine. It was only when the program was running that a problem occurred. While syntax errors are usually caught by developers (this would be you when you are building you own testing application), runtime errors sometimes slip past them. As a tester, you no doubt find ways of breaking what the developer thought was working. Seeing how the application will respond to invalid data and unusual responses is vital to good testing.

One classic example of a runtime error is where you divide a number by zero and the computer does not know how to handle it. The code may look something like this:

VB .NET

```
Dim Mileage, Distance, Gallons As Decimal
'Add code to set these values from the UI
Mileage = Distance / Gallons
```

C#

```
Decimal Mileage, Distance, Gallons
//Add code to set these values from the UI
Mileage = Distance / Gallons
```

Of course, when the developer tested the code with correct values, it would have worked fine. The Divide by Zero error only shows up if a 0 value is entered into the Gallons variable. A good tester will find an error like this pretty quickly using common testing techniques.

Although testers do not always have access to the code directly, you do you have more options. For example, when you are White Box testing and can see the code, you can use the Visual Studio debugging tools to locate the real problem and give a more detailed description in your bug reports. If you are developing your own testware, then you can fix these types of errors by finding the boundaries of invalid responses and providing an appropriate error message to the user.

Working with Logic Errors

With logic errors, you test the application and never see an error message or disruptive behavior. However, you may find that the data being returned, or the process being completed, is invalid. Traditionally, these can be the hardest problems for a tester to track down. Even the developer that wrote the code can be puzzled when it does not work as intended. Once again, if you have access to the code, the debugging tools in Visual Studio can be very handy for these types of errors. You can set *breakpoints*, and then step through the code line-by-line evaluating the expressions and variables to determine where the problem lies.

Note Before you begin debugging, you need to make sure that the application you are working with is being built in Debug mode—not Release mode. If you are using a version of Visual Studio other than Express, you can change between Release and Debug modes by using the drop-down menu at the top of the Visual Studio Development window. When the program is built in Release mode, it will not be able to access all of the debugging items. The .NET compiler removes many of these debugging features to speed up the execution of the program. If you are using a Visual Studio Express edition, you are already in Debug mode, as it is the only mode it comes with.

Working with Breakpoints

Even if you have never tested with the debugger in Visual Studio, you will find it easy to use. To get started, you need to have your application enter Break mode while it is running. *Break mode* is when the application pauses running temporarily and lets you examine what is occurring in the program at that time. There are a number of ways you can have the program break, but let's focus on the most common one: setting a breakpoint.

With a project open and the Code Editor window displayed, you can set a breakpoint by clicking in the left-hand margin of that window. You will know you have it set when a red dot appears. In Figure 4-4, we have set the breakpoint on line 11, which is the beginning of a method called GetAnswer(). You can only set breakpoints on executable lines of code. For example, if you try to set a breakpoint on line 12 where there is no code, Visual Studio .NET will just ignore you.

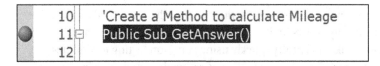

Figure 4-4. *Setting a breakpoint*

As long as you begin running the program in Debug mode, it will pause when it comes to any line with a breakpoint. With the program paused in Break mode, you can hover over variables and expressions to see what values they evaluate into at this point in the program. As you advance the program through the other lines of code, you can watch as the program values change. In Figure 4-5, you can see that the value of Distance is 100 (the "D" indicates that it is a decimal value). Notice the arrow on the far left; this indicates the line that the program is currently about to process. The program will not actually process this code until you move the arrow off of it and onto the next line. So, if you were to hover over the Mileage variable right now, you would see the value that was set earlier in the code. It is only when you move to the next line of code that the program will divide Distance by Gallons and fill Mileage with its new value.

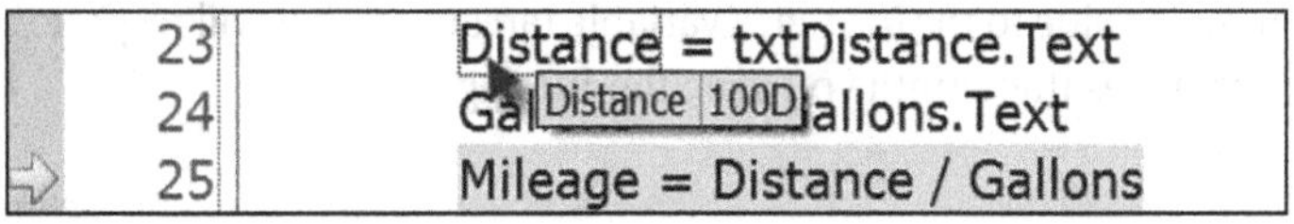

```
23   Distance = txtDistance.Text
24   Ga Distance 100D allons.Text
25   Mileage = Distance / Gallons
```

Figure 4-5. *Looking at the current value*

To advance the program line-by-line, you can use the Debug toolbar. Most of the time, you will see it once you enter Break mode, but you can also display it by selecting View ➤ Toolbars and then clicking on Debug.

This toolbar allows you to process the code line-by-line, skip over sections of code you have already looked at, and open other windows related to debugging. In Figure 4-6, the three most frequently used options are circled: Step Into (left), Step Over (middle), and Step Out (right).

Figure 4-6. *The Debug toolbar*

Step Into

Step Into is the button you will use most often, since it advances to the next line being executed each time you press it. You can press F8 on the keyboard (using the default setting) to do the same thing, or use the Debug menu at the top of VS .NET as well. If you open that menu, you will see the other toolbar options listed too, but let's use the toolbar as in our examples.

One thing that confuses first-time programmers is that Step Into skips over some lines of code. For example, if you have the following lines of code (see Figure 4-7) . . .

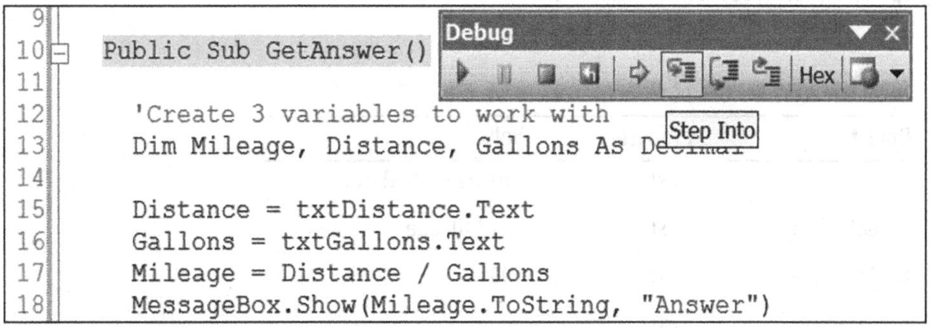

```
 9
10 ⊟  Public Sub GetAnswer()
11
12      'Create 3 variables to work with
13      Dim Mileage, Distance, Gallons As Decimal
14
15      Distance = txtDistance.Text
16      Gallons = txtGallons.Text
17      Mileage = Distance / Gallons
18      MessageBox.Show(Mileage.ToString, "Answer")
```

Figure 4-7. *Stepping into code*

. . . and you had stopped on line 10, then clicking Step Into would advance to line 15—not to line 12 or 13. Step Into always skips over blank lines, variable declarations, and comments. These neutral lines of code are always skipped, while the debugger pauses on all active lines of code. Line 15 is an instruction to set a value to the Distance variable (an action that will respond to a breakpoint), so the program pauses there until you use Step Into again.

Step Over

Similar to the Step Into button, when you click the Step Over button, it will advance to the next line of code. The big difference is that if the next line to run is a call to a method, then it will not jump to the other method. Instead, will "step over" the line with the method call and continue to the next line afterward. Oh, .NET will still run the code that was in the called method, it will just not show you each line being processed within it. This is convenient when you are working with methods that you have already debugged and you do not wish to go though all of the code again.

Step Out

Sometimes you will continue to click the Step Into button and find that you have entered into a method that you have already tested. In essence, you forgot to click Step Over and now you want to "step out" of that method being processed. When this happens, just click the Step Out button to exit this method. As always, .NET will continue running all the code in the method, but you won't have to watch as it does. Your program will, once again, pause on the next line after the method was called. Let's see how these options work in Exercise 4-1.

Exercise 4-1: Using the Debugger

As you have seen, the debugger is an important tool for testers. Let's take a look at some of the debugger's options.

1. Create a new Windows application called MileageCalculator. On Form1, add two textboxes, two labels, and one button. Then, change the names of each and set their properties, as shown in Table 4-2, to end up with the result, as shown in Figure 4-8.

Table 4-2. *Properties to Set*

Object	Property	Value
Form1	Text	MileageCalculator
btnGetMileage	Text	Get Mileage
txtDistance	Text	100
txtGallons	Text	10
lblDistance	Text	Distance
lblGallons	Text	Gallons

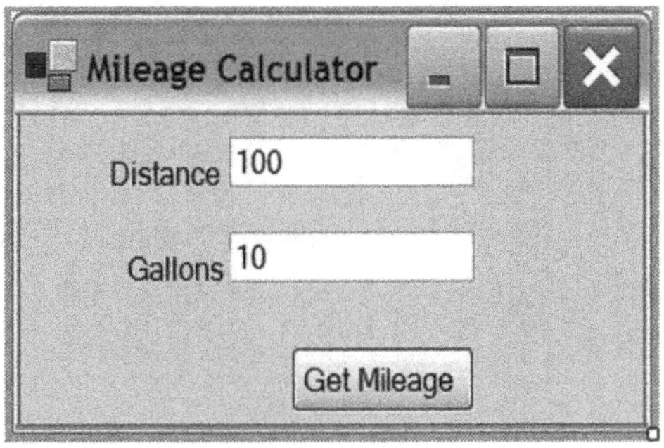

Figure 4-8. *Form1*

2. Double-click the button to create an event procedure for the btnGetMileage_Click event, and fill in the missing code (see Listing 4-1) to complete the Form1 class.

Listing 4-1. *Code Used in Form1*

VB .NET

```
Public Class Form1

Private Sub btnGetMileage_Click _
  (ByVal sender As System.Object, ByVal e As System.EventArgs) _
  Handles btnGetMileage.Click

  'Call the GetAnswer Method
  GetAnswer()
  MessageBox.Show("Done")

End Sub

'Create a Method to calculate Mileage
Public Sub GetAnswer()

  'Create three variables to work with
  Dim Mileage, Distance, Gallons As Decimal
  'Add code to set these values from the UI
  Distance = txtDistance.Text
  Gallons = txtGallons.Text
  Mileage = Distance / Gallons
  MessageBox.Show(Mileage.ToString,"Answer")

End Sub

End Class
```

C#

```csharp
#region using directives

using System;
using System.Collections.Generic;
using System.ComponentModel;
using System.Data;
using System.Drawing;
using System.Windows.Forms;

#endregion

namespace MileageCalculator
{
partial class Form1 : Form
{
  public Form1()
  {
    InitializeComponent();
  }

  private void btnGetMileage_Click(object sender, EventArgs e)
  {
    GetAnswer();
    MessageBox.Show("Done");
  }

  //Create a Method to calculate Mileage
  public void  GetAnswer()
  {
    //Create three variables to work with
    Decimal Mileage, Distance, Gallons;
    //Add code to set these values from the UI
    Distance = Convert.ToDecimal(txtDistance.Text);
    Gallons = Convert.ToDecimal(txtGallons.Text);
    Mileage = Distance / Gallons;

    MessageBox.Show(Mileage.ToString(), "Answer");
  }
} //End of Class
}//End of Namespace
```

3. Set a breakpoint on the btnGetMileage_Click() method, then run the program.

4. Using 100 in txtMiles and 10 in txtGallons, click btnGetMileage and step through the code line-by-line using the Step Into button. Notice that when GetAnswer() is called, the program jumps to that method.

■**Note** You may notice that, right now, you do not have any error handling code, so just use the values noted in step 4. You will try other values that will cause errors and then see options to handle these problems later in this chapter.

5. Hover over the variables and read the ToolTip that pops up. Notice that the values will not change until you leave the line of code that changes the values—not while you are on that line.

6. Continue stepping into the lines of code until you see the GetAnswer() method end and the program jump back to the line after the GetAnswer() method call.

7. Close any message box that pops up, and click the btnGetMileage button again.

8. This time click the Step Over button on the Debug toolbar. You will still see the message box with the answer, but you will not pause on each line in the GetAnswer() method.

9. Close any message box that pops up and click btnGetMileage once again. This time use Step Into until you get to the line where the Distance variable is set to values of the txtDistance.Text. Now use Step Out to stop pausing on each line of the GetAnswer() method. The program jumps back to the line after the GetAnswer() method call.

10. Stop the application—but don't close the project yet, you have more to do!

In this exercise, you created a simple application and tested it using breakpoints and the Debug toolbar. As you can see, each of the buttons of the toolbar is useful. When combined with breakpoints, they provide an easy way to pause and examine your code while you run an application.

The Debugging Windows

The Debug toolbar also provides a number of debugging windows (see Figure 4-9). Microsoft also calls these the "Variable Windows" in some of their documentation. Some of these you will use more than others, but let's take a look some common ones and what they do.

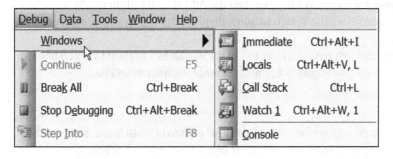

Figure 4-9. *The debugging windows*

The Locals Window

This window shows information about all the values that are "in scope." For example, before you enter into a method, like GetAnswer() from Exercise 4-1, you would not see the variables inside that method, like Distance, Gallons, or Mileage. Once you enter the method, they would all show up in the Locals window automatically (see Figure 4-10). Like many other debugging windows, this window also allows you to change the values. The Locals window also has a line that says "Me" in VB .NET (in C#, you will see the word "this"). This line refers to the Form1 object. Since this object is "in scope," it shows up in the Locals window. You can expand its "tree" of information by clicking on the plus sign next to it; however, most of the time it is more information than you need—and so, by default, the tree is collapsed.

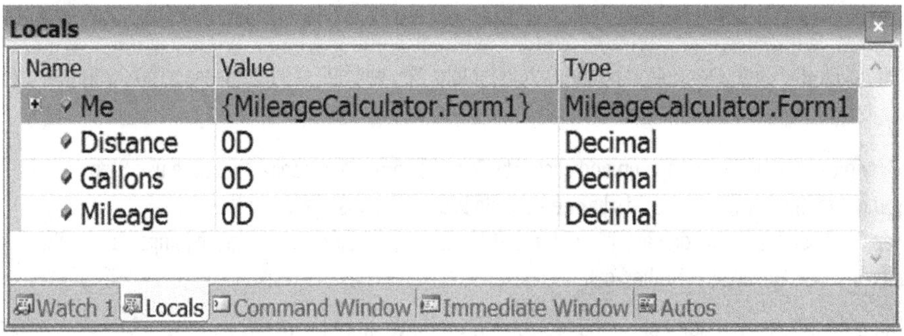

Locals			
Name	Value	Type	
☐ ✓ Me	{MileageCalculator.Form1}	MileageCalculator.Form1	
✦ Distance	0D	Decimal	
✦ Gallons	0D	Decimal	
✦ Mileage	0D	Decimal	

Watch 1 | Locals | Command Window | Immediate Window | Autos

Figure 4-10. *The Locals window*

The Watch Window

You can use the Watch window to create your own list of variables and expressions that you wish to watch. By default, nothing will show up in this window until you add an item to watch, like so:

1. Highlight the variable you wish to watch and right-click.

2. Select Add Watch from the pop-up menu.

For example, in Figure 4-11, we have right-clicked on the Distance variable, highlighted in gray, to access the pop-up menu. We then clicked the Add Watch option to add it to the Watch window. Once completed, the Watch window displays the name, value, and type of the Distance variable.

In addition, you can also just type in the names of the variables you want to watch or even type in expressions, like 5 + 5 (see Figure 4-12), and see what the answer will be.

■**Note** Although most of the debugging windows are found in all editions of Visual Studio, some are not. For example, the next window discussed, called Autos, is not included with the Express editions.

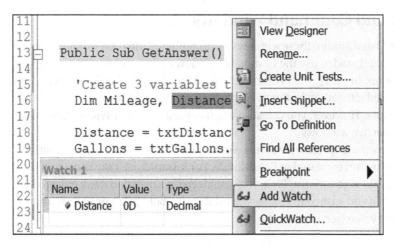

Figure 4-11. *The Watch window*

Name	Value	Type
Distance	100	Integer
5 + 5	10	Integer
Distance/10	10.0	Double

Watch 1

Autos Locals Watch 1

Figure 4-12. *Adding your own expressions*

The Autos Window

The Autos window automatically shows variable names and values based on what line you are paused on. It also shows information about values from three lines before and after that line (see Figure 4-13). As you step though your code, you can even use it to change the values of the variable, if you wish. This can be very handy if you want to test "what if" scenarios.

```
10    Public Sub GetAnswer()
11
12        'Create 3 variabl
13        Dim Mileage, Dist
14
15        Distance = txtDis
16        Gallons = txtGall
17        Mileage = Distanc
18        MessageBox.Show(M
19
20    End Sub
```

Autos

Name	Value	Type
Distance	0D	Decimal
Gallons	0D	Decimal
Mileage	0D	Decimal
txtDistance	Nothing	System.Windows.Forms.TextBox
txtGallons	Nothing	System.Windows.Forms.TextBox

Autos Locals Watch 1

Figure 4-13. *The Autos window*

The Immediate and Command Windows

In previous versions of Visual Studio, these windows were combined into one window. You would type in the command >cmd to use the Command window option, or immed to use the Immediate window option. In the Express editions of Visual Studio 2005, the Command window has been removed altogether, but both are available in the other versions, just not in the same window anymore. However, you can still switch between them by typing these two commands in their respective windows.

Let's look at the Immediate window first. This window allows you to add programming instructions while the program is paused in Break mode. For instance, let's say you wanted to find out the value of the Distance variable. First, you would type in a question mark followed by the name of the variable. If you wished to change the value, you would just type in the name of the variable and the new value (see Figure 4-14).

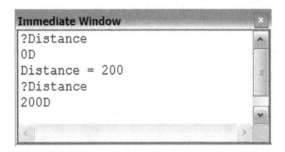

Figure 4-14. *The Immediate window in Immediate mode*

If you are not using the Express editions, you can use the Command window to issue commands that interact with Visual Studio .NET itself. This includes menu items such as the Open File option under the File menu. You can even use commands that do not appear in any menus, such as nf, which creates a new file, or the command open, which opens a file directly without the Open File dialog (see Figure 4-15).

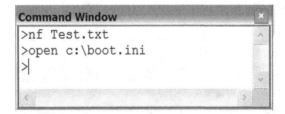

Figure 4-15. *The Command window*

The Call Stack Window

The Call Stack window allows you to see which methods are currently being run. It shows the name and the programming language of each method, but you may also see optional information as well. This includes line numbers or the parameter names, types, and values. The display of this optional information can be turned on or off by right-clicking and selecting your choices from the pop-up menu (see Figure 4-16). Also note in the figure that you can see two methods listed: the first one is GetAnswer(), which is followed by the method that called it, btnGetMileage_Click(). On the left, the dot with an arrow indicates the method that is currently running. The line number is also noted, but it is not really needed in this case since you can double-click on the method's name and the editor will jump the cursor to that line.

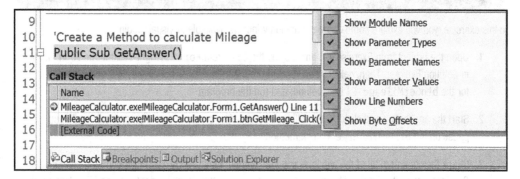

Figure 4-16. *The Call Stack window*

The Data Tips Window

Although it's not really one of the debugging windows, the Data Tips window is a nice, new feature in 2005. When Visual Studio finds an error in your code, it will offer a Data Tip like the one shown in Figure 4-17. In the figure, you may notice that we have attempted to divide by zero again, but this time outside of a Try-Catch block. We did this because the Data Tips window will not show up if the error happens inside a Try-Catch block, only when outside of one. The data tip describes the error it found, gives you advice on what to do about it, and offers more detailed information if you click the View Detail link at the bottom of the dialog window. The View Details dialog window provides much more detailed information, which is useful when the troubleshooting tips are not enough.

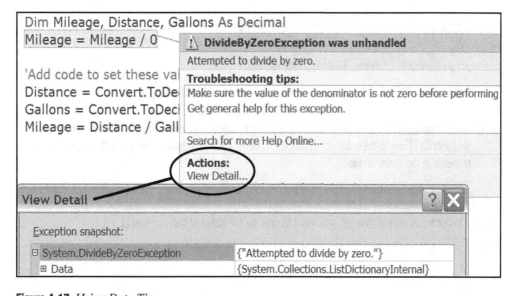

Figure 4-17. *Using Data Tips*

As you can see, there are a lot of windows and options. The best way to get to know when and how to use these is it to take some time to work with them. In Exercise 4-2, you will do just that.

Exercise 4-2: Using the Debugging Windows

In this exercise, you will explore some of the debugging windows available in Visual Studio.

1. Open the project from Exercise 4-1 and display the code from Form1 by right-clicking the Form1 icon in Solution Explorer. Then, select View Code from the menu. If it is not already set, add a breakpoint for the btnGetMileage_Click method, and run the program.

2. Start the application and click the Get Mileage button. Your program should enter Break mode and pause on the btnGetMileage_Click method.

3. Check the content of all of the windows you just learned about: Autos, Locals, Watch, Immediate, and Call Stack. Note that some of the windows do not have anything in them right now, and the Command and Data Tips windows we talked about are not involved at all.

4. Step into the code a line or two, then look at each window again. Notice how some windows change and some do not.

5. With the Locals window open, move to the line where the Mileage variable is set to Distance/Gallons. The value of Mileage will still be 0 until you move off this line and onto the next. Note how when the value of Mileage changes, the Locals window changes the value to red text.

6. Step out of the method and close any message box that has opened. Now click the button again to reenter Break mode. Once your application pauses, highlight the Gallons variable and add it to the Watch window. Since Gallons is part of the GetAnswer() method, it will not have a value or even exist in memory right now. A red dot with an "x" on it shows up in the Watch window to indicate this (see Figure 4-18).

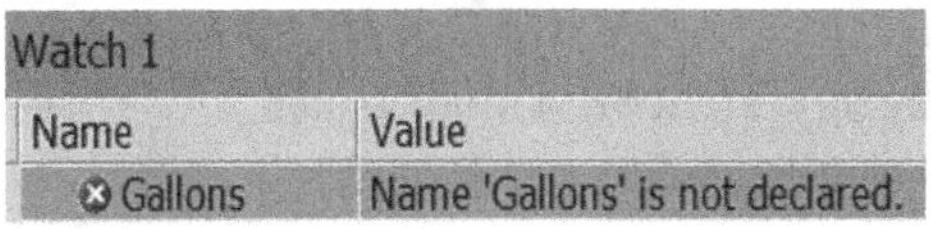

Watch 1	
Name	Value
⊗ Gallons	Name 'Gallons' is not declared.

Figure 4-18. *The Watch window shows when a variable is out of scope.*

7. Keep stepping into the code until Gallons comes into scope. Continue until just before the line of code that sets Gallons to the value in txtGallons.text. Click Step Into and watch as the changes are reflected in the Watch window.

■**Note** Do not move off this line yet, you want to change the value of Gallons next.

---

8. Click the Value, and manually change the value of `Gallons` to 100. Then press Enter (see Figure 4-19).

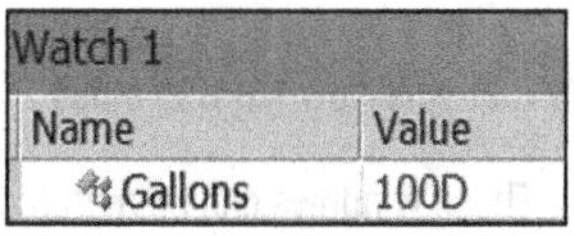

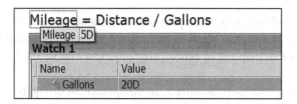

Figure 4-19. *Changing the value of Gallons*

9. Step into the next line. When the message box pops up, verify that it now says 5, and not 10, to prove that the value of `Gallons` was updated before the calculation was performed (see Figure 4-20).

Figure 4-20. *Verifying the change of Gallons*

10. Stop the program and restart it again. Step into the lines of code until you come to the line highlighted in Figure 4-21. Change the value of `Gallons` once again, but this time to zero. Beneath that type in **Distance/0** and press Enter. You will see an error message telling you about what error you will receive if you run this calculation.

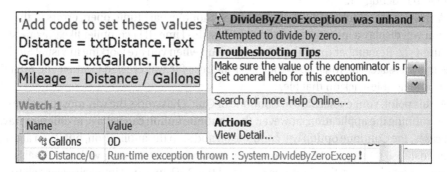

Figure 4-21. *Verifying the change of Gallons*

11. Try to step into the next line and a Data Tip pops up telling you that an error has occurred.

12. Change the value of `Gallons` back to 20, and step into the rest of your code.

13. Click on the Immediate window, and type in this command:

```
>nf "NotesToSelf.txt"
```

A new Text window will appear. Just type a note that says **Add a Try-Catch statement to your code later to handle Divide by Zero and other errors**. Once you type out your note, save the file to C:\.

14. Now type in the following:

```
>File.OpenFile
```

When the Open File dialog box pops up, navigate to C:\ and verify that your new file was made.

In this exercise, you looked at how to use some of the debugging windows. These windows can be a great help not only to developers, but also to all testers that engage in White Box testing or in developing testware.

The Just-In-Time Debugger

Often the developer only tests his code within a development environment like Visual Studio, but what happens after the product is released? Microsoft must have asked this question too, because they added some features that help you to debug programs even without the full development tools.

Normally, when a programming error is encountered, the operating system will try to find a debugging tool installed on that computer. You will find that there are a number of these tools on most computer systems added by one software program or another. If you have tested on a computer that offers a list of installed debuggers when an error happens, then you have seen these yourself.

You may have noticed that selecting a debugger from the list will not always help you if that debugger is not compatible with the code that has thrown the error. Of course, Microsoft's .NET Framework helps by including its own debugging option for .NET applications: the Just-In-Time (JIT) debugger.

When you are running a .NET application without Visual Studio open, errors in the program will display a message from the .NET Just-In-Time (JIT) compiler like the one shown in Figure 4-22. Remember that this will not show up when you are working in Visual Studio; so to see this message, you must go to the folder the .exe file was created in when you built the project and double-click on that file.

At this point, your choices are to Continue or Quit. Quit works the way most people expect, it stops running the application; however, the Continue option can behave in different ways. In most cases, the Continue option will continue on and stop the application, but it can also enter into an installed debugger. When a program is running on a computer without Visual Studio and encounters an error, the Continue option of the .NET Just-In-Time debugger will try to ignore the error by not running any code after the error was found. It will not shut down, but will keep running the program so that you can try again. This can change if you have Visual Studio .NET installed and configured a certain way. In this case, the Just-In-Time debugging feature can launch the Visual Studio Debugger automatically, allowing you to step through the code and query values.

In order to see this, you must configure VS .NET to open up the VS .NET Debugger. You do this from VS .NET, as seen in Exercise 4-3.

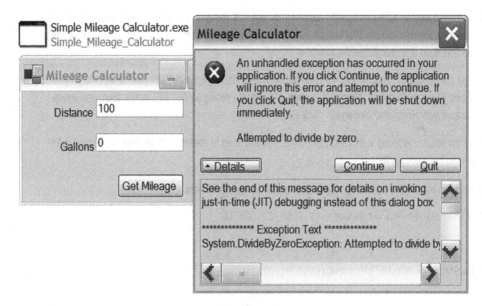

Figure 4-22. *The Just-In-Time debugger dialog window*

Exercise 4-3: Setting Up the Just-In-Time Debugger

Note This option doesn't exist in the Express editions, so if you are using one of those versions, then you will want to skip this exercise. Don't worry—it will not impact later exercises.

1. When you completed Exercise 4-2, your project was complied into an `.exe` file. This file can be found in the bin folder where your project was saved. Copy the `MileageCalculator.exe` file from the bin folder of Exercise 4-2 and place it on your desktop.

2. Double-click the `.exe` file to start the application. Once it displays, put **0** in the Gallons textbox. Press the `btnGetMileage` button and verify that the JIT Debug dialog box pops up (again, see Figure 4-22).

3. Click the Details button and review what kinds of information are given to you.

4. Scroll down to the end of the message. At the end, you'll see that this section looks like the following:

```
************** JIT Debugging **************
```

Read it carefully, as it explains some of what you need to do to set JIT debugging to use Visual Studio .NET.

5. Open your Solution from Exercise 4-2 using Visual Studio. Select Tools ➤ Options.

6. On the left-hand side of the Options dialog box, expand the Debugging option. If you don't see this option, then look at the bottom of the Options window for the Show All Settings check box and check the box.

7. In the Debugging folder, select the Just-In-Time page. If you do not see this, then you are most likely using the Express edition. This will not impact the rest of this chapter, but if you are using an Express edition, then this completes the exercise.

8. You should see the Enable Just-In-Time Debugging of These Types of Code box. Select the program types you want to debug: Managed, Native, or Script (to debug an ASP.NET application, you would choose both Script and Managed). Click OK.

9. When you are working with Windows Forms, you will need to enable Just-In-Time debugging in the `machine.config` file.

You will find the `machine.config.` file in one of the following folders:

`C:\WINNT\Microsoft.NET\Framework\v2.0.50727\CONFIG`

or

`C:\WINDOWS\Microsoft.NET\Framework\v2.0.50727\CONFIG`

■**Note** The `machine.config` file is used to control the way .NET programs run on a particular computer. You will find this file in a subfolder of the C:\WINDOWS\Microsoft.NET\Framework or C:\WINNT\Microsoft.NET\ Framework folders of your hard drive (where C:\ is the drive your operating system is installed on). The actual file you need will be inside a subfolder with a version number as its name. For example, if the application you are trying to configure was written in .NET 2003, you would use this path: C:\WINDOWS\Microsoft.NET\ Framework\v1.1.4322. The newer versions of .NET will start with 2.0. At the time of this writing, the latest version was C:\WINDOWS\Microsoft.NET\Framework\v2.0.50727. If you are unsure which version you used for the previous exercises, just use the latest version you can find and that will likely be the correct one.

---

10. Open the file called `machine.config.Comments` with a text editor, such as Notepad or Visual Studio. This file explains the settings available in the actual `machine.config` file. You will use this to add a new setting to the `machine.config` file without having to type out the new setting by hand. In the Comments version of the file, search for `system.windows.forms jitDebugging=`. What you should see is a set of XML tags like the following:

```
<!--
    <system.windows.forms
         jitDebugging = "false" [true|false]
    />
-->
<system.windows.forms jitDebugging="false" />
```

The `<!--` and `-->` indicate an XML comment; whatever is inside of these tags is ignored. That being the case, what you are seeing inside of this comment is the syntax example for the statement below the comment. This example details the default setting, `false`, and the optional settings, `[true|false]`. Note that XML is case sensitive, so you must be sure to use lowercase when setting these options.

11. Copy the line of code that looks like this: `<system.windows.forms jitDebugging="false" />`. Now open the actual `machine.config` file in the same folder.

12. Paste the code you copied at the bottom of the file and change the setting from `false` to `true`, as shown here:

```
<system.windows.forms jitDebugging="true" />
</configuration>
```

13. Save the `machine.config` file and close both documents. Open the MileageCalculator program again and test the Divide by Zero error again. Now when an error occurs, a different dialog box opens—one which allows you to debug the program (see Figure 4-23).

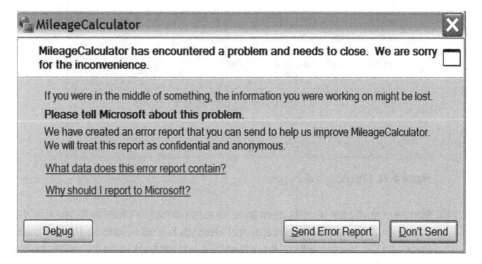

Figure 4-23. *Debug screen when JIT debugging is on*

14. Press the Debug button and you will be presented with a list of debugging tools to choose from (see Figure 4-24). From here, you can choose either Visual Studio or the Common Language Runtime (CLR) debuggers. If you choose CLR, you will see a tool that looks and acts much like Visual Studio. Choose that one now and a new message box opens with a Break, Continue, and Ignore button. Click Continue to stop the program (we know, that is not very intuitive).

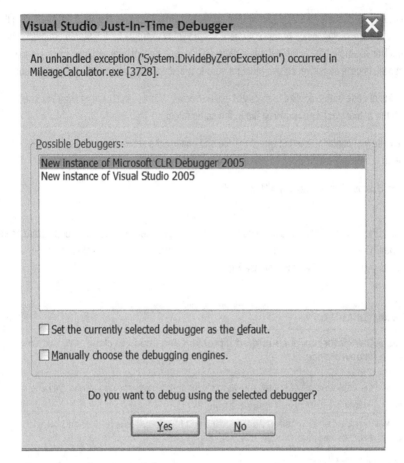

Figure 4-24. *Choosing a debugger*

15. Start the program again using the green arrow, as you do normally in Visual Studio, and enter the zero value again. A message box appears again that allows you to Break or Continue. This time choose Break—the CRL debugger will load the code on the screen and break on the line causing the problem (see Figure 4-25).

16. Step though the code and use the different debugging windows as you did earlier. You should notice that you do not have as many options as when debugging with Visual Studio and the actual project files, but this tool may provide all you need for a bug report.

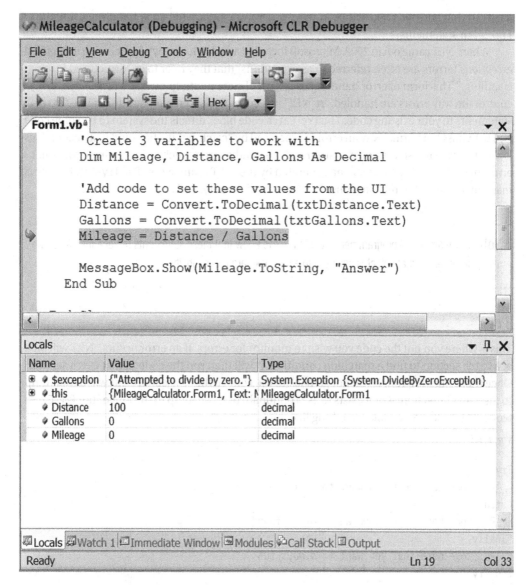

Figure 4-25. *Using the CLR debugger*

In this exercise, you saw how to set up the Just-In-Time debugger. This option allows you to debug applications without the use of Visual Studio.

Using the Try-Catch Statements

Setting up Try-Catch statements on a development or test lab PC is useful, but it is not something the end user would get much benefit from. What most users need is a clear message explaining how an application should be used. A developer needs to give useful messages that either let users know how to fix the problem or, even better, have the application fix the problem itself. To that end, let's take a look at ways programs can provide error handling using the Try-Catch statements.

When .NET came out in 2002, Microsoft included an advanced way of processing unhandled *exceptions* (errors are often referred to as exceptions) that they refer to as "Structured Error Handling." This form of error handling uses a set of statements, known as a *code block*, to control the way errors are handled. In .NET, this code block is created by adding Try-Catch statements to your existing code. The Try-Catch code block directs the system to try some code and to bypass the normal way an error is processed by "catching" it when, and if, it occurs. This is a simple way to use your own custom code to handle errors, such as just giving a friendlier error message than the normal one generated by the .NET Framework. The Try-Catch block is made up of three different sections: Try, Catch, and Finally. Let's take a look at each.

■**Note** If you are a VB6 programmer, you will want to know that these statements replace the use of the err object; however, that object is still available for backward compatibility.

Try

This is where you put the code you wish to monitor for errors. If an error occurs, .NET will look at a Catch section to find a matching condition. It will then run the code in that Catch section. Once those lines are run, it will not go back to the code in the Try section, but will either jump to the Finally section, if one exists (this is optional), or it will jump to the end of the Try-Catch block. The code would look something like this prototype:

VB .NET

```
Try
    'Add code here that you want to test
Catch
    'Put code here; runs when an error is found
Finally
    'Put code here that you want to always run
End Try
```

C#

```
try
{
    //Add code here that you want to test
}
catch
{
    //Put code here; runs when an error is found
}
finally
{
    //Put code here that you want to always run
}
```

Catch

The Catch section is where you put your custom error messages or code to handle the error. It is possible to use one or more Catch clauses in the same Try-Catch statement. Each Catch will refer to a predefined type of exception. Microsoft has defined common exceptions like DividingByZeroException and FileNotFoundException for you, but you can make your own as well. If an error occurs, .NET examines the Catch statements in the order they appear. Using a Catch statement without specifying a type of exception to match will catch any type of error. You should have one of these "generic" statements to catch errors you did not plan for, as shown in the following code. Whenever .NET finds a Catch statement that matches the generated exception, it executes the code for that Catch clause.

VB .NET

```
Catch ex As DivideByZeroException
  MessageBox.Show("Don't use Zero for Gallons")
Catch
  MessageBox.Show("Your Friendly Message here")
```

C#

```
catch( DivideByZeroException ex)
  {
    MessageBox.Show("Don't use Zero for Gallons");
  }
catch
  {
    MessageBox.Show(ex.Message);
  }
```

> **Note** Once the system finds a matching Catch block, it will not keep searching for more matching Catch statements. For this reason, it is important to put the generic Catch clause at the end. If you put it at the beginning, it will always consider that one a match, run its code, then jump to Finally or the end of the Try-Catch statement.

Finally

No matter if your code runs with or without an error, it always executes any code you put in the Finally section. Developers will often put "clean-up code" in this section. *Clean-up code* includes things like closing files you have opened or database connections you have been using. If you do not have any code like that, you don't need to add this section—Finally is an optional clause.

In summary, when you use a Try-Catch block:

- You can have one or more Catch statements.

- You can also choose to include or omit a Finally statement.

- For each Try there must be at least one Catch statement (if you don't use a Finally statement).

- There will be only one Finally statement, and it runs regardless of any errors.

Scope Issues

Take a look at Listing 4-2. Notice that we have declared local variables Mileage, Distance, and Gallons inside the Try block. Since they are in the Try block, they will only be available while running code in that Try block. For example, if we try to access Mileage in a MessageBox after the Try-Catch block, we will get an error.

Listing 4-2. *Try-Catch Blocks Have Their Own Scope*

VB .NET

```
Public Sub GetAnswer()
  Try
    'Create three variables to work with
    Dim Mileage, Distance, Gallons As Decimal

    'Add code to set these values from the UI
    Distance = txtDistance.Text
    Gallons = txtGallons.Text
    Mileage = Distance / Gallons
  Catch
    MessageBox.Show("Your Friendly Message here")
  Finally
    'Put code here that you want to always run
  End Try

  MessageBox.Show(Mileage.ToString, "Answer") 'GIVES ERROR
End Sub
```

C#

```
public void  GetAnswer()
{
  try
  {
    //Create three variables to work with
    Decimal Mileage = 0 , Distance = 0 , Gallons = 0;

    Distance = Convert.ToDecimal(txtDistance.Text);
    Gallons = Convert.ToDecimal(txtGallons.Text);
    Mileage = Distance / Gallons;
  }
```

```
catch
{
  //Catch any other type of Exception
  MessageBox.Show("Your Friendly Message here");
}
finally
{
  //Put code here that you want to always run
}

MessageBox.Show(Mileage.ToString(), "Answer"); //Give Error
} //End of GetAnswer()
```

This error is caused because Mileage is no longer available when the code tries to use it in the MessageBox.

Note If you want to use a variable outside of a Try-Catch block, you must declare the variable outside of the Try-Catch-Finally block.

Exception Classes

When Microsoft included the Try-Catch option, they also included a way to get lots of information about the errors that cause the Catch code to run. How they did this was to create an object in memory whenever an error, or exception as it's referred to in most of the documentation, is encountered.

An object is made and placed in memory much like a simple variable is. Both a simple variable, like Gallons from our example, and an object are really just ones and zeros in memory. Both can be filled with data that may be used later in a program. The difference is that objects can do and hold more than simple variables. For one thing, you can store more than one piece of data in an object. For another, you can also store functions or subroutines in them as well. Two of the best things about objects are that they are easy to make and just as easy to use.

The first step in making an object is to create a template that outlines what data or *methods* (the generic term used for functions and subroutines) you want to store in it. In .NET, you have two basic types of templates. The first one is a called a structure. *Structures* allow you to create a simple object template. They have some restrictions about what they can and cannot do, but these restrictions keep others from using your code in ways you didn't intend. The second template type is a class. *Classes* are the most flexible choice, but to get the most out of them, you need to design them carefully. We will talk about both of these in more detail in Chapter 6, but for now it really does not matter which one you use. Just so you get a visual of what we mean, Listing 4-3 shows examples of each. Note how alike they look. Again, both can be used to create objects.

Listing 4-3. *Classes and Structures Can Look Similar.*

VB .NET

```
Class MyExceptionTemplate1
  Public Message As String
  Public ErrorNumber As Int16
End Class

Structure MyExceptionTemplate2
  Public Message As String
  Public ErrorNumber As Int16
End Structure
```

C#

```
class MyExceptionTemplate1
{
  public string Message;
  public Int16 ErrorNumber;
}

struct MyExceptionTemplate2
{
  public string Message;
  public Int16 ErrorNumber;
}
```

While there are differences in the way .NET treats classes and structures internally, if your template is simply holding data, then you can choose either one. Again, we will talk more about the differences between them in Chapter 6.

Making an Exception Object

While it is possible to use the code you type into a class or structure directly, most of the time they are just used as templates for making objects. You can think of each object you make as having a copy of the template code, but these objects each have their own space in memory. For example, to create an object from either the class or structure you just looked at, you would type in the following code:

VB .NET

```
Dim objMyCustomExceptionA As New MyExceptionTemplete1
Dim objMyCustomExceptionB As New MyExceptionTemplete2
```

C#

```
MyExceptionTemplate1 objMyCustomExceptionA =
  new MyExceptionTemplate1();
MyExceptionTemplate2 objMyCustomExceptionB =
  new MyExceptionTemplate2();
```

Once your objects, objMyCustomExceptionA and objMyCustomExceptionB, are made in memory, you can fill them up with data. When we created the templates, we designed the Message and ErrorNumber variables as places to hold the data for each object. Since each object is just a copy of the class that is its template, you can make one or more copies as needed. Each will have its own space in memory and each can hold different data. Changing the values of one object will not affect another. Nor will it affect the class or structure at all, because their code is held in their own memory spaces separate from the objects you create from them.

When you work with the data in an object, like the Message and ErrorNumber variables here, most programmers refer to these as an object's "properties." This may be familiar to you since, by now, you have set the Text property of a Textbox object many times, and a Textbox object is one made from Microsoft's Textbox class. You set and read the properties of the objects you create just as you would set and read the properties of a Textbox object.

VB .NET

```
objMyCustomExceptionA.Message = "Your Friendly Message here"
objMyCustomExceptionA.ErrorNumber = 123
MessageBox.Show(objMyCustomException.Message)
```

C#

```
objMyCustomExceptionA.Message = "Your Friendly Message here";
objMyCustomExceptionA.ErrorNumber = 123;
MessageBox.Show(objMyCustomException.Message);
```

Using Exception Objects

Microsoft made a number of predefined classes for common errors. These are collectively referred to as the Exception classes. When .NET comes across an error, like trying to divide by zero, the .NET Framework automatically creates an object in memory based on the appropriate Exception class.

If your code includes a Catch statement in its Try-Catch block, you can include a variable in the Catch statement that will allow you to access the Exception object that was created. Since variables act as named placeholders that point to a memory address, this variable will then be linked to the address of the object created by the .NET Framework when that type of error happens. For example, in Listing 4-4, the ex variable will be mapped to an object made from the DivideByZeroException class if you set the value of Gallons to zero and try to divide Distance by Gallons.

Listing 4-4. *Typical Try-Catch Block*

VB .NET

```
Try
  'Add code to set these values from the UI
  Distance = txtDistance.Text
  Gallons = txtGallons.Text
  Mileage = Distance / Gallons
Catch ex As DivideByZeroException
  MessageBox.Show(ex.Message)
```

```
Catch ex as Exception
  MessageBox.Show(ex.Message)
End Try
```

C#

```
try
{
  Distance = txtDistance.Text;
  Gallons = txtGallons.Text;
  Mileage = Distance / Gallons;
}
catch (DivideByZeroException ex)
{
  MessageBox.Show(ex.Message);
}
catch (Exception ex)
{
  MessageBox.Show(ex.Message);
}
```

The ex variable automatically points to the object created when the error happened, thanks to the way .NET handles errors. However, .NET can only point a variable to an Exception object if the data type of the variable, in this case ex, is compatible with the error object.

For example, if an Exception object is made from the DivideByZeroException class and you create a Catch clause that has the same data type (as in Catch ex As DivideByZeroException), then .NET considers this a match, and the code for that particular Catch block runs. As it turns out, Microsoft allows the data type of Exception to point to any of the Exception objects. So, if your Catch statement does not specify an exception type, or uses the Exception class as the data type, then any exception is considered a match. That is why it's important that these generic versions should be the last Catch statement of that Try-Catch block; otherwise, it will match any exception that you did not "catch" in the preceding Catch blocks.

Once a variable, like ex in our example, points to an object, it will now be able to access the properties Microsoft created in that Exception class, such as its Message property.

Creating Your Own Exception Class

Microsoft allows you to create your own custom Exception classes and your own custom error messages inside of them. To do so, you would first create a new class and "inherit" all the code from Microsoft's Exception class. Once this is done, you need to tell .NET that your new class is going use its own version of the Message property and set the value for the new message you want. When creating your own user-defined exceptions, it is good coding practice to end the class name with the word Exception. Listing 4-5 shows an example of this.

Listing 4-5. *Creating a Custom Exception Class*

VB .NET

```
Class MyCustomException
    Inherits Exception
    Public Shadows Message As String = "Your Friendly Message here"
End Class
```

C#

```
class MyCustomException: System.Exception
{
    public new string Message = "Your Friendly Message here";
}
```

Classes that inherit code from Microsoft's Exception class all have a Message property. Of course, this property is used to inform the user of what kind of error happened, and it may even suggest actions to take when resolving the problem.

Each Exception object will also have a ToString() method, which will usually show a lot of additional information about the error that just happened. The ToString() method is really handy when you are testing because of the additional information, but this information is often too much when an application is ready to be released to the end users. When creating your own testware applications, you might want to design them so that the user is presented with the simple error message at first. Then you can give them an option to look at the more complex message the ToString() method offers.

Throwing Exceptions

When an error happens in .NET, an Exception object will be "thrown" into memory by the .NET Framework. You can explicitly throw your own custom exception using the Throw statement. This can be useful in combination with a conditional statement, as shown in Listing 4-6.

Listing 4-6. *Throwing an Exception*

VB .NET

```
  If Gallons = 0 Or Distance = 0 Then
    'Cause an Exception to be Thrown
    Throw New MyCustomException
  End If
```

C#

```
  if (Distance == 0)
  {
    //Cause an Exception to be Thrown
    throw new MyCustomException();
  }
```

In this example, if either Gallons or Distance has been set to zero, then a new MyCustomException object will be created in memory automatically. When this is used with a Try-Catch block, you can Catch the error and use the properties of that object to let the user know what happened (see Exercise 4-4).

Exercise 4-4: Using a Try-Catch Block

In this exercise, you will add on to the code you created in Exercise 4-1 to create a Try-Catch block that captures any errors that occur. You will also create a very simple custom Exception class that holds a custom error message. Then, you will step through your code and verify that the specific, generic, and custom exceptions are being caught.

1. In Solution Explorer, right-click on the MileageCalculator project and add a new class using the menu option shown in Figure 4-26.

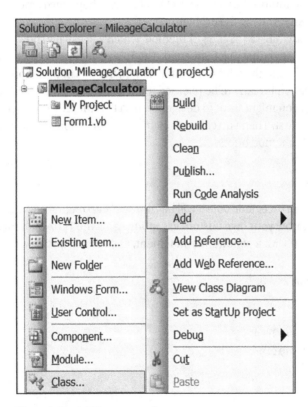

Figure 4-26. *Adding a new class*

2. A dialog window will open that allows you to name the new class. In the Name textbox at the bottom of this dialog window, type **MyCustomException.vb** or **MyCustomerException.cs**, as shown in Figure 4-27.

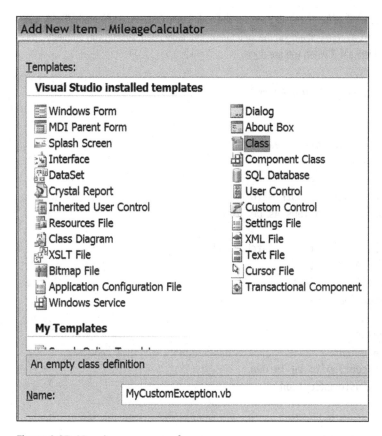

Figure 4-27. *Naming your new class*

3. When the code window opens, add the following code to your new class. Note that by using `Inherits`, in VB .NET, or `: System.Exception`, in C#, you are letting .NET know that you want to inherit all of the properties and methods found in Microsoft's `Exception` class in your new custom `Exception` class.

VB .NET

```
Class MyCustomException
  Inherits Exception
  'This Class demos how to make a simple Custom Exception Class
  Public Shadows Message As String = "Your Friendly Message here"
End Class
```

C#

```
class MyCustomException : System.Exception
{
  //This Class demos how to make a simple Custom Exception Class
  public new string Message = "Your Friendly Message here";
}
```

4. Open the code window for Form1 and replace the code in the GetAnswer() method with code that includes a Try-Catch block around the statements that have been causing you problems. Your code will look like Listing 4-7 when you are done.

Listing 4-7. *Using Your Own Custom Class*

VB .NET

```
'Create a Method to calculate Mileage
Public Sub GetAnswer()

  'Create three variables to work with
  Dim Mileage, Distance, Gallons As Decimal

  Try 'Add this line to start Try-Catch Block
    ' Set values from the UI
    Distance = txtDistance.Text
    Gallons = txtGallons.Text

    'Check for zeros
    If Distance = 0 Then
      'Cause an Exception to be Thrown
      Throw New MyCustomException
    End If

    'Calculate the mileage
    Mileage = Distance / Gallons

  Catch ex As DivideByZeroException
    'Catch Divide by Zero errors and use the object from Microsoft's
    'DivideByZeroException Class to show a Message
    MessageBox.Show(ex.Message)

  Catch ex As MyCustomException
    'Catch all MyCustomException errors,
    'Use the Object to show a Custom error Message
    MessageBox.Show(ex.Message)

  Catch
    'Catch any other type of Exception
    MessageBox.Show("There was an Error")

  Finally
    'Put code here that you want to always run
    MessageBox.Show("Inside Finally")
  End Try
  MessageBox.Show(Mileage.ToString, "Answer")

End Sub
```

C#

```csharp
//Create a Method to calculate Mileage
public void  GetAnswer()
{
  //Create three variables to work with
  Decimal Mileage = 0, Distance = 0, Gallons = 0;

  try
  {
    //Add code to set these values from the UI
     Distance = Convert.ToDecimal(txtDistance.Text);
    Gallons = Convert.ToDecimal(txtGallons.Text);

    //Check for zeros
    if (Distance == 0)
    {
      //Cause an Exception to be Thrown
      throw new MyCustomException();
    }

    Mileage = Distance / Gallons;
    }//end if

    catch (DivideByZeroException ex)
    {
     //Catch Divide by Zero errors and use the object from Microsoft's
      //DivideByZeroException Class to show a Message
      MessageBox.Show(ex.Message);
    }
   catch (MyCustomException ex)
   {
     //Catch all MyCustomException errors,
     //Use the Object to show a Custom error Message
     MessageBox.Show(ex.Message);
    }
    catch
    {
      //Catch any other type of Exception
      MessageBox.Show("There was an Error");
    }
    finally
    {
      //Put code here that you want to always run
      MessageBox.Show("Inside Finally");
    } //End Try-Catch Block
```

```
MessageBox.Show(Mileage.ToString(), "Answer");
```

```
}//end of GetAnswer
```

5. With a breakpoint set on the start of the GetMileage() method, start the application and step into the code using the default values, Distance being 100 and Gallons being 10. The application should work as expected and give you an answer of 10. Note that the code in the Finally clause still runs even though there were no errors.

6. Change the value of Gallons to 0 in the txtGallons textbox and click the button again. Step into the code line-by-line and watch how it jumps to the DivideByZeroException Catch clause when the application attempts to divide by zero. Note that the Finally clause still runs its code.

7. Change the value of Distance to 0 and click the button again. Step into the code line-by-line until it enters the If statement block and throws the error. Continue stepping into the code and watch how, this time, it jumps to the Catch clause that matches your custom Exception. The Finally block will run once again.

In this exercise, you saw how the Try-Catch-Finally statement block is used to catch errors. You also saw how you can create your own custom Exception class, how to throw that Exception, and how to catch it. As you go through the book, you will see more of these types of statements, which will help you understand when and how to use this knowledge in practice.

Using Debug and Trace

In addition to using Visual Studio to debug applications, Microsoft has long had a set of Debug commands that you could use to get information about what is happening in your program while it is running.

The way it works is this: You put Debug commands in your code to print out information about what is going on at specific points in your code. This information can be things like line numbers reached, the value of variables, or the status of a conditional statement.

These types of statements can be used while you have Visual Studio open in front of you, but you already have breakpoints for that. The Debug messages really come in handy when you have just merged two or more code files, like an .exe and a .dll, and you want to see how they work together. This works even when you have access to some or none of the actual code files.

TESTER'S TIP: WHY USE TRACE AND DEBUG?

Testing individual parts of an application is one way to find errors in applications; this is usually referred to as *unit testing*. Most applications are made up of multiple files, or units. This often takes the form of one .exe file accessing code in another .exe or .dll file. Unit testing is commonly considered the developer's domain, along with *integration testing*, which is what you do when you combine multiple units together and test their interaction. This integration testing provides another opportunity to find mistakes that may have slipped past while unit testing. However, when the developer performs unit tests and/or integration tests, she usually doesn't do enough of both the positive and negative testing that a good test professional would employ. This is because the developer's goal is to ensure functionality of the units, not to try to break them. (We testers try our best to break them before the customer/user does!) A good test professional can employ knowledge of testing techniques, such as boundary analysis and equivalence class partitioning, to round out the developer's efforts.

The Debug and Trace classes are features of .NET intended for developers, but they are very useful in testing situations as well. You can use these two classes to return information about the application as it runs. For example, if an application is having performance issues, memory management issues, or problems with additional application files, then they may not be detected until runtime. With these classes, you can gather information about what is happening during runtime. If the developer prepared for these tests by adding Debug or Trace statements to the code, you can test how an application handles issues like these to document what is needed for improvement. If they did not, then it may fall to you, the tester, to add these statements. Presuming you have access to the source code, you can use Visual Studio for this. You can make a copy of the source project and then insert your Debug and Trace class coding into that copy. This is called *instrumenting* the code. In this section, you will learn how to do this not only for the applications you test, but also for your own testing applications.

The Debug class has been used in Visual Studio a long time, but Microsoft added the Trace class beginning with Visual Studio .NET. This new class has additional commands and features that you will find quite useful. Both Trace and Debug classes can be used to gather information about what is going on in your program while it's running. You can elect to use one or both of these classes. Both are identical in many ways, but here are some important differences:

- Debug commands are removed when you compile your program in Release mode; Trace commands are not. This is important because it means that adding Trace commands will allow applications to be debugged even after release. Debug commands are only used during software development.

- Debug commands need Visual Studio installed in order for them to run; Trace commands only need the .NET Framework.

- You can turn tracing on and off for an application, one or more web pages, or even an entire computer. This isn't so with the Debug option.

- Trace has both a web version and a Windows version. Each of these provides unique options for their specific environment. Debug does not have different versions.

The Debug Class

The Debug class allows you to send out messages to text files, to the command console (which can be the DOS prompt or one of the Debug windows), or to a Windows Event log. This class is found in the System.Diagnostics namespace, so you must either refer to it by its full name or have an Imports statement (using in C#) at the beginning of your code.

VB .NET

```
Imports System.Diagnostics
```

C#

using System.Diagnostics;

The Debug commands use "debug symbols" to track which lines of code are running and what objects, functions, and variables are available. Keeping this extra debug code makes the output file a bit larger and slower, so Microsoft recommends that you build your application in Release mode after you have finished programming your application.

■**Note** As of this writing, the Express editions do not allow you to choose Release mode.

The Visual Studio Debugger uses a program database (.pdb) file to hold the debugging instruction for Visual Studio—these are known as the *debug symbols.* You can use Notepad to open it if you are curious to see what is inside. The file is found in the bin folder next to your .exe or .dll file (see Figure 4-28). Be warned, it's not designed to be pretty to humans, just functional for the Visual Studio Debugger.

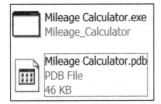

Figure 4-28. *The .pdb file*

This file will not be used when you compile your program in Release mode. This means that any Debug commands are ignored when the program runs using Release mode. In fact, the final .exe or .dll file will not even contain those commands since the compiler now removes them from the original code. You can change the mode from Release to Debug again, and the command will be added back in when the files are recompiled (which happens each time you run and/or build the program in Visual Studio). You can select between the two modes by using the drop-down box next to the blue arrow on the toolbar that you have been using the run your programs.

■**Note** In previous versions of Visual Studio, the breakpoint would be ignored when the application was built in Release mode; however, in Visual Studio 2005, the breakpoints will still function.

The Trace Class

The Trace and Debug classes are almost identical, but one big difference is that the Trace class commands are still included in the .exe or .dll when you build your program using Release mode. However, a developer can control this also by turning these off when manually building the .exe or .dll from your code files.

To build manually, you would open a command prompt (Start ➤ Programs ➤ Microsoft Visual Studio 2005 ➤ Visual Studio Tools ➤ Visual Studio 2005 Command Prompt) and add the TRACE compiler directive.

■**Note** If you are using the Express versions, you will not see the command prompt option in the menu, so you will have to find these command utilities another way. Open the c:\WINDOWS\Microsoft.NET\Framework or c:\WinNT\Microsoft.NET\Framework folder and look for the folder with the highest version number. This is the place where you will find the commands for the C# and the VB .NET compilers. Navigate to this folder with a command prompt and you will be able to run these commands, as shown later in Exercise 4-5. For more information on how to use the command console, see Chapter 7.

Here is an example of two files, called MyApp.vb and MyApp.cs, being compiled using the VB .NET and the C# compilers, respectively. These commands will create a new file, called MyApp.exe (since .exes are the default), with the Trace and Debug commands disabled.

VB .NET

```
vbc /d:TRACE=FALSE /d:DEBUG=FALSE MyApp.vb
```

C#

```
csc /d:TRACE=FALSE /d:DEBUG=FALSE MyApp.cs
```

■**Note** When the TRACE directive is set to false, all tracing code is excluded in the executable code. The same is true in the case of Debug for debug code. The reason we are bringing this up is that the next items we talk about will not work if the developer stripped out the Trace and Debug commands using this option. Also, just so you know, options specified at the command prompt are case sensitive. So both the TRACE and DEBUG option must be typed in uppercase.

Another difference between Trace and Debug is that the Trace object does not require Visual Studio to be installed on the PC running your program. Since this is how it would run normally anyway, it is a useful way to test how code will run in a production environment. Having Trace statements hidden in the code allows you to test it after it is deployed, but it is usually intended to allow administrators and tech-support personnel to monitor a program while it is in use. Adding this as an option is often referred to as *instrumentation*.

TESTER'S TIP: INSTRUMENTATION

Providing instrumentation for your own applications is very useful when those applications are divided among multiple files, and those files are divided among multiple computers. These *distributed applications* cannot easily be debugged with Visual Studio, but the proper use of Trace statements can make it much easier. Using Trace statements, you can display information not only about errors, but also about performance and statistical information. Examples include counters of how often an error occurred or how many times a function was called.

Trace and Debug Methods

Both Trace and Debug classes have a number of methods you can work with. Microsoft designed these methods to be used directly from the class without having to create an object first (which is the same thing they did with the MessageBox.Show() method). Let's look at some of the more common methods you might find useful.

Assert()

Assert() allows you to pause the program much like setting a breakpoint does. When this happens, a dialog box pops up to display a message for the user (see Figure 4-29).

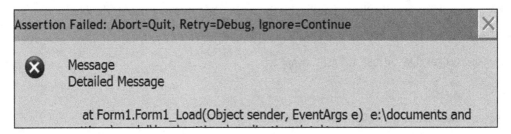

Figure 4-29. *The Assert dialog box*

To get the dialog box to display, you have to add a Debug.Assert() or Trace.Assert() command to your code. You also need to set the condition that will cause it to display, a short message, and a more detailed message. These last two items are optional; however, the information that the system gives you will not be very useful to most people, so providing your own custom message makes more sense.

■**Note** The condition you are asserting must evaluate to false, not true, in order for the dialog to display. Most people expect the opposite.

VB .NET

```
Dim boolContinue As Boolean = False
'Stop if the answer is false
Debug.Assert(boolContinue, "Message", "Detailed Message")
Trace.Assert(boolContinue, "Message", "Detailed Message")
```

C#

```
bool boolContinue = false ;
//Stop if the answer is false
Debug.Assert(boolContinue, "Message", "Detailed Message")
Trace.Assert(boolContinue, "Message", "Detailed Message");
```

WriteIf() and WriteLineIf()

WriteIf() and WriteLineIf() only show a message when the condition is true, and they do not show it in a dialog box. Instead, they send the message to a "trace listener." This built-in feature will send out messages for both Debug and Trace messages. There is always one default trace listener when your code starts up, but you can add others as needed. You will see how in just a bit. The arguments for these are different from Assert(). For one thing, the "detailed message" is not used; instead, a "category" is used in its place. The category can be used to organize your messages if you have a lot of them. The difference between WriteIf() and WriteLineIf() is that the latter adds a carriage return to the message. This can make your messages more readable.

VB .NET

```
Dim boolContinue As Boolean = True
'Stop if the answer is True
Debug.WriteIf(boolContinue, "Message", "Category")
Trace.WriteIf(boolContinue, "Message", "Category")
```

C#

```
bool boolContinue = true;
//Stop if the answer is true
Debug.WriteIf(boolContinue, "Message", "Category");
Trace.WriteIf(boolContinue, "Message", "Category");
```

Write() and WriteLine()

Write() and WriteLine() are the same as WriteIf() and WriteLineIf(), but you don't specify any condition to decide when they will write, they just write it.

VB .NET

```
Debug.Write(boolContinue, "Message", "Category")
Debug.Write(boolContinue, "Message", "Category")
```

C#

```
Debug.Write(boolContinue, "Message", "Category");
Debug.Write(boolContinue, "Message", "Category");
```

Flush()

A trace listener holds the messages you send it in memory until you Flush() it to its destination. By default, these messages show up in one of the debugging windows. Depending on the version of Visual Studio you are using, this will be either the Output window or the Immediate window. There is always a default listener, but you can add additional listeners, as you will see in a moment. If you have more than one listener, then you can choose to flush them individually by specifying which one you want, or all of them, by calling the Flush() method directly on the Trace or Debug object. There is even an AutoFlush option, which will flush the message for you after any of the previously mentioned Write statements are called.

VB .NET

```
Trace.Listeners("MyListener").Flush()
Trace.Flush()
Debug.Listeners("MyListener").Flush()
Debug.Flush()
Trace.AutoFlush = True
```

C#

```
Trace.Listeners["MyListener"].Flush();
Trace.Flush();
Debug.Listeners["MyListener"].Flush();
Debug.Flush();
Trace.AutoFlush = true;
```

Close()

The Close() method flushes out the data and then turns off one or more listeners. Like the Flush() method, you can choose to close only one listener, by specifying which one you want, or all of them, by calling the Close() method directly on the Trace or Debug object. Once the Close() method is called, you cannot call any other methods on the closed objects, so always put this at the end of your code.

VB .NET

```
Trace.Listeners("MyListener").Close()
Trace.Close()
Debug.Listeners("MyListener").Close()
Debug.Close()
```

C#

```
Trace.Listeners["MyListener"].Close();
Trace.Close();
Debug.Listeners["MyListener"].Close();
Debug.Close();
```

TraceListeners

When a .NET application starts up, there are lots of built-in classes and objects that get loaded for you behind the scenes. Three examples of these are the Trace, Debug, and TraceListenersCollection classes. The TraceListenersCollection class is used to hold one or more TraceListeners. A *TraceListener* is an object that is used to direct where and when your messages will be sent. These TraceListeners must be added to the TraceListenersCollection before they can be used. As mentioned previously, there is a default listener added to the collection when your program starts, but you can add others.

To do this, you would first create a new object from either the TextWriterTraceListener or EventLogTraceListener class. As their names suggest, one writes out text and one sends messages to the Windows Event log. The one that sends text can be directed to write to either the console or a file. After you have created a listener, you need to add it to the collection before you can start sending your messages. Your code would look like the following:

VB .NET

```
Dim objTWFile As New TextWriterTraceListener("c:\Trace.log")
Dim objTWCon As New TextWriterTraceListener(Console.Out)
Dim objEL As New EventLogTraceListener("Mileage Calculator")
Trace.Listeners.Add(objTWFile)
Trace.Listeners.Add(objTWCon)
Trace.Listeners.Add(objEL)
```

C#

```
TextWriterTraceListener objTWFile =
  new TextWriterTraceListener("c:\\Trace.log");
TextWriterTraceListener objTWCon =
  new TextWriterTraceListener(Console.Out);
EventLogTraceListener objEL =
  new EventLogTraceListener("Mileage Calculator");
Trace.Listeners.Add(objTWFile);
Trace.Listeners.Add(objTWCon);
Trace.Listeners.Add(objEL);
```

When that is done, you would use Write(), WriteLine(), WriteIf(), and WriteLineIf() statements to send the messages to memory, and then use the Flush method to send them on to their final destination.

As you will see in Exercise 4-5, the Trace and Debug objects share the same Listeners collection. So, if you want to send out both Trace and Debug messages, you just add one listener, not two. When any of the Trace or Debug methods are called, the message will be sent to all of the listeners in the Listeners collection.

Exercise 4-5: Debugging with Listeners

In this exercise, you will learn how to use the Trace and TraceListener classes to help debug an application. You'll do this by modifying the existing code from Exercise 4-4 to send messages to the Output window, a text file, and the Windows Event Log.

■Note Before you begin this section, make sure the System.Diagnostics namespace is referenced at the top of your C# code page by adding using System.Diagnostics; if it is not there. This is not needed with VB .NET.

---

1. Open the project for the MileageCalculator program you made in Exercise 4-4 and locate the Catch block with your custom exception called MyCustomExecption. So far, you have been using a MessageBox to display the error message, but now you want to use a TraceListener instead.

2. Comment out the MessageBox code and add the following comments to the code (see Listing 4-8), which outline the steps you will take to implement the trace listeners.

Listing 4-8. *Using TraceListeners*

VB .NET

```
Catch ex As MyCustomException
    'Catch all MyCustomException errors,
    'Use the Object to show a Custom error Message
    'MessageBox.Show(ex.Message) < -- This line is no longer needed
    'Step a: Create the TraceListener Objects
    'Step b: Add the Objects to the Listeners collection
    'Step c: Set the system to automatic mode
    'Step d: Set the message you want to send
    'Step e: Send the message to all of the listeners, including the default
    'Step f: Close the file in the file version and clear all the Listeners
```

C#

```
catch (MyCustomException ex)
{
    //Catch all MyCustomException errors,
    //Use the Object to show a Custom error Message
    //MessageBox.Show(ex.Message); <-- This line is no longer needed
```

```
//Step a: Create the TraceListener Objects
//Step b: Add the Objects to the Listeners collection
//Step c: Set the system to automatic mode
//Step d: Set the message you want to send
//Step e: Send the message to all of the listeners, including the default
//Step f: Close the file in the file version and clear all the Listeners
}
```

3. Locate step A and add the code needed to create three new TraceListener objects, as shown here:

VB .NET

```
'Step a: Create the TraceListener Objects
Dim objTWFile As New TextWriterTraceListener("c:\Trace.log")
Dim objTWCon As New TextWriterTraceListener(Console.Out)
Dim objEL As New EventLogTraceListener("Mileage Calculator")
```

C#

```
//Step a: Create the TraceListener Objects
TextWriterTraceListener objTWCon =
  new TextWriterTraceListener(Console.Out);
TextWriterTraceListener objTWFile =
  new TextWriterTraceListener("c:\\Trace.log");
EventLogTraceListener objEL =
  new EventLogTraceListener("Mileage Calculator");
```

4. Add each of the new Trace objects to the TraceListeners collection, as shown here:

VB .NET

```
'Step b: Add the Objects to the Listeners collection
Trace.Listeners.Add(objTWFile)
Trace.Listeners.Add(objTWCon)
Trace.Listeners.Add(objEL)
```

C#

```
//Step b: Add the Objects to the Listeners collection
Trace.Listeners.Add(objTWFile);
Trace.Listeners.Add(objTWCon);
Trace.Listeners.Add(objEL);
```

5. Set the AutoFlush option to on, as shown in the following code. This will automatically call the Flush() method for you when you send a message with one of the Write() commands. Remember, when you want to have the messages show up in a file, you must Flush() the them from memory to the file. AutoFlush will do this for you.

VB .NET

```
'Step c: Set the system to automatic mode
Trace.AutoFlush = True
```

C#

```
//Step c: Set the system to automatic mode
Trace.AutoFlush = true;
```

6. Create a message to be sent. Include a header in the message so that it will be easy to see where your message starts, and add the current time to this header as well. After the header, add the short message coming from the exception thrown, and then add the longer message using the ToString() method, as shown here:

VB .NET

```
'Step d: Set the message you want to send
Dim strMessage As String
strMessage = "======( Trace Info: " + Now() + " )======" + vbCrLf
strMessage += ex.Message + vbCrLf
strMessage += ex.ToString()
```

C#

```
//Step d: Set the message you want to send
string strMessage;
strMessage = "======( Trace Info: " + DateTime.Now + " )======" + "\n";
strMessage += ex.Message + "\n";
strMessage += ex.ToString();
```

7. Send out the message using the WriteLine method, as shown here:

VB .NET

```
'Step e: Send the message to all of the listeners, including the default
Trace.WriteLine(strMessage)
```

C#

```
//Step e: Send the message to all of the listeners, including the default
Trace.WriteLine(strMessage);
```

8. Close up the text file listener so that the file does not remain locked for writing. Then clear out all the listeners, removing them from memory, since you will not be using them after this code ends:

VB .NET

```
'Step f: Close the file in the file version and clear all the Listeners
objTWFile.Close()
Trace.Listeners.Clear()
```

C#

```
//Step f: Close the file in the file version and clear all the Listeners
objTWFile.Close();
Trace.Listeners.Clear();
```

■Note When completed, your final code should look like Listing 4-9.

Listing 4-9. *Debugging with TraceListeners*

VB .NET

```
Catch ex As MyCustomEException
   'Catch all MyCustomException errors,
   'Use the Object to show a Custom error Message
   'MessageBox.Show(ex.Message) < -- This line is no longer needed

   'Step a: Create the TraceListener Objects
   Dim objTWFile As New TextWriterTraceListener("c:\Trace.log")
   Dim objTWCon As New TextWriterTraceListener(Console.Out)
   Dim objEL As New EventLogTraceListener("Mileage Calculator")

   'Step b: Add the Objects to the Listeners collection
   Trace.Listeners.Add(objTWFile)
   Trace.Listeners.Add(objTWCon)
   Trace.Listeners.Add(objEL)

   'Step c: Set the system to automatic mode
   Trace.AutoFlush = True

   'Step d: Set the message you want to send
   Dim strMessage As String
   strMessage = "======( Trace Info: " + Now() + " )======" + vbCrLf
   strMessage += ex.Message + vbCrLf
   strMessage += ex.ToString()

   'Step e: Send the message to all of the listeners, including the default
   Trace.WriteLine(strMessage)

   'Step f: Close the file in the file version and clear all the Listeners
   objTWFile.Close()
   Trace.Listeners.Clear()
```

C#

```
catch (MyCustomException ex)
{
   //Catch all MyCustomException errors,
   //Use the Object to show a Custom error Message
   //MessageBox.Show(ex.Message); <-- This line is no longer needed
```

```
//Step a: Create the TraceListener Objects
TextWriterTraceListener objTWCon =
  new TextWriterTraceListener(Console.Out);
TextWriterTraceListener objTWFile =
  new TextWriterTraceListener("c:\\Trace.log");
EventLogTraceListener objEL =
  new EventLogTraceListener("Mileage Calculator");

//Step b: Add the Objects to the Listeners collection
Trace.Listeners.Add(objTWFile);
Trace.Listeners.Add(objTWCon);
Trace.Listeners.Add(objEL);

//Step c: Set the system to automatic mode
Trace.AutoFlush = true;

//Step d: Set the message you want to send
string strMessage;
strMessage = "======( Trace Info: " + DateTime.Now + " )======" + "\n";
strMessage += ex.Message + "\n";
strMessage += ex.ToString();

//Step e: Send the message to all of the listeners, including the default
Trace.WriteLine(strMessage);

//Step f: Close the file in the file version and clear all the Listeners
objTWFile.Close();
Trace.Listeners.Clear();
}
```

9. If the error happens again, your code will just remake them when that code runs again. So start the program and set the value of Distance to Zero, as you did to test the MyCustomException class in Exercise 4-4, and verify that this is what happens. Make sure that you set the value of Distance and not Miles this time, or you will only see the Divide by Zero message again and not your new custom exception.

■**Note** If you have time, try changing the references to the Trace over to Debug instead. Then, test that the Trace commands work when you build in both Release and Debug modes, but that the Debug commands do not. Answers to this and all exercises in this book will be located in the DownloadFiles\ChapterX\ folder (substitute the number of the chapter for the letter X in the path). These files are available for download from the Source Code section of the Apress website (www.apress.com). See Appendix A for more details.

In this exercise, you saw how to use the Trace class, along with TraceListeners, to send error messages to the Output window, a text file, and the Windows Event log.

Turning On Trace After an Application Is Deployed

When you use the Write() and WriteLine() methods in your code, the messages will show up unconditionally whenever that line of code runs. When you use the Debug statements, you can turn these messages off by building the application in Release mode. However, the Trace statements are still there even when built in Release mode. Of course, you could just remove them, but it might be better to have them available in your released application. That way you will be able to turn them on or off at will. Microsoft thought of this as well, so they included a couple options that allow you to do just that.

One simple option is a BooleanSwitch that, when used with the WriteIf() and WriteLineIf() statements, turns tracing either on or off. The Boolean option works well for simple applications and it's easy to implement.

A second choice is similar, but it also allows you to specify different levels of tracing—it's called a TraceSwitch. The TraceSwitch levels let you display only the tracing information you want to look at for a specific problem. You can tell .NET that you only want to see error messages, warning messages, informational messages, verbose tracing messages, or no message at all. Each level of message has a number associated with it, like 1 for "error" and 2 for "warning." One interesting fact is that .NET does not check to see how you use the definitions in your code. Because of this, you could use all 1s in the .exe part of you application and 2s in the .dll part of your application, and then turn on only one or the other. This is a very nice feature, but you had better document your choices well or you may confuse people troubleshooting your applications later.

To use these options, and turn them either on or off, you need to add a configuration file to your project. This file needs to be stored in the folder as your executable file. To make things easier, Visual Studio can create a new configuration file for you. Select the Project ➤ Add New Item menu, and choose an Application Configuration File from the offered templates. Once you do that, Visual Studio will add a file called App.config. This is where you would type your configuration options, such as a BooleanSwitch.

However, when the project is built, Visual Studio will create an new file called the same name as your application plus .exe.config added at the end. For example, if an application is called BooleanSwitchDemo, the new configuration file will be named BooleanSwitchDemo.exe.config. This new file will be placed in the same folder as the .exe, as shown in Figure 4-30.

Remember, that file is only a text file, which allows you to change it even after you deploy the application. Be careful though, it is typed in an XML format, so be sure you pay attention to the syntax and case sensitivity. Also, don't forget to keep the proper filename, as mentioned previously, and place the file in the same folder as the .exe file. The file extension is required to be .exe.config by .NET. If it is not named correctly, then .NET acts as if it were not there at all.

In Figure 4-30, we have set up a BooleanSwitch by adding new XML tags. Notice that the name of the new switch is "MySwitch" and its value is set to 0. When the value is set to 0, all the WriteIf() and WriteLineIf() statements connected to this switch will be turned off. To turn them on again, you would change the value to any non-zero number, like 1.

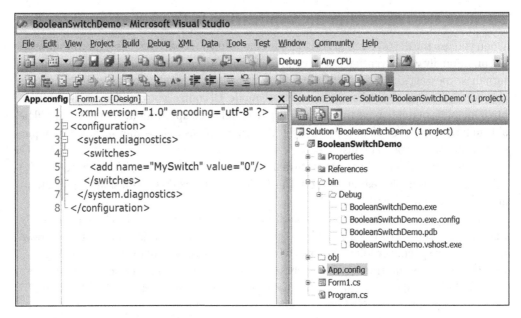

Figure 4-30. *Creating a configuration file*

Note We are showing the C# version of this file; the VB .NET version includes many other setting and it looks pretty messy. If you are using VB .NET, you need to find the <switches> section and just add another tag inside of it, like the one shown previously. We have provided a demo of both the C# and VB .NET versions in the DownloadFiles\Chapter4\Exercises\DemoCode folder. You can find this folder on the Apress website (www.apress.com) in the Source Code section. See Appendix A for more download details.

Of course, adding a switch to the configuration file will not have any impact if you do not associate the switch to a WriteIf() and WriteLineIf() statement. To do this you must create a new BooleanSwitch object and then provide the exact name of your switch from your configuration file (see Listing 4-10). You also must provide a description of the switch right after that, so that somebody looking at the configuration file later will know what it does.

Lastly, you need to use the BooleanSwitch as the conditional of your WriteIf() and WritelineIf() statements. Since both of these statements will only run when a condition is true, all you need to do is check the status of the switch, as shown in Listing 4-10. You may also add new Listeners if you'd like, as you did in Exercise 4-5.

Listing 4-10. *Using Switches*

VB .NET

```
Private Sub Button1_Click _
    (ByVal sender As System.Object, ByVal e As System.EventArgs) _
    Handles Button1.Click
```

```vb
  Dim BS1 As BooleanSwitch = New _
    BooleanSwitch("MySwitch", "Decription: Toggles Trace")

  Dim objTWFile As TextWriterTraceListener = New _
    TextWriterTraceListener("c:\SwitchDemo.txt")

  Trace.Listeners.Add(objTWFile)
  Trace.AutoFlush = True
  Trace.WriteLineIf(BS1.Enabled = True, "MyMessage", "MyCatagory")
  MessageBox.Show("Now look in SwitchDemo.txt when switch is on")
  objTWFile.Close()
  Trace.Listeners.Clear()
  End Sub
```

C#

```csharp
private void button1_Click(object sender, EventArgs e)
{
  //make sure to add using System.Diagnostics; at the top of the code file
  BooleanSwitch BS1 = new
    BooleanSwitch("MySwitch", "Decription: Toggles Trace");

  TextWriterTraceListener objTWFile = new
    TextWriterTraceListener("c:\\SwitchDemo.txt");

  Trace.Listeners.Add(objTWFile);
  Trace.AutoFlush = true ;

  Trace.WriteLineIf(BS1.Enabled == true, "MyMessage", "MyCatagory");
  MessageBox.Show("Now look in SwitchDemo.txt when switch is on");
  objTWFile.Close();
  Trace.Listeners.Clear();
}
```

One last note, when you are ready to deploy the .exe file for you application, you would send the configuration file along with it. When the .exe file and the configuration file are in the same folder, the Trace switch will be read and set to whatever value you have typed in. To change this setting later on, you would just open the file in a text editor, like Notepad, and change the 0 to 1. In this case, your Trace messages would then show up in the Windows Event log, but you could also make a Listener that sends it to a text file.

If a developer includes these, you can easily continue testing and troubleshooting applications in a production environment. Since you may be the developer of your testware, you may want to include these features as well.

Summary

In this chapter, you looked at several different debugging tools that you can use in your test projects. These range from built-in windows and features of Visual Studio to customizations you can add to your testware. If you would like to learn more on this subject, check out the references in Appendix C for further information. There you will find a reference to Dan Appleman's *Trace and Logging in .NET* booklet, which we believe you will find quite good.

Tester's Checklist
☑ Use breakpoints to pause your program.
☑ Use the debugging windows to help you test in Visual Studio.
☑ Use Debug and Trace to get debugging information after an application is deployed.
☑ Use Try-Catch blocks to handle exceptions in your applications.
☑ Use the built-in Exception classes for standard error handling.
☑ Use custom build Exception classes to provide your own error handling.
☑ Create code to throw exception errors when non–.NET errors are encountered.

CHAPTER 5

▪▪▪

Creating a Testing Framework

On any automated testing project, if you have to write every line of code from scratch every time, you'll never finish. If you start early in the project to identify tasks that can be written and stored as utilities and used repeatedly, it will save you time and prevent headaches. An additional benefit is that some of these utilities are usable on other projects. Remember from Chapter 1 that one of the goals of good software is *reuse*? Actually, the whole reason you are automating testing in the first place is to increase your testing capabilities with code and to avoid doing certain tests over and over manually, right? So, it makes sense to create pieces of code generic enough to be used more than once. In fact, it makes even more sense to create a reusable *framework* of test routines and utilities that you can use from test project to test project. These framework routines can include all of your favorite code for doing common tasks on a test project. Common tasks on a test project can include actual tests, but since those will often be very specific to your test project, your test utilities most often will include tasks that support your tests—tasks such as:

- Setting up test logging routines to report test results

- Creating application start-up and shut-down routines

- Creating platform reset routines, such as uninstalling or reinstalling programs to prepare for a test run

- Writing code to report platform statistics, such as the operating system version, installed hardware and software, computer name, etc.

- Creating routines to monitor system performance and state—for example, monitoring memory usage

This list is just the beginning. You will find many routines that you will find valuable and want to keep.

To create and use these utilities, you use a common programming structure called the *procedure*. Appendix B covers the basic idea of a procedure, and we also used this structure in Chapter 3. In this chapter, we will cover procedures formally, both subroutine and function procedures, and show you how to put them to good use in your test utilities. To create a test framework, you will need to learn about the various ways to create libraries of routines. In this chapter, you'll learn how to create a static library that you can take with you from test project to test project. Along the way, you will learn some additional techniques to round out your test, like adding timing and using the SendKeys() statement to send keystrokes to an application.

After that, the sky is the limit! You can create many different kinds of utilities, and you can set up a sophisticated, reusable test framework with the techniques you will learn in this chapter.

Objectives

By the end of this chapter, you will be able to do the following:

- Explain why the creation of utilities is important on a testing project

- Explain the term *test framework* and how utilities can be incorporated into a framework for your tests

- Build test utilities using procedures

- Describe the purpose and scope of Shared, static, and Form classes

- Add a new Form and a new Shared/static class to your .NET testware application

- Use the MenuStrip control to add menus to your testware

- Add code for simple timing to your test script

- Use the SendKeys() command to simulate user input

Using Procedures to Create Test Utilities

Many lines of code are useful enough to be used more than once—not just in one project, but in others as well. Rather than cutting and pasting, it makes sense to write the steps down and put them in a library where they can be accessed or called repeatedly. After all, the idea behind automated testing is to avoid duplication of labor. This same philosophy can be applied to reusing code—why reinvent the wheel?

Frequently, you might find yourself writing the same code and then copying and pasting it into new projects. When you find yourself doing that, you should consider creating a procedure for those statements. You write a procedure once, but you can use it (or "call" it) multiple times, which saves you from copying and pasting. Procedures, when created correctly, can be used in many of your projects by saving them into a library.

There are two kinds of procedures: ones that return a value and ones that don't. In Visual Basic .NET, subroutine procedures don't return values, while function procedures do. However, in C#, you just specify the data type you want to return, or use the keyword "void" if you do not want to return a value. You have already worked with a special-purpose subroutine procedure, the *event procedure*, many times; and in Exercise 3-3, you created your own function to write test results to a database. In VB .NET, all event procedures have the keyword "Sub" in their first line (Sub is short for *subroutine*); in C#, you will always see "void" as the return type if there is no return value. Listing 5-1 shows the subroutine procedure you used in Chapter 3 to write test results to a database.

Listing 5-1. *A Subroutine Procedure for Writing Test Results to a Database (see Chapter 3)*

VB .NET

```vbnet
Sub TestLog(ByVal tid As Integer, ByVal testdate As Date, _
    ByVal reqmt As String, ByVal Tester As String, ByVal result As Boolean)
  Dim cnTestResults As New OleDbConnection( _
    "Provider=Microsoft.jet.oledb.4.0;Data Source=TestResultsDB.mdb")
  Dim iRet As Integer
  cnTestResults.Open()
  Dim cmd As New OleDbCommand( _
    "Insert into TestResults (TestID, TestDate, Reqmt, Tester, Result) " & _
    " Values (" &   tid & ", '" & testdate & "', '" & _
      reqmt & "', '" & Tester & "', " & result & ")", cnTestResults)
        iRet = cmd.ExecuteNonQuery
        cnTestResults.Close()
End Sub
```

C#

```csharp
void TestLog(int tid, System.DateTime testdate,
             string reqmt, string Tester, bool result)
{
  OleDbConnection cnTestResults = new OleDbConnection(
    "Provider=Microsoft.jet.oledb.4.0;Data Source=TestResultsDB.mdb");
  int iRet;
  cnTestResults.Open();
  OleDbCommand cmd = new OleDbCommand(
    "Insert into TestResults (TestID, TestDate, Reqmt, Tester, Result) " + _
    " Values (" + tid + ", '" + testdate + "', '" + reqmt + "', '" +
      Tester + "', " + result + ")", cnTestResults);
  iRet = cmd.ExecuteNonQuery();
  cnTestResults.Close();
}
```

The TestLog procedure uses routines from the System.Data.OleDB namespace. So, you imported that namespace at the start of your program, and then you were able to call the TestLog routine to handle the job of opening a database, writing your test results, and then closing the database again. Now that you've gone to all the trouble of creating this routine, why not save this code in a location so that you can use it again? This procedure is not attached to any specific event or control so it can be executed any time you call it. To make it accessible, you will want to place it in a library of your own along with other useful procedures. Generic procedures, such as this one, will prove to be a very powerful way to expand the efficacy of your code. Before you do, though, you need to engage in some planning to make sure you are headed in the right direction.

Planning Your Procedures

Each procedure you create should be about doing one task. So, before actually sitting down and writing a bunch of routines, you need to do some planning. What exactly is the task you are trying to accomplish? How can you organize this task into manageable parts and write the code to implement it? Your initial task definition will either come from the Test Plan or from your Test Lead in the form of a test case. Then, assuming the test case you have been given includes automating all or part of the test case, you will have to sit down and plan how to write the code to accomplish it. In general, you will want to do what is done on, essentially, all software projects:

1. Analyze requirements (from the Test Plan and/or your Test Lead)

2. Design your automated tests

3. Write the test code

4. Test the test code—yes, you must test your tests!

5. Deliver (implement the test)

6. Maintain the test code

Depending on the task, you may have to repeat these steps many times to get your procedures just right, but in the end your goal is to have a solid, reusable set of statements. The procedures that you create will be grouped yet again, but this time into classes, structures, or code modules. You can think of these as subparts of the larger program. Like many subcontractors working on a big construction project, each class, structure, or module will have a specialty and will perform the tasks of that specialty though its procedures.

The code in our TestLog procedure is a bit complex, so for now let's take a step back and start a little more simply. In most tests that you will automate, there will be some essential starting tasks to perform, such as checking system statistics and then properly starting the application under test. At the end, there will be some clean-up tasks—for example, shutting down the application and printing out test results. In the next few sections, we will show you how to create some simple routines to start your application and to log test results. So your current design might be the following:

1. StartProgram

2. RunTest1

3. LogTests

Launching One Program from Another

One way to test an application is to start that application with a *test harness*. A test harness is a program that runs another program or part of another program. The test harness is generally used to run the application you are testing, and it includes codes to both launch and run some tests against that application. In .NET, you use the Process.Start() command to start another application from within an application. You first used the Process.Start() command in Chapter 3 to run the Notepad utility. In that code, you weren't testing Notepad, so your code really couldn't be considered a test harness; you launched the Notepad utility for another reason—i.e., so you could display the file into which you had written your test results. You'll use similar code, though, to launch the applications you want to test. The Process.Start() method will come in handy for that.

The Process.Start() method launches a *process*. Each application running on a computer will use at least one process. There is a built-in cycle of time that each process has in order to access the resources of the computer, such as the RAM, hard drives, and processor. This happens so fast that you don't notice it—to the computer user it seems that all applications are accessing the computer hardware at the same time. Think of how a motion picture seems to be one smooth-running image but is really made up of individual pictures displayed rapidly one after another and you will have an idea of how these processes allow a computer to appear to run multiple programs simultaneously.

Each process is further divided by its *threads*. A thread can execute any part of the code of the process, including parts currently being executed by another thread in the same process. Many applications work just fine with one thread, but some, like Microsoft Word, which runs a spell checker in the background while you type, will have more. That's right, the spell checker in Word runs as a separate, independent thread. Again, you cannot tell that there are many threads taking their turn at the hardware because the cycle is so fast. To start a new process and the first thread associated with it, all you need to do is call the Process.Start() method. The code in Listing 5-2 shows how to start the Calculator using the Process.Start() method.

Listing 5-2. *Starting a New Process and Its First Thread*

VB. NET

```
Private Sub Button1_Click(ByVal sender As System.Object, _
    ByVal e As System.EventArgs) Handles Button1.Click
  Process.Start("Calc.exe")
End Sub
```

C#

```
private void button1_Click(object sender, EventArgs e)
 {
   Process.Start("Calc.exe");
 }
```

This code will open up the Calculator when button1 is clicked. You can make this code more flexible by creating an additional procedure with the same code and calling the new procedure from this button's Click event procedure.

Moving this code to its own procedure will make it independent of any particular events. This means that you can call the procedure from different places in your application. At this stage, you should write out comments about what you want the procedure to do. This will help you focus your efforts and keep your routines simple and direct. Listing 5-3 shows some sample pseudocode comments.

Listing 5-3. *Pseudocode for Running an Application*

VB .NET

```
Public Class Form1
  Public Sub StartProgram(ByVal strAppname As String)
   'This routine will start a new process with the name and
   'path contained in strAppname.
   'TODO If a log file does not exist, it will create one

    Process.Start(strAppname)

    'TODO Add code to log start time.
  End Sub
```

C#

```
public void StartProgram(string strAppName)
{
  //This routine will start a new process with the name and
  //path contained in strAppname .
  //TODO If a log file does not exist, it will call a routine to create one.


  Process.Start(strAppname);

  //TODO Add code to log start time.
}
```

Most of the preceding comments are a form of *pseudocode*. Only the call to Process.Start() and the start and ending lines of the routine are actual code. The rest is pseudocode, which is just what it sounds like—code that isn't real. Pseudocode isn't executable code, but it includes statements in plain English (or your native language) descriptive enough to allow you to plan how you will organize and write real code. This is part of the planning and design process that developers use to help write organized code. When you have everything listed that needs to be done, you go back and add the code that really does the task you outlined in your notes. The pseudocode can be left as documentation (i.e., comments) to remind you in plain language what it is you're doing. This just helps you organize your intent.

By the way, the use of TODO is not accidental. The .NET IDE will recognize the 'TODO (or //TODO in C#) and will place that entire statement in the Task List for your application. You can then refer to that list to remind you to finish the code you have written in pseudocode, or for anything else you want to remind yourself "todo." In fact, you can double-click on the TODO lines in the Task List window and your cursor will move to that exact line in the code. It's a great way to get to the place you've been working. Figure 5-1 shows the Task List window with a few TODOs.

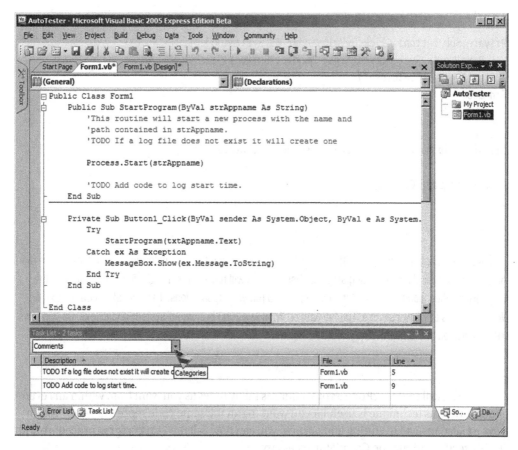

Figure 5-1. *The Task List window displaying a TODO list*

To display the Task List window, select View ➤ Other Windows ➤ Task List (in Visual Studio 2005, select View ➤ Task List). In order to see your TODO list, you will need to select Comments from the Task List window's Categories drop-down list as shown in Figure 5-1 as well.

Now, the question is when and how will this new procedure run? Event procedures run in response to an event. Since the StartProgram procedure you just wrote is not an event procedure, and is therefore not associated with any control, there is no event that will automatically cause it to run.

When you want the StartProgram procedure to run, the first thing you must ask yourself is *when?* This is event-driven programming, remember? Once you have determined when you want it to run, choose the correct event procedure from which to run it, and then you can simply type the name of your StartProgram procedure into that event procedure. Using programming terms, we say we are *calling* the procedure when we do this. The generic procedures you create yourself won't run unless called. In this case, you want your new StartProgram procedure to run when the user clicks a button. To call the new procedure, create a button and type the name of the procedure you want to call into the Click-event code of the button. Since the program requires an argument (i.e., the name of the program to run), you must provide that argument. In the following code, you pass the name of the Calculator application:

VB .NET

```
Private Sub Button1_Click(ByVal sender As System.Object, _
    ByVal e As System.EventArgs) Handles Button1.Click
  StartProgram("Calc.exe")
End Sub
```

C#

```
private void button1_Click(object sender, EventArgs e)
{
  StartProgram("Calc.exe");
}
```

Note This snippet of code is written using the knowledge that the Calculator accessory is located in the default path for Windows operating systems. Usually, you will have to provide the full pathname, i.e., the directory location along with the filename, in order to run your applications. The full path to Calc.exe on Windows NT is c:\winnt\calc.exe. The full path on Windows 2000 is c:\winnt\system32\calc.exe. On Windows XP, it is located in C:\WINDOWS\System32\calc.exe.

You can call the StartProgram procedure as many times as you want from within any event procedure. This technique is useful if you want to run the same code more than once within your project. Instead of cutting and pasting, you can now call the StartProgram procedure and it will execute and run the Calculator accessory.

Exercise 5-1 is a simple exercise designed to give you the feel of writing a short procedure that can be called many times.

Exercise 5-1: Creating a StartProgram Routine

1. Create a new Windows application (Windows Forms) project and name it AutoTester.

2. Place a button on the Form1 and change its properties to match Table 5-1.

Table 5-1. *Properties to Set for the AutoTester Application*

Object	Property	Value
Form1	Text	AutoTester
textBox1	Name	txtAppname
textBox1	Text	(leave this blank)
button1	Name	btnStartApp
button1	Text	Start Application

Your form should look similar to Figure 5-2.

Figure 5-2. *The AutoTester form*

3. In the form's Code window, type in the following code for the btnStartApp_Click event and the StartProgram procedure:

VB .NET

```
Public Sub StartProgram(ByVal strAppname As String)

  Process.Start(strAppname)

End Sub

Private Sub Button1_Click(ByVal sender As System.Object, _
  ByVal e As System.EventArgs) Handles btnStartApp.Click
  Try
    StartProgram(txtAppname.Text)
  Catch ex As Exception
    MessageBox.Show(ex.Message.ToString)
  End Try
End Sub
```

C#

```
using System.Diagnostics;
/* The above line goes in the directives section */
public void StartProgram(string strAppname)
{
  Process.Start(strAppname);
}


private void btnStartApp_Click(object sender, EventArgs e)
{
  try
  {
    StartProgram(txtAppname.Text);
  }
```

```
catch (Exception ex)
{
  MessageBox.Show(ex.Message.ToString());
}
}
```

4. Press F5 to run your program. Enter **Calc** in the textbox, then click the button. What happens? (You should see the Calculator program run.) Try it again, this time typing **Notepad** and then clicking the button. Now try it one more time using the following full path: **C:\Program Files\Internet Explorer\ iexplore.exe.** (This assumes you have Internet Explorer installed in this location.) To see the information written into the Debug object, select Debug ➤ Windows ➤ Immediate from the main menu.

In this exercise, you have written a simple, general procedure called StartProgram. You could call it again from any other spot in your code by simply typing its name and providing the full path to an executable file in the textbox.

In Exercise 5-1, it might have struck you that it would have been easier, and less code, just to call Process.Start() from within the button's Click event, rather than pass the name of the application to the procedure. And you would be right, for this short example, but what you're doing is setting up the StartProgram procedure so that it's available and ready once you decide you need, or want, to put more code around the start of your application. As you learn and know more about what you'd like to do as an application starts, you can add that code to the StartProgram routine and only have to type it there once. You will modify the StartProgram routine to be more useful, but first you'll learn a little more about some procedure basics, such as when and how you can access procedures, and how to place them in a library.

Using Function Procedures

Functions, like subs, are also procedures. The main difference between functions and subs is that a function *always* returns a value. Another difference is that functions can be used in an arithmetic expression. For example, the following is a function for calculating the average of three numbers. It takes three arguments and returns a value representing the average of those three numbers.

VB .NET

```
Private Function AvgSize(ByVal F1 As int16, ByVal F2 As int16, _
    ByVal F3 As int16) As int32
  Return (F1 + F2 + F3) / 3
End Function
```

C#

```
private int32 AvgSize(int16 F1 , int16 F2 , int16 F3 )
{
  return (F1 + F2 + F3) / 3;
}
```

Notice that in the C# example, the word Function does not exist. This is because C# does not make a formal distinction between subs and functions. They are both procedures, it's just that some do return a value and some don't. In both of these examples, you are telling the system that you wish to return a 32-bit integer. So, a function, unlike a procedure, has a single value that it returns (in VB .NET, the extra As int32 indicates the data type of that return value). This function has declared three parameters; each is specified with its name and data type and separated from the others by commas. The parameters listed inside the parentheses list what must be *passed to* the function (F1 As int16, F2 As int16, F3 As int16) and the As int32 is what the function *gives back*.

TESTER'S TIP: AVERAGE VALUES

Taking an average value is a common testing task. For example, you may test the performance of a certain task of an application (such as logging into an application) by measuring how long it takes to complete. How can you be certain that the performance you saw is typical? Often you will perform the test multiple times and then take an average. This is just one example; you will likely find many others.

Another difference between procedures and functions is that somewhere within the body of the function you will see the word Return. On the right-hand side will be the value that the function returns. Since the function must return a value, you must assign the function a value in the body of the code. Leaving this out will cause an error. Also, any code after the Return statement runs will not be processed. The following is the line that does this for the AvgSize function:

VB .NET

```
Return (F1 + F2 + F3) / 3
```

Note In VB. NET, you may see the name of the function on the left-hand side of an equal sign instead of return, for example:

```
AvgSize = (F1 + F2 + F3) / 3
```

It's just another way of setting the return value for the function. The benefit of doing it this way is that you can set the value many different times. The function does not end on this line, but only on a line with a Return command, or when the end of the function is reached. It's the only way it could be set in VB6, so you may see this format a lot in older code that has been converted to .NET. While this is still allowed for backward compatibility, you should use the word Return instead.

Procedure Accessibility

You may have noticed that when an event procedure is created, it has the Private keyword preceding the word "Sub". We also used this Private keyword when we created our own procedures. The Private keyword is actually called an *accessibility modifier*. Accessibility modifiers are used to affect the *scope* of the routine—i.e., from where in the application it can be called.

Every procedure or function must be declared with a modifier to indicate its scope, or else its scope will be `Public` by default. If a procedure is declared `Private`, then that procedure can only be called from within the form in which it is declared. So far, you have been working with an application that only has one form, so it really hasn't been an issue. However, you will soon be adding new forms and other kinds of modules to your application. If you want to call your new general routines from code in some other part of the application, you need to make sure that the routine is declared with the appropriate access modifier and placed in the proper location. Table 5-2 shows the access modifiers available in .NET.

Table 5-2. *Access Modifers in .NET*

VB .NET	C#	Description
Public	Public	Available anywhere inside a project and to other projects that reference the project
Private	Private	Available only inside the class (or module or structure) in which it's declared
Friend	Internal	Available inside the project, but not to projects that reference the project
Protected	Protected	Available inside the class in which it's declared and to any derived classes
Protected Friend	Protected Internal	Available inside the project and to any derived classes

We've listed all of the access modifiers for completeness, but the only ones that make sense for you right now are `Public`, `Private`, and `Friend/Internal`. The other modifiers are applicable when we start talking about creating classes that inherit from another class. We'll cover inheritance in Chapter 6, so we'll leave discussion of those access modifiers until then.

For the routines written so far, you've used only the `Private` access modifier, which means that you can only use the procedures inside the form in which they were declared. In order to make them more accessible and more reusable, you'll learn to place them inside a specially created class.

Building a Testing Framework Using a Static Class

Once you start to amass useful functions and procedures, like the simple `StartProgram` procedure and some of the things you learned in Chapter 3 (like working with the Registry and Regular Expressions), you will likely find that you want to use them in more than one test project. So far, you have written procedures and functions (in Chapter 3) inside of one form class and have declared them with the `Private` keyword. If you create the routines with a `Public` scope, you can access them from anywhere in your .NET application. Rather than have `Public` procedures in a `Form` module though, it makes sense to move your general functions and subroutines to a general location—a sort of library file. There, they will be easier to locate and maintain. In .NET, one place to store general routines is in a static class module.

To create a new class, select Project ➤ Add Class from the main menu. The Add New Item dialog will display, as shown in Figure 5-3. (Actually, if you select Add User Control, Add New Item, or Add Windows Form, then the same dialog displays, just with a different icon selected.) Here VB .NET and C# differ in the templates provided for your use, so Figure 5-3 shows both dialogs.

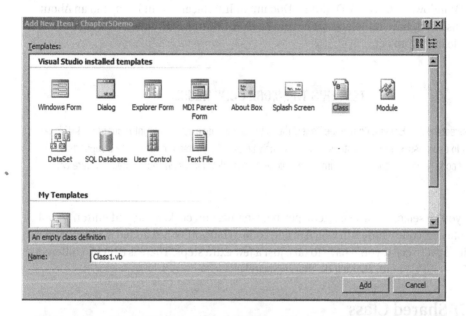

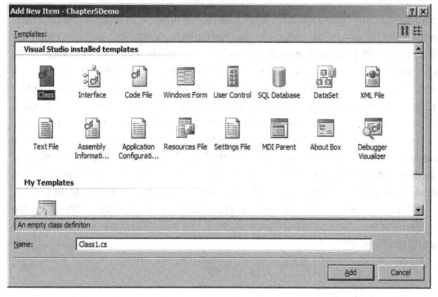

Figure 5-3. *The Add New Item dialogs for both VB .NET and C# display a different set of templates.*

Note These templates also differ between versions. Visual Studio has many other installed templates. Those shown are from the Beta Express edition for C# and VB .NET.

Notice that there are quite a few items that you can add to a project. VB .NET and C# provide many of the same templates—for example, they both have templates for adding forms including an additional Windows Form, an MDI (Multi-Document Interface) Parent form, and an About box. They also both have templates for creating a User Control, SQL database, DataSet, Class, and Text File in the project.

TESTER'S TIP: MORE CODE REUSE

You can select the Add Existing Item of the Project menu to add already existing files into your project. This will allow you to use classes, forms, controls, etc., previously created by yourself or others. This supports the concept of code reuse—a good programming technique for both developers *and* automated testware writers.

Once you've selected the class item, given it a name, and clicked the Add button, you'll have a whole new code window in which to add code. What you've just added is a regular class. To make it a `static` class, you'll have to take just a few extra steps. There is a bit of a difference in VB .NET versus C# here, so we'll do this separately.

VB .NET Shared Class

VB .NET doesn't specifically have a special `static` class as C# does; so in order to create a class which can be used simply as a code receptacle, you have two options. First, you can create a VB .NET code module. VB6 programmers will remember the module structure as a place where they could place general routines. A VB .NET code module is similar to a C# `static` class. You can create a code module by selecting Project ▶ New Module from the main menu. This should make former VB6 programmers happy. If you're not a former VB6 programmer, don't bother. The second way of creating a `static` class is more compatible with the other .NET languages, so that's what you're going to work with here. You create a regular class, as you learned how to do in the previous section, and then you just fill it with shared members. A shared member of a class is a member that can be used directly with the class name without having to first declare a member of the class (you'll see what we mean when we use this class in code). Listing 5-4 shows a VB .NET "Static" class already loaded with the `StartProgram` procedure, and also with a couple of procedures you can use to log information out to a file. This code is very similar to what you learned in Chapter 3.

Listing 5-4. *Shared Class in VB .NET with Some Useful Procedures*

```vb
Imports System.Diagnostics
Imports System.IO

Public Class TestLib
  Public Shared Logfile As String = "c:\testlog.txt"

  Public Shared Sub StartProgram(ByVal strAppname As String)
    'This routine will start a new process with normal focus.
    'Allow the user to choose the path of the application
    'and log the starting time to a file. If the logfile does not
    'exist the CreateLog routine is called.

    Process.Start(strAppname)
    If Not File.Exists(Logfile) Then
      CreateLog("Starting Log file " & DateTime.Now)
    End If
    LogtoFile("Application " & _
        strAppname & " Started at: " & DateTime.Now)
  End Sub

  Public Shared Sub CreateLog(ByVal strHeader As String)
    Dim Writer As StreamWriter
    Writer = File.CreateText(Logfile)
    Writer.WriteLine(strHeader)
    Writer.Close()
  End Sub

  Public Shared Sub LogtoFile(ByVal strLog As String)
    Dim Writer As StreamWriter
    Writer = File.AppendText(Logfile)
    Writer.WriteLine(strLog)
    Writer.Close()
  End Sub
End Class
```

Note the following about the code in Listing 5-4:

- There are two imported libraries: System.Diagnostics and System.IO. System.Diagnostics gives you access to the Process class that you use to launch an application in your StartProgram routine. The System.IO library provides access to the routines you need so you can write to the log file.

- The `StartProgram` subroutine has a call to a new routine named `CreateLog` and another call to a routine named `LogtoFile`. You'll notice that both the `CreateLog` and `LogtoFile` routines are created in the class as well. It's possible to call one routine from another—this technique is called *procedure nesting*. Both of these routines contain code that will be very familiar to you if you've read Chapter 3, since it's basically the same code but written inside of a reusable subroutine.

- The keyword `Shared` is included in the first line of each subroutine in this class.

To call this from anywhere within the project, all you have to do is use the name of the class, as shown in the following code snippet:

```
TestLib.Logfile = "c:\TestLog.log"
TestLib.StartProgram("Calc.exe")
```

Next, you'll see how to create a similar class in C#.

C# Static Class

A `static` class in C# is specifically intended to hold only `static` members, i.e., members that can be accessed directly with the class name. It's just what you need to hold a library of your basic test routines. It is similar in function to what you created for VB .NET in the preceding section. Listing 5-5 shows a C# `static` class.

Listing 5-5. *Static Class in C# with Some Useful Procedures*

```csharp
using System.Diagnostics;
using System.IO;

static class TestLib
  {
    public static string Logfile = "c:\\logfile.txt";

    public static void StartProgram(string strAppName)
    {
      if (!(File.Exists(Logfile)))
      {
       CreateLog("Starting Log file " + DateTime.Now);
      }
      Process.Start(strAppName);
      LogtoFile("Application " + strAppName + "
         Started at: " + DateTime.Now);
    }
```

```
private static void CreateLog(string strHeader)
{
  StreamWriter Writer;
  Writer = File.CreateText(Logfile);
  Writer.WriteLine(strHeader);
  Writer.Close();
}

private static void LogtoFile(string strLog)
{
  StreamWriter Writer;
  Writer = File.AppendText(Logfile);
  Writer.WriteLine(strLog);
  Writer.Close();
}
}
```

In Exercise 5-2, you're going to create a static class library and add in some useful routines to get started on a testing framework.

Exercise 5-2: Creating a Testing Framework

1. If necessary, reopen the AutoTester application created in Exercise 5-1.

2. From the main menu, select Project ➤ Add Class. Be sure the class icon is selected and change the name of the class from the default name, Class1.vb, to TestLib.vb (for VB .NET) or from Class1.cs to TestLib.cs (for C#). Then click the Add button. The TestLib code window will display.

3. Within the TestLib class, you will add a number of functions and procedures as Shared (VB .NET) or static (C#) members of the class. Add the code from Listing 5-4 (VB .NET) or Listing 5-5 (C#) so that your code window looks the same as the appropriate listing.

4. Return to the Form1.vb code window and delete the code for the StartProgram subroutine. You'll now see a blue squiggly line under the call to the StartProgram routine in the btnStartApp (button1) Click event. This is because the .NET IDE cannot find the StartProgram routine even though it is listed as public in the class you added. In order to find it, you'll have to help out by indicating where it's located. You'll do that in the next step.

5. Modify the code in the button's Click event so that it looks like the following:

VB .NET

```
Try
  TestLib.Logfile = "c:\testlog.log"
  TestLib.StartProgram(txtAppname.Text)
Catch ex As Exception
  MessageBox.Show(ex.Message.ToString)
End Try
```

C#

```
try
{
    TestLib.Logfile = "c:\\testlog.log";
    TestLib.StartProgram(txtAppname.Text);
}
catch (Exception ex)
{
  MessageBox.Show(ex.Message.ToString());
}
```

In this code, you have really only added one line and modified one other. The first line, after the `Try`, sets a variable from your `TestLib` that will be used to create the log file. In the next line, the `StartProgram` routine is called exactly the same as before except you told the system to look in the `TestLib` to find it.

6. Try out your new program and verify that the `Logfile` was created and the correct information was added into it.

In this exercise, you created a `static/Shared` class. The true value of creating and using such a class is demonstrated when you have another project that needs to use the same code. In the next section, you'll see how to reuse this library.

Adding Existing Classes to Projects

Another great benefit of all classes is the ability to add them to other projects. Once you have created a set of useful utilities in a `Shared/static` class, you can import that class into other projects. There are a number of ways to do this. We want to share the choices with you so that you can choose the best way for your project. In Chapter 6, we'll show you how to create a full class library of routines for your test project while taking advantage of the full object-oriented capabilities of .NET. In this chapter, we'll show you the uncomplicated approach of simply adding an existing file into your project. One advantage to this simple approach is speed. It's easy to do and may be the fastest way to get the job done in certain situations.

Here's how you can add an existing class to a .NET project: Select Project ➤ Add Existing Item. The Add Existing Item dialog displays (see Figure 5-4). Navigate to the item you want to add, select it, and click Open. The class is now added to your Project window. Class files in VB .NET will have a `.vb` extension, and class files in C# will have a `.cs` extension. (Note that this process is the way you add any kind of item to a .NET project, whether or not it is a class.)

Caution If the class you are adding has the same name as another class in your project, you will get an error message. The solution is to rename the class in your application first (change its Name property in the Properties window) and then import the new one.

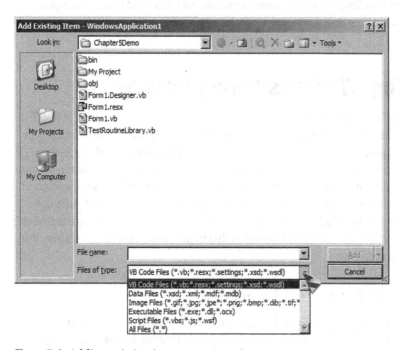

Figure 5-4. *Adding existing items to your project*

In Figure 5-4, the Files Of Type drop-down list is displayed showing the file extensions of all the kinds of existing items you can add to your project. Remember that when you created a class file in Exercise 5-2, it had an extension of .vb or .cs. Form files have this extension also and so do a few other types of files as well. As you can see, there are many other kinds of items you can add. You will explore many of these different files as you proceed.

Once you have imported your static/Shared class file, your new project now has the power of the procedures and variables you created earlier. All you have to do to use them is add the appropriate declarations and calls to the routines using the format *classname.item*. This is why it is critical to make sure your procedures and variables are properly scoped in all classes—i.e., declared with the correct access modifier. You need to plan your class carefully to make sure that you can access the things you need to.

This is also why good documentation in the form of well-thought-out, relevant comments will become your friend—it may seem hard to imagine but, in the future, you could have tens or hundreds of files you've written and keeping them straight (project management) is difficult! That's why good commenting is a great habit to have.

TESTER'S TIP: VERSION CONTROL

You should enforce version control for your files. It can quickly become chaotic trying to remember which .NET script goes with which product build—especially when you have a lot of people writing them! Microsoft's Visual SourceSafe is software that can provide this kind of version management. There are other software packages that will do the same thing. Or, you can enforce version control yourself, but it can become quite complicated very quickly in a large project.

Understanding Windows Forms Classes

You may have noticed that forms are also classes. If you didn't notice that, just look at the first few lines of the code window for any form. Form classes and other classes work identically in the way that variables, constants, procedures, and functions are declared and used within them.

The major difference between a Form class and any other class is that the Form class contains a visual interface—i.e., it contains a screen that the user can see at runtime. As we mentioned earlier, Shared/static classes are code storage areas and are never actually seen by the user. You can think of them as a library where general code is stored. Form classes, in contrast, have a specific use, and that is to store the information needed to properly process and display the form and its associated controls.

Adding Additional Forms to a Project

Each Windows project contains one default form. You can create additional forms for your projects, as well as add in existing forms that have already been created, in much the same way you did in the static/Shared class example. To add a new form, select Project ➤ Add Windows Form. The same Add New Item dialog displays, and the only difference from selecting this and having selected Add Class is that this time the Windows Form icon is highlighted. Notice that you can create a couple of forms based on templates, as shown in Figure 5-3. For example, you can create an About Box, an MDI Parent Form (used for multidocument, interface applications, i.e., applications that need multiple child forms within a parent, like Microsoft Word), or a Splash Screen (VB .NET) by selecting these icons. You will find that these templates come complete with default controls and code. The idea is that you will modify these templates to your needs. Selecting the Windows Form icon adds another empty Windows Form just like the default one the application starts with.

In Exercise 5-3, you'll use one of these templates, the Windows Form template, to add a new form to an application. You'll also see how to properly reference this new form in your code.

Exercise 5-3: Adding a New Form

In Exercise 5-3, you will add a Form module to an existing .NET application. You can use the application you worked on from Exercise 5-2 or you can use any existing or new .NET application to do this. (There is no template or exercise files for this exercise.)

1. Open the AutoTester application from Exercise 5-2, then select Project ➤ Add Windows Form. The Add New Item dialog appears. Select the About Box form template and click the Add button. A new form called AboutBox1.vb or AboutBox1.cs now appears in your Project window, and the new Form object appears in the Form Designer window.

2. In the Form Designer window, right-click anywhere on your new form and select View Code from the pop-up menu. Review the code behind the form. Notice, first, that it represents a new class called AboutBox1. Within the code for this class, you'll see that VB .NET uses a new namespace called My. The My namespace is a very useful one for VB .NET programmers. It is, essentially, a one-stop shop for returning information about the system—something you always need to do. You'll learn more about this namespace in Chapter 7. C# uses the this keyword to get to similar information contained within the Form class. Although you can customize the values for the labels of the form, such as Product Name, Version, Copyright, and Company Name, these values will be consistent with other locations in your application if you change them from the My Project folder.

3. In the Project Designer window, click the Assembly Information button. The Assembly Information dialog is displayed. Figure 5-5 shows the Project Designer window within the VB .NET IDE and the Assembly Information dialog as well. (C#'s window will be slightly different, but we will use only the common items.)

Make changes to the Assembly Information dialog similar to what you see in Figure 5-5. For example, change the File Version number to 1.5.5.5 by placing those four numbers, respectively, in the Major, Minor, Build, and Revision boxes. (Do not change the GUID number.) When done, click OK on the Assembly Information dialog. You might want to spend some time perusing the rest of the information on the other tabs within the Project Designer, but you won't change any other values.

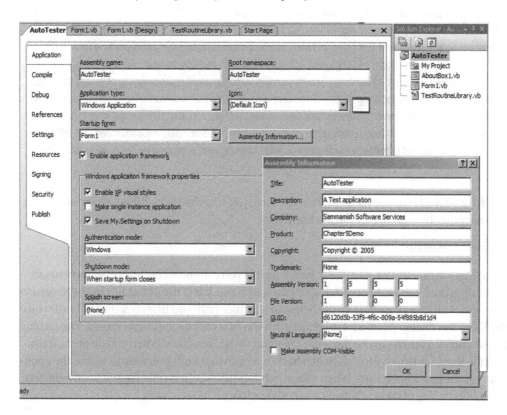

Figure 5-5. *The Project Designer window and the Assembly Information dialog*

4. Make other changes to the About Box form by returning to the Form Designer window and using the Properties window. For example, you can change the height, width, and back color of the form from here. Save your work when you're finished, but do not close the application. You'll use it for the next exercise.

In this exercise, you've learned how to add a form, modify it, and display it as the start-up form.

Now you know how to create a new form from a template and edit it—so how do you determine when and how to display it? In the next section, you'll learn about the commands to move from one form to another in an application. You'll also learn about adding menus using a new control: the MenuStrip.

Displaying Forms

Once you have a new Form module and you've added code and controls to customize it, you might think you can just run your program and this new form will appear automatically. Forms don't just appear on their own. You must write code to manage when and how the new form will display in the program.

TESTER'S TIP: CREATING TEST DRIVER SOFTWARE VS. QUICK TEST SCRIPTS

Managing the display of multiple forms on an application usually takes a lot of analysis and thought. For most of your testware applications, try not to worry about creating a fabulous user interface; you will not usually be creating software for wide public distribution, but just for your own purposes. In some cases, test teams will choose to build sophisticated Test Driver software, which can mean creating user interfaces for a large number of testers. These systems can be very useful, but you will need to carefully consider whether you want to spend the time and budget to build one. You may end up finding yourself in the business of writing test tools and not have much time for actual testing. So be careful to really consider how many forms you need and how much time you want to spend on the interface, because the more you add, the more you will have to determine how to manage. For that reason, in this book, we try not to focus on developing a sophisticated user interface with fancy controls, but to create as much useful code for retrieving system information and running actual tests.

To display a form, you have two choices. First, you can choose to display a form as a dialog box using the ShowDialog method as shown here:

Formname.ShowDialog

When a form displays as a dialog box, it means you cannot access any other form in the application until you've dealt with it. For example, if you select the About Box in the Notepad accessory, you cannot go back to the Notepad interface until you first click the OK button on the About Box dialog. When a form behaves this way, it is called *application modal*. The second way to display a form is to use the Show() method of the Form class. When you display a form with the Show() method, you can switch back and forth to it from other forms within the application as the application runs. When a form behaves this way, it is called *application modeless*. The following line of code will display a modeless form:

Formname.Show

Although you really don't want to spend a lot of time learning how to create fancy interfaces, up to this point you've only created applications with the most simple controls, buttons, textboxes, and labels. In Exercise 5-4, you'll display the new form you added in Exercise 5-3 using a menu.

Exercise 5-4: Displaying a Form

1. If necessary, reopen the AutoTester application from Exercise 5-3. Select Form1 in your application. Open the Toolbox window and locate the MenuStrip control. Double-click it to add it to your form. A menu is added to the form (displaying the text "Type Here"), and the MenuStrip control is added to the *component tray* (see Figure 5-6).

   What's the component tray? The component tray shows a list of controls that are attached to the form that either don't display (as you'll see with the Timer control soon) or, in the case of the MenuStrip control, can have more than one in the same location on the form. It allows you to easily locate the control and click on it to view its properties, whereas it might be difficult to find the control otherwise. Up to this point, you have created controls that do not use the component tray; but many controls do get added to this tray, so you'll see more as you create more testware.

▮**Caution** Now that you have two forms, be careful to place the MenuStrip on the correct form. Place it on the main form (Form1) in your application—do *not* place the menu on your new AboutBox1 form!

   This new menu will be used to show the AboutBox1 form and also to exit the program in the standard Windows way. In the next steps, you'll add code to do that.

2. Locate where the "Type Here" text is displayed on the MenuStrip in the Form Designer window. (If you don't see it, all you need to do is to click the MenuStrip control in the component tray once again and you will.) Click the displayed text, then type **&File**. This creates a top-level menu item. Click the next box under that one, then type **E&xit**. This creates a submenu item underneath &File. Now click just to the right of where you originally typed &File and create a second top-level menu item by typing **&Special**. Click just below that and create a submenu item under this one by typing **Start &Application**. Now, using the same process, add a third top-level menu item called **&Help** and a submenu item underneath it called **&About**. Table 5-3 shows the menu items to create.

Table 5-3. *Menu Items to Create*

Top-Level Menu	Submenu Item
&File	E&xit
&Special	Start &Application
&Help	&About

Figure 5-6 shows the `MenuStrip` control on the `AutoTester` form filled with these menu items (the `Exit` submenu item is not shown, but it is there!). Be sure your `MenuStrip` looks similar to this.

It may seem strange, but each time you typed in some text into the `MenuStrip` control, you were creating a separate control. Each menu item has its own set of properties. You'll see each menu item by opening the Properties window and clicking on each Menu Item in the drop-down list. For example, the Help menu item will show up in the Properties box as `HelpToolStripMenuItem` and the File menu item will show up as `FileToolStripMenuItem`. Note that you can change some of the properties of these controls, including their long and cumbersome names, just as you have done with other controls. For now, you will leave them as is. You'll write code for the Click event of these menu items in the next steps.

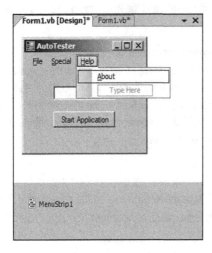

Figure 5-6. *The AutoTester form*

3. To write code for a menu item, you simply double-click it as you would any other control. Once in the code window, type the following line of code for the `exitToolStripMenuItem_Click` event.

VB .NET

```
Me.Close()
```

C#

```
this.Close();
```

Yes, that's all there is to it! One line closes the form.

4. Return to the Form Designer window and select the Help ➤ About menu item. Write the following code for its `AboutToolStripMenuItem_Click` event:

VB .NET

```
AboutBox1.ShowDialog()
```

C#

```
AboutBox1 aForm = new AboutBox1();
aForm.ShowDialog();
```

This code will display the About box. Notice that for C# you have a little more work than VB .NET. In C#, you must create a new instance of the form before you can show it. So in the C# code, you create a new form called aForm that will look exactly like the AboutBox1 form you created. In earlier versions of VB .NET, you had to do this as well, but now they've made it a bit easier and you can show the form in one line, as done previously in VB6.

5. Return to the Form Designer once again, and this time select the Special ➤ Start Application menu item. Write the following code for the StartApplicationToolStripMenuItem_Click event:

```
btnStartApp.PerformClick()    ' for C# add the semicolon at the end!
```

This line of code saves you from copying and pasting the same code from the button into the menu control. This is more reusable also, so that if you decide to change the code for the button's Click event, this code will not have to change.

Listing 5-6 shows the full code for this exercise.

Listing 5-6. *Full Code for Exercise 5-4*

VB .NET

```
Public Class Form1

  Private Sub Button1_Click(ByVal sender As System.Object, _
      ByVal e As System.EventArgs) Handles btnStartApp.Click
    Try
      TestLib.Logfile = "c:\testlog.log"
      TestLib.StartProgram(txtAppname.Text)
    Catch ex As Exception
      MessageBox.Show(ex.Message.ToString)
    End Try
  End Sub

  Private Sub AboutToolStripMenuItem_Click(ByVal sender As System.Object, _
    ByVal e As System.EventArgs) Handles AboutToolStripMenuItem.Click
    AboutBox1.ShowDialog()
  End Sub

  Private Sub ExitToolStripMenuItem_Click(ByVal sender As System.Object, _
    ByVal e As System.EventArgs) Handles ExitToolStripMenuItem.Click
    Me.Close()
  End Sub

  Private Sub StartApplicationToolStripMenuItem_Click( _
      ByVal sender As System.Object, ByVal e As System.EventArgs) _
      Handles StartApplicationToolStripMenuItem.Click
    btnStartApp.PerformClick()
  End Sub
End Class
```

C#

```csharp
using System;
using System.Collections.Generic;
using System.ComponentModel;
using System.Data;
using System.Drawing;
using System.Text;
using System.Windows.Forms;
using System.Diagnostics;

namespace AutoTester
{
public partial class Form1 : Form
 {
    public Form1()
    {
        InitializeComponent();
    }

    private void btnStartApp_Click(object sender, EventArgs e)
    {

        try
        {
            TestLib.Logfile = "c:\\testlog.log";
            TestLib.StartProgram(txtAppname.Text);
        }
        catch (Exception ex)
        {
            MessageBox.Show(ex.Message.ToString());
        }
    }

    private void exitToolStripMenuItem_Click(object sender, EventArgs e)
    {
        this.Close();
    }

    private void aboutToolStripMenuItem_Click(object sender, EventArgs e)
    {
      AboutBox1 aForm = new AboutBox1();
      aForm.ShowDialog();
     }
```

```csharp
private void startApplicationToolStripMenuItem_Click(
    object sender, EventArgs e)
{
    btnStartApp.PerformClick();
}

    }
}
```

6. Build and run the application. Try every menu item to be sure all the code functions properly.

7. Save your work.

Adding Timing to Your Tests

Adding code to time the length of actions can be an important task on any testing project. Why? You can use the time a task takes to complete as a measure of performance for that task. In addition, you can use timing statistics to compare times for common tasks from build-to-build of the applications you test, which can give you a feel for the relative improvement or degradation of performance as the system progresses to completion. Hence, in this section, you'll learn how to take time measurements in .NET. First, you'll do basic timing using the DateTime and TimeSpan classes. Next, you'll look at a VB .NET command that you can also use from C#, then the Shell() command for synchronous timing, and, finally, you'll explore the use of the Timer control for testing.

Basic Test Timing

Determining how long a segment of code takes to process is simple using the DateTime and TimeSpan classes provided by .NET.

For VB .NET, first declare three variables for holding start, end, and elapsed time values:

```vbnet
Dim StartTime As DateTime
Dim EndTime as DateTime
Dim Interval As TimeSpan
```

Set the values for StartTime and EndTime at the appropriate times—before and after the critical action(s):

```vbnet
StartTime = DateTime.Now 'capture current seconds
' do critical task that needs timing
EndTime = DateTime.Now
```

Then calculate the difference:

```vbnet
Interval = EndTime - StartTime
```

For C#, the following code will do the same thing:

```
DateTime StartTime;
DateTime EndTime;
TimeSpan Interval;

StartTime = DateTime.Now;
' do critical task that needs timing
EndTime = DateTime.Now;

Interval = EndTime - StartTime;
```

Keep in mind that what is being clocked with these statements is only the time it takes to execute the code. If another process is started, as happens with the Process.Start() method, then you are *not* timing the execution of that process and how long it takes to complete. This kind of timing is appropriate for White Box testing of certain actions that you know the application code itself will undertake. Say, for example, that the code you are interested in is the time it takes to open a database connection or to open and read the contents of a file. In this case, using the code in the previous snippets would be appropriate. This method of timing can help establish the approximate time, given the correct platform and configuration, that it would take to perform these tasks. Then, perhaps, a comparison could be made to other ways of performing that same task.

Listing 5-7 uses this simple timing process to clock the execution of a subroutine to find Hrefs.

Listing 5-7. *Timing the Execution of an Algorithm*

VB .NET

```
Imports System.Text.RegularExpressions

Private Sub Button1_Click(ByVal sender As System.Object, _
    ByVal e As System.EventArgs) Handles Button1.Click
  Dim StartTime As DateTime
  Dim EndTime As DateTime
  Dim Interval As TimeSpan
  Dim numHrefs As Int16

  StartTime = DateTime.Now 'capture current seconds
  numHrefs = FindHref(txtSource.text) 'routine being timed
  EndTime = DateTime.Now

  lblHrefs.Text = numHrefs.ToString
  Interval = EndTime - StartTime  ' calculate time elapsed
  lblTime.Text = Interval.ToString()
End Sub

Public Function FindHref(ByVal strSource As String) As Integer
  Dim r As Regex
  Dim m As Match
  Dim iCount As Integer
```

```vbnet
  r = New Regex("href\s*=\s*(?:""(?<1>[^""]*)""|(?<1>\S+))", _
  RegexOptions.IgnoreCase Or RegexOptions.Compiled)

  m = r.Match(strSource)
  While m.Success
    iCount += 1
    m = m.NextMatch()
  End While
  Return iCount
End Function
```

C#

```csharp
using System.Text.RegularExpressions;
// the line above goes at the top with the other directives

private void button1_Click(object sender, EventArgs e)
{
  DateTime StartTime;
  DateTime EndTime;
  TimeSpan Interval;
  Int16 numHrefs;
  StartTime = DateTime.Now;
  numHrefs = FindHref(txtSource.Text);
  EndTime = DateTime.Now;
  lblHrefs.Text = numHrefs.ToString();
  Interval = EndTime - StartTime;
  lblTime.Text = Interval.ToString();
}

public Int16 FindHref(string strSource)
{
  Regex r;
  Match m;
  Int16 iCount = 0;
  r = new Regex("href\\s*=\\s*(?:\"(?<1>[^\"]*)\")\"|(?<1>\\S+))",
      RegexOptions.IgnoreCase | RegexOptions.Compiled);
  m = r.Match(strSource);
  while (m.Success)
  {
    iCount += 1;
    m = m.NextMatch();
  }
  return iCount;
}
```

You may recognize the code in the FindHref procedure from the "Using Regular Expressions to Read From a file" section in Chapter 3. It's the same code we used to count Hrefs in a file, but in this case we've converted the code into a function procedure that returns an integer value indicating how many Hrefs were found. Let's imagine that this code to find Hrefs is an important algorithm used in an application you are testing. Let's imagine that it's the first time the developers have used something new they've heard about, Regular Expressions, and you're going to time this algorithm and compare it to a value for the previous way it was done.

The timing in Listing 5-7 measures how long it takes to execute this code in the FindHref function. If another algorithm is substituted for this routine, say using something other than Regular Expressions (such as regular string functions, perhaps), then the timing between the two algorithms could be compared to see which performs better (see the following Tester's Tip on controlling timing variables).

TESTER'S TIP: CONTROLLING TIMING VARIABLES

When you time tests, you will want to eliminate other variables that can impact the recorded times. For example, timing the same task on one platform versus another might vary significantly due to the differing device configurations. When running timing tests, you'll want to standardize on a particular platform and platform configuration. Often, you may want to do the same timing tests on high-priority target platforms and configurations. This is a very good use of automated tests because you can write the code once and run it on multiple platforms, thus recording the differences in timing. This gives the test team a feel for the relative performance of the application from one platform to the next.

Synchronous Timing Using the Shell() Method

Now that you know how to time tasks, let's say that you now want to time how long it takes to launch an application. You might try what we've done in the following code snippet. It uses the same method for timing a task, but this time it places a line of code between the setting of the StartTime and EndTime variables that calls the Process.Start() method:

VB .NET

```
StartTime = DateTime.Now
Process.Start("notepad")
EndTime = DateTime.Now
Interval = EndTime - StartTime
Messagebox.Show (Interval.ToString())
```

C#

```
StartTime = DateTime.Now;
Process.Start("notepad");
EndTime = DateTime.Now;
Interval = EndTime - StartTime;
MessageBox.Show(Interval.ToString());
```

There's a problem here—the code in this snippet is *not* timing how long it takes to launch Notepad. If you try this code, you'll find that the message box displaying the time interval frequently shows up before the Notepad window does! This is because Notepad runs in a separate process, so it runs asynchronously to your code. If you want to launch an application within the same process (i.e., that runs synchronously with your test code), then there is another method available. The Shell() method has the option of launching an application with a wait option.

The Shell() method is located within the Microsoft.VisualBasic namespace. It is still available to C# though. All C# programmers need to do is use the using directive for this namespace to gain access to it (and in most versions they'll also have to set a reference to it; see the "Setting a Reference to the VB .NET Namespace from C#" sidebar).

SETTING A REFERENCE TO THE VB .NET NAMESPACE FROM C#

In order to access VB routines from C# code (such as the Shell() method mentioned in this chapter), execute the following steps from within a C# application:

1. Select Project ➤ Add Reference. The Add Reference dialog will display, as shown in Figure 5-7.

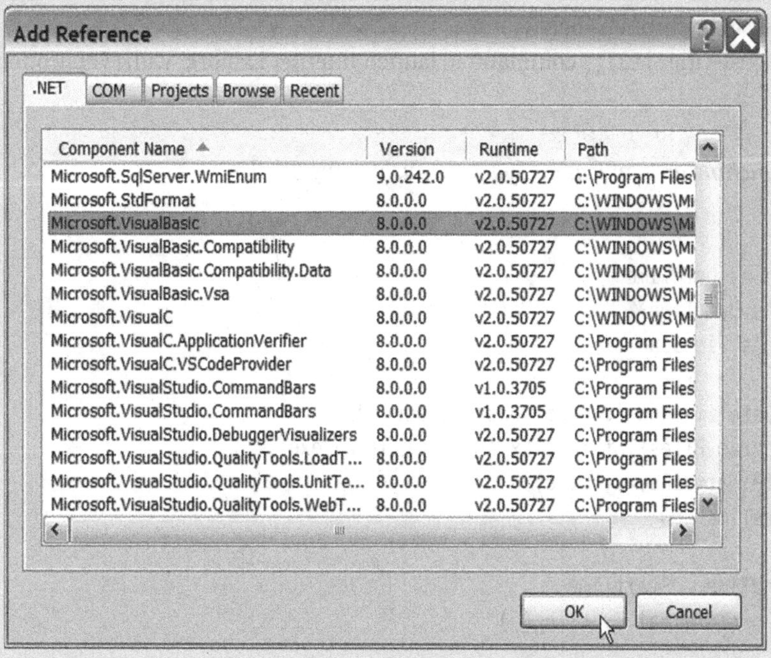

Figure 5-7. *The Add Reference dialog with the Microsoft.VisualBasic component selected*

2. From the .NET tab, scroll down until you see the Microsoft.VisualBasic component. Click it to select it.

3. Click OK. The dialog will close and the reference will be added to your project automatically. All you will need to do from here is put the following using directive at the top of your code, and then you will be able to use features from Microsoft Visual Basic within C#:

```
using Microsoft.VisualBasic;
```

The following line of code uses the Shell() method to launch the Notepad accessory:

VB .NET

```
Shell("C:\Program Files\Internet Explorer\iexplore.exe", _
      AppWinStyle.NormalFocus, True)
```

C#

```
Interaction.Shell("C:\\Program Files\\Internet Explorer\\iexplore.exe",
                  AppWinStyle.NormalFocus, true, -1);
```

The first argument of the Shell() method shown in this code snippet is a string where you put the full path of the application you want to launch. In this short code example, you launch Internet Explorer. The second argument determines the way the window will display with the AppWinStyle enumeration. The possible values for this argument will allow you to display the window maximized, minimized, hidden, or with normal focus, as shown. The third argument is a Boolean value, True or False, which indicates whether you want the current process (i.e., your code) to wait until the process launched by the Shell() command completes. False, which is the default, means that your code won't wait, and the launched process will run asynchronously to your code (just like the Process.Start() method). However, providing True for this argument instead will cause synchronous behavior.

Listing 5-8 uses the Shell() command to launch Internet Explorer with synchronous behavior.

Listing 5-8. *Launching an Application Synchronously Using Shell()*

VB .NET

```
Dim StartTime As DateTime
Dim EndTime As DateTime
Dim Interval As TimeSpan

StartTime = DateTime.Now 'capture current seconds
Shell("C:\Program Files\Internet Explorer\iexplore.exe", _
   AppWinStyle.NormalFocus, True)
EndTime = DateTime.Now

Interval = EndTime - StartTime
MessageBox.Show(Interval.ToString())
```

C#

```
DateTime StartTime;
DateTime EndTime;
TimeSpan Interval;
StartTime = DateTime.Now;
Interaction.Shell
    ("C:\\Program Files\\Internet Explorer\\iexplore.exe",
      AppWinStyle.NormalFocus, true, 5000);
EndTime = DateTime.Now;
Interval = EndTime - StartTime;
MessageBox.Show(Interval.ToString());
```

■**Note** When calling the `Shell()` method in C#, you must provide a fourth argument, which is the number of maximum milliseconds the system will wait until it returns control to your original program code. If you make this argument a fairly large number (this example shows 5 seconds, which is a long time to a computer), then this code will behave as it does it VB .NET—it will wait until the program completes or is dismissed. This argument is optional in VB .NET.

If you try this code, you will find that the message box does not appear until you have dismissed the Notepad window. The `Shell()` method is actually a function that will return the process ID of the launched application. Every application gets its own process identifier number. In this case, you don't need it, but the process ID can be handy to have if you want to manipulate the process, such as set or unset the focus or even kill it. (By the way, the `Process.Start()` method can also access the process ID, as you'll see in Exercise 5-5.)

You can use the `Shell()` method when you would like to determine how long it takes to launch another task and run it to completion. Both of these methods of launching applications, the `Process.Start()` and the `Shell()` method, are valuable when running and timing tests.

Using the Timer Control

Although employing the `DateTime` and `TimeSpan` classes is useful for many kinds of time tests, there are other test situations when it makes sense to perform a task repeatedly at a specified interval—for example, pinging a server or a website to determine its state or availability. To do this kind of timing, .NET contains a control, called the `Timer`, that you can place on your form to trigger an event at a timed interval. You can add this control to the form by double-clicking it (see Figure 5-8).

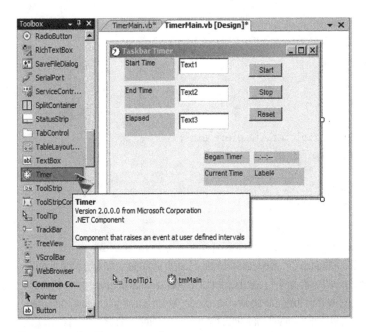

Figure 5-8. *The Timer control*

The Timer control will not display to the user at runtime. It's a hidden object during Run mode, so you will only see it in Design mode. Like the MenuStrip used earlier, it displays in the component tray in Design mode.

The purpose of the Timer control is to add a link to the system timer. It will fire off an event at an interval you specify. Once you place a timer on the form, you can set the interval for it by using its properties. The Timer object has one event: the Timer event that fires whenever the specified interval elapses.

The code in Listing 5-9 enables the Timer when a button is clicked. The interval property is set to 1 second so that the code in the tick event of the Timer will get executed every second.

Listing 5-9. *Code for Working with the Timer Control*

VB .NET

```
Private Sub Button1_Click(ByVal sender As System.Object, _
    ByVal e As System.EventArgs) Handles Button1.Click
  Timer1.Interval = 1000 '1000 milliseconds = 1 second
  Timer1.Enabled = True
End Sub

Private Sub Timer1_Tick(ByVal sender As Object, _
    ByVal e As System.EventArgs) Handles Timer1.Tick
  If My.Computer.Network.Ping("198.01.01.01") Then
    MessageBox.Show("Server pinged successfully.")
  Else
    MessageBox.Show ("Ping request timed out.")
  End If
End Sub
```

■**Note** For the following code to work, you must first follow the steps to reference the `Microsoft.VisualBasic` namespace, see the "Setting a Reference to the VB .NET Namespace from C#" sidebar.

C#

```
private void button1_Click(object sender, EventArgs e)
{
  timer1.Interval = 1000;    //1000 milliseconds = 1 second
  timer1.Enabled = true;
}

private void timer1_Tick(object sender, EventArgs e)
  Microsoft.VisualBasic.Devices.Network myNetwork = new
      Microsoft.VisualBasic.Devices.Network();
  if (myNetwork.Ping("198.01.01.01"))
  {
    MessageBox.Show("Server pinged successfully.");
  }
  else
  {
    MessageBox.Show("Ping request timed out.");
  }
}
```

To stop the Timer, you set the Timer's enabled property to false. In this example, this could be done in another button or could be set with a line of code after determining the server was successfully pinged.

Another demonstration of the Timer control's use is contained in the Demo Files folder for this chapter (see DownloadFiles\Chapter5\DemoFiles\TaskBarTimer in the Source Code folder of the Apress website at www.apress.com). The TaskBarTimer folder contains code for a stopwatch-type program called TaskBarTimer. The TaskBarTimer program can come in handy for the simple timing of manual tasks whenever you can't find your stopwatch. The code in this program uses the standard .NET Timer object.

Simple GUI Testing Using SendKeys()

One task you may want .NET to support is simulated user action on the application's Graphical User Interface (GUI). Extensive GUI testing can be tricky and time-consuming so you may want to consider more sophisticated tools if you want to automate testing of the GUI. However, if you choose to do some simple and short GUI tests, .NET does provide functions for doing so. You have already seen the Process.Start() and Shell() methods to launch an application, but how about performing some simple user tasks such as clicking buttons and typing text?

GUI TESTING TOOLS

There are many tools on the market for performing automated testing. Some are expensive and some are free (*shareware*). Most of these tools provide a way to manipulate an application's Graphical User Interface (GUI) by pointing, clicking, dragging, typing into textboxes, and so on, in an application's windows—just as a user might. In fact, some of these tools provide sophisticated recording of your own actions and then produce a script that will repeat those actions, thus reporting results and providing many options. You could write similar tools in .NET, but it is not a simple task and would take a significant investment of time and resources. Again, you may find yourself in the business of writing test tools rather than actually testing. There are new open-source test tools available regularly. To find out more about the tools already available, you should become a member of Quality Assurance (QA) forums at www.QAForums.com. This is a great resource for testers for many reasons, but the main reason is to get information from other test professionals. For information on other QA tools, you can also try ApTest's website at www.aptest.com/resources.html.

The SendKeys() statement does just what it implies, it sends keyboard commands to a window. The following line of code sends the characters *H-e-l-l-o-sp-T-h-e-r-e-!* from the keyboard to the screen. If a window on the screen (such as Notepad) has the focus, it types the words "Hello There!" into it:

```
System.Windows.Forms.SendKeys "Hello there!"
```

Since you'll be using the SendKeys() method to simulate a user's keystrokes, you'll need to be able to delay data entry the way a user would when he is thinking, reading, and responding to screens; otherwise, the computer will enter the keystrokes too quickly. .NET also provides a Sleep() statement that can come in very handy for this purpose. The following line of code will delay your process for 1,000 milliseconds, which is 1 second:

```
System.Threading.Thread.Sleep(1000)
```

Listing 5-10 demonstrates using the SendKeys() method to automate Notepad.

Listing 5-10. *Using the SendKeys() Command to Manipulate the Notepad Accessory*

VB .NET

```
Dim ProcessID As Integer
ProcessID = Shell("notepad.exe", 1) ' Run Notepad.

System.Threading.Thread.Sleep(1000) 'Give Notepad a chance to launch
AppActivate(ProcessID) ' Give focus to the Notepad.

System.Threading.Thread.Sleep(1000)

SendKeys.SendWait("Hello there!")
System.Threading.Thread.Sleep(1000)
```

```
SendKeys.Send("%{F4}") ' Send ALT+F4 to close Notepad.
SendKeys.Send("{tab}")
SendKeys.Send("{enter}")
```

Note In order for the following C# code to use the `Shell()` command as shown here, you will have to first follow the steps in the "Setting a Reference to the VB .NET Namespace from C#" sidebar.

C#

```
int ProcessID;
ProcessID =
    Interaction.Shell("notepad.exe", AppWinStyle.NormalFocus, true, 5000);
System.Threading.Thread.Sleep(1000);
Interaction.AppActivate(ProcessID);

System.Threading.Thread.Sleep(1000);

SendKeys.SendWait("Hello there!");

System.Threading.Thread.Sleep(1000);

SendKeys.Send("%{F4}");
SendKeys.Send("{tab}");      //What do you suppose this code does??
SendKeys.Send("{enter}");
```

The code in Listing 5-10 was written in a Windows Forms application, so the `System.Windows.Forms` namespace designation was not needed. However, if you use this in the console, you would have to use the namespace or else import that library. Consider the fourth line of code in this listing:

```
AppActivate(ProcessID) ' Give focus to the Notepad.
```

The `AppActivate()` method will ensure that the application you're sending keystrokes to is the active application and has the focus. This method is contained within the `Microsoft.VisualBasic.Interaction` class. So you will also have to import the `Microsoft.VisualBasic` namespace if you are attempting to use this method from within C#.

In Exercise 5-5, you will use the `SendKeys()` statement, along with all you have learned about creating utilities, to set up some simple GUI manipulation of the Calculator accessory and to execute a verification test against its Addition capability.

Note It is possible to get more sophisticated GUI tests using calls to the Windows API libraries if necessary. However, this will take a significant amount of coding effort, and we don't recommend doing much GUI testing this way (see the "GUI Testing Tools" sidebar earlier in this chapter).

Exercise 5-5: Testing the Calculator

In this exercise, you will write a program to automate a test of the Calculator accessory. You will start with a template that has much of the code already written. You'll then add an existing library to the application, and then add procedures to this library. You will also add code to test the Addition capability of the Calculator using the SendKeys() method.

Figure 5-9 shows how your program should look when it's complete.

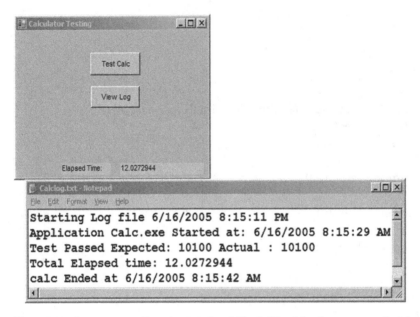

Figure 5-9. *The answer to Exercise 5-5 should look like this when you are finished.*

(The complete answer to this exercise is in the Download Files folder for this chapter, which is available from the Apress website (www.apress.com). Check it if you need a hint!)

1. Launch Visual Studio .NET, either VB .NET or C#, and use the File ➤ Open menu item to navigate to the Download Files folder. Double-click on the Chapter5\VB\Exercise5-5\CalcTestTemplate\CalcTest.sln (or replace VB with C#) file to open it.

■**Caution** This template program will *not* run without error until you complete it by following the remaining steps.

For C# only, add the following using statement at the start of the code window:

```
using Microsoft.VisualBasic;
```

Note For C# only, you will *also* need to follow the steps in the "Setting a Reference to the VB Namespace from C#" sidebar.

2. Take some time to explore the existing application controls and code. You will find some errors in the Task List because this code is not complete. Locate the comment in the code window that says "ADD CODE HERE!".

3. Directly under the line that says "Add Code Here", add code to sleep for 1 second (1,000 milliseconds). This is necessary because the line just above the comment has launched the Calculator accessory, and we need to make sure that it has had a chance to launch before sending keystrokes to it.

```
System.Threading.Thread.Sleep(1000)
```

You can type this line of code or you can write the code at the top of the file to import the System.Threading.Thread namespace, and then simply call the Sleep() method by itself: Sleep(1000).

Note Depending on the speed of your computer, you may want to adjust this time between 1,000 and 3,000 milliseconds.

4. Next, add code to record the starting time into the StartTime variable that has already been created. Add another line to set the focus to the Calculator application. You'll use the AppActivate() command for this. AppActivate() takes a single argument, which has to be the process ID number of a running process. The StartProgram function returns the process ID number of the instance of the calculator that it starts. That value has been returned into the CalcProcessID integer variable:

VB .NET

```
StartTime = DateTime.Now 'capture current seconds
AppActivate(CalcProcessID)
```

C#

```
StartTime = DateTime.Now;
Interaction.AppActivate(CalcProcessID);
```

5. The next lines of code you'll add will send keystrokes to test the Addition capability of the Calculator accessory. You are simply summing the numbers from 1 to 100. This test ends up clicking every button on the numeric keypad, so it's a good basic test. The statement SendKeys({+}) essentially clicks the plus sign on the Calculator keypad. The SendWait() command waits until the keystroke has been processed before proceeding:

VB .NET

```
for I = 1 To 100 ' Set up counting loop.
   SendKeys.SendWait(I & "{+}") ' Send keystrokes to Calculator
Next I ' to add each value of I.
SendKeys.SendWait("=") ' Get grand total.
SendKeys.SendWait("^c") 'copy result to the clipboard
```

C#

```
for (I = 1; I <= 100; I++)
{
  SendKeys.SendWait(I + "{+}");
}
SendKeys.SendWait("=");
SendKeys.SendWait("^c");
```

The last two lines are SendWait() method calls that send an equal sign (=) to retrieve the total value, and then send a Ctrl+c (^c) to copy the resulting value to the clipboard. These are keystrokes that the Calculator accessory recognizes. Be sure to add these lines directly under the lines from step 4.

6. The last line you will add into this file will go directly after the lines added in step 5. This line will retrieve the information that was loaded into the clipboard in the last line of step 5. (Working with the clipboard can be an efficient way to retrieve information from applications.)

```
strTotal = Clipboard.GetData(DataFormats.Text).ToString()
```

Note   For C#, you'll need to add the semicolon at the end of this line!

The Clipboard class is a member of the Windows.Forms.Form namespace, so it doesn't need to be imported into a Windows Forms application. The GetData() method of the Clipboard class is used to retrieve data from the clipboard, and the DataFormats.Text argument ensures that you are retrieving only data from the clipboard and not another kind of item, like an image.

You've added all code into the Form class, but there are still a lot of squigglies—indicating errors—in the code. To fix these, you need to add your test library to give you the routines for starting the program and performing test logging.

Adding the TestLib library

7. There is a TestLib file that you can add into your program. To add this file, select Project ➤ Add Existing Item from the main menu. In the Add Existing Item dialog, if necessary, navigate to the CalculatorTestingTemplate folder and add in the TestLib.vb (or TestLib.cs) file by selecting it and clicking the Add button.

8. Review the code in the `TestLib` file. Notice that the `StartProgram` routine has changed from a subroutine to a function—that is, it returns a value. This routine is used to launch the Calculator accessory. The code now returns the value of the process ID of the launched application. This way you'll be able to use that process ID to manipulate the program once it's running. It's not necessary to pass the whole process back and forth between routines, just passing the process ID will allow you to access it.

9. Build the project. You should find that most of the tasks are gone—all except two. You need to add code for closing the program and for viewing the `Logfile`.

10. Go to the code window for the `TestLib` class. Add a public `Shared/static` subroutine called `Readlog` that takes no arguments. This subroutine should use the `Process.Start()` method to launch the Notepad application with the contents of the `Logfile` displayed.

VB .NET

```
Public Shared Sub Readlog()
  Dim myProcess As Process = Process.Start("Notepad", Logfile)
End Sub
```

C#

```
public static void Readlog()
{
  Process myProcess = Process.Start("Notepad", Logfile);
}
```

11. Add one more public `Shared/static` subroutine called `CloseProgram` that takes a single string argument. This routine should use the `SendKeys()` method to send an Alt+F4 command to the Calculator window.

VB .NET

```
Public Shared Sub CloseProgram(ByRef App As String)
  System.Windows.Forms.SendKeys.SendWait("%{F4}")
  LogtoFile(App & " Ended at " & DateTime.Now)
End Sub
```

C#

```
public static void CloseProgram(string App)
{
    System.Windows.Forms.SendKeys.SendWait("%{F4}");
    LogtoFile(App + " Ended at " + DateTime.Now);
}
```

12. Run the application and click the Test Calc button. (You'll notice that the View Report button is not enabled; it won't be until the test has been run at least once—do you understand how the code works to make this happen?) You should see the Calculator appear and the Addition test will take a few seconds to run.

■**Caution** Do not touch the mouse or keyboard while the test is running! You might interfere with the test.

Once the test is complete, the View Report button will be enabled. Click it to see the results of the test. Dismiss the CalcTest window and return to the code window.

13. In the code window, change the value 10100 to 5000. Build the application and run it again. This time when you run the test and view the report, you should see a test failure reported in your test results. It's important to test both the pass and failure branches of your tests, even with bogus data, to ensure that your test is written properly. Before exiting the application, be sure to change this value back to 10100.

Question: What does the "time elapsed" value in this test really represent?

In this exercise, you've written a test of the Addition function on the Calculator accessory. Sure the Calculator accessory has been well tested prior to this, but this test has given you the .NET tools, from start to finish, in order to accomplish a similar test on another system. In the process, you used many of the commands and objects discussed in this chapter, including static/Shared libraries, procedures, test timing, and GUI testing techniques. The full code for this exercise (except for the TestLib) is displayed in Listing 5-11.

Listing 5-11. *Full Code for Exercise 5-5*

VB .NET

```vbnet
Friend Class frmTestCalc
    Inherits System.Windows.Forms.Form
    ''************************************
    '*  Name:      CalcTest
    '*  Purpose:   This application contains code to
    '*             test the calculator accessory addition capability.
    '*
    '*             It is the answer for the Chapter 5-5 Exercise.
    '*
    '*  Author:    M. Sweeney
    '*  Date Created: 6/15/2005
    '*  Inputs:
    '*  Expected Result: That the calculator
    '*  Modification History:
    '*  Name:      Date:      Purpose:
    '*
    '************************************


Private Sub cmdLog_Click(ByVal eventSender As System.Object, _
    ByVal eventArgs As System.EventArgs) Handles cmdLog.Click
    TestLib.Readlog()
End Sub
```

```vb
Private Sub cmdTest_Click(ByVal eventSender As System.Object, _
    ByVal eventArgs As System.EventArgs) Handles cmdTest.Click
  Dim StartTime As DateTime
  Dim Interval As TimeSpan
  Dim strTotal As String
  Dim CalcProcessID As Integer
  Dim I As Short

  TestLib.Logfile = "c:\Calclog.txt"
  CalcProcessID = TestLib.StartProgram("Calc.exe") ' Run Calculator.
  System.Threading.Thread.Sleep(1000) 'let calc start before proceeding

  StartTime = DateTime.Now 'capture current seconds
  AppActivate(CalcProcessID)
  For I = 1 To 100 ' Set up counting loop.
    SendKeys.SendWait(I & "{+}") ' Send keystrokes to Calculator
  Next I ' to add each value of I.
  SendKeys.SendWait("=") ' Get grand total.
  SendKeys.SendWait("^c") 'copy result to the clipboard
  strTotal = Clipboard.GetData(DataFormats.Text).ToString()

  If Convert.ToInt32(strTotal) = 10100 Then
    TestLib.LogtoFile("Test Passed Expected: 10100 Actual : " & strTotal)
  Else
    TestLib.LogtoFile("Test Failed Expected: 10100 Actual : " & strTotal)
  End If

  Interval = DateTime.Now - StartTime 'find elapsed time
  lblTime.Text = Interval.TotalSeconds.ToString 'report to test bed
  TestLib.LogtoFile("Total Elapsed time: " & lblTime.Text) 'report to file

 TestLib.CloseProgram("calc") 'close the calculator program


  cmdLog.Enabled = True 'enable the View Report button
End Sub

  Private Sub frmTestCalc_Load(ByVal eventSender As System.Object, _
      ByVal eventArgs As System.EventArgs) Handles MyBase.Load
    cmdLog.Enabled = False
  End Sub

End Class
```

C#

```csharp
using System;
using System.Collections.Generic;
using System.ComponentModel;
using System.Data;
using System.Drawing;
using System.Text;
using System.Windows.Forms;
using Microsoft.VisualBasic;

namespace CalcTest
{
  public partial class Form1 : Form
  {
    public Form1()
    {
      InitializeComponent();
    }
//     ''*************************************
//     '*  Name:        CalcTest
//     '*  Purpose:     This application contains code to
//     '*              test the calculator accessory addition capability.
//     '*
//     '*              It is the answer for the Chapter 5-5 Exercise.
//     '*
//     '*  Author:     M. Sweeney
//     '*  Date Created: 6/15/2005
//     '*  Inputs:
//     '*  Expected Result: That the calculator
//     '*  Modification History:
//     '*  Name:        Date:       Purpose:
//     '*
//     '*************************************
    private void cmdTest_Click(object sender, EventArgs e)
    {
      DateTime StartTime;
      TimeSpan Interval;
      String strTotal = "";
      Int32 CalcProcessID;
      Int16 I;

      TestLib.Logfile = "c:\\Calclog.txt";
      CalcProcessID = TestLib.StartProgram("Calc.exe");
      System.Threading.Thread.Sleep(1000);
```

```
    StartTime = DateTime.Now;
    Interaction.AppActivate(CalcProcessID);
    for (I = 1; I <= 100; I++)
    {
        SendKeys.SendWait(I + "{+}");
    }
    SendKeys.SendWait("=");
    SendKeys.SendWait("^c");
    strTotal = Clipboard.GetData(DataFormats.Text).ToString();

     // if statement
    if (Convert.ToInt32(strTotal) == 10100)
    {
      TestLib.LogtoFile("Test Passed Expected: 10100 Actual : " + strTotal);
    }
    else
    {
      TestLib.LogtoFile("Test Failed Expected: 10100 Actual : " + strTotal);
    }
    Interval = DateTime.Now - StartTime;

    lblTime.Text = Interval.TotalSeconds.ToString();
    TestLib.LogtoFile("Total Elapsed time: " + lblTime.Text);

    TestLib.CloseProgram("calc");
    cmdLog.Enabled = true;
}

private void cmdLog_Click(object sender, EventArgs e)
{
  TestLib.Readlog();
}

private void Form1_Load(object sender, EventArgs e)
{
//don't allow access to View Report button until test runs at least once
  cmdLog.Enabled = false;
  }
 }
}
```

Summary

In this chapter, you've learned how to set up a framework for your tests, including creating additional classes to contain libraries of your reusable test procedures. You've learned how to create both functions, when you need a value returned, and subroutine procedures within your testware applications. You've also covered adding new items to your applications, including new forms and classes, as well as existing items. And you've learned some important ways to use timing in your tests, including using the DateTime and TimeSpan classes, as well as the Timer control. You also looked at two ways to launch applications—synchronously and asynchronously—using the Shell() and Process.Start() methods, respectively.

What we hope you will take away from this chapter is that every time you create, or run across, a useful procedure for testing, you'll throw it into a library for your future use and that of your test team. Having a code repository that you can use to quickly get yourself ready to run actual tests is one of the most important things you can create for yourself. You don't have time to write every line of code from scratch, so you'll find that you'll often leverage the code from other projects to get your automated tests written quickly. So, in other words, not only should your test project have a test framework, in the form of prewritten code libraries of common and useful routines, but also so should *you*! You can take these libraries from project-to-project and job-to-job to add your own value to any automated test project.

The kind of class you focused on in this chapter is the static/Shared class that can simply function as a code repository. In the next chapter, you'll learn how to make and test fully object-oriented applications using standard classes and the object-oriented concepts of encapsulation, inheritance, and polymorphism.

Tester's Checklist

When performing code reviews, look for the following in a well-written .NET application:

Does the project

- ☑ Use Shared or static classes to contain logically related reusable routines?

- ☑ Properly manage forms and their display?

Does the code

- ☑ Use understandable names for functions and procedures?

- ☑ Create functions and procedures that are single-purpose? (Large, cumbersome procedures are less reusable and intelligible. Routines should have a single, clear purpose.)

- ☑ Correctly distinguish between synchronous and asynchronous timing?

- ☑ Consistently document all files?

CHAPTER 6

■ ■ ■

Creating Testware Components

As you know, testing jobs are becoming more demanding every day. Employers demand that their testers be more productive, which often translates into having to know not only testing and documenting, but also how to automate testing procedures and programs in general. In the last chapter, you saw how to create simple automations. Automation is a very important tool for testers, but creating good automation tools, or *testware*, takes time. When you do write these testware applications, it is vital that you get the most benefit for your efforts. This means first identifying tasks that can be automated and then creating code that can be reused. It also means designing your code to be simple enough that it can be modified for other projects without a great deal of time and expense.

To create efficient testing utilities, you need to learn to break your tasks into small, reusable components. The term *components* can mean a number of things, but it all comes down to creating small, reusable sections of code. You can accomplish this by creating sets of programming statements and saving them in one or more files.

With the proper use of components, the individual parts of your applications can be created and tested before they are combined into a whole application. This is just what is done in the applications you may be asked to *unit test*. In fact, unit testing is such an important part of testing nowadays because the use of components is so prevalent.

In this chapter, you will examine some important principals of how modern applications are programmed into components, and how you can use these same principals to create your own reusable testware components. You will see how your components can use the principals of OOP to allow your future projects to take advantage of your earlier work.

To do this, you will first build a simple bug-reporting application with all the programming statements in one code file. You will then separate these statements into sets of reusable statements, called *methods*. These methods will be reorganized again into a set of methods and placed into classes. Later, these classes themselves will be divided into different code files at first and then into different component files (`.exes` and `.dlls`) after that. Finally, you will see how you can reuse these methods and classes in these component files for other projects by changing (or "morphing") them into slightly different versions of your original design.

Objectives

By the end of this chapter, you will be able to

- Explain unit, component, and integration testing

- Explain White Box and Black Box testing

- Explain how and why applications are broken into components

- Define what classes and objects are

- Identify the difference between properties and methods

- Explain what `.dll` and `.exe` files are

Defining Properties and Methods

As mentioned earlier, your goal is to build a component based on a bug-reporting application. Along the way, you will use a lot of terms found in OOP. These are very important in .NET since all of the documentation, and most of the articles, you read about OOP will use these terms.

To start with, in the OOP terms, the actions that a program can do are accomplished by its *methods*, while the data that a program holds is found in its *properties*.

In .NET, the way to create properties and methods is to first create a container to hold them in. Although there are a few other options, most of the time this container will be a *class*. When your program starts running, it will load the code from your classes into the computer's memory automatically using .NET's Class Loader program. Then you will be able to use the methods and properties that you typed in your classes while the code is running.

You should be aware that the properties and methods of a class can also be called a lot of other names in the software industry. Unfortunately, most people find this confusing—especially when they start programming. To make matters worse, these names change when you are talking about them at different stages of the development process. For example, the name of a property will often change from when the class is designed to when that same class is later used to create objects. As you continue through the chapter, we will use the different terms in their proper places, since seeing the different terms in use will make it easier to read existing code and documentation.

THE INCONSISTENCY OF TERMS

Before we go any further with defining terms, we have to caution you that there is a lot of inconsistency in how terms are used in the industry. Not everyone agrees on which term to use and when to use it, which really makes learning these terms difficult for a beginner. However, we offer the following examples as a guideline.

When a developer is at the planning phase of designing a class, he might call the data of a class its *attributes*. After the class has been planned and the actual coding begins, he may still use the term *attribute*, but often you will hear him switch to the term *properties* for that same data. Finally, when programmers are discussing an object, and not the class the object is made from, you will usually hear the object's data called its *properties*, and seldom called its *attributes*. The following are some of the names you will hear data called:

- Attributes

- Properties

- Data members

- Fields

- Variables

- Constants

- Arrays, hashes, or collections

- Enums (or enumerations)

- Arguments

- Parameters

Believe it or not, there are even more out there, but by now you should be getting the idea that there are lots of names for data and you should pay attention to when these terms are used. In addition, you should know that different geographical locations favor one term over another. When you are testing, keep an eye out for anything that holds some kind of data. As mentioned earlier, the basic design of a program will involve its use of properties and methods. Identifying the properties and methods will help you decide what the application does and how the different parts of an application work together.

Most people will search the Internet for code examples to help them build their projects. This is especially true of people that do not code everyday for a living, like testers. The good news is that there are a lot of free code examples out there; the bad news is that it takes time and patience to know what code examples do and determine if you can make them work for your needs. Since the description of what the code does can be written by many people, learning the different names for things and how they are used will help out immensely.

Classes and Objects

When you design your classes, you will have decide if you want other people to access the properties and methods directly from the class or whether they have to create an object of the class first and then access them. Most of the time, you will choose to create objects first. An object is created by taking a copy of all the class's code from memory and putting that copy into its own memory space. Any changes to this copy will not affect the original class, so you can change the properties without fear that it will affect other areas of your program without you telling it to. Also, you can make as many copies as you need from the class. Each of these copies will be an "object instance" of that class.

Planning Your Bug-Reporter Application

Now that you know what properties and methods your application needs, you can start to design it. To start with, let's make a list of what data this application needs and what it is going to do.

Examples of data that needs saving are

- Tester's name

- Application's name

- Build number

- Date reported

- Description

- Filename

Examples of things that need doing are

- Getting data from the user about the bug

- Saving the data to a file

Here are a couple more questions you should ask yourself when you are designing a program: First, "What data will you collect from the user?" This will translate into what textboxes and other controls you add. And second, "What data will the application provide for the user?" This will translate into what labels and text you use.

Once you have examined these questions, then you would sketch out what the User Interface (UI) would look like. Since testware must be built quickly and is usually rather simple, don't spend too much time on this part of the process. Most testware applications are very small—at least when you compare them to something like the next version of Microsoft's Office Suite. Months of planning go into something like Office before a single line of code is written. When planning testware, your goal should be to list the properties, methods, and basic design quickly. As you create your application, you will often find that you missed something at first. This is a natural part of creating testware, so don't stress over getting it perfect the first time. Your first goal should be to create a "working model" of the testware, and then make improvements later—after you have a better picture of what you really need to accomplish your goals. Once you can prove how your goals can be accomplished, then you can go back and improve your code as needed. At that point, your new goals will be the following:

- Add properties and methods that you did not think of before.

- Add error handling. Yes, testware need error handling, too (if for no other reason than other testers can use your testware without having to learn the inner workings of your code).

- Add validation to the UI to keep your fellow testers from using your application incorrectly.

- Separate the different parts of your application into different self-contained sections so that you can reuse these sections on different testware projects.

In Exercise 6-1, you will start the process of building a simple, component-based application. As you progress through this chapter, you will continue improving on this initial design.

■**Note** See Appendix A for instructions on how to download the solutions to these exercises.

Exercise 6-1: Creating the Bug-Reporter Application

In this exercise, you will create a simple bug-reporting application. The focus, at this stage, is to create a preliminary application that identifies the basics of how to make the program you need. To start out, here is a bullet-point list of what you will be doing:

- Get the tester's name, the application's name and build number, the date the bug is reported, the bug description, and the name of the file that stores the bug report.

- Collect all the data and format it into a string before you save it.

- Open a file and save the data.

1. Create an initial interface design on paper. Figure 6-1 shows the design we came up with for a simple bug-reporting application. While your application can look different, please do not add additional items at this stage.

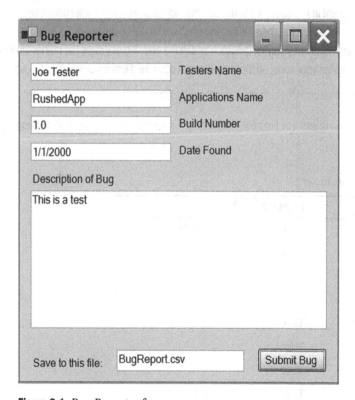

Figure 6-1. *Bug Reporter form*

2. Now that we have created a preliminary design, create a new .NET project named **BugReporter**.

3. Although Visual Studio always starts you off with a form called Form1, please rename this form to **BugReporterForm.vb** or **BugReporterForm.cs**, depending on the language you are using. You can change the name of the file to match the new class name by right-clicking and renaming it in Solution Explorer (see Figure 6-2): Rename in VB .NET, and Refactor ➤ Rename in C#.

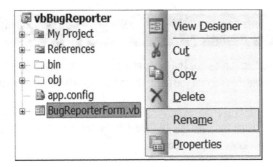

Figure 6-2. *Renaming the BugReporterForm.vb*

Note Using one of the new features in Visual Studio 2005, you could have also gone to the code view of the form, right-clicked on the name of the class, and chosen to Rename in VB .NET or Refactor ➤ Rename in C# from the pop-up menu. The problem is that this option does not change the filename. Choosing to rename the code file instead is convenient in this case, but there are times when one code file will contain two or more classes. If a second class is in the same file, then the second class would not be renamed. So, you would have to manually change it yourself. Either way works, though—and in the end, it really does not matter too much. When Visual Studio 2005 compiles your code, all the code files are combined into an .exe or .dll output file.

---

4. Add controls to the form (again, see Figure 6-1), and set the properties for these controls as shown in Table 6-1.

Table 6-1. *Properties to Set*

Object	Property	Value
BugReporterForm	Text	Bug reporter
txtTester	Text	
txtAppName	Text	
txtBuildNumber	Text	
txtDateReported	Text	
txtDescription	Text	
txtFileName	Text	
btnSubmitBug	Text	Submit bug
lblTester	Text	Tester's name
lblAppName	Text	Application's name
lblBuildNumber	Text	Build number
lblDateReported	Text	Date found
lblDescription	Text	Description of bug
lblFileName	Text	Save to this file

> **Note** We are using a Comma Separated Value (CSV/.csv) file because it is so useful in actual production applications. CSV files are really just text files. So, you can open them with Notepad if you like. Still, they are more useful when working with spreadsheet programs (like Microsoft Excel) or database programs (like Microsoft Access or SQL Server). For instance, if you have Excel installed on your computer, you will notice that double-clicking on the CSV file opens a new spreadsheet.

    5. Add the following code to respond to the Click event for the btnSubmitBug button:

VB .NET

```
Private Sub btnSubmitBug_Click _
(ByVal sender As System.Object, ByVal e As System.EventArgs) _
 Handles btnSubmitBug.Click

  '---- Declare Variables Section ----
  Dim strTester As String
  Dim strApplicationName As String
  Dim strBuildNumber As String
  Dim strDateReported As String
  Dim strDescription As String
  Dim strFileName As String
  Dim strData As String

  '---- Get Data Section ----
  'Create string variables and get the data from the user
  strTester = txtTester.Text
  strApplicationName = txtAppName.Text
  strBuildNumber = txtBuildNumber.Text
  strDateReported = txtDateReported.Text
  strDescription = txtDescription.Text
  strFileName = txtFileName.Text

  'Pull data out of the variables above and put it into a string
  strData = strTester + ","
  strData += strApplicationName + ","
  strData += strBuildNumber + ","
  strData += strDateReported + ","
  strData += strDescription

  '---- Save Data to File Section ----
  'Create a variable that will hold a reference to a file
  Dim objWriter As System.IO.StreamWriter
```

```
  If (System.IO.File.Exists(strFileName) = False) Then
    'Make a new file, open it, and have objWriter reference it
    objWriter = System.IO.File.CreateText(strFileName)
  Else
    'Open an existing file, set "True" for Append,
    'and have objWriter reference it
    objWriter = New System.IO.StreamWriter(strFileName, True)
  End If

  objWriter.WriteLine(strData)
  objWriter.Close()
  objWriter = Nothing
End Sub
```

C#

```
private void btnSubmitBug_Click(object sender, EventArgs e)
{
  //---- Declare Variables Section ----
  string strTester;
  string strApplicationName;
  string strBuildNumber;
  string strDateReported;
  string strDescription;
  string strFileName;
  string strData;

  //---- Get Data Section ----
  //Create string variables and get the data from the user
  string strTester = txtTester.Text;
  string strApplicationName = txtAppName.Text;
  string strBuildNumber = txtBuildNumber.Text;
  string strDateReported = txtDateReported.Text;
  string strDescription = txtDescription.Text;
  string strFileName  = txtFileName.Text;
  string strData ;

  //Pull data out of the variables above and put it into a string
  strData = strTester + ",";
  strData += strApplicationName + ",";
  strData += strBuildNumber + ",";
  strData += strDateReported + ",";
  strData += strDescription;

  //---- Save Data to File Section ----
  //Create a variable that will hold a reference to a file
  System.IO.StreamWriter objWriter;
```

```
if (System.IO.File.Exists(strFileName) == false)
{
  //Make a new file, open it, and have objWriter reference it
  objWriter = System.IO.File.CreateText(strFileName);
  }
else
{
  //Open an existing file, set "True" for Append,
  //and have objWriter reference it
  objWriter = new System.IO.StreamWriter(strFileName, true);
}
objWriter.WriteLine(strData);
objWriter.Close();
objWriter = null;
}
```

6. Run the application to see that it works and, of course, test where it fails as well. The first thing you may notice is that there is no feedback to the user when the method is called. You will change this later in Exercise 6-3. To verify that the program works, open the BugReport.csv file. You will find the BugReport.csv file by looking in the same folder as your .exe file. Open this file with Notepad and review its contents.

■**Note** You can find the path to the .exe file by using the Show All Files button in Solution Explorer, expanding the bin folder until you see the .exe file, right-clicking to access the pop-up menu, and selecting Properties. After you run the program, you can also open the BugReport.csv file from Solution Explorer; you will just have to use the Refresh button before it will display.

In this exercise, you created a new application, designed the UI, and added code to a single procedure. You then tested the new application to see that it worked as expected. You will now want to reexamine your testware application to improve its usability.

Creating and Using Procedures

In the last exercise, all the code you typed was in one procedure. While this worked, it does not provide you with the most flexible approach. Instead, you should break the code into separate procedures based on functionality. Using separate procedures makes your code much easier to debug and reuse.

For example, think about how you would create another application that writes data to a file and then ask yourself how you could reuse this code. As it is now, the code that collects data from the UI is mixed in with the data processing code. While this works OK for this project, if you were to copy and paste this code into another application, one that has a different UI, would it still work as well? Of course, you could make it work with the new UI by modifying your code, but then you would have to test it all over again to make sure that the modified code still worked as designed. Now, consider what would happen if the code had been divided into different procedures: one for gathering data from the UI and one for processing the data. If the processing data procedure code never changed, you would not have to retest that code to know it works. When you put the same data into the same procedure, you expect it to perform the same way and return the same results consistently. Now your focus would be on how to integrate all of the other methods with this one.

Of course, if you change code that has already been passed as bug free, you are forced to retest that code for any new bugs that are introduced. If you don't, you might easily assume that the code will work fine when, in fact, you have missed a newly created bug. If you have ever wondered how developers could miss some pretty obvious errors, this is one common explanation for it. This can be especially true of testware since, typically, it will not have a formal design process to catch the errors.

Note We are using "procedure" as a generic term. Just like data, procedures have many names. Some common ones include functions, subroutines, behaviors, operations, and methods. When to use these terms is, once again, dependent on which stage of development you are in when you are referring to them. As you build your application for this chapter, we will point out where these terms are most likely used.

When you want to break your code into smaller, reusable procedures, start by identifying which statements should be grouped together. For instance, take a look at the code in Exercise 6-1 and you will see that there are really two distinct sections. The first part of the code is about gathering data from the UI while the second part is about storing that data into a text file. From this observation, you may have guessed that you can create two procedures instead: one to collect the user's data, and one to save that data to the file.

Looking at Exercise 6-1, you think about creating a procedure to get the data from the UI data that is separate from the btnSubmitBug_Click() method. The idea would be to call that new procedure when the button was clicked (see Listing 6-1).

Listing 6-1. *Separating Processing and UI code*

VB .NET

```
Private Sub btnSubmitBug_Click(ByVal sender ...
  GetUIData() 'This calls the method below
End Sub

Private Sub GetUIData()
  'Add code to get UI data
End Sub
```

C#

```
private void btnSubmitBug_Click(object sender ...
{
  GetUIData(); //This calls the method below
}


private void GetUIData()
{
  //Add code to get UI data

}
```

When you review the code in the previous exercise, you will see that the "get data" code is strongly dependent on the UI design. As such, the code will not be reuseable in another application (or even in another Windows Form in the same application)—at least, not without many modifications.

However, in the case of the "save data" section, you see a different pattern. Since the data sent to this section inside of the strData variable does need to follow the same pattern each time, the UI that gathers this data could look quite different. Say, for example, that you created a web page that captured the same input from the user; as long as you filled strData with this data you could still use the same "save data" code without having to modify it to fit the change in the UI. This means that the "save data" section is processing code and is a good indication that it should be included in its own procedure.

Moving the code to a procedure called Save() would make it easier to reuse in other projects. However, the procedure must be designed correctly. One feature of a correct design is to have your procedures inform the program upon completion or failure of the action it is performing. In Exercise 6-2, you will move the "save data" code to a Save() procedure and add this notification code.

Exercise 6-2: Using Multiple Procedures

In this exercise, you'll start with the results of Exercise 6-1 and create a new procedure to save data to a file. This will separate the processing and UI code. If you didn't do Exercise 6-1, you will find a completed version of the files in the Chapter 6 Exercise folder (see Appendix A for download instructions).

1. Cut and paste the Declare Variables Section out of the btnSubmitBug_Click() event procedure and into the body of the class itself. You are doing this so that they, the variables, can be used by both procedures. If you are using VB .NET, remove the word *Dim* and replace it with the word *Private*. If you are using C#, just add the word *private* in front of the variables. Although this last step is not truly necessary (since it will behave the same with the original code), it is considered better to mark your variables explicitly with the word Private when you declare them outside of a method. The modified code should look like this:

VB .NET

```
'---- Declare Variables Section ----
Private strTester As String
Private strApplicationName As String
Private strBuildNumber As String
Private strDateReported As String
Private strDescription As String
Private strFileName As String
Private strData As String
```

Private Sub btnSubmitBug_Click(ByVal sender ...

C#

```
//---- Declare Variables Section ----
private string strTester;
private string strApplicationName;
private string strBuildNumber;
private string strDateReported;
private string strDescription;
private string strFileName;
private string strData;
```

private void btnSubmitBug_Click(object sender ...

2. Create a new method called Save() just after the btnSubmitBug_Click() method ends. Then cut and paste "Save Data to File Section" of btnSubmitBug_Click() to the new Save() procedure:

VB .NET

End Sub

```
Public Sub Save()
  '---- Save Data to File Section ----
  'Create a variable that will hold a reference to a file
  Dim objWriter As System.IO.StreamWriter

  If (System.IO.File.Exists(strFileName) = False) Then
    'Make a new file, open it, and have objWriter reference it
    objWriter = System.IO.File.CreateText(strFileName)
  Else
    'Open an existing file, set "True" for Append,
    'and have objWriter reference it
    objWriter = New System.IO.StreamWriter(strFileName, True)
  End If
```

```vbnet
   objWriter.WriteLine(strData)
   objWriter.Close()
   objWriter = Nothing
End Sub

End Class
```

C#

```csharp
}//end of btnSubmitBug_Click()

public void Save()
{
  //---- Save Data to File Section ----
  //Create a variable that will hold a reference to a file
  System.IO.StreamWriter objWriter;

  if (System.IO.File.Exists(strFileName) == false)
  {
    //Make a new file, open it, and have objWriter reference it
    objWriter = System.IO.File.CreateText(strFileName);
  }
  else
  {
    //Open an existing file, set "True" for Append,
    //and have objWriter reference it
    objWriter = new System.IO.StreamWriter(strFileName, true);
  }
  objWriter.WriteLine(strData);
  objWriter.Close();
  objWriter = null;
}//end of Save()

}//end of BugReporterForm class
```

3. Add a call to Save() in your btnSubmitBug_Click() event. This method should now look like this:

VB .NET

```vbnet
Private Sub btnSubmitBug_Click _
(ByVal sender As System.Object, ByVal e As System.EventArgs) _
 Handles btnSubmitBug.Click

  '---- Get Data Section ----
  'Create string variables and get the data from the user
  strTester = txtTester.Text
  strApplicationName = txtAppName.Text
  strBuildNumber = txtBuildNumber.Text
```

```
    strDateReported = txtDateReported.Text
    strDescription = txtDescription.Text
    strFileName = txtFileName.Text

    'Pull data out of the variables above and put it into a string
    strData = strTester + ","
    strData += strApplicationName + ","
    strData += strBuildNumber + ","
    strData += strDateReported + ","
    strData += strDescription

    'Call the Save method
    Save()
End Sub
```

C#

```csharp
private void btnSubmitBug_Click(object sender, EventArgs e)
{
    //---- Get Data Section ----
    //Create string variables and get the data from the user
    strTester = txtTester.Text;
    strApplicationName = txtAppName.Text;
    strBuildNumber = txtBuildNumber.Text;
    strDateReported = txtDateReported.Text;
    strDescription = txtDescription.Text;
    strFileName  = txtFileName.Text;

    //Pull data out of the variables above and put it into a string
    strData = strTester + ",";
    strData += strApplicationName + ",";
    strData += strBuildNumber + ",";
    strData += strDateReported + ",";
    strData += strDescription;

    // Call the Save method
    Save();
}//end of btnSubmitBug_Click()
```

4. Run the program and verify that it still works as it did in Exercise 6-1.

In this exercise, you separated the data *gathering* code from the data *processing* code. This makes it easier to reuse the data processing code in other projects.

Adding Error Handling to Methods

Although your bug-reporter testware now has separate procedures, you still need to make some additions. For instance, so far you have not added any code that would catch any errors that might occur. At the end of Exercise 6-1, you may have tested the application and found that there were a number of things that could break it. Things you might have noticed may have included the fact that you are accepting empty input from the textboxes and/or that you are allowing numbers where the tester's name should go. In fact, you could end up needing quite a lot of extra code if you consider all of the things that might go wrong. In a production application, it is estimated that 60 percent of a program's code is devoted to error handling.

Since our bug reporter is being used for demonstration purposes, it may not be appropriate to handle all the possible errors, but you should take a look at one example to give you an idea how you could implement your actual testware later. With that in mind, let's examine how you could include error handling within the Save() method.

If you review the code in the Save() method, you may notice that we did not place a Try-Catch block around the code creating the .csv file. This is a mistake, since there are a number of issues that could go wrong at this point. For one, what if the operation system does not allow the user to create new text files? The answer is simple—she will get an error. In fact, this could even shut down the application if not handled correctly. As you might imagine, this would not make for a happy user.

There are many theories about how to create well-designed, and bug-free, methods. One theory states that all methods should have only one exit point. This means that if you find an error, your code should not immediately exit the method but, instead, should continue on to the normal exit point. One way to do this is to create a variable that is used as a status "flag." When an error occurs, you would set the value of the flag to indicate that an error has been found.

For instance, say that you wanted to indicate that a method was successfully completed by setting a variable called blnCompleted to True. You could also set the value to False if any errors were found—an indication that the method did not complete successfully. That code would look something like Listing 6-2.

Listing 6-2. *Using a Status Flag*

VB .NET

```
Dim blnCompleted As Boolean
Try
    'Try somthing
    'if if worked
    blnCompleted = True
Catch ex As Exception
    'if it had an error
    blnCompleted = False
End Try
Return blnCompleted
```

C#

```csharp
bool blnCompleted;
    try
    {
      // try something
      // if it worked
      blnCompleted = true;
    }
    catch
    {
      // if it had an error
      blnCompleted = false;
    }
    return blnCompleted;
```

In this code, notice that we are returning the results of the completion status back to whatever code called this method, but we are not including any actual message back to the UI here. The theory goes that you use the UI code for creating a message to the user and just send back the status from the processing procedures. In this case, we are only indicating success or failure, but not the reason for the error. In actual practice, you will often see specific status numbers returned. These numbers, often referred to as *return codes*, should be identified at the beginning of a project. For example, the design specifications might indicate that return code 100 indicates that a security violation has happened.

As a tester, you know that you do not always have the source code available, so all you see are the error messages. Some error messages will present you with just error numbers. When that happens, you may have to track down the list of return codes in order to identify what is happening inside of a method. You will add this kind of error handling to the bug-reporter application in Exercise 6-3.

Exercise 6-3: Adding Error Handling to Methods

In this exercise, you will modify the application you made in Exercise 6-2 to include error handling using a Try-Catch block. You will also add a Boolean flag to indicate the status of the method and return the outcome at the end of the method. Finally, you will add a message to let the user know when the method succeeded or failed. If you didn't do Exercise 6-2, you will find the appropriate files in the following folder: DownloadFiles\Chapter6\Exercise6-2. These files are available for download from the Source Code section of the Apress website (www.apress.com).

1. Delete the Save() method and replace it with this new version:

VB .NET

```vbnet
Public Function Save() As Boolean
    '---- Save Data to File Section ----
    'Create a variable that will hold a reference to a file
    Dim objWriter As System.IO.StreamWriter
    Dim blnCompleted As Boolean
```

```vb
Try
  If (System.IO.File.Exists(strFileName) = False) Then
    'Make a new file, open it, and have objWriter reference it
    objWriter = System.IO.File.CreateText(strFileName)
  Else
    'Open an existing file, set "True" for Append,
    'and have objWriter reference it
    objWriter = New System.IO.StreamWriter(strFileName, True)
  End If
  objWriter.WriteLine(strData)
  objWriter.Close()
  objWriter = Nothing
  txtDescription.Clear()
  'if it made it this far without an error
  blnCompleted = True
Catch ex As Exception
  'if it had an error
  blnCompleted = False
End Try
Return blnCompleted

End Function
```

C#

```csharp
public bool Save()
{
  //---- Save Data to File Section ----
  //Create a variable that will hold a reference to a file
  System.IO.StreamWriter objWriter;
  bool blnCompleted;
  try
  {
    if (System.IO.File.Exists(strFileName) == false)
    {
      //Make a new file, open it, and have objWriter reference it
      objWriter = System.IO.File.CreateText(strFileName);
    }
    else
    {
      //Open an existing file, set "True" for Append,
      //and have objWriter reference it
      objWriter = new System.IO.StreamWriter(strFileName, true);
    }

    objWriter.WriteLine(strData);
    objWriter.Close();
    objWriter = null;
    txtDescription.Clear();
```

```
    //if it made it this far without an error
    blnCompleted = true;
  }
  catch
  {
    // if it had an error
    blnCompleted = false;
  }
  return blnCompleted;
}//end of Save()
```

2. Next, you need to replace the line of code that calls the Save() method in the btnSubmitBug_Click() method. The new version of this line will check the Boolean value returned from the Save() method. If the value is True, you will use a MessageBox to indicate success of the Save() method. If the returned value is False, you need to use a MessageBox to indicate failure. Your code should look like this:

VB .NET

```
'Call the Save() method
If Save() = True Then
  MessageBox.Show("Bug reported!")
Else
  MessageBox.Show("There was an error!")
End If
```

C#

```
// Call the Save() method
if (Save() == true)
{
  MessageBox.Show("Bug reported!");
}
else
{
  MessageBox.Show("There was an error!");
}
```

3. Run the application and test that your testware works when you add correct data.

4. Now, you will test what happens when there is an error. To create an error, you can change the file to "read only." To do this, open Windows Explorer and navigate to the BugReport.csv file. Now, highlight the file and right-click on it to access the pop-up menu. In the menu, choose Properties and a Properties dialog will appear.

5. In the Properties dialog, enable the Read Only check box to stop your application from writing to this file (see Figure 6-3). Now when the Save() method is called, it will fail.

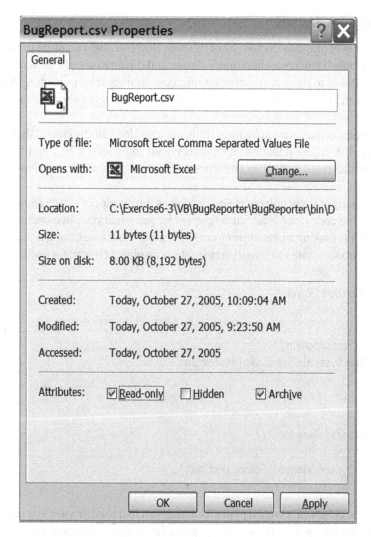

Figure 6-3. *Setting the file to Read Only*

6. Click OK to close the dialog and then test your application again. This time you should see the message indication that the bug was not saved.

In this exercise, you added simple error handling to the Save() procedure. In actual testware, you might want to create a set of error numbers to provide more detailed information about the error.

Because you modified the methods, you had to go through the testing process again. As you can see, it would have saved time if you made these modifications the first time. This goes to show that a well-designed program will need less rewrites and, therefore, less retesting.

Next, you will look at another way to make your code more reusable—by grouping methods into separate classes.

Creating Reusable Classes

So far, the bug reporter uses one class to hold all of its code. However, you can often increase the reusability of your code if you create additional classes and divide your code between them. This process is similar to the way you divided your code into separate procedures in Exercise 6-2. Of course, in order to do this you will have to understand more about classes and how they are used.

As mentioned before, when your application starts up, it will load all the classes that are required into memory. After a class is loaded into memory, your code can tell .NET to construct an *object instance* from that class. Each object instance can be thought of as a stand-alone copy of a class's code.

You can make as many of these objects as you need or as the developer's code allows. For example, if you look at the code that Visual Studio creates for you when you put a textbox on a form, you will see that it is making a new object from the TextBox class (see Listing 6-3). If you drag and drop more textboxes onto the form, you would see an object created for each.

Listing 6-3. *Creating a TextBox Object*

VB .NET

```
  Private Sub InitializeComponent()
    Me.txtTester = New System.Windows.Forms.TextBox
...
```

C#

```
    private void InitializeComponent()
    {
this.txtTester = new System.Windows.Forms.TextBox();
...
```

You can think of the class as if it were a paper form that you had to write your bug reports on. Would you use the original paper? Or, would you go to the copier, make some copies, and then write on one of the copies? Even if you had only one bug report to make, you might still make a copy for yourself and keep the template from being used directly. In the software world, you do much the same thing. You make classes to act as templates and then create objects to do the actual work.

Just like a paper original, you must design your template well in order for it to be useful. The process of creating useful classes begins with separating procedures and data into one or more classes.

Another way you can think of a *class is* as a programming tool used to group data and actions into different classifications based on what they have in common. Many times, the point of these classes is to create reusable components of code. One benefit that applies to using both multiple procedures and multiple classes is that self-contained code can be reused without exhaustive retesting—at least as long as it is not modified. You can write it once, test it toughly, and then reuse it in many places without a lot of extra development time. Better yet, you can use someone else's toughly tested classes in your own testware without having to do the development work yourself!

One of the tenets of good software design is that one developer should be able to use another developer's code without having to know all the details of that code. Oh, it is true that she will need to know something about it, but only in the abstract. Perhaps that is why, in object-oriented terms, this design theory is called *abstraction.*

To understand this concept, think about what happens when you want to use a class that someone else wrote. You might need to look for documentation on what a class does, what kind of data can be passed to its methods, and what kind of data those methods will return. But once you determine this, you can use another developer's classes in your own program without having to know the details about how the other person's code works.

Abstraction is a concept you have been working with all along. You have used it each time you have typed out MessageBox.Show(). When Microsoft made the MessageBox class, they programmed its Show() method to create a small window with a label and a button on it. The data you pass into the Show() method is the text you wish to have the label's text property display. You do not need to know, and probably don't care, how Microsoft's code does this—as long as it works consistently in every application you use it in. When you consider that there are likely more than 100 lines of code in this class and that more than 1 million people will use it, that is over 100 million lines of code that developers don't have to rewrite! From this, you can see what powerful tools abstraction and classes can be.

To create you own classes, start by dividing your data and actions into different classifications of code. First, you would look at a list of all the data your testware is working with and divide that up into different groups based on how it is used. Then, you would do the same for the actions your testware will perform.

Table 6-2 shows some of the classifications of data you have used in the BugReporter testware example.

Table 6-2. *Classifications of Data*

Data Members	Example
Data for the UI	lblTester.text
Data the software needs to save	ApplicationName
Data for messages to user	"There was an error"

Data for the UI should be kept in the class that creates the UI, but the data that the "software needs to save" can be moved into its own section without affecting the UI code. You started grouping this data when you created the Save() procedure in Exercise 6-1. Now you would move this data into a different class. Any "data that needs to be saved to file" would go into this new class while the "data needed for the UI" would stay behind. The "data for messages to the user" must be divided between the two classes—depending on how strongly they were dependent on the action in those classes.

While we are thinking about it, a common term for data when you are designing your classes is *attributes.* This is because the data in the class is thought to describe the class. For example, .NET has a button class, and the text attribute of a button is one way to describe it, just as its width and height attributes do.

As for the actions your program would take, you would divide these into separate classes as well. The proper term used for these actions when a developer is at the designing stage of a class is *behaviors.* You would examine these behaviors to decide what should stay with the UI class and what should be moved to a different class. Ask yourself a question like, "What actions could be created independent of the UI class?" In the bug-reporter example, the Save() method is an obvious choice. Your classifications of behaviors might look something like Table 6-3.

Table 6-3. *Classifications of Behaviors*

Behaviors	Example
Gather data from UI	strTester = txtTester.Text
Save data to file	Save()
Send message to user	MessageBox.Show("There was an error")

In the BugReporter application, you end up with at least two possible classes: one to interact with the user and one to save the data. The first class was created for you when you started making the BugReporter Windows Form. Visual Studio creates a new class for each Windows Form file, in this case the BugReporterForm class. However, now you would have to make the new class—one that we will call the ReportToFile class.

While you could just type the new class into the BugReporterForm file, this is usually not your best choice. Instead, we recommend that each class have its own file. Having each class in its own file makes it easier to organize your code. To create the new class, you would right-click on the project and use the pop-up menu to add the new class file (see Figure 6-4).

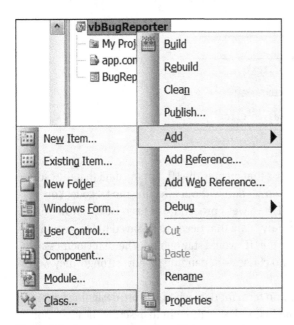

Figure 6-4. *Creating a new class file*

TESTER'S TIP: WHAT ABOUT STRUCTURES AND MODULES?

In Chapter 4, we focused on using classes, but you can also use both *structures* and VB .NET *modules* (C# does not have modules) to create reusable components. Both of these items are similar to a class in some ways. For example, they all organize data and procedures and they are all loaded into memory by the Class Loader as a .NET program needs them. Of course, they are different in a number of important ways as well. First, neither a structure nor a module can be used for inheritance. *Inheritance* is where you write a class with code to perform some basic tasks, and then create another class that inherits this code and adds additional code to perform tasks that are more specific. We will look at an example of inheritance at the end of this chapter. A second difference is that objects made from structures are stored in memory as *value types* whereas objects made from classes are *reference types*. If these terms are not familiar to you, take a look at Appendix B for a quick overview of the subject. A third difference (which affects the VB .NET module only) is that they cannot be used to create objects; instead, you use the code inside of a module directly just like you do with the Show() method of the MessageBox class. While you can make classes and structures behave this way, with a module you have no other choice. For the most part, you can just use classes in your testware applications. Although, in terms of computer resources, classes have a slightly higher overhead and they also provide the most flexibility.

Creating Class Members

Once you have a new class file made, you would need to create the members of the class. Most classes you will make should have the following types of members:

- Fields

- Properties

- Constructors

- Methods

Let's take a few moments to examine how each is used.

Fields

Fields are the data your class will work with. These usually take the form of variables and constants that you place at the beginning of your class (see Listing 6-4). For each piece of data you wish to work with, you would identify each field and mark it as being private. Making fields private allows only the code inside the same class the ability to use them. This stops other classes from using the field's data directly. We take a closer look at why this is considered a good design strategy in the next section; but for now, here is the syntax you use to create a field.

Listing 6-4. *Declaring the strTester Field*

VB .NET

```
Public Class ReportToFile
  '---- Declare Data Section ----
  Private strTester As String
```

C#

```
public class ReportToFile
  {
    //---- Declare Variables Section ----
    private string strTester;
```

Properties

One of the rules of designing a well-made class is that you should not allow direct access to fields. Instead, you should create a special type of procedure to access and modify each field indirectly. These special procedures are known as *property procedures*. Each property procedure provides controlled access to your fields from outside the class. To understand why this is considered better, let's look at one example.

Say that you wanted to allow a user of your BugReporter testware to choose a number between bug severity level 1 and 5, and the field that would hold this data would be called intSeverity. If you let the user set the value directly to the field, then it could be any valid integer—well beyond the range you want the user to choose from. To fix this, you set intSeverity to "private" and create a "public" property. You would include code to check that the user was assigning a value within the specified range (see Listing 6-5). This is a much better solution in at least three ways: it allows you to validate data before it is set to your fields; it allows you to send error messages to the user when they get it wrong; and it allows the user to assign a value, just as if they were assigning it directly to the field.

Listing 6-5. *Creating Properties*

VB .NET

```
Private intSeverity As Integer

Public Property Severity() As Integer
  Get
    Return intSeverity
  End Get
  Set(ByVal value As Integer)
    If value > 0 And value < 6 Then
      intSeverity = value
    Else
      MessageBox.Show("Severity must be between 1 and 5")
    End If
  End Set
End Property
```

C#

```csharp
private int intSeverity;

public int Severity
{
  get
  {
    return intSeverity;
  }
  set
  {
    if (value > 0 & value < 6)
    {
      intSeverity = value;
    }
    else
    {
      MessageBox.Show("Severity must be between 1 and 5");
    }
  }
}
```

Looking at Listing 6-5, you may notice that the Property procedure is divided into two sections. The Get portion of the procedure runs when your code tries to read, or "access," the value of the Severity property, like this:

VB .NET

```
lblSeverity.Text = Severity
```

C#

```csharp
lblSeverity.Text = Severity;
```

The Set portion is used when your code tries to change, or "mutate," the value of the Severity property, as follows (if you're a beginning programmer, remember that what is on the right side of the equals sign is always placed into what is on the left side):

VB .NET

```
Severity = txtSeverity.Text
```

C#

```csharp
Severity = txtSeverity.Text;
```

When the Set portion of the code runs, it will use a built-in variable "value" to hold the incoming data. You can then check this value variable for its data and decide if you wish to allow it to set the field's data or reject it. If you reject it, you can choose to notify the user that this was an incorrect value or just set the value to some default you think would be acceptable.

In fact, you could choose to do both—it is really up to you to decide what kind of error handling you would like to enforce.

Using properties is a common practice in OOP. If fact, you have been using them for a while now. Whenever you have used syntax like `lblTester.text = "Joe Tester"`, you were setting a `Property`. While the code inside of a `Property` procedure is similar to code you find in other procedures, the `Property` procedure allows the user to set a field's value by using the assignment operator (=), while still allowing you to add additional code for validation of formatting as you would in a normal procedure.

■**Note** Properties are sometimes called *accessors* or *mutators*—because you are "accessing" the data in the field using `Get`, and you are "mutating" the value of the field using `Set`.

Constructors

A *constructor* is a special type of procedure that runs first whenever an object is made from the class. You can use a constructor to set the initial values of the properties and fields, as well as run any other code you think would be useful when starting to work with a brand new object. Since the construct's code runs every time an object is made from the class, this is a perfect place for code that will "initialize" the new object instance.

Every object will have a constructor—even if you do not make one yourself. In fact, if you do not create a constructor in your class, .NET will create one for you; however, this one is invisible to you, and invisible code is notorious for creating strange bugs. We recommend that you create your own constructor even if it would do the same thing that the invisible one would do. For example, in .NET's invisible constructor, all strings are set to "empty" in VB .NET or "null" in C#. We recommend that you have your constructor perform the same tasks, but now the code would be visible and, thus, clearer. To make a constructor, you create a procedure called New when using VB .NET, or one with the same name as the class when using C#. In either language, a constructor is not allowed to return a value, so you must make it a Sub in VB .NET. However, in C#, this is implied and you do not need to indicate that the return type is void— in fact, it will give you an error if you try (see Listing 6-6).

Listing 6-6. *Creating a Constructor*

VB. NET

```
Public Sub New() 'constructor is always named New
  strTester = ""
  strApplicationName = ""
  strBuildNumber = ""
  strDateReported = ""
  strDescription = ""
  strFileName = ""
  strData = ""
End Sub
```

C#

```csharp
public ReportToFile() //constructor is always the same name as the class
{
  strTester = "";
  strApplicationName = "";
  strBuildNumber = "";
  strDateReported = "";
  strDescription = "";
  strFileName = "";
  strData = "";
}
```

Common Terms for Methods

You covered these in Chapter 5 so, no doubt, you understand how to create these. You may remember that in that chapter we indicated that *method* is another word for *procedure*. However, this may be a good time to tell you about other names used in the industry.

Although *method* is perhaps the most common term you'll see, there are a number of other names that you'll want to become familiar with—such as behaviors, operations, and functions. Since both of us are teachers as well as consultants, we have heard students ask, "When do you use which term?" To help with that, here is an overview of the most common usage.

When you are in the process of designing a class, it is appropriate to say that you have to include a "behavior" like Save() in the class. It would also be OK to call it an "operation" at this point. Depending on which part of the country you are in, you would hear a preference toward one or the other; but until the class was actually at the coding stage, you would be less likely to hear it called a "method." We sometimes call the Save() "method" a "procedure" in this chapter, but "function" would have worked as a generic term if this book had only used C# (since only VB .NET has both subs and functions). In the end, it really does not matter too much. If you wish to speak about it formally, like in a bug report, you may wish to keep in mind some of these common uses:

- When the class is being designed, use "behaviors" and "operations."

- When the classes have been coded, use "operations" and "methods."

- When you are talking about an object, use "methods."

- When talking as a generalization, use "methods," "procedures," or "functions."

Since it is important to be consistent in your reports, adjust your choice depending on region and corporate culture—as each may have its own preferences.

■**Note** Classes may contain other programming items, such as enumerations, delegates, events, structures, and even other classes. However, until you have time to learn about these other useful tools, you can still build powerful and reusable testware using a combination of fields, properties, constructors, and methods.

Creating a Class

Now that you know what a class is, and what kind of code goes into those classes, you would next create your classes with all of the appropriate members. The best way to learn how to do this is to actually do it yourself. In Exercise 6-4, you will modify the BugReporter project to include a new, reusable class to process your bug reports.

Exercise 6-4: Using Multiple Classes

In this exercise, you'll create a new class that includes a list of private fields, public properties, a constructor, and the Save() method you have been using.

1. To start, open the project from Exercise 6-3.

2. Add a new class to the project by right-clicking the project icon in Solution Explorer. In the pop-up menu, select Add ➤ Class, and name the new class **ReportToFile**.

3. At the beginning of the ReportToFile class, you need to create private variables to hold the data used in the Save() method. In the ReportToFile class, add the following code:

VB. NET

```
  Public Class ReportToFile
'---- Declare Fields Section ----
  Private strTester As String
  Private strApplicationName As String
  Private strBuildNumber As String
  Private strDateReported As String
  Private strDescription As String
  Private strFileName As String
  Private strData As String
End Class
```

C#

```
class ReportToFile
{
  //----Declare Fields Section ----
  private string strTester;
  private string strApplicationName;
  private string strBuildNumber;
  private string strDateReported;
  private string strDescription;
  private string strFileName;
  private string strData;
}
```

■**Note** Since the lines of code you just typed in are the same ones you used in the BugReporterForm class in Exercise 6-1, you could cut them from the BugReporterForm and paste them into the new ReportToFile class. However, it is good practice to copy the original code, paste it in its new place, and comment out the original code instead of deleting it. This way you can compare what you had before the move to what you have now. This often makes it easier to figure out how to fix a problem if one shows up after you move the code. Keep the original commented code until you have tested that your changes work as intended, then go back and remove the original code.

4. Go back to the BugReporterForm class and find the lines of code that look like those you just typed in step 3. You should find them all in the Declare Variables Section. Comment out each of these lines of code since you will no longer need them in the BugReporterForm class.

5. *Under* the fields you just created, add public properties for *each* field. To keep the code simple, you are not adding any validation code at this time. Your code will look like this:

VB. NET

```
'----Properties Section ----
  Public Property Tester() As String
    Get
      Return strTester
    End Get
    Set(ByVal value As String)
      strTester = value
    End Set
  End Property
  Public Property ApplicationName() As String
    Get
      Return strApplicationName
    End Get
    Set(ByVal value As String)
      strApplicationName = value
    End Set
  End Property

  Public Property BuildNumber() As String
    Get
      Return strBuildNumber
    End Get
    Set(ByVal value As String)
      strBuildNumber = value
    End Set
  End Property
```

```vb
    Public Property DateReported() As String
      Get
        Return strDateReported
      End Get
      Set(ByVal value As String)
        strDateReported = value
      End Set
    End Property

    Public Property Description() As String
      Get
        Return strDescription
      End Get
      Set(ByVal value As String)
        strDescription = value
      End Set
    End Property

    Public Property FileName() As String
      Get
        Return strFileName
      End Get
      Set(ByVal value As String)
        strFileName = value
      End Set
    End Property

    Public Property Data() As String
      Get
        Return strData
      End Get
      Set(ByVal value As String)
        strData = value
      End Set
    End Property
```

C#

```csharp
    //----Properties Section----
    public string Tester
    {
      get
      {
        return strTester;
      }
```

```
    set
    {
      strTester = value;
    }
}

public string ApplicationName
{
  get
  {
    return strApplicationName;
  }
  set
  {
    strApplicationName = value;
  }
}

public string BuildNumber
{
  get
  {
    return strBuildNumber;
  }
  set
  {
    strBuildNumber = value;
  }
}

public string DateReported
{
  get
  {
    return strDateReported;
  }
  set
  {
    strDateReported = value;
  }
}

public string Description
{
  get
  {
    return strDescription;
  }
```

```
    set
    {
      strDescription = value;
    }
  }

  public string FileName
  {
    get
    {
      return strFileName;
    }
    set
    {
      strFileName = value;
    }
  }

  public string Data
  {
    get
    {
      return strData;
    }
    set
    {
      strData = value;
    }
  }
```

6. *Beneath* the code for your properties, add a constructor to set initial values. Your code should look like the following:

VB .NET

```
'---- The Constructor Section ----
Public Sub New()
  strTester = ""
  strApplicationName = ""
  strBuildNumber = ""
  strDateReported = ""
  strDescription = ""
  strFileName = ""
  strData = ""
End Sub
```

C#

```
//---- The Constructor Section ----
public  ReportToFile()
{
   strTester = "";
   strApplicationName = "";
   strBuildNumber = "";
   strDateReported = "";
   strDescription = "";
   strFileName = "";
   strData = "";
}
```

7. Now, you need to move the Save() method from the BugReporterForm class to the ReportToFile class. Place the method directly *below* the constructor you just made. You can do this by copying and pasting this time, but remember to modify the BugReporterForm by commenting out the Save() method or you will have one in each class. Once the code is moved to the ReportToFile class, modify the Save() method so that it uses the new property procedures you just made instead of the fields. Your code should look like this:

VB .NET

```
'----The Methods Section ----
Public Function Save() As Boolean
   '---- Save Data to File Section ----
   'Create a variables that will hold a reference to a file
   Dim objWriter As System.IO.StreamWriter
   Dim blnCompleted As Boolean

   Try
      If (System.IO.File.Exists(FileName) = False) Then
         'Make a new file, open it, and have objWriter reference it
         objWriter = System.IO.File.CreateText(FileName)
      Else
         'Open an existing file, set "True" for Append,
         'and have objWriter reference it
         objWriter = New System.IO.StreamWriter(FileName, True)
      End If
      objWriter.WriteLine(Data)
      objWriter.Close()
      objWriter = Nothing

      'if it made it this far without an error
      blnCompleted = True
   Catch ex As Exception
      'if it had an error
      blnCompleted = False
   End Try
   Return blnCompleted
End Function
```

C#

```csharp
public bool Save()
{
  //---- Save Data to File Section ----
  //Create a variable that will hold a reference to a file
  System.IO.StreamWriter objWriter;
  bool blnCompleted;
  try
  {
    if (System.IO.File.Exists(FileName) == false)
    {
      //Make a new file, open it, and have objWriter reference it
      objWriter = System.IO.File.CreateText(FileName);
    }
    else
    {
      //Open an existing file, set "True" for Append,
      //and have objWriter reference it
      objWriter = new System.IO.StreamWriter(FileName, true);
    }

    objWriter.WriteLine(Data);
    objWriter.Close();
    objWriter = null;

    //if it made it this far without an error
    blnCompleted = true;
  }
  catch
  {
    // if it had an error
    blnCompleted = false;
  }
  return blnCompleted;
}//end of Save()
```

8. Next, you are going to move the code that formats the data in the BugReporter class to a different method in the ReportToFile class. This new method is different in that it will access the properties and not the fields themselves. Since the code will be different as well, you cannot simply copy and paste the code. So, start this process by looking in the btnSubmitBug_Click() method, locating the formatting code, and commenting out that section so that it looks like this:

VB .NET

```vbnet
'Pull data out of the variables above and put it into a string
'strData = strTester + ","
'strData += strApplicationName + ","
'strData += strBuildNumber + ","
```

```
'strData += strDateReported + ","
'strData += strDescription
```

C#

```
//Pull data out of the variables above and put it into a string
//strData = strTester + ",";
//strData += strApplicationName + ",";
//strData += strBuildNumber + ",";
//strData += strDateReported + ",";
//strData += strDescription;
```

9. You are replacing the code in step 8 with a new method called FormatData(). Add this method to the ReportToFile class using the following code:

VB .NET

```
Public Sub FormatData()
  Data = Tester + ","
  Data += ApplicationName + ","
  Data += BuildNumber + ","
  Data += DateReported + ","
  Data += Description
End Sub
```

C#

```
public void FormatData()
{
  Data = Tester + ",";
  Data += ApplicationName + ",";
  Data += BuildNumber + ",";
  Data += DateReported + ",";
  Data += Description;
}
```

10. Going back to the BugReporterForm class, add this code just *above* the btnSubmitBug_Click() method to create a new object from the ReportToFile class with this code:

VB .NET

```
Dim objReport As New ReportToFile
```

C#

```
ReportToFile objReport = new ReportToFile();
```

11. With the object made, you will now need to set the properties of the objReport object with the UI data. To do this, look *inside* the btnSubmitBug_Click() method, comment out the section of code that was used to set the variables you moved in step 3, and set the properties of objReport using the values in the textboxes, as shown here:

VB .NET

```
'Create string variables and get the data from the user
'strTester = txtTester.Text
'strApplicationName = txtAppName.Text
'strBuildNumber = txtBuildNumber.Text
'strDateReported = txtDateReported.Text
'strDescription = txtDescription.Text
'strFileName = txtFileName.Text

objReport.Tester = txtTester.Text
objReport.ApplicationName = txtAppName.Text
objReport.BuildNumber = txtBuildNumber.Text
objReport.DateReported = txtDateReported.Text
objReport.Description = txtDescription.Text
objReport.FileName = txtFileName.Text
```

C#

```
//Create string variables and get the data from the user
//strTester = txtTester.Text;
//strApplicationName = txtAppName.Text;
//strBuildNumber = txtBuildNumber.Text;
//strDateReported = txtDateReported.Text;
//strDescription = txtDescription.Text;
//strFileName = txtFileName.Text;
objReport.Tester = txtTester.Text;
objReport.ApplicationName = txtAppName.Text;
objReport.BuildNumber = txtBuildNumber.Text;
objReport.DateReported = txtDateReported.Text;
objReport.Description = txtDescription.Text;
objReport.FileName = txtFileName.Text;
```

12. Now you need to change the way you call the Save() method in the BugReporterForm. Since the Save() method has been moved to objReport, you need to add code that will call the method in that object. Once again, comment out the code you used previously and add this new version to the BugReporterForm class:

VB .NET

```
'Call the Save() method
'If objReport.Save() = True Then
' MessageBox.Show("Bug reported!")
'Else
' MessageBox.Show("There was an error!")
'End If

If objReport.Save() = True Then
  MessageBox.Show("Bug recorded")
  txtDescription.Text = ""
```

```
  Else
    MessageBox.Show("There was an error")
  End If
```

C#

```
// Call the Save() method
// If objReport.Save() = True Then
// MessageBox.Show("Bug reported!")
// Else
// MessageBox.Show("There was an error!")
// End If
 if (objReport.Save() == true)
 {
    MessageBox.Show("Bug recorded");
    txtDescription.Text = "";
 }
 else
 {
    MessageBox.Show("There was an error");
 }
```

13. Add code that calls the `FormatData()` method just *before* you call the `Save()` method:

VB .NET

```
    'Call the FormatData() method
    objReport.FormatData()
```

C#

```
//Call the FormatData() method
objReport.FormatData();
```

14. Run the program and verify that it still saves the bug report data when the `BugReport.csv` file is not in Read Only mode and gives an error when it is.

15. Once you have verified that that program is working as it was before you moved the code, go back and remove all of the code you commented out.

In this exercise, you saw how to create a new class that included fields, properties, a constructor, and a method. You also saw how to create an object from your class, set the properties, and call the methods. While you have not fundamentally changed the way the program behaves, you have made it easier to reuse the code in the `ReportToFile` class in another project. For example, you could create a web application and use the `ReportToFile` class in that project without modifications. You will learn more about web applications in Chapter 9, but if you would like to see an example, you will find the completed version of the files in the Chapter 6 DemoCode\Exercise6-4WebSite folder (see Appendix A for download instructions).

Separating Different Classes into Different Files

No doubt, you are starting to see a pattern to this chapter. You have been taking your code, deciding which parts are alike and which are dissimilar, and then placing that code into different, reusable containers. First came the procedure, then the class files, and now you will divide the classes into different files. One file will hold the UI code in an .exe file and one will hold the data processing code in a .dll (dynamic link library) file. Each of these files is considered a component of the bug-reporter application.

The reason for doing this is much the same as it was in the last two sections: self-contained code can be reused without exhaustive retesting as long as it is not modified. Using different files can save you time and money when making your testware applications, just like using procedures and different classes. As a bonus, creating testware in this way lets you see how the applications you test are made. That's right, most modern programs are made up of multiple files, so learning how to do this yourself will give you a better understanding of what potential problems to test for.

Testing a file while other people are still working on another part of the project becomes a reality when using separate files. As a tester, you can test these components by creating a small testware program referred to as a *test harness*. Creating a test harness is an important part of unit testing. Unit testing helps you prove that one component of the application works as expected, or not. In other words, when you add data and call the methods, its code works as you predicted. Unit tests are run as a White Box test or a Black Box test.

TESTER'S TIP: BLACK BOX AND WHITE BOX TEST METHODS

Black Box and White Box are test-design methods. Black Box test design treats the system as a "black box," so that you don't need to know the internals of the actual code you are testing. Black Box test design is usually described as focusing on testing functional requirements, not on the code itself (without knowledge of how the internal code works). You may also hear Black Box called things like functional, behavioral, opaque-box, and closed-box testing. Unlike Black Box testing, with White Box testing you do have access to the code. This allows you to see inside the "box" and is also called glass-box, clear-box, or structural testing.

Let's look at two component examples you could create for the bug-reporting application. The first is a completely new component file that will hold some validation code. The second will take the ReportToFile class and move it to its own .dll file. Both components will be reusable in other applications.

Validation Code

To create good testware, you need to add code for validating user input. When we first started this chapter, we didn't add validation code to the Click event procedure, but in the real world we would have. When all the code in a testware application is used only by that application, its validation code can be added directly to the event procedure that starts processing your data. For example, in Exercise 6-1, we collected the tester's name from the UI, but we did not add code that checked if the user put his name in the textbox. At the least, we should have checked that the textbox was not left empty. We could even have gone as far as looking up a list of tester names in a database and comparing it to the textbox data. We chose not to add this code because, in a book, we really need to keep the examples as small as possible—while still keeping relevance. Not showing all the validation code required is one way to keep examples small. Still, when you are designing your testware, you will want to add validation logic.

TESTER'S TIP: SHORT-TERM VS. LONG-TERM TESTWARE

Many of our students have asked, "Isn't it the developer's job to create validation code?" While this is true, when you are creating testware who is the developer then, if not you? All applications, including testware, can benefit from adding reusable validation code. Keep in mind also that how much effort you put into validation coding will have to do with what you expect the lifetime of the testware to be. Some testware will be quick, throwaway scripts to satisfy a one-time-only requirement (or changing requirements), and some testware you will want to keep around longer—from build to build of the software, and even between test projects. This longer-term testware, which is the kind we discuss in this chapter, would mostly be your test drivers and test harnesses. In this type of testware, you'll want to put more effort into adding robust validation coding. Putting a lot of validation code into short test scripts will waste the limited time you have on a test project. This is a major difference between creating testware and creating other software applications. So, it's okay to throw away and cut and paste when creating quick testware! You'll find you end up with both kinds, long- and short-term testware, and that figuring out which is which is a skill you'll gain with experience.

To identify what validation code you will need, ask yourself what kind of data could the users put in—or forget to put in—that would cause an error. This one is intuitive for most testers. As you know, data should only be used in the manner it was designed for. If you can fill up a textbox with incorrect text, such as putting character data into a field that should be only numbers, and it goes into the application without throwing an error, then you assume that the programmer missed adding validation for this and write it up as a defect. With these issues, it is easy to prove that there is a bug even if you do not have access to the application's code. Certainly, leaving the textboxes empty is something that could happen. So, you could write some code that will check for empty textboxes (see Listing 6-7).

Listing 6-7. *Testing for an Empty String*

VB .NET

```
If (txtTester.Text = "") Then
  MessageBox.Show("All textboxes must have values")
  Return
End If
```

C#

```
if (txtTester.Text == "")
{
  MessageBox.Show("All textboxes must have values");
  return;
}
```

For a more complex example, consider an application that allows you to fill up a textbox with a word or words and then searches a database for information about those words. Most of us have used these types of applications while doing web page searches. However, did you know that these simple applications are susceptible to a very serious problem called *SQL injection attacks*? Here is how it works.

Most database programming uses Structured Query Language (SQL). One SQL command is the ; `DROP TABLE` command—for example, ; `DROP TABLE Customers`, where `Customers` is a table in the database. This statement will remove the `Customers` table from the database. If the textbox on an application permits it, and the security of that database allows it, a tester (or hacker) could type this statement in the textbox of an application and the code will drop the table (see Figure 6-5). When this slips past development and test teams and a hacker inserts this kind of command, then it's called a SQL injection attack.

How could you stop this from happening using *validation* in your application? Since the semicolon (;) indicates the end of one SQL statement and the beginning of another, you could do something as simple as checking if a semicolon is in the text and, if you find one, remove any text after it. Although there are a number of ways to stop this at the database level as well, it's considered good practice to place validation at multiple levels.

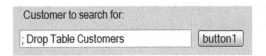

Figure 6-5. *A SQL injection attack*

Looking for a specific combination of characters is also a common validation task. Character data going into the application needs to be in the correct format and contain only acceptable values. As a tester, you know these "boundary analysis" issues come up when there is a fixed range of values that are acceptable to the program and you verify that it will not exceed these boundaries—for example, ensuring that a salary field does not allow 0 or negative values. While choosing the proper size or type for a variable can help with this, when working with character data you may need tools that are more powerful. Classic examples of this are when working with dates or when someone enters **1**, **2**, or **3** when they should a have typed **Good**, **Better**, or **Best**. If these incorrect values are accepted and stored, the data is now a mix of both acceptable and unacceptable values and, thus, should be considered corrupt data. You want to make sure that the data being entered is a match for that data you want.

You saw Regular Expressions in Chapter 3 and how they are used to find, and sometimes replace, a searched-for value. Most modern programming languages have Regular Expressions support. In .NET, Regular Expressions support is built into the `System.Text.RegularExpressions.Regex` class. For example, if you wanted to force a report file to end with `.csv`, you could create a validation method like the one shown in Listing 6-8.

Listing 6-8. *Using Regular Expressions*

VB .NET

```
Dim strPattern As String = "^.+\.[c][s][v]$"

If (System.Text.RegularExpressions.Regex.IsMatch(strTempString, strPattern)) Then
  Return True
Else
  Return False
End If
```

C#

```
// use the @ symbol to make sure C# uses the string exactly as typed
string strPattern = @"^.+\.[c][s][v]$";

if (System.Text.RegularExpressions.Regex.IsMatch(strTempString, strPattern))
  { return true; }
else
  { return false; }
```

Most likely, this code seems a bit confusing; but trust us, you don't have to be an expert in Regular Expressions to use them. You can simply copy this example—or one of the many other examples in Microsoft's documentation and on many Internet websites. These examples can be used to find common patterns, such as e-mail addresses and phone numbers. A complete discussion of Regular Expressions is beyond the scope of this book, but take a look at how we used one in Listing 6-8 using the breakdown in Table 6-4.

Table 6-4. *Looking for .csv*

Symbol	Meaning
@	This is for C# and is *NOT* part of the Regular Expressions.
^	Find a match where the beginning of a line is . . .
.	followed by any one character . . .
+	and that character repeats one or more times . . .
\.	then is followed by a literal dot . . .
[c][s][v]	which is followed by c, then an s, then a v . . .
$	and v is at the end of the string.

Using Regular Expressions can provide your testware with powerful validation logic. This validation code is vital to creating reusable components. Good testware should be

- *Bug free*: Bug free is easier to accomplish if the components of your application are kept small and hold to only one task.

- *Made up of small, reusable pieces*: Small and focused components are easier to add to other applications.

- *Simple to use*: Applications are simple to use if the users are protected from entering data that would corrupt their work, and if the application gives them consistent feedback.

- *Simple for others to add to their testware*: Bug-free components with good validation code are easier for others to add to their testware applications.

Creating all this validation code seems like a lot of work—and it is! However, one of the great things about creating components is that, once made, they can be used repeatedly in many testware applications. Validation may cost you time and money to create up front, but is vital to good reusable testware solutions for your long-term testware.

You will better understand how to create a validation component after you complete Exercise 6-5. So, let's do that now.

Exercise 6-5: Creating a Validation Class Library

In this exercise, you will create a new `.dll` component file that holds your validation's classes. To keep the exercise small, you will be creating only one class with one string validation. After you have created this class, you will test it by creating a simple test harness application to make sure it performs the validation task as expected.

First, you will create the `Validations.dll`:

1. Create a new Project.

2. In the New Project dialog box, choose the Class Library template and name the new project **Validations**.

3. In Solution Explorer, you will see that a new `Class1.cs` or `Class1.vb` file was created. Right-click on that file and choose Rename from the pop-up menu. Change the name to **Strings.cs** or **Strings.vb**.

4. Add the following code to this class:

VB .NET

```
Public Class Strings
   'This class is designed to validate strings

   Public Shared Function TestForEmptyStrings(ByVal strData As String) As Boolean
      'This function tests for a simple pattern
      Dim strPattern As String = ""
      If (strData = strPattern) Then
         Return True
```

```
      Else
        Return False
      End If
  End Function
End Class
```

C#

```
public static class Strings
{
  //This class is designed to validate string data

  public static bool TestForEmptyStrings(string strData)
  {
    //This function tests for a simple pattern
    string strPattern = "";
    if (strData == strPattern)
    {
      return true;
    }
    else
    {
      return false;
    }
  }//end of TestForEmptyStrings
}//end of class
```

■**Note** Notice that in this code we have chosen to make the method static or Shared. Doing this allows you to call these methods directly from the class without making an object first. Without this, you would have to make an object from the class first, and then call the method on that object.

---

5. Build the project to create the dynamic linked library (Validations.dll). This component file now holds your Strings class. You will find this file in one of the folders inside your project's bin folder. You will need this .dll file for step 10.

■**Note** One way to find out where the project is saved on the hard drive is to select the File ➤ Save As menu option. This will bring up a dialog box that allows you to save the file; but more importantly, it also shows you what folder the current file is in. Be warned that you should *NOT* use this feature to try to move your project, as it will only move the file you are currently working with. This makes your project have files in many places, which ends up being very confusing! Another way to find your .dll file is to right-click the file in the Solution Explorer window and look at its properties. However, you will have to use the Show All Files button at the top of this window before you will see your file.

With the `Validations.dll` created, you now want to build a test harness and test it before you try using it with the `BugReporter`.

6. Create a new Project.

7. In the New Project dialog box, choose the Windows Application template and call the new project **TestHarness**.

8. Add a textbox and two buttons to the `Form1` the project created. It should like something like Figure 6-6.

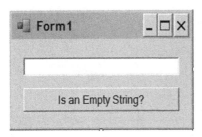

Figure 6-6. *The test harness form*

9. Set the properties based on Table 6-5.

Table 6-5. *Properties for the Test Harness Form*

Object	Property	Value
Textbox1	text	
btnEmptyString	text	"Is an Empty String?"

10. Add a reference to the `Validations.dll` by selecting Project ➤ Add Reference and browsing to the `Validations.dll` you just created in step 5.

11. Create a Click event procedure for the button by double-clicking it and then adding the following code:

VB .NET

```
Private Sub btnEmptyString_Click _
(ByVal sender As System.Object, ByVal e As System.EventArgs) _
Handles btnEmptyString.Click

  If Validations.Strings.TestForEmptyStrings(TextBox1.Text) = True Then
    MessageBox.Show("it was empty")
  Else
    MessageBox.Show("it was not empty")
  End If

End Sub
```

C#

```
private void btnEmptyString_Click(object sender, System.EventArgs e)
{
 if (Validations.Strings.TestForEmptyStrings(textBox1.Text) == true) {
   MessageBox.Show("it was empty");
 } else {
   MessageBox.Show("it was not empty");
 }
}
```

12. Run your test harness application and verify that your .dll is working correctly by *evaluating* the test case in Table 6-6.

Table 6-6. *Test Case for the Empty String Validation Component*

Control	Value	Pass/Fail
btnEmptyString	"test"	Pass
btnEmptyString		Fail

In this exercise, you created a new validation component. You then created a test harness and verified that the component worked. In Exercise 6-6, you will use this component with your BugReporter testware. In the real world, you would continue to add validation logic as needed. For example, you might also want to add a class that checked numbers or dates. Then you would be able to use all of these classes as your validation component for other testware applications without having to rewrite and retest the validation code. This is a perfect example of the kind of code you'll want to keep around for the long term.

Although we used only one validation here, you can add other ones on your own if you would like an extra challenge. For each property in your application, think about what kinds of validations you could use. Use your knowledge of boundary analysis (such as submitting maximum and minimum values, etc.) to test the functionality of each property within the object.

Separating the UI and Processing Components

As stated before, the big advantage of components is the ability to use them in multiple projects. You will find that your testware is more flexible when you separate the UI code from the processing code into these different components. For example, let's say that you wanted the ReportToFile class to be used in both a Web- and a Console-based version of the BugReporter application. While you could just copy and paste the code or add the code files into both of the applications, creating a separate .dll file like you did for the validation code has a number of advantages.

One issue that comes up is that a project and its output file, the .exe or .dll, can only use one programming language at a time. If your ReportToFile code was written in C# and another tester on your team wanted to use your code but only knew VB .NET, what would you do then? You could decide to teach him C# or just convert your code to VB .NET—but this takes time away from your main job, which is actually testing. Since your development skills are considered secondary to your primary job, your allotment of development- and code-maintenance time reflects this. So, getting the most out of what time you are given is vital to your career.

In this scenario, using components allows you to reuse your existing code without extra expense because C# and VB .NET components can work together. You can write a component in C# and compile it into a .dll file, then let the other tester that uses VB .NET reference your .dll file from his .exe file without having to rewrite any code.

TESTER'S TIP: MARSHALLING

It's the nature of a tester's job to come across a lot of developer terms; one of these is *marshalling*. This term refers to sending data between component objects, like the ones you just made in the .exe and .dll files. Marshalling is an advanced concept beyond the scope of this book, but be aware that common bugs occur when the data types in the .exe and .dll files are not the same. For example, if the .exe code thinks that an integer takes up 4 bytes in memory but the .dll code thinks that it should really be only 2 bytes, then there is a problem. Since all .NET languages share a common description of data types, you can communicate between C# and VB .NET components without having to perform some kind of translation. This is not always the case in traditional COM objects, like the ones you create with C++ or VB6. Applications like these often use components called *wrappers*, which act as translators between components used in traditional COM applications.

So far you have created a component .dll that holds some validation logic, but you could also create a new .dll that would hold the ReportToFile class that you have been using in the exercises. In fact, you could use all three separate component files for an application. The Validations.dll would be used from a new component file called ReportMaker.dll that held your ReportToFile class; and the BugReporter application would hold your UI code (see Figure 6-7).

Figure 6-7. *The component files*

Not all validations have to go into a separate file; if you were making actual testware, you would perform additional testing to determine what validations should be added to one or both component files. If you found validations that would be useful in other testware applications, you would add them to the Validations.dll. If the validations were specific to the ReportMaker.dll, you would only need to add them to that component. If the validations were specific to this particular user interface, you would include them in the BugReporter.exe.

For example, say that you want to make sure that the description of the bug is never allowed to be blank. You know that you have a method in the Validations.dll that tests for empty strings. This method returns true when the string is empty and false when it has something in it. So, you would reference the Validations.dll from your ReportMaker.dll and call the TestForEmptyStrings() method as you did in Exercise 6-5. You would use an If statement to determine the outcome of the method and throw an exception when the string was empty (exceptions were covered in Chapter 4). Your code would look something like Listing 6-9.

Listing 6-9. *Processing Validations*

VB .NET

```
'Test if description was left blank.
Dim blnIsEmpty As Boolean
blnIsEmpty = Validations.Strings.TestForEmptyStrings(Description)

If blnIsEmpty = True Then
  Throw New Exception("Description cannot be empty")
Else
  strData += Description
End If
```

C#

```
bool blnIsEmpty;
blnIsEmpty = Validations.Strings.TestForEmptyStrings(Description);
if (blnIsEmpty == true)
{
 throw new Exception("Description cannot be empty");
}
else
{
 strData += Description;
}
```

Here is a summary of the process that would happen inside your application:

1. When you click the Submit Bug button, your code would call the Save() method, which is now inside of the ReportMaker.dll. This causes .NET to load this file into memory.

2. When the Save() method starts to process, it calls the validation methods, which causes the code from Validations.dll to load into memory.

3. The code in ReportMaker.dll checks with the validation component for empty strings. If the validation comes back as true, the code throws an exception (again, see Listing 6-9). This exception gives a more detailed message than the generic message we have been using (i.e., "There was an error").

4. If an exception is thrown, a Try-Catch block placed in the UI component (the BugReporter.exe) would be able to catch this error and display a message to the user (see Listing 6-10).

5. If all the validations pass, your ReportMaker.dll will then make the BugReport.csv file as expected.

If this seems hard to follow, draw it out (like we did in Figure 6-7) and think about how the different components work together to create one testware application.

Listing 6-10. *Catching Exception Errors from Your Component*

VB .NET

```
Try
  If objReport.Save() = True Then
    MessageBox.Show("Bug recorded")
  Else
    'Show generic error message
    MessageBox.Show("There was an error")
  End If
Catch ex As Exception
  'Show specific error message
  MessageBox.Show(ex.ToString)
End Try
```

C#

```
try
{
  if (objReport.Save() == true)
  {
    //Show generic error message
    MessageBox.Show("Bug recorded");
  }
  else
  {
  MessageBox.Show("There was an error");
  }
}
catch (Exception ex)
{
  //Show specific error message
  MessageBox.Show(ex.ToString);
}
```

Private and Shared Assemblies

Because you have kept the UI, processing, and validation separate, you can use the same code in many testware applications. Each one of these components is referred to in .NET terminology as an *assembly*. Assemblies can be used by applications in one of two ways. The first way uses private assemblies and the second uses shared assemblies.

Private assemblies keep the .exe and the .dll component files together in the same folder. The big advantage of this option is simplicity. If you ever have to fix a bug in one of these components (heaven forbid!), you would only need to place the new version of the file in the folder and test that the new fix did not break anything.

Shared assemblies are a bit more complex, but are useful when you have many programs using the same components. Microsoft created a special place where you can register common components called the Global Assembly Cache (GAC). If you were to register the ReportMaker.dll in the

GAC, you could use it from a Console, Web, and Windows application all at the same time without having to have a separate copy of the file in each application's folder. Each application would ask .NET to create objects from the classes in ReportMaker.dll, but each object would be used independently by the different applications. Setting the properties of one of these objects would not influence another because each is in its own unique space in memory. This memory is associated with the individual applications that are using it. When objects are associated with a particular application, there are said to be within that application's *domain*.

Many of the larger applications that you test may be built this way, but most testware applications are too small to take advantage of this. So, in our examples, we are choosing to keep the .exe and .dll in the same folder and not use the GAC. This is a very easy way to create your testware components. Since most of these components are small in size, having multiple copies of the .dll on the hard drive will not take up much space. Also, when your testware is done and ready to distribute, all you need to do is copy and paste all the .exe and .dll files for your applications. You can save then to a floppy, burn them onto a CD, place them on a network share, or even e-mail them. As long as the PC they are copied to has the .NET Framework (note: Visual Studio is not required, just the Framework), you will be able to run your application.

Copying and pasting component files to another computer or folder and having them run without having to create a fancy install program is known as *XCOPY deployment*. You will find that this is a simple and effective choice for most of your testware applications. In fact, you can try this out at the end of Exercise 6-6.

Exercise 6-6: Separating the UI and Processing Components

In this exercise, you will move your ReportToFile class from your BugReporter.exe to a new ReportMaker.dll component file. Next, you will reference the new ReportMaker.dll from your BugReporter.exe project. Then, you will reference the Validations.dll from ReportMaker.dll (again, see Figure 6-7). Lastly, you will add code to the Description property to demonstrate how validations can be implemented in this program.

1. Create a new Project.

2. In the New Project dialog box, choose the Class Library template and name the new project **ReportMaker**.

3. In Solution Explorer, you will see that a new Class1.cs or Class1.vb file was created, but you do not need this file. So, right-click on that file and choose Delete from the pop-up menu.

4. Using the Project ➤ Add Existing Item menu selection, add the ReportToFile.vb or ReportToFile.cs class file from the BugReporter project you made in Exercise 6-4 to your new project .

5. Like the test harness you used in Exercise 6-4, you want the ReportToFile class to use the Strings class in the Validations.dll. So, add a reference from the ReportMaker project to the Validations.dll by selecting Project ➤ Add Reference and browse to the Validations.dll you created in Exercise 6-5.

6. Locate the Description property in the ReportToFile class and add code to validate that this property is not blank. Your code should look like this:

VB .NET

```vbnet
Public Property Description() As String
  Get
    Return strDescription
  End Get
  Set(ByVal value As String)
    Dim blnIsEmpty As Boolean
    blnIsEmpty = Validations.Strings.TestForEmptyStrings(value)
    If blnIsEmpty = True Then
      Throw New Exception("Description cannot be empty")
    Else
      strDescription = value
    End If
  End Set
End Property
```

C#

```csharp
public string Description
{
  get
  {
    return strDescription;
  }
  set
  {
    //Test if Description was left blank.
    bool blnIsEmpty;
    blnIsEmpty = Validations.Strings.TestForEmptyStrings(value);

    if (blnIsEmpty == true)
    {
      throw new Exception("Description cannot be empty");
    }
    else
    {
      strDescription = value;
    }

  }
}
```

   7. If you are using C#, change the namespace and access modifier of the `ReportToFile` class as follows:

C#

```csharp
namespace ReportMaker
{
  public class ReportToFile
  {
```

8. Now, go to the Build ➤ Build ReportMaker menu item and have Visual Studio create the ReportMaker.dll.

9. Open the BugReporter solution you created in Exercise 6-4 and delete the ReportToFile class file from this project. It is no longer needed since this code was moved into the ReportMaker.dll.

10. Add a reference to the ReportMaker.dll by selecting Project ➤ Add Reference and browsing to the ReportMaker.dll you created in step 6.

11. Modify the line that creates the ReportToFile object to use the ReportMaker.dll. The new code should look like this:

VB .NET

```
Dim objReport As New ReportMaker.ReportToFile
```

C#

```
ReportMaker.ReportToFile objReport = new ReportMaker.ReportToFile();
```

12. Modify the code in the btnSubmitBug_Click() to include a Try-Catch block that captures any validation errors when the property values are set. Your final code should look like this:

VB .NET

```
Try
  'Create string variables and get the data from the user
  objReport.Tester = txtTester.Text
  objReport.ApplicationName = txtAppName.Text
  objReport.BuildNumber = txtBuildNumber.Text
  objReport.DateReported = txtDateReported.Text
  objReport.Description = txtDescription.Text
  objReport.FileName = txtFileName.Text
Catch ex As Exception
  MessageBox.Show(ex.ToString())
End Try
```

C#

```
try
{
  //---- Get Data Section ----
  objReport.Tester = txtTester.Text;
  objReport.ApplicationName = txtAppName.Text;
  objReport.BuildNumber = txtBuildNumber.Text;
  objReport.DateReported = txtDateReported.Text;
  objReport.Description = txtDescription.Text;
  objReport.FileName = txtFileName.Text;
}
catch(Exception ex)
{
  MessageBox.Show(ex.ToString());
}
```

13. Run your test harness application and verify that your `.dll` is working correctly by *evaluating* the test case in Table 6-7.

Table 6-7. *Test Case for Your Validation Component*

Control	Value	Pass/Fail
txtDescription	"Some data"	Pass
txtDescription		Fail

14. If you have another computer with the .NET Framework installed on it, try copying all of the files in the bin folder to that computer, and verify that the program still works as it does here.

In this exercise, you moved your `ReportToFile` class from your `BugReporter.exe` to a new `ReportMaker.dll` component. Then, you created references between `BugReporter.exe`, `ReportMaker.dll`, and `Validations.dll` to demonstrate how components are used together to form one complete testware application. You also added validation code to two of the properties. If this were production code, you would add validations to all of the properties as needed. Next, you will look at how these same components can be enhanced using more principles of OOP.

Extending and Changing Your Components

In this chapter, you have been introduced to a number of OOP concepts already, but now you will look at two OOP concepts that allow you to extend and change your components without having to rewrite a lot of code. These two concepts are *polymorphism* and *inheritance*.

Polymorphism

Imagine that your bug reporter is a success with the team, but another tester is creating an ASP.NET application and asks if your `ReportMaker.dll` is able to save the report file to an XML or HTML file instead. At first, you might be inclined to just hand over the code and let her figure out how to do this. However, since you created it, you are really the only person who knows this code well. Having her do it would be like having her start from scratch, costing the team time it really does not have. Instead, you realize that you'll just need to build a new version of the `FormatData()` method. This new version will be almost like the original version, but will allow you to choose `.csv`, `.html`, or `.xml` files. Once created, you can hand over the `.dll` to the other tester for use in her ASP.NET application.

So now you need to decide how to go about this task. The original `Save()` method was not really designed with XML or HTML in mind. You could make two new versions of this method and call them `FormatToXML()` and `FormatToHTML()`, rebuild the `ReportMaker.dll`, and redistribute the new version of the `.dll`. If you choose this option, the other tester could then call these new methods as needed.

While this would work, perhaps a better way would be to create a new version of the `FormatData()` method itself. This one would have a parameter used to determine what type of file the user wants to make. The new version might look something like Listing 6-11 (which is used in Exercise 6-7).

Once this new version is made, the old version will still exist, and any application that uses the original version will still work. When the new ASP.NET testware calls the Save() method without any arguments, the original (default) version runs; however, if it used FormatData("xml") or FormatData("html"), it will run the new version. If someone else wants a new format later, you can easily add a new "case" statement to match the new format.

Creating multiple versions of a method in a single class is one form of *polymorphism*. Although the name sounds intimidating, it just means that the method has been changed ("morphed") into many ("poly") versions. Instead of using many different names for methods that do almost the same thing, it is good practice to use one name and create different overloads of that method. *Overloading* is the fancy term used when polymorphing a method in the same class.

Microsoft leads by example in .NET—as they use overloaded methods everywhere. Take, for example, the MessageBox.Show() method. As of this writing, there are 21 overloaded versions of the Show() method. If Microsoft had chosen to create a new method for each combination of parameters, that would have been 20 more method names you would have to know. As it is, all you need to know is that the Show() method can be used in many ways.

One more thought, since you did not change the original FormatData() method, it still exists unaltered. So, you will only need your newest version of the ReportMaker.dll to work with both your existing and new applications. Reducing the number of file versions needed for your applications makes keeping track of testware files much easier.

So, in the end, we recommend that you make your testware more developer friendly (that's friendly for you and your follow testers) and use polymorphism when you need to add new features. To get some practice, you will build the example we just talked about in Exercise 6-7.

Exercise 6-7: Polymorphic Components

In this exercise, you will change your ReportMaker.dll component file so that is has a new version of the FormatData() method. This new method will have one parameter that is used to set a choice between .xml, .html, and .csv files. After you have changed this class, you will want to test it by creating a simple test harness to make sure it does the job as expected.

■**Tip** Before you begin, make a back-up copy of the ReportMaker folder before you start. To do this, just use Windows Explorer and copy the whole ReportMaker solution folder you created in Exercise 6-6. Now paste this folder to a safe location. You should always make a backup of the old version of the files in case you ever need it again. Visual Studio will not do this for you, so you must do it manually. Also, remember that the *Save As* features will not accomplish this either. You must copy the whole folder

---

1. Open the ReportMaker solutions and add a new version of the Save() method beneath the old version using the code in Listing 6-11.

Listing 6-11. *An Overloaded Version of FormatData()*

VB .NET

```vb
Public Sub FormatData(ByVal FileType As String)
  'To keep the code simple our XML and
  'HTML files will only have one report each
  If (System.IO.File.Exists(FileName) = True) Then
    System.IO.File.Delete(FileName)
  End If

  Select Case FileType
    Case "xml"
      'Pull data out of the variables above and put it into a string
      'Notice we are using "" to escape the dbl-quote in the xml attributes
      strData = "<?xml version=""1.0"" encoding=""utf-8"" ?>"
      strData += "<root>"
      strData += vbCrLf
      strData += "<Tester>" + Tester + "</Tester>"
      strData += vbCrLf
      strData += "<ApplicationName>" + ApplicationName + "</ApplicationName>"
      strData += vbCrLf
      strData += "<BuildNumber>" + BuildNumber + "</BuildNumber>"
      strData += vbCrLf
      strData += "<DateReported>" + DateReported + "</DateReported>"
      strData += vbCrLf
      strData += "</root>"

    Case "html"
      strData = "<html><head>"
      strData += "<title>" + Description.Substring(1, 5) + "...</title>"
      strData += "</head><body>"
      strData += "<hr />"
      strData += "<b>Testers Name: </b>" + Tester
      strData += "<br />"
      strData += "<b>ApplicationName:</b>" + ApplicationName
      strData += "<br />"
      strData += "<b>BuildNumber:</b>" + BuildNumber
      strData += "<br />"
      strData += "<b>DateReported:</b>" + DateReported
      strData += "<hr />"
      strData += "</body></html>"

    Case Else
      FormatData() 'call the original version
  End Select
End Sub
```

C#

```csharp
public void FormatData(string FileType)
{
  //To keep the code simple our XML and
  //HTML files will only have one report each

  if ((System.IO.File.Exists(FileName) == true))
  {
    System.IO.File.Delete(FileName);
  }
  if (FileType == "xml")
  {
    //Pull data out of the variables above and put it into a string
    //Notice we are using \ to escape the dbl-quote in the xml attributes

    strData = "<?xml version=\"1.0\" encoding=\"utf-8\" ?>";
    strData += "<root>";
    strData += "\r\n";
    strData += "<Tester>" + Tester + "</Tester>";
    strData += "\r\n";
    strData += "<ApplicationName>" + ApplicationName + "</ApplicationName>";
    strData += "\r\n";
    strData += "<BuildNumber>" + BuildNumber + "</BuildNumber>";
    strData += "\r\n";
    strData += "<DateReported>" + DateReported + "</DateReported>";
    strData += "\r\n";
    strData += "</root>";
  }
  else if (FileType == "html")
  {
    strData = "<html><head>";
    strData += "<title>" + Description.Substring(1, 5) + "...</title>";
    strData += "</head><body>";
    strData += "<hr />";
    strData += "<b>Testers Name: </b>" + Tester;
    strData += "<br />";
    strData += "<b>ApplicationName:</b>" + ApplicationName;
    strData += "<br />";
    strData += "<b>BuildNumber:</b>" + BuildNumber;
    strData += "<br />";
    strData += "<b>DateReported:</b>" + DateReported;
    strData += "<hr />";
    strData += "</body></html>";
  }
```

```
  else
  {
    FormatData();
  }
}//end of FormatData
```

2. Now, build the project to create the new version of `ReportMaker.dll`.

3. Create a new project to use as a test harness (you need to test it before you give it to the other tester to make sure it works and to use as an example of how to use it).

4. In the New Project dialog box, choose the Windows Application template and call the new project **Test Harness**.

5. Add a textbox, a label, and one button to the `Form1` that the project created. It should look something like Figure 6-8.

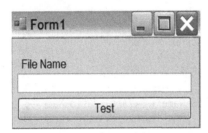

Figure 6-8. *The test harness form*

6. Set the properties based on Table 6-8.

Table 6-8. *Properties for the Test Harness Form*

Object	Property	Value
txtFileName	text	
btnTest	text	"Test"
lblFileName	text	"File Name"

7. Add a reference to the new `ReportMaker.dll` by selecting the Project ➤ Add Reference menu and browsing to the `ReportMaker.dll` you created in step 2.

8. To test what file extension is being used, you can use Regular Expressions. Add an `Imports` or `using` statement to the top of the `Form1` file so that you will not have to type out the full name later.

VB .NET

```
Imports System.Text.RegularExpressions
```

C#

```csharp
using System.Text.RegularExpressions;
```

9. Create an event procedure by double-clicking on the button and adding the following code:

VB .NET

```vbnet
Private Sub btnTest_Click _
(ByVal sender As System.Object, ByVal e As System.EventArgs) _
Handles btnTest.Click
  Dim objReport As New ReportMaker.ReportToFile

  objReport.Tester = "Joe tester"
  objReport.ApplicationName = "Test App"
  objReport.BuildNumber = "1.1"
  objReport.DateReported = Date.Today.ToShortDateString()
  objReport.Description = "This is a test Bug"
  objReport.FileName = txtFileName.Text

  Dim strTempString As String

  'Convert to lowercase to make the RegEx simpler
  strTempString = txtFileName.Text.ToLower()

  Dim strXMLPattern As String = "^.+\.[x][m][l]$"
  Dim strHTMLPattern As String = "^.+\.[h][t][m][l]$"

  Try

    If (Regex.IsMatch(strTempString, strXMLPattern)) Then
      objReport.FormatData("xml")
    ElseIf (Regex.IsMatch(strTempString, strHTMLPattern)) Then
      objReport.FormatData("html")
    Else
      objReport.FormatData()
    End If
    objReport.Save()
    MessageBox.Show("Saved")

  Catch ex As Exception
    MessageBox.Show(ex.ToString)
  End Try

End Sub
```

C#

```csharp
public void FormatData(string FileType)
{
  if ((System.IO.File.Exists(FileName) == true))
  {
    System.IO.File.Delete(FileName);
  }
  if (FileType == "xml")
  {
    strData = "<?xml version=\"1.0\" encoding=\"utf-8\" ?>";
    strData += "<root>";
    strData += "\r\n";
    strData += "<Tester>" + Tester + "</Tester>";
    strData += "\r\n";
    strData += "<ApplicationName>" + ApplicationName + "</ApplicationName>";
    strData += "\r\n";
    strData += "<BuildNumber>" + BuildNumber + "</BuildNumber>";
    strData += "\r\n";
    strData += "<DateReported>" + DateReported + "</DateReported>";
    strData += "\r\n";
    strData += "</root>";
  }
  else if (FileType == "html")
  {
    strData = "<html><head>";
    strData += "<title>" + Description.Substring(1, 5) + "...</title>";
    strData += "</head><body>";
    strData += "<hr />";
    strData += "<b>Testers Name: </b>" + Tester;
    strData += "<br />";
    strData += "<b>ApplicationName:</b>" + ApplicationName;
    strData += "<br />";
    strData += "<b>BuildNumber:</b>" + BuildNumber;
    strData += "<br />";
    strData += "<b>DateReported:</b>" + DateReported;
    strData += "<hr />";
    strData += "</body></html>";
  }
  else
  {
    FormatData();
  }
}//end of FormatData
```

10. Run your test harness application and verify that your .dll is working correctly by *evaluating* the following test case:

   a. *Test Case*: Test the .xml, .csv, and .html filenames.

   b. *Test Setup*: Check the number of rows in table.

   c. *Test Procedure*:

   • Add test.xml, test.html, and test.csv to the File Name textbox.

   • Open the folder and check that the files are made (see Figure 6-9).

   • Open the file and check that it contains proper formatting.

   d. *Expected*: File is made and in proper format.

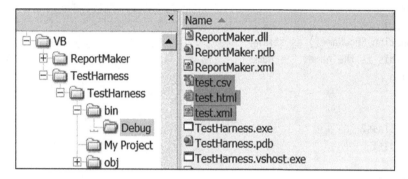

Figure 6-9. *Verifying that the files were made*

In this exercise, you saw how you overload methods to create new versions without changing the original versions. This is important—since any changes to the original mandate additional testing. On a live project, you would now need to document the new features and tell the other tester that the new .dll version is ready to use in her testware project.

Inheritance

We have one more tool from OOP to discuss: the concept of *inheritance*. Using inheritance, you can create newer versions of not just one method in the ReportMaker.dll, but a completely new version of the ReportToFile class inside of it. This can be handy when a class you know about already has much of the properties and methods you need for a new project.

For example, let's say that your bug reporter has received a lot of attention and other test teams are starting to adopt it. The problem is that your current version of ReportMaker only saves to local files; and with so many testers using your testware, it would be nice to store these bug reports in a central location. A database would be a good idea; so you might make a new ReportToDatabase class with similar properties and methods as your ReportsToFile class. Inheritance will let you do this without having to rewrite a lot of your previous code.

Here's a simple example of how inheritance works; consider this simple class in Listing 6-12.

Listing 6-12. *Using Inheritance*

VB .NET

```
Public Class Class1
  Private strName As String

  Public Property Name() as string
    Get
      Return strName
    End Get
    Set(ByVal value as string)
      strName = value
    End Set
  End Property

  Public Function ShowName() as string
    Return "This is the name: " + Name
  End Function
End Class

Public Class Class2
  Inherits Class1
End Class
```

C#

```
public class Class1
{
 private string strName;

 public string Name {
   get {
     return strName;
   }
   set {
     strName = value;
   }
 }

 public string ShowName()
 {
   return "This is the name: " + Name;
 }
}
public class Class2 : Class1
{
}
```

As you can see, Class1 has a field, a property, and a method. We have also created a second class called Class2, but you will notice that there is no code inside it. However, since this class is marked up as "inheriting" from Class1, the code you see in Class1 is automatically available to Class2.

In fact, if you created a Button1_Click() event handler, you could make an object from Class2 and still access the properties and methods inherited from Class1:

VB .NET

```
Private Sub Button1_Click _
(ByVal sender As System.Object, ByVal e As System.EventArgs) _
 Handles Button1.Click
    Dim x As New Class2
    x.Name = "Joe"
    MessageBox.Show(x.ShowName())
End Sub
```

C#

```
private void Button1_Click(object sender, System.EventArgs e)
{
 Class2 x = new Class2();
 x.Name = "Joe";
 MessageBox.Show(x.ShowName());
}
```

You can do this same thing with the ReportToDatabase class. By inheriting the code from the ReportToFile class, you will not have to re-create the field or properties. However, you will need to add additional fields and properties, as well as change the way the Save() method works.

Adding the additional fields and properties will be easy. All you need to do is add them into the *child* class. That's the class that is inheriting code from the *parent* class. For example, if you wanted to add a PhoneNumber property to the code in Listing 6-12, it would look like Listing 6-13.

Listing 6-13. *Adding a New Field and Property*

VB .NET

```
Public Class Class2
 Inherits Class1
 Private strPhoneNumber As String

  Public Property PhoneNumber()
    Get
      Return strPhoneNumber
    End Get
    Set(ByVal value)
      strPhoneNumber = value
    End Set
  End Property
End Class
```

C#

```csharp
public class Class2 : Class1
{
  private string strPhoneNumber;

  public string PhoneNumber
  {
    get
    {
      return strPhoneNumber;
    }
    set
    {
      strPhoneNumber = value;
    }
  }
}
```

Now you could use the additional property just like the other properties that came from the parent class:

VB .NET

```vbnet
Dim x As New Class2
x.Name = "Joe"
x.PhoneNumber = "555-1212"
```

C#

```csharp
Class2 x;
x.Name = "Joe";
x.PhoneNumber = "555-1212";
```

Changing a method in the child class is almost as easy; but for that, you need to use another form of polymorphism called *overriding*.

Overriding a method is done when you have a method in a parent class that you need changed in the child class. It is similar to overloading the method, but overloads are when the new version of the method has additional parameters and/or the parameters are using different data types. In contrast, overrides happen when you already have a matching version in the parent class and you need the child class version to do something else.

Consider the ShowName() method in the Class1 example. If you wanted to add a new version of this method to Class2, it might look something like Listing 6-14.

Listing 6-14. *Overload vs. Override*

VB .NET

```vbnet
'This is an overload because it has different parameters as the parent
Public Function ShowName(ByVal message As String) as string
  Return "message: " + Name
End Function
```

```
'This is an override because it has the same parameters as the parent
Public Function ShowName() as string
  Return Name + ": " + PhoneNumber
End Function
```

C#

```
//This is an overload because it has different parameters as the parent
public string ShowName(string message)
{
 return "message: " + Name;
}
//This is an override because it has the same parameters as the parent
public string ShowName()
{
 return Name + ": " + PhoneNumber;
}
```

Note If you type out the examples in Listings 6-12, 6-13, and 6-14, you will see a warning about how the ShowName() method "hides" or "shadows" another method in Class1. While it will work as shown, to design this properly we would need to prepare our parent class methods to be overloaded by adding additional instructions to the method. Using overriding is an advanced feature that needs more discussion than we have room for in this book. You may wish to read Matt Weisfeld's *Object-Oriented Thought Process, 2nd Edition* (Sams Publishing, 2003) for a language-neutral look at this and other OOP topics. For now, don't worry about the warning. Testers do not need to know every detail about OOP before they can make use of this type of polymorphism; but if you find yourself creating lot of testware, consider looking into this further.

In the ReportToDatabase class, you would need to override the Save() method to send the bug report to a database. The code would look something like Listing 6-15.

Listing 6-15. *Overriding the Save() Method*

VB .NET

```
Imports System.Data.SqlClient
Public Class ReportToDatabase
  Inherits ReportToFiles

Public Shadows Function Save() As Boolean

  Dim myConn As SqlConnection = New SqlConnection()
  myConn.ConnectionString = "SSPI=true;Initial Catalog=TestDB;Data Source=TestSvr;"
  myConn.Open()
```

```
    Dim myCmd As New SqlCommand
    myCmd.Connection = myConn

    Dim strSQLCommand As String
    strSQLCommand = "exec insBugReports "

    'Pull data out of the fields and put it into a string
    strSQLCommand = Tester + ","
    strSQLCommand += ApplicationName + ","
    strSQLCommand += BuildNumber + ","
    strSQLCommand += DateReported + ","
    strSQLCommand += Description

    myCmd.CommandText = strSQLCommand
    myCmd.ExecuteNonQuery()

    myConn.Close()
    myConn = Nothing
    myCmd = Nothing
End Function

End Class
```

C#

```
using System.Data.SqlClient;
public class ReportToDatabase : ReportToFiles
{

  public new bool Save()
  {
    SqlConnection myConn = new SqlConnection();
    myConn.ConnectionString =
      "SSPI=true;Initial Catalog=TestDB;Data Source=TestSvr;";
    myConn.Open();
    SqlCommand myCmd = new SqlCommand();
    myCmd.Connection = myConn;
    string strSQLCommand;
    strSQLCommand = "exec insBugReports ";
    strSQLCommand = Tester + ",";
    strSQLCommand += ApplicationName + ",";
    strSQLCommand += BuildNumber + ",";
    strSQLCommand += DateReported + ",";
    strSQLCommand += Description;
```

```
    myCmd.CommandText = strSQLCommand;
    myCmd.ExecuteNonQuery();
    myConn.Close();
    myConn = null;
    myCmd = null;
  }
}
```

This code accesses Microsoft SQL Server—but after we had tested that the testware was working, we could go back and overload the Save() method (yet again) to include a version for Access or Oracle.

Summary

Applications are often divided between what the human user sees (the User Interface or UI), and the code in the background that the UI works with. The UI is typically stored in an .exe file while the background code is stored in a .dll file. These .dll files are sometimes referred to as class libraries because they will be made up of one or more classes. Classes are used to organize code by data and functionality. The data stored in a class may be referred to as the class's properties, attributes, or—sometimes—fields. Methods provide the functionality (i.e., the behavior) of a class. Procedures are sometimes called functions, operations, or behaviors, but methods is the most common developer term. It is somewhat confusing that there are many names for the same thing, but with practice, the names will all make sense. Creating testware using OOP can save your testing team time and money. You have seen that components and OOP make testware easier to make and more flexible in use. While mastering OOP and components will take lot of study and practice, hopefully this chapter has shown you just how and why these concepts are important to testers. For further resources on OOP, see Appendix C.

Tester's Checklist

☑ Use procedures to group statements together.

☑ Use classes to group field, properties, and methods together.

☑ Never allow direct access to the field from outside of the class.

☑ Use properties to let code access and change fields.

☑ Use overloading instead of using different method names for similar methods.

☑ Create reusable components to make your testing more productive.

CHAPTER 7

###

Automation with Console-Based Testware

Although Console applications don't seem like much fun to make, they can be very useful when creating testing automation software. One reason they are often overlooked is that they do not have an attractive interface; instead, the user looks at a command prompt (i.e., the DOS window). For many users, this window is not something they are familiar with, so they find it intimidating. In fact, many developers purposely create these types of applications to hide the more powerful programs on a PC from casual users.

In this chapter, you will look at two Console applications—ones that you may find useful in just about any test lab. The first application gathers information about the computer you are testing and creates a report. The second application will review this report for requirements, download an application from a network share, and upload a status report about the computer and the installation to another network share. In addition, we will talk about how you can use the Windows Scheduler to run these programs automatically.

Objectives

By the end of this chapter, you will be able to do the following:

- Discuss how Console applications are used in testing

- Write code to report information about the PC you are testing on

- Write code to read the report information and verify requirements

- Write code to download testware from a network share

- Write code to send a simple report to a network share

- Create a schedule to run an application

Using Console Applications

If you are used to working with Windows applications, then Console applications may seem confusing at first. You have to think differently about how you capture the data from your users and display messages back to them. When programming Windows applications, you build all your code behind a graphical UI, load it into memory, and respond to events that happen. Console applications are used mostly for simple tasks where the amount of interaction you need is greatly reduced. With a Console application, you start the program, proceed through the code until the end, and then close the program. You do not wait to respond to events, and you seldom query the user about their choices while the program is running. Still, you will usually want some initial data sent to the program. Let's review how you can add input and output interaction with Console applications.

Using Arguments

As you saw in Chapter 2, Console applications run by calling the .exe file from a command prompt. To add additional instruction to the application, you include a space-separated list of arguments after the file's name. These arguments are then passed into the program's Main() method as an array of values. You would add code to separate each array element and place them into separate variables; then you would use these to process the various instructions inside your application. Listing 7-1 shows an example of a Main() method printing out the various elements of the array.

Listing 7-1. *Processing Command-Line Arguments with the Main() Method*

VB .NET

```
Public Shared Sub Main(ByVal args() As String)
  Dim command As String
  For Each command In args
    Debug.Write(command)
  Next
End Sub
```

C#

```
public static void Main(string[][0] args)
{
  string command;
  foreach (int command in args)
  {
    Debug.Write(command);
  }
}
```

In Listing 7-1, we chose to write out the arguments using Debug.Write(), but another choice would be to use the Console.WriteLine() method or an output file. Console.WriteLine() prints the message to the command-prompt screen, while the output file option is used to record messages to a text file. Using a text file quietly lets the program perform its tasks in the background. You would check on the status of how the tasks completed by reviewing the text file at a later time. In many cases, especially when working with testware automation, this may be all you need or want.

To test a Console application with some arguments, you have two options: you can compile and run it from the command prompt, or set the Command-Line Arguments option in Visual Studio and run it right in the development environment.

For the first option, open the Command window by selecting the Windows Start menu ➤ Run option. From there, type the **cmd** command (see Figure 7-1).

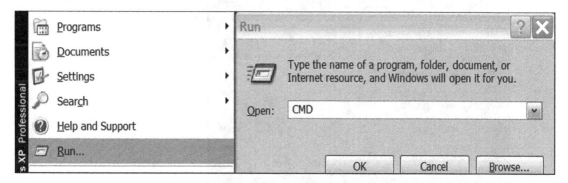

Figure 7-1. *Starting the Command Console*

■**Note** The Windows operating system is not case-sensitive in most cases. So, commands such as **cmd** or **cd** can also be entered as **CMD** or **CD**. However, this is seldom true of the arguments you pass into these commands. For the most part, arguments are case-sensitive.

You can also type **command** instead of **cmd**, as each will open a Command window. However, the Command option opens up an older version of the Command Console window. Although this older version works much like the newer one, not all the newer commands will run from it. It is used to running older programs and is provided for backward compatibility. If you look closely at Figure 7-2, you will see that the older Command window reports that it is for Microsoft's Windows DOS. You can also see that it does not display long folder names, but rather places a ~ and a number in place of the rest of the folder name. While there is nothing strictly wrong with this window, you would not use it unless you were running a rather old piece of software—one that would not run in the standard Command window. You would also run it on Windows 98 or ME, since both of these operating systems do not use the newer one.

Once you have opened the Command window, you need to navigate to your application's folder. Start by changing to the correct drive letter. Typing **C:** or **D:**, or whatever your drive letter is, will take you to the root folder of that drive. Next, you need to change from this root folder to the one that holds your .exe file. You can use the Change Directory command (cd) for this purpose. Finally, type the name of the program's executable file, a space, and then any arguments you want to pass into the Main() method to finally run your application.

For instance, in Figure 7-2 you can see that we have changed to the root of the C:\ drive and then to the TestApp folder. Once we are in the correct folder, we send two arguments, Some and Data, into the program MyApp.exe.

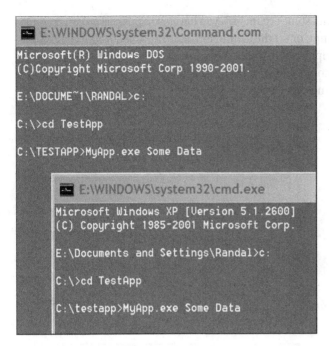

Figure 7-2. *Using the Command Console*

Using spaces to separate the arguments instead of commas may seem odd at first, but it is all part of the mystery that makes Console applications so much . . . ah . . . fun? Seriously though, working with Console applications is not all that hard to get used to—and they are quite simple once you do.

As mentioned earlier, you can also pass in arguments to the program from Visual Studio. This is pretty important since you can use this option to run and debug your testware as you develop it. You will find this option by right-clicking on the project's name in Solution Explorer and choosing Properties from the pop-up menu. When the Properties tab displays, use the Debug section to add your command-line arguments (see Figure 7-3). You can also access the Properties tab by using the Project menu and selecting the Properties option at the bottom of the menu.

Start Options

Command line arguments: Some Data

Figure 7-3. *Using Visual Studio to add arguments*

Creating a Simple Example

To get a better understanding about how Console applications work, you really need to build one. So, let's start with a simple application that gathers data from a computer using some of the built-in objects that .NET provides.

Often a developer needs to know how a computer was set up when a bug was recorded. This can be a tedious job if done manually. What if you could run a program and have it gather all of the information you need into a simple report file—would that save you time? If you think so too, then take a look at three samples that demonstrate how this could be achieved.

The first is the My.Computer object. (You first encountered the My namespace in Exercise 5-3, but here we'll cover it in more detail.) This built-in object is created for you automatically when your application starts up. This means that you do not have to create the object in your code; you only need to call the methods the object contains. This object provides general information about the operating system and settings on the computer that the program is running on.

Here are some things My.Computer is useful for:

- To determine if the network connection is working

- To download a remote file from an HTTP site

- To upload a file to an HTTP site

- To get software settings (such as the operating system version and computer name)

- To get hardware information about the keyboard, mouse, and physical memory

Listing 7-2 shows an example of getting basic information about the operating system using the My.Computer object.

Listing 7-2. *Getting Operating System Data*

VB .NET

```
Sub Main()
  Dim strPCInfo As String = ""
  strPCInfo += My.Computer.Name + ", "
  strPCInfo += My.Computer.Info.OSFullName + ", "
  Console.WriteLine(strPCInfo)
End Sub
```

C#

```
static void Main(string[] args)
{
  Microsoft.VisualBasic.Devices.Computer mc;
  mc = new Microsoft.VisualBasic.Devices.Computer();
  string strPCInfo = "";
  strPCInfo += mc.Name + ", ";
  strPCInfo += mc.Info.OSFullName + ", ";
  Console.WriteLine(strPCInfo);
}
```

___

■**Note** At the time of this writing, My.Computer is not directly available in C#, so you will need to add a reference to it through VB .NET before you can use the simple methods in the My.Computer object. To add a reference in your project, you would use the Project ➤ Add Reference menu in Visual Studio. From the .NET tab, scroll down until you see the Microsoft.VisualBasic component name and double-click on that. You would also have to make a new object from VB .NET as we have done in Listing 7-2.

___

While this example gathers only software settings, you can also get data on hardware—at least in some cases. We say "some cases" because the My.Computer object does not provide a complete listing of all methods to all resources. My.Computer is a wrapper used to call methods and properties in other objects and classes for you. Microsoft only included a selection of methods and properties, not all possible ones. Still, the selection includes things like how much memory is on the system and how much of that is available, which is data that testers often use. As you know, showing a developer that there is a problem with his application and providing information about things like memory usage at the time the problem occurred can really be useful in solving the problem. Listing 7-3 gathers such data.

Listing 7-3. *Getting Information About Memory*

VB .NET

```
Sub Main()
  Const MEGABYTES As Int32 = 1024000
  Dim strMemoryInfo As String = ""
  Dim intTPhysicalMem As UInt64 = My.Computer.Info.TotalPhysicalMemory
  strMemoryInfo = (intTPhysicalMem / MEGABYTES).ToString + " MB , "
  Console.WriteLine(strMemoryInfo)
End Sub
```

C#

```
static void Main(string[] args)
{
  const Int64 MEGABYTES = 1024000;
  Microsoft.VisualBasic.Devices.Computer mc;
  mc = new Microsoft.VisualBasic.Devices.Computer();
  string strMemoryInfo = "";
  UInt64 intTPhysicalMem = mc.Info.TotalPhysicalMemory;
  strMemoryInfo = (intTPhysicalMem / MEGABYTES).ToString() + " MB , ";
  Console.WriteLine(strMemoryInfo);
}
```

As useful as the My.Computer class is, it cannot call all the information methods provided with .NET. That is not really a problem though; you can just use these classes directly.

For example, the System.IO namespace contains a number of useful classes for getting information about the hard drive (see Listing 7-4). This information can be about both the local and network drives or even files and folders.

Listing 7-4. *Using System.IO.DriveInfo*

VB .NET

```
  Sub Main()
    Const MEGABYTES As Int32 = 1024000
    Dim strHDInfo As String = ""
```

```
    'Get Drive Info
    Dim objDI As System.IO.DriveInfo
    Dim strDL As String
    For Each objDI In System.IO.DriveInfo.GetDrives()
      strDL = objDI.Name.Substring(0, 1)
      strHDInfo += strDL + ": "

      If objDI.DriveType = IO.DriveType.Fixed Then
        strHDInfo += objDI.DriveFormat + ", "
        strHDInfo += (objDI.AvailableFreeSpace / MEGABYTES).ToString + " MB, "
        strHDInfo += objDI.DriveType.ToString()
      End If
      strHDInfo += vbCrLf
    Next
    Console.WriteLine(strHDInfo)
  End Sub
```

C#

```
static void Main(string[] args)
{
  const Int64 MEGABYTES = 1024000;
  Microsoft.VisualBasic.Devices.Computer mc;
  mc = new Microsoft.VisualBasic.Devices.Computer();
  string strHDInfo = "";

  //Get Drive Info
  string strDL;
  foreach (System.IO.DriveInfo objDI in System.IO.DriveInfo.GetDrives())
  {
    strDL = objDI.Name.Substring(0, 1);
    strHDInfo += strDL + ": ";
    if (objDI.DriveType == System.IO.DriveType.Fixed)
    {
      strHDInfo += objDI.DriveFormat + ", ";
      strHDInfo += (objDI.AvailableFreeSpace / MEGABYTES).ToString() + " MB, ";
      strHDInfo += objDI.DriveType.ToString();
    }
    strHDInfo += "\r\n";
  }

  Console.WriteLine(strHDInfo);
}
```

Including this data along with your bug reports lets developers know what the conditions were on the computer when the bug occurred. While these listings are all useful separately, you could combine these to make a simple report about a computer you are testing. You might also want to send them to a file instead of to the Command Console. You will see how to do that in Exercise 7-1.

Exercise 7-1: Gathering PC Data

In this exercise, you will create a simple testware application that records information about a computer. First, you will create a new Console project, add code to gather the information you need, and, finally, send the data to the output file. Since the output file will be in a comma-separated-values (.csv) file, you can use Microsoft Excel to review the report. You can also use Notepad to view the file if you do not have Excel.

■**Note** At the time of this writing, My.Computer is not directly available in C#, so you will need to add a reference to it through VB .NET before you can use the simple methods in the My.Computer object. To add a reference in your project, you would use the Project ➤ Add Reference menu in Visual Studio. From the .NET tab, scroll down until you see the Microsoft.VisualBasic component name and double-click on that (see Figure 7-4). You would also have to make a new object from VB .NET as we have done in Listing 7-4.

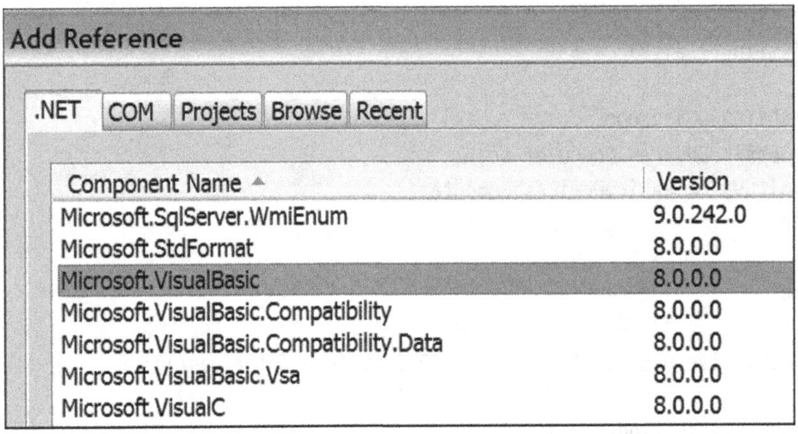

Figure 7-4. *Adding a reference to VB .NET*

1. Create a new project and choose the Console application template. Name your application **InspectPC**.

2. Delete the Module1.vb or Program.cs file and create a new Class file called **PCInfo**. Call the new class file **PCInfo.vb** or **PCInfo.cs** depending on the language you are using.

   VB .NET will add a file called Module1.vb while C# will add a file called Program.cs. While nothing is wrong with these files, let's start from scratch so that both the VB .NET and C# examples will be very similar. To do this, delete the file you have now and add a new Class file to the project.

3. Remove any extra code Visual Studio gives you, such as comments and namespaces. This is so that you are dealing with a blank code file.

4. Add an Imports/using statement to reference the System namespace. Also, add a constant called MEGABYTES as an Int32 data type.

The memory and drive-space data reports in bytes, but most users are not used to seeing so small a measurement in a report. Converting the display to show megabytes will make the report more understandable. Your code should now look like Listing 7-5.

Listing 7-5. *Defining the Class-Level Data Members*

VB .NET

```
Imports System
Public Class PCInfo
 Const MEGABYTES As Int32 = 1024000

End class
```

C#

```
using System;
using Microsoft.VisualBasic.Devices;
class PCInfo
{
  const Int64 MEGABYTES = 1024000;
  static Computer mc;

}
```

5. In PCInfo, create a Main() method. Console applications need a Main() method to start from, so you need to add this to the new class (see Listing 7-6).

    This method, as well as the other methods in this class, should be Shared (VB .NET) or static (C#). You can use non-Shared/static methods in a Console application, but since you seldom use more then one instance of a Console application's classes, it is more common to use Shared/static ones instead. Notice that you need to add an extra using statement and variable to the C# code to work with the My.Computer class.

Listing 7-6. *Creating the Main() Method*

VB .NET

```
Imports System
Public Class PCInfo
  Const MEGABYTES As Int32 = 1024000

  Shared Sub Main(ByVal args() As String)
  End Sub

End class
```

C#

```csharp
using System;
using Microsoft.VisualBasic.Devices;
class PCInfo
{
    const Int64 MEGABYTES = 1024000;
    static Computer mc;

    static void Main(string[] args)
    {
    }
}
```

6. Just under the `Main()` method, create four functions (as shown in Listing 7-7). You want to get information about the computer, its drives, and its memory and then write that information to a file. These methods will hold that code.

Listing 7-7. *Creating the Class's Methods*

VB .NET

```vbnet
Shared Sub Main(ByVal args() As String)
End Sub

Private Shared Function GetPCInfo() As String
End Function

Private Shared Function GetDriveInfo() As String
End Function

Private Shared Function GetMemoryInfo() As String
End Function

Private Shared Sub WriteReport(ByVal Data As String)
End Sub
```

C#

```csharp
static void Main(string[] args)
{
}

private static string GetPCInfo()
{ }

private static string GetDriveInfo()
{ }
```

```
private static string GetMemoryInfo()
{ }

private static void WriteReport(string Data)
{ }
```

7. Add code to the GetPCInfo() method to retrieve information about the computer's name, OS, OS version, language settings, and time. Your code should look like Listing 7-8.

Listing 7-8. *Getting Operating System Data*

VB .NET

```
Private Shared Function GetPCInfo() As String
  Dim strPCInfo As String = ""
  Dim strHeading As String = ""

  'Make column heading
  strHeading += "Computer Name,  "
  strHeading += "Operating System,  "
  strHeading += "Operating System Version,  "
  strHeading += "UI Culture,  "
  strHeading += "Time on PC"
  strPCInfo += strHeading + vbCrLf

  'Get column data
  strPCInfo += My.Computer.Name + ", "
  strPCInfo += My.Computer.Info.OSFullName + ", "
  strPCInfo += My.Computer.Info.OSVersion + ", "
  strPCInfo += My.Computer.Info.InstalledUICulture.EnglishName + ", "
  strPCInfo += My.Computer.Clock.LocalTime
  strPCInfo += vbCrLf
  Return strPCInfo
End Function
```

C#

```
private static string GetPCInfo()
{
  string strPCInfo = "";
  string strHeading = "";
  strHeading += "Computer Name, ";
  strHeading += "Operating System, ";
  strHeading += "Operating System Version, ";
  strHeading += "UI Culture, ";
  strHeading += "Time on PC";

  strPCInfo += strHeading + "\r\n";
  strPCInfo += mc.Name + ", ";
```

```
strPCInfo += mc.Info.OSFullName + ", ";
strPCInfo += mc.Info.OSVersion + ", ";
strPCInfo += mc.Info.InstalledUICulture.EnglishName + ", ";
strPCInfo += mc.Clock.LocalTime;
strPCInfo += "\r\n";
return strPCInfo;
}
```

8. Add code to the GetDriveInfo() method to retrieve information about the drive's letter, format, free space, and type. Your code should look like Listing 7-9.

Listing 7-9. *Using the System.IO.DriveInfo Class*

VB .NET

```
Private Shared Function GetDriveInfo() As String
  Dim strHDInfo As String = ""
  'Dim objDI As New System.IO.DriveInfo()
  Dim strHeading As String = ""

  'Make column headings
  strHeading += "Drive Letter,  "
  strHeading += "File Format,  "
  strHeading += "Free Space,  "
  strHeading += "Drive Type"
  strHDInfo += strHeading + vbCrLf

  'Get Drive Info
  Dim objDI As System.IO.DriveInfo
  Dim strDL As String
  For Each objDI In System.IO.DriveInfo.GetDrives()
    strDL = objDI.Name.Substring(0, 1)
    strHDInfo += strDL + ":, "

    If objDI.DriveType = IO.DriveType.Fixed Then
      strHDInfo += objDI.DriveFormat + ", "
      strHDInfo += (objDI.AvailableFreeSpace / MEGABYTES).ToString + " MB, "
      strHDInfo += objDI.DriveType.ToString()

    ElseIf objDI.DriveType = IO.DriveType.CDRom Then
      strHDInfo += "NA,"
      strHDInfo += "NA,"
      strHDInfo += objDI.DriveType.ToString()

    ElseIf objDI.DriveType = IO.DriveType.Removable Then
      strHDInfo += "NA,"
      strHDInfo += "NA,"
      strHDInfo += objDI.DriveType.ToString()
```

```vb
    ElseIf objDI.DriveType = IO.DriveType.Network Then
      strHDInfo += objDI.DriveFormat + ", "
      strHDInfo += (objDI.AvailableFreeSpace / MEGABYTES).ToString + " MB, "
      strHDInfo += objDI.DriveType.ToString()
    End If
    strHDInfo += vbCrLf
  Next
  Return strHDInfo
End Function
```

C#

```csharp
private static string GetDriveInfo()
{
  string strHDInfo = "";
  string strHeading = "";

  //Make column headings
  strHeading += "Drive Letter, ";
  strHeading += "File Format, ";
  strHeading += "Free Space, ";
  strHeading += "Drive Type";
  strHDInfo += strHeading + "\r\n";

  //Get Drive Info
  // System.IO.DriveInfo objDI;
  string strDL;
  foreach (System.IO.DriveInfo objDI in System.IO.DriveInfo.GetDrives())
  {
    strDL = objDI.Name.Substring(0, 1);
    strHDInfo += strDL + ":, ";
    if (objDI.DriveType == System.IO.DriveType.Fixed)
    {
      strHDInfo += objDI.DriveFormat + ", ";
      strHDInfo += (objDI.AvailableFreeSpace / MEGABYTES).ToString() + " MB, ";
      strHDInfo += objDI.DriveType.ToString();
    }
    else if (objDI.DriveType == System.IO.DriveType.CDRom)
    {
      strHDInfo += "NA,";
      strHDInfo += "NA,";
      strHDInfo += objDI.DriveType.ToString();
    }
    else if (objDI.DriveType == System.IO.DriveType.Removable)
    {
      strHDInfo += "NA,";
      strHDInfo += "NA,";
      strHDInfo += objDI.DriveType.ToString();
    }
```

```
    else if (objDI.DriveType == System.IO.DriveType.Network)
    {
      strHDInfo += objDI.DriveFormat + ", ";
      strHDInfo += (objDI.AvailableFreeSpace / MEGABYTES).ToString()  + " MB, ";
      strHDInfo += objDI.DriveType.ToString();
    }
    strHDInfo += "\r\n";
  }
  return strHDInfo;
}
```

9. Add code to the GetMemoryInfo() method to retrieve information about the physical and virtual memory. You want both total and available values. Your code should look like Listing 7-10.

Listing 7-10. *Getting Information About Memory*

VB .NET

```
Private Shared Function GetMemoryInfo() As String
  'Get Memory info
  Dim strMemoryInfo As String = ""
  Dim strHeading As String = ""

  'Make column heading
  strHeading += "Total Phyical Memory,  "
  strHeading += "Total Virtual Memory,  "
  strHeading += "Available Phyical Memory,  "
  strHeading += "Available Virtual Memory  "
  strMemoryInfo += strHeading + vbCrLf

  Dim intTPhysicalMem As UInt64 = My.Computer.Info.TotalPhysicalMemory
  Dim intTVirtualMem As UInt64 = My.Computer.Info.TotalVirtualMemory
  Dim intAPhysicalMem As UInt64 = My.Computer.Info.AvailablePhysicalMemory
  Dim intAVirtualMem As UInt64 = My.Computer.Info.AvailableVirtualMemory

  strMemoryInfo += (intTPhysicalMem / MEGABYTES).ToString + " MB , "
  strMemoryInfo += (intTVirtualMem / MEGABYTES).ToString + "MB , "
  strMemoryInfo += (intAPhysicalMem / MEGABYTES).ToString + " MB , "
  strMemoryInfo += (intAVirtualMem / MEGABYTES).ToString + "MB "
  strMemoryInfo += vbCrLf
  Return strMemoryInfo
End Function
```

C#

```csharp
private static string GetMemoryInfo()
{
  string strMemoryInfo = "";
  string strHeading = "";
  strHeading += "Total Phyical Memory, ";
  strHeading += "Total Virtual Memory, ";
  strHeading += "Available Phyical Memory, ";
  strHeading += "Available Virtual Memory ";
  strMemoryInfo += strHeading + "\r\n";
  UInt64 intTPhysicalMem = mc.Info.TotalPhysicalMemory;
  UInt64 intTVirtualMem = mc.Info.TotalVirtualMemory;
  UInt64 intAPhysicalMem = mc.Info.AvailablePhysicalMemory;
  UInt64 intAVirtualMem = mc.Info.AvailableVirtualMemory;
  strMemoryInfo += (intTPhysicalMem / MEGABYTES).ToString() + " MB , ";
  strMemoryInfo += (intTVirtualMem / MEGABYTES).ToString() + "MB , ";
  strMemoryInfo += (intAPhysicalMem / MEGABYTES).ToString() + " MB , ";
  strMemoryInfo += (intAVirtualMem / MEGABYTES).ToString() + "MB ";
  strMemoryInfo += "\r\n";
  return strMemoryInfo;
}
```

10. Create a folder on your C drive called **PCInfo** and then add code to the WriteReport() method to record the information you gathered into a file inside of this folder. Your code should look like Listing 7-11. You only need to create the folder manually, since this method will create the file for you.

■**Caution** Please use the file and folder names as shown in the code. If the file c:\PCInfo\PCInfo.csv is not created, you will not be able to make the next exercise work.

Listing 7-11. *Writing the Report*

VB .NET

```vbnet
Private Shared Sub WriteReport(ByVal Data As String)
  Dim objSW As System.IO.StreamWriter
  Try
    objSW = New System.IO.StreamWriter("c:\PCInfo\PCInfo.csv", False)
    objSW.Write(Data)
    objSW.Close()
  Catch ex As Exception
    ex.ToString()
  End Try
End Sub
```

C#

```csharp
private static void WriteReport(string Data)
{
  System.IO.StreamWriter objSW;
  try
  {
    objSW = new System.IO.StreamWriter("c:\\PCInfo\\PCInfo.csv", false);
    objSW.Write(Data);
    objSW.Close();
  }
  catch (Exception ex)
  {
    ex.ToString();
  }
}
```

11. Now you add code to the Main() method to call the other methods you just created. You will also want to capture any arguments passed in from the command line. Use these to determine if the information you gathered should be saved to a file or shown on the screen. Finally, use a Try-Catch block to handle errors if the user does not provide your program with arguments. Your code should look Listing 7-12.

Listing 7-12. *Calling the Methods and Checking for Errors*

VB .NET

```vbnet
Shared Sub Main(ByVal args() As String)
  if args.Length = 0 then
  Console.WriteLine("You must pass in a arugment of Y or N ")
  end if

  Dim strData As String = ""

  'a) Check PC Hardware and OS info
  strData += "PC Information" + vbCrLf
  strData += GetPCInfo() + vbCrLf

  strData += "Drive Information" + vbCrLf
  strData += GetDriveInfo() + vbCrLf

  strData += "Memory Information" + vbCrLf
  strData += GetMemoryInfo() + vbCrLf

  Try
    'Get user arguments
    'y = save to file.
    'n = do not save to file.
```

```vb
        If args(0) = "y" Then
          'b) Create folder and store setup info
          'in a .csv for easy import to a database.
          Dim DI As New System.IO.DirectoryInfo("c:\PCInfo")
          If Not DI.Exists Then
            DI.Create()
          End If


          WriteReport(strData)
        ElseIf args(0) = "n" Then
          Console.WriteLine(strData)
        Else
          Console.WriteLine("You must chose to write to file or not.")
          Console.WriteLine("Add y or n after the program name")
        End If
    Catch ex As Exception
        Console.WriteLine(ex.ToString)
    End Try
End Sub
```

C#

```csharp
static void Main(string[] args)
{
  if (args.Length == 0)
  {
    Console.WriteLine("You must pass in a arugment of Y or N ");
  }
  mc = new Computer();

  string strData = "";
  strData += "PC Information" + "\r\n";
    strData += GetPCInfo() + "\r\n";
    strData += "Drive Information" + "\r\n";
    strData += GetDriveInfo() + "\r\n";
    strData += "Memory Information" + "\r\n";
    strData += GetMemoryInfo() + "\r\n";
    try
    {
      if (args[0] == "y")
      {
        System.IO.DirectoryInfo DI = new System.IO.DirectoryInfo("c:\\PCInfo");
        if (!(DI.Exists))
        {
          DI.Create();
        }
        WriteReport(strData);
      }
```

```
     else if (args[0] == "n")
     {
       Console.WriteLine(strData);
     }
     else
     {
       Console.WriteLine("You must chose to write to file or not.");
       Console.WriteLine("y or n after the program name");
     }
   }
   catch (Exception ex)
   {
     Console.WriteLine(ex.ToString());
   }
}
```

12. Set the command-line argument to y so that the program will write to the file. To do so, select the Project ➤ InspectPC Properties menu option. View the Debug tab and add the lowercase y command, as shown in Figure 7-5.

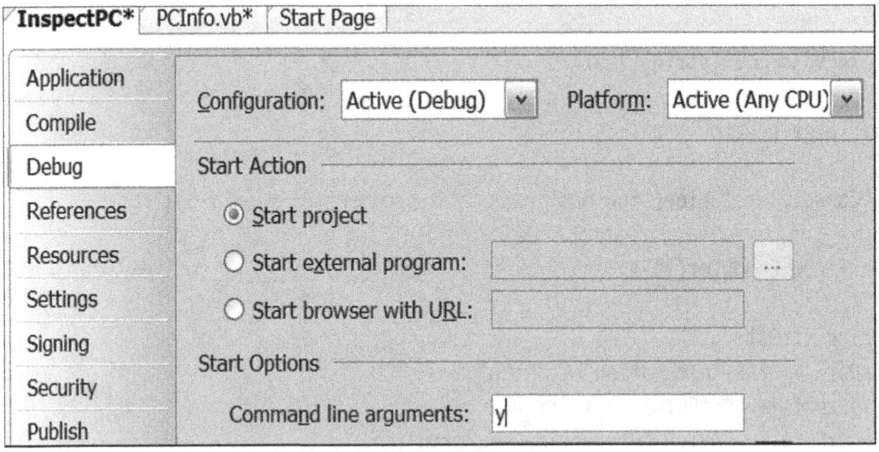

Figure 7-5. *Setting the project's Debug arguments*

13. Start the program and create the file. You can use Ctrl+F5 to start the Console application, and it will leave the Command window open when it's done running your program. Make sure you open the file to see what is saved. You can use Notepad or Excel to do this (although, Excel will look nicer).

14. Go back and change the argument from y to n and test that the program shows the results onscreen instead of to a file.

15. You should also test from the Command window. Copy the InspectPC.exe file from your project's bin folder to your C:\PCInfo folder and test it again.

■Note You will use the `InspectPC.exe` file from the C:\PCInfo folder in Exercise 7-2.

In this exercise, you created an application that records information about a computer. From here, you could add improvements, such as letting the user choose where the file is saved or getting additional data.

Creating a Test Lab Setup

An automated lab setup is a common task in many test projects. In Chapter 5, we talked about the importance of creating a testing framework, which includes set-up and take-down software for your tests, as well as other useful routines that support your tests. Console applications are a good choice for these types of applications, since they are designed to run with minimal interaction from the user .

In this section, you will look at an example of automated lab setup using a Console application. To start, let's list what we want to accomplish:

- Get a report on the PC using the `InspectPC` testware

- Compare the report against the requirements of the application being installed

- Download the new application's files from a network share

- Report the install status and upload that report to a network share

While there might be more things to add, this will give us enough to start.

■Note In the next few sections, we will be discussing code used in Exercise 7-2. While that exercise will include both VB .NET and C# code, we are conserving paper and only showing the VB .NET versions here.

Running One Program from Another

A common task before installing software is to check that the minimal requirements are met. You might check this yourself manually, but this is a good thing to automate. Since the `InspectPC` testware you created in Exercise 7-1 gathers system data, you can start the `InspectPC.exe`, generate the report file, and then review it to verify these requirements. The code you would use might look like Listing 7-13.

Listing 7-13. *Checking for Install Requirements*

VB .NET

```
Public Shared Function GetPCData(ByVal RunReport As String) As String
  Dim strStatus As String = ""
  Dim objProc As New System.Diagnostics.Process
  objProc.StartInfo.FileName = "C:\PCInfo\InspectPC.exe"
  objProc.StartInfo.Arguments = "y"
  objProc.StartInfo.CreateNoWindow = True
  objProc.StartInfo.ErrorDialog = True

  Try
    objProc.Start()
    strStatus = "Completed"
  Catch ex As Exception
    Console.WriteLine(ex.ToString + vbCrLf + "Press any key to continue...")
    strStatus = "Failed"
  End Try
  Return strStatus
End Function
```

This listing introduces a couple of new classes we should talk about. The first one you see is the Process class. This class allows you to run other programs from inside of your own program using the Start() method. Before the Start() method is called, you supply the various starting information by defining the properties found in the StartInfo class. Instead of using the StartInfo class directly, this class is accessed indirectly though the Process class (which may explain the way the code looks in Listing 7-13).

Using StartInfo, you set the arguments needed by this program. You pass in a y to indicate that you wish to create the report file. You also tell the system to run this silently, not popping open an additional Command window, by setting the CreateNoWindow property to True. Next, you indicate that you would like an error message dialog box to show up, if there is an error, by setting the ErrorDialog property also to True.

Once your settings are done, you call the Start() method to run the external program and use a Try-Catch block to capture any errors. If there are no errors, you return a status of Completed; otherwise, you display the error and return a status of Failed.

Checking for Software Requirements

With the report created, you need to read the report to determine if the requirements are met. To do this part, let's review a trick you learned in Chapter 3—where you opened a file and used a Regular Expression to find if it contained a particular string. For example, in Listing 7-14, you are checking to see if the operating system is either Windows XP or 2003.

Listing 7-14. *Checking for Windows XP or 2003*

VB .NET

```
Private Shared Function CheckForOS(ByVal ReportData As String) As Boolean
    Dim r As Regex
    Dim m As Match

    r = New Regex("XP | 2003", RegexOptions.IgnoreCase Or RegexOptions.Compiled)
    m = r.Match(ReportData)
    If m.Success Then
      Return True
    Else
      Return False
    End If

  End Function
```

To enhance your applications, you could use other functions to check additional requirements, and you would likely want to create a separate .dll file to hold your collection of "requirements" methods. Each method should return a standard status message, such as True/False or Passed/Failed. For instance, Listing 7-15 opens a report file, fills a string with the contents, and runs the string through the CheckForOS() function to make sure that either Windows XP or 2003 is listed in the string.

Listing 7-15. *Validating the OS Version*

VB .NET

```
Public Shared Function CheckPCData(ByVal CheckReport As String) As String
    Dim strStatus As String = ""
    Dim objSR As System.IO.StreamReader
    Dim strReportData As String

    Try
      'Open file to read
      objSR = New System.IO.StreamReader("c:\PCInfo\PCInfo.csv")
      strReportData = objSR.ReadToEnd
      objSR.Close()

      'Check for the following requirements
      '1) OS must = XP
      If CheckForOS(strReportData) = True Then
        strStatus = "Passed"
      Else
        strStatus = "Failed"
      End If
```

```
Catch ex As Exception
  Console.WriteLine(ex.ToString + vbCrLf + "Press any key to continue...")
  Console.ReadLine()
  strStatus = "Failed"
End Try

Return strStatus
End Function
```

Note that after the `CheckPCData()` method calls the `CheckForOS()` method, it determines if the result was either `True` or `False`. `CheckPCData()` itself reports back its `Passed` or `Failed` status to the code that will call it. In this case, you report `Passed` when successful and `Failed` when not to indicate the outcome of this part of the installation process. If you had more requirements to check, you would also call them from this same method. After the `CheckPCData()` method has finished running all the validation checks, you return the final status.

Installing Application Files from a Network Share

With the requirements checked, you begin the installation. Microsoft .NET has included two standard installation processes: the use of a set-up program and XCOPY deployment.

With a typical Windows set-up program, you ask the users for required information and then inform them of the progress. You have, no doubt, used these many times since this is the standard installation process for Microsoft Windows applications. Using this option, you normally just click the `Setup.exe` file to begin the installation. The `Setup.exe` file checks that the Microsoft Windows Installer (MSI) software is on that particular PC and then begins the actual installation by using the MSI file. These files have an `.msi` extension. In fact, you can just click the `.msi` file directly. This works, but it does not verify that the MSI is installed on that particular PC, and you may receive an odd error if it is not. It is the `.msi` file that contains the actual installation instructions. This includes things like where to put the `.exe` or `.dll` files, what additional files should be copied over to the program's folder, and what Registry entries (if any) should be made. (The *Windows Registry* is a Windows database where many software applications store information—including installation information, such as version numbers, etc. Chapter 3 covers working with the Windows Registry in more detail.)

Network administrators use `.msi` files to "push" down installations to the entire network. This is a great time-saver when you have hundreds of computers that need the same software. They do this using group policies or custom administration software like Microsoft's System Management Server (SMS). While these are powerful tools, they take time to learn and can be quite confusing if you don't work with them all the time. Microsoft's .NET provides a simpler approach as well, called XCOPY deployment. Although this other option is less powerful, it is easy to learn and use.

With XCOPY deployment, you only need to copy the needed files from one place to the other. If additional set-up instructions need processing, like adding Registry entries, it is up to you to make them. Although this option is not as fancy as the set-up program, it basically does the same thing.

To use XCOPY deployment, you first create a folder for your testware files. In a test lab, this would normally be on a central network share on one of your test lab PCs. If this was not already set up for you, you would pick one computer to put the files on, make a network share, and fill the folder with your files. You can use the `System.IO.Directory.GetFiles()` method to get a list of all the files in that particular folder when you want to copy them later.

Since many testers are not specifically trained on networking per se, let's review the process of setting up a network share.

Creating a Network Share

One way to create a network share is to use Windows Explorer, but you can also use OS `Shell` commands. With the Windows Explorer option, you navigate to the folder you want and right-click on that folder.

█Note Many of the following security options may not be found on a home PC. This is because many home computers are not set up to for security, but for ease of use. One example of this is the file system. Microsoft offers two basic versions of this: the File Allocation Table (FAT) system and the New Technologies File System (NTFS). While both allow you to set security on a network share, only NTFS allows you to configure security at the file and folder level. You can tell which file system a drive uses by reviewing its properties in Windows Explorer. If you are using FAT and not NTFS, the following instructions will not apply, but since the default FAT security options are very relaxed, you should be able to make a share and complete Exercise 7-2 anyway. If you have problems or would just like to know more on this subject, the help files that come with Windows are quite good on this subject. You can access the help files from the Windows Start menu, under "Help and Support." Use the Search feature along with the keywords **Sharing**, **FAT**, and **NTFS**.

In Windows 2000, XP, or 2003, you should see an option for sharing and security. However, since Microsoft decided this was an advanced option, Explorer hides the option by default, so you may need to configure Explorer before it will display this. If you cannot see this option, follow these steps:

1. Change the settings by going to the tools menu in Windows Explorer and selecting Folder Options.

2. From there, you can scroll down to the bottom of the Advance Settings listbox until you see the Use Simple File Sharing option (see Figure 7-6).

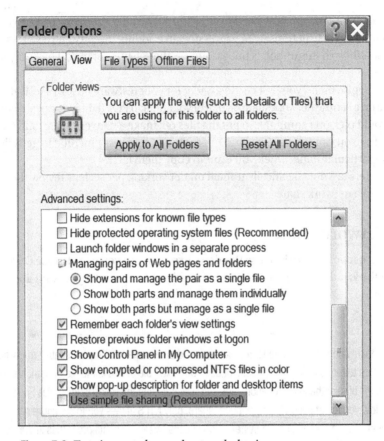

Figure 7-6. *Turning on advanced network sharing*

3. *Uncheck* this option to turn off the Simple mode. Once this is done, right-clicking on the folder allows you to choose the Sharing And Security menu selection (see Figure 7-7).

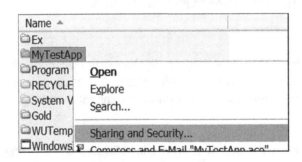

Figure 7-7. *Sharing a folder with Windows Explorer*

After clicking this menu item, you should be looking at the dialog window on the left in Figure 7-8. Locate the Share This folder radio button. Select this option, give the share a name, and then click the Permissions button to set the permissions required. In the Share Permissions dialog box, shown in the dialog window on the right in Figure 7-8, you would verify that permissions were set for your needs. In this example, the special built-in Windows group called Everyone is allowed read permissions, but is not allowed to write to the share. For that, you would need to give them Change permissions by checking the Change check box.

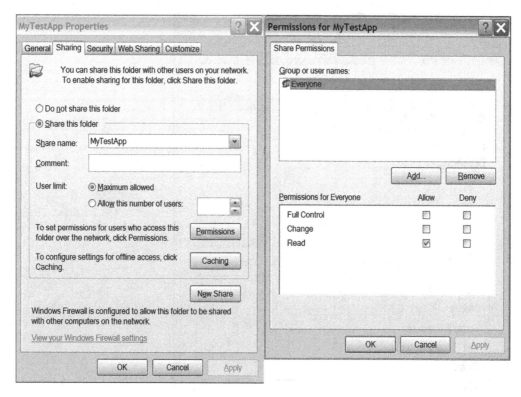

Figure 7-8. *Creating the share*

■**Note** The Everyone group consists of anyone that has access to that computer. Using the Everyone group is not considered very secure. Instead, you should create a specific group and give permissions to it. Still, in a test lab environment, simplicity may be more important than security. If that is the case, then you can go ahead and use this group to assign permissions. If, however, you need more security, you will need to decide what strategy is best to take. You may need to ask someone knowledgeable in Windows security to assist you in this task, or learn more about this subject yourself.

In addition to setting the security for the share itself, you may need to set it on the individual files and folders themselves. To do this, click the Security tab at the top of the Properties dialog form (the one you were using to create the share) and you will see something like Figure 7-9. If you do not see this, then your hard drive partition is not using the NTSF file structure and you will not need to worry about this step.

If you look closely at Figure 7-9, you can see that the Administrators group is allowed full control of this folder. This will also provide full control of the files inside the folder by default. When you are able to, logging in as the administrator when you run your test lab set-up application should provide you with all the permissions you need. Once again, this is not the most secure option. If security is important to the needs of your test project, you must take the time to formulate a security plan. Unfortunately, that is something outside the scope of this book. For now, make life easy by logging into your computer with administrative rights and allowing the Everyone group access to the share. This way, Exercise 7-2 should work without a problem.

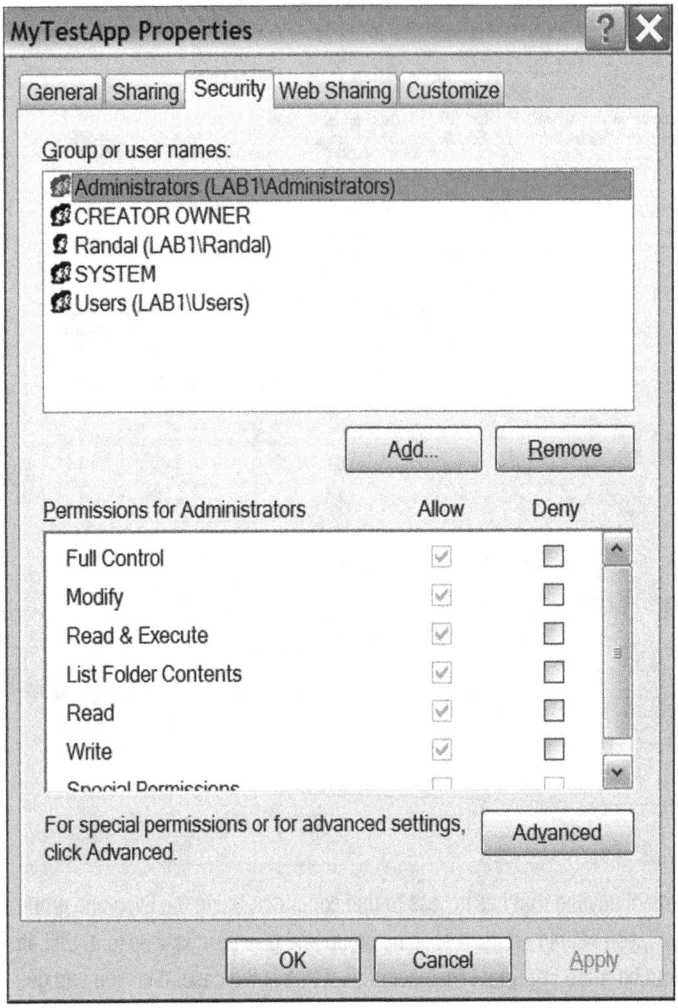

Figure 7-9. *The Security tab*

■**Caution** From our experience as teachers and consultants, we know that many people may have problems with this next section. While we have tried to make this example as simple as possible, a variety of issues may still cause problems. If you cannot get Exercise 7-2 to work, just get the concepts involved with creating a network share and then talk to a coworker or instructor who has more networking experience. Try not to get too bogged down with these technical difficulties since the *concepts* are more important. These concepts are the primary building blocks used to accomplish many automation scenarios.

With the folder shared and the security set, you can now use a method to copy all the files from the share. Of course, you need to provide the method with the proper path to find the files using code similar to this:

VB .NET

```
Dim strAppPathAndName As String = ""
strAppPathAndName = args(0) 'example "\\Lab1\Share\FolderWithFiles"
strInstallStatus = DownloadAppFiles(strAppPathAndName)
```

Note that, in this example, args(0) will contain the server name, share name, and folder name. To visualize how this would be used, we provide the following example.

Let's say that you have created a new testware application called TestApp.exe. You would create a share on a central network computer and place in it a folder holding all of the files you needed for that particular testware.

In Figure 7-10, we show a share being accessed on a computer called lab1 with a share we named "share". Not a very original name, but it works. Our application files are in a subfolder called TestApp. We are using Windows Explorer to navigate to that share and list the files inside of it using the Universal Naming Convention (UNC). The UNC path is made up of two backward slashes followed by the server name and then a backward slash followed by the share name. This is commonly referred to in networking slang as *Wack Wack Server Wack Share*. After the path to the share, you can specify any subfolders you need. In this example, we are calling the folder the same name as the application: TestApp.

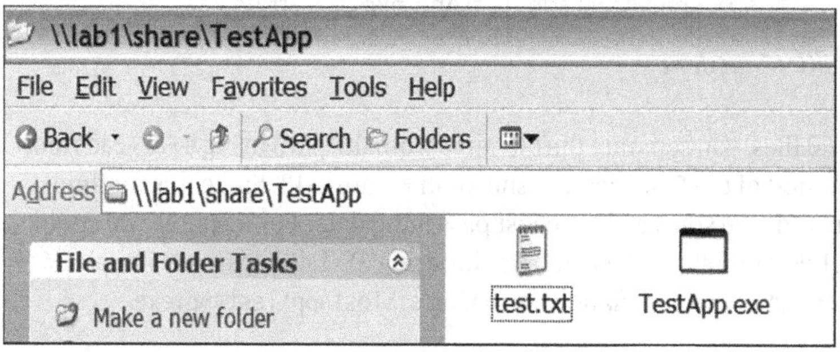

Figure 7-10. *Navigating to the install folder*

When your installation application runs, you could pass in the full pathname and just separate the individual parts that you needed by searching though the string for backward slashes. The characters after the last backward slash in the address would define the name of the folder holding your application files. Since the pathname would be a string and strings act like an array of characters, you can use the LastIndexOf() method to find the index value of the last backward slash and the Substring() method to copy the all the characters after this into a new string (see Figure 7-11).

```
intIndex = PathAndName.LastIndexOf("\")
strAppName = PathAndName.Substring(intIndex + 1)
        ● strAppName ⌕ ▾ "testapp"
```

Figure 7-11. *Extracting the folder name*

Note For an overview on arrays, please see Appendix B.

Copying the Files from the Share

Once you have identified the folder on the share, you should write some code that will get a list of all the files in the folder automatically. The GetFiles() method in the System.IO.Directory namespace can do just that. It returns an array of the filenames it finds in the folder you specify. This array contains an element for each file found. It also includes the full path as well, as noted in Figure 7-12.

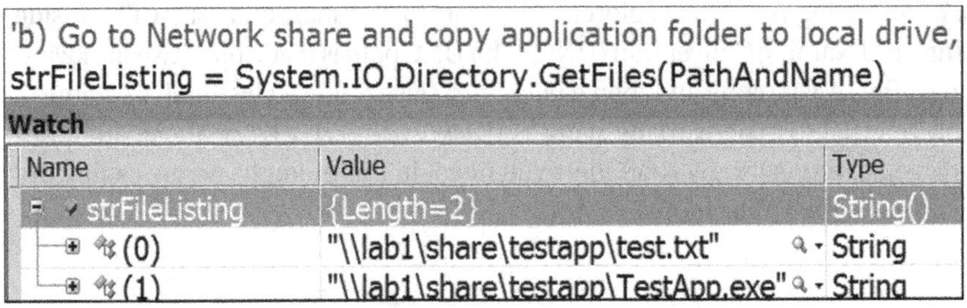

```
'b) Go to Network share and copy application folder to local drive,
strFileListing = System.IO.Directory.GetFiles(PathAndName)
```

Watch		
Name	Value	Type
⊟ ✓ strFileListing	{Length=2}	String()
⊞ ⁗ (0)	"\\lab1\share\testapp\test.txt" ⚲ ▾	String
⊞ ⁗ (1)	"\\lab1\share\testapp\TestApp.exe" ⚲ ▾	String

Figure 7-12. *Using the GetFiles() method*

To copy the individual files, you separate the filename from the path using a For-Each loop along with the Copy() method of the File class, as shown in Figure 7-13. Since this method requires the full pathname for the source file, we just pass it the data. For instance, we could create a variable called strFullFileName, have it hold the string "\\lab1\share\testapp\ TestApp.exe", and indicate what the destination would be: c:\TestApp\TestApp.exe.

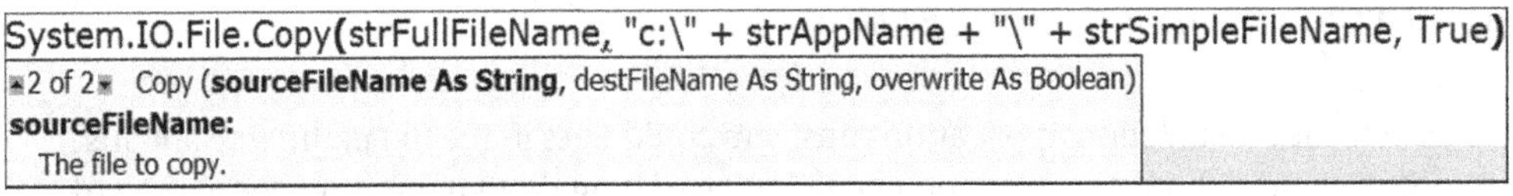

```
System.IO.File.Copy(strFullFileName, "c:\" + strAppName + "\" + strSimpleFileName, True)
▲2 of 2▼  Copy (sourceFileName As String, destFileName As String, overwrite As Boolean)
sourceFileName:
  The file to copy.
```

Figure 7-13. *Using the Copy() method*

To review the process, you create a folder with all the files you need, place it on the network share, pass in the correct name and path to your installer program, and, when the process succeeds, return a status of Completed. Listing 7-16 is an example of what that code would look like.

Listing 7-16. *Downloading Application Files*

VB .NET

```vbnet
Public Shared Function DownloadAppFiles(ByVal PathAndName As String) As String
    Dim strStatus As String = ""
    Dim strFileListing() As String
    Dim strFullFileName As String
    Dim strSimpleFileName As String
    Dim strAppName As String
    Dim intIndex As Int32

    'Get only the folders name from the full name
    intIndex = PathAndName.LastIndexOf("\")
    strAppName = PathAndName.Substring(intIndex + 1)

    Try
      'a) Create a folder for your Testware as needed
      Dim DI As New System.IO.DirectoryInfo("c:\" + strAppName)
      If Not DI.Exists Then 'Find out if there already is a folder by that name
        DI.Create()
      End If

      'b) Go to Network share and copy the files in
      'the application folder to local drive, overwrite as needed
      strFileListing = System.IO.Directory.GetFiles(PathAndName)
      For Each strFullFileName In strFileListing
        intIndex = strFullFileName.LastIndexOf("\")
        strSimpleFileName = strFullFileName.Substring(intIndex + 1)
        System.IO.File.Copy _
        (strFullFileName, "c:\" + strAppName + "\" + strSimpleFileName, True)
      Next

      'c) Indicate the errors status
      strStatus = "Completed"
    Catch ex As Exception
      Console.WriteLine(ex.ToString + vbCrLf + "Press any key to continue...")
      Console.ReadLine()
      strStatus = "Failed"
    End Try

    Return strStatus
  End Function
```

Saving Testware Reports to a Central Network Share

As you may have noticed, the last three examples each returns the status of Completed or Failed. Along with the actual installation, you could automate a report being created and sent to a share for viewing later. To demonstrate this, we have created the ReportOnInstall() method (see Listing 7-17).

Listing 7-17. *Creating an HTML Report*

VB .NET

```
Public Shared Function ReportOnInstall(ByVal ReportFileName) As String
    Dim strStatus As String = ""
    Dim objSR As System.IO.StreamReader
    Dim objSW As System.IO.StreamWriter
    Dim strReportData As String = ""
    Dim strComputer As String = My.Computer.Name

    Try
      'Open PCInfo.csv and Append the install info
      objSR = New System.IO.StreamReader("c:\PCInfo\PCInfo.csv")
      strReportData = "<b>*** " + strComputer + " = Done ***</b><p> "
      strReportData += objSR.ReadToEnd
      strReportData += "<hr>"
      objSR.Close()

      objSW = New System.IO.StreamWriter(ReportFileName, True)
      objSW.Write(strReportData)
      objSW.Close()
      strStatus = "Completed"

    Catch ex As Exception
      Console.WriteLine(ex.ToString + vbCrLf + "Press any key to continue...")
      Console.ReadLine()
      strStatus = "Failed"
    End Try

    Return strStatus
  End Function
```

The first part of the ReportOnInstall() method gets a StreamReader, a StreamWriter, and the computer's name. Then, within the Try-Catch block, we add some very basic formatting we wanted to see in our report heading by using stars and the computer's name. Next, we read the contents of the .csv file we received from Exercise 7-1 and place it into a text string. We also add some HTML tags, such as <hr/>, which create a "horizontal rule" across the screen of a web browser. From this, you may have guessed that we are saving our report to a file with an .html extension. Once we have the report data and some basic formatting, we are ready to write the contents to the report file on a network share.

Our goal is to create a web page that can be viewed by all the testers on the team. This way, anyone can see which installations have been completed and which have not. Since the report contains data on more then one installation, we create a new StreamWriter and open with the Append option set to True (again, see Listing 7-17). This will allow us to add more reports to the same file. We have included a picture of the web page in Figure 7-14 where you can see that the installations on two computers, Lab2 and Lab3, are done. The report also shows the information gathered from our InspectPC testware application.

> **Note** On an actual project, you would want to add more formatting to make your report more professional looking. We have chosen not to do too much because we wanted to simplify the code as much as possible.

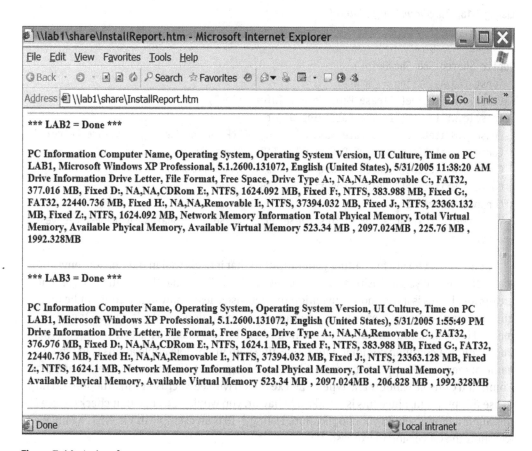

Figure 7-14. *A simple report*

Completing the Application

With the ReportOnInstall() method created, you have most of the ingredients to complete your application. Now you just have to link them all together. To do this, you would create code in the Main() method that will call each of these methods in turn. It would need to get arguments from the user and feed them into the various methods when required. Table 7-1 displays a list of the arguments you will need.

Table 7-1. *Arguments for Your Application*

Argument	Value	Required
Application path and name	Name and path of folder	Required
Run report	Yes/No	Optional
Check report	Yes/No	Optional
Upload report	Yes/No	Optional

With this many arguments, you really should add a way to let the users know what arguments to pass in. Listing 7-18 shows an additional method called ShowHelp() that outlines how to use your testware.

Listing 7-18. *The ShowHelp() Method*

VB .NET

```
Public Shared Sub ShowHelp()
  Const TAB As String = ChrW(9)
  Console.WriteLine("Please Provide All Information")
  Console.WriteLine("In The Following Order...")
  Console.WriteLine(" Testware Name =" + TAB + "(Path and Name of Testware Folder)")
  Console.WriteLine(" Run PC Report =" + TAB + "[Yes/No]")
  Console.WriteLine(" Check Report =" + TAB + TAB + "[Yes/No]")
  Console.WriteLine(" Upload Report =" + TAB + "[Yes/No]")
  Console.WriteLine _
  (" Example: " + TAB + TAB + "TestLabSetup.exe \\Server1\ShareWithApp yes yes yes")
End Sub
```

Remember, you are formatting your output so that it reads well in the Console environment. Notice that you are using square brackets, [ ], to indicate that the last three arguments are optional. This is a common convention that lets users learn how to use your application quickly. It is also a good idea to show an example, so this is done on the last line. Once this method is created, you would call the method when the user makes a mistake or requests help information. A common command for requesting help in Console applications is to type the name of the Console application and add a /? or -? argument. For example if you open up a Command Console window and type **Time.exe /?**, you will see Microsoft's instructions on how to use this program. Since this is standard behavior, you would add code that checks to see if this argument was sent to your application. Listing 7-19 is an example in VB .NET. Again, we will show the C# version in Exercise 7-2.

Listing 7-19. *Checking If Help Was Asked For*

VB .NET

```
    If args(0) = "-?" Or args(0) = "/?" Then
      Console.WriteLine("Test Lab Setup Application Help")
      ShowHelp()
      Return
    End If
```

As mentioned, you would also want to show the help message if there was some kind of error in the entry. Using the Try-Catch block again, your code would respond by showing the help when an error happened (see Listing 7-20).

Listing 7-20. *Evaluating the Arguments*

VB .NET

```
'Get Argument data
   Try
     'Get required argument
     strAppPathAndName = args(0)
     'Get optional arguments
     If args.Length = 2 Then
       strRunReport = args(1)
     ElseIf args.Length = 3 Then
       strRunReport = args(1)
       strCheckReport = args(2)
     ElseIf args.Length = 4 Then
       strRunReport = args(1)
       strCheckReport = args(2)
       strUploadReport = args(3)
     End If
   Catch ex As Exception
     Console.WriteLine("Please Check Your Arguments And Try Again")
     ShowHelp()
     Return
   End Try
```

Reporting Status on the Local Computer

One last chore is needed—you need to let the user know what the status of the install was if they are running your application manually. To do this, we have created a method called ReportToUser(), as shown in Listing 7-21. This method displays the status of each of the four installation steps. Calling this function would be the last thing you do in the Main() method.

Listing 7-21. *Reporting to an Interactive User*

VB .NET

```
Private Shared Sub ReportToUser _
  ( _
  ByVal Report As String, _
  ByVal Requirements As String, _
  ByVal Install As String, _
  ByVal Uploaded As String _
  )
    Dim strStatusReport As String = ""
```

```
      strStatusReport = " *** Status Report ***" + vbCrLf
      strStatusReport += "Check Report: " + Report + vbCrLf
      strStatusReport += "Check Requirements: " + Requirements + vbCrLf
      strStatusReport += "Install Testware: " + Install + vbCrLf
      strStatusReport += "Install Report Uploaded: " + Uploaded + vbCrLf
      Console.WriteLine(strStatusReport)
   End Sub
```

In Exercise 7-2, you will combine all of the preceding examples into an automated testware application.

Exercise 7-2: Automating Testware Setup

In this exercise, you will create a custom installation program that downloads files from a network share and reports the success or failure of this process. You will create the share, create all the methods you need, and add code to these methods. Lastly, you will fill in the code of the Main() method to process the program's arguments, call the methods, and report the status to the user.

■**Caution** Before you get started, you should also test that you can run the InspectPC.exe from the C:\PCInfo folder. This is the program you made in Exercise 7-1.

---

1. Open Windows Explorer and create a new folder on your C:\ called **Share**. Then make this folder into a new network share, as shown in the "Creating a Network Share" section of this chapter.

2. Create a new project and choose the Console application template. Name your application **TestLabSetup** and place it on the C:\ drive as well.

3. Delete the code files and create a new class in your project called **SetUp**.

   VB .NET will add a file called Module1.vb, while C# will add a file called Program.cs. While there is nothing wrong with these files, let's start from scratch so that both the VB .NET and C# examples will be very similar.

4. Remove any code that Visual Studio adds to the SetUp class.

5. With the SetUp class now empty, create the following methods and any Imports/using statements, as shown here:

VB .NET

```
Imports System.Text.RegularExpressions

Public Class SetUp

   Shared Sub Main(ByVal args() As String)
   End Sub
```

```
Public Shared Sub ShowHelp()
End Sub

Public Shared Function GetPCData(ByVal RunReport As String) As String
End Function

Public Shared Function CheckPCData(ByVal CheckReport As String) As String
End Function

Private Shared Function CheckForOS(ByVal ReportData As String) As Boolean
End Function


Public Shared Function DownloadAppFiles(ByVal PathAndName As String) As String
End Function

Public Shared Function ReportOnInstall(ByVal ReportFileName) As String
End Function

Private Shared Sub ReportToUser _
( _
ByVal Report As String, _
ByVal Requirements As String, _
ByVal Install As String, _
ByVal Uploaded As String _
)
End Sub
End Class
```

■**Note** At the time of this writing, My.Computer is not directly available in C#, so you will need to add a reference to it through VB .NET. My.Computer really is just providing a simple means to class other classes from one central class. This is convenient, but not strictly necessary. Still, it is an example of how you can use class in one language from another—and it is easy to do as well! So if you are using C#, add a reference to Microsoft.VisualBasic.dll using the Project ➤ Add Reference, as you did in Exercise 7-1.

C#

```
using System;
using System.Text.RegularExpressions;
using Microsoft.VisualBasic.Devices;

public class SetUp
{
  static Computer mc;
```

```
static void Main(string[] args)
{ }

public static void ShowHelp()
{  }

 public static string GetPCData(string RunReport)
 {  }

 public static string CheckPCData(string CheckReport)
 {  }

 private static bool CheckForOS(string ReportData)
 {  }

 public static string DownloadAppFiles(string PathAndName)
 {  }

 public static string ReportOnInstall(object ReportFileName)
 {  }

private static void ReportToUser
 (string Report, string Requirements, string Install, string Uploaded)
 {  }

}//end of class
```

6. Add the following comments to the Main() method. The Main() method will call each of these other methods in turn. Since this is a complex program, it is best that we outline the steps before we continue.

VB .NET

```
Shared Sub Main(ByVal args() As String)
  '---- Required Variables Section ----
    'Variables for general data
    'Variables to collect Switches
    'Variable to collect Function Status

  '---- Help Section ----

  '---- Get Arguments Section ----

  '----Commands and Report Status Section ----
   '1)Get PC Data Report = GetPCData()
   '2) Check Requirements Report = CheckPCData()
   '3) Download Testware = DownloadAppFiles()
   '4) Append Install Status and Upload to Report Share = ReportOnInstall
   '5) Print install Status to the Command Console = ReportToUser
End Sub
```

C#

```csharp
static void Main(string[] args)
{
  //---- Required Variables Section ----
    //Variables for general data
    //Variables to collect Switches
    //Variable to collect Function Status

  //---- Help Section ----

  //---- Get Arguments Section ----

  //----Commands and Report Status Section ----
  //1)Get PC Data Report = GetPCData()
  //2) Check Requirements Report = CheckPCData()
  //3) Download Testware = DownloadAppFiles()
  //4) Append Install Status and Upload to Report Share = ReportOnInstall
  //5) Print install Status to the Command Console = ReportToUser
}
```

7. Add the following code to the ShowHelp() method to display help information:

VB .NET

```vbnet
Public Shared Sub ShowHelp()
  Const TAB As String = ChrW(9)
  Console.WriteLine("Please Provide All Information")
  Console.WriteLine("In The Following Order...")
  Console.WriteLine(" Name =" + TAB + "(Path and Name of Testware Folder)")
  Console.WriteLine(" Run PC Report =" + TAB + "[Yes/No]")
  Console.WriteLine(" Check Report =" + TAB + TAB + "[Yes/No]")
  Console.WriteLine(" Upload Report =" + TAB + "[Yes/No]")
  Console.WriteLine(" Example: " + TAB + TAB + _
    "TestLabSetup.exe \\Server1\ShareWithApp yes yes yes")
End Sub
```

C#

```csharp
public static void ShowHelp()
{
  const string TAB = "\t";
  Console.WriteLine("Please Provide All Information");
  Console.WriteLine("In The Following Order...");
  Console.WriteLine(" Name =" + TAB + "(Path and Name of Testware Folder)");
  Console.WriteLine(" Run PC Report =" + TAB + "[Yes/No]");
  Console.WriteLine(" Check Report =" + TAB + TAB + "[Yes/No]");
  Console.WriteLine(" Upload Report =" + TAB + "[Yes/No]");
  Console.WriteLine(" Example: " + TAB + TAB +
  "TestLabSetup.exe \\\\Server1\\ShareWithApp yes yes yes");
  }
```

8. Add the following code to the GetPCData() method to run InspectPC.exe to gather the PC information:

VB .NET

```
Public Shared Function GetPCData(ByVal RunReport As String) As String
  Dim strStatus As String = ""
  Dim objProc As New System.Diagnostics.Process
  objProc.StartInfo.FileName = "C:\PCInfo\InspectPC.exe"
  objProc.StartInfo.CreateNoWindow = True
  objProc.StartInfo.ErrorDialog = True

  Try
    objProc.Start()
    strStatus = "Completed"
  Catch ex As Exception
    Console.WriteLine(ex.ToString + vbCrLf + "Press any key to continue...")
    Console.ReadLine()
    strStatus = "Failed"
  End Try
  Return strStatus
End Function
```

C#

```
public static string GetPCData(string RunReport)
{
  string strStatus = "";
  System.Diagnostics.Process objProc = new System.Diagnostics.Process();
  objProc.StartInfo.FileName = "C:\\PCInfo\\InspectPC.exe";
  objProc.StartInfo.Arguments = "y";
  objProc.StartInfo.CreateNoWindow = true;
  objProc.StartInfo.ErrorDialog = true;
  try
  {
    objProc.Start();
    strStatus = "Completed";
  }
  catch (Exception ex)
  {
    Console.WriteLine(ex.ToString() + "\r\n" + "Press any key to continue...");
    strStatus = "Failed";
  }
  return strStatus;
}
```

9. Add the following code to the CheckPCData() method. Notice that this method to calls the CheckForOS() method to check for the OS requirement. This is the only validation method we have created, but you could create others and use them here as well:

VB .NET

```
Public Shared Function CheckPCData(ByVal CheckReport As String) As String
  Dim strStatus As String = ""
  Dim objSR As System.IO.StreamReader
  Dim strReportData As String

  Try
    'Open file to read
    objSR = New System.IO.StreamReader("c:\PCInfo\PCInfo.csv")
    strReportData = objSR.ReadToEnd
    objSR.Close()

    'Check for the following requirements
    '1) OS must = XP
    If CheckForOS(strReportData) = True Then
      strStatus = "Completed"
    Else
      strStatus = "Failed"
    End If

  Catch ex As Exception
    Console.WriteLine(ex.ToString + vbCrLf + "Press any key to continue...")
    Console.ReadLine()
    strStatus = "Failed"
  End Try

  Return strStatus
End Function
```

C#

```
public static string CheckPCData(string CheckReport)
{
  string strStatus = "";
  System.IO.StreamReader objSR;
  string strReportData;
  try
  {
    //--- Gather System Data Section --
    objSR = new System.IO.StreamReader("c:\\PCInfo\\PCInfo.csv");
    strReportData = objSR.ReadToEnd();
    objSR.Close();
```

```
  // ---- Call The Verification Methods ---
  // This demo inlcudes only one
  if (CheckForOS(strReportData) == true)
  {
    strStatus = "Completed";
  }
  else
  {
    strStatus = "Failed";
  }
}
catch (Exception ex)
{
  Console.WriteLine(ex.ToString() + "\r\n" + "Press any key to continue...");
  Console.ReadLine(); //Pauses console until someone hit Enter
  strStatus = "Failed";
}
return strStatus;
}
```

10. Add the following code to the CheckForOS() method to check that the OS is either Windows XP or 2003:

VB .NET

```
Private Shared Function CheckForOS(ByVal ReportData As String) As Boolean
  Dim r As Regex
  Dim m As Match

  r = New Regex("XP | 2003", RegexOptions.IgnoreCase Or RegexOptions.Compiled)
  m = r.Match(ReportData)
  If m.Success Then
    Return True
  Else
    Return False
  End If
End Function
```

C#

```
private static bool CheckForOS(string ReportData)
{
  Regex r;
  Match m;
  r = new Regex("XP | 2003", RegexOptions.IgnoreCase | RegexOptions.Compiled);
  m = r.Match(ReportData);
  if (m.Success)
  {
    return true;
  }
```

```
   else
   {
     return false;
   }
}
```

   11. Add the following code to the DownloadAppFiles() method to XCOPY the files from the share:

VB .NET

```
Public Shared Function DownloadAppFiles(ByVal PathAndName As String) As String
  Dim strStatus As String = ""
  Dim strFileListing() As String
  Dim strFullFileName As String
  Dim strSimpleFileName As String
  Dim strAppName As String
  Dim intIndex As Int16
  intIndex = PathAndName.LastIndexOf("\")
  strAppName = PathAndName.Substring(intIndex + 1)


  Try
    'a) Create folder for your Testware
    Dim DI As New System.IO.DirectoryInfo("c:\" + strAppName)
    If Not DI.Exists Then
      DI.Create()
    End If

    'b) Go to Network share and copy
    'application folder to local drive, overwrite as needed
    strFileListing = System.IO.Directory.GetFiles(PathAndName)

    For Each strFullFileName In strFileListing
      intIndex = strFullFileName.LastIndexOf("\")
      strSimpleFileName = strFullFileName.Substring(intIndex + 1)
      System.IO.File.Copy _
      (strFullFileName, "c:\" + strAppName + "\" + strSimpleFileName, True)
    Next
    strStatus = "Completed"
  Catch ex As Exception
    Console.WriteLine(ex.ToString + vbCrLf + "Press any key to continue...")
    Console.ReadLine()
    strStatus = "Failed"
  End Try


  Return strStatus
End Function
```

C#

```csharp
public static string DownloadAppFiles(string PathAndName)
{
  string strStatus = "";
  string[] strFileListing;
  string strSimpleFileName;
  string strAppName;
  Int32 intIndex;
  intIndex = PathAndName.LastIndexOf("\\");
  strAppName = PathAndName.Substring(intIndex + 1);
  try
  {
    //a) Create folder for your Testware
    System.IO.DirectoryInfo DI =
      new System.IO.DirectoryInfo("c:\\" + strAppName);
    if (!(DI.Exists))
    {
      DI.Create();
    }

    //b) Go to Network share and copy
    //application folder to local drive, overwrite as needed
    strFileListing = System.IO.Directory.GetFiles(PathAndName);
    foreach (string strFullFileName in strFileListing)
    {
      intIndex = strFullFileName.LastIndexOf("\\");
      strSimpleFileName = strFullFileName.Substring(intIndex + 1);
      System.IO.File.Copy(strFullFileName, "c:\\" +
                        strAppName + "\\" + strSimpleFileName, true);
    }
    strStatus = "Completed";
  }
  catch (Exception ex)
  {
    Console.WriteLine(ex.ToString() + "\r\n" + "Press any key to continue...");
    Console.ReadLine();
    strStatus = "Failed";
  }
  return strStatus;
}
```

12. Add the following code to the ReportOnInstall() method to upload report data about the installation:

VB .NET

```
Public Shared Function ReportOnInstall(ByVal ReportFileName) As String
  Dim strStatus As String = ""
  Dim objSR As System.IO.StreamReader
  Dim objSW As System.IO.StreamWriter
  Dim strReportData As String = ""
  Dim strComputer As String = My.Computer.Name

  Try
    'Open PCInfo.csv and Append the install info
    objSR = New System.IO.StreamReader("c:\PCInfo\PCInfo.csv")
    strReportData = "<b>*** " + strComputer + " = Done ***</b><p> "
    strReportData += objSR.ReadToEnd
    strReportData += "***" + strComputer + "***" + "<hr>"
    objSR.Close()

    objSW = New System.IO.StreamWriter(ReportFileName, True)
    objSW.Write(strReportData)
    objSW.Close()
    strStatus = "Completed"

  Catch ex As Exception
    Console.WriteLine(ex.ToString + vbCrLf + "Press any key to continue...")
    Console.ReadLine()
    strStatus = "Failed"
  End Try

  Return strStatus
End Function
```

C#

```
public static string ReportOnInstall(string ReportFileName)
{
  string strStatus = "";
  System.IO.StreamReader objSR;
  System.IO.StreamWriter objSW;
  string strReportData = "";
  string strComputer = mc.Name;
  try
  {
    objSR = new System.IO.StreamReader("c:\\PCInfo\\PCInfo.csv");
    strReportData = "<b>*** " + strComputer + " = Done ***</b><p> ";
    strReportData += objSR.ReadToEnd();
    strReportData += "<hr>";
    objSR.Close();
    objSW = new System.IO.StreamWriter(ReportFileName, true);
```

```
    objSW.Write(strReportData);
    objSW.Close();
    strStatus = "Completed";
  }
  catch (Exception ex)
  {
    Console.WriteLine(ex.ToString() + "\r\n" + "Press any key to continue...");
    Console.ReadLine();
    strStatus = "Failed";
  }
  return strStatus;
}
```

13. Add the following code to the ReportToUser() method to display the status information:

VB .NET

```
Private Shared Sub ReportToUser _
( _
ByVal Report As String, _
ByVal Requirements As String, _
ByVal Install As String, _
ByVal Uploaded As String _
)
  Dim strStatusReport As String = ""

  strStatusReport = " *** Status Report ***" + vbCrLf
  strStatusReport += "Check Report: " + Report + vbCrLf
  strStatusReport += "Check Requirements: " + Requirements + vbCrLf
  strStatusReport += "Install Testware: " + Install + vbCrLf
  strStatusReport += "Install Report Uploaded: " + Uploaded + vbCrLf
  Console.WriteLine(strStatusReport)
End Sub
```

C#

```
private static void ReportToUser
(string Report, string Requirements, string Install, string Uploaded)
{
  string strStatusReport = "";
  strStatusReport = " *** Status Report ***" + "\r\n";
  strStatusReport += "Check Report: " + Report + "\r\n";
  strStatusReport += "Check Requirements: " + Requirements + "\r\n";
  strStatusReport += "Install Testware: " + Install + "\r\n";
  strStatusReport += "Install Report Uploaded: " + Uploaded + "\r\n";
  Console.WriteLine(strStatusReport);
}
```

14. Now you need to complete the code to the Main() method to call the methods you just created and capture any arguments passed in from the command line. Fill in the missing code until your main method looks like this:

VB .NET

```
Shared Sub Main(ByVal args() As String)
  '---- Required Variables Section----
  'Variables for general data
  Dim strAppPathAndName = ""

  'Variables to collect Switches
  Dim strRunReport As String = "no" 'optional
  Dim strCheckReport As String = "no" 'optional
  Dim strUploadReport As String = "no"   'optional

  'Variable to collect Function Status
  Dim strReportStatus As String = ""
  Dim strRequirementsStatus As String = ""
  Dim strInstallStatus As String = ""
  Dim strReportUploadStatus As String = ""

  '---- Help Section ----
  If args(0) = "-?" Or args(0) = "/?" Then
    Console.WriteLine("Test Lab Setup Application Help")
    ShowHelp()
    Return
  End If
  '---- Get Arguments Section ----
  Try
    'Get required argument
    strAppPathAndName = args(0)
    'Get optional arguments
    If args.Length = 2 Then
      strRunReport = args(1)
    ElseIf args.Length = 3 Then
      strRunReport = args(1)
      strCheckReport = args(2)
    ElseIf args.Length = 4 Then
      strRunReport = args(1)
      strCheckReport = args(2)
      strUploadReport = args(3)
    End If
  Catch ex As Exception
    'If there was a problem with the arguments
    Console.WriteLine("Please Check Your Arguments And Try Again")
    ShowHelp()
    Return
  End Try
```

```
'----Commands and Report Status Section ----
'1)Run PCData Report
If strRunReport.ToLower = "yes" Then
  strReportStatus = GetPCData(strRunReport)
Else
  strReportStatus = "Skipped"
End If


'2) Check Requirements Report
If strCheckReport.ToLower = "yes" Then
  strRequirementsStatus = CheckPCData(strCheckReport)
Else
  strRequirementsStatus = "Skipped"
End If


'3) Download Testware
strInstallStatus = DownloadAppFiles(strAppPathAndName)

'4) Append Install Status and Upload to Report Share
If strUploadReport.ToLower = "yes" Then
  strReportUploadStatus = ReportOnInstall("\\Lab1\Share\InstallReport.htm")
Else
  strReportUploadStatus = "Skipped"
End If


'5) Print install Status to the Command Console
ReportToUser(strReportStatus, strRequirementsStatus, _
  strInstallStatus, strReportUploadStatus)

End Sub
```

C#

```
static void Main(string[] args)
{
  //---- Required Variables Section ----
  //Variables for general data
  mc = new Computer();
  string strAppPathAndName = "";

  //Variables to collect Switches
  string strRunReport = "no";
  string strCheckReport = "no";
  string strUploadReport = "no";
```

```
//Variable to collect Function Status
string strReportStatus = "";
string strRequirementsStatus = "";
string strInstallStatus = "";
string strReportUploadStatus = "";

//---- Help Section ----
if (args[0] == "-?" | args[0] == "/?") {
  Console.WriteLine("Test Lab Setup Application Help");
  ShowHelp();
  return;
}


//---- Get Arguments Section ----
try
{
 //Get required argument
  strAppPathAndName = args[0];

  //Get optional arguments
  if (args.Length == 2)
  {
    strRunReport = args[1];
  }
  else if (args.Length == 3)
  {
    strRunReport = args[1];
    strCheckReport = args[2];
  }
  else if (args.Length == 4)
  {
    strRunReport = args[1];
    strCheckReport = args[2];
    strUploadReport = args[3];
  }
}
catch (Exception ex)
{
  //If there was a problem with the arguments
  Console.WriteLine("Please Check Your Arguments And Try Again");
  ShowHelp();
  return;
}
```

```csharp
//----Commands and Report Status Section ----
//1)Get PC Data Report
if (strRunReport.ToLower() == "yes") {
  strReportStatus = GetPCData(strRunReport);
}
else
{
  strReportStatus = "Skipped";
}

//2) Check Requirements Report
if (strCheckReport.ToLower() == "yes") {
  strRequirementsStatus = CheckPCData(strCheckReport);
}
else
{
  strRequirementsStatus = "Skipped";
 }

//3) Download Testware
strInstallStatus = DownloadAppFiles(strAppPathAndName);

//4) Append Install Status and Upload to Report Share
if (strUploadReport.ToLower() == "yes")
{
  strReportUploadStatus =
    ReportOnInstall("\\\\Lab1\\Share\\InstallReportCS.htm");
}
else
{
  strReportUploadStatus = "Skipped";
}

//5) Print install Status to the Command Console
ReportToUser(strReportStatus, strRequirementsStatus,
            strInstallStatus, strReportUploadStatus);
}
```

■**Note** The full code for the finished exercise is in the DownloadFiles\Chapter7\VB\Exercise7-2 folder
(or replace the VB with C#). These files are available for download from the Source Code section of the Apress
website at www.apress.com. See Appendix C for download details.

---

15. Compile your TestLabSetup program to create the TestLabSetup.exe file. Copy this file to the root of
    C:\ drive so that it is easy to find later.

16. Now, create a new simple Windows application called **TestApp**. It does not matter what it does; what
    you want is to test that it downloaded from a share. We have provided you with one in the aforemen-
    tioned exercise folder. Build the application to create a TestApp.exe file.

17. Create a new *folder* called **TestApp** within the share you made earlier and move the TestApp.exe file
    to this new folder. Also, use Notepad to create a simple text file in this same folder, so that you can test
    that your application will copy multiple files from this folder. Your folder's contents should look like
    Figure 7-15.

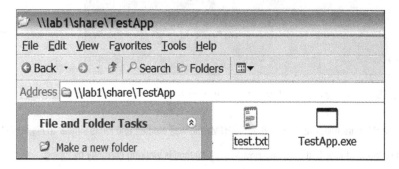

Figure 7-15. *The Application files*

18. Open a command prompt and navigate to your TestLabSetup.exe file you placed on the root of
    C:\ drive. (This is similar to Figure 7-2, using the Command Console). Execute your program adding the
    following arguments:

TestLabSetup.exe \\lab1\share\testapp yes yes yes

19. The program should copy the files from the share and place them in a folder called C:\testapp. Verify
    that all the steps where completed successfully, as shown in Figure 7-16.

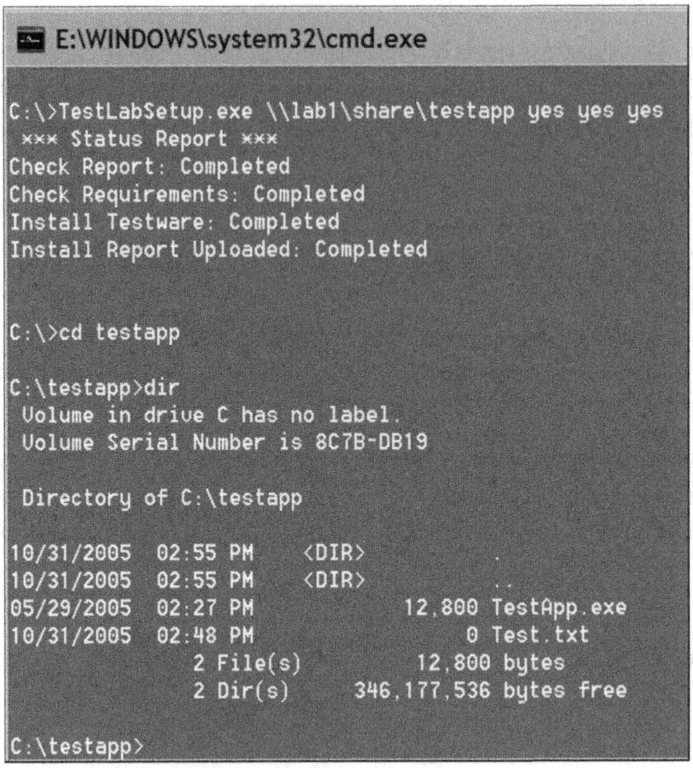

Figure 7-16. *Running the TestLabSetup application*

20. Look in the C:\Share folder and verify that the HTML file was created and looks similar to Figure 7-14.

21. From the command line, test that the ShowHelp() method is working correctly by typing **c:\TestLabSetup.exe /?**.

In this exercise, you created an application that downloads an application from a network share. From here, you could add improvements, such as letting the user have more options, checking for more requirements, or creating a better report. Another thing that you might consider is automating the execution of this program, which is what we will talk about next.

■**Note** Now that the application is working, you could go through it again and redesign it into reusable component files like those you did in Chapter 6. We have chosen to create only one class and file here for simplicity's sake.

Using Batch Files

With the install program complete, all the user needs to do to install a set of testware files is open a Command window and tell your program from which folder to download. This is pretty easy, but you can make it even easier by creating a batch file. A *batch file* is a simple text file that contains simple instructions for the OS to process. They are used for quite a number of tasks, but one task is to run a program and pass arguments to it.

To make a batch file, open Notepad (or any other text editor) and save a file with the .bat extension. Now you would add your instructions into the file. In this case, you would add instructions like the ones shown in Figure 7-17.

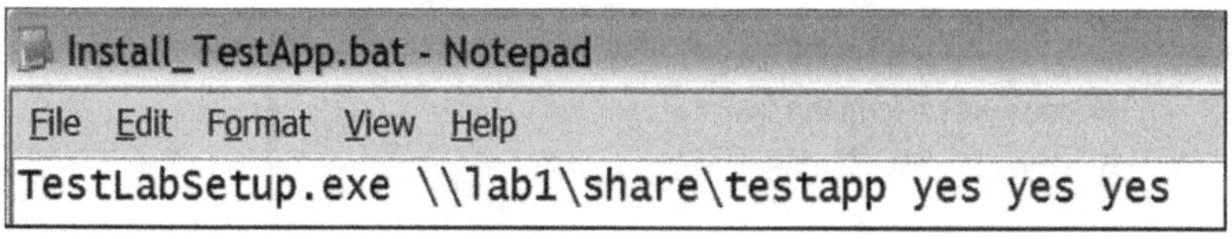

Figure 7-17. *Creating a batch file*

With the batch file made, all you need to do is use Windows Explorer to navigate to this file and double-click it. The OS will run the TestLabSetup.exe program with the specified parameters.

If you are going to run a program with the same arguments more than once, using a batch file is easier than typing them repeatedly in the Command window. Add that to the fact that you can make a different batch file for each program and argument combination and then run the batch file, and you have a simple-to-use test lab setup. As an example, say you have five commonly used testware applications, but you do not need all of these on each lab setup. You can create a folder for each application on a share and create a new batch file for each of these as well. Next, you just tell the team where the batch files are found and what they do. You can either place these batch files on a central network share or, if you use imaging technology on your lab PCs, add these batch files to the master image.

Some tests you might want to regularly automate using batch files are Build Verification Tests (BVTs) or Smoke Tests. *BVTs* are those tests that are run by the Test Team after initial build release to ensure that development has released a testable build. They test very basic functionality and are run frequently enough that automating them makes sense. *Smoke Tests* are somewhat random tests just to ensure that all parts of the system are working. They are often run after integration testing just to "smoke" out any potential problems. These examples are the type of tests that you might want to keep and run regularly from a batch to check on the validity of the builds at any given time. They lend themselves quite well to automating with batch files. Installing software for test setup and removing software to reset the platform are also excellent tasks to automate on a test project since batching them can save you tons of time.

Using Windows Scheduler

Microsoft has long included a program that runs commands at a given time. In the current version of Windows, this program is called Scheduled Tasks and can be found in the Control Panel. When you open this folder, you will see the Add Scheduled Task icon, and you would click on this to start the wizard.

The wizard walks you through the process and is very easy to use. You just pick the program file you wish to run—either the TestLabSetup.exe or TestApp.bat file in this case. Then, you choose a date and time you wish it to run and finish the wizard. You can edit the settings the wizard configures by double-clicking on the file it creates or by checking the Advanced Properties check box on the wizard's final screen (see Figure 7-18).

Figure 7-18. *Completing the Scheduled Task Wizard*

When the Advanced Properties window opens, you will see four tabs. You use these tabs to control the way your program will run. One important option is the Run textbox on the Task tab. If you are not using the Batch File option, you will need to add the arguments into this textbox (see Figure 7-19).

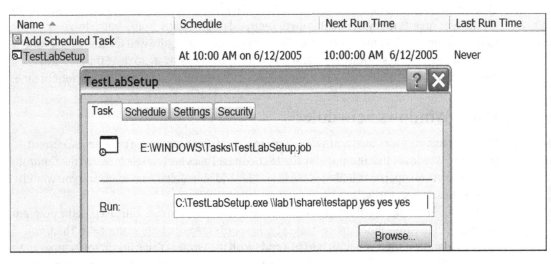

Figure 7-19. *Modifying the Task settings*

All that you need to do now is test it, of course. When the scheduled time comes, your installation should automatically start and the install report should show up on the network share for you to review later.

Summary

In this chapter, you have seen that a Console application can be a useful tool when you want to automate test lab setups. You saw two examples: one that created a useful report about the PC itself and one that automated an installation after it checked this report. You also saw how to work with command-line arguments and how to create your own. Finally, you saw how by using a combination of simple tools, such as batch files and the Task Scheduler, you can create a system that will automate lab setups—a process that can save your company time and money.

Of course, this example used text files to save both the report data from the InspectPC and the SetUp testware applications. In many professional testing suites, you will find that they use a database to store this kind of data instead. You can build your testware to do this as well, but you will need more experience with database programming. To get started, you will take a look at databases and how to work with them in Chapter 8.

Tester's Checklist

On a test project,

☑ Create automation tools that are simple and reusable.

☑ Use the Console application whenever you do *not* need a lot of user interaction.

☑ Use network share to access common files needed in a test lab.

☑ Create reports on your automations that can be reviewed and verified.

CHAPTER 8

■■■

Introduction to Database Testing

Testing software applications usually includes accessing and verifying data of some kind. This is true of any kind of software application you can think of these days, including, of course, web applications. In fact, out of necessity, more focus is being placed on end-to-end testing of large software applications. *End-to-end testing* traces the flow of information and any bugs encountered from the user of the system (the client) all the way through to any data accessed and then back again to the original client. Going through the entire system may include passing through multiple servers and accessing heterogeneous data stores. For example, a client system (such as a browser on a home computer) accesses an application stored on a web server. This web server, in turn, passes the client's request for information—say, a price on a product—to a database server. The database server returns the request back to the web server, which, in turn, passes the information back to the client. Testing this kind of arrangement can be complex as the tester tries to determine the source of bugs in the system's multiple layers (see Figure 8-1).

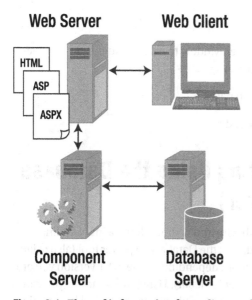

Figure 8-1. *Flow of information from client to database*

It is important to understand and work with all types of data to be effective at end-to-end testing. This data can be stored in many ways—for example, spreadsheets, text files, and databases. Relational Database Management Systems (RDBMSs) such as Oracle, SQL Server, Informix, DB2, etc. are used to store data for large, client/server-type systems. However, many applications include data from older, nonrelational database systems. Because of this exceedingly wide field of possible data sources, we will have to limit the focus in this chapter to data stored in relational databases. By far, this is the storage option widely favored for today's systems due to the proven consistency and reliability of relational databases.

Understanding data testing involves more than can be presented in one book. To be effective at database application testing, you will also need a database background—in other words, a thorough knowledge of database design and SQL, as well as practical training and experience with a DBMS. There are a number of ways to get this knowledge; some resources are provided in Appendix C. Meanwhile, there is still much you can do with the basics that you will learn in this chapter.

.NET can be a very functional means to access and verify data in a database in several ways. First, the .NET IDE contains a number of useful tools to reference and view a database and even modify its structure and data. In addition, .NET languages can be used to programmatically access data using a variety of data access methods. It's great that .NET provides these capabilities because, as test professionals, you need to get into the database to do important testing tasks, such as verify the correctness of application functionality with respect to the data, as well as insert and remove test data. In this chapter, you will start by exploring the use of the Database Explorer tools for data access and then use ADO.NET programming to manipulate and verify data in a database.

Objectives

At the end of this chapter, you will be able to

- Use the Database Explorer tools to access databases.

- Use the Database Explorer tools' Query Builder window to execute queries to retrieve information and insert and remove test data.

- Employ the new data source controls for web pages.

- Create access to databases using ADO.NET code.

Database Application Testing Using the Database Explorer (or Server Explorer)

.NET can be used to support database testing both with and without doing a lot of coding. A tool you can use that doesn't involve a lot of coding is the Database Explorer tool (also called the Server Explorer tools and the Visual Database tools, depending on the .NET version you are using; see the "Database Explorer and Server Explorer" sidebar). Using this window, you can connect to a database and display its structure and contents. This can be very useful for ensuring application functionality. For example, you can enter data from the front end, or presentation layer, of your application and then view it using the Database Explorer window to be sure it made it through the application software and all physical servers into the database back end correctly and without corruption. For Microsoft databases, including Access and SQL Server, you can modify structure by adding tables—perhaps to load in test data or test results and add and remove rows of data using the Database Explorer.

Using the Database Explorer Window for Field-Level Integrity Testing

Creating a connection in the Database Explorer window is an easy way to quickly set up access to a database. Then, once the database is open, you will be able to inspect and interrogate database objects including tables, stored procedures, and views. Figure 8-2 shows the Database Explorer window displaying Microsoft Access' Northwind sample database.

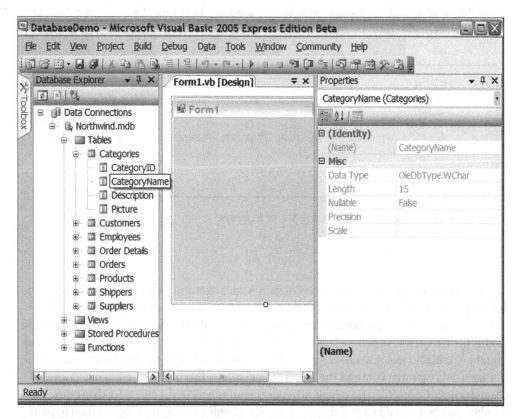

Figure 8-2. *The Database Explorer window in the .NET IDE displaying the Northwind database*

What you are viewing in the Database Explorer window is essentially the *schema*, or structure, of the database itself. A database schema contains the names of the tables within the database and the columns within those tables, including the *data types* of those columns. Even at this point you can see a lot of useful information. Within the Database Explorer window, you can expand icons to look at the entire spectrum of database objects. One of the common test cases regarding databases is to verify that all the database objects (such as tables, views, and stored procedures) that are supposed to be there are actually there. Is anything missing? If so, you already have a defect to report. So, the Database Explorer window allows you to visually verify that the database structure is correct.

DATABASE EXPLORER AND SERVER EXPLORER

If you are using the full version of Visual Studio and not just the Express version, you will need to use Server Explorer instead. Database Explorer only exists in the Express product; all other Visual Studio products use Server Explorer. (Since the Express Editions are in Beta as of this writing, this may change). Still, the process of opening up a connection is similar in either window; you just have to click the Connect To Database button, which looks like a cylinder with a power cord (see Figure 8-3), and choose the correct Data Source from the list. Once you do that, you will have to point to the server and database you wish to open. Although Database Explorer is a bit easier to use, both work about the same way. We chose to use the Express versions of Visual Studio 2005 because they have most of the features needed and are inexpensive for our readers (free at the time of this writing). That being the case, we concentrate on pointing out important features of using Database Explorer in this chapter, but you should be able to follow along with Server Explorer without much trouble.

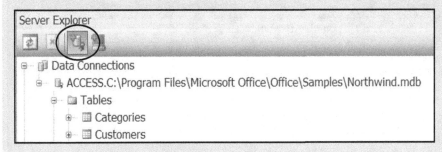

Figure 8-3. *Opening a connection using Server Explorer*

In Figure 8-2, we have expanded the Categories table icon and clicked on the CategoryName field. If you look at the Properties window in Figure 8-2, you can see that properties of the CategoryName field are displayed. (The properties appear grayed out only because you cannot modify them from this window.) This tells you the data type—i.e., the kind of data this field can contain. The OleDbType.WChar data type might not mean a lot to you at first; however, any time you see a data type that contains the letters "Char" means this field may contain any kind of character data. Character data means any letters or numbers (so in character data types, the numbers will be treated just as if they are characters, which means that you can't do numeric operations on them, like adding or subtracting). Other kinds of data types will indicate numeric fields, such as integer (whole numbers) or floating-point numbers, or other kinds of data such as currency, binary, or date fields. All databases have a rich variety of data types for developers to choose from. The correct choice of data type for fields is very important in good database design. Seeing the choices of data types can help you choose the correct kinds of data with which to test the fields in your application; this is often referred to as field-level integrity testing.

Note that the field's size is also indicated in the Properties window of Figure 8-2. The CategoryName field is 15 characters long. This is helpful in creating appropriate test data for this field. It also is important to note any differences in the sizes listed in the database for fields and their sizes in the presentation layer of the application. For example, what if the application you're testing has a web page that allows for 20 characters in the CategoryName field, but you can see here that the database allows only 15? Here you could create a test case to input 20 characters into the web application's CategoryName field and see what happens to it in the database. Very likely you would see data truncation, and you could then report that as a defect. Of course, it's also possible you would see a worse error, too, such as an error message or even a failure! So viewing data types and sizes in the Database Explorer window is an important way to help verify data integrity at the field level.

Exercise 8-1 is a short exercise that shows you the steps for connecting to and inspecting a database and its objects.

Exercise 8-1: Database Component Verification Using the Database Explorer

In this exercise, you'll use the Database Explorer window to connect to a database and perform some component verification testing.

Test Case Set Up:

Assume you're testing an application that uses the Northwind database (a copy of the Microsoft Access Northwind database is included in the exercise folder for this chapter), your application is in version 3.0 and some database structure changes have been made in this build, the Orders table has been modified to update the ShipName column from 25 characters to 40 characters, and a Manager's table has been added.

Your task is to verify the following about these database components:

- Does this Orders table exist in the database?

- Does this Manager's table exist in the database?

- Assuming the Orders table exists, verify that the size of the ShipName column is 40 characters.

To accomplish these tasks, execute the following steps:

1. Launch Visual Studio .NET. From the View menu, select the Database Explorer (or Server Explorer) menu item. The Database Explorer window appears.

■**Note** Depending on the .NET software you are using, you may be working with the Server Explorer rather than the Database Explorer. These will operate similarly (see the "Database Explorer and Server Explorer" sidebar). If you *do* have the Server Explorer rather than the Database Explorer, then for the remainder of this exercise simply substitute Server Explorer whenever Database Explorer is indicated.

---

2. Right-click the Connections icon in the Database Explorer (or select Tools ➤ Add Connection from the Visual Studio main menu). The Choose Data Source dialog appears (see Figure 8-4).

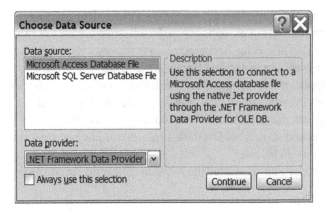

Figure 8-4. *Choosing a data source*

3. Choose the Microsoft Access Database File from the Data Source listbox. Uncheck the Always Use This Selection box and then click the Continue button.

   The Add Connection dialog appears (see Figure 8-5).

Figure 8-5. *The Add Connection dialog*

4. In the Add Connection dialog under Database File Name, browse to the location that contains the Northwind database. A copy of the Microsoft Access Northwind sample database is contained in exercise folder for this chapter.

▪**Note** If you have Microsoft Office installed, you can also access this same database in the following location: C:\Program Files\Microsoft Office\Office10\Samples\Northwind.mdb.

---

5. Click the Test Connection button at the bottom of the Add Connection dialog to ensure that you entered a correct database file. A message box will display indicating that your selection is correct. If it does not, be sure you have typed a correct path and filename into the Database File Name textbox. Be sure you have not changed anything else on the dialog, then try again. Once you have a successful connection, click OK to close that dialog and click OK again to dismiss the Add Connection dialog. You will see the new connection appear in the Database Explorer window.

6. Expand your new connection icon in the Database Explorer window until it looks like Figure 8-2. Now you can perform the tasks indicated at the start of this exercise. Does the Orders table exist? Pass or Fail? How about the Manager's table? In the Orders table, what is the length of the ShipName column? After answering these questions, continue to explore the Northwind database. One of your first tasks in any test project involving a database is to become familiar with the database components, so spend some time getting comfortable with the objects in the Northwind database. You will use it for future exercises in this chapter.

If you close and reopen Visual Studio, you will notice that the connection you created doesn't go away. To remove a connection, you can right-click it in the Database Explorer window and select Delete from the submenu. This connection does not affect your projects in any way (except that the project can use the connection if desired), but just having the connection there doesn't hurt anything so you can leave it for now. Keep in mind, you didn't have to create a project for this exercise!

In this exercise, you learned how to use the Database Explorer window to create a database connection and verify database components. This tool also comes in handy when writing code to access databases, since it provides the correct names of database components. For this reason alone, it's a good idea to set up a connection to your application's database and have it available whether you are manually testing or using automated testing.

Creating a database connection, investigating the database structure, and reviewing its contents are valuable first steps in database application testing. You can follow pretty much all of the same steps from the last section to access any database. This gives you a common way to access databases so it isn't always necessary to learn each one of their individual database software packages. For example, once you have a username and password to an Oracle database that's available from your location, you can create a connection to this database using the Database Explorer and explore its components. This saves you from downloading and spending time learning specialized tools used to work with an Oracle database, especially when doing quick and simple tasks. Of course, the Database Explorer is no substitute for the professional database administration tools that all DBMSs have, but it can be useful for many of the tasks you need to perform. Note that you will need to get proper permissions to access all database components. Obtaining a username, password, and proper permissions is something you will get from your project's database administrator.

TESTER'S TIP: CHANGING DATABASE STRUCTURE FOR TESTING SQL SERVER DATABASES

With Visual Studio 2005, in addition to exploring database components and data, you can also create, add to, and delete SQL Server databases and their components (which is necessary to set up test databases) as long as you are given the proper permissions from your database administrator. Unfortunately, this ability will not apply to non-Microsoft databases such as Oracle and DB2. This is because the driver software that is supplied by these vendors does not allow it.

Executing Database Queries Using the Query Designer

As valuable as it is to view and verify database components, it can be even more valuable to execute queries against the database directly. This can help you verify application functionality and the existence of correctly entered test data. You can use the connection(s) you set up using the Database Explorer window to generate tabs that contain data and allow you to enter SQL queries. Figure 8-6 shows the multiple panes you can use to view and access data.

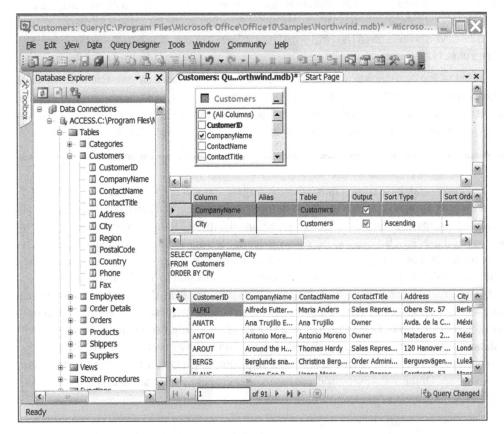

Figure 8-6. *The Query Designer showing multiple panes for retrieving and viewing data*

Note You can go quickly to the query window for entering SQL statements by right-clicking the table name in the Database Explorer and selecting New Query from the context menu. You will then be presented with a dialog to select the tables you want to work with. When you have selected one or more, then click Add Table and you will, again, see all of the panes displayed in Figure 8-6.

In Exercise 8-2, you'll learn how to use the Query Designer panes to enter SQL queries useful on a test project.

Exercise 8-2: Executing Database Queries

In this exercise, assume you are testing an application that uses a Microsoft Access database to store its data. You will enter and remove test data and execute other queries using the Query Designer.

1. Launch Visual Studio .NET, if necessary. Make sure you have created the data connection from Exercise 8-1.

2. Expand the Access Connection icon, then expand the Tables icon and within it, the Customers icon (see Database Explorer window in Figure 8-6).

Note If you see a red X near the Access Connection icon, don't worry, this isn't a problem. It just means that the connection was released; connections are not constantly held. Just clicking to expand the icon will reestablish the connection.

3. Place your cursor on the Customers table icon and right-click it. Select Show Table Data from the context menu (in older versions of Visual Studio you will select Open). A new tab will appear in the Designer window with a list of the records from the Customers table. This tab is scrollable; to see all the data, you'll have to scroll down to the bottom. You'll also have to scroll horizontally to see all the fields in each record. Explore this table and its data. If you change any values, keep in mind that these changes are saved into the database and are permanent!

Changing Data Values:

4. Scroll down to the very last record. Change the value in the ContactName field to your own name. Now close the tab (click the X in the upper, right-hand corner) and reopen it by repeating step 3. Scroll down again to the last record in the table and you'll see your name is still there as the contact for the last record. This means you can change data values for testing field level integrity. Keep in mind that you will have to conform to the rules set for that field—i.e., you will have to understand the type and length of the values required. Taking a look at the field's data type may be necessary. To do that you only need to select the field in the Database Explorer window and view its properties in the Properties window.

Adding Test Data:

5. Scroll down to the very last line in the Customers tab. This line has "null" in every field. This row doesn't represent a row in the table; it is there to allow you to add new data values. Enter the following values into this row for each field, as shown in Table 8-1.

Table 8-1. *Test Data Values*

Field Name	Value
CustomerID	SWMAR
CompanyName	Sammamish Software
ContactName	Mary R. Sweeney
ContactTitle	Owner
Address	555 SE 42nd Court
City	Issaquah
Region	WA
PostalCode	98029
Country	USA
Phone	425-466-5555
Fax	

Once all values are entered, press the Enter key. This enters the row into the table. Feel free to add more rows of test data by following the same process again and making up your own values. However, if you add data that doesn't meet field requirements, you will get an error. You won't usually get the error until you move off of the row by attempting to place your cursor in another row. For example, if you type a letter into a field that accepts only numbers, you'll get an error. The only way to fix the error is to type correct data into that field, *or* you can cancel the entire record entry by pressing the Esc key.

Removing Test Data:

6. Usually, once you add data for a test case, you'll want to clean it up by removing it. You've only been adding single rows of data at a time so far. To remove a single row of data, all you need to do is place your cursor all the way to the left of the row, right-click, and select Delete from the context menu. A dialog will ask if you really want to delete the row. If you do, click OK. The row is then permanently deleted from the database.

■**Caution** You will be able to delete any row that you have added during this exercise; however, you will not be allowed to delete most of the already existing rows because there are links between that data and the data in other tables.

Delete the row of test data you added using the values in Table 8-2 by right-clicking in the box to the left of the row and selecting Delete from the context menu.

Executing SQL Queries:

To execute SQL queries, you need a place to add SQL statements, so you'll bring up the SQL pane in the next steps.

7. Place your cursor anywhere in the data values in the Customer table data tab. Select the Query Designer ➤ Pane ➤ SQL menu item from the main menu. This is the only pane you'll need to enter SQL statements; however, just for fun let's display the other panes as well. Select Query Designer ➤ Pane ➤ Diagram from the menu and then Query Designer ➤ Pane ➤ Criteria. Now your IDE should look exactly like Figure 8-6.

8. In the SQL pane, find the lines that read `select * from customers` and replace them with the following query:

```
SELECT CompanyName, ContactName
FROM  Customers
WHERE (Country = 'USA')
```

Once this query has been entered into the SQL pane, select Query Designer ➤ Execute SQL from the menu (or press Ctrl+R). In the Results pane (the bottom pane), you will see that you only have a subset of the rows returned and only two columns. In the Select statement you issued, only two columns were requested: the CompanyName and ContactName columns. This statement also requested only rows for those customers who live in the USA by using the Where clause, which performs a filter on the query.

In this exercise, you've learned how to use the Query Designer and the multiple panes it contains for viewing and accessing data. These panes include the Results, Diagram, SQL, and Criteria panes. One of the best things about using the Query Designer is that working with any kind of database is the same—i.e., you can work with Oracle, SQL Server, Access, etc. in the same way using these panes. This sure beats having to download multiple vendor tools to work with all the different kinds of databases. So the .NET Query Designer gives you a common front end for accessing databases.

If you are more proficient with SQL, you can continue to execute SQL statements here. If you are not proficient in SQL, you can formulate a query using the Criteria pane. It works much like similar database systems. You can select the columns you'd like to see and the criteria for specifying rows. The SQL pane will be updated with the correct SQL statement based on your selections in the Criteria pane. This can be a good learning tool for those who already know a little SQL and can use some help formulating the queries. For more information about how to use the Criteria pane, search for "Criteria Pane" in Visual Studio Help.

SQL Statements for Testing

There are a number of SQL statements that are valuable for testing. The following are just a sample using the data in the Northwind database (to try them, repeat step 8 from Exercise 8-2):

- To return the number of rows in the Customers table:

```
SELECT Count(*) FROM Customers
```

TESTER'S TIP: AGGREGATE QUERIES

This query is one of the five ANSI standard *aggregate* queries contained in all language versions of SQL. These aggregate queries give you summary information about the data, which can be particularly useful to the test professional. The other four aggregate queries are the Sum, Avg, Max, Min aggregates. These are worth paying special attention to when you take a course on SQL.

- To return the most recently ordered items from the Orders table:

```
SELECT *
FROM Orders
WHERE orderdate =
        (SELECT MAX(orderdate) FROM orders)
```

- To find records with duplicate primary keys in a table (there are no such duplicate records in Northwind tables; however, this is a good check for other databases where referential integrity of the data is suspect):

```
SELECT employeeid
FROM employees
GROUP BY employeeid
HAVING COUNT(employeeid) > 1
```

- To find orphan records—i.e., orders that have no employee assigned [again, this result should yield zero rows (no data) in the Northwind database]:

```
SELECT e.EmployeeID, o.Orderid
FROM employees e RIGHT OUTER JOIN
    orders o ON e.employeeid = o.employeeid
WHERE e.employeeid IS NULL
```

- You can also drag tables and views from the Database Explorer window and drop them onto the Diagram pane of the Query Designer. This is a quick way to run predefined queries without knowing a lot of SQL. To give this a try, place your cursor on any table in the Data View window, click it once, drag it just over the Diagram pane of the Query Designer window, and let go. From there, you can modify the SQL statement if desired.

To get the most out of these tools, you should learn more about SQL. There are many excellent books on SQL. For further information on learning this language, see Appendix C.

RELATIONAL DATABASE OBJECTS PRIMER

If you are unfamiliar with relational databases, you will need to get up to speed on the basics before doing any significant amount of testing. There are courses available at community colleges and many good books that can help you. Appendix C of this book lists some good resources.

To get you started, here is a description of some of the major objects in a relational database:

- *Tables*: All data in relational databases is stored in table format. The rows of the table represent one record's worth of data. For example, each row in a Customers table would contain information about a single customer. The columns of the table represent individual pieces of data about the customer, such as the customer's name, address, and so on.

- *Views*: A view is an alternate way to look at data from one or more tables in the database. A view's contents are generated by a query and usually contain a subset of columns and rows from one or more tables. A view is considered a virtual table because it can be treated as though it were a table even though it isn't. For example, a view can store the SQL code to find all customers in the Customers table who live in Washington. That information actually resides in the Customers table, but since it is defined in a view, you can look at it in the view as though the view is a table itself. So, a view is really just a query that is stored and has a name.

- *Stored procedures*: A stored procedure allows the database programmer to write a set of SQL statements and give it a name so that it can be used over and over without having to rewrite it each time it is needed. Stored procedures usually contain multiple SQL statements and can be used to perform simple or complex database tasks.

Database References vs. Database Connections

There is another way to refer to and use databases within .NET, and that is by setting a database reference within the Solution Explorer. Database connections created in the Database Explorer, as you saw in the preceding section, are not associated with any project and will stay until the connection is removed. (Although, these connections can be referenced in certain controls, as you'll see later in this chapter.) In contrast, database references can be created in the Solution Explorer that *will* be associated with the project. When you reopen the project, the database references are still there and are available to you.

Using the Solution Explorer to maintain a set of database references can be very useful on a test project. You can maintain several database references that are kept with the project. As you develop and test your project, you might choose to keep one reference to a personal test database on your own machine and another reference to a group-wide test database that you share with your colleagues.

To create a database reference in Solution Explorer (assuming you already have an open project), follow these steps:

1. Select the Data ➤ Add New Data Source menu item. The Data Source Configuration Wizard will display (see Figure 8-7).

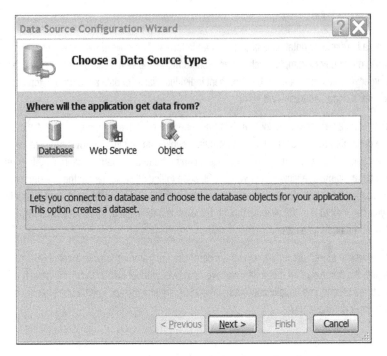

Figure 8-7. *Using the Data Source Configuration Wizard*

2. Click the Database icon and click Next. In the next dialog, the Wizard will ask you to choose an existing connection (like the ones we have created in this chapter so far) or to create a new connection. If you choose to create a new connection, the New Connection dialog box will display just as you saw earlier in Figure 8-5. Use an existing connection or use the New Connection dialog box to create a new one.

3. Once you have established a connection using the Wizard, you will be prompted to choose which database object (i.e., tables, views) you want to include. Choose a table and click Finish. A DataSet filled with the database objects you chose will be created for you when you finish the Wizard. This dataset will be displayed in the Solution Explorer window.

To perform programmatic access to this DataSet, you will use the classes found in the ADO.NET class library. The ADO.NET library provides great flexibility and power without having to write large amounts of code. Before you work with your new DataSet, let's take some time to learn the basics of ADO.NET.

Automated Database Testing Using ADO.NET

So far in this chapter, you've learned how to manually access and manipulate databases using Visual Studio's Database Explorer. If you want to set up automated tests to do similar actions programmatically, you'll need to write some code. Microsoft provides the ADO.NET class libraries to create programmatic connections to access and manipulate database components. In Chapter 3, you used ADO.NET without much explanation or fanfare to write test results into a database. In Chapter 9, you will see this same approach used to store test data from a web-based application. You may notice that we use much of the same code in both cases. This same code can be used to write test data into many different application databases. This means that without much more work than just changing the database and table names, you can use ADO.NET to perform many different testing tasks. To really understand what needs to change and what remains the same when programming these tasks, we should first take a step back and formally introduce ADO.NET.

ADO.NET Basics

In VB6, we had ADO, but not ADO.NET. ADO.NET is about as similar to VB6's ADO as VB .NET itself is to VB6, which means that it's completely revamped but sort of familiar. ADO.NET is way more flexible and powerful, but perhaps not as easy to learn at first. Once you do learn it, however, it'll be worth it. It's actually simpler to do many tasks once you understand how to work with the ADO.NET core objects.

What was wrong with ADO? Many of us spent a lot of time coding and becoming proficient in ADO because it had a lot of nice features. The problem was that although ADO had a simple and elegant model and it was straightforward to learn, it simply didn't scale reasonably for large systems and didn't work well with Internet applications. Also, many of the objects performed the same task, which was sometimes confusing when choosing which one to use. The new ADO.NET model has more objects to learn, but allows for much more efficient transfer of data across the Internet and is more flexible *and* very powerful. Of course, the reason for the flexibility and scalability is to provide a set of libraries that will be effective for complex development tasks. You won't necessarily need to use all of the complex capabilities of ADO.NET in order to access and retrieve important data for your tests. You want to get up and running quickly so, in this section, you'll get started with some simple and effective basics.

The ADO.NET programming model has four core objects: the Connection object, the Command object, the DataReader object, and the DataAdapter object. Figure 8-8 displays these major ADO.NET objects, arranged at a high level, to represent the order in which they interact with the database and the target system.

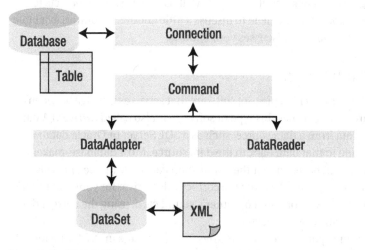

Figure 8-8. *ADO.NET classes*

The database itself is accessed via the Connection object, while the Command object provides methods to retrieve and manipulate data. Once the data is retrieved, it can either be used immediately using a DataReader or stored locally in a DataSet. A DataSet uses XML (eXtensible Markup Language) to organize the data in memory, but for the most part you will not notice this.

To help you to understand these different classes a little better, Table 8-2 lists each of the four core classes used with ADO.NET.

Table 8-2. *The Core ADO.NET Classes*

Object	Description
Connection	Establishes a connection to a specific data source.
Command	Executes a command against a data source.
DataReader	Reads a forward-only, read-only stream of data from a data source (very useful for retrieving information quickly).
DataAdapter	Populates a DataSet and resolves updates with the data source.

Note A fifth class you might consider as a core member would be the DataSet class. While not truly part of ADO.NET, it is most often used with the DataAdapter to hold an updateable copy of the results from a query. In fact, the DataAdapter is really not much use without it. Updates to the results in a DataSet can be sent back to the original data source or saved to a local XML file.

We'll use the Connection object first to establish our link to the database programmatically, the Command object to execute queries, and the DataReader to retrieve the information. The DataAdapter can be used for more complex tasks that require synchronization between a local database and a host data source. Although we will talk about this later, we'll use the first three objects to get up and running quickly. Before we start, we need to discuss a little about the libraries available for data access in .NET. The next section discusses your choices.

Choosing the Correct .NET Data Provider

What's a data provider? A *data provider* is a piece of software that serves as a bridge between an application and a data source. (Sometimes this type of software is also called a *driver*.) A data provider is used to retrieve data from a data source, such as a SQL Server or Oracle database, and to reconcile changes made to that data back to the data source. Most database-makers create data providers for their databases so that the application can serve up (i.e., provide) their information in a common way. Just like using the correct video driver for your computer's video card or the correct sound driver for your computer's sound card, using the correct data provider to connect to your database is important.

You are actually given four separate provider libraries for data access in .NET: one for Microsoft SQL Server; one for Oracle; one for databases that provide OLE DB drivers; and, finally, one for all other ODBC-compliant databases. You could choose to access everything, including SQL Server, using the generic ODBC libraries; however, that wouldn't necessarily be the most efficient way to do it. The four libraries are provided to give you the most efficient access to the database you use. Each library contains all the core objects you looked at in the preceding section, so once the proper library is imported, you'll have very similar code to write no matter which you choose.

Of course, if you are accessing a SQL Server or Oracle database, for greater efficiency you'll want to choose the libraries provided for them since they're optimized for best performance. For all other databases, the next to choose would be the OLE DB library since these libraries are the most current. The ODBC libraries are provided for any database that has not yet created a provider for the new, more efficient OLE DB. Once you've determined which library you want to use, you'll need to create the correct statement to import the library. Table 8-3 lists the four providers and the namespace you'll need to import to use it.

Table 8-3. *The Four .NET Data Provider Libraries*

.NET Framework Data Provider	Namespace to Import
SQL Server	System.Data.SqlClient
Oracle	System.Data.OracleClient
OLE DB	System.Data.OleDB
ODBC	System.Data.Odbc

Using the Connection and Command Objects

The Connection class sets up the information necessary to attach to a database. It has a number of properties available to specify this information, such as username and password, as well as, of course, the location of the database. After creating (often called *instantiating*) the Connection object and setting its properties correctly, you'll call the Open() method of the Connection object, which actually creates the connection to the database and opens it.

Let's recall the code in Chapter 3 to write out test data into a database. Listing 8-1 and Listing 3-10 are essentially the same listing. At that time, we used this code for writing test results into a database. (Notice that we chose to use the System.Data.OleDb libraries since we were writing to a Microsoft Access database.)

Listing 8-1. *Writing Test Results to a Microsoft Access Database*

VB .NET

```
Imports System.Data.OleDb
…
Dim cn As New OleDbConnection _
    ("Provider=Microsoft.jet.oledb.4.0;Data Source=TestResultsDB.mdb")
Dim intRet As Integer
cn.Open()
Dim cmd As New OleDbCommand( _
    "Insert into TestResults (TestID, TestDate, Reqmt, Tester, Result) " & _
    "Values (3, '01-Jan-2006', 'Test Reqmt ABC', 'M. Sweeney', 1)", cn)
```

```
intRet = cmd.ExecuteNonQuery
cn.Close()
```

C#

```
using System.Data.OleDb
...

OleDbConnection cn = new OleDbConnection
    ("Provider=Microsoft.jet.oledb.4.0;Data Source=TestResultsDB.mdb");
int intRet;
cn.Open();
OleDbCommand cmd = new OleDbCommand(
    "Insert into TestResults (TestID, TestDate, Reqmt, Tester, Result) " +
    "Values (3, '01-Jan-2006', 'Test Reqmt ABC', 'M. Sweeney', 1)", cn);
intRet = cmd.ExecuteNonQuery();
cn.Close();
```

This time, we'll focus our attention on the ADO.NET classes used to create this code:

- The first line imports the correct library where the ADO.NET classes reside: System.Data.OleDb.

- The second line declares our ADO.NET Connection object and names it cn. It is in this line that you will need to provide all information necessary to access the database. Any username and password information will be inserted here, depending on the type of database. (This code presumes the default set up for Microsoft Access installations, i.e., no password.) Listing 8-2 displays connection declarations for Oracle and SQL Server databases for both VB .NET and C#.

- The line cn.open will establish the connection to the database using the criteria set up in the preceding line.

- The statement following the Open() method of the Connection object creates a Command object called cmd. This declaration also loads this new Command object with a SQL statement to insert values into the TestResults table. Notice that the very last part of this statement specifies that the cn Connection object is to be used. This is because a Command object can be associated with any connection. This is part of the flexibility of ADO.NET.

- After the Command object is created, it is executed with its ExecuteNonQuery() method, as shown in the following code line:

  ```
  intRet=cmd.ExecuteNonQuery()
  ```

- The ExecuteNonQuery() method is used for queries that will not return any rows from the database. In this case, the Insert method is used. The ExecuteNonQuery() method will return an integer that represents the number of rows affected. In this case, if the Insert executes without error, then a return value of 1 will be returned into the intRet variable.

In Listing 8-1, we imported the OleDb libraries. Listing 8-2 gives you similar code for the other three data providers: Oracle, SQL Server, and ODBC.

Listing 8-2. *Connection String Examples for Various Databases*

VB .NET, SQL Server Connection

```
Imports System.Data.SQLClient
…
Dim nwindConn As SqlConnection = New SqlConnection _
("Data Source=localhost;Integrated Security=SSPI;Initial Catalog=northwind")
nwindConn.Open()
```

VB .NET, Oracle Connection

```
Dim nwindConn As OracleConnection = _
New OracleConnection("Data Source=MyOracleServer;Integrated Security=yes;")
nwindConn.Open()
```

VB .NET, ODBC Connection

```
Dim nwindConn As OdbcConnection = New OdbcConnection _
("Driver={SQL Server};Server=localhost; Trusted_Connection=yes;Database=northwind")
nwindConn.Open()
```

C#, SQL Server Connection

```
using System.Data.SQLClient;
…
SqlConnection nwindConn =
    new SqlConnection("Data Source=localhost; Integrated Security=SSPI;" +
    "Initial Catalog=northwind");
nwindConn.Open();
```

C#, Oracle Connection

```
using System.Data.OracleClient
…
OracleConnection nwindConn =
new OracleConnection("Data Source=MyOracleServer;Integrated Security=yes;");
nwindConn.Open();
```

C#, ODBC Connection

```
using System.Data.Odbc
…
OdbcConnection nwdCn = new OdbcConnection("Driver={SQL Server};Server=localhost;" +
  "Trusted_Connection=yes;Database=northwind");
nwdCn.Open();
```

Although the ODBC connections shown in Listing 8-2 access a SQL Server database, they use a format that can be used with any ODBC-compliant database.

■**Note** For more information on the keywords used for various database systems, go to `http://msdn.` `microsoft.com/library` and do a search on the term *sqldriverconnect.*

Wherever you see the words *localhost* or *MyOracleServer* in the connection strings in Listing 8-2, replace them with the name of your own server. All SQL Server connections are shown using `Trusted_Connection=yes` or `Integrated Security=SSPI`. Both of these will log onto the server using Windows Authentication, which means your Windows logon rather than using a username/password combination. This is a more secure way of coding so that you don't have to embed password information into your code, as long as your database administrator has created a logon for you that maps to your Windows account.

Of course, in order for all of this to work, you must have the appropriate database either installed or accessible across a network. Your project's database administrator will need to create a logon and permissions for you to access the database using your Windows system account or provide a username and password.

Using the DataReader Object

Rather than insert, delete, or update records as you can do with the `Command` object, you may just want to retrieve information about what's in the database. For example, if you've entered some test data from the application's front end, you might want to verify it's really there and in the proper locations in the database. The `DataReader` object can be used to process the results of a SQL statement issued by a `Command` object. (For those of you familiar with previous versions of ADO, this object is the one most similar to the now-obsolete `Recordset` object.) Once you have a set of records for the `DataReader`, you can think of them like a card file of index cards: you can count them, or you can process them one-by-one and look up information in them; or you can print them all out to a file or a form to see what you have. Listing 8-3 shows code to retrieve data from the Customers table in SQL Server's Northwind sample database.

■**Note** With the `DataReader`, it is not necessary to use a `DataSet` as it is when you are using a `DataAdapter`.

Listing 8-3. *Using the DataReader Object*

VB .NET

```
Dim cn As New SqlConnection _
    ("Data Source=localhost;Database=Northwind;Trusted_Connection=Yes")
Dim dr As SqlDataReader
Dim cmd As New SqlCommand( _
    "Select * from customers where ContactName like 'M%' ", cn)
```

```
cn.Open()
dr = cmd.ExecuteReader
if dr.HasRows then
   Do While dr.Read
      Debug.WriteLine(dr.Item("ContactName"))
   Loop
Else
   MessageBox.Show("no rows returned")
End If
dr.Close()
cn.Close()
```

C#

```
//Note: Add a using System.Diagnostics and a using System.Data.SqlClient;
// to the top of your code page.

SqlConnection cn = new SqlConnection
   ("Data Source=localhost;Database=Northwind;Trusted_Connection=Yes");
SqlDataReader dr;
SqlCommand cmd = new SqlCommand
      ("Select * from customers where ContactName like 'M%' ", cn);

cn.Open();
dr = cmd.ExecuteReader();
if (dr.HasRows)
   while (dr.Read()==true)
   {
      Debug.WriteLine(dr.GetString(dr.GetOrdinal("ContactName")));
   }
else
   MessageBox.Show("no rows returned");
dr.Close();
cn.Close();
```

___

Note We had to add the using System.Diagnostics and using System.Data.SqlClient; directives to the top of our code page when using C#, but not when coding in VB .NET. Also, C# cannot access the Item property as VB .NET can. So, we had to call the GetOrdinal() method along with the GetString() method to accomplish the same task. This same code also works in VB .NET, but calling the Item property was less cumbersome.

___

The code in Listing 8-3 first declares a Connection object, and then a DataReader and Command object in the next two lines. Notice that after the connection is opened, the ExecuteReader() method of the Command object is called. This method creates a DataReader object in memory.

■**Note** It may seem a bit odd, but you cannot create a new DataReader object directly from the DataReader class. That is why you do not see the new keyword used when we declared the dr variable. We can, however, reference the object that ExecuteReader creates for us by assigning the dr variable to it. This is a behavior you may see in a number of places throughout .NET.

Using the DataReader object, you can execute a loop to run through each row retrieved by the SQL query "Select * from customers where ContactName like 'M%' ". This SQL query, by the way, will return all rows in the Customers table for which the ContactName column has a value that starts with the letter "M". Using the Debug.WriteLine() method, the results are printed into the Immediate window, but you could use this data in many different ways by capturing it into a string variable. The complete syntax for all of the properties and methods of the DataReader and Command objects can be found by exploring the ADO.NET type library in the Object Browser. Although, to use these properly, you will have to spend considerable time studying more about them (see Appendix C for good sources to learn more).

Listing 8-3 used the ExecuteReader() method of the Command object to give us a set of records. In Exercise 3-3, you were introduced to the ExecuteScalar() method of the Command object without much fanfare. Let's revisit the ExecuteScalar() method and see how it can be used in a test situation.

Suppose that one test requirement is to determine that a certain number of rows exist in a table within the database. The code in Listing 8-4 will open the database, count the number of rows in a table, and determine whether or not the actual number of rows found is equivalent to what is expected.

Listing 8-4. *Testing the Northwind Sample Database by Verifying Rowcount in the Customers Table*

VB .NET

```
Dim cn As New SqlConnection( _
    "Data Source=localhost;Database=Northwind;Trusted_Connection=Yes")
Dim intRet As Int16
Dim cmd As New SqlCommand("Select count(*) from customers", cn)
Const EXPECTED As Integer = 91 'set number of expected items
cn.Open()
intRet = cmd.ExecuteScalar
If intRet = EXPECTED Then
    MessageBox.Show("Test passed; Expected: " & EXPECTED & " Actual: " & intRet)
Else
    MessageBox.Show("Test failed; Expected: " + EXPECTED + " Actual: " + intRet)
End If
cn.Close()
```

C#

```
//Note: Add a using System.Diagnostics and a using System.Data.SqlClient;
// to the top of your code page.
```

```
SqlConnection cn = new SqlConnection
    ("Data Source=localhost;Database=Northwind;Trusted_Connection=Yes");
Int16 intRet;
SqlCommand cmd = new SqlCommand("Select count(*) from customers", cn);
const int EXPECTED = 91;
cn.Open();
intRet = Convert.ToInt16 (cmd.ExecuteScalar());
if (intRet == EXPECTED)
{
    MessageBox.Show("Test passed; Expected: " + EXPECTED + " Actual: " + intRet);
}
else
{
    MessageBox.Show("Test failed; Expected: " + EXPECTED + " Actual: " + intRet);
}
cn.Close();
```

The code in Listing 8-4 is pretty simple, yet effective. It calls the ExecuteScalar() method of the Command object. The ExecuteScalar() method returns an integer value that is the result of the SQL statement executed. In this case, the SQL statement is one that returns the number of rows in the Customers table. This value is compared to an expected value that is loaded into a constant called EXPECTED. If the two values are the same, then the program indicates a pass result; otherwise, it returns a failure. Keep in mind that you could use the logging techniques learned in Chapter 3 to also log this result to a file or a database. We're keeping it simple here for demonstration purposes. Another upgrade for this code would be to read the expected value from a textbox rather than use a constant—this would make the code more flexible.

Now you're ready to try out another example of working with ADO.NET. Exercise 8-3 will help cement your knowledge of ADO.NET for test situations. There will be many times, if you do a significant amount of work with the database, that you will find yourself using both the Database Explorer window and ADO.NET code in conjunction with each other. In Exercise 8-3, you will practice doing both.

Exercise 8-3: Querying a Database Using ADO.NET

The purpose of Exercise 8-3 is to increase your familiarity with ADO.NET programming and the use of the Database Explorer. You will write ADO.NET code to accomplish a simple test to verify the existence and amount of test data added into your database. You will also modify the data in the database directly by adding some test data using the database and then rerunning your ADO.NET code to verify the new data entered correctly.

1. Start a new Visual Studio Windows Forms project and name it **MaxOrdersTest**.

2. Add one button and a listbox control to the form. In the Properties window, change the following properties of these two new buttons and the listbox according to Table 8-4. You can arrange and size these controls any way you like but be sure to enlarge the listbox so that it's relatively large and wide.

Table 8-4. *Controls and Associated Properties for Exercise 8-3*

Control	Name Property	Text Property
listBox1	lstResults	
Button1	cmdADO	Start test

■**Caution** The listbox name starts with the letter l, not the number 1!

---

3. Open the code window for the form. On the top of the code window, you will need to add the following statements (in their usual locations):

VB .NET

```
Imports System.Data.OleDb
```

C#

```
using System.Data.OleDb;
```

4. Now you will need to move the Microsoft Access database into the correct location. Chapter 8's exercise folder contains a copy of the Northwind.mdb database. Locate this file, then copy and paste it into the bin directory of your project. You can accomplish this several ways, including just copying and pasting the file using Windows Explorer. However, the easiest way to accomplish this is to click Show All Files in the Solution Explorer window, then locate the bin folder and the Debug folder within it. Right-click the Debug folder and choose Add Existing Item. Navigate to the exercise folder for Chapter 8 and select the Northwind.mdb database. This will add the database to your project. (You will possibly have a Wizard dialog display. You can simply dismiss this dialog by clicking Cancel.)

5. Next, you will add ADO code to the Click event of the cmdADO button to open a connection to the Microsoft Access Northwind sample database. You will then add code to execute a SQL statement that will return the most recently ordered items from the Orders table into the Listbox control (see the "*SQL Statements for Testing*" section earlier in this chapter), as well as add code to report the number of records found into a message box.

   Type the code in Listing 8-5 into to the cmdADO_Click event.

Listing 8-5. *Code to Add to the cmdADO_Click Event*

VB .NET

```
Dim cn As New OleDbConnection _
 ("Provider=Microsoft.jet.oledb.4.0;Data Source=Northwind.mdb")
Dim dr As OleDbDataReader
Dim intCount As Int16 = 0

cn.Open()
Dim cmd As New OleDbCommand
```

```vbnet
cmd.CommandText = _
  "SELECT Orderid, Orderdate FROM Orders " & _
  "WHERE orderdate=(SELECT MAX(orderdate) FROM orders)"
cmd.Connection = cn
dr = cmd.ExecuteReader
If dr.HasRows Then
  Do While dr.Read
    lstResults.Items.Add(dr.Item("OrderID").ToString + " " + _
    dr.Item("Orderdate").ToString)
    intCount += 1
  Loop
  MessageBox.Show(intCount.ToString & " rows qualified")
Else
  MessageBox.Show("no rows returned")
End If
dr.Close()
cn.Close()
```

C#

```csharp
OleDbConnection cn = new OleDbConnection(
    "Provider=Microsoft.jet.oledb.4.0;Data Source=Northwind.mdb");
OleDbDataReader dr;
Int16 intCount = 0;
cn.Open();
OleDbCommand cmd = new OleDbCommand();
cmd.CommandText = "SELECT Orderid, Orderdate FROM Orders " +
    "WHERE orderdate = (SELECT MAX(orderdate) FROM orders)";
cmd.Connection = cn;
dr = cmd.ExecuteReader();
if (dr.HasRows)
{
    while (dr.Read())
    {
        lstResults.Items.Add
          (dr.GetInt32(dr.GetOrdinal("OrderID")) +
            " " + dr.GetDateTime(dr.GetOrdinal("Orderdate")));
        intCount += 1;
    }
    MessageBox.Show(intCount + " rows qualified");
}
else
{
    MessageBox.Show("no rows returned");
}
dr.Close();
cn.Close();
```

6. Compile, test, debug, and run your new application.

7. Now open the Database Explorer window. Use the existing connection you created earlier in this chapter to access the same database (see Exercise 8-1) and display the SQL pane in the Database Explorer window.

8. You will enter a new row into the Orders table using a SQL statement. This row will have an OrderDate column equal to today's date so it will show up in your query to return most recent orders. Erase whatever value is in the SQL pane and type the following SQL Insert statement into the SQL pane:

```
INSERT INTO Orders
    (orderid, customerid, employeeid, orderdate, requireddate, shipvia )
VALUES (77777, 'BONAP', 7, Now, Now+2, 2)
```

Note The Now function is specific to Microsoft Access. It returns today's date. Now+2 would insert today's date plus two days (or the day after tomorrow) into the required date field.

---

9. Right-click in the SQL pane and select Execute SQL from the pop-up menu to execute this query (or you can select this command from the Query Designer menu). If you have any problems, check the syntax and try again. Once the query has successfully run, you will receive a message box saying, "1 row affected by last query." This means the new row was inserted correctly. Click OK to dismiss this message box.

   Try inserting again by simply changing the values in the SQL Insert statement. Be sure to change the first value (77777) to something else. This value is associated with the primary-key field and can't be duplicated in the table. You can also try adding rows to the table by simply adding them to the last row in the Query Designer's Results pane.

10. Now run your project again. Your test results should now show a number that verifies the number of rows *you* inserted today via the Database Explorer window.

Once again, you can add test logging and error handling to make this code more useful and robust.

In this exercise, you wrote a program that accessed a database and executed a SQL query to return the most recently entered data. You then compared this result to the rows entered into the database. With only a little modification, you can change this code to access your own database. Then you could use this as a little utility to verify the entry of test data into the database from the application's front end.

The code in Listing 8-6 shows the same functionality for your code in Exercise 8-3 only it uses a Microsoft SQL Server connection.

Listing 8-6. *SQL Server Code for the MaxOrdersTest*

VB .NET

```vbnet
Dim cn As New SqlConnection( _
    "Data Source=localhost;Database=Northwind;Trusted_Connection=Yes")
Dim dr As SqlDataReader
Dim intCount As Int16 = 0

cn.Open()
Dim cmd As New SqlCommand
cmd.CommandText = _
 "SELECT Orderid, Orderdate FROM Orders " & _
         "WHERE orderdate=(SELECT MAX(orderdate) FROM orders)"
cmd.Connection = cn
dr = cmd.ExecuteReader
If dr.HasRows Then
    Do While dr.Read
        lstResults.Items.Add(dr.Item("OrderID").ToString + " " + _
            dr.Item("Orderdate").ToString)
            intCount += 1
    Loop
    MessageBox.Show(intCount.ToString & " rows qualified")
Else
    MessageBox.Show("no rows returned")
End If
dr.Close()
cn.Close()
```

C#

```csharp
SqlConnection cn = new SqlConnection
  ("Data Source=localhost;Database=Northwind;Trusted_Connection=Yes");
SqlDataReader dr;
Int16 intCount = 0;
cn.Open();
SqlCommand cmd = new SqlCommand();
cmd.CommandText = "SELECT Orderid, Orderdate FROM Orders " +
    "WHERE orderdate = (SELECT MAX(orderdate) FROM orders)";
cmd.Connection = cn;
dr = cmd.ExecuteReader();
if (dr.HasRows)
{
```

```
    while (dr.Read())
     {
        lstResults.Items.Add
            (dr.GetInt32 (dr.GetOrdinal("OrderID"))
                + " " + dr.GetDateTime(dr.GetOrdinal ("Orderdate")));
        intCount += 1;
        }
      MessageBox.Show(intCount + " rows qualified");
 }
 else
 {
      MessageBox.Show("no rows returned");
   }
dr.Close();
cn.Close();
```

There's much more to learn about ADO.NET, how much you need to learn will depend on the complexity of the application you are testing and the test requirements. There are more references for ADO.NET in Appendix C. You are not quite done learning about ADO.NET though. There are some new controls available in Visual Studio's web applications that can be very useful. You'll look at those next.

Database Testing Using the ASP.NET Data Source Controls

So far, all of your database testing has used a Windows Form application. Of course, you can do essentially the same tasks using a Console or Web application. Additionally for Web applications, there are a few new controls available for web development that make database access a lot easier. As you will see in Chapter 9, a .NET web application can use scripts to link to, open, extract, and iterate records in a database, but all of this processing has been encapsulated in single controls coded declaratively on the web page. You can add these data source controls directly to your web page and set properties that they will use to handle retrieving and displaying the data you want.

The available data source controls are the following:

- Access data source control

- SQL data source control

- XML data source control

- Object data source control

The Access data source control is used specifically to connect to Microsoft Access databases. The SQL data source control, however, isn't just for Microsoft SQL Server databases; you can also use it for any database. It can be set up to use any of the four connection libraries: OleDb, ODBC, SqlClient, and OracleClient. The XML data source control can be used with XML data stores. The Object data source control is intended for use with middleware objects, such as classes and class libraries and other components.

To give you a feel for using these data source controls, in this section we'll demonstrate using the Access data source control.

Using the Access Data Source Control

The easiest way to see how to use these source controls is to try them. To try the Access data source control, follow these steps:

1. Create a new web page application (see Exercise 2-4).

2. Switch to Design view. In the Toolbox window, collapse the Standard Tools tab and then expand the Data Tools tab (see Figure 8-9).

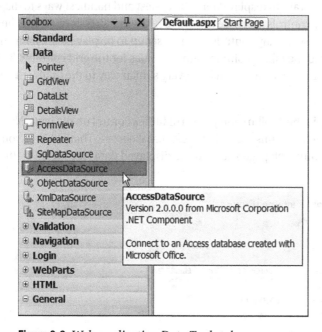

Figure 8-9. *Web application Data Tools tab*

Adding a data source control to a web page adds an unremarkable gray box to the form that will not display when the page is rendered. This gray box contains more power than it appears to! It provides hooks into ADO.NET so that all you'll have to do is set a few key properties in order to get into a database.

3. Next, you'll set the necessary properties, as shown in Table 8-5.

Table 8-5. *Properties to Set for the AccessDataSource Control*

Property	Value
Datafile	~/Northwind.mdb
SelectCommand	Select CompanyName, Country from Customers where Country = 'USA'

If you look at this in Source mode, you'll see the following HTML code:

```
<asp:AccessDataSource ID="AccessDataSource1" runat="server"
    SelectCommand="Select CompanyName, Country from Customers where Country = 'USA'"
    DataFile="~/Northwind.mdb">
</asp:AccessDataSource>
```

Notice that the DataFile parameter is set up to access the Northwind database, but the tilde (~) indicates that the file will be residing within this application. To make this happen, take the Northwind.mdb file that is located in the Chapter8\Exercises folder, copy it, and paste it into the folder for this web site.

All you've done is set up access to a data source. Next, you'll need a control for displaying the data. There's a lot of ways to display data—the easiest and handiest ways to display it are to use the display controls available in ASP.NET. The GridView is one of the best and easiest to use of these display controls since it's set up to display all the data and even automatically grab the table's column names as titles for the grid columns. The other display controls bind to a data source in a very similar way to the GridView, so it's a good one to learn.

Return to the Data tab in the Toolbox and place a GridView control on the page. Now set the DataSourceID property for this control to AccessDataSource1. That's it! Now you should be able to run your web page and view the displayed data (see Figure 8-10).

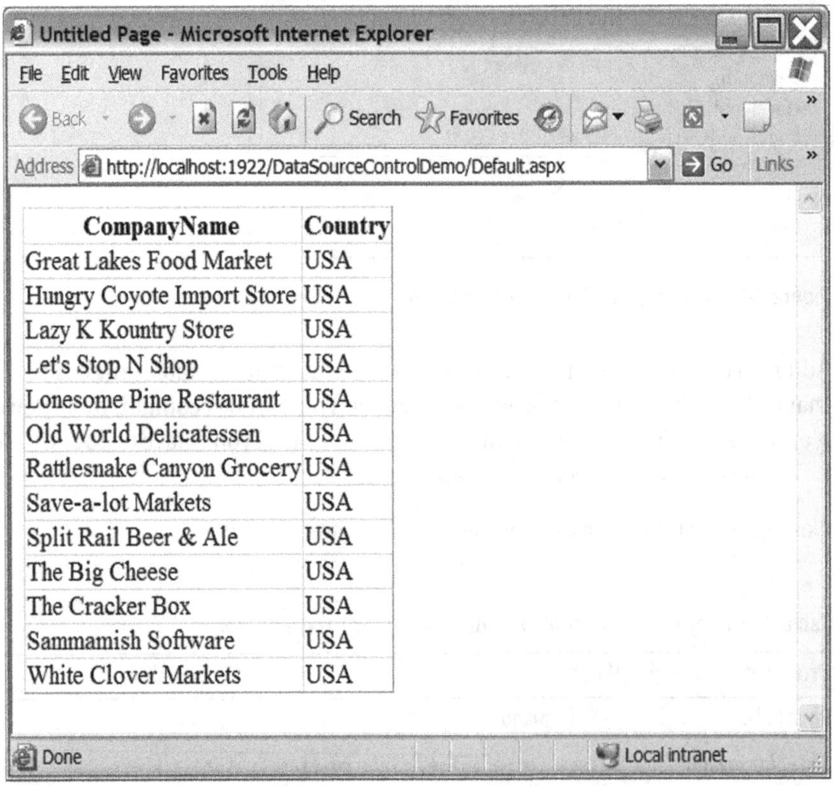

Figure 8-10. *Displaying data with the AccessDataSource and GridView controls*

As you can see, these controls can be an efficient way to work with data. Simply changing the SQL statement can retrieve the information you want. This is an excellent way to set up and work with data without having to learn a formalized tool interface.

Working with DataGrids

Although the ASP.NET data source control is an easy way to add data connectivity to a web page, it does not work with Windows applications. Not to worry though, with just a bit of extra work you can include a DataGrid in your Windows applications that will perform just as well, if not better. In fact, DataGrids come in many different versions for both Web and Windows applications. All the versions of DataGrids are simple to use and have advanced features that do not exist in the ASP.NET data source control. Although the different versions may have other names, like DataGridView for one, they all work pretty much the same. To make things simple, we will collectively refer to the different versions as DataGrids.

DataGrids use a DataSet as the source of their data. A DataSet is an object that can hold one or more DataTable objects. Each DataTable object is connected to the original data source, most often a relational database table, by an individual DataAdapter object. The DataAdapter itself uses four ADO.NET Command objects to work with the data source. Each of these Command objects are mapped to a SQL statement that provides the function of a Select, Insert, Update, or Delete statement. These DataTable objects can be used to fill not only DataGrids, but also ComboBoxes and ListBoxes as well (see Figure 8-11).

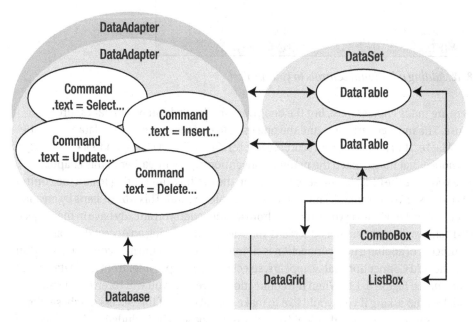

Figure 8-11. *DataAdapters and the DataSet*

Setting Up the DataAdapter

Although it may *look* complex, actually using a DataAdapter and DataSet is quite easy once you know where to find the proper controls. To start with, you will need to add a DataAdapter to the toolbox. This is different than in previous versions of Visual Studio where this control is in the toolbox by default. To add an item to the toolbox, use the Tools ➤ Choose Toolbox Items menu item. It may take a few seconds for the dialog box to open, but when it does you will be able to add a number of .NET (and earlier COM) controls to your project (see Figure 8-12). As you scroll thorough the items in the dialog box, you will also see various DataGrids that you can reference as well. Depending on the version of Visual Studio you have, these may or may not be added to the toolbox already. Items that are already added have a check mark next to them.

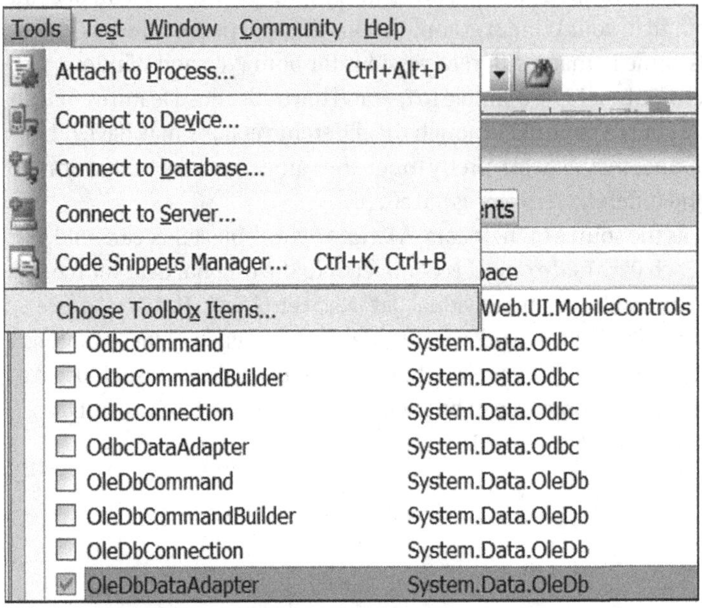

Figure 8-12. *Adding additional controls to your project*

There are many choices here, but the one you want depends on which data source you want to use. The most generic one, and the one used to connect to an Access database, is the OleDbDataAdapter, but there is also an OdbcDataAdapter, OracleDataAdapter, and SQLDataAdapter. You may notice that these match the naming conventions you saw earlier in this chapter.

Once you have the OleDbDataAdapter control in the toolbox, attempting to add the control to your Windows or Web Form will launch the Data Adapter Wizard. This wizard starts by creating a Connection object or allowing you to choose from a connection you already have in the project. Figure 8-13 shows the different dialog screens you will see when using an Access database.

The process of adding a new connection is simple. Just click on the new connection button and when the Add Connection dialog appears, select the proper provider from the Data Source listbox (again, see Figure 8-13). When the connection is created, you will receive a message from Visual Studio asking if you would like to make a local copy of this Access database. You will choose Yes if you want an individual copy of this database to be included with all copies of your testware program. If you expect there to be a copy already on the computer or if a single file will be accessed over a network share, you'll choose No (see Figure 8-14).

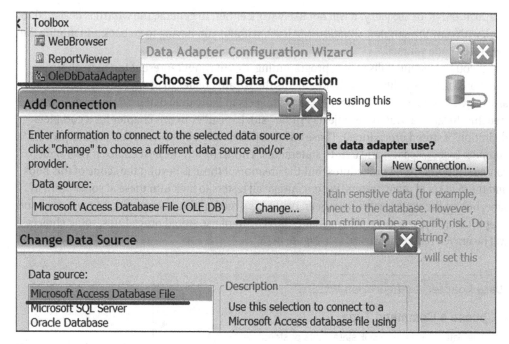

Figure 8-13. *Starting the Data Adapter Configuration Wizard*

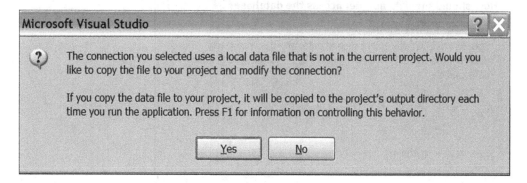

Figure 8-14. *Choosing to create a local copy*

Now that the connection is established, the wizard will move you on to the next choice—that of the data you wish to access. The data will be accessed though a Command object whose CommandText property is set to a SQL Select command. When the wizard is done, it will also have created three other Command objects, unless you tell it otherwise. Modifications are done through these other Command objects, which are set to use an individual Insert, Update, or Delete SQL statement—one for each object.

Although you may not know much about all of these types of statements, the wizard can create them for you so you don't have to. It does so by examining the query you use and creating the appropriate SQL code to match it. You should be aware that although this is a time-saver for the beginner, it will only work when you use a relatively simple table or query, such as one that accesses a single table. However, if the table has complex data types or uses complex database objects for validation logic, the wizard will not be able to create SQL code that actually works without modification. Also, if the query you use involves a complex SQL statement, such as a Join, Union, or Subquery, it will not likely work either. In general, the wizard is designed to work with only the simplest situations. At least, without you having to go back and modify the generated code yourself.

If you have some skills in SQL programming, this may not represent too big a chore for you. You can just modify the SQL statements the wizard creates to fit your needs. The wizard also allows you to map the different Command objects to individual database *stored procedures* (see the "Relational Database Objects Primer" sidebar earlier in this chapter for a complete definition of stored procedures). These advanced database objects are often used to process complex Insert, Update, and Delete statements. This is, by far, the best choice if your data source supports stored procedures, but the creation of these is beyond the scope of this book and the skill set of many testers. We encourage all testers to look into these at some point in time, but for the examples we have been using, it's a moot point anyway, since Access does not support stored procedures. When a data source cannot use stored procedures, some choices will be grayed out in the wizard (see Figure 8-15).

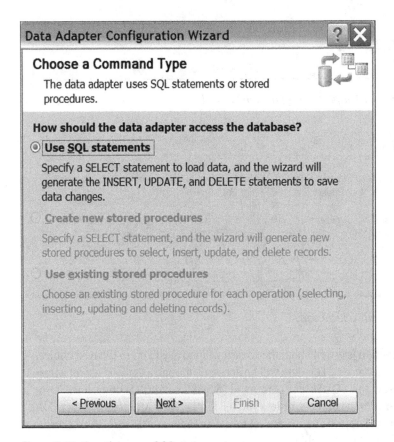

Figure 8-15. *Creating your SQL statements*

When you click the Next button, you will find a window that allows you to type in a SQL Select statement. If you know the syntax for the statement you want, you can just type it in; If you do not, then you can click on the Query Builder button (see Figure 8-16). This button takes you to the Query Builder dialog screen you saw earlier in this chapter.

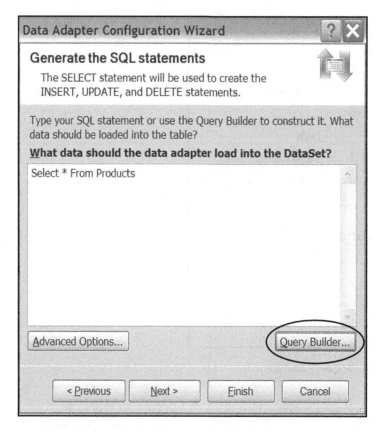

Figure 8-16. *Writing the SQL Select statement*

If you click the Query Builder button and the screen is blank, you can add the table you want to query by right-clicking the upper area and selecting the Add Table menu item (see Figure 8-17). When the table appears, you can choose to return all of the columns or only a select few. As you make your selections, you will see a SQL statement created in the lower pane.

When you're done using the Query Builder, you will be returned to the previous screen. At the bottom of that screen, you will see an Advanced button. This button opens yet another dialog screen that allows you to disable the creations of the Insert, Update, and Delete commands we mentioned earlier (see Figure 8-18). This is a good option when you want your DataGrid to display information, but not allow users to change the data. This choice seems pretty easy to understand, but the additional options on this screen may be a little more confusing. For instance, the Use Optimistic Concurrency check box allows you to change the way certain errors are reported to the application. It is an advanced concept dealing with database locking behavior and not something you need to worry about right now. The Refresh The DataSet option adds a SQL Select in addition to the Insert, Update, and Delete commands the wizard normally utilizes. This means that after each of the statements, the Command object would also run a Select statement that would refresh the DataGrid. Both of these options should be left as they are until you become more experienced with these types of applications.

Figure 8-17. *Adding a table to the Query Builder*

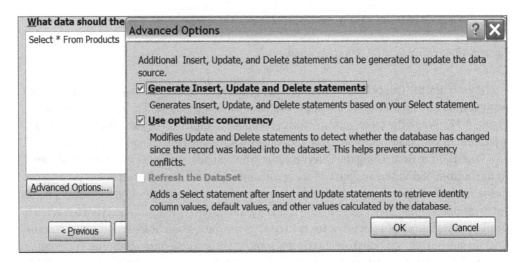

Figure 8-18. *Using the Advanced options*

After closing the Advanced Options dialog, clicking the Next button will take you to a Summary dialog, and clicking the Finish button there completes the configurations you have chosen.

Filling the DataSet

With the DataAdapter configured, you are ready to create a DataSet. The DataSet is an object that holds the result of your Select statement in memory. Each DataSet can hold one or more results using a collection of DataTable objects. These DataTable objects are designed to mimic the way tables in a database are used.

Just as in a relational database, the creation of a table starts by defining one or more columns. Each column of the table needs to describe what type of data is allowed within itself. This is done by specifying the data type of the column.

You can set the data types of these columns in one of two ways. The first way is to let .NET figure it out for you as it loads the data into the DataSet. The second way is to predefine it yourself. This second way takes a bit more work, but it allows you to restrict what is legal to load into the column.

For example, let's say you have an application that creates a DataTable with two columns: one for Id, and one for Severity. (This DataTable might hold a list of Severity levels your test lab uses to describe the bugs you find.) It would be natural to have a restriction that only numbers can be loaded into the Id column and only character data can be loaded into the Severity column. If you choose the first option mentioned, then .NET chooses the column data types when the data is loaded into the DataTable. This being the case, you might end up with different data types being chosen if the data sources are changed between tests. Any errors in this example will not happen upon loading the data; the DataTable will just contain columns with data types based on the new data source and not necessarily the ones you had originally intended. Depending on how the application is programmed, this may or may not cause an error. Still it does introduce the possibility of a bug in you program, so you may want to avoid this option for anything but very simple testware.

The better option is to define the data types for your columns when you design the DataTables. In .NET, this is done by creating an XML schema. DataSets that have a schema are referred to as *typed* DataSets; ones that do not are referred to as *untyped*.

An *XML schema* is a text file that describes the order and data types of XML elements. XML elements are what make up an XML document, such as the following example. Looking at this, you can see that the Id and Severity elements are defined in the schema as using an int and a string, respectively.

An XML Document

```
<?xml version="1.0" encoding="utf-8" ?>
<root>
  <Id>100</Id>
  <Severity>Bad</Severity>
  <Id>200</Id>
  <Severity>Really Bad</Severity>
  <Id>300</Id>
  <Severity>OMG</Severity>
</root>
```

An XML Schema

```xml
<?xml version="1.0" encoding="utf-8"?>
<xs:schema attributeFormDefault="unqualified" elementFormDefault="qualified"
 xmlns:xs="http://www.w3.org/2001/XMLSchema">
  <xs:element name="root">
    <xs:complexType>
      <xs:sequence>
        <xs:choice maxOccurs="unbounded">
          <xs:element name="Id" type="xs:int" />
          <xs:element name="Severity" type="xs:string" />
        </xs:choice>
      </xs:sequence>
    </xs:complexType>
  </xs:element>
</xs:schema>
```

Microsoft utilizes both XML and XML schemas when creating the DataSet by creating all of the objects inside of it using an XML format. Using XML has a number of advantages. For one, you can load an XML document directly into a DataSet by using the DataSet's ReadXML() method. You can also save the contents of your DataSet to an XML document by using the WriteXML() method. This handy feature also allows you to load data from a relational database into a DataSet and save that data into an XML file. The XML file can, in turn, be loaded back into the DataSet at a later date, and changes to the XML file can be updated back into the original database. While you may not create this type of application for your testware, you can bet that developers of data-driven applications find this an attractive option.

Although you may not know how to create an XML schema yourself, Visual Studio can create one for you with just a few mouse clicks. To have Visual Studio create a schema, all you need to do is right-click on the DataAdapter in the component tray and select Generate DataSet. You have to do this after you run its configuration wizard so that .NET knows what data to expect. The component tray is the area at the bottom of the Form Designer screen—right below your Windows or Web Form (see Figure 8-19). This area is the place Visual Studio puts controls that have no visual representation on the loaded form.

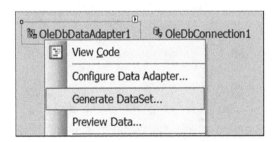

Figure 8-19. *Creating a DataSet*

After you click on this menu item, you will be presented with the Generate DataSet dialog (see Figure 8-20). This screen lets you specify a name for your DataSet and the DataTables within it by checking the tables mapped to one or more DataAdapters. Each DataTable is connected to only one DataAdapter. So, if you have two tables you want loaded into the DataSet, you should create both DataAdapters before launching this dialog and checking both of them from the list of DataAdapters. However, you can also start this dialog twice: the first time creating the new DataSet, and the second time using the existing one.

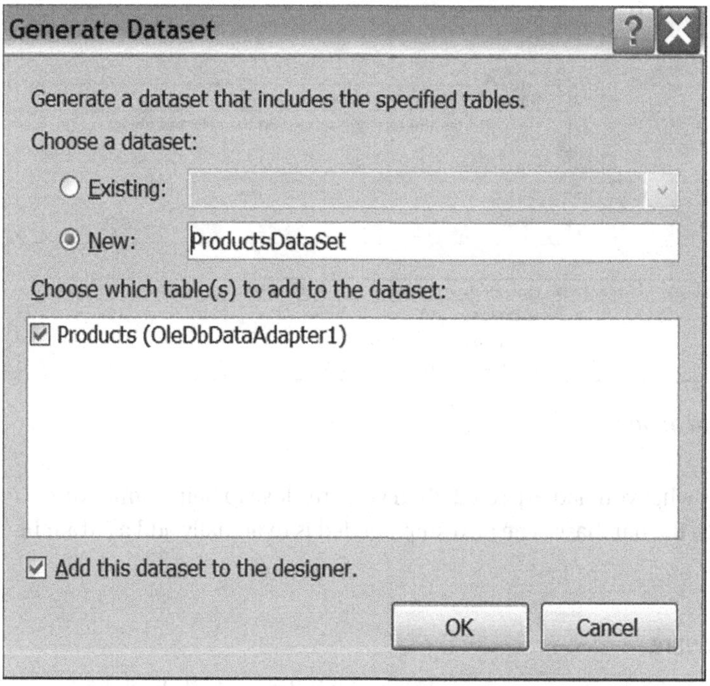

Figure 8-20. *Using the Generate DataSet dialog*

Loading multiple results into one DataSet provides you with several powerful options. Options you could use to create a whole relational database within a DataSet if you worked hard enough. Still, if you are just starting out using DataSets, it may be best to use only simple options until you gain more programming experience.

You may notice that in Figure 8-20, we are using only one DataAdapter, which will create a single DataTable within the DataSet, called the Products table. We even named the DataSet ProductsDataSet to indicate that it holds only product information.

Once the DataSet is created, you will see an icon for it in the component tray. Note that the name of this icon is called ProductsDataSet1 and not ProductsDataSet. This is because Visual Studio created a new class called ProductsDataSet and added it to the project, but this icon is representing an object made from the new class. This class inherits from Microsoft's generic DataSet class, but contains the customization needed to work with your DataAdapters. The class file, along a new XML schema file, is normally hidden from sight in Visual Studio. If you would like to see what they look like, clicking the View All button in Solution Explorer will display these files. Be aware, that these files are quite advanced so, again, we caution you not to work with them directly until you have more skills in this area.

When you have completed making the DataSet, you will want to test it to make sure all of your steps have been successful. Microsoft includes a Preview Data menu option (again, see Figure 8-19), when you right-click the DataAdapter, that is perfect for this task. Selecting this option shows a new dialog that allows you to load the results from the query into a temporary

DataSet (see Figure 8-21). You can choose to load it as a typed or untyped DataSet. Clicking the Preview button allows you to see if the data you are going to get back is consistent with what you had planned.

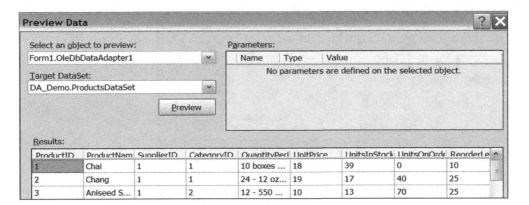

Figure 8-21. *The Preview Data dialog*

If the previewed data is what you had expected, then you are close to being done with linking a DataGrid control to the database. The next step needed is to actually add a DataGrid control to the form.

Adding a Grid to Your Testware

We have been using the DataGrid class as an example because it is the original class of this type used in the previous versions of Visual Studio .NET. In truth, however, there are now a number of similar controls included with Visual Studio 2005. These new controls have additional features, and they allow you to configure them easier than before. You can choose to add both the old and new versions to the toolbox just as you did with the DataAdapter (see Figure 8-22).

Name	Namespace	Assembly Name
☐ DatabaseLogOnList	CrystalDecisions.Reporting.WebCo...	CrystalDecisions.Web (10.2.3600.0)
☑ DataGrid	System.Windows.Forms	System.Windows.Forms.DataGrid (1.0.500...
☑ DataGrid	System.Windows.Forms	System.Windows.Forms.DataGrid (2.0.0.0)
☐ DataGrid	System.Windows.Forms	System.Windows.Forms (2.0.0.0)
☐ DataGrid	System.Web.UI.WebControls	System.Web (2.0.0.0)
☑ DataGridView	System.Windows.Forms	System.Windows.Forms (2.0.0.0)

Figure 8-22. *Selecting from the various DataGrids*

By default, the control that comes in the toolbox is the new DataGridView for Windows applications and the GridView for Web applications. We showed you an example using the GridView earlier in the "Using the Access Data Source Control" section, so let's look at how to use the DataGridView now.

The first step is to add the DataGridView to the form you are using. After you add this control, Visual Studio will display a configuration pop-up menu. If you click away from this control without using the menu first, it will disappear. You can display it again by clicking on the very small arrow at the upper-right corner of the DataGridView control (see Figure 8-23).

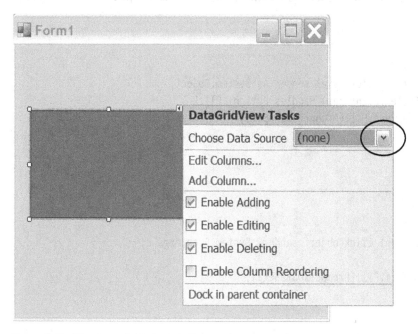

Figure 8-23. *The DataGridView Tasks menu*

From the pop-up menu, you can map a data source to the DataGridView by opening the drop-down menu You want to use the Products table in our example, so you would click on the Project Data Sources in the tree view then expand the DataSet icon until you see the Products table listed (see Figure 8-24).

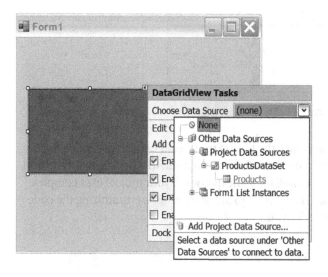

Figure 8-24. *Choosing a data source*

Once the DataGridView is mapped to a data source, in this case the Products table in the DataSet, you need to tell the DataAdapter to fill up the table. You can do this simply by adding a button to the form and having it run the Fill() method of the DataAdapter class. If you had created other controls on the form, such as a ComboBox or a ListBox, and mapped them to the Products table as well, you would see these controls fill with data too, just using this single command.

VB. NET

```
Public Class Form1
  Private Sub Button1_Click(ByVal sender As System.Object, _
    ByVal e As System.EventArgs) Handles Button1.Click
      OleDbDataAdapter1.Fill(ProductsDataSet1)
  End Sub
End Class
```

C#

```
public class Form1
{
  private void Button1_Click(object sender, System.EventArgs e)
  {
    OleDbDataAdapter1.Fill(ProductsDataSet1);
  }
}
```

One final thing you might want to do is anchor the DataGridView to the four sides of the Windows Form. This will make it expand along with the Form, thereby allowing you to see more of the data. To set this, right-click the DataGridView and select Properties from the menu. Then, locate the Anchor property and use the visual control to set the property, as shown in Figure 8-25.

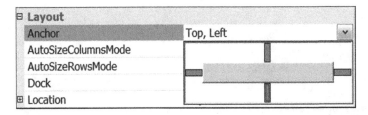

Figure 8-25. *Setting the Anchor property*

When all is set, run the project and click the button to see your results (see Figure 8-26). The data should display within the DataGridView. You can even edit that data from this control, but keep in mind this option only works well for some queries. If your project uses complex SQL queries to create your DataSets, you will have to invest more time customizing the code the wizards and dialog screens created for you.

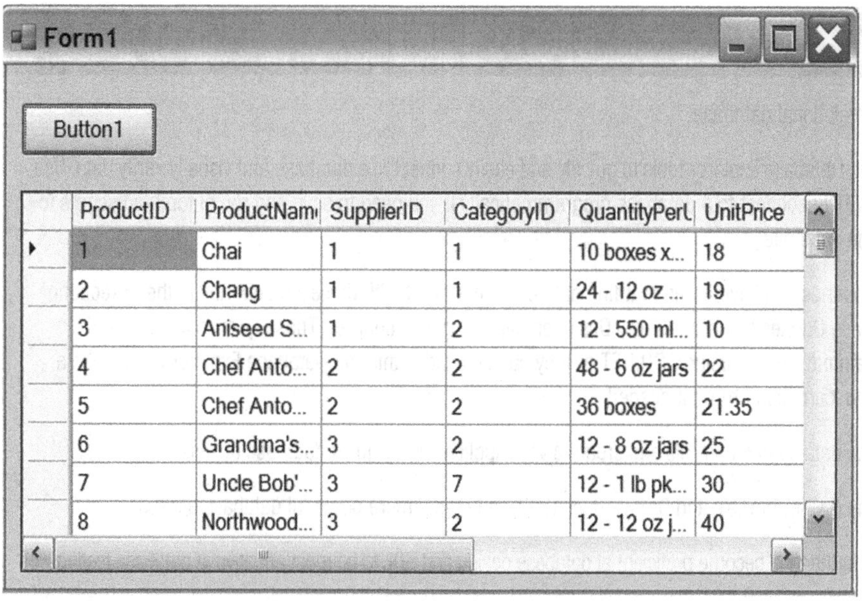

Figure 8-26. *The completed DataGridView form*

As you can see, DataGrids make it easy to display data from a database. Since storing and retrieving data from a database is a common testing task, and since testware development budgets are usually tight or nonexistent, you may find these tools both quick and useful.

Summary

This chapter has been an introduction to using the power of .NET and Visual Studio to access and work with databases on a test project. In the process, you've been introduced to the Database Explorer tool, a few of ADO.NET's major objects, and both the ASP.NET data source controls and the more advanced DataAdapter/DataSet controls. With all of this, you've still only just touched the tip of the iceberg. This topic is large enough to span an entire book. We encourage you to follow up our primer with continued practice and study. There are more resources for the database application tester and, specifically, the .NET tester. Check out QA Forums (www.qaforums.com) and other testing groups for links to database testing resources. Our resource list in Appendix C will help you in this next step.

Tester's Checklist

When testing a relational database,

☑ Use the Database Explorer tools to quickly and easily connect to a database and visually verify data. Use ADO.NET to connect to a database programmatically if you need to save and run automated scripts to test the database.

☑ Save queries you have found that find data problems. Start with those SQL queries in the "Executing Database Queries Using the Query Designer" section of this chapter. These queries can be used programmatically by using ADO.NET or they can be used within the Database Explorer tools. Take a class to learn about more if needed.

☑ Use the data source controls and create a web application for quick database access.

☑ Use the `DataAdapter` and `DataSet` controls and create more powerful database access.

☑ Study further and become proficient at database design and SQL to be most effective at database testing.

∎∎∎

CHAPTER 9

Creating Web-Based Testware

Web-based testware can be a useful addition to any test lab. On top of that, they are fun to make! The downside is that in order to build web-based testware you need to have skills in a number of different technologies. In addition, to be an effective web tester, you really need to know a number of fundamental concepts involving how these web technologies work.

Even though, nowadays, web applications are used all of the time, not many people understand what is actually happening when they use them. In this chapter, you will look at how web applications work. You will see how multilayered applications are designed and how the different layers affect testing professionals. Of course, you will also see how you can build web-based testware and then add database connectivity and validation components to it.

Objectives

By the end of this chapter, you will be able to do the following:

- Explain how web pages run on a web server

- Explain what 2-tier, 3-tier, and N-tier applications are

- Create a data-driven ASP.NET web application

- Explain how components are used with web applications

- Use tracing commands with your web pages

- Deploy an ASP.NET web application

Web Technology Overview

Using a web application has its advantages: you get interactions similar to a Windows application, but the application is installed on a single web server and used by multiple computers at the same time; web-based applications do not have to be installed on each individual computer (unlike Windows applications); and computers using your web-based application only need a web browser, which is pretty standard on most operating systems today. In fact, the operating system can be anyone that supports a web browser. This gives you maximum flexibility within your test lab. With all this goodness, there must be a downside—and, of course, there is. To create anything but very simple web applications requires a lot of additional skills and time. This is mainly because these applications rely on several different components on a number of computers. To make matters worse, each component is often coded in different languages.

In the simplest model, a web page is a file that can be loaded into a web browser. The web browser's job is to interpret the code in the file and display the contents to the user. With this scenario, a web server is not required; all you need is a file with code that a browser can understand.

You can try this out by opening a text editor like Notepad, typing the code in Listing 9-1, and then saving the file as test.htm. When you are done, you can open a web browser and then type the path and filename to your file in the address bar. The browser will read the file and a simple web page with a silver background will appear. (In most cases, you can also double-click the file to open it in a web browser and see the results.)

Listing 9-1. *A Very Simple Web Page*

```
<html>
  <head> <title></title> </head>
  <body bgcolor='silver'>Test Text</body>
</html>
```

The color is added because the web browser understands the command bgcolor='silver'. This example should always work, but if the browser you are using is very old, it might ignore this command altogether. In fact, in the future, your browser might ignore it as well, since this HTML command has been deprecated. *Deprecated commands* are commands that have been slated for removal from the standard syntax of that language.

This brings up the first issue you should know about when testing web applications: you must plan for different types of browsers. This means that when you are testing web applications, you should use multiple browsers as part of your Test Plan. However, if you are creating testware that will only be used in your own lab, you will likely be able to dictate which browser is used and not have to worry about this issue.

Although you can run simple web pages directly from a hard drive, most of the time you will not want to. Using this option would force you to install a copy of your web files on every computer that needed them. Although this is what you do with a Windows application, with web applications you normally create a share on a central computer and have all the other computers run the web files from that share.

Oh, it's true that Windows applications can do this to some degree by using a standard network share, but all computers using that share would require direct access to the shared folder where the application files are. Instead of allowing that, Windows applications that share code from a central server usually take the form of an .exe file on the local PC and a .dll file on the remote server. An application built like this is said to use *remoting* and it typically uses software called a *component server* to access the shared .dll files. This is not a bad option if all the computers involved are within the same company, but for security reasons companies seldom open up their file shares and component servers to the general public. Instead, companies consider it a much better option to install web-server software on a computer and allow external users only limited access to that web server. The users cannot get direct access to the company shares or component servers, but they can access these indirectly through the web pages of a web server (see Figure 9-1). It is the web server's job to access internal resources for the users. Consider this analogy of asking for your medical records from a health clinic and having the person behind the counter get them for you, but not letting you go back and get them yourself.

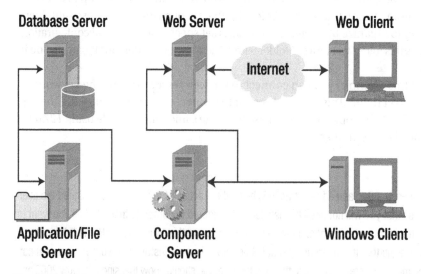

Figure 9-1. *Web vs. Windows applications*

To set up a website, you need to configure the web server to use a particular folder as a *web share* and then place the files you want shared into that folder. If you install Microsoft's free web server, Internet Information Server (IIS), a default web share is created for you in a folder called wwwroot. You can find this folder on the same drive that the operating system is installed on; in most cases, this drive is usually C:\. The folder itself is a subfolder of another folder called Inetpubs. Any files you place in here will be accessible through the web server by typing out the proper address.

As an example, let's say you've made the test.htm file mentioned earlier and placed it in this folder. Using your local computer, you could request the test.htm file from IIS by typing the http://LocalHost/test.htm address (see Figure 9-2). The web server would find the file, read it, and send back to your browser the contents of the file.

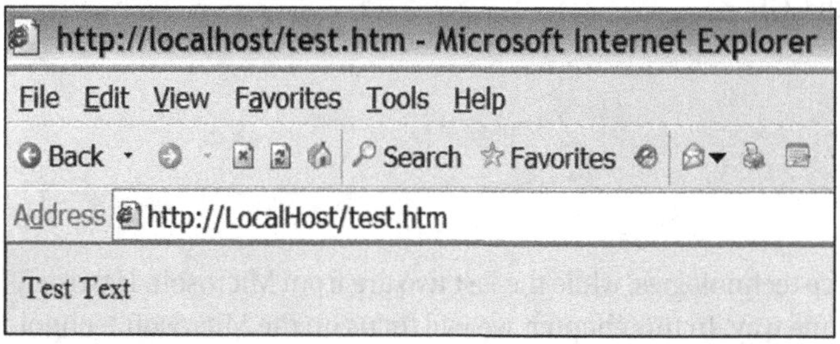

Figure 9-2. *Browing the web page*

To understand the address, consider that when viewing web pages you use the HyperText Transport Protocol (HTTP) and not something like the File Transfer Protocol (FTP). Since most browsers are capable of using more than one transport protocol, most require that you specify which protocol you want to use.

Of course, you also need to specify the file you want. However, in this case, you do not need to specify in which share the file is found. This is because the web server will use the default share, wwwroot, if you do not specify otherwise. When your web application is made up of a set of web pages, it is common to create a separate folder for that set of pages. Using these subfolders allows a webmaster to organize the web files, as well as set specific security and configuration settings. Sometimes this folder will be a subfolder within the wwwroot folder, but it can also be in other folders as well.

As you saw in this example, you can connect to the web server by using the keyword *LocalHost* for the server name. This tells the browser to connect to the same computer the web browser is running on. Other options you can use to do the same thing include using *127.0.0.1* or the actual name of the computer.

Note Since web-server setup and administration is beyond the scope of this book, we designed the exercises in this chapter so that you will not need IIS installed or configured to complete them. Still, if you want to investigate some of the features we mention in this chapter, be aware that Windows XP Home Edition does not support IIS. This means that if you are using that OS or if IIS is just not installed on your PC, you will not be able to duplicate some of the screens shown in this chapter. Also, you should know that since Window 2000 and XP Professional come installed with IIS by default; hackers the world over have had great fun creating viruses that infect computers using IIS. Make sure you always update IIS with the latest security patches to avoid potential virus attacks. Lastly, Windows 2003 include a newer, more secure version of IIS, but this new version is not installed by default—and even after it is, some of the features mentioned in this chapter may be turned off. The Help files that come with Windows 2003 are quite useful in configuring and troubleshooting this version of IIS.

As mentioned earlier, when your web pages contain only simple text and HTML code, you only need a web browser to process the HTML instructions. However, when accessing other programs through a web server, such as a database application, you need specialized technologies to get the job done. Common ones you may have heard of include these:

- Perl, in combination with CGI

- PHP

- ASP

- ASP.NET

The first two are open source technologies, while the last two are from Microsoft. However, all four are used in much the same way. In this chapter, we will focus on the Microsoft technologies, but no matter which of these you use, the methods and properties in these technologies will be accessed through some kind of .exe or .dll file using languages other than HTML. Because of this, you need to tell the web server which .exe or .dll file to reference when it needs to process commands. The most common way to do this is to configure the web server to reference the correct file based on the different file extensions. For example, when a file with the .asp extension is requested, the web server will send the code in the file over to a .dll called ASP.dll for processing. This mapping to an extension is configured through one of the settings in IIS, as shown in Figure 9-3. (We will talk more about how to get the IIS management tools later in this chapter, within the "Deploying an ASP.NET Application" section.)

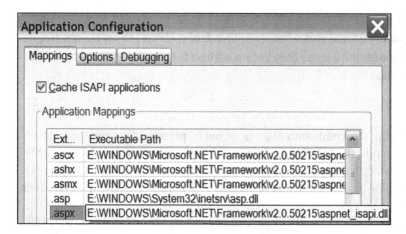

Figure 9-3. *Application mappings*

Looking at Figure 9-3, you'll see that there are a number of extensions mapped to .dlls. We hovered over the .aspx extension so that you could see the ToolTip. It indicates that ASP.NET pages, which use the .aspx extension, are mapped to the aspnet_isapi.dll. ASP.NET applications run differently than the traditional ASP applications, in part because they use two different sets of processing instructions. However, keep in mind that the process involved with using these two types of files is much the same. You request the file by name, the server loads the file's code into memory, and then the server calls any methods it needs from the mapped .dll. When the processing is done, the web server sends the results back to the browser.

Two-Tier Applications

In most cases, you will have the web-server software and the web-browser software running on two different computers. This type of architecture is often referred to as *2-tier* architecture (see Figure 9-4). Although the server software and the client software work together to form a whole application, they are really two distinct components of software involved. Still, to the user, they act like a single application.

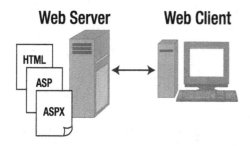

Figure 9-4. *Two-tier architecture*

While the web server use the file extension to map to the .exe or .dll for general processing instructions, internally those files may need to call additional .exes and .dlls for specific processing. One example of this is the use of Visual Basic Scripting Edition (VBS) commands in a traditional ASP web page.

Note We are talking about the model used in traditional ASP instead of ASP.NET for two reasons: first, it's a slightly simpler model; and second, it is very likely that you will have to deal with ASP as well as ASP.NET pages for some time to come.

In traditional ASP, the VBS commands make up about 80 percent of the code in an `.asp` file. To run these commands, the ASP library file (`ASP.dll`) must reference the VBS library file and call the methods inside of it. Once done, it sends the processed results back to the `ASP.dll`. In ASP.NET, the same thing happens; but instead of using VBS, it uses C# or VB .NET as the bulk of its code.

The code found in the ASP or ASP.NET pages can be a mixture of HTML, JavaScript, ASP, VBS, C#, VB .NET, and others. So how, you may ask, does the web server know where to send each line of code?

When a web server loads these pages, it starts by sending code to a processing file based on the extensions. These processing files look for special symbols within the code to determine how to process each line. For example, the <%%> symbols define the *server-side script blocks* of an ASP web page. When the web server finds the <%%> symbols in an ASP web page, it starts to process each line inside these tags through the `ASP.dll`. After the web server processes the ASP code, the results of this processed code will be sent back to the browser along with any other code found in that web page. HTML and JavaScript are the two most common examples of this additional code. Since this *client-side* code is found outside of the server-side script blocks, it must be processed by the web browser.

What this all means, is that your web applications may use many pieces of software to process your programming statements. For instance, consider that you will often find the `Response.Write()` command inside of a server-side script block. This is an ASP command, which outputs additional text to the non-processed, client-side code. You may also find functions like `UCase()`, which changes text to uppercase text. This is not a true ASP command—in that it is not in the ASP.dll, but rather is a VBS command. ASP will forward this call to VBS for processing. When VBS is done with it, it will send the results back to ASP and continue to the next line of code (see Figure 9-5).

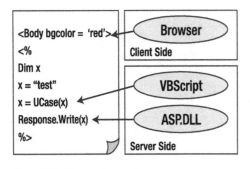

Figure 9-5. *Processing code*

Although ASP was created to use VBS commands by default, you can use other languages if you wish. Of course, any `.dll` for these languages has to be installed and you would have to include code that tells ASP what language you are using. You can do this by adding a Language attribute to a script tag, as shown in Listing 9-2. The first line of this sample indicates that this script block will use JavaScript instead of VBScript.

Listing 9-2. *Using the Script Tag*

```
<SCRIPT LANGUAGE="javascript" RUNAT="Server">
//Make some variables
var objconn, objrs, strquery, strconnection;

//Create an ADO Connection object
objconn = server.createobject("adodb.connection");

//Connect to the DB
strconnection = "dsn=pubs;database=pubs;uid=sa;pwd=password;"
objconn.open (strconnection);

//Get some data from the DB
strquery = "select title, price from titles order by title";
objrs = objconn.execute(strquery);
</SCRIPT>
```

You may have noticed that this code creates an object using the `adodb.connection` class. This class is located in an additional library file called `ADO.dll`. This particular `.dll` is installed as part of many Microsoft products and is likely installed on any PC you use. Here, we created a variable called `objconn` and set a reference to a connection object made by the ASP method `server.createobject()`. This method allows you to create objects from classes not normally mapped by the `ASP.dll`. In this case, it is utilizing ADO's `Connection` class, but it can also be used with classes found in other `.dlls`. The ability for the `ASP.dll` to work with another `.dll` is governed by the specifications of the Component Object Model (COM). You will learn more about COM objects and how .NET can interoperate with them in Chapter 10.

Three-Tier Applications

Most web applications today have connections to a database on some, if not all, of their pages. When using this option, the database stores the dynamic content of the web pages, the web server will process the data, and the web client will present the data to the user. These types of web applications use three distinct pieces of software divided into three distinct layers, or *tiers*. The first layer is for presenting the results to the user, the second is for processing the instructions, and the third is for holding the data (see Figure 9-6).

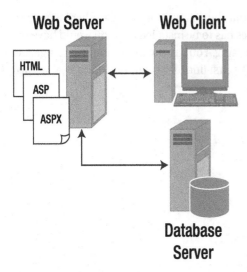

Figure 9-6. *Three-tier architecture*

In most cases, you can expect validation to take place on the web browser first. For example, a developer will add code to check if all the textboxes are filled in before the page's data can be sent back to the server for processing. Listing 9-3 is an example of client-side validation code using JavaScript. Notice that since the script tag shown here does not include the RUNAT="Server" attribute, the ASP processor will ignore the code in the script block and pass all of its code on to the browser for processing. Both traditional ASP and ASP.NET work this way, as well as most other similar technologies.

Listing 9-3. *Client-Side Validation Code*

```html
<html>
<head><title></title>
    <!-- Adding Validation Script -->
<script language="JavaScript">
 function Validate()
 {
```

```
  if (ValidForm.Name.value !== "" && ValidForm.Email.value !== "")
    { ValidForm.submit(); }
  else
    if (ValidForm.Name.value == "" )
    { window.alert("Please enter your \nFirst and Last name");}
    if (ValidForm.Email.value == "")
    { window.alert("Please enter your \nEmail address");}
  }
</script>
</head>
<body>
<form action="http://localhost/CheckWithDB.asp" method="POST"
 name="ValidForm">
Name:  <input name="Name" type="Text" size="20" maxlength="50"><br>
Email: <input name="Email" type="Text" size="20" maxlength="100"><br>
       <input type="button" value="Send" onclick="Validate()">
</form>
</body>
</html>
```

In Listing 9-3, the Validate() method is called whenever the button is clicked. Although written in JavaScript, this code is similar to C# so you may have figured out that it will check to see if the value of either textbox is left blank and alert the user if either is empty.

It is common programming practice that when a Submit button is clicked, values from the textboxes and other controls on the web page are normally gathered up and sent to a JavaScript method for local validation processing. The data is sent to the web server only after it passes local validation.

The web browser sends data to the web server in one of two ways: by GET or by POST. The developer makes this choice by setting the method attribute in the <form> tag. Using the GET option, the name and the value of each textbox are sent to the web server as part of the page's address. It is easy to spot a web page that uses this option because you will see name and value pairs in the address bar, as shown in Figure 9-7.

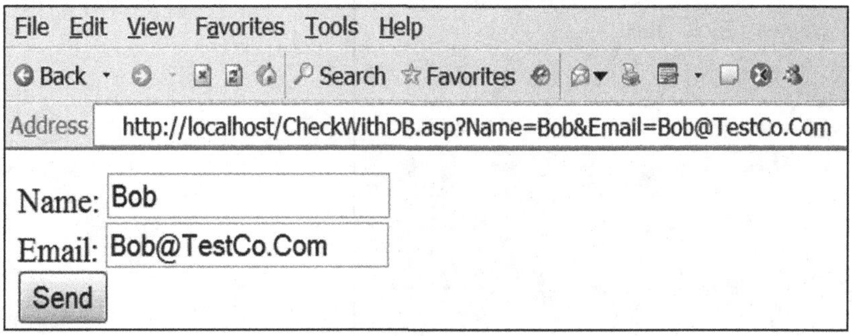

Figure 9-7. *Sending data to the server using GET*

One thing that most people find very confusing is that POST and GET are really doing the same thing. Even though POST and GET seem to mean opposite things; in both cases the data is being sent by the web browser to the web server for processing.

In cases where the data is sent using the POST method, you will not see the text in the address; instead, the name and value pairs are hidden from sight. Oh, they are still accessible if you know where to look, you just won't be able to see them so casually. Although this may appear safer, rest assured that a hacker can read and even modify this data. So, it is not really much more secure then using GET.

TESTER'S TIP: POST AND SSL

When using POST, someone standing behind you will not see your data in the address bar. However, this does not mean that it is encrypted in any way; it just means that someone behind you cannot snoop as easily. When web technology was first coming out, this was considered a minor security upgrade from GET. It seems much too simple now, since security requirements have become so complex in today's world. To be secure, additional technologies, like Secure Sockets Layer (SSL), are used to provide encryption on most commercial websites. If security is on your list of things to test, don't assume that data is safe just because it can't be seen.

Looking back at Listing 9-3, find the action attribute. This attribute tells the browser to pass the data from the current web page to another web page. In this case, that web page is called CheckWithDB.asp. When performance will allow it, a well-designed web application includes validation logic at all levels. When you create the CheckWithDB.asp page, you would add code to validate the client's data yet again and then pass the valid data on to a database server. In fact, even the database would have additional validation inside of it!

To highlight why redundant validation code is important, consider how a hacker can submit data directly to the server page. In Figure 9-8, a web tester is trying to send a name to the CheckWithDB.asp processing page by modifying the address directly. If this works (in other words, no server-side validation catches the fact that the e-mail address is left blank), then it's time to create a bug report. (Mark this down as a one of your basic web test cases!)

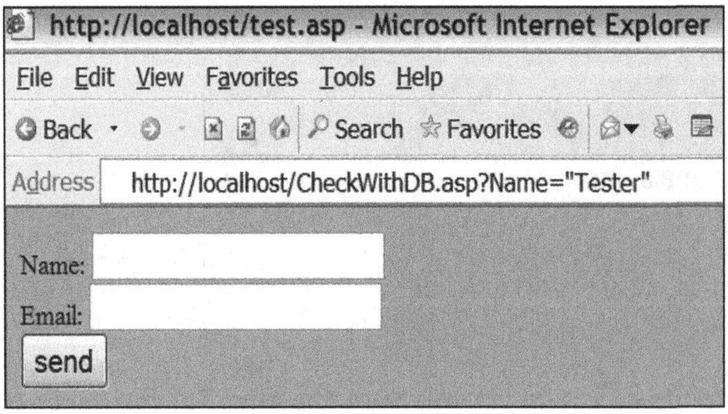

Figure 9-8. *Hacking around client validation*

■**Note** When Microsoft designed ASP.NET, they included special web controls that automatically generate both the server- and client-side code for you. Of course, to take advantage of this feature, you must use the Microsoft web-server controls instead of the standard HTML ones; but, they work just as well if not better for most web pages. You can find the web-server controls in the Visual Studio toolbox under the heading by that name. They look very much like the ones you use when you are building Windows applications; however, they are actually enhanced versions made especially for ASP.NET.

N-Tier Applications

Larger websites may have additional layers of processing code added to the design. In fact, there may be many additional layers added on very large sites. This expansion of layers can be carrier out to the "Nth" degree. Perhaps that is why you sometimes hear it referred to as N-tier architecture (see Figure 9-9). As you might imagine, these types of websites will have validation code at the web-client, web-server, database, and component-server levels. Once again, this means that a thorough Test Plan must test all levels.

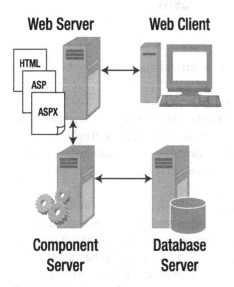

Figure 9-9. *N-tier architecture*

Special component servers are used to host these additional processing layers. These servers have .dlls that are specifically designed for a business's custom logic. Because of this, it is not surprising that this component layer is often called the *business layer*.

Sometimes, .dlls of this sort contain methods that may be useful to other business applications as well. So, it is common to see both Windows and web applications using these same component servers within one company.

In cases where you have many clients using the same code on one server, the workload can exceed what that computer's hardware can handle. One solution for this is to add duplicate servers and redirect some of the clients to the various replicas (see Figure 9-10). This is also considered a form of N-tier architecture, but on a larger scale.

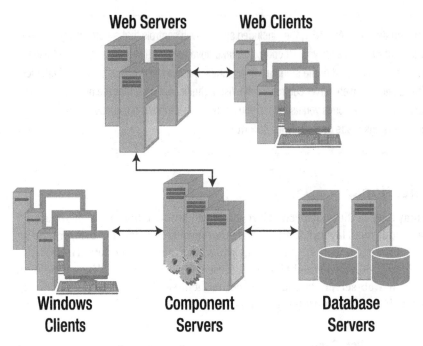

Figure 9-10. *Large scale N-tier architecture*

As a test professional, you need to be aware that bugs can show up in the system when these replicas are not exactly the same. These bugs can be hard to spot, since some layers are very sensitive to these synchronization issues and others are not.

For example, the data layer is one that is very sensitive to these errors. If not designed well, the delay (or *latency*) between changes made in one replica of the database will collide with changes made in another. These issues may be difficult to resolve since it is not always practical to keep all copies synchronized in real-time. Thus, the developer may determine it to be an unavoidable design trait and not an actual bug.

From our discussion so far, you can see that web development in the real world is complicated. Another area where this is demonstrated is in the deployment of the web application once it is finished. Both Console and Windows applications use a simple deployment model. Often, all you need to do for those applications is copy the .exe file to a computer and run the executable. This differs from a web application, which, at a minimum, deploys on the web server but runs on the web browser.

In summary, when testing web applications, here are some items to keep in mind:

- Instructions are divided into UI languages (HTML and CSS) and processing languages (VB .NET, C#, JavaScript, etc.).

- There can be many layers involved and each one needs to be tested.

- The UI may be expected to work on many different browsers. So different browsers must be tested for compatibility.

- Security takes place on the operating system, web server, and web browser. So, security must be tested at all levels as well.

- The browser disconnects from the web server every time the UI is loaded on the screen. Settings and data are sent back to the web server repeatedly, which means that performance testing is a must for all but the simplest web application.

Note Although there is a lot more we would like to tell you about web technology, we will have to stop here. To cover all aspects of creating web applications, along with the details of troubleshooting and debugging them, would likely take another 500 pages. If you find this subject as interesting as we do, check out some of Apress's other books specifically about this topic (www.apress.com).

Creating Web-Based Testware

By now, it is clear that web applications take more effort to develop and to test. The good news is that Microsoft has done a lot toward making web development simpler. They have also made it very easy to reuse existing components along with your web applications. To give you a feel for this, let's discuss how you could build your own web-based testware application.

Note We have used the Visual Web Developer 2005 Express Edition for our following examples. We did this for a few reasons: 1) because it provides all the functionality we need for simple testware; 2) as of this writing, it is free, and although Microsoft may end up charging a small fee for it at the end of 2006, it's the least expensive choice; and 3) it was designed to be the easiest version to use, and to get for that matter. If you are following along using a more advanced version of Visual Studio, your screens may vary, but all the steps and code should be similar. If you have not downloaded and installed this software, please refer to the Appendix A for instructions.

The first thing you need to do is to open up the Visual Studio 2005 or Visual Web Developer 2005 Express Edition. When Visual Web Developer opens up, you will see the Start page. To create your website, select File ➤ New Web Site. You will now see a dialog box that lets you choose between standard and customized templates (see Figure 9-11). The two typical choices are ASP.NET Web Site or an ASP.NET Web Service. The Web Service option is similar to creating a class library (see the "Testing COM and Web Services" section in Chapter 10 for more information). The Web Service option is used to allow software to talk to software, while the Web Site option provides interaction between software and humans. For this example, you want to choose the Web Site option since you will be creating a bug-reporting website.

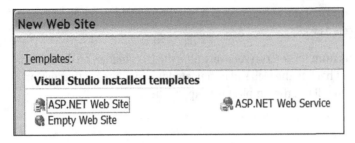

Figure 9-11. *Starting a new website*

At the bottom of this same screen, you will also see two important drop-down boxes (see Figure 9-12). The first one lets you pick the location for your new website. The second one lets you pick the language you'd like to use. You can use any .NET language installed, but C# and VB .NET are, by far, the most common choices.

A blank ASP.NET Web site		
Location:	File System ▾	C:\WebSites\WebSite1
Language:	Visual C# ▾	

Figure 9-12. *Choosing a location and language*

In the Location combo box, you will see three choices: File System, HTTP, and FTP. Both HTTP and FTP allow you to create a new website directly on a web server. The only web server that .NET supports is Microsoft's IIS. So, in order to use either the FTP or HTTP options, IIS must be installed on either your own desktop PC, another server on your network, or a server at an Internet Service Provider (ISP) where you have an account.

To make web development easier, Microsoft now provides a built-in web server with all of the Visual Web Developer 2005 Editions. This greatly simplifies development and is a welcome addition.

To use this feature, choose the File System option in the Location combo box and specify not a web server's name but a folder on the local hard drive. Visual Studio will use this folder to store your web files while you are developing them, and the built-in web server will treat your application just as if it were on an IIS server. This lets you easily browse and debug the application as you develop it. When you are done with the development of your website, you can simply copy, or *upload* as it is called, your files to an actual production web server.

Understanding the Default Web Page Code

Once you have selected your choices and clicked the Add button, Visual Studio will create a new website along with an initial page called default.aspx. Using the Source view on this page, you can begin to add your own code. Listing 9-4 is an example of what the default code looks like. Note, in this example, we have also added a button to the page called Button1 that we will talk about later.

Listing 9-4. *The default.aspx Page*

```
<%@ Page Language="C#" AutoEventWireup="true"
CodeFile="Default.aspx.cs" Inherits="_Default" %>

<!DOCTYPE html PUBLIC "-//W3C//DTD XHTML 1.1//EN"
"http://www.w3.org/TR/xhtml11/DTD/xhtml11.dtd">

<html xmlns="http://www.w3.org/1999/xhtml" >
<head runat="server">
    <title>Untitled Page</title>
</head>
<body>
    <form id="form1" runat="server">
    <div>
      <asp:Button ID="Button1" runat="server"
        OnClick="Button1_Click" Text="Button" />
    </div>
    </form>
</body>
</html>
```

If you already program in HTML, you may recognize many of the tags, but some of the tags are purely for ASP.NET. Although all of this code will be sent to ASP.NET, as we discussed earlier, some of these instructions will be solely processed on the web server and others will be sent along to a web browser for processing afterward.

Unlike traditional ASP, ASP.NET will still process the HTML commands shown here. It does this so that ASP.NET can do things like change the HTML code to match the type of web browser that is requesting the page. For example, if the browser is an older one, many of the newer HTML commands will be converted to the older syntax. This automated feature saves a developer from having to write multiple output functions to match each type of web browser, which is a common task with non-ASP.NET technologies.

Since Listing 9-4 consists of several different sections, let's review these sections before you move on, beginning with this first one:

```
<%@ Page Language="C#" AutoEventWireup="true"
CodeFile="Default.aspx.cs"
Inherits="_Default" %>
```

This code includes a number of optional attributes. The <% %> symbols you see here are similar to the command for a <script> block. They are used to group server-side commands together and indicate that they should be processed only on the server. The Language attribute instructs ASP.NET as to which language the page uses. The AutoEventWireup states that events, like the Click event of a button, should be automatically associated to a method with a predefined Microsoft name. This means that as long as you create event handlers with the correct name, you will not have to manually map the event to the method that will handle that event. Although set to true by default in Visual Studio, Microsoft does not consider this a good option to have turned on when you want the best performance. Still, you will not see much, if any, impact from setting this to either `true` or `false` with smaller websites; so, for most common testware, just leave it at the default.

The `CodeFile` attribute tells ASP.NET that an additional C# or VB .NET file is actually part of this code file as well. This option allows you to place your server-processed code in a separate file from the broswer-processed code that describes how to display the web form. `Inherits` specifies that the code in this file inherits all the code you will find in the `_Default` class, found inside of the file indicated by the `CodeFile` attribute..

A while ago, the World Wide Web Consortium (W3C) came out with a recommendation for a stricter version of HTML, called *XHTML*. The recommendation dictates that many of the rules for creating well-formed XML documents should be used when creating HTML files. The following section denotes that this web page uses this recommendation:

```
<!DOCTYPE html PUBLIC "-//W3C//DTD XHTML 1.1//EN"
"http://www.w3.org/TR/xhtml11/DTD/xhtml11.dtd">
<html xmlns="http://www.w3.org/1999/xhtml" >
```

In HTML, the `<head>` (or *header*) section holds general processing instructions. While you can place these instructions in other areas as well, most are found here. The header often includes blocks of server-side and client-side code. With ASP.NET, the server-side code will be in languages like C# or VB .NET, while the client-side code will be in JavaScript since almost all browsers can run that language.

```
<head runat="server">
    <title>Untitled Page</title>
</head>
```

With so many options to choose from, we know that this can be very confusing at first. However, all you really need to specify is the language option. Deciding if you need the other attributes is mostly determined by your choice of using the code-behind or single-file option. Let's take a look at the differences between these options next.

Code-Behind vs. Single-File Options

When you first start a project in Visual Web Developer, an initial web form is created for you. This first page is automatically configured to use the code-behind option. However, when you create additional web forms, you are asked to decide which option you want. For example, if you use the menu item Web Site ➤ Add New Item to add a new web form to the project, you will see two check boxes at the bottom of the page: Place Code In Separate File and Select Master Page (see Figure 9-13).

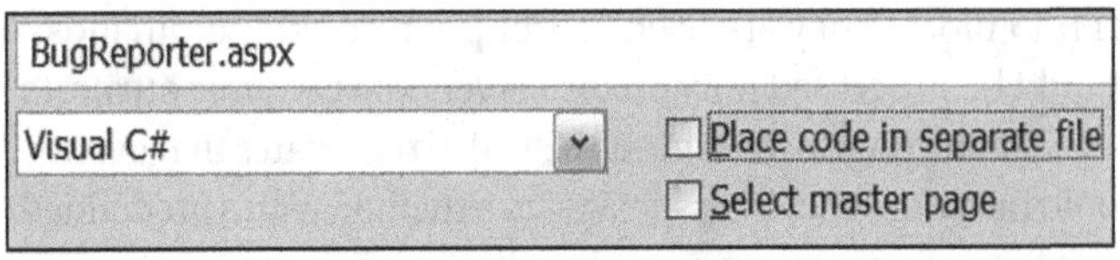

Figure 9-13. *The code-behind and single-file check boxes*

When Place Code In Separate File is checked, a code-behind file is added to the project. This additional file holds the C# or VB .NET code used along with your `.aspx` page. When the check box is unchecked, Visual Web Developer uses the single-file option instead. This option demands that you place all of your VB .NET and C# code in the same single file as the rest of the page's code. In the end, both will process the code in exactly the same way; so your choice is not as important as you might think. The single-file option is similar to the way most other common web technologies, like PHP and traditional ASP, work.

The Select Master Page option allows developers to create a master page as a template to use for other web pages in that website. This helps larger website projects define a consistent look and feel for all the web pages.

Leaving both options unchecked will make a new web form with initial code that looks slightly different than the first example you saw. Notice that in this new sample (see Listing 9-5), only the Language attribute is specified in the first line. Also note that a <script runat="server"> tag is included for you as a place for your server-side VB .NET and C# code.

Listing 9-5. *Using the Single-File Option*

```
<%@ Page Language="C#" %>
<!DOCTYPE html PUBLIC "-//W3C//DTD XHTML 1.1//EN"
  "http://www.w3.org/TR/xhtml11/DTD/xhtml11.dtd">
<script runat="server">
    protected void Button1_Click(object sender, EventArgs e)
    {
      //add event handling code here
    }
</script>
<html xmlns="http://www.w3.org/1999/xhtml" >
<head runat="server">
    <title>Untitled Page</title>
</head>
<body>
 <form id="form1" runat="server">
  <div>
  <asp:Button ID="Button1" runat="server" OnClick="Button1_Click"
  Text="Button" />
  </div>
 </form>
</body>
</html>
```

As in Listing 9-4, we added a button to the web form. We did this to highlight one of the major differences between the code-behind and the single-file options. Since Listing 9-4 used the code-behind option, code handling for the button's Click event will be within the Default.aspx.cs file. However, looking at the single-file example (Listing 9-5), you can see that the code for the Click event now goes within the server-side script block.

In summary, when you use the code-behind option, you place event handling code in a separate code file not in the .aspx page. This file will be named whatever you named the .aspx file, but with a .vb or .cs extension added on at the end.

In general, the single-file approach is simpler, while the code-behind option is better if you want to organize the browser and server code into distinct files. In Exercise 9-1, we will use the code-behind option so that you can see what both files look like.

Exercise 9-1: Starting the BugReporter Application

In this exercise, you will create a new web application that will later become a web-based, bug-reporting application. Follow these steps to complete the exercise:

1. Create a new ASP.NET website with a location set to c:\WebSites\BugReporter (again, see Figure 9-11). This will create a new folder and add a new default web form called Default.aspx. A window with code that looks like Listing 9-4 should appear. This web form will become the menu page for your website.

2. Add a heading and two buttons to the body of the document by typing code into the web page, as shown here:

```
<form id="form1" runat="server">
<div>
  <h1>Bug Reports Web Site</h1>
  <asp:Button ID="btnReportBug" runat="server"
    Text="Report a Bug" Width="226px" />
  <p />
  <asp:Button ID="btnViewBugs" runat="server"
    Text="View Reported Bugs" Width="226px" />
</div>
</form>
```

3. At the bottom of Visual Studio, you will see two buttons labeled Design and Source. You are looking at the Source option now; switch to the Design option by clicking the word *Design*. You should see a heading and the two buttons (see Figure 9-14).

■**Note** Typing the code in the Source view adds the buttons in the Design view, but the opposite is true as well. While in Design view, you can add buttons, textboxes, and other controls from the toolbox just as you do with Windows applications.

Figure 9-14. *The default web page in Design view*

4. Using the Design view, double-click on each button to create an event handler method just as you would do in a Windows applications. Notice that the editor is now using a new file for your code. This new file is the code-behind page.

5. Add the code in Listing 9-6 to these methods.

Listing 9-6. *Testing That the Buttons Work As Expected*

VB .NET

```
Partial Class _Default
  Inherits System.Web.UI.Page

  Protected Sub btnReportBug_Click _
  (ByVal sender As Object, ByVal e As System.EventArgs) _
  Handles btnReportBug.Click
    Response.Write("Test Stub")
  End Sub

  Protected Sub btnViewBugs_Click _
  (ByVal sender As Object, ByVal e As System.EventArgs) _
   Handles btnViewBugs.Click
    Response.Write("Test Stub")
  End Sub
End Class
```

C#

```
public partial class _Default : System.Web.UI.Page
{
  protected void btnReportBug_Click(object sender, EventArgs e)
  {
    Response.Write("Test Stub");
  }
  protected void btnViewBugs_Click(object sender, EventArgs e)
  {
    Response.Write("Test Stub");
  }
}
```

6. Run the application by pressing the green start arrow or the F5 key. If this is the first time you have done so, you will see the screen in Figure 9-15. Clicking OK will create a web configuration file that has the debugging option turned on. As the dialog box tells you, this is not recommended for a production website, but you are in the development phase now so this is fine. Click OK now.

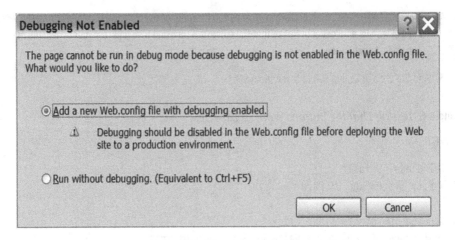

Figure 9-15. *Choosing to enable debugging*

7. When the web page displays, test the buttons and close the web page. This will only display Test Stub right now, but in Exercise 9-2 you will use these buttons to interact with a database. Note that each press of a button is going back to the server for processing. This is why you are seeing only one instance of the message. After each click of a button, a completely new page is being displayed—you are not just adding more text to the same page.

In this exercise, you created a simple web page that uses the code-behind option. You created two event handler methods that will be modified in Exercise 9-2. Before we start those modifications, you will need to take a look at how databases and web pages interact.

Inserting Data to a Database

When you want to save data from a website, a database is a logical choice. Microsoft has made it easy to do this by using the classes found in ADO.NET.

The first thing you need is a database. Microsoft has two standard choices for this: Access and SQL Server. We are using a pre-made Access database for the examples in this chapter, so we have included a database file called BugData.mdb in the DownloadFiles\Chapter9\ folder. This file is available for download from the Source Code section of the Apress website (www.apress.com). See Appendix A for more download details.

■**Note** We must confess, SQL Server is our favorite choice between the two. SQL Server is also the more common choice for production databases. However, since Access would be sufficient for many testware applications, and it is more commonly installed on home and classroom computers, we have chosen to use this for our examples. If you have experience with SQL Server, you will find the following example directly applicable with only a few minor changes.

If you have Microsoft Access XP or newer, you can open the file and see the one table we have inside of it. As shown Figure 9-16, the table, called ReportedBugs, is very simple. The Design view of the table shows that it contains a field for each of the textboxes we used in the Chapter 6's Windows version of the BugReporter.

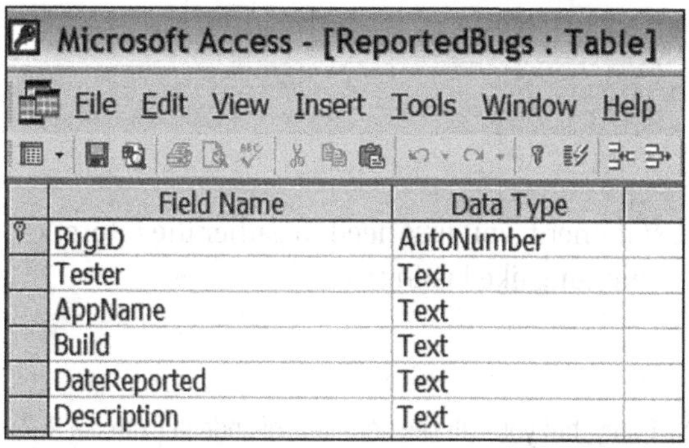

Figure 9-16. *The Design view of the ReportedBugs table*

When you are using a database and want to add data to a table, you commonly use a SQL Insert statement. SQL is an industry-standard language for working with databases. Microsoft's SQL Server used the languages acronym for its name, which can be confusing. Although Microsoft's SQL Server certainly runs SQL commands, so do most other database programs, like Microsoft's Access and Oracle. So, when someone tells you an application is working on a SQL Server, you might have to clarify the term.

To add data from the web page to the database, you must pass the Insert statement to the database and let the database execute the statement for you. The Insert statement you need for this example will look like Listing 9-7.

Listing 9-7. *Inserting into the ReportedBugs Table*

```
Insert Into ReportedBugs
(Tester, AppName, Build, DateReported, Description)
Values
( 'JoeTester', 'BuggyApp', '1.0', '11/07/2005', 'One Bad Bug')
```

As you can see, the Insert statement maps a value to each of the five columns. Note that it skips over the first column, the BugID. This is because it is an autonumber field and an ID number will automatically be added for you by Access. Another thing to note is that SQL uses single quotes (') to indicate string data, not double quotes (").

When the statement runs, the new values will be added to the table so that now the data in the table will look like Figure 9-17.

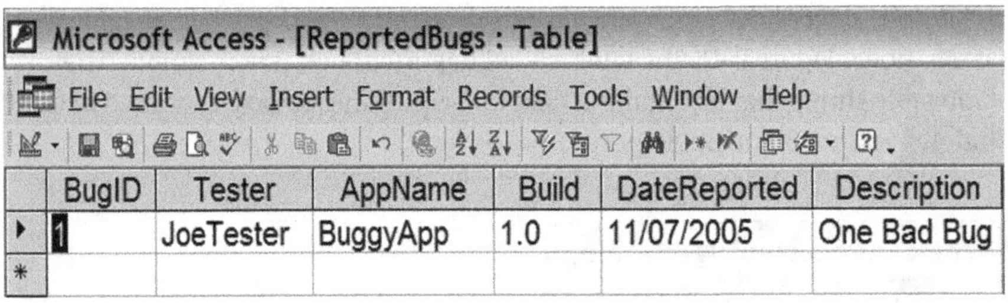

Figure 9-17. *Inserted data*

Of course, before you can run the Insert statement, you first need to gather the informa-tion from a web page. Your code would look something like Listing 9-8.

Note The following examples are shown in VB .NET only, but you will see both sets of code in Exercise 9-2.

Listing 9-8. *Gathering the Web Form Data*

VB .NET

```
'---- Get Data Section ----
'Create string variables and get the data from the user
Dim strTester As String = txtTester.Text
Dim strApplicationName As String = txtAppName.Text
Dim strBuildNumber As String = txtBuildNumber.Text
Dim strDateReported As String = txtDateReported.Text
Dim strDescription As String = txtDescription.Text

'Pull data out of the variables above and put it into a string
Dim strData As String = ""
strData += "'" + strTester + "',"
strData += "'" + strApplicationName + "',"
strData += "'" + strBuildNumber + "',"
strData += "'" + strDateReported + "',"
strData += "'" + strDescription + "'"

'---- Save Data to Database Section ----
AddBug(strData)
```

From this example, you can infer that you need to build the string of values used in the Insert statement and then pass the string on to the database. Again, note the use of single quotes. We have seen both novice and expert struggle with these. As you saw in the SQL state-ment in Listing 9-7, all the string values are enclosed in single quotes. Leaving just one of these quotes off would cause a SQL syntax error. Whenever you are building a string to send to a SQL statement, pay special attention to the use of single quotes.

TESTER'S TIP: SPECIAL CHARACTERS

One common test procedure when working with any database-driven application is to test how the application handles the use of special characters, like the single quote in the name O'day. If the system cannot process this entry, you have found another bug. In both SQL Server and Access, you can solve this by adding another single quote directly after the first one, like this: O''day. Although that may *look like* a double quote, it is really two single ones and, as such, will be recorded in the database just fine. Testing for special characters should be a basic test case for all data-driven applications. Included in that should be other SQL special characters including the semicolon (;), the slash (/), and the double hyphen (--) because these have special meaning in SQL and can be used to attempt a SQL injection attack.

Once the data is gathered from the textboxes and placed into a string, the code at the end of Listing 9-8 continues on to the next step, which is passing this string to a new method we call AddBug(), as shown in Listing 9-9. We use the data we collected in the variable strData as an argument to the BugData parameter in AddBug(). This method then connects to the database and executes an SQL Insert statement.

Listing 9-9. *Inserting the Web Form Data*

VB .NET

```
Protected Sub AddBug(ByVal BugData As String)
Dim objBuilder As Data.OleDb.OleDbConnectionStringBuilder
Dim objCon As Data.OleDb.OleDbConnection
Dim objComm As Data.OleDb.OleDbCommand
Dim strInsert As String = ""

'Create a connection to the database
objBuilder = New Data.OleDb.OleDbConnectionStringBuilder
objBuilder.ConnectionString = "Data Source= C:\BugData.mdb"
objBuilder.Add("Provider", "Microsoft.Jet.Oledb.4.0")
objBuilder.Add("Jet OLEDB:Database Password", "")
'Set up row-level locking.
objBuilder.Add("Jet OLEDB:Database Locking Mode", 1)

objCon = New Data.OleDb.OleDbConnection(objBuilder.ConnectionString)

'Build the Insert SQL command
'Note the spaces are important!
strInsert = " Insert Into ReportedBugs "
strInsert += " (Tester, AppName, Build, DateReported, Description) "
strInsert += " Values( " + BugData + " ) "

'Build a Command object to send your command
objComm = New Data.OleDb.OleDbCommand()
objComm.Connection = objCon
```

```
objComm.CommandType = Data.CommandType.Text
objComm.CommandText = strInsert
'Response.Write(objComm.CommandText.ToString)

'Open the connection and run the command
Try
objCon.Open()
objComm.ExecuteNonQuery()
objCon.Close()
Response.Redirect("Default.aspx")

Catch ex As Exception
Response.Write(ex.ToString)
End Try
End Sub
```

Looking at the Data Source property in Listing 9-9, you will notice that it points to an .mdb file on the hard drive. Although it could be in any folder, we have placed this file on the C:\ drive just to make the path easy to type. Next, we set the provider (which acts like a driver) to use the Microsoft Jet data engine. This is the provider used in a number of Microsoft products including Access and Excel. After that, we set the Password to blank, which is the default in Access, and specify row-level locking so that other users of the web application will not find the entire table locked when one user runs the Insert command.

Listing 9-9 is using ADO.NET 2.0, which is the newest version at the time of this writing. This version has a number of new features that makes connecting to a database easier than ever. One of these is the new OleDbConnectionStringBuilder class. This class allows you to make connection strings by setting the properties of the class. While this may not seem like much at first, you will appreciate it when Visual Studio displays the properties and values that are commonly used with IntelliSense.

Once the connection string was made, we used it to create a new Connection object. We chose to use a variable called objCon to point to this object using this code:

```
objCon = new Data.OleDb.OleDbConnection(objBuilder.ConnectionString)
```

Next, we built our SQL Insert statement using the data passed into the BugData parameter, as shown here:

```
strInsert = " Insert Into ReportedBugs "
strInsert += " (Tester, AppName, Build, DateReported, Description) "
strInsert += " Values( " + BugData + " ) "
```

To issue the SQL command, we created a Command object from the ADO Command class and set the Connection, CommandType, and CommandText properties as needed:

```
objComm = new Data.OleDb.OleDbCommand()
objComm.Connection = objCon
objComm.CommandType = Data.CommandType.Text
objComm.CommandText = strInsert
```

■**Note** You may notice that we are using a `Try-Catch` block around the code that opens the connection and executes the query. If there is an error, using the `Catch` block provides an error message to help with troubleshooting. One common issue happens when the application does not find the database file. We have chosen to place the file on the root of the C:\ drive to make this less likely to happen; but when testing real applications, this is something to watch for.

When the `ExecuteNonQuery()` method is called, the `Insert` statement is sent to Access. After it completes, we close the connection and redirect the user back to the default web page using ASP.NET's `Response.Redirect()` method.

This example only allows the user to submit bug reports, but more features could be added later (such as the ability to edit and remove a bug report). To allow changes like these, you would use this same code, but modify the statements to delete and update the bug reports by executing those types of SQL statements.

Viewing Data from a Database

Displaying the contents of the ReportedBugs table is another example of where this code can be reused. To do this, you need to execute a SQL `Select` statement indicating which columns and rows you would want returned. Once you retrieve data from your database to your web server, you need to store these results in memory, at least temporarily. In ADO.NET, you have two choices: the `DataReader` and the `DataSet`. Both of these classes are used to make an object that holds the results coming back from a SQL `Select` statement, but the `DataSet` has a lot more features while the `DataReader` takes up less memory.

Additionally, the `DataSet` can be added easily to the web server's cache, where it will be used repeatedly by many web page requests. The `DataReader`, on the other hand, cannot be cached directly. Oh, you can build an array, pour the contents of the `DataReader` into the array, and cache the array yourself, but this seems like a lot of extra work when the `DataSet` class is already available.

A cached `DataSet` is often used on websites that have a lot of traffic. To understand why this is, consider that, unlike a Windows application, the objects created on a web page are destroyed and re-created each time the page is refreshed. As you might imagine, this creates a lot of extra work on the web server. To counter this, web developers will often hold a copy of data in local memory of the web server. These caches of data are useful because they are not destroyed for each page request, but, instead, are reused until the developer thinks that new or updated data is required.

However, where it gets tricky is deciding how often the cached data needs refreshing. Some items, like a list of all the states a company ships to, is seldom updated and is a prime candidate for caching. Some data, like an inventory list, must be up to date every time the user needs to know how many items are still in stock. If this data was cached and only updated every 30 minutes, you can image that at some point someone would think an item was in stock when it was actually sold out almost a half hour ago.

Although caching is a powerful feature, if you want to simply issue a SQL `Select` statement and display the result to a web page, it's hard the fault the use of a `DataReader`. It has low memory requirements and is easy to use.

To understand how a DataReader pulls data into a web page, consider the code in Listing 9-10.

Listing 9-10. *Selecting Data into a Web Page*

VB .NET

```
Protected Sub Page_Load _
(ByVal sender As Object, ByVal e As System.EventArgs) Handles Me.Load

  Dim objBuilder As System.Data.OleDb.OleDbConnectionStringBuilder
  Dim objCon As System.Data.OleDb.OleDbConnection
  Dim objComm As System.Data.OleDb.OleDbCommand
  Dim strSelect As String = ""

  'Create a connection to the System.Database.
  objBuilder = New System.Data.OleDb.OleDbConnectionStringBuilder
  objBuilder.ConnectionString = "Data Source= C:\BugData.mdb"
  objBuilder.Add("Provider", "Microsoft.Jet.Oledb.4.0")
  objBuilder.Add("Jet OLEDB:Database Password", "")
  ' Set up row-level locking.
  objBuilder.Add("Jet OLEDB:Database Locking Mode", 1)
  objCon = New System.Data.OleDb.OleDbConnection(objBuilder.ConnectionString)

  'Build the SQL Select command.
  'Note the spaces are important!
  strSelect = " Select "
  strSelect += " Tester, AppName, Build, DateReported, Description "
  strSelect += " From ReportedBugs"

  'Build a Command object to send your command.
  objComm = New System.Data.OleDb.OleDbCommand()
  objComm.Connection = objCon
  objComm.CommandType = System.Data.CommandType.Text
  objComm.CommandText = strSelect
  'Response.Write(objComm.CommandText.ToString)

  'Create a System.DataReader variable to referance the results
  'we get back from the System.Database.
  Dim objDR As System.Data.OleDb.OleDbDataReader
  'Open the connection and run the command.
  Try
    objCon.Open()
    objDR = objComm.ExecuteReader()

    Response.Write("<table border='1'>")
    Response.Write("<tr>")
    Response.Write("<th>Tester</th>")
    Response.Write("<th>App Name</th>")
```

```
    Response.Write("<th>Build</th>")
    Response.Write("<th>DateReported</th>")
    Response.Write("<th>Description</th>")
    Response.Write("</tr>")

    'Print out the results
    While objDR.Read = True
      Response.Write("<tr>")
      Response.Write("<td>" & objDR("Tester") & "</td>")
      Response.Write("<td>" & objDR("AppName") & "</td>")
      Response.Write("<td>" & objDR("Build") & "</td>")
      Response.Write("<td>" & objDR("DateReported") & "</td>")
      Response.Write("<td>" & objDR("Description") & "</td>")
      Response.Write("</tr>")
    End While

    Response.Write("</table>")
    objDR.Close()

  Catch ex As Exception
    Response.Write(ex.ToString)
  Finally
    If objCon.State = System.Data.ConnectionState.Open Then
      objCon.Close()
    End If
  End Try
End Sub
```

Much like Listing 9-9, this code starts out with a connection being made to the database. This time though, we are building a Select statement, not an Insert. The Select retrieves the content of the Tester, AppName, Build, DateReported, and Description columns from every row in the ReportedBugs table. When the SQL statement is built, it will look like this:

```
"Select Tester, AppName, Build, DateReported, Description From ReportedBugs"
```

TESTER'S TIP: CHECKING SQL FORMATTING

Note how there are spaces between all keywords and names. One of the most common errors with Select statements is not allowing for these spaces. If you are having problems getting a SQL statement to work, you may find it useful to test if the string variable is holding correctly formatted data. In traditional ASP, you would commonly do this by printing out the SQL statement on the web page using the Response.Write() method.

```
Response.Write(objComm.CommandText.ToString)
```

Of course, with Visual Studio, you can use the debugging tools to examine the string; however, using something like Response.Write() is still a common practice whenever these debugging tools are unavailable.

Once the Select statement is ready, you will need to execute the query. Since Select statements bring back a set of results you need to decide how you are going to process these results. In this example, we chose to use the ExecuteReader() method, which creates a DataReader object in memory. Note that the objDR variable uses the DataReader class as its type, but does not create a new object. It is the ExecuteReader() method that creates the object for you, so you only need a variable of the same type to act as a pointer to the object. As such, you just reference the one made by the Command object with this code:

```
Dim objDR As Data.OleDb.OleDbDataReader
objDR = objComm.ExecuteReader()
```

With the object referenced, you can now process the returned results by using the Read() method of the DataReader object. When you use the method, it retrieves one row of the results at a time. If you call the method and there are no more rows to retrieve, the Read() method returns false. Listing 9-10 takes advantage of this and uses a While loop to continue processing the results as long are there are rows to read.

Once you have processed all of the records, you use the DataReader's Close() method followed by the Connection class's Close() method to complete the data retrieval.

Now, let's take a look at how all of these pieces work together to create a web application that can both read from and write to a database (see Exercise 9-2).

Exercise 9-2: Saving a Bug Report to a Database

In this exercise, you will expand the functionality of the website you built in Exercise 9-1. You will build one web page to save your bug report data to a database and another that allows you to view the saved data.

1. If you have closed Visual Studio 2005 or Web Development Express after the last exercise, reopen it since you are going to *add on* to that website. Use the File ➤ Open Web Site menu selection. The Open Web Site dialog will display (see Figure 9-18). You want to open the folder Visual Studio made in the last exercise. So, in this dialog, choose the File System option on the left side of the screen. Then select the BugReporter folder on the right.

Figure 9-18. *Opening an existing website*

2. Add a new web form by selecting Web Site ➤ New Item.

3. When the dialog screen shows up, make sure to choose the Web Form icon from the list of templates. At the bottom of the Add New Item dialog screen, change the name of the web form to **BugReporter.aspx**, Make sure to select the language you wish to use, and the Place Code In Separate File checkbox is *checked* (see Figure 9-19). Now, click the Add button.

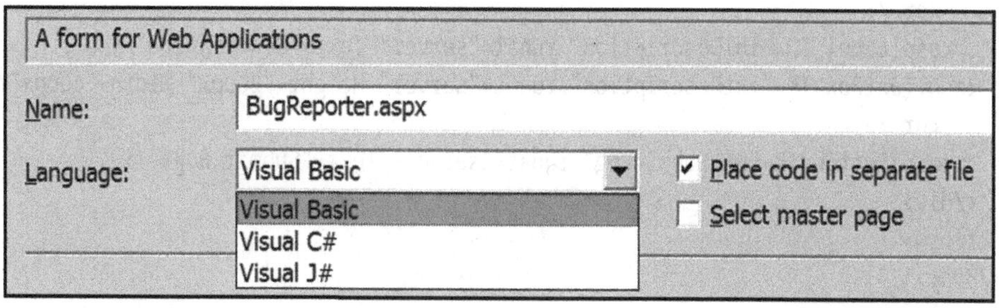

A form for Web Applications	
Name:	BugReporter.aspx
Language:	Visual Basic ▼ ☑ Place code in separate file
	Visual Basic
	Visual C# ☐ Select master page
	Visual J#

Figure 9-19. *Starting the BugReporter web page*

4. You should now see an HTML code page. Right below the first line of code, replace the current code with the following code. It will add all of the controls for you.

■**Note** Make sure that you leave the first line that identifies the Language attribute for VB .NET or C# and add this code after that line.

HTML

```html
<!DOCTYPE html PUBLIC "-//W3C//DTD XHTML 1.1//EN"
"http://www.w3.org/TR/xhtml11/DTD/xhtml11.dtd">
<script runat="server">
</script>
<html xmlns="http://www.w3.org/1999/xhtml" >
<head runat="server">
    <title>Bug Reporter</title>
</head>
<body>
 <div>
  <h1>Bug Reporter</h1>
  <p> Please enter the following information to report a bug:</p>
 </div>
 <form id="form1" runat="server">
  <div>
    <asp:TextBox ID="txtTester" runat="server"></asp:TextBox>
    <asp:Label ID="lblTester" runat="server" Text="Testers Name" />
    <br />
    <asp:TextBox ID="txtAppName" runat="server"></asp:TextBox>
    <asp:Label ID="lblAppName" runat="server" Text="Application Name"/>
    <br />
```

```
     <asp:TextBox ID="txtBuildNumber" runat="server"></asp:TextBox>
     <asp:Label ID="lblBuildNumber" runat="server" Text="Build Number"/>
      <br />
     <asp:TextBox ID="txtDateReported" runat="server"></asp:TextBox>
     <asp:Label ID="lblDateReported" runat="server" Text="Date Reported"/>
      <br />
     <asp:Label ID="lblDescription" runat="server" Text="Description"/>
  <asp:TextBox ID="txtDescription" runat="server" Height="200px" Width="400px"/>
      <br />
     <asp:Button ID="btnSubmitBug" runat="server" Text="Submit Bug" />
   </div>
 </form>
</body>
</html>
```

5. After adding is code, use the Design button at the bottom of the editor to verify your form looks like Figure 9-20.

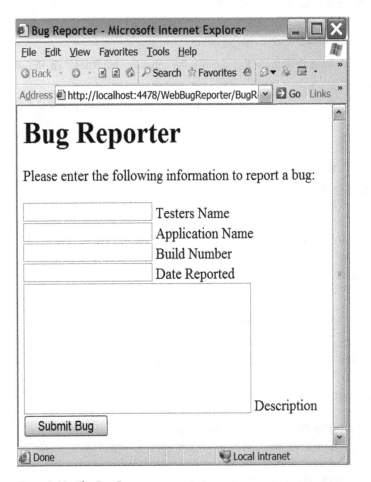

Figure 9-20. *The BugReporter page*

6. Although they should be correct now, verify that the properties for the controls are correct per Table 9-1 using the Property window. Notice that you can change the properties in either the `.aspx` page or the Property window.

Table 9-1. *Properties to Set*

Object	Property	Value
txtTester	Text	(Leave this blank)
txtAppName	Text	(Leave this blank)
txtBuildNumber	Text	(Leave this blank)
txtDateReported	Text	(Leave this blank)
txtDescription	Text	(Leave this blank)
	Height	200
	Width	400
btnSubmitBug	Text	Submit bug
lblTester	Text	Tester's name
lblAppName	Text	Application's name
lblBuildNumber	Text	Build number
lblDateReported	Text	Date found
lblDescription	Text	Description of bug

7. From the Design view, double-click btnSubmitBug to create a new event handling method called btnSubmitBug_Click() in the `.aspx.vb` or `.aspx.cs` page. This code collects the data from the textboxes, adds the commas, and adds single quotes around each string value as needed to be used in the SQL Insert statement. Once the data is collected and formatted, pass it to a method we will create next called AddBug():

VB .NET

```
Protected Sub btnSubmitBug_Click(ByVal sender As Object, _
ByVal e As System.EventArgs) Handles btnSubmitBug.Click
'---- Get Data Section ----
'Create string variables and get the data from the user
Dim strTester As String = txtTester.Text
Dim strApplicationName As String = txtAppName.Text
Dim strBuildNumber As String = txtBuildNumber.Text
Dim strDateReported As String = txtDateReported.Text
Dim strDescription As String = txtDescription.Text
```

```
'Pull data out of the variables above and put it into a string
Dim strData As String = ""
strData += "'" + strTester + "',"
strData += "'" + strApplicationName + "',"
strData += "'" + strBuildNumber + "',"
strData += "'" + strDateReported + "',"
strData += "'" + strDescription + "'"

'---- Save Data to Database Section ----
AddBug(strData)
Response.Redirect("default.aspx")
End Sub
```

C#

```
protected void btnSubmitBug_Click(object sender, System.EventArgs e)
{
//---- Get Data Section ----
//Create string variables and get the data from the User
string strTester = txtTester.Text;
string strApplicationName = txtAppName.Text;
string strBuildNumber = txtBuildNumber.Text;
string strDateReported = txtDateReported.Text;
string strDescription = txtDescription.Text;

//Pull data out of the variables above and put it into a string
string strData = "";
strData += "'" + strTester + "',";
strData += "'" + strApplicationName + "',";
strData += "'" + strBuildNumber + "',";
strData += "'" + strDateReported + "',";
strData += "'" + strDescription + "'";

//---- Save Data to Database Section ----
AddBug(strData);
Response.Redirect("default.aspx");
}//end of btnSubmitBug_Click()
```

8. Create a new method called AddBug() just below the btnSubmitBug_Click() method, as shown next. This code uses ADO.NET to connect to the database and execute the Insert statement:

VB .NET

```
Protected Sub AddBug(ByVal BugData As String)
    Dim objBuilder As System.Data.OleDb.OleDbConnectionStringBuilder
    Dim objCon As System.Data.OleDb.OleDbConnection
    Dim objComm As System.Data.OleDb.OleDbCommand
    Dim strInsert As String = ""
```

```
'Create a connection to the database
objBuilder = New System.Data.OleDb.OleDbConnectionStringBuilder
objBuilder.ConnectionString = "Data Source= C:\BugData.mdb"
objBuilder.Add("Provider", "Microsoft.Jet.Oledb.4.0")
objBuilder.Add("Jet OLEDB:Database Password", "")
' Set up row-level locking.
objBuilder.Add("Jet OLEDB:Database Locking Mode", 1)

objCon = New System.Data.OleDb.OleDbConnection(objBuilder.ConnectionString)

'Build the Insert SQL command(
'Note the spaces are important!
strInsert = " Insert Into ReportedBugs "
strInsert += " (Tester, AppName, Build, DateReported, Description) "
strInsert += " Values( " + BugData + " ) "

'Build a Command object to send your command
objComm = New System.Data.OleDb.OleDbCommand()
objComm.Connection = objCon
objComm.CommandType = System.Data.CommandType.Text
objComm.CommandText = strInsert
'Response.Write(objComm.CommandText.ToString)

'Open the connection and run the command
Try
    objCon.Open()
    objComm.ExecuteNonQuery()
    objCon.Close()
    Response.Redirect("Default.aspx")

Catch ex As Exception
    Response.Write(ex.ToString)
End Try
End Sub
```

C#

```
protected void AddBug(string BugData)
{
    System.Data.OleDb.OleDbConnectionStringBuilder objBuilder;
    System.Data.OleDb.OleDbConnection objCon;
    System.Data.OleDb.OleDbCommand objComm;
    string strInsert = "";

    objBuilder = new System.Data.OleDb.OleDbConnectionStringBuilder();
    objBuilder.ConnectionString = "Data Source= C:\\BugData.mdb";
    objBuilder.Add("Provider", "Microsoft.Jet.Oledb.4.0");
    objBuilder.Add("Jet OLEDB:Database Password", "");
```

```
objBuilder.Add("Jet OLEDB:Database Locking Mode", 1);
objCon = new System.Data.OleDb.OleDbConnection(objBuilder.ConnectionString);

strInsert = " Insert Into ReportedBugs ";
strInsert += " (Tester, AppName, Build, DateReported, Description) ";
strInsert += " Values( " + BugData + " ) ";
objComm = new System.Data.OleDb.OleDbCommand();
objComm.Connection = objCon;
objComm.CommandType = System.Data.CommandType.Text;
objComm.CommandText = strInsert;

try
{
  objCon.Open();
  objComm.ExecuteNonQuery();
  objCon.Close();
  Response.Redirect("Default.aspx");
}
catch (Exception ex) {
  Response.Write(ex.ToString());
}
}//end of AddBug()
```

9. Place the BugData.mdb file on the root of C:\. You can find this file in the DownloadFiles\Chapter9\ folder. This file is available for download from the Source Code section of the Apress website (www. apress.com). See Appendix C for more download details. If you have not downloaded the files and you are familiar with Microsoft Access, then you can make this table yourself. Just refer back to the table structure shown in Figure 9-16.

10. Now, you are going to create the page that selects the bug report data. To do this, add a new web form by selecting Web Site ➤ New Item.

11. When the dialog screen shows, make sure to choose the Web Form icon from the list of templates. At the bottom of the Add New Item dialog screen, change the name of the web form to **BugViewer.aspx**, select the language you wish to use, and *check* the Place Code In Separate File check box. Now, click the Add button. This will bring up the screen shown in Figure 9-21.

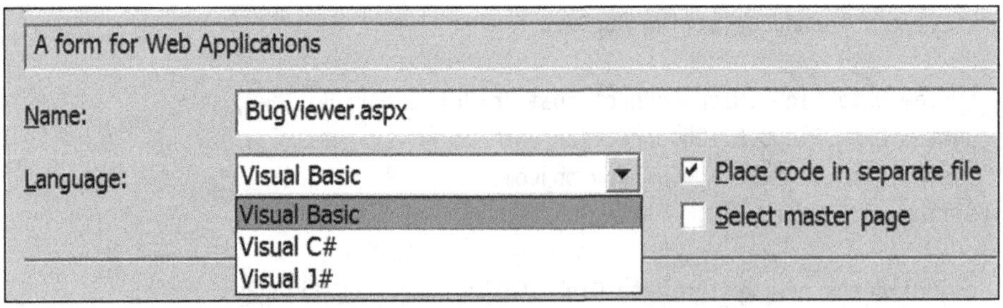

Figure 9-21. *Starting the BugViewer web page*

12. Click the Design button to display the Design view of your web form. Although there is nothing on the page yet, you will add code to show the bug report data when the page loads.

13. Switch to the Design view of this page and double-clicking on the blank page to add an event handler for the Page Load event.

14. You want to connect to the database, retrieve the reported bug, and display them on the web page. So, add the following code to the Page Load event procedure:

VB .NET

```
Protected Sub Page_Load(ByVal sender As Object, ByVal e As System.EventArgs)

  Dim objBuilder As System.Data.OleDb.OleDbConnectionStringBuilder
  Dim objCon As System.Data.OleDb.OleDbConnection
  Dim objComm As System.Data.OleDb.OleDbCommand
  Dim strSelect As String = ""

  'Create a connection to the System.Database
  objBuilder = New System.Data.OleDb.OleDbConnectionStringBuilder
  objBuilder.ConnectionString = "Data Source= C:\BugData.mdb"
  objBuilder.Add("Provider", "Microsoft.Jet.Oledb.4.0")
  objBuilder.Add("Jet OLEDB:Database Password", "")
  ' Set up row-level locking.
  objBuilder.Add("Jet OLEDB:Database Locking Mode", 1)
  objCon = New System.Data.OleDb.OleDbConnection(objBuilder.ConnectionString)

  'Build the SQL Select command
  'Note the Spaces are important!
  strSelect = " Select "
  strSelect += " Tester, AppName, Build, DateReported, Description "
  strSelect += " From ReportedBugs"

  'Build a Command object to send your command
  objComm = New System.Data.OleDb.OleDbCommand()
  objComm.Connection = objCon
  objComm.CommandType = System.Data.CommandType.Text
  objComm.CommandText = strSelect
  'Response.Write(objComm.CommandText.ToString)

  'Create a System.DataReader variable to referance the results
  'we get back from the System.Database.
  Dim objDR As System.Data.OleDb.OleDbDataReader
  'Open the connection and run the command
  Try
    objCon.Open()
    objDR = objComm.ExecuteReader()
```

```vb
      Response.Write("<table border='1'>")
      Response.Write("<tr>")
      Response.Write("<th>Tester</th>")
      Response.Write("<th>App Name</th>")
      Response.Write("<th>Build</th>")
      Response.Write("<th>DateReported</th>")
      Response.Write("<th>Description</th>")
      Response.Write("</tr>")

      'Print out the results
      While objDR.Read = True
        Response.Write("<tr>")
        Response.Write("<td>" & objDR("Tester") & "</td>")
        Response.Write("<td>" & objDR("AppName") & "</td>")
        Response.Write("<td>" & objDR("Build") & "</td>")
        Response.Write("<td>" & objDR("DateReported") & "</td>")
        Response.Write("<td>" & objDR("Description") & "</td>")
        Response.Write("</tr>")
      End While

      Response.Write("</table>")
      Response.Write("Use the back button to return to the default page")

      objDR.Close()

    Catch ex As Exception
      Response.Write(ex.ToString)
    Finally
      If objCon.State = System.Data.ConnectionState.Open Then
        objCon.Close()
      End If
    End Try
End Sub
```

C#

```csharp
protected void Page_Load(object sender, System.EventArgs e)
{
  System.Data.OleDb.OleDbConnectionStringBuilder objBuilder;
  System.Data.OleDb.OleDbConnection objCon;
  System.Data.OleDb.OleDbCommand objComm;
  string strSelect = "";

  //Create a connection to the database
  objBuilder = new System.Data.OleDb.OleDbConnectionStringBuilder();
  objBuilder.ConnectionString = "Data Source= C:\\BugData.mdb";
  objBuilder.Add("Provider", "Microsoft.Jet.Oledb.4.0");
  objBuilder.Add("Jet OLEDB:Database Password", "");
```

```
objBuilder.Add("Jet OLEDB:Database Locking Mode", 1);
objCon = new System.Data.OleDb.OleDbConnection(objBuilder.ConnectionString);

//Build the SQL Select command
//Note the spaces are important!
strSelect = " Select ";
strSelect += " Tester, AppName, Build, DateReported, Description ";
strSelect += " From ReportedBugs";

//Build a Command object to send your command
objComm = new System.Data.OleDb.OleDbCommand();
objComm.Connection = objCon;
objComm.CommandType = System.Data.CommandType.Text;
objComm.CommandText = strSelect;
//Response.Write(objComm.CommandText.ToString)

//Create a DataReader variable to reference the results
//we get back from the database.
System.Data.OleDb.OleDbDataReader objDR;

//Open the connection and run the command
try
{
  objCon.Open();
  objDR = objComm.ExecuteReader();

  //Print out the results
  Response.Write("<table border='1'>");
  Response.Write("<tr>");
  Response.Write("<th>Tester</th>");
  Response.Write("<th>App Name</th>");
  Response.Write("<th>Build</th>");
  Response.Write("<th>DateReported</th>");
  Response.Write("<th>Description</th>");
  Response.Write("</tr>");

  while (objDR.Read() == true)
  {
    Response.Write("<tr>");
    Response.Write("<td>" + objDR["Tester"] + "</td>");
    Response.Write("<td>" + objDR["AppName"] + "</td>");
    Response.Write("<td>" + objDR["Build"] + "</td>");
    Response.Write("<td>" + objDR["DateReported"] + "</td>");
    Response.Write("<td>" + objDR["Description"] + "</td>");
    Response.Write("</tr>");
  }
```

```
    Response.Write("</table>");
    Response.Write("Use the back button to return to the default page");
    objDR.Close();
  }
  catch (Exception ex)
  {
    Response.Write(ex.ToString());
  }
  finally
  {
    if (objCon.State == System.Data.ConnectionState.Open)
    {
      objCon.Close();
    }
  }
}//end of Page_load
```

15. Reopen the Default.aspx page. This is the page you worked with in Exercise 9-1. You are going to add code that redirects the user from the Default.aspx to the BugReporter.aspx and BugViewer.aspx pages when the buttons are pressed. Since you used the code-behind option in Exercise 9-1, this code will be in the Default web page's code-behind page (default.aspx.vb or default.aspx.cs). Modify the code you created in Listing 9-6 to look like the following:

VB .NET

```
Protected Sub btnReportBug_Click(ByVal sender As Object, _
ByVal e As System.EventArgs) Handles btnReportBug.Click
  Response.Redirect("BugReporter.aspx")
End Sub


Protected Sub btnViewBugs_Click(ByVal sender As Object, _
ByVal e As System.EventArgs) Handles btnViewBugs.Click
  Response.Redirect("BugViewer.aspx")
End Sub
```

C#

```
protected void btnReportBug_Click(object sender, EventArgs e)
{
  Response.Redirect("BugReporter.aspx");
}
protected void btnViewBugs_Click(object sender, EventArgs e)
{
  Response.Redirect("BugViewer.aspx");
}
```

16. Start the application and test the web pages for the following:

- Can you navigate from the Default page to the other pages?

- Can you submit data to the database?

- Can you view the data from the database?

You may want to test how and when the application fails and ask yourself what properties, methods, and validation code you might want to add later.

In this exercise, you created two new web pages: one to gather and insert a bug report into a database and one to display the reports. You probably noticed that there are still features missing from this application, like validation code. We will talk about that in the next section.

Adding Validation Code

As you know, testing often involves proving that validation code exists and that it is working correctly. As mentioned earlier, most web pages will provide validation code in a client-side script block, but since it is possible to go around this code and send data directly to the server, this code is repeated in a server-side script block.

Many software companies now sell pre-packaged websites for things like order tracking and customer relationship management (CRM). These sites contain validation code the developers thought would be needed for most circumstances. However, most companies find that they require additional validations to match their individual needs. These types of validations are referred to as *business rules*. Since these validations may be used by the other applications a company has, they are often placed into a .dll and that .dll is placed on a central server. In a web application, these component servers often sit between the web server and a database server, and are commonly referred to as *middle-tier servers*. Other common terms you may have heard include, biz-layer servers or COM servers. Whatever it's called, it represents a place to store reusable components.

■**Note** When we wrote this book, we assumed that most readers would have a single computer to study with and not a network of servers. As such, you will not need to set up a component server or a separate database server to follow the next topics. However, be aware that while all the presentation, business, and database layers can be on a single computer as we have here, in most production applications these would exist on separate computers.

If it exists, a web page will run client-side validation code before the web browser sends data to the server. Since this client-side code is processed by the web browser, it must be in a language that the browser understands. At the time of this writing, no browser can process either C# or VB .NET; so, instead, you need to use a scripting language like VBS or JavaScript. Since only Microsoft web browsers support VBS, JavaScript is the logical choice for this task. Listing 9-11 is an example in JavaScript that checks to see if a textbox is still empty when the on_Submit() method is called.

Listing 9-11. *Checking for an Empty Textbox with JavaScript*

JavaScript

```
<script language="javascript" type="text/javascript" >
function on_Submit()
 {
  if(document.form1.txtTester.value == "")
  {
   alert("You must provide a tester name");
   return false;
  }
}
</script>
```

Since you need to perform this validation on the web server as well, you also add server-side code to the web page that the web server understands. In ASP.NET, this will most commonly be either VB .NET or C#. Listing 9-12 shows an example in each of these languages.

Listing 9-12. *Checking for an Empty String with VB .NET or C#*

VB .NET

```
Public Shared Function TestForEmptyStrings(ByVal strData As String) As Boolean
    Dim strPattern As String = ""
    If (strData = strPattern) Then
      Return True
    Else
      Return False
    End If
End Function
```

C#

```
public static bool TestForEmptyStrings(string strData)
{
  string strPattern = "";
  if (strData == strPattern)
  {
    return true;
  }
  else
  {
    return false;
  }
}
```

Reusing Existing Components

You may recognize Listing 9-12 as code we used it in Chapter 6. However, in that chapter, we placed this code in a .dll file and referenced it from a Windows application. We can do this same thing from a web application by referring to that same .dll file. There are two ways this can be done: one, by making a copy of the .dll file for both the Windows and web applications; and two, by reusing the same file from both applications.

In the first option, all you would do is locate the .dll file and copy it to the web server. Although this is very easy to do, it does have some drawbacks. For example, you have to keep track of the version numbers and location of all copies of the .dll so that you can apply updates when needed.

To combat issues like these, larger applications will host these .dll files on a central component server (again, see Figure 9-1). These types of servers often have advanced capability for managing security and workloads built into them. Advanced features include things like transaction management and a form of caching that you may have heard of called *object pooling*. Object pooling is used when you know that clients will be repeatedly creating objects from the classes in your .dlls, so you create a number of the objects ahead of time. These objects are collected into a pool of objects, allowing the client to reference one of the objects from the pool and, thereby, offsetting the cost of creating a new object with each request.

No matter which option you choose, adding a reference to a .dll from a web application is fundamentally the same as from a Windows application. In both types of projects, Visual Studio lets you use either the Web Site ➤ Add Reference menu or just right-click on the project's name within Solution Explorer and choose to add a reference from the pop-up menu (see Figure 9-22).

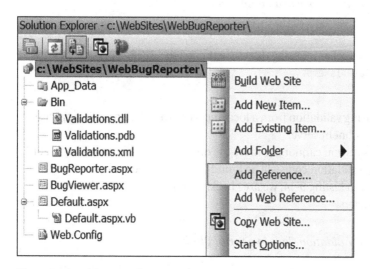

Figure 9-22. *Adding a reference to a .dll*

As an example, let's say that you wanted to use the methods you made in Chapter 6's Validatations.dll. When adding a reference to local file like this one, Visual Studio will make a copy of the .dll file and add it to the bin folder of your current project. Once that is done, you can right-click on this file in Solution Explorer and use the Open With menu item to exam the .dll with the Object Browser. The Object Browser reveals the namespaces, classes, properties, and methods within your .dll (see Figure 9-23).

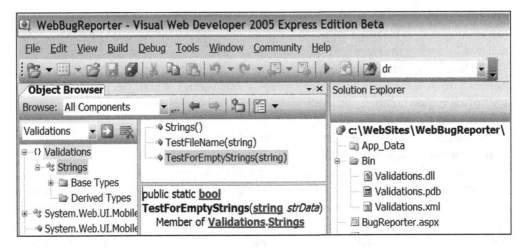

Figure 9-23. *Using the Object Browser*

In Figure 9-23, you can see a method called TestForEmptyStrings(). This method takes a string for its argument and returns a Boolean value for true if the string is empty. You could call this function from your web page using code like what you see in Listing 9-13.

Listing 9-13. *Using Server Validation Code in a Component*

VB .NET

```
If Validations.Strings.TestForEmptyStrings(Data.Text) = True Then
  strProblem = "Textbox data is empty."
End if
```

While this example is using validation from a local file, you would use a similar process with a .dll located on a component server.

Be aware that nothing says you cannot use more the one option within a web page. For example, not all server-side validation code will be found in .dll components, so it may be added in the web page itself. In Listing 9-14, we are checking that a string value has not exceeded a limit of 20 characters.

Listing 9-14. *Using Server-Side Validation Code in a Script Block*

VB .NET

```
<title>Bug Reporter</title>
<script runat="server">

Protected Function MoreThenTwenty(ByVal strData As String) As Boolean
 If strData.Length > 20 Then
   Return True
 Else
   Return False
 End If
End Function
```

You can also combine the two validation methods to form your complete server-side validation logic, as shown in Listing 9-15. Note how both the code from the component and the script block are used. If either one finds a problem, the strProblem variable will be filled with a message to indicate the issue and a false value will be returned to indicate that the entry is not complete.

Listing 9-15. *Combining the Different Types of Server-Side Validation Code*

VB .NET

```
Protected Function IsComplete(ByRef Data As TextBox) As Boolean
If Validations.Strings.TestForEmptyStrings(Data.Text) = True Then
  strProblem = "is empty."
  Return False
ElseIf MoreThenTwenty(Data.Text) = True _
  And Not Data.ID = "txtDescription" Then
  strProblem = "has more the 20 characters."
  Return False
Else
  Return True
End If
End Function
```

Looking closely, you may notice that we have exempted the txtDescription textbox from the 20-character limit, but are still checking that it is not empty. Did you also notice that the code passes in a reference to the textbox object and not just the text from these controls? This is done so that you can examine some of the other properties of the textboxes, such as the ID.

To evaluate each textbox, you would call the IsCompete() method and pass in a reference of that textbox. Since you would do it for each of the textboxes on the page, you may find it handy to organize your code in something like If-Else or Select case statement, whichever you find easier to read. We show an example in Listing 9-17.

TESTER'S TIP: BUILT-IN VALIDATION TOOLS

To make developing faster, Microsoft has included a number of built-in features with ASP.NET that we have not looked at. These other options include the set of validators found in the Validation tab of the toolbox. These are very handy features, but other technologies, like traditional ASP and PHP, do not have these. We chose to use more traditional examples to point out common ways validation code is implemented in the industry.

Although all the examples in this section have dealt with validation logic, be aware that validation code is not the only code inside of the components at the middle tier. Other uses include financial calculations and code used to access database resources. Both of these are a natural choice since many applications in a company can use the same calculation functions and feed into the same corporate database.

Exercise 9-3 shows how to update the application you made in Exercise 9-2 to include both client-side and server-side validations.

<table>
<tr><td>

Exercise 9-3: Reusing Components

</td></tr>
</table>

In this exercise, you will add validation logic to your web page from the Validations.dll component you created in Chapter 6. If you did not complete Chapter 6, we have included this file with the Download Files\Chapter6 folder in the Source Code area of the Apress website (www.apress.com).

1. If you closed Visual Studio after Exercise 9-2, you will need to reopen it since you are going to add on to that website. To do this, use the File ➤ Open Web Site menu selection. The Open Web Site dialog will display. You want to open the folder Visual Studio made in Exercise 9-2. So, in this dialog, choose the File System option on the left side of the screen, then select the BugReporter folder on the right, as you did in step 1 of Exercise 9-2 (again, see Figure 9-18).

2. You will be adding code to the BugReporter.aspx webpage, so double-click that page in Solution Explorer and choose the Source button at the bottom of Visual Studio to see the HTML code. If you find that you are looking at VB .NET or C# code, then please switch from the aspx.vb or aspx.cs to the .aspx page.

3. When the editor opens, locate the <head> and <title> tags in the HTML.

4. Create a JavaScript, client-side function called on_Submit() that verifies that the txtTester textbox is not empty and returns an error message if it is:

Note You must make sure that the server-side code will not still run if the textbox is empty. You can do this by using the return false; command. (Tip: JavaScript is a case-sensitive language, so be careful as you type.)

```
<head runat="server">
   <title>Bug Reporter</title>
   <script language="javascript" type="text/javascript" >
   function on_Submit()
   {
      if(document.form1.txtTester.value == "")
      {
         alert("You must provide a tester name");
         //stop the sever-side code from running
         return false;
      }
   }
   </script>
```

5. The on_Submit() JavaScript function needs to run when the Submit button is clicked. So, locate the code that creates the button and add an OnClientClick attribute to it. It will be in the same web page, BugReporter.aspx, but toward the bottom:

Note This attribute uses the `return` keyword to stop the server-side function `btnSubmitBug_Click()` from running if a `false` values is returned from `on_Submit()`.

```
<asp:Button ID="btnSubmitBug" runat="server" Text="Submit Bug"
OnClick="btnSubmitBug_Click" OnClientClick="return on_Submit()" />
```

6. View the web page to see the results of these changes. You can do this by right-clicking the page in Solution Explorer and choosing View In Brower from the pop-up menu. When the page loads, clicking the Submit button should show the alert message if the `txtTester` textbox is empty.

   While this validation was completed on the web browser, you will now add validation code that runs on the web server. This validation code will use the `Validations.dll` you created in Chapter 6.

7. Use the Design view to create a label on the web page, as you would with a Windows application. This label will be used to display an error message to the user. Set the ID property of the label to **lblErrorMessage** and position it next to the button on the page (see Figure 9-24).

Figure 9-24. *Adding a new Error Message label*

8. Create a reference to the `Validations.dll` on your hard drive. You can do this by right-clicking on the project's name within Solution Explorer and choosing to add a reference from the pop-up menu (again, see Figure 9-22).

9. Open the BugReporter.aspx.vb, or the BugReporter.aspx.cs, code file and add a string variable called strProblem and a function called IsComplete() that returns a Boolean value between the beginning of the class and the btnSubmitBug_Click() method. Your code should like Listing 9-16.

Listing 9-16. *Creating the IsComplete() Method*

VB .NET

```
Partial Class BugReporter
    Inherits System.Web.UI.Page

  Dim strProblem As String

  Protected Function IsComplete(ByRef Data As TextBox) As Boolean
    If Validations.Strings.TestForEmptyStrings(Data.Text) = True Then
      strProblem = "is empty."
      Return False
    Else
      Return (True)
    End If
  End Function

  Protected Sub btnSubmitBug_Click ...
```

C#

```
public partial class BugReporter : System.Web.UI.Page
{
  protected void Page_Load(object sender, EventArgs e)
  {
  }

  string strProblem;

  protected bool IsComplete(ref TextBox Data)
  {
    if (Validations.Strings.TestForEmptyStrings(Data.Text) == true)
    {
      strProblem = "is empty.";
      return false;
    }
    else
    {
      return (true);
    }
  }//end of IsComplete()

  protected void btnSubmitBug_Click ...
```

10. Locate the btnSubmitBug_Click() method, and add the following validation code to the beginning of that method. Your code should look like Listing 9-17.

Listing 9-17. *Validating Each Textbox*

VB .NET

```
Protected Sub btnSubmitBug_Click _
(ByVal sender As Object, ByVal e As System.EventArgs)
  '---- Server Side Validation Section ----
  If False = IsComplete(txtTester) Then
    lblErrorMessage.Text = "*Testers Name " + strProblem
    Return
  ElseIf False = IsComplete(txtAppName) Then
    lblErrorMessage.Text = "*Application Name " + strProblem
    Return
  ElseIf False = IsComplete(txtBuildNumber) Then
    lblErrorMessage.Text = "*Build Number " + strProblem
    Return
  ElseIf False = IsComplete(txtDateReported) Then
    lblErrorMessage.Text = "*Date " + strProblem
    Return
  ElseIf False = IsComplete(txtDescription) Then
    lblErrorMessage.Text = "*Description " + strProblem
    Return
  End If

'---- Get Data Section ----
```

C#

```
protected void btnSubmitBug_Click(object sender, EventArgs e)
{
  //---- Server Side Validation Section ----
  if (false == IsComplete(ref txtTester))
  {
    lblErrorMessage.Text = "*Testers Name " + strProblem;
    return;
  }
  else if (false == IsComplete(ref txtAppName))
  {
    lblErrorMessage.Text = "*Application Name " + strProblem;
    return;
  }
  else if (false == IsComplete(ref txtBuildNumber))
  {
    lblErrorMessage.Text = "*Build Number " + strProblem;
    return;
  }
```

```
else if (false == IsComplete(ref txtDateReported))
{
  lblErrorMessage.Text = "*Date " + strProblem;
  return;
}
else if (false == IsComplete(ref txtDescription))
{
  lblErrorMessage.Text = "*Description " + strProblem;
  return;
}

//---- Get Data Section ----
```

11. View the web page to see the results of these changes. You can do this by right-clicking the page in Solution Explorer and choosing View In Brower from the pop-up menu. When the page loads, clicking the Submit button should show the alert message if the `txtTester` textbox is empty. However, if the `txtTester` textbox it filled, then the other textboxes will be tested server side. When all of the textboxes are filled in, the web page should add the bug report to the database.

In this exercise, you saw how components are used in web applications. You also saw that validation logic can be added at many levels within these applications. If this had been a production application, you would have to continue to add even more validation code, but this time at the database level. Of course, the more validations added to a project, the more test cases have to be examined. As we have stated many times before, web applications are more complex when it comes to testing and debugging them. Next, you will take a look at some simple tools to assist you with the debugging process.

Debugging a Web Application

Although test professionals are often asked to test an application's UI without access to the code underneath, when you write your own custom testware, you now become the developer and will need to know how to debug your code. With web applications being distributed over many computers, there are unique issues to be aware of when trying to debug them. In fact, there are so many issues that there are whole books devoted to the subject of debugging ASP.NET applications. If your life is like ours, there always seems to be so much to learn with so little time to learn it. You'll be glad to know there are some easy things you can do to start debugging your web applications.

Often, debugging distills down to two questions: "Did my program reach the line of code intended?" and "What were the values in the variables when it did reach this line?" One common way web developers answer these questions is to use a temporary "print" statement. In a web application, these print statements are added at one of the layers of code and then printed out on the web page when it is browsed. A developer knows that that particular line was reached when the printed statement displays in the page. If she has decided to print out the contents of a variable, then she can examine the output, decide if it is correct, and then remove the print statement from the code when done.

While these types of statements can be used at all tiers of the application, to do so you need to use a different syntax for each language. For example, if you want test the web browser's client-side script block, you would print a message using the write() method of a browser's document object, as shown in Listing 9-18.

Listing 9-18. *Printing from the Client*

```
<script language=javascript >
document.write("Made it to this line");
</script>
```

The write() method can be used in most modern web browsers because this method is actually part of a browser's Document Object Model (DOM). The web browser's DOM is not part of a particular language, and so the object's properties and methods can be called from any language that the browser understands. To understand the mechanics of how you access the properties and methods of these objects, consider that all web pages loaded into browsers automatically have a document object created for them. The document object of the page may contain slightly different code depending on who wrote the web browser; however, the two main browsers in the industry, Netscape and Internet Explorer, have tried to keep their object models fairly close to each other. As such, most methods and properties are accessed the same way in either of them.

Although client-side script blocks can use the browser's DOM, is not available to server-side script blocks. The reason for this is that the code on the web server does not have access to the browser's objects. Since methods and properties must be loaded into a computer's memory before they can be used, and the document.write() method is loaded into the memory of the client's computer, the web servers memory has no knowledge of them. To print out a message from the server-side script block, you need to use a similar type of print command—but one loaded on the web server.

The method you call will depend on the server-side technology you are using. But as you have seen in our earlier examples, when you are using traditional ASP or ASP.NET, you can print out a message using the Write() method of the Response object. This is such a common command that Microsoft included a shorter version of the command that looks like Listing 9-19.

Listing 9-19. *Using the Shortened Version of Response.Write()*

```
<% Response.Write("Made it to this line") %>
<%=("Made it to this line")%>
```

Both of these statements work on the web server because the web server has access to the Response object, which is part of ASP and ASP.NET. However, once you get past the web server and are working with the component layer, the commands will change yet again. The component layer will not have access to either the browser's DOM or the web server's ASP commands. Since these components are not intended for direct interaction with a person, they don't usually have a simple built-in print statement as there is on the browser and the web server layers. Instead, you must use the commands and object that exist within the component to pass a message on to the previous layers. Although this may sound complex, you can simply send return values back to the web server and have the web server process the actual printing onto the web page. A common way to do this is to add a temporary variable or property to the component for this sole purpose. When you want to verify that your code reached a particular line, you set the value of this variable to indicate this event, as shown in Listing 9-20.

Listing 9-20. *A Simple Way to Add a Print Message in a .dll*

```
Public Class Class1
  Public strDebugMessage

  Public Sub DoStuff()
    strDebugMessage = "Made it to this line"
  End Sub
End Class
```

To verify that the line was processed, you display the value of the variable with a Response.Write() statement like the one in Listing 9-21.

Listing 9-21. *Displaying the .dll Print Message with an ASP.NET Page*

```
Dim c1 As New ClassLibrary1.Class1()
Response.Write(c1.strDebugMessage)
```

Of course, this assumes that you have access to the code in the component .dll and can remove these messages once you have completed your debugging. While this would be true when you are writing your own custom piece of testware, if you are just testing someone else's component, then you are left looking at a Black Box. If the developers did not document that there are hidden variables, sometimes called *trace flags*, you have no way to probe the component in this manner.

To make accessing these types of messages more consistent, most languages have added some type of print command that can be turned on and off from outside of the .dll. As we discussed in Chapter 4, .NET includes the Debug and Trace statements for this purpose.

As you can imagine, database servers have their own ways to print out messages. In fact, the SQL command for this is easy to remember since it is actually called Print. Just as in the other technologies, you add the Print command to verify that a particular line was reached or that a particular value was set.

SQL Print statements are often used to test stored procedures. Stored procedures are like methods in that they allow you to store a set of one or more SQL commands on the database server. Just like methods in a Windows or web application, the store procedure is called when you want to run the code inside of it. Of course, it is necessary to debug and test these just like any other method since they contain processing and validation statements. Listing 9-22 is a very simple example that gives you an idea of what this would look like.

Listing 9-22. *Printing from a SQL Stored Procedure*

```
Create Proc DoSQLStuff
As
 Begin
  Print 'Got to this line'
 End
```

To forward this print message from the database, you must pass it through all of the layers up to the browser. Microsoft's ADO.NET will help you capture SQL `Print` messages and then you can pass them on to the web browser by using the `Response.Write()` method yet again. Although ADO.NET's `SqlConnection.InfoMessage` event can be used to do this, it is not exactly simple, and would take us too far off topic.

TESTER'S TIP: SIMPLE DEBUGGING

By now you're probably convinced that multitiered web applications are just harder to test and develop. Perhaps it is easy to understand why developers sometimes skip over some of the debugging chores they should do and pass them along to the testing team. Although the debugging tools in a Windows application are usually easy to use, they can be very complex in a web application. One big problem is that developers need different debuggers for the web browser, the web server, the components, and the database. Microsoft has integrated these different debuggers within Visual Studio, but they don't always work well together, nor are they intuitive to set up. This will likely change one day, but until then, using print statements for trouble-shooting and debugging are common tasks even today.

The Trace Class

With ASP.NET, Microsoft created a more sophisticated version of the print statement using the `Trace` class. Although similar, this is not the same the `Trace` class you saw for Windows applications in Chapter 4. Instead, this one is focused solely on ASP.NET applications and designed to be a more practical debugging tool than using `Response.Write()`.

One advantage of this class is that you can turn the messages on and off for a page, website, or even a whole web server. This helps alleviate a common mistake—where the developer does not find and remove all of the print statements from the code after debugging.

Tracing can be toggled on and off in three distinct ways: page level, application level, and machine level.

To turn tracing on and off at the page level, you add a command at the very top of the ASP.NET page, like the one shown in Listing 9-23.

Listing 9-23. *Turning On Page-Level Tracing*

```
<%@ Page Trace="true" %>
<html>
<script language="VB" runat="server">
```

To turn tracing on and off at the website level, you add commands within a file called web.config. You then place this configuration file within the same folder as the web pages with your Trace statements. The code inside the web.config file would look like Listing 9-24.

Listing 9-24. *Turning On Application-Level Tracing*

```
<configuration>
  <system.web>
    <trace
      enabled="true"
      pageOutput="false"
      localOnly="true"
    />
  </system.web>
</configuration>
```

The localOnly attribute, shown in Listing 9-24, allows you to display the results only when you are using a web browser on the web server itself. Since tracing can sometimes reveal sensitive information, you may not want other computers to see this content. This is a handy option to have on when you are a web server administrator trying to troubleshoot a problem. Of course, if you are a tester trying to get trace information from a remote web server, it will stop you from doing so—as you would have to be using the actual web server to see it.

You may also have noticed that the pageOutput attribute is set to false. Setting this option to true will cause the print messages to show up on the individual pages just as they would when using Response.Write(). However, when pageOutput is set to false, the trace information will not show up on the individual page, but rather can be seen on a special hidden page called trace.axd. This hidden page is created automatically whenever the pageOutput is set to false.

The trace.axd page is among a number of pages that ASP.NET can create dynamically in memory. Because of this, it is not physically stored in an .axd file on the hard drive. So you won't find this file in the web folder; however, it can be accessed like a normal web page by typing in the name of the web server, the name of the web folder, and the name of the page itself:

http://localhost/BugReporter/**trace.axd**

You can also turn tracing on and off at the machine level by adding this command in the Machine.Config file. This file contains thousands of lines of instructions and should be modified with caution. Changing the settings here will affect all websites on that server and allow any trace messages of the individual web pages to start printing out their values. We recommend that you avoid this option and, instead, turn tracing on at either the page or the application level as needed. Also, remember to turn tracing off once you are done with your tests. In Exercise 9-4, you will see an example of both page- and application-level tracing using your bug-reporting application.

Exercise 9-4: Adding Tracing to Your Web Pages

In this exercise, you will add tracing statements to your web pages and then review the output. Specifically, you will be printing out the SQL Select statement to verify what is being sent to the database. This is something you may find useful in the future, since it is a common place for syntax errors to occur.

First, let's look at using the page-level option.

1. If you closed Visual Studio after the Exercise 9-3, you will need to reopen it since you are going to add on to that website. To do this, use the File ➤ Open Web Site menu selection. The Open Web Site dialog will display. You want to open the folder Visual Studio made in Exercise 9-3. So, in this dialog, chose the File System option on the left side of the screen, then select the BugReporter folder on the right.

2. You will be adding code to the BugViewer.aspx web page, so right-click that page in Solution Explorer and choose View Code from the pop-up menu.

3. At the top of this page, find and edit the Page directive by adding the Trace option right after the Language attribute. Actually, you could put in that line anyway and it will work; but for now, please add it as shown here:

```
<%@ Page Language="VB" Trace="true" ...
```

4. Now, switch over to the BugViewer.aspx.vb or BugViewer.aspx.cs file so that you can add the Trace.Write() command to print out the SQL Select statement. Scroll down until you find the code that builds a string to hold the SQL Select statement and *add* a trace statement that prints out the content of the string to the web page, like the text in bold here:

VB .NET

```
'Build the SQL Select command
'Note the spaces are important!
strSelect = " Select "
strSelect += " Tester, AppName, Build, DateReported, Description "
strSelect += " From ReportedBugs"
Trace.Write(strSelect)
```

C#

```
//Build the SQL Select command
//Note the Spaces are important!
strSelect = " Select ";
strSelect += " Tester, AppName, Build, DateReported, Description ";
strSelect += " From ReportedBugs";
Trace.Write(strSelect);
```

5. View the web page to see the results of this statement. You can do this by right-clicking the page in Solution Explorer and choosing View In Brower from the pop-up menu. The bottom of the page will now look similar to what you see in Figure 9-25.

Trace Information	
Category	**Message**
aspx.page	Begin PreInit
aspx.page	End PreInit
aspx.page	Begin Init
aspx.page	End Init
aspx.page	Begin InitComplete
aspx.page	End InitComplete
aspx.page	Begin PreLoad
aspx.page	End PreLoad
aspx.page	Begin Load
	Select Tester, AppName, Build, DateReported, Description From ReportedBugs
aspx.page	End Load

Figure 9-25. *Viewing the Trace message within the web page*

Note Using the Write() method will print out the message in black, while using the Warn() method will print it out in red. You can try adding both to the code so that you will see the difference.

Now let's see how you can use the web.config file to turn on tracing at the application level.

6. Find the web.config file in Solution Explorer and double-click it to open it in the code editor.

7. Toward the middle of this file, you will see a *compilation* tag. Add a new tag that turns on tracing for the whole web application, as shown here:

VB .NET

```
<compilation debug="true" strict="false" explicit="true"/>
<trace enabled="true" localOnly="true" pageOutput="false"/>
```

C#

```
<compilation debug="true"/>
<trace enabled="true" localOnly="true" pageOutput="false"/>
```

8. Save your changes and browse to the trace.axd page. You can do this by right-clicking the BugViewer.aspx in Solution Explorer and choosing View In Brower from the pop-up menu. Once that page is open, you will need to add **trace.axd** to the end of the address line of the browser, like this:

```
http://localhost:1111/BugReporter/trace.axd
```

■**Note** The number after `localhost`, in this case `1111`, is the port number and will likely be different on your own computer. Port numbers are used to identify the application you wish to talk to on a particular machine. A computer's IP address can include a port number much like an address of an office building can include a suite number. The IP address would be analogous to the street address of the building, and the port number would be analogous to the suite number of an actual office in the building.

When you want to connect to the standard port of the web server, you just need to type in the computer's name or the nickname of `localhost`. This name is then translated to an IP address by the computer behind the scenes. If you do not indicate a port number, most software will just use a default port number. In web browsers, the default port for HTTP requests is port 80. Since Visual Web Developer is using its own built-in web server, it uses a different port number than the standard web port used by IIS. The port number may be different each time you use Visual Studio; but, not to worry, Visual Studio will include the correct port number for you.

9. When the `trace.axd` page appears, you should see a dialog display like the one in Figure 9-26. Note the View Details link in the lower, right-hand corner. Click this link to see the detail for that particular request.

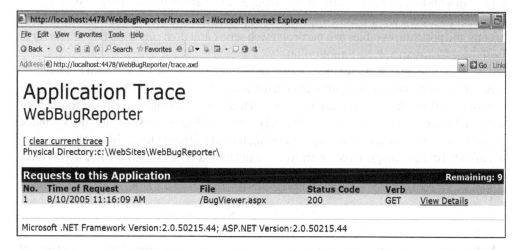

Figure 9-26. *Browsing the trace.axd page*

Each time you make additional requests for the `BugViewer.aspx` page, you will see additional lines added to this page.

10. Go back and edit the `BugViewer.aspx` page by setting the `Trace` option to `false`:

```
<%@ Page Language="VB" Trace="false" %>
```

11. Right-click the `BugViewer.aspx` page in Solution Explorer again, and choose View In Brower from the pop-up menu. Notice that the trace messages are no longer appearing on that page.

12. Browse to the Trace.axd page again and note that a new line has *not* been added to the list of requests. This is because the more specific command at the page level overrides the command at the application level.

13. Close this web page and browse the Default.aspx web page instead. Try each button, using the web browsers "Back" button to navigate back and forth.

14. Once that page is open, add **trace.axd** to the end of the address line of the browser, like this:

```
http://localhost:1111/BugReporter/trace.axd
```

15. When the trace.axd page appears, note that the request to both the default.aspx and BugReporter.aspx shows up on the list of requests, but any *new* visits to the BugViewer.aspx do not.

In this exercise, you saw how to enable tracing for a web page and a web application. When you are writing your web-based testware, you may find it a useful tool in the process of debugging your code. When you are testing someone else's application, these trace messages may provide additional information about the web page if they exist.

Deploying an ASP.NET Application

With your web-based testware written and debugged, you are ready to deploy it. Although, Microsoft provides a few different ways to do this, perhaps the most educational way would be to copy and paste the web files to a particular web server and then configure the web server to treat these files as an ASP.NET application.

This is really what the other methods are doing for you, they just are doing it behind the scenes using additional commands added to the web server, collectively known as *Web Server Extensions*. Microsoft chose to reuse some commands they had made for another one of their web development products called FrontPage. These "Front Page Extensions" let you command a remote web server to upload files and set configuration on those files. If these extensions are not installed or not configured correctly, you will not be able to use the automated deployment options that come with Visual Studio. So let's take a look at how to manually deploy your web application next.

Note Although it is not necessary in order to get the concepts we are discussing here, you must have IIS installed if you want to follow along with this section of the chapter.

First, you will need a web share to hold your files. Web shares are also called *virtual directories*. For example, you can make a folder within the wwwroot folder and paste the files from BugReporter into the new folder. In Figure 9-27, we have done just that by creating a folder called _DemoFolder. The name looks kind of strange since we used an underscore to make the folder show up at the top of the tree view, but normally you would call it something that makes more sense for a real application.

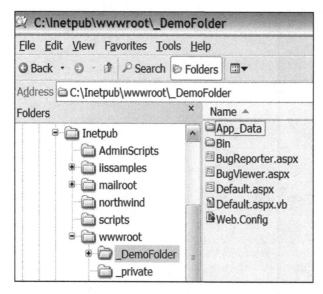

Figure 9-27. *Creating a web share*

Even though the files are in place and it is now an official web share, you still need to configure the web server to treat the files in this particular folder as an ASP.NET application. If you do not do this, it's just a standard web share but not a web application.

You can access the administration console for IIS in a few ways:

- Go to Start ➤ Control Panel ➤ Administrative Tools, and then click Internet Information Services (IIS) Manager.

- From the Start menu, click Run option, type in **inetmgr**, and then click OK.

- Open the Computer Management window by right-clicking My Computer on your desktop, then click Manage in the pop-up menu. Accessing IIS in this way does not show you all of the options offered by IIS, but will be sufficient for most of things.

No matter which way you get into the IIS Manager, you should see something like Figure 9-28. Note, you may have to click the + symbols within the tree a few times before it expands enough to see the folder you have created in the wwwroot folder. Once you find your folder, you can right-click it and use the pop-up menu to access that folder's Property window.

When the Property window opens, you can set the folder to be an ASP.NET application by clicking the Create button shown in Figure 9-29.

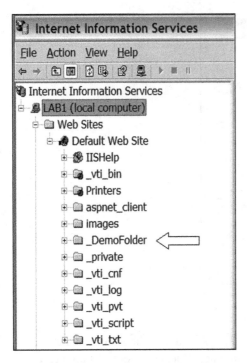

Figure 9-28. *Using the Internet Service Manager*

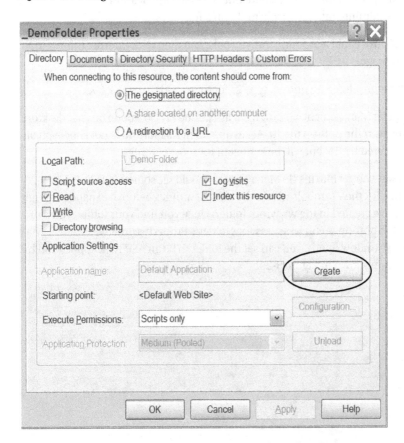

Figure 9-29. *Click the Create button to create a web application.*

In Figure 9-29, the application has not been made yet. You can tell because the application configuration options are grayed out. If you try to browse the ASP.NET web pages at this point, you get an error message. However, after you click the Create button, the application will be created and you will be able to browse the pages successfully.

Once you have set up the application, the button's text changes and you will have access to the additional configurations through the Configuration button (see Figure 9-30). While these additional configurations are beyond the scope of this book, you should know that this is where the application mapping for the file extensions are found. We discussed these mappings at the beginning of the chapter (again, see Figure 9-3).

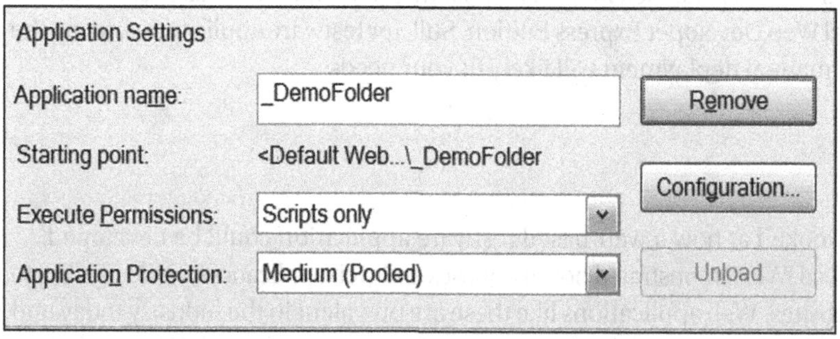

Figure 9-30. *After you create the web application*

To browse the site, you type the address shown in Figure 9-31. It will open up the website you have just configured and display the default.aspx page. Note that this page is displayed even though the address does not include it. This is because IIS is normally set up to look for a file called default.aspx when you install ASP.NET on it. This default page can be changed to another page if you'd like, but many developers will just use this as the name of the first page in their applications.

Figure 9-31. *Browsing the deployed web application*

Using the Copy Web and the Publish Web Options

While deploying a website manually is not hard, you may want to investigate the automatic tools Microsoft has in Visual Studio. In Visual Web Developer 2005, these include the Copy Web and the Publish Web options.

The Copy Web tool in Visual Web Developer will copy the current website you have been working on directly to the IIS web server you specify. You can use either your own computer or on another computer that you have administrative rights to.

The Publish Web utility will do much the same thing, but it includes more advanced features as well, such as compiling your website files and then copying the needed files to the target web server. This option is intended for professional web developers and, as such, is not available in the Visual Web Developer Express Edition. Still, for testware applications, using the Copy Web option or manual deployment will likely fit your needs.

Summary

In this chapter, you looked at how a web-based testware application could be developed, debugged, and deployed. We demonstrated how databases and web applications work together to form data-driven websites. Web applications like these are prevalent in the industry today and can range from quite simple, as in our example, to complex N-tier commercial sites.

While web development is a topic that cannot be fully discussed in only a few pages, we hope this chapter has given you a better understanding of how web applications work. Although professional web developers need years of experience to master their craft, a tester can still create web-based testware quite easily using Visual Web Developer 2005.

Also, remember that testware by its nature is often used for only one project before it needs to be reworked for the next project that comes along. While it is fun to create fancier websites, you may find it more cost effective to keep your web-based testware simple.

Tester's Checklist

When building web-based testware,

- ☑ Use Visual Web Developer to create and debug you testware.

- ☑ Reuse preexisting testware components to lower development costs.

- ☑ Use `Trace` to print debugging messages instead of `Response.Write()`.

- ☑ Keep the website code and design as simple as you can while still getting the job done.

■ ■ ■

CHAPTER 10

Testing COM and Web Services

You learned in Chapter 6 that most software systems are built using components rather than all at once. In that chapter, we showed you how to create and test components using classes and class libraries. In today's complex software systems, there are still other kinds of components you'll need to understand and test. Your software development team has many issues to consider in determining the type of components to use. These issues include performance, cost, interoperability with other systems (including legacy systems), and team expertise—just to name a few of the important ones. Two important, and common, types of components you need to examine are Web Services and Common Object Model (COM) objects. Many established Windows systems use COM, a technology developed by Microsoft that's been in use in Microsoft systems for many years. Web Services is another technology that has been around for a while but is new to .NET. Web Services have many advantages, including the ability to work well with the Internet. In this chapter, you'll examine both of these technologies to determine how to create and test them and, in the process, you'll also learn a bit about their comparative benefits and liabilities.

Objectives

By the end of this chapter, you will be able to do the following:

- Create a Web Service

- Create a .NET application to test a Web Service

- Set a reference to a COM library

- Write code to test a COM component

- Discuss the types of components available to .NET systems

Web Services vs. COM Components

Prior to .NET, Microsoft component–based systems were built using COM. Thus, many existing systems use COM architecture and components. With .NET, the emphasis has moved from COM architecture to Service-Oriented Architecture (SOA), which leans heavily toward the use of Web Services. Although the movement may be away from COM, the testing community will continue to need to understand and test COM objects for existing applications and for interoperability (interop). To that end, we will address referencing and testing COM libraries in this chapter using the COM interop libraries. We will also, of course, address Web Services.

Web Services technologies have been used successfully by the software industry in general for many years as a way to leverage the Web to distribute information, data, and software components. Microsoft systems prior to .NET used remoting to interact with other systems' Web Services. .NET remoting is a complex way of accessing Web Services, but it is workable. Microsoft's .NET makes interacting with Web Services much easier, as we'll see in the next section. We'll examine both types of components, COM and Web Services, in more detail in the following sections.

Understanding Web Services

Web Services are, essentially, web pages that are not intended for human consumption (i.e., they do not require visual, manual operation) as on a regular web page, but can be used by software to gain information programmatically. In other words, Web Services are web-based information that you must write code to access. Since so many applications are web-enabled, Web Services provide a consistent and standardized way to transfer information that lends itself well to working across the Internet.

It's a lot easier to explain Web Services by illustration. The classic example of a Web Service, and a good one, is the Web Service provided by an airline to a travel company. As you know, there are many online companies, such as Expedia and Travelocity to name two, that provide information about airlines and even allow you to reserve and pay for flights. These travel companies receive current information about flights directly from Web Services provided by the airlines. The travel companies have an agreement with airlines, and also with hotel and car rental agencies, to get access to their most current information via the Web. These travel companies then create their own websites to programmatically access the airline, hotel, and car information provided by the airlines in the form of Web Services. They then turn around and display that information on their own web pages. If travel companies can consume and transform information in this manner, certainly any kind of data can be provided this way. Even internally, corporations can provide information to their employees via a Web Service on their own company intranets. More and more companies are using this strategy to provide (or *serve*) information. For another example, weather information can be provided this way by forecasting experts and this information can be consumed by anyone, such as newspapers and radio stations. Figure 10-1 displays a simple graphic illustrating how Web Services work at a high level.

One of the really nice things about Web Services is that they are programming language– and operating system–independent because the information is transported via a protocol called SOAP (Simple Object Access Protocol) that is also language-independent. Web Services are flexible enough that users can even access some Web Services through a peer-to-peer arrangement rather than by going to a central server. Today, services that were previously possible with only the older, standardized service known as Electronic Data Interchange (EDI) are increasingly likely to become Web Services instead. Web Services are also increasingly enabled by the use of the XML as a means of standardizing data formats and exchanging data. XML is the foundation for the Web Services Description Language (WSDL) that describes a Web Service and how to communicate with it.

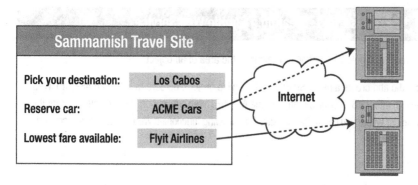

Figure 10-1. *Web Services provide data that can be accessed via the Web*

It's also still possible to access Web Services using .NET remoting; however, it's not recommended. See the "XML Web Services vs. .NET Remoting" sidebar.

SOA (SERVICE-ORIENTED ARCHITECTURE)

A service-oriented architecture (SOA) defines how two computing entities interact in such a way as to enable one entity to perform a unit of work on behalf of another entity. The unit of work is referred to as a service, and the service interactions are defined using a description language. Each interaction is self-contained and loosely coupled, so that each interaction is independent of any other interaction. Simple Object Access Protocol (SOAP)-based Web services are becoming the most common implementation of SOA.

——From TechTarget (www.techtarget.com)

XML WEB SERVICES VS. .NET REMOTING

XML Web Services and .NET remoting are both services for exposing an API to remote clients across a network. The main difference is that .NET remoting can be faster and, therefore, can be a good choice for company intranets; however, it is technology-specific: the client must be running .NET to receive the messages. XML Web Services are technology-agnostic: any client can receive the message. .NET remoting is outside the scope of this book; however, there is an excellent white paper available called "Performance Comparison: .NET Remoting vs. ASP.NET Web Services" available on the Microsoft Developer's Network (MSDN) that can help you choose which is the best option for your system.

Creating a Web Service

The best way to fully understand the power of Web Services is to create one for yourself (see Exercise 10-1). Although the process will likely seem fairly straightforward, it does include a number of important steps that do a lot behind the scenes—including creating a WSDL and a SOAP envelope for the Web Service.

Exercise 10-1: Creating a Simple Web Service

In this exercise, you'll create a simple Web Service to calculate the area of an object.

1. Start Visual Studio and create a new ASP.NET Web Service project. Be sure to select an ASP.NET Web *Service* project (in either VB .NET or C#) and not the ASP.NET Web *Site* option. Also, be sure to note the location of the folder where you create the website. The following functioning Web Service code is created for you:

VB .NET

```
Imports System.Web
Imports System.Web.Services
Imports System.Web.Services.Protocols

<WebService(Namespace := "http://tempuri.org/")> _
<WebServiceBinding(ConformsTo:=WsiProfiles.BasicProfile1_1)> _
Public Class Service
    Inherits System.Web.Services.WebService

    Public Sub Service

    End Sub

    <WebMethod()> _
    Public Function HelloWorld() As String
        Return "Hello World"
    End Function

End Class
```

C#

```
using System;
using System.Web;
using System.Web.Services;
using System.Web.Services.Protocols;

[WebService(Namespace = "http://tempuri.org/")]
[WebServiceBinding(ConformsTo = WsiProfiles.BasicProfile1_1)]
public class Service : System.Web.Services.WebService
{
    public Service () {

    }
```

```
[WebMethod]
public string HelloWorld() {
    return "Hello World";
}
}
```

Notice that this class inherits from System.Web.Services.WebService. The code provides a simple Web Service for you called *Hello World*. The namespace that is created by this code is called tempuri.org. Tempuri stands for "Temporary Uniform Resource Information" and it is intended to be a temporary namespace, provided by the W3C, which you can use for Web Service development until you locate your Web Service on its own deployment server. (It'll do for our purposes, so we won't change it.)

2. To see this Web Service work, right-click its name (Service.asmx) in the Solution Explorer window and select View In Browser, as shown in Figure 10-2.

■**Note** Be patient! It takes a few moments to launch the browser and display the Web Service even on a speedy system.

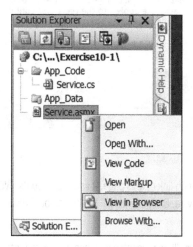

Figure 10-2. *Launching the default Web Service*

Assuming all goes well, in a few moments the window in Figure 10-3 will display.

■**Note** If you have difficulty starting the Web Service, you may need to follow the steps in Appendix A for setting up your computer to run a website.

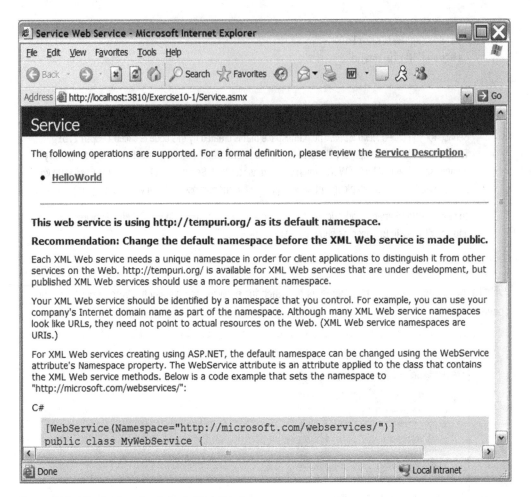

Figure 10-3. *Displaying the default Web Service*

Before going to the next step, click the Service Description link on this page. It will show you the WSDL document created in XML that describes your Web Service. Click the "back" button on your browser to return to this page before continuing.

3. Click the Hello World link on this page. The next page you'll be presented with has an Invoke button on it. Click this button. You will see the following XML code displayed regardless of whether you created this Web Service in VB .NET or C#:

```
<?xml version="1.0" encoding="utf-8" ?>
<string xmlns="http://tempuri.org/">Hello World</string>
```

This is the information that will be returned to any program calling this Web Service. The XML code uses *tags* to describe the contents it is serving. The first line of this code is an XML version tag that tells the version of the XML being used (in this case 1.0) and the encoding. (The encoding is important to the code that will eventually consume this service; but for you, at this point, it doesn't really matter.) The second line describes the data type of the return value as string. It also gives the actual value returned by the service, Hello World. Not very useful, is it? It is still a working Web Service; in later steps, you'll make it more useful.

4. Close all web browser windows (there might be two) and return to Visual Studio. Replace the code for the Hello World web method in the Code window with the following code:

VB .NET

```
<WebMethod(Description:= _
"This service calculates the area of a rectangle")> _
Public Function RectangleArea(ByVal length As Single, ByVal width As Single)  _
        As Single
    Return length * width
End Function
```

C#

```
[WebMethod(Description =
"This service calculates the area of a rectangle")]
    public Single RectangleArea(Single length, Single width) {
        return length * width;
    }
```

The first two lines of code comprise an *attribute* that declares the function following it as a WebMethod that will be exposed by the Web Service. We've added a description that is useful to have attached to the Web Service in order to describe its functionality to those wishing to use it. It is included in the Service Method help page. Additionally, in this code, the Web Service function, RectangleArea, has been changed to take two arguments, one for length and one for width, and return the corresponding area.

5. Right-click Service.asmx in the Solution Explorer window, and select View In Browser, as shown in Figure 10-2, just as you did in step 2. The same window (as shown in Figure 10-3) will display once again, but this time, of course, the name of the web method will be RectangleArea—and notice that just below the name, the description will also display.

6. Click the RectangleArea link; a browser window similar to Figure 10-4 displays.

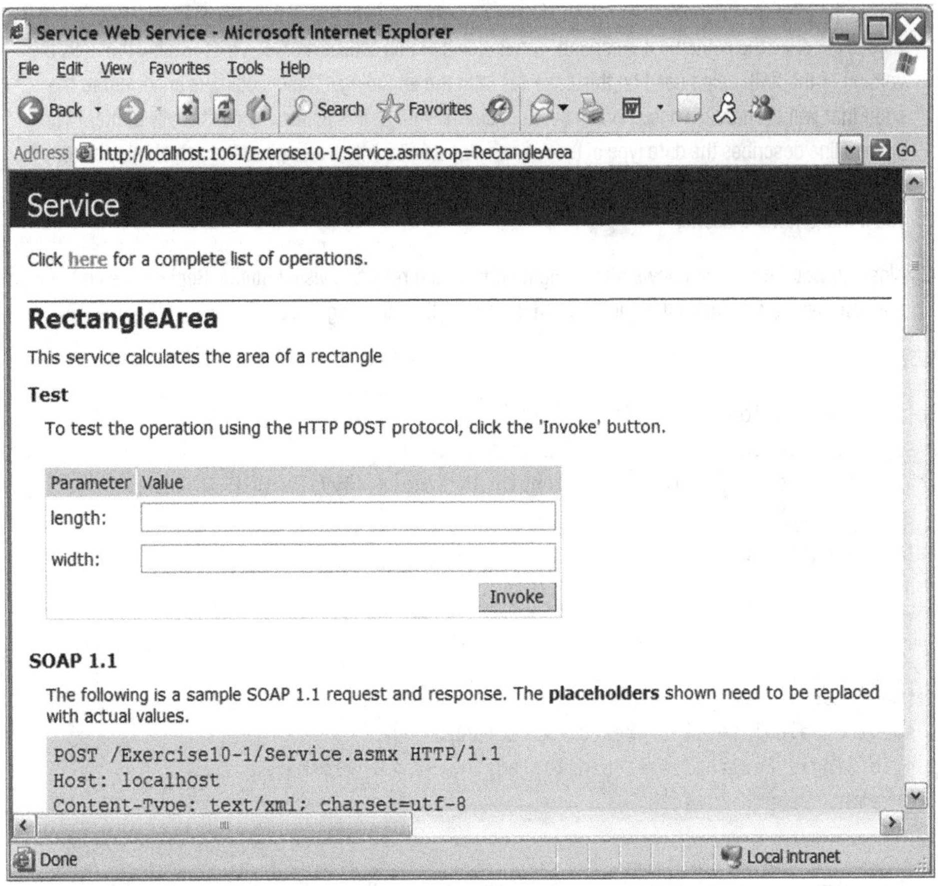

Figure 10-4. *Entering the Web Service parameters*

This browser window now contains two boxes for you to enter the `length` and `width` parameters that the Web Service will use to calculate an area. Before taking the next step, scroll down and read the section titled SOAP 1.1 in this window. This describes the SOAP envelope in which your Web Service will be enclosed. This envelope and the WSDL document provided with the Web Service have been created for you.

7. Enter two values, such as **7** and **2**, in the `length` and `width` parameters and click the Invoke button. You will see the following XML code appear:

```
<?xml version="1.0" encoding="utf-8" ?>
<float xmlns="http://tempuri.org/">14</float>
```

Of course the value 14 in this code represents the result of 2 × 7, which are the numbers you entered in the example. The `<float` is the part of the tag that tells what kind of data the result will be. Recall that when we wrote the code, we specified that the return value would be of type *double*, which means a double-precision floating point number. This XML code specifies that the return value will be a *float*. This is the floating point data type that is generic to Web Services, and so this makes this Web Service consumable by programs written in other languages, as you will see in the next section.

8. Save your work.

The Web *Service* you created in the preceding exercise has just one web *method*. Actually, Web Services can expose multiple web methods. So you could create additional routines for calculating other areas and circumferences, for example, thus creating a math-based Web Service for use, perhaps, by construction engineers. Web Services can be about anything, really. There are Web Services providing weather information, cookbook recipes, price lists for just about any product, and pretty much any other service you can imagine. They can get very sophisticated and complex depending on the type of Web Service. Web Services can have much more complex code than what you saw in Exercise 10-1, of course. For example, the Web Service can have code to access databases and to read and write to and from files, the Registry, etc., using the same kinds of calls you have seen in earlier chapters. They can also call other Web Services.

Testing Web Services

Now that you've had a chance to create a Web Service, it's time to pursue your true objective— to learn how to *test* one. You can test a Web Service by creating a program to access it. You could do that in many different languages since Web Services are created generically using XML and SOAP and their implementation code is hidden. Of course, since .NET is your focus, you'll create a test bed for your Web Service using .NET languages. You can consume this Web Service in any .NET language regardless of what .NET language you create it in. So, yes, you can create your Web Service in VB .NET and consume it in C#, and vice versa. It's also possible to consume the Web Service using any of the .NET applications: Console, Web, or Windows Forms.

Since Web Services can be about anything, how can you specify a single way to test them? What you'll do is learn how to create a *test bed* in .NET (see Exercise 10-2). A test bed is simply code you'll create to access the Web Service. In order to determine what inputs to use to effectively test this service, you'll need to learn how to read and inspect the Web Service, its methods, and their parameters. You'll get a chance to do all of that in Exercise 10-2.

Exercise 10-2: Consuming a Simple Web Service

In this exercise, you'll access and test the Web Service you created in Exercise 10-1.

1. Restart Visual Studio and create a new Windows Forms application in either C# or VB .NET. (Do *not* create another Web Service!) Name this new application **WebServTestBed**. Click OK to create the project.

2. From the toolbox, drag two textboxes, three labels, and a button control to the form's Designer window and set their properties according to Table 10-1.

■**Note** Label3 will not display since its text property is blank; but, don't worry, it's still there. Also, you will want to size the button wider, by dragging, so that you can see all of its text.

Table 10-1. *Property Settings for Exercise 10-2*

Control	Property	Value
Label1	Text	Length
Label2	Text	Width
Label3	Name	lblArea
	Text	(Leave this blank)
Textbox1	Name	txtLength
	Text	(Leave this blank)
Textbox2	Name	txtWidth
	Text	(Leave this blank)
Button1	Name	btnCalculate
	Text	Click to Calculate Area

In addition, change the text property of the form to read **Web Service Test Bed**.

Arrange the six controls according to Figure 10-5.

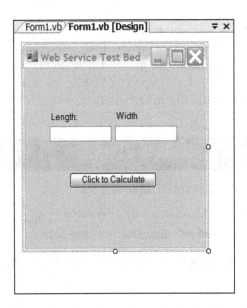

Figure 10-5. *The Design form for the Web Service test bed*

3. On the Project menu, click the Add Web Reference submenu item. The dialog box in Figure 10-6 appears.

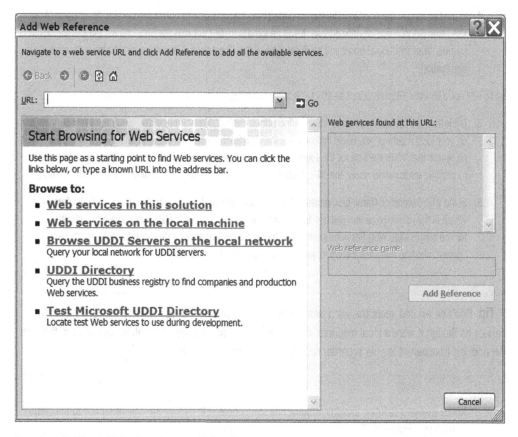

Figure 10-6. *The Add Web Reference dialog box*

This dialog box gives you options for where to locate your web reference. The one we will locate and test is on our local machine; however, notice that you can browse multiple locations including the entire local network and also the UDDI directory on the web. (See the following sidebar on the UDDI.)

THE UDDI (UNIVERSAL DESCRIPTION, DISCOVERY, AND INTEGRATION) DIRECTORY

UDDI (Universal Description, Discovery, and Integration) is an XML-based registry for businesses worldwide to list themselves on the Internet. Its ultimate goal is to streamline online transactions by enabling companies to find one another on the Web and make their systems interoperable for e-commerce. UDDI is often compared to a telephone book's white, yellow, and green pages. The project allows businesses to list themselves by name, product, location, or the Web services they offer. Although Microsoft, IBM, and Ariba spearheaded UDDI, the project now includes 130+ companies.

*——From TechTarget (*www.techtarget.com*)*

4. In the URL box of the Add Web Reference dialog box, type the URL to obtain the service description of the XML Web Service you want to access. It will be similar to, but not *exactly* the same as, the following (the number after the `localhost` will be different and the directory will be wherever you have created your application):

`http://localhost:3810/Exercise10-1/Service.asmx`

5. Click the "Go" button to retrieve information about the XML Web Service. (*Or*, since the Web Service is on your local machine, you could instead click the Web Services On The Local Machine link in the Browser pane and then click the link for the Exercise10-1/Service.asmx XML Web Service from the list provided to retrieve information about the XML Web Service. However, doing it this way can take a bit longer.)

6. In the Web Reference Name box, rename the web reference that now reads "localhost" to **CalculateArea**, which is the namespace you will use for this web reference. Click Add Reference to add a web reference for the target XML Web Service. Visual Studio downloads the service description and generates a "proxy" class to interface between your application and the XML Web Service.

■**Tip** Don't be excited about the word *proxy* here. It simply means that you will now be referencing this service as though it were a local resource, when it actually is going to be information coming from the Web Service. It's transparent to your program code so the reference is called a "proxy."

Notice that your Solution Explorer window has been updated to include the new reference to the Web Service (see Figure 10-7).

Figure 10-7. *The newly added Web Service reference displays in the Solution Explorer.*

7. Double-click the Click To Calculate Area button on the Designer window to create an event-handling method for this button. Modify this `button1_Click()` event so that it looks like the following code:

VB .NET

```
Dim AreaServ As New CalculateArea.Service
Dim sngLength As Single
Dim sngWidth As Single
Dim sngArea As Single

sngLength = Convert.ToSingle(txtLength.Text)
sngWidth = Convert.ToSingle(txtWidth.Text)
sngArea = AreaServ.RectangleArea(sngLength, sngWidth)

lblArea.Text = sngArea.ToString
```

C#

```
CalculateArea.Service AreaServ = new CalculateArea.Service();
float sngLength;
float sngWidth;
float sngArea;
sngLength = Convert.ToSingle(txtLength.Text);
sngWidth = Convert.ToSingle(txtWidth.Text);
sngArea = AreaServ.RectangleArea(sngLength, sngWidth);
lblArea.Text = sngArea.ToString();
```

Caution If you are using the Express Editions, you will need to ensure that the Web Service from Exercise 10-1 is running by launching that Web Service application before executing the next step. In other words, the Web Service from Exercise 10-1 must be running in the background before you proceed only if you are using the Express Editions (at the time of this writing, the Express editions are in Beta and this may change in the final release).

---

8. Run the application and test the operation by entering values for `length` and `width`. Save your work.

Challenge: If you've been following all of this code in either VB .NET or C#, you should try accessing the Web Service in the opposite language of the Web Service you created. This will demonstrate the language independence of Web Services.

In this exercise, you created an application to attach to the Web Service and input its parameters. How is this testing? To make this a more effective test bed, you would now apply your knowledge of testing input values to read inputs from a file or from a database (as you learned in Chapters 3, 5, and 8) and your basic testing knowledge of boundary value analysis and equivalence classing (see "Tester's Tip: Equivalence Class Partitioning and Boundary Value Analysis" next) to ensure proper functioning of the Web Service with different kinds of inputs. What you have now is a skeleton test bed that you can round out with your knowledge of effective test values.

TESTER'S TIP: EQUIVALENCE CLASS PARTITIONING AND BOUNDARY VALUE ANALYSIS

These are essential techniques for every tester, whether automated or not:

- *Equivalence classing* means to partition the input domain for your test cases into classes of input, including valid and invalid classes. For example, a numeric field could be easily partitioned into three classes: negative, zero, and positive values. Of course, a good tester will try all three of these classes by selecting at least one input from each one, knowing that, of course, zero is in a class all by itself! An experienced tester would also use ingenuity and experience to come up with other classes of input, such as the highest possible number and the lowest possible number for the value, and also other interesting classes of input such as text values and special characters. Each of these can be considered a class and should be tested.

- *Boundary value analysis* uses the partitions created in equivalence classing but, rather than choose just any value from within a class, focuses on values that exist around the boundaries of the classes. For example, with our numeric field, boundary value analysis would not choose −75 as a negative value to try but would select −1 instead, and +1 for a positive value since these are just around the boundary of the classes. The analysis would continue by carefully examining each class and selecting inputs above and below the boundaries. Test professionals know that examining the boundaries of input can produce a higher yield of bugs. Just by nature, humans make mistakes when they code around the boundaries. It's very common to be "one off" in programming arrays, lists, and reading files.

For more information on these techniques and others, see the basic testing books by Kaner and Myers listed in Appendix C.

Now you've learned how to create *and* consume a simple Web Service. This basic knowledge should help you get started with understanding and testing these essential components. Architectures involving Web Services can get quite complex since, as we mentioned before, one Web Service can call others and those in turn can call still other Web Services. One possible strategy for testing these complex Web Services architectures is to diagram it out, and then test at the lowest level, i.e., furthest from the human consumer or other end consumer (for non-human interfaces) as possible and then work your way out, creating test beds at each level. Some excellent white papers for testing web services architectures are available on the MSDN (`http://msdn.microsoft.com`).

Database Access with Web Services

In this book, we've covered accessing databases many times and in many ways starting in Chapter 3 and continuing in most of the remaining chapters. This is because testing database systems is a critical task in most testing projects, and also because it's required to effectively store and report on test data. You can use the techniques in previous chapters to add database access to the simple Web Service you've created. In order to help you in that effort, Listing 10-1 shows how it can be done.

Listing 10-1. *Returning a DataSet from a Web Service*

VB .NET

```
<WebMethod()> _
Public Function GetProductList() As DataSet
'Be sure to copy the nwind.mdb file to c:\ for this demo
  Dim strConn = _
  "Provider=Microsoft.Jet.OLEDB.4.0;" & _
"Data Source=c:\nwind.mdb;Persist Security Info=False"
  Dim strSQL As String = _
    "SELECT ProductName, ProductID, UnitPrice FROM Products"
  Dim oConn As New OleDbConnection(strConn)
  oConn.Open()
  Dim oDA As New OleDbDataAdapter(strSQL, oConn)
  Dim oDS As New DataSet()
  oDA.Fill(oDS, "Products")
  Return oDS
End Function
```

C#

```
[WebMethod()]
public DataSet GetProductList()
{
 object strConn = "Provider=Microsoft.Jet.OLEDB.4.0;" +
  "Data Source=c:\\nwind.mdb;Persist Security Info=False";
 string strSQL = "SELECT ProductName, ProductID, UnitPrice FROM Products";
 OleDbConnection oConn = new OleDbConnection(strConn);
 oConn.Open();
 OleDbDataAdapter oDA = new OleDbDataAdapter(strSQL, oConn);
 DataSet oDS = new DataSet();
 oDA.Fill(oDS, "Products");
 return oDS;
}
```

The code in Listing 10-1 declares a web method that you could create within a Web Service. Essentially this code creates and fills a DataSet with a list of product names from a database (in this case the NWind sample database from Microsoft Access). This web method could be called by another program and used to fill a grid or create a report in that program with the data pulled from this table. If you compare this code with the code we used in Chapter 8 to access databases, you can see it's essentially the same way we accessed databases there using ADO.NET objects.

Running Remote Testware with Web Services

At the end of Chapter 7, you saw how you can use a batch file to start an automated setup. That batch file was a simple text file that launched an executable file while passing arguments into it. While that example only works when you are at the computer with the executable file, you could use a Web Service to launch this setup remotely.

To start with, you would need to have the Web Service execute the TestLabSetup.exe and include the proper arguments. If you remember, we did something similar to this when we had the TestLabSetup.exe call the InspectPC.exe to generate the report file. The TestLabSetup.exe then reviewed this report to verify the installation requirements. Listing 10-2 is the VB .NET example you used in that chapter.

Listing 10-2. *Checking for Install Requirements*

VB. NET

```
Public Shared Function GetPCData(ByVal RunReport As String) As String
  Dim strStatus As String = ""
  Dim objProc As New System.Diagnostics.Process
  objProc.StartInfo.FileName = "C:\PCInfo\InspectPC.exe"
  objProc.StartInfo.Arguments = "y"
  objProc.StartInfo.CreateNoWindow = True
  objProc.StartInfo.ErrorDialog = True
  Try
    objProc.Start()
    strStatus = "Completed"
  Catch ex As Exception
    Console.WriteLine(ex.ToString + vbCrLf + "Press any key to continue...")
      strStatus = "Failed"
    End Try
    Return strStatus
  End Function
```

You can use a modified version of this code in a web method to run the TestLabSetup program. Your goal would be to have your Web Service call this GetPCData() method, and the TestLabSetup.exe would then call the InspectPC.exe and all the other methods you used to create the Chapter 7 automated install.

The easiest way to set this up would be to install a Web Service and the TestLabSetup.exe on one computer. This computer would access a share that holds the applications you want to install. Other computers, either desktops or laptops, would host your Web Service client application and you would start the installations by calling the web method from these. Once the web method was called, the TestLabSetup would use the InspectPC program to gather information from the individual lab computers, validate the installation requirements, and start the installations. This setup would look something like Figure 10-8.

Notice that the figure shows multiple TestLabSetup programs in a folder. Each of these represents a different type of setup you use around the lab. In this example, if you wanted to have the TestLabSetup1.exe run, you would execute a Web Service method, like the one in Listing 10-3, and it would execute the TestLabSetup1.exe for you.

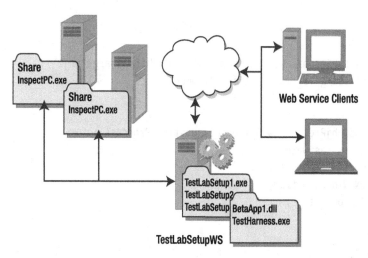

Figure 10-8. *Calling TestLabSetup from the Web Service*

Listing 10-3. *Calling a Setup Program from a Web Service*

VB. NET

```
<WebMethod _
(Description:= "Example: TestLabSetup1.exe, \\Server1\ShareWithApp arg1 arg2")> _
Public Function RunLabSetup _
  (ByVal Testware as string,  Arguments As String) As String

  Dim strStatus As String = ""
  Dim objProc As New System.Diagnostics.Process
  objProc.StartInfo.FileName = Testware
  objProc.StartInfo.Arguments = Arguments
  objProc.StartInfo.CreateNoWindow = True
  objProc.StartInfo.ErrorDialog = True

  Try
    objProc.Start()
    strStatus = "Completed"
  Catch ex As Exception
      strStatus = "Failed"
  End Try
  Return strStatus
End Function
```

C#

```
[WebMethod
(Description="Example: TestLabSetup1.exe, \\\\Server1\\ShareWithApp arg1 arg2")]
public string RunLabSetup(string Testware, string Arguments)
{
 string strStatus = "";
 System.Diagnostics.Process objProc = new System.Diagnostics.Process();
 objProc.StartInfo.FileName = Testware;
 objProc.StartInfo.Arguments = Arguments;
 objProc.StartInfo.CreateNoWindow = true;
 objProc.StartInfo.ErrorDialog = true;
 try {
   objProc.Start();
   strStatus = "Completed";
 } catch (Exception ex) {
   strStatus = "Failed";
 }
 return strStatus;
}
```

As you can see, the parameters of the RunLabSetup() method collects the application's name and arguments and then uses these to set the properties of the StartInfo class. The FileName property identifies which automation testware you would like to start. The Arguments property holds all of the arguments needed by the automation program. Once your settings are done, you call the Start() method to run the program and use a Try-Catch block to capture any errors. If there are no errors, we return a status of "Completed"; otherwise, we display the error and return a status of "Failed".

One thing to note: when creating testware that is used by a Web Service, you must write your error handlers to respond to other software and not to a person. In other words, you write the testware so that it throws an exception when an error happens. If the testware just prints a message to the screen, the Web Service will not see it. However, if you throw an exception the Web Service will be able to use a Try-Catch block catch it. You would then add code to the Try-Catch block to send status information back to the Web Service client. This client could then display an error message to the user or use this information to create a report on the lab setup.

One advantage of this scenario is that you could start this process from any client PC that had access to the Web Service. It would not matter if the computer were in the same room or at a remote location. In addition, the client application could be any type of the standard interfaces: Console, Windows, or Web.

In the end, you could create a number of small test lab utilities, place them in a folder, and have a simple way to execute these—independent of a particular user interface. This gives you a lot of flexibility without a whole lot of development time. Moreover, the best part would be that you could change out the different components as your needs change.

Next, we turn your attention to another important component—the COM object.

Understanding and Testing COM

COM is a system that Microsoft created for defining software objects that can interact with one another. This model proliferates throughout existing Windows software and in many Windows-based applications. Although COM is a good model and will be around for a long time, one problem with COM is that it doesn't map very well to the Internet; thus, Microsoft has turned more to Web Services and SOA, while continuing to support COM architecture. Consequently, we will be operating under the COM architecture model along with other architectures, including SOA, for a long time. In this section, you will learn how to reference and access COM objects for testing purposes.

COM, like .NET, is also built on the idea of classes and their objects and methods, and it arranges objects in a similar way (it just doesn't automatically translate as easily into web-consumable objects). In order to work between the legacy COM libraries and .NET Framework libraries, Microsoft provides some interop libraries that you'll make use of to attach and work with COM objects.

Referencing a COM Library

To set a reference to an existing COM library, you'll access the Add References dialog box. To do that, all you'll need to do is select Project ➤ Add Reference from within any .NET application. Figure 10-9 shows the Add Reference dialog box with the COM tab selected.

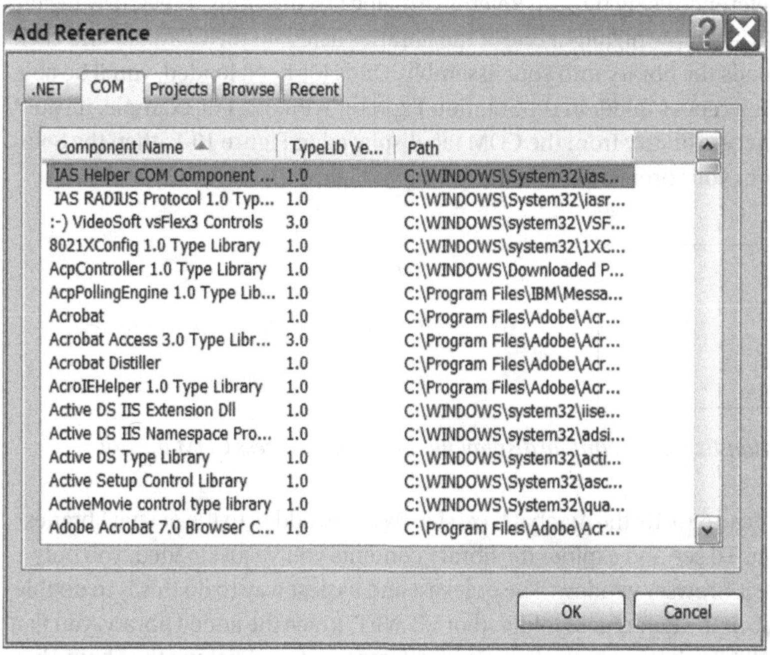

Figure 10-9. *The Add Reference dialog box*

Notice that there are other tabs on the Add Reference dialog box. The .NET tab will list a number of useful libraries that you can reference as needed. The COM tab is the one we're interested in, however, since it will list all installed COM libraries. As you scroll through this window, you'll find COM libraries provided not only by Microsoft, but also by third-party companies that have libraries written to help you access their software. It's a long list that gets installed by default when you install the .NET Framework. For example, Figure 10-9 shows COM libraries for Adobe's Acrobat software. If you have software you work with regularly that you might want to access programmatically, it'd be worth it to investigate if the software vendor has existing libraries installed by default for your use. Even if these libraries do not automatically install with .NET, it is still possible that libraries are provided by the software vendor. You will have to contact the vendor directly to answer that question. Of course, to access these libraries, you will have to write code.

For those familiar with earlier versions of Visual Basic, the process of referencing COM libraries in .NET code is similar; however, .NET adds the creation of an interop assembly to the procedure. References to the members of the COM object (library) are routed to the interop assembly and then forwarded to the actual COM object. Likewise, responses from the COM object are routed to the interop assembly and then forwarded to your .NET application. In other words, the interop assembly acts as a translator between your .NET code and the COM component. This translation won't affect how you work with the COM library, however, since the interop assembly handles it all for you, as you'll see in the next section.

Accessing and Testing a COM Library

Given today's complex systems with multiple kinds of components, it's highly likely in your testing endeavors that you'll eventually encounter a COM library. To access and test these libraries, you'll set a reference using the Add Reference dialog box described previously (again, see Figure 10-9). You will simply highlight one of the libraries listed on the COM tab and click the OK button. This loads the library into your assembly. Once it's been loaded, you'll be able to see it listed in the References folder in the Solution Explorer window. For example, if you selected the Acrobat Access library from the COM tab displayed in Figure 10-9, then the Solution Explorer window in your project would look similar to Figure 10-10.

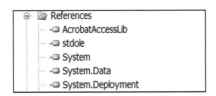

Figure 10-10. *The Solution Explorer window displaying the Acrobat Access COM library*

As you can see in Figure 10-10, the AcrobatAccessLib has been added to the default libraries loaded into the project. To see and explore the library contents you've just loaded, you only need to open the Object Browser window. The quickest and easiest way to do this is to double-click AcrobatAccessLib in the References folder. (For VB .NET, to see the added library, you first must click the Show All Files button in the Solution Explorer window. Clicking the Show All Files button displays the References folder in the Solution Explorer window. Expand this folder to see the library. C# always displays the References folder.)

This will open the Object Browser with the library contents already displayed, as in Figure 10-11.

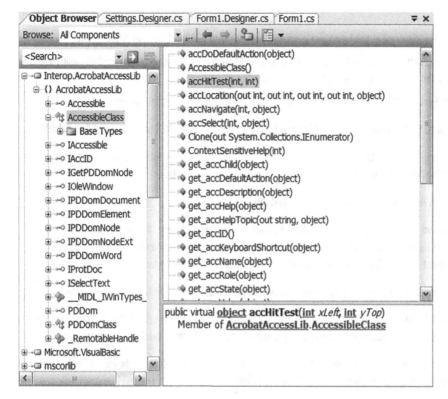

Figure 10-11. *The Object Browser window displaying the Acrobat Access library contents*

Of course, the next question is, "How do you know what's in this library and how it works?" The Object Browser will show you the contents and you can explore the methods and classes within the library, but you'll get only limited information about them (similar to what you see in Figure 10-11). In order to test this library, you'll have to be very familiar with the software already or you'll need to have a software requirements document or Test Plan to guide you. Chances are you aren't an expert at the internals of Adobe Acrobat software, so this particular library won't be easy to reference and test without the associated planning documentation you should have on any good automated test project. Still, you want to get a feel for how to work with these libraries, so in Exercise 10-3 you'll reference and test a method of a library many of us are more familiar with—the Excel spreadsheet library.

Exercise 10-3: Testing COM

In this exercise, you'll access and test the Excel COM library.

Important Note In order to complete this exercise, you *must* have Microsoft Excel installed.

Test Setup:

Assume that you are assigned to the Excel test team and your job is to test the following requirement:

Test Requirement: Test the principal interest formula within the Microsoft Excel object library. Test its basic functionality by providing simple inputs and testing the output to verify correct results.

Expected Result: Excel's PMT formula for calculating interest will return a correct calculation.

1. Start Visual Studio and create a new Windows Forms application in VB .NET or C#. Name it **ComTestBed**.

2. Set a reference to the Microsoft Excel COM library by selecting Project ➤ Add References from the main menu. The Add Reference dialog box will display (again, see Figure 10-9)

3. In the Add Reference dialog box, click the COM tab.

4. Scroll down in the dialog until you find the Microsoft Excel Object Library. (If you have more than one version of this library available, select the highest version number. This code was written using the Excel 10.0 Object Library.) Click OK to add this library to your list of references for this project.

5. To see the library you just added, expand the References folder in the Solution Explorer window.

   (For VB .NET: To see the added library, you must click the Show All Files button in the Solution Explorer window. Clicking the Show All Files button displays the References folder in the Solution Explorer window.)

6. Place a button on the form and set its text property to `Automate`. Place three textboxes on the form and change their name properties to `txtInterest`, `txtMonths`, and `txtPrincipal`, respectively.

7. For each textbox, add a label control and change the text properties of these labels to read **Interest**, **Months**, and **Principal**, respectively. Arrange the textboxes and label controls as desired. Your form should look similar to Figure 10-12.

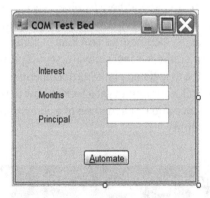

Figure 10-12. *Layout of controls for the COM test bed*

8. Now, add the following code to the Click event of your new button:

VB .NET

```
Dim xlApp As New Excel._ExcelApplication

Dim loanpayment As Decimal
Dim dblInterest, dblMonths, dblprincipal As Double

dblprincipal = Convert.ToDouble(txtPrincipal.Text)
dblMonths = Convert.ToDouble(txtMonths.Text)
dblInterest = Convert.ToDouble(txtInterest.Text)
loanpayment = xlApp.WorksheetFunction.Pmt _
  (dblInterest / 12, dblMonths, dblprincipal)
MessageBox.Show("the monthly payment is: " & _
  Format(Math.Abs(loanpayment), "$#.##"), "Mortgage")
```

C#

```
Excel.Application xlApp = new Excel.Application();
double loanpayment;
double dblInterest;
double dblMonths;
double dblprincipal;
dblprincipal = Convert.ToDouble(txtPrincipal.Text);
dblMonths = Convert.ToDouble(txtMonths.Text);
dblInterest = Convert.ToDouble(txtInterest.Text);
loanpayment =
   xlApp.WorksheetFunction.Pmt(
     dblInterest / 12, dblMonths, dblprincipal, 0, 0);
MessageBox.Show("the monthly payment is: " +
   Convert.ToString(Math.Abs(loanpayment)), "Mortgage");
```

9. Run the application by pressing F5. Enter some data to verify the code works. This is not a test at this point. So far, you're just verifying functionality. In the next step, you'll set this up as a test.

10. Return to the Code window and, following the information below, write code to return a *test pass* or *test fail* condition using a branching statement, such as an If-Then-Else or a Select-Case statement. The principal interest formula is the following:

P = Principal: the initial amount of the loan

I = The annual interest rate (from 1 to 100 percent)

L = Length: the length (in years) of the loan, or at least the length over which the loan is amortized

J = Monthly interest in decimal form = **I / (12 x 100)**

N = Number of months over which loan is amortized = **L x 12**

So, given the variable definitions here, the monthly payment (**M**) formula is

$$M = P \times J/(1-(1+J)^\wedge - N$$

This is the formula we use in the following code. Add this code to the end of the button1 Click event to calculate the principal interest formula programmatically:

VB .NET

```
Dim myPayment as Decimal
myPayment = _
  Convert.ToDouble(dblprincipal) * _
    -((dblInterest / 12) / _
        (1 - (1 + (dblInterest / 12)) ^ (-Convert.ToDouble(dblMonths))))
```

C#

```
double myPayment;
myPayment =
  Convert.ToDouble(dblprincipal) *
   -((dblInterest / 12) / (1 - Math.Pow((1 + (dblInterest / 12)),
     (-Convert.ToDouble(dblMonths)))));
```

11. To write the test comparison, you will need to round to an appropriate number of digits. You can use the round function from the Math library as follows:

VB .NET

```
If Math.Round(loanpayment, 5) = Math.Round(mypayment, 5) Then
        Debug.WriteLine("Test passed: formula correct")
        Messagebox.Show("Test passed: formula correct")
 Else
        Debug.WriteLine("Test failed: incorrect formula result")
        Messagebox.Show("Test failed: incorrect formula result")
End If
```

■**Note** C# code will need to use the using directive to import the System.Diagnostics namespace. This is needed for the Debug.WriteLine statement since it comes from that namespace.

C#

```
using System.Diagnostics;
/* add above line to directives list at top of code window */

if (Math.Round(loanpayment, 5) == Math.Round(myPayment, 5))
  {
    Debug.WriteLine("Test passed: formula correct");
    MessageBox.Show("Test passed: formula correct");
  }
else
  {
    Debug.WriteLine("Test failed: incorrect formula result");
    MessageBox.Show("Test failed: incorrect formula result");
  }
```

The full code for the button1 Click event should look like Listing 10-4.

Listing 10-4. *Full Code for Exercise 10-3*

VB .NET

```vb
Public Class Form1

Private Sub Button1_Click(ByVal sender As System.Object, _
        ByVal e As System.EventArgs) Handles Button1.Click
    Dim xlApp As New Excel._ExcelApplication

    Dim loanpayment As Decimal
    Dim dblInterest, dblMonths, dblprincipal As Double

    dblprincipal = Convert.ToDouble(txtPrincipal.Text)
    dblMonths = Convert.ToDouble(txtMonths.Text)
    dblInterest = Convert.ToDouble(txtInterest.Text)

    loanpayment = xlApp.WorksheetFunction.Pmt _
        (dblInterest / 12, dblMonths, dblprincipal)
    MsgBox("the monthly payment is: " & _
        Format(Math.Abs(loanpayment), "$#.##"), , "Mortgage")

    '***** Begin Test of PMT formula:
    Dim myPayment As Decimal
    myPayment = Convert.ToDouble(dblprincipal) * -((dblInterest / 12) / _
        (1 - (1 + (dblInterest / 12)) ^ (-Convert.ToDouble(dblMonths))))

    If Math.Round(loanpayment, 5) = Math.Round(myPayment, 5) Then
        Debug.WriteLine("Test passed: formula correct")
        MessageBox.Show("Test passed: formula correct")
    Else
        Debug.WriteLine("Test failed: incorrect formula result")
        MessageBox.Show("Test failed: incorrect formula result")
    End If


    End Sub
End Class
```

C#

```csharp
using System;
using System.Collections.Generic;
using System.ComponentModel;
using System.Data;
using System.Drawing;
using System.Text;
using System.Windows.Forms;
using System.Diagnostics;
```

```csharp
namespace ComTestBedx
{
    public partial class Form1 : Form
    {
        public Form1()
        {
            InitializeComponent();
        }

        private void button1_Click(object sender, EventArgs e)
        {
            Excel.Application xlApp = new Excel.Application();
            double loanpayment;
            double dblInterest;
            double dblMonths;
            double dblprincipal;
            dblprincipal = Convert.ToDouble(txtPrincipal.Text);
            dblMonths = Convert.ToDouble(txtMonths.Text);
            dblInterest = Convert.ToDouble(txtInterest.Text);
            loanpayment = xlApp.WorksheetFunction.Pmt
              (dblInterest / 12, dblMonths, dblprincipal, 0, 0);
            MessageBox.Show("the monthly payment is: " +
                Convert.ToString(Math.Abs(loanpayment)), "Mortgage");

            /* begin test of PMT formula: */
            double myPayment;
            myPayment =
              Convert.ToDouble(dblprincipal) * -((dblInterest / 12)/
              (1 - Math.Pow((1 + (dblInterest / 12)),
                (-Convert.ToDouble(dblMonths)))));

            if (Math.Round(loanpayment, 5) == Math.Round(myPayment, 5))
            {
                Debug.WriteLine("Test passed: formula correct");
                MessageBox.Show("Test passed: formula correct");
            }
            else
            {
                Debug.WriteLine("Test failed: incorrect formula result");
                MessageBox.Show("Test failed: incorrect formula result");
            }

        }
    }
```

12. Run the program again. Enter test data according to Table 10-2.

Table 10-2. *Data for Exercise 10-3*

Interest	Months	Principal	Expected Result	Actual Result
34	34	34	96.333	
.04	5	1200	212.405	
.25	100	100000	2386.978	

13. Record your results for all test data entries in the Actual Result column of Table 10-2. Would entering text data be a proper test of Excel's PMT function? Why or why not?

What other enhancements could you add to this test? One enhancement would be to enter the data using a file or a database table filled with test data entries. How about structured exception handling? How about Debug and/or Trace class enhancements? How about adding appropriate comments to the test to indicate what it's doing and why?

14. Stop the program. Save your work and quit Visual Studio.

In this exercise, you've looked at accessing and testing a function within the Excel COM library. You took the common definition of the PMT function and tested Excel's function to be sure it behaved as expected. Chances are you found that the Excel PMT function works fine. Excel has already been well-tested, so that's not surprising. What you have learned how to do, though, is set up and run a basic test of a function within a COM library. You can use this program as a test bed (i.e., a template) for testing functions in other COM libraries you encounter.

Finding Your Project's COM Libraries

Many applications make extensive use of COM libraries. These libraries are not necessarily provided by Windows software, as is the one from Excel you tested in Exercise 10-3. It's possible that your software project has extensive libraries written by your own developers. These libraries may not show up in the COM tab on the Add Reference dialog box. So how would you find them? You can use the same dialog box to browse for additional COM libraries. Figure 10-13 shows the Browse tab of the Add Reference dialog box.

Notice that the file filter for this dialog allows you to browse for files with the following extensions: .dll, .tlb, .olb, .ocx, .exe, and .manifest. All of these extensions indicate files that can contain libraries of components. To find and reference your own application's components, you'll need to know the names and locations of these files. Then, you can browse to them and add them to your project, view them in the Object Browser, and set up a test bed to access them, much as you did in Exercise 10-3.

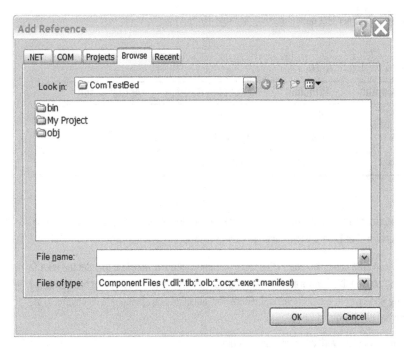

Figure 10-13. *The Browse tab of the Add Reference dialog box allows you to browse for other components.*

Summary

In this chapter, you've explored two kinds of possible components you may encounter in your testing projects: Web Services and COM components. You've seen how to reference, attach, and set up simple tests for both of these kinds of objects. In both situations, you've set up a program, often called a test bed or a *test bench* (to represent the bench you may see in hardware workshops), to reference and then attach to the component in code. You've then used program code to send values to the component to test it. In this way, you've separated the component from the other components in the application and tested it separately, which is a good strategy. We've mentioned in previous chapters that this is a form of *unit testing*. When you combine this method with the reporting techniques learned in Chapters 3, 5, and 6, you'll find you can create a reusable test bed for accessing these new components. This can save you a tremendous amount of time on a testing project.

Now that you've gotten a handle on how to work with COM and Web Services components in a basic way, you'll want to explore more in-depth information about each of them for more specifics on how to work with them on your test projects. Still, another large issue is accessing components across distributed systems. To accomplish this, developers also have a few strategies to choose from, including COM+ and .NET remoting. Your primary concern is to learn how to work with and to test whatever components are chosen. Since distributed systems architecture, and testing these systems, is a large topic that would need an entire book in itself to discuss, we have presented some basics here and now refer you to other sources for further information.

For more information on these technologies, see these websites:

- COM technologies: `http://www.microsoft.com/Com/default.mspx`

- SOA technologies: `http://msdn.microsoft.com/architecture/soa/`

As we explained earlier in this chapter, architecture choice is a complex exercise. You will want to be as familiar as you can with the variety of technologies and architectures available.

Tester's Checklist

When testing Web services or COM components,

☑ Set a reference and attach to the component and test its capabilities separately from other components.

☑ Create a reusable test bed (or test bench) in .NET code in order to test this same component from build-to-build of your project.

☑ Use the Project ➤ Add References menu item to locate the Add References dialog box. Use this dialog box to reference COM libraries.

☑ Study further on Web Services and COM (see this chapter's "Summary" section and Appendix C).

■■■

CHAPTER 11

An Introduction to Visual Studio Team Test

Throughout this book we've concentrated on educating you, the software test professional, on the programming skills and techniques needed to help you do effective technical testing in a .NET environment. We felt it important that these skills and techniques be independent of the version of Visual Studio you are using. In fact, Chapters 1 through 10 present knowledge, techniques, and code that you can use with *any* version and in a wide variety of test situations, including the Express Editions that are available for free download (at the time of this writing) from the Microsoft website. This is *not* a book about the feature set of the newest Visual Studio product because we wanted to teach you skills that will be applicable for a long time to come no matter what the version. However, with the release of Visual Studio 2005, Microsoft has integrated a significant amount of test capability into Visual Studio with its Visual Studio Team Test software. Although this software is not available to those using the Express Editions, it is significant to the software test community using .NET and so we believe it's important to address it here.

The intent of this chapter is to provide an overview of the features available in Visual Studio's Team Test software. We will *not* be covering the entire feature set of this new addition, but we will cover some basics in order to give you a feel for its power and capabilities, as well as to compare and contrast it to what you've learned up to this point. Appropriately, there are numerous books planned for publication on this topic at this writing (see Appendix C for specific references) for those who need a more in-depth treatment.

Objectives

At the end of this chapter, you will be able to do the following:

- Understand the core windows used in Team Test

- Discuss the types of tests available in Team Test

- Create a test project that contains multiple types of tests

- Create a test list and assign tests to it

- Create, run, and evaluate a unit test

- Create and run basic ordered, manual, and web tests

- Add data access to a test for data-driven testing

- Work with the Test Manager, Test Results, Test Run Configure, and Test View windows to manage, organize, and evaluate test runs

Team Test Edition Overview

The idea behind the Team Test software is the integration of testing tools into the software development environment. Microsoft's intent is to create a setting where information can be shared across all the groups involved in software development. Tests and their results can then be shared and managed across the organization—from management to the development and test teams, and back again. In Team Test, there are a variety of test types to address different organizational processes and software development methodologies, including Agile, Extreme, and Test First testing methods, as well as the traditional software lifecycle model. Types of tests you can create and support include unit, web, load, and even manual testing. In addition, there's an extensibility option in the creation of a generic test type so that you can even include tests created in other tools. In the Enterprise Edition, the test results can be published to a database from which you can generate trend and historical reports and publish bug reports.

To do all of this, Microsoft maintains that they analyzed the requests of testers via public forums and studied existing technologies used in testing, including use of nUnit (www.nUnit.org) and other popular open source tools as well as common features in commercial-based tools. As a result, they've produced a fairly comprehensive combined test and development environment. However, as we mentioned, this environment is not available to all Visual Studio editions. In fact, to get all of the capabilities just discussed, a company must purchase the Visual Studio Team System. You have no capability for test creation in the Standard, Professional, Architect, and Express Editions. You can get test creation capability, although no ability to publish test results and produce bug reports, by purchasing the Visual Studio Team Edition for Software Testers (VSTEST). It is this edition that we will focus on in this chapter because our intent is to focus on the capability of test creation and management in the broadest way possible without requiring extensive set up. Even if you don't have the correct edition installed, we hope to give you a feel in this chapter for the overall testing capabilities of this software.

To access the Team Test software, you will open the Test menu item from the main menu in the Visual Studio Development environment. Figure 11-1 shows the Test menu opened and the Windows submenu items expanded. Team Test has a number of windows you can use to set up and view existing tests.

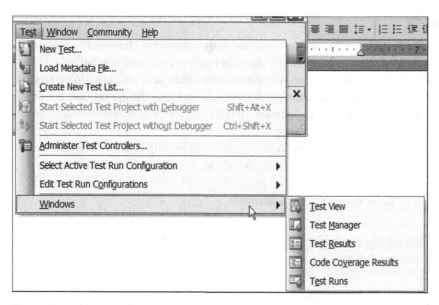

Figure 11-1. *Accessing the Team Test software via the Test menu*

Team Test Windows

Team Test provides a number of new windows that you'll need to learn about in order to understand what the tool can do for you:

- Test View window

- Test Manager window

- Test Results window

- Test Run Configuration window

- Code Coverage windows

A typical way you could use these windows is to first create a test from a template using the Test menu. After creating the test, you can view the test and edit it and its properties as necessary from the Test View window. You can use the Test Results window to, of course, view the results of your test(s). After creating a number of tests you can manage, organize them into a variety of test suites and run them using the Test Manager window. You'll use the Test Run Configuration window to set properties for your test runs (such as deployment options), and whether or not you want to review code coverage on the tests. If you have specified you want code coverage results (i.e., which lines of source code were touched during your tests) in your Test Run Configuration options, then you will be able to view the results of that code coverage analysis in the Code Coverage Results window. Let's take a look at each of these basic windows and then you'll have a chance to use most of them in Exercise 11-1.

Test View Window

The purpose of the Test View window is to allow you to quickly access your tests for authoring and editing. Figure 11-2 shows a number of tests including both unit and manual tests. From this window, you can double-click any test to open its editor and make changes. Unit test types will open the code window, whereas manual test types will open into the appropriate editor for manual tests, either Microsoft Word or Notepad. In the same way, opening web or load tests will open a custom editor for those test types.

You can also right-click the tests, and from the resulting pop-up menu you can not only edit the test, but also run the test or even create an entirely new one. The Test View window allows you to customize the columns you see and sort (group) the tests by any column or a variety of other criteria, including priority and owner.

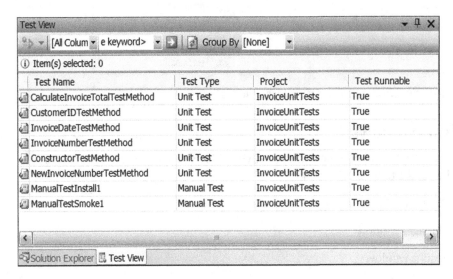

Figure 11-2. *The Test View window displays tests and makes them readily available for modification.*

The Test View window is a very useful and easy to get started with. However, the main window intended for running your tests is the Test Manager window.

Test Manager Window

The Test Manager window is just what it sounds like—it's an overall location for managing test runs. From here you can categorize your tests into lists of your choosing and customize the test run by selecting which to run. Figure 11-3 shows some tests organized into a list called "InvoiceLibUnitTests," while two other manual tests are part of a category called "Tests Not in a List." (Creating and managing lists will be covered in the "Organizing Tests and Managing Test Runs" section later in this chapter.) As you will see, the system is very flexible, allowing you to run only those tests you have selected by checking their box. You can also select all tests in a list to run. Lists can be created from here and these lists can contain any number of tests and any test type. By the way, a test can also be a part of multiple lists. In this way, you can organize and run a variety of tests in different combinations without having to duplicate effort by writing a test twice.

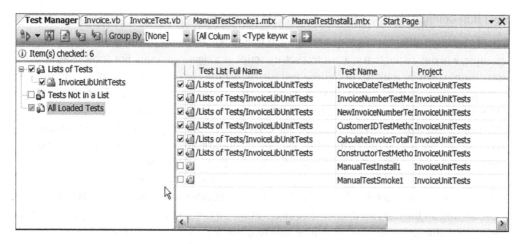

Figure 11-3. *The Test Manager window allows you to organize and manage your tests and test runs.*

In Figure 11-3, the tests within the InvoiceLibUnitTests list (created by your authors) are selected and will run when the user clicks the right-facing arrow in the upper-left corner of the Test Manager window. From the Test Manager window, like the Test View window, you can also filter and sort by columns, keywords, or by owner, priority, etc.

Test Results Window

Once you've run some tests from the Test Manager or Test View windows, you'll immediately get a Test Results window that will, by default, dock itself onto the bottom of your Visual Studio IDE and provide information about the tests as they run and give, of course, results (hence, the name) about the tests when they are complete. Figure 11-4 shows the Test Results window after a test run. When the tests are complete, this window will report a pass, fail, or inconclusive result for each test.

	Result	Test Name	Project	Error Message
☐	Passed	ManualTestInstall1	InvoiceUnitTests	
☐	Passed	ManualTestSmoke1	InvoiceUnitTests	
☑	Inconclusive	InvoiceDateTestMethod	InvoiceUnitTests	Assert.Inconclusive failed. Verify the correctness of this
☑	Failed	InvoiceNumberTestMethod	InvoiceUnitTests	Assert.AreEqual failed. Expected:<0>, Actual:<2>. Inv
☑	Failed	NewInvoiceNumberTestMethod	InvoiceUnitTests	
☑	Inconclusive	CustomerIDTestMethod	InvoiceUnitTests	Assert.Inconclusive failed. Verify the correctness of this
☑	Inconclusive	CalculateInvoiceTotalTestMethod	InvoiceUnitTests	Assert.Inconclusive failed. Verify the correctness of this
☑	Inconclusive	ConstructorTestMethod	InvoiceUnitTests	Assert.Inconclusive failed. TODO: Implement code to ve

Figure 11-4. *The Test Results window after a test run*

In addition, you'll get an error message, depending on the reason for failure and how you've written or coded the tests.

Test Run Configuration Window

There are many different kinds of settings you might like to specify during a test run—for example, whether or not to run a pre-test set-up script or a clean-up script. For another example, sometimes you may want to configure a test run to include code coverage. Allowing options for settings such as these allows for flexibility in your test runs and can help eliminate duplication of a test; plus, it can just save you some time. In Team Test, you can configure your test runs for all kinds of different options including Code Coverage, Deployment, Timing, Host settings, and Set-up/Clean-up scripts using the Test Run Configuration window. You can also save these configurations into a file and apply them as needed to different test runs.

To create and specify test run configuration settings, select Test ➤ Edit Test Run Configurations. Figure 11-5 shows the dialog box highlighting the Code Coverage page. In this example, we're setting up the test run to enable code coverage on the `InvoiceLib.dll` component. This means that after our tests run, we will be able to observe code coverage results.

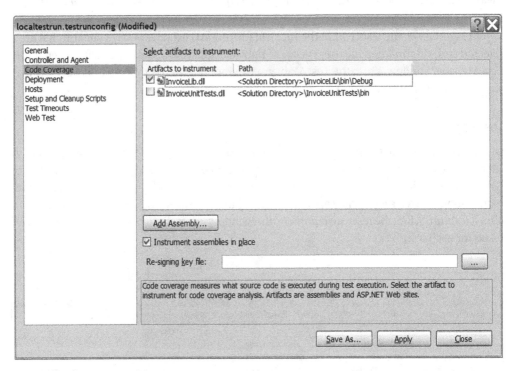

Figure 11-5. *The Test Run Configuration dialog box allows you to specify multiple types of settings to apply to your test runs.*

Notice that the Test Run Configuration dialog box also has a Save As button. This will save the settings under a name of your choice (with an extension of `.testrunconfig`) so that you can apply these settings to other test runs. For example, we might be focusing on code coverage on a particular system and will want to save a test run configuration that always includes instrumentation for code coverage. If so, we can save this into our project and use it again. We can also use it as the default test run configuration, or choose another configuration file for the standard or default configurations. This allows groups to set up standard and consistent configurations across the team, but also allows for individuals to modify certain test runs now and then for specific reasons.

Once you have saved multiple test configurations, you can switch between them on your test run by selecting Test ➤ Select Active Test Run Configuration and then selecting the configuration you want from the resulting menu.

Note If you select Test ➤ Select Active Test Run Configurations or Test ➤ Edit Test Run Configuration and all you see is the message "No configuration available," it means that you haven't yet created a test project. You can create a test project in a couple of ways. The easiest way is to simply create a single test of any type, then a test project will be automatically created as a container for that test. Or you can select File ➤ New Project and select a test project template from the New Project dialog box.

Code Coverage Windows

While your tests run, you can use the Code Coverage windows to gauge the percentage of lines of code covered by the test and even view exactly which lines were touched and which were not. Figure 11-6 shows the Code Coverage Results window (bottom half of the figure) with the Code window above it. The Code window displays blue for the lines that it touched during the test run. You can scroll through the windows to see exactly which lines. Untouched lines will be highlighted in red. You can also view the percentage of lines touched in each code block. In our example in Figure 11-6, all lines were covered so the percentage of Not Covered is 0.

You must specify that you want to instrument your code in this way by selecting it in the Test Run Configuration dialog box.

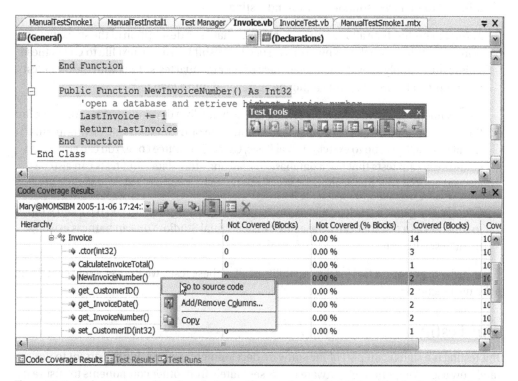

Figure 11-6. *Code Coverage Results window with tested code highlighted in the Code window*

One item for test professionals to note about code coverage in team test is that it reports any line that has been executed as the code runs, but does not report anything about path coverage. Path coverage goes further than code coverage in that it reports whether each branch of a condition is covered at least once. There are other tools to report path coverage, so if that kind of testing is needed, you will need to look for other tools. For more information on test tools, see Appendix C.

Types of Tests Available

There are a number of different test categories you can create and integrate into your software test process. The intent is to give a flexible approach for those who already have existing tests of their own, such as those written similarly to the other chapters in this book, or those written through the use of third-party software. The following are the current types of tests available:

Web: With a web test, you can verify the functionality of your web applications. You can navigate through the site, clicking on different buttons, links, forms, etc. and all the web traffic gets saved and can then be played back and verified without your writing code to do so.

Load: Load tests allow you to take other tests (except manual tests) and run them simultaneously under simulated load using virtual users. This type of test allows you to set thresholds and to see where performance points you have identified have failed. You can collect and evaluate the resulting performance data.

Ordered: You can place a set of existing tests in an ordered container so that they will run in an order you specify. This is important where certain kinds of tests are dependent on others. Ordered tests support end-to-end testing.

Manual: This test type allows you to create tests that are a description of the steps that you want a tester to manually follow. You can use Microsoft Word or a text file to create these. This feature simply allows you to keep track of your manual tests along with the other tests in your project. A manual test cannot be aggregated into a load test.

Unit: Sometimes called White Box testing, this is typically a development task or a task for the technical tester, especially those involved in Agile or Extreme testing environments. A unit test can be set up to exercise Visual Basic, C#, or C++ source code. You can also create data-driven unit tests that use a database to read and store data. Unit tests can also be created for ASP.NET applications.

Generic: The generic test type allows you to take an existing program you have and wrap it to function as a test that can be executed inside Visual Studio. You can harness existing nUnit tests this way.

In order to give you a feel for the capability of all of these tests, we'll cover a subset of them in the next sections.

Unit Testing

Unit testing is a significant part of the software development process. It's important to understand how each component in software works separately from other components to ensure its basic functionality requirements are met. Eventually, integration testing is performed to ensure they all work together. Traditionally, unit testing and integration testing have been the domain of the software developer and not the software test engineer. However, as software has become more complex, the industry has found a greater need for test support at a lower level. Having professional testers support the unit and integration testing allows the developer the chance to do more development, and also separates the development team from the bias that can naturally occur when one tests one's own code. This is part of the spirit behind the Agile and Extreme testing methods. Of course, not only those companies using these methods are seeing a need for more technical testers—it's becoming an industry-wide requirement due not only to the complexity of the software, but also simply to the volume of software today and the need to ensure quality at every level.

TESTER'S TIP: TEST TEAM SUPPORT FOR UNIT TESTING

We are frequently asked, "Why should anyone from the test team get involved in unit testing? That's the developer's job." Unit testing is traditionally considered the domain of the development team. No one is suggesting that developers stop doing unit testing; however, a test professional can support the unit testing process greatly by incorporating additional knowledge of test essentials into the unit testing process. Here's an example: A developer friend of ours created his own extensive unit testing framework using software called nUnit. His unit testing framework was similar in many ways to what can be generated in Team Test. He was very proud of it, but asked for our support in making it better. Upon evaluating his code, we added data-driven tests, including many more inputs to his software components than he had originally planned. We included tests using our knowledge of boundary value analysis and equivalence partitioning, as well as performing much more negative testing than his original specification provided. This is analogous to the support a professional, technical tester can provide to the development team. The developer often does not have the time and certainly does not always have the correct mindset to perform thorough Quality Assurance testing.

In this book, we've showed many ways that testers can write code to attach to components at a fairly low level, including attaching to Web Services and COM objects (see Chapter 10), databases (see Chapter 8), as well as class libraries (see Chapter 6). The new integration of Microsoft's Team Edition allows your organization a predefined and relatively easy way to attach to some of these same objects and create a test project that generates unit testing code.

The `Microsoft.VisualStudio.TestTools.UnitTesting` namespace contains the methods to create the unit tests for the software you test.

In Exercise 11-1, you'll create a unit test and, in the process, explore the use of the basic windows and other functionality just described.

Exercise 11-1: Creating a Unit Test

In this exercise you'll create a class, generate unit test code for that class, then execute and run unit tests. You'll then round out these tests by adding test data and customizing them to meet your own test criteria.

1. Launch Visual Studio 2005 and create a new Class Library project (be sure not to create any other kind of project!) and name it **InvoiceLib** (see Figure 11-7).

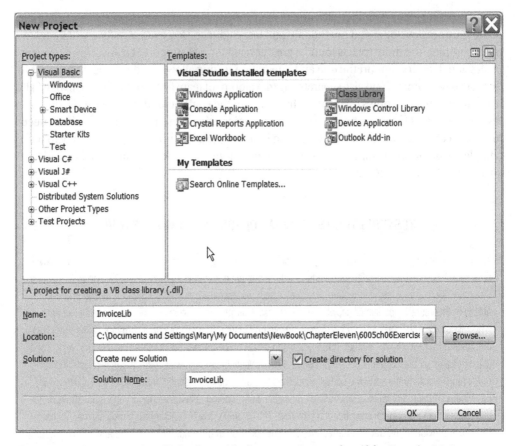

Figure 11-7. *The New Project dialog box with the correct items selected for Exercise 11-1*

By default, the Create Directory For Solution check box is enabled. Leaving this option as is will create the test project in a separate directory alongside the InvoiceLib project. (Unchecking this box will place the test project into a subdirectory of the InvoiceLib project when it is saved. Either way is fine, but for this exercise leave it checked.)

2. In the Solution Explorer window, right-click the existing class, *class1*, and rename it to **Invoice.vb** or **Invoice.cs**. This will also change the code associated with the class to the same name. Add code to the class so that it looks like following:

VB .NET

```vb
Public Class Invoice
  Private _InvoiceNumber As Int32
  Private _InvoiceDate As Date
  Private _CustomerID As Int32
  Private Shared LastInvoice As Int32

  Public Sub New(ByVal CustID As Int32)
    _CustomerID = CustID
    _InvoiceNumber = NewInvoiceNumber()
  End Sub
```

```vb
  Public ReadOnly Property InvoiceNumber() As Int32
    Get
      Return _InvoiceNumber
    End Get
  End Property
  Public Property InvoiceDate() As Date
    Get
      Return _InvoiceDate
    End Get
    Set(ByVal value As Date)
      _InvoiceDate = value
    End Set
  End Property
  Public Property CustomerID() As Int32
    Get
      Return _CustomerID
    End Get
    Set(ByVal value As Int32)
      _CustomerID = value
    End Set
  End Property

  Public Function CalculateInvoiceTotal() As Decimal
    'We will add code to this in the next exercise for now just leave as is
  End Function

  Public Function NewInvoiceNumber() As Int32
    'open a database and retrieve highest invoice number
    LastInvoice += 1
    Return LastInvoice
  End Function
End Class
```

C#

```csharp
public class Invoice
{
  private Int32 _InvoiceNumber;
  private System.DateTime _InvoiceDate;
  private Int32 _CustomerID;
  private static Int32 LastInvoice;

  public Invoice(Int32 CustID)
  {
    _CustomerID = CustID;
    _InvoiceNumber = NewInvoiceNumber();
  }
```

```csharp
    public Int32 InvoiceNumber
    {
      get
      {
        return _InvoiceNumber;
      }
    }

    public System.DateTime InvoiceDate
    {
      get
      {
        return _InvoiceDate;
      }
      set
      {
        _InvoiceDate = value;
      }
    }

    public Int32 CustomerID
    {
      get
      {
        return _CustomerID;
      }
      set
      {
        _CustomerID = value;
      }
    }

    public decimal CalculateInvoiceTotal()
    {
      //We will add code to this in the next exercise for now just leave as is
    }

    public Int32 NewInvoiceNumber()
    {
      LastInvoice += 1;
      return LastInvoice;
    }
}
```

3. Place your cursor anywhere in the Code window for the Invoice class, then right-click and select Create Unit Tests from the pop-up window (see Figure 11-8). This action automatically creates a new test project that is added to your solution. You'll use this test project for testing your Invoice class in the remaining exercise steps.

```
Public Class Invoice
    Private _InvoiceNumber As Int32
    Private _InvoiceDate As Date
    Private _CustomerID As Int32
    Private _Remarks As String
    Private Shared LastInvoice As Int32

    Public Sub New(ByVal CustID As Int32)
        _CustomerID = CustID
        _InvoiceNumber = NewInvo                    Rename...
    End Sub                                    🔲  Create Unit Tests...
                                                   Create Private Accessor  ▶
    Public ReadOnly Property Inv     🔲  Insert Snippet...
        Get
            Return _InvoiceNumbe     🔳  Go To Definition
        End Get                          Find All References
    End Property
    Public Property InvoiceDate (        Breakpoint              ▶
        Get                          ◆🔳  Run To Cursor
            Return _InvoiceDate      🔲  Cut
        End Get
        Set(ByVal value As Date)     🔲  Copy
```

Figure 11-8. *Selecting the Create Unit Tests option*

The Create Unit Tests dialog box will appear. All of the properties and methods of the InvoiceLib class are displayed in a tree structure with check boxes. What's going to happen is that any item that is checked in this dialog box will have a test created for it. Go ahead and click all of the check boxes except the My box (for VB .NET), as shown in Figure 11-9, so that all of your properties and methods will get a corresponding test method.

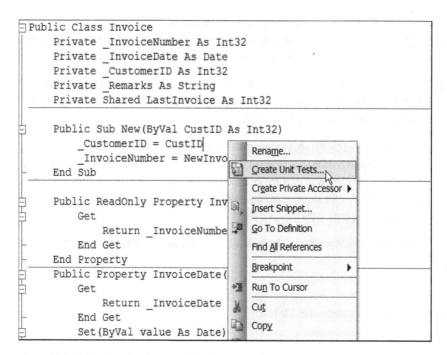

Figure 11-9. *The Create Unit Tests dialog box*

Notice that the Output Project box will, by default, create a Visual Basic test project. Leave this default if you want to continue in VB .NET. C# people can choose the C# option, but do not *have* to. Note that you can also create the test project in C++ or C#, regardless of which language the project you are testing was written.

4. Click OK to begin creating the tests. You will be presented with a dialog box asking you to name your test project. Remove the default name and type **InvoiceUnitTests** (if you missed this dialog box, the default name for the test project is also fine to use).

Once the test project creation has been completed, you'll see your new test project, InvoiceUnitTests, in the Solution Explorer and the Code window for the new test class, InvoiceTestClass, will be displayed. Scroll through this window to view and examine just how much code has been generated for you. This code contains merely the structure and the shells of the actual tests. To turn them into useful tests, you will customize this code in the following steps.

5. In the Code window, locate the test for the NewInvoiceNumber() method; it will start with these lines:

VB .NET

```
<TestMethod()> _
Public Sub NewInvoiceNumberTestMethod()
```

C#

```
[TestMethod()]
public void NewInvoiceNumberTestMethod()
```

The first line of this code, <TestMethod()> (VB .NET) or [TestMethod()] (C#), is what tells the compiler that the method following it is part of the test and will be flagged as a test by Team Test software (i.e., that means it will show up in the appropriate windows). If this first line is taken off, the method will still reside in the test class, but won't be considered a test.

Modify the code in the NewInvoiceNumberTestMethod() to set the initial value for the CustID variable to **0** (in C#, this is already done for you) and modify the actual variable so that its initial value is **75**. Delete the line that starts with Assert.Inconclusive. When you're finished, the full method will look like the following (including preliminary comments):

VB .NET

```
<summary>
'''A test for NewInvoiceNumber()
'''</summary>
<TestMethod()> _
Public Sub NewInvoiceNumberTestMethod()
  Dim CustID As Integer = 0
  Dim target As Invoice = New Invoice(CustID)

  Dim expected As Integer = 75
  Dim actual As Integer
  actual = target.NewInvoiceNumber

  Assert.AreEqual(expected, actual, _
  "InvoiceLib.Invoice.NewInvoiceNumber did not return the expected value.")
End Sub
```

C#

```
/// <summary>
///A test for CalculateInvoiceTotal ()
///</summary>
[TestMethod()]
public void NewInvoiceNumberTestMethod ()
{
  int CustID = 0;
  Invoice target = new Invoice(CustID);

  decimal expected = 75;
  decimal actual;
  actual = target.NewInvoiceNumberTestMethod ();

  Assert.AreEqual(expected, actual,
    "InvoiceLib.Invoice.NewInvoiceNumberTestMethod " +
      "did not return the expected value.");
}
```

This test, when run, will create an instance of the InvoiceLib class, which is referred to as target in the code. When the instance is created, the constructor of the InvoiceLib class runs first (that's the job of the constructor). Looking back at the code, you'll see that the constructor of the Invoice class calls the NewInvoiceNumber() method, which in turn initializes the _InvoiceNumber variable to 1. Then the code calls target.NewInvoiceNumber. So the actual value of the InvoiceNumber after the test runs should be 2, not 75. You'll see how this is handled when the test is run in the next steps, and then later you'll modify the test to check for 2 and not 75. First, let's see what happens when the test fails.

6. Rebuild the test solution, InvoiceUnitTests, by selecting Build ➤ Rebuild InvoiceLib from the main menu.

■**Important Note** Any time you make a modification to the test project, you should rebuild it for the changes to take effect.

---

7. Next, open the Test View window by selecting Test ➤ Windows ➤ Test View from the main menu. The Test View window displays as a tab in the same area as the Solution Explorer. Examining the list of tests in the Test View window, you can see that all of the test shells for the InvoiceLib's properties and methods are listed. However, the only one we've modified to be a test is the NewInvoiceNumberTestMethod().

8. Right-click the NewInvoiceNumberTestMethod() and select Run Selection from the pop-up menu, as shown in Figure 11-10.

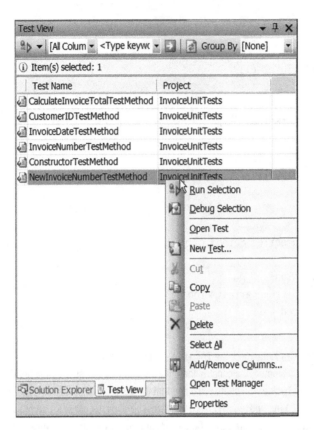

Figure 11-10. *Selecting and running a test from the Test View window*

The test will run in the background. As it runs, the Test Results window will automatically display at the bottom of the Visual Studio development environment. While it's running, it will report that it is pending. In a short time the test will complete (since this isn't a very complex test) and, in this case, the test will report a failure. This is because the actual result, which should be 2, won't match what you coded for the value of the expected result: 75 (see Figure 11-11).

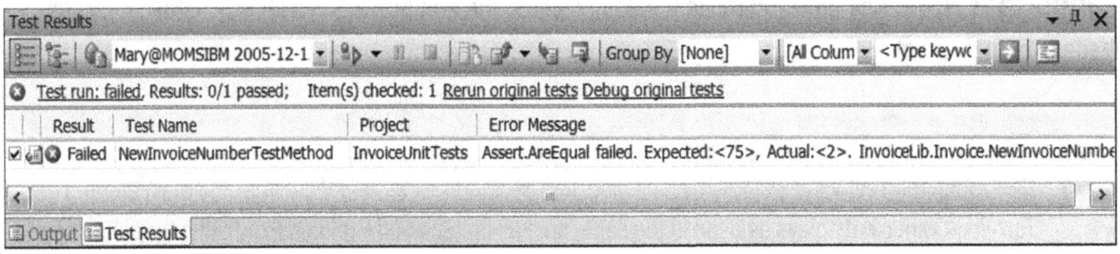

Figure 11-11. *The Test Results window with a failed test displayed*

9. Return to the code window and the NewInvoiceNumberTestMethod(). Change the code so that the Expected variable is set to 2. Save and rebuild the test project solution. Run the test again by right-clicking it in the Test View window, as you did earlier. This time the Test Results window should indicate that the test passed. (If you receive an inconclusive result, it probably means you forgot to comment out

the Inconclusive line as indicated in step 5. Ensure your code looks exactly like step 5!) To view additional details on the test, double-click on it to open up the Common Results window (see Figure 11-12).

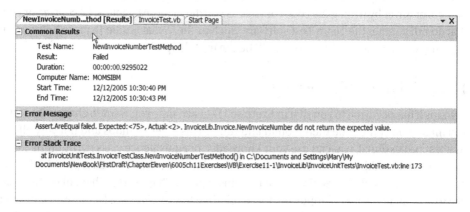

Figure 11-12. *Viewing additional test details*

10. Optional: For more practice, continue modifying tests for the other methods in the test project. Of course, you'll want to make the other methods in the Invoice class functional in some way before you code a test for them, just be sure to keep things simple. Remember to rebuild each time you make a change to the Invoice class and to your test project so the changes will take effect.

In this exercise, you've learned how to create a basic unit test for a class. In the process, you used the Test View and Test Results windows. You've also learned how to modify and rerun tests using these windows and the code available in your test class. You observed how the software responded when tested with both valid and invalid data.

TESTER'S TIP: USING THE DEBUGGER

If something goes wrong during your test run, or you're unsure how the tests are processing through, you can set a breakpoint in either the application code or your own test code and walk through the whole test step-by-step using the Visual Studio Debugger, just as you did in Chapter 4. One of the nice features of the Team Test tool is that it is fully integrated with the Visual Studio Debugger so this works very well. Using the debugger is useful for ensuring your test code is working properly, of course, but is also very instructive for analyzing how the code under test is operating as well.

It would be useful now to go back and compare the code generated in Exercise 11-1 to the code used in some of our earlier chapters—for example, Chapters 6 and 10—to create test harnesses for component access. In many cases, it will be faster and easier to create a quick test harness or driver by writing the code yourself, as you did in those chapters. Of course, for editions that do not contain the Team Test software (such as the Visual Studio Express Editions), the information in these earlier chapters will be the most helpful.

Data-Driven Unit Testing

Perhaps it has occurred to you that in Exercise 11-1 each time you want to change the test input you must modify the code then rebuild and run it. This is very tedious and not very effective. As a test professional, you can use your knowledge of equivalence class partitioning for input values to create additional test cases (for a discussion of equivalence class partitioning and boundary value analysis, see the sidebar on this topic in Chapter 10). Then, of course, you'd like to automate the task of inputting these multiple test data values. Data-driven testing can greatly increase the efficiency of your testing by allowing many test values to be input into an application in a short period of time. This kind of data-driven testing is available using the Team Test software.

Two properties are provided for each unit test that allow you to associate that test with a database and a table within the database. These two properties are Data Connection String and Data Table Name (see Figure 11-13). Since these two properties are associated with each unit test, this means that you can independently associate each separate unit test with a different database and database table, if desired. This allows for a very flexible approach to your data-driven testing.

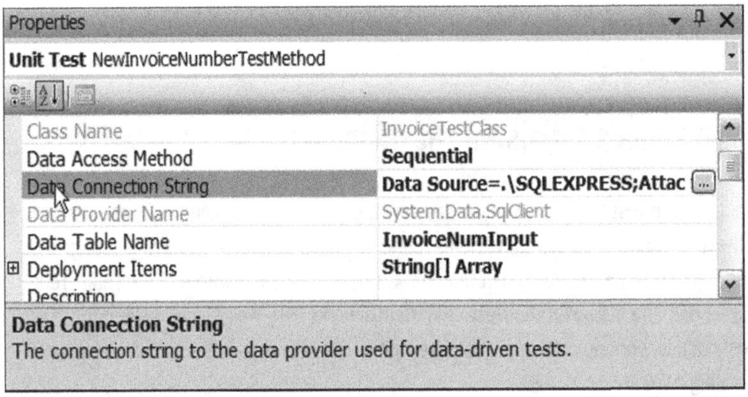

Figure 11-13. *The Data Connection String and Data Table Name properties for a unit test*

To add data-driven inputs to the unit test you created in Exercise 11-1, you will need to add access to a database. There are a few ways this can be done:

- If you have SQL Server or Microsoft Access installed, you can attach to an available database by selecting it from the Data Connection String property of your test. This is a good option if there is already a test database set up.

- You can create a new database on an available server from the Server Explorer window by right-clicking on the Data Connections icon and selecting the Create New SQL Server Database menu item from the pop-up menu. This also presumes SQL Server is installed. This option will create a new local database on your own system or on another server.

- You can select Project ➤ Existing Item from the Visual Studio main menu to insert a SQL database file into the project. This way the test data will be directly attached to the test project; however, a downside to this option is that this file can't get too large. Still, this option is best for most data-driven tests. For larger test databases, you will need to work with a larger database located on a global server.

For Exercise 11-2, we have provided a SQL Server file containing a table with sample test data for your use. You'll use this file and the first option from the previous bulleted list in Exercise 11-2 to add data-driven input to your unit tests.

Exercise 11-2: Adding Data-Driven Inputs to Your Unit Test

In this exercise, you'll continue working with your unit tests from Exercise 11-1. You'll add a SQL Server database file called `InvoiceTestDB_Data.MDF` (provided in the Download Files for this chapter; see Appendix A for details) into your project. This database file contains a table called SalesTest loaded with some sample test data. If you prefer, you can select one of the other options in the previous bulleted list to create this table and load the data yourself using your choice of databases (for those who prefer, a Microsoft Access file is also included).

Note You may want to move the exercise files from the Exercise folder to the C:\ drive. It makes things easier, and some things still choke on long pathnames.

In case you'd like to try using a different database than SQL Server, the table structure and data values are listed in Figures 11-14 and 11-15.

	Column Name	Data Type	Length	Allow Nulls
▶	SaleAmount	decimal	9	✓
	Expected	decimal	9	✓
	isValid	bit	1	✓

Figure 11-14. *The structure of the test data table, SalesTest, used in this exercise*

	SaleAmount	Expected	isValid
1	−1	0	0
2	500	500	0
3	0	500	0

Figure 11-15. *The Test Data table*

> ■**Note** If you have SQL Server (or SQL Server Express) installed locally, you *may* have to stop the SQL Server Service temporarily prior to executing the following set-up steps to connect to the InvoiceTestDB_Data.MDF data file. Otherwise, you will get an error message indicating that the file is "already in use," especially if you've previously attached to this file using any of SQL Server's tools, such as Query Analyzer or Enterprise Manager. Usually, you will use the SQL Server Service Manager tool to shut down the SQL Server service. To access this tool from a local installation, click the Windows Start button then go to All Programs and select the SQL Server program group. Click the Service Manager icon and then click the Stop button on the Service Manager dialog box. (You can also often access the SQL Server Service Manager from the system tray as well.) Once access to the file has been set, you can restart the service again, if desired, by following the same steps except clicking Start (instead of Stop) once in the Service Manager dialog box.

Be sure you are in the InvoiceLib project created in Exercise 11-1 before continuing with this exercise.

1. First, you'll need to add a little more code worthy of testing to your application. So, return to the code window for the Invoice class in the InvoiceLib project. Add the following bolded declaration to the Invoice class just before the other declarations at the top of the Invoice class:

VB .NET

```
Public Class Invoice
  Private _TotalSales As Decimal
```

C#

```
Public class Invoice
  {
    private decimal _TotalSales;
```

And, modify the function CalculateInvoiceTotal so that it looks like the following:

VB .NET

```
Public Function CalculateInvoiceTotal(ByVal Sale As Decimal) As Decimal
  Return _TotalSales + Sale
End Function
```

C#

```
public decimal CalculateInvoiceTotal(decimal Sale)
{
  return _TotalSales + Sale;
}
```

2. Open the Test View window and right-click the CalculateInvoiceTotalTestMethod(). Select Properties from the pop-up menu.

3. From the Properties window of the CalculateInvoiceTotalTestMethod(), click the Data Connection String property and click its ellipsis. When the Add Connection dialog box displays, you will click the Change button, which will, in turn, display the Change Data Source dialog box (see Figure 11-16).

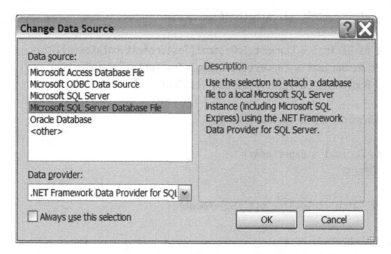

Figure 11-16. *The Change Data Source dialog box*

From the Change Data Source dialog box, select the Microsoft SQL Server Database File option from the Data Source list (again, see Figure 11-16) and click OK. You will be returned to the Add Connection dialog box again. From there, you will select the Browse button. Browse to the Chapter 11 Exercises folder (provided within the Download Files for this book; see Appendix A). Select the InvoiceTestDB_Data.MDF file and click Open. Your connection is now set up.

4. Click the Data Table Name property in the Properties window, and select the SalesTest table from the drop-down list. (Note: If the table doesn't show up in the list, it likely means your connection didn't work, so try steps 2 and 3 again.)

5. Return to the code window for this test by right-clicking the CalculateInvoiceTotalTestMethod() test in the Test View window and selecting Open Test. Notice that a new attribute, similar to the following, has been added to the top of your test (your attribute will be on a single line; ours needs to break for printing purposes):

```
<DataSource("System.Data.SqlClient",
"Data Source=.\SQLEXPRESS;AttachDbFilename="
"C:\\InvoiceTestDB_Data.MDF"";
Integrated Security=True;Connect Timeout=30;User Instance=True",
 "SalesTest", DataAccessMethod.Sequential)>
```

■**Note** The path to the database file will be different depending on where you placed the download files for this chapter and, of course, also will be different if you chose to link to a different type of database.

Change the code in the `CalculateInvoiceTotalTestMethod()` to look like the following (the added and changed areas are bolded in the code shown here):

VB .NET

```
Public Sub CalculateInvoiceTotalTestMethod()
  Dim CustID As Integer  = 0
  Dim SaleAmount As Decimal = Convert.ToDecimal(TestContext.DataRow(0))
  Dim ExpectedAmt As Decimal = Convert.ToDecimal(TestContext.DataRow(1))
  Dim isvalid As Boolean = Convert.ToBoolean(TestContext.DataRow(2))

  Dim target As Invoice = New Invoice(CustID)

  Dim expected As Decimal = ExpectedAmt
  Dim actual As Decimal

  actual = target.CalculateInvoiceTotal(SaleAmount)

  Assert.AreEqual(expected, actual, _
    "InvoiceLib.Invoice.CalculateInvoiceTotal did not " + _
      "return the expected value.")
'Assert.Inconclusive("Verify the correctness of this test method.");
End Sub
```

C#

```
public void CalculateInvoiceTotalTestMethod()
{
  int CustID = 0;
  decimal SaleAmount = Convert.ToDecimal(TestContext.DataRow[0]);
  decimal ExpectedAmt = Convert.ToDecimal(TestContext.DataRow[1]);
  bool isvalid = Convert.ToBoolean(TestContext.DataRow[2]);

  Invoice target = new Invoice(CustID);
  decimal expected = ExpectedAmt;
  decimal actual;
  actual = target.CalculateInvoiceTotal(SaleAmount);
  Assert.AreEqual(expected, actual,
    "InvoiceLib.Invoice.CalculateInvoiceTotal didn't return expected value.");
//Assert.Inconclusive("Verify the correctness of this test method.");

}
```

■**Important Note** You *must* comment out (or delete) the line that begins with `Assert.Inconclusive`; otherwise, your test will always return `Inconclusive`!

In the previous code, the three added declarations for the variables, SaleAmount, ExpectedAmt, and isvalid, have the effect of linking the three columns in the table (again, see Figure 11-15) each, in turn, to the three declared variables using a property called TestContext that was created automatically for you when you linked the test to the database.

6. Now you're ready to build the project and run the test. Select Build ➤ Build Solution. Then right-click the CalculateInvoiceTotalTestMethod test in the Test View and select Run Selection. The Test Results window will display "pending" as the test runs, and finally will report a failure. This is because if even one test fails, the whole test run will report as failed.

To see the test result details, right-click the test in the Test Results window and select the View Test Results Details menu item (see Figure 11-17).

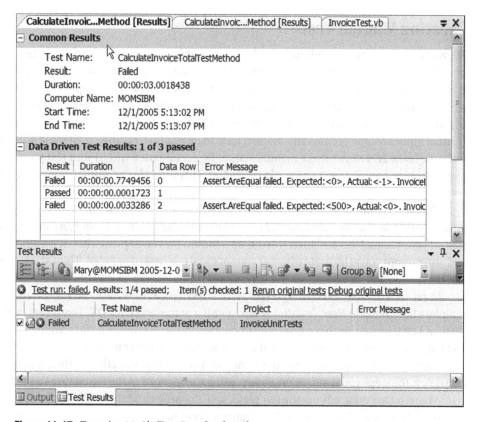

Figure 11-17. *Exercise 11-2's Test Results details*

Notice that the first and last test failed, while the second test passed. Review the values in Figure 11-15. The first test failed because we input a negative value (−1) and then expected that the CalculateInvoiceTotal() function would not return a negative value, but it did. That's because we wrote it that way. However, it would be reasonable to expect such a function to refuse a negative input. If this were a real application, we could report this failure as a defect. The next test correctly added 0 to 500 with a result of 500, so it passed. The third test failed because we passed in a 0 value, but expected a result of 500. This indicates a problem with our test value. We shouldn't expect 0 plus 0 to equal 500. So this one failed; however, not because of a problem with the method we're testing, but because our test values for this test are bogus. This underscores the point that you must carefully analyze what you're testing and be sure your inputs make sense. Tests can appear to fail simply because you've made an error in input!

In this exercise, you've seen how to use the Team Test software to add multiple input values from a database into your unit tests to create a data-driven test run. We hope you noticed that this software makes this process relatively easy to connect your unit tests to a database and to loop through the data values without your having to write a loop to do so.

There is also an excellent tutorial available showing how to do data-driven unit testing in the MSDN at `http://msdn.microsoft.com/library/default.asp?url=/library/en-us/dnvs05/html/ vstsunittesting.asp`.

Creating Manual Tests

Manual tests are the most traditional and, in many companies, are still the most common kind of tests run on a test project. A manual test is simply one that is not automated in any way but is followed step-by-step by a tester, usually directly interacting with an application's screens similar to the way the end user would. Since this kind of test is, by definition, not automated, why does Team Test have an option to create one? Many kinds of automated tests require some manual input or some preliminary manual tests to be run first, during, or after the automated test run. Team Test allows these manual tests to be documented within your test projects so that all tests can be managed and tracked together. This allows for a common approach to your test project.

It's relatively simple to set up a manual test within the Team Test environment. If you create a list of tests that include a manual test when your other tests run, Team Test can prompt you to start your manual test and then will put up a button for you to push when it is complete. It will also prompt you to indicate whether your manual test passed or failed. Then, the test result for that manual test can be added to the results of the other tests in the run.

To create a manual test in your test project, select Test ➤ New Test. Click the Manual Test template from the Add New Test dialog box, give it a name, and click OK. Team Test creates a Manual Test template file that contains instructions and a textual template for creating a manual test that you can edit to create the set of steps you'd like the tester to follow.

Figure 11-18 shows a portion of this template. You can type directly into this page, and add and delete the steps you need, as necessary, using the sections of the template as a guide.

When you are done editing the template, save the project. You can view and run the new test in the Test View window or the Test Manager window.

When you run your new manual test, you will be prompted with a dialog box indicating that your test run contains manual tests. You can click OK to dismiss this dialog box. The Test Results window will briefly show a pending designation as your test begins to process, and then you will be prompted with a dialog box indicating that your manual test is "ready for execution." This is your cue to perform the manual test. So you'll dismiss this dialog box as well and then perform the test by following the steps you wrote in your manual test. Visual Studio presents a window awaiting your input to indicate whether the manual test passed or failed (see Figure 11-19).

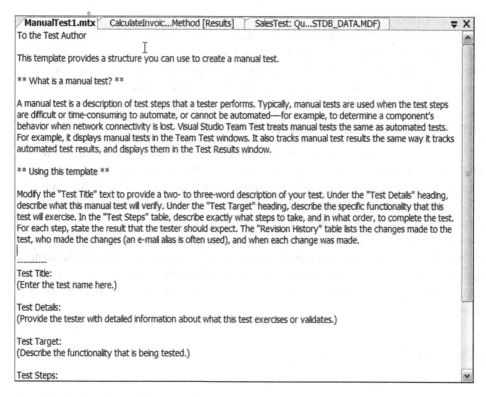

Figure 11-18. *The Manual Test template*

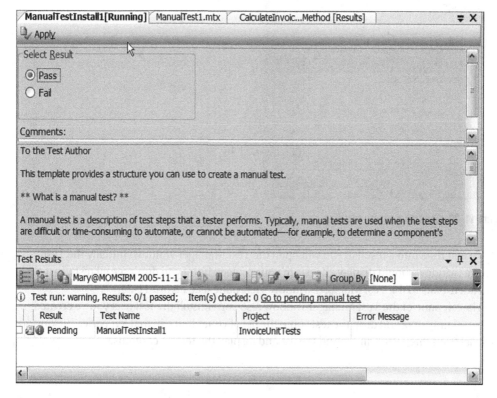

Figure 11-19. *Visual Studio waits for you to complete your manual test.*

Figure 11-19 shows the Pass result option button selected. Selecting either the Pass or Fail result option will enable the Apply button at the top-left corner of this window. Once you click this Apply button, your test result is recorded. If you have run this test along with others (as you will learn how to do in the next section), the test run will continue with your remaining tests and then report the results of your manual tests along with their results.

Organizing Tests and Managing Test Runs

One of the more useful features of the Team Test software is the ability to create lists of tests that allow you to organize your test project into a variety of flexible test runs. (By the way, a test list in Team Test is similar to a test "suite"; a common term in testing. The Microsoft Team Test developers intentionally avoided the word "suite" because of its multiple definitions in the industry, but it might make more sense to experienced testers.)

To create test lists of the tests you've created, select Test ➤ Create New Test List. The Create New Test dialog box that displays allows you to name and describe the list you want to create (see Figure 11-20). You can also use it to create a hierarchy of test lists. You can't add tests to the list from the Create New Test List dialog box, however; you will simply create the empty test list here.

Figure 11-20. *Creating a new test list*

To add tests into a test list, you will open the Test Manager window. Initially the Test Manager window should display all tests in your project; but if you don't see all tests, just click All Loaded Tests in the Test Manager window's left pane (see Figure 11-21).

The left pane of the Test Manager window also contains all the test lists you've created. You can simply drag and drop the tests onto the list of your choice in that left pane. Clicking on a test list from this pane will expand the list and display the tests it contains.

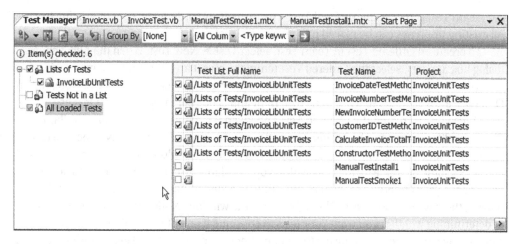

Figure 11-21. *All Loaded Tests in the Test Manager window*

To run the tests in a test list, you will simply check the boxes of the lists you want to run and then click the arrow in the upper-left corner of the Test Manager window (hovering over this arrow will produce the tip "Run Checked Tests"). You can also drill down into a test list from the left pane containing the lists to run only a selected few of the tests, as desired.

Creating Ordered Tests

There are times when a prescribed order or sequence is required for your tests. This is true especially for those test methodologies that include *end-to-end testing* (taking the system through an entire user sequence from start to finish) and for those who employ *Use Cases* as a requirements development or test technique (see the following sidebar).

USE CASES AS A TEST TECHNIQUE

A Use Case is a methodology used in system analysis to identify, clarify, and organize system requirements. The Use Case is made up of a set of possible sequences of interactions between systems and users in a particular environment and related to a particular goal. It consists of a group of elements (for example, classes and interfaces) that can be used together in a way that will have an effect larger than the sum of the separate elements combined. The Use Case should contain all system activities that have significance to the users.

—From TechTarget (www.techtarget.com)

Although Use Cases are primarily used as a system requirements development technique, the scenarios that are developed are also very useful for the test team as test scenarios. Ordered tests and test sequencing can be based on these Use Cases.

Team Test provides the Ordered Test type to create an ordered test out of existing tests. All existing test types can be placed into an ordered test.

To create an Ordered Test in Team Test, select Test ➤ New Test. When the Add New Test dialog box appears, select the Ordered Test template, give it an appropriate name (it will have the extension .OrderedTest and will be saved into your test project), and click OK. Note that an Ordered Test is considered a test in its own right and is not the same thing as a test list!

Once you've created the Ordered Test and given it a name, a new window similar to Figure 11-22 will appear. This window is pretty straight-forward, you simply select the tests you want from the Available Tests list on the left side of this window. You can navigate around and select some of your existing tests within your available test lists. When you've selected all you want in your Ordered Test, you can modify the order of them in the Selected Tests list by moving them with the arrows on the right side of the window. Notice that you have the option of determining whether you want your tests to continue if one of them fails or if you want to stop by checking or not checking the Continue After Failure check box. There is no Save button on this dialog box, but clicking the Save button on the Visual Studio toolbar will have the effect of saving your new test. Now you can select it and run it from the Test Manager or Test View window as you would any other test.

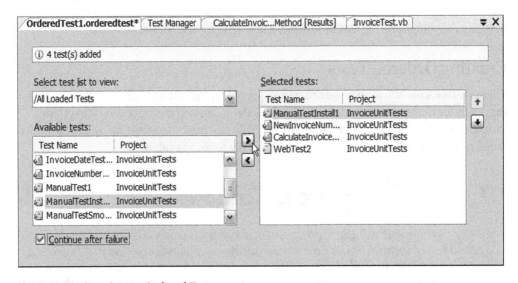

Figure 11-22. *Creating an Ordered Test*

Web Testing

Testing a web application is a common and important task in the testing industry. All websites need to be tested for functionality, as well as tested for performance, during stress and load situations. Tools for this are abundant and therein lies a lot of the problem we've had in the test industry to date: determining which tools work well and which are appropriate for your site.

The Team Test software includes support for web testing, and one big advantage to them over others will be that they are integrated into the Visual Studio development environment. In this section, you'll examine some of the basics of what you can do with web testing with the Team Test software, and then you will want to compare what you learn to what you've already used and what's available. Keep in mind that many web testing tools are available as open source (i.e., no cost), but investigating their effectiveness and applicability can be very time consuming.

In Team Test, a web test is a series of HTTP requests. Team Test's web testing tools test at the HTTP layer so that they do not exercise browser code per se, but they do exercise server-side logic. Web tests can be used to test web application basic functionality and also to test web applications under load and stress situations.

You create web tests in Team Test by recording your activities in a browser session as you navigate through a web application, or you can also build web tests manually using the Web Test Editor.

Once you have a set of web tests, you can then assemble them along with unit tests, if desired or required, into load tests (see the "Load Testing" section later in this chapter). Exercise 11-3 presents the basic steps for testing a website.

■**Caution** This exercise presumes you have a nonproduction, or test, website to use for testing purposes. Please be careful not to perform extensive tests on production sites, for obvious reasons!

Exercise 11-3: Recording a Basic Web Test

1. Create a new Visual Studio test project by selecting File ➤ New ➤ Project, and then selecting Test Project from the Project Types and Test Project from the templates.

2. Select Test ➤ New Test. The Add New Test dialog box will display. From here, select Web Test. In the Test Name box, type an appropriate name or just leave the default. (Do not change the `.webtest` extension though.) When finished, click OK.

   At this point, the Web Test Recorder will open inside an instance of Internet Explorer. Navigate to the site you want to test and, as you do so, observe the URLs that are listed in the Web Test Recorder.

3. Navigate around the site, clicking more links. Notice that as you click links, the URLs are added to the list of recorded URLs on the left side of the Web Test Recorder pane (see Figure 11-23).

   When you navigate to a place that requires user input, you'll notice that the URL will get a "+" in the recorder, which means you can open the URL in the recorder and view the Query String and Form Post Parameters (see Figure 11-24).

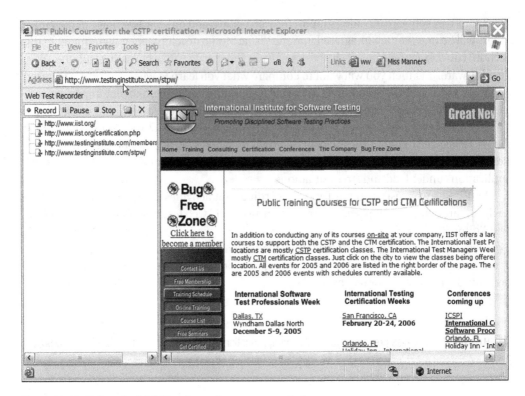

Figure 11-23. *Using the Web Test Recorder to test a website*

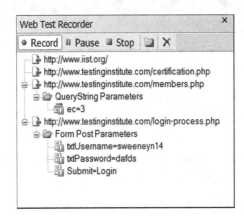

Figure 11-24. *The Web Test Recorder showing Query String and Form Post Parameters*

There are actually two windows of interest at this point. Internet Explorer is displaying the website and the URLs, but the Visual Studio IDE also displays the recorded web test in the Web Test Editor as it is being recorded (see Figure 11-25). After you stop the recording, you will be able to edit the test.

4. To stop the recording, you can either click the Stop Recording link in the Visual Studio Web Test Editor (again, see Figure 11-25), or you can click the Stop button in the Web Test Recorder window (again, see Figure 11-24).

5. To save your newly recorded web test, select File ➤ Save. The new web test will show up in your Test View and Test Manager windows.

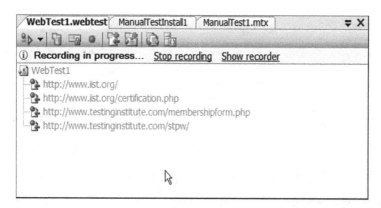

Figure 11-25. *The Web Test Editor displays URLs as they are recorded.*

In this exercise, you learned how to record a basic web functionality test—navigating through the site while the Web Test Recorder logged your actions. Although you exercised the site by clicking links and typing in data, the recorder is performing more than a simple link-check, as you'll see in the continuing discussion in this section.

The Web Test Recorder doesn't capture all traffic sent between client and server, so requests for picture files, Cascading Style Sheets (CSS), and JavaScript code aren't recorded. The Web Test Viewer determines these dependent requests at runtime when you execute the test. The upside is that this makes your web tests more robust in that they are not muddied with requests for all kinds of images and will be less likely to fail for that reason. The downside to this is that any JavaScript code you may have isn't exercised. So if your site issues JavaScript requests, you'll have to manually add these requests to the recorded web test later in the Web Test Editor.

To run your new web test, you can simply select it from the Test View or Test Manager window, right-click it, and select Run as you would with any other test. As your test runs, you'll be able to see the pages of your website as they are navigated to in real time (see Figure 11-26). By default, you can see the HTTP Status, Response Time, and Size of the request.

Notice that the version of Internet Explorer used in this test run is 6.0. Naturally, you'll want to test for the target varieties of browsers and connections that your users will. You can change these settings in the Test Run Configuration dialog box (select Test ➤ Edit Test Run Configurations) on the Web Test tab.

You might want to edit your web test for a number of reasons, including the following:

- To add the missed JavaScript, CSS, or picture file requests not recorded

- To add or remove URLs

- To add data-driven capability for the Query String or Form Post Parameters

To edit your web test, you can right-click it and select Open Test from the Test View window. This will open the Web Test Editor. You can right-click the Web Test in the editor to see the variety of options you have for modifying your test (see Figure 11-27).

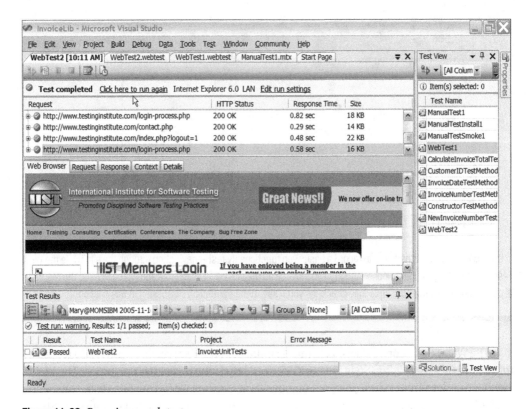

Figure 11-26. *Running a web test*

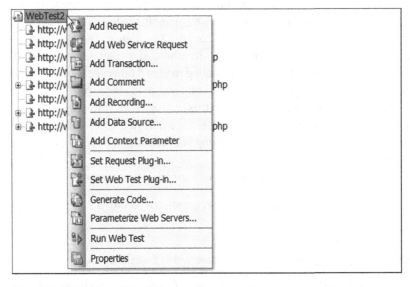

Figure 11-27. *Options for editing a web test*

There is much more to performing the extensive web testing that a good website needs. We include references for Team Test resources at the end of this chapter and in Appendix C.

Load Testing

Team Edition for Testers provides a tool for creating and running *load tests*. In the test industry, the term "load test" can have a variety of definitions, meaning different things to different people. So before discussing the method for creating load tests, let's look at the definition of load test used by Microsoft from their Visual Studio Team System glossary:

> *Load test: A test type that contains other test types and exercises them with simulated user settings to perform a predefined load scenario.*

In Team Test then, the primary goal of load tests is to simulate numerous users accessing a server simultaneously. Using Team Test software, you can add unit and web tests to a load test. When you add web tests to a load test, you are simulating multiple users connecting to a server and making multiple HTTP requests. When you add unit tests to a load test, you are examining the performance of non–Web-based components (for example, database access components).

Load tests are used in several different types of testing:

■**Note** These definitions come from Microsoft documentation; these terms are not defined uniformly across the industry; however, for simplicity, we will use the definitions as defined by Microsoft for this section so that we can understand their application of these terms within the Team Test software.

- *Smoke*: How your application performs under light loads for short durations

- *Stress*: To determine if the application will run successfully for a sustained duration under heavy load

- *Performance*: To determine how responsive your application is

- *Capacity planning*: How your application performs at various capacities

The Load Test Wizard will be helpful in specifying your initial settings. You'll be able to change these settings later with the Load Test Editor. To create a load test, you'll create a new test within an existing test project just as you've done with the other test types. Within the Add New Test dialog box, you'll give the test an appropriate name (it will have a .loadtest extension) and click OK. This will immediately launch the Load Test Wizard, which will walk you through the following settings:

- *Think Time*: Think time is defined as the time a user takes to view a web page and determine the next action to take. When you initially record a web test, your think times are recorded for each web page. Then, when the web test is run, those think times between pages are repeated again, or ignored, based on what you choose in this setting.

- *Load Pattern*: The load pattern for a test refers to the number of users you want to simulate and the time periods and rates for adding these users. You can select the number of users and you can also determine whether the load is *constant* (same number of users the whole time) or *stepped* (starting with a certain amount and increasing or decreasing).

- *Test Mix*: The test mix allows you to add an assortment of unit or web tests to your load test. You can also specify distribution rates for these tests; for example, you can select three different existing tests and specify that one will be run 40 percent and the others at 30 percent each. This ability allows you to select a distribution of tests close to what you expect your actual users would perform on your application (see Figure 11-28).

Caution Although the documentation said to add only unit and web tests to the load test, we tried adding an ordered test that included manual tests. Our recommendation: Don't try this at home! The addition of manual tests (which was silly anyway) managed to hang the load test. Stick to adding to your load tests what the documentation recommends: only unit and web tests. (The final release of the software will not allow manual tests in a load test.)

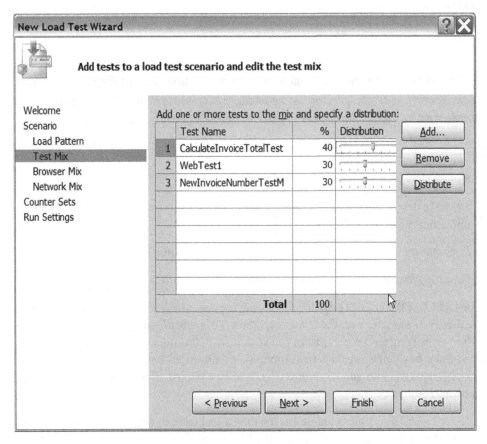

Figure 11-28. *Specifying a mix and distribution of tests in the Load Test Wizard*

- *Browser Mix*: The browser mix setting allows you to select from a predefined set of browsers (Netscape 6.0, Internet Explorer (IE) 5.5 and 6.0, Smartphone, and Pocket IE) and also specify the distribution of use of those browsers during the test. For example, if your user demographics show that most of your users use Netscape 6.0, but some do use

Internet Explorer, you can select both Netscape and IE and give a higher distribution to the Netscape browser to more closely simulate your actual users.

- *Network Mix*: You can select from a set of network settings to simulate during the load test. The selection includes a variety of settings including several each for dial-up, high speed cable, and DSL, as well as LAN and T1. As with the browser mix, you can also specify a percentage distribution rate for them.

- *Counter Sets*: The Team Test tools provide a set of selected performance counters that the tool will track and graph as the tests run. To use this option, you'll select which computers on your network you want to track (see Figure 11-29).

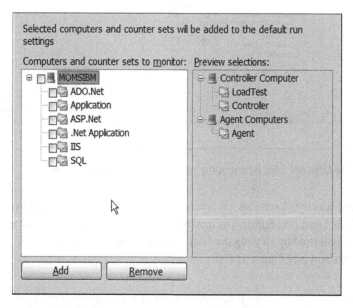

Figure 11-29. *Performance counters available for load testing*

Notice that these performance counter sets include SQL, IIS, ADO, and ASP counters, among others. You can add counters for multiple computers by selecting the Add button. The counter set selection is not the complete set of counters available on a Windows operating system, but a selection of those considered most important by the Team Test developers based on user-request.

- *Run Settings*: Using run settings, you can specify the total duration of the load test, the *warm-up duration* (the time to wait before data samples are taken), and the *sampling rate* (the rate at which performance counters are measured).

After the Load Test Wizard walks you through all of these settings, click Finish to create the test. You'll then be presented with the Load Test Editor where you can modify the settings, as desired, by right-clicking them (see Figure 11-30).

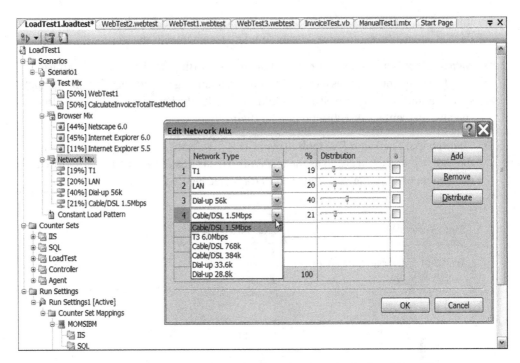

Figure 11-30. *Modifying the Network Mix setting for a load test in the Load Test Editor*

When you're finished specifying settings, you can run the load test by clicking the arrow in the upper-left corner of the Load Test Editor. The load test will run and you can view the performance counter values in real time by viewing the Load Test Monitor, which displays automatically as your tests run (see Figure 11-31).

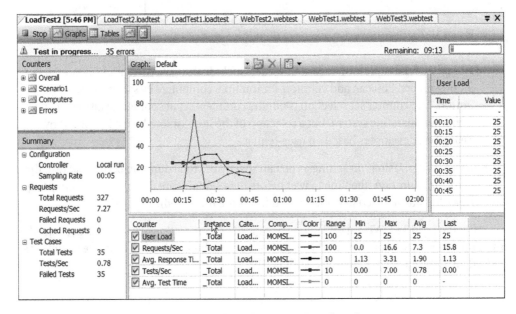

Figure 11-31. *The Load Test Monitor displays, showing selected performance counters as your load test runs.*

The Load Test Monitor's default configuration is displayed in Figure 11-31 as well. You can also select from a variety of graphs and tables that provide further detail about the settings you selected when setting up the test.

To view load test results for completed test runs, you'll open the Load Test Analyzer. The Analyzer is basically the same window as the Load Test Monitor. It just has a different name depending on whether you're viewing it as you run your test or not.

These results are easily copied into Microsoft Word or Excel documents to share with your test team. In the Enterprise editions, you can publish these results to a SQL Server database and create reports from them.

Summary

In this chapter, you've explored a sampling of the test types available in Team Test and the windows that comprise the core of the Team Test software. This overview has only touched upon the basic capabilities of the Team Test tool. Our hope is that this discussion will give you an idea of the capabilities so that you can compare it with other test tools and your team's coding capabilities. This software is new and its usefulness will be determined in the months and years to follow this initial release. However, the usefulness looks promising for companies that choose to purchase the Visual Studio Team Edition software. As we've mentioned, these features are not available, at the time of this writing, to any of the other editions, including the Professional Edition. Thus, larger software development companies can make effective use of these tools to save a lot of coding time for automated tests in Visual Studio that will integrate nicely with the software development project. However, these tools may not be necessary for smaller organizations and individual testers who want to write quick and simple tests. The techniques used and learned in the first ten chapters of this book will be the most useful for those using other than the Visual Studio Team Edition software. We do not necessarily advocate one edition or version over another, but instead recommend careful analysis in determining what is right for you and your company.

To help you in your analysis of which product is right for your organization, Microsoft provides a Product Line Overview web page at `http://msdn.microsoft.com/vstudio/ products/compare/default.aspx`. This page is useful for comparing the features of the Visual Studio 2005 products.

For more information on these technologies, see these resources:

- Microsoft Visual Studio Team Edition for Software Testers forum: `http:// forums.microsoft.com/msdn/showforum.aspx?forumid=19&siteid=1`

- Microsoft Events and Webcasts that give detailed demonstrations of the products by senior team members: `www.microsoft.com/webcasts`

Tester's Checklist

When testing with Visual Studio 2005 Team Test software,

☑ Use the Visual Studio Team Test tools to create tests and metrics that can be shared with development and management.

☑ Use the Visual Studio Team Test tools to save time on coding automated tests.

☑ Create unit tests to attach to class libraries to test the functionality of the software at the class and method levels.

☑ Use the techniques in Chapters 1 through 10 to attach to components if your Visual Studio Edition (i.e., Express, Standard, or Professional) does not contain Team Test software.

Setting Up Your Computer

We tried to keep the requirements for this book as simple and inexpensive as we could. For example, we wrote as if your computer would be a stand-alone PC and not necessarily part of a network. This way you can easily complete the exercises in this book at work, home, or in a classroom environment. Of course, there are some minimum requirements you will need and here is some information to help you to determine those requirements.

Hardware Requirements

We recommend that your computer meet the following *minimum* configuration:

- Pentium 750 MHz processor, 1.5 GHz or better recommended

- 192MB physical memory, 1GB or better recommended

- 3GB of free space on installation drive, with 1GB of that on the system drive for the full versions of Visual Studio

- 1.5GB on the installation drive, with 500MB on the system drive for the Expess Editions of Visual Studio

- Super VGA (800 × 600) or higher resolution monitor with 256 colors

- Microsoft mouse or compatible pointing device

■**Note** We have found that increasing your computer's RAM will improve Visual Studio's performance—more so than a faster processor.

Software Requirements

We recommend that your computer to meet the following *minimum* configuration:

- *Microsoft's Windows 2000, Windows 2000 Professional, or Windows XP Professional Editions with the latest service packs for each*: We do not recommend using XP Home Edition since is has a reduced feature set by design, but most of the book's examples will work anyway. If that is what you have, there certainly is no need to upgrade for this one book. We also do not recommend using Windows Server 2003 as is has a number of enhanced security features that may confuse and impede you as you work through the examples. However, if you have experience administering and troubleshooting Windows Server 2003, there should be no problem using it.

- *Microsoft Visual Studio Express Editions, Visual Studio Standard Edition, Visual Studio Professional Edition, Visual Studio Tools for Office, or Visual Studio Team System*: We recommend using the Express or Standard Editions, as they are the least expensive for you and will often have all the features you will need for smaller testware projects. There is a 90-day evaluation version that you can send for at http://msdn.microsoft.com/vstudio/products/trial. However, be aware that only the Team Test version has all of the new Team Test tools discussed in Chapter 11.

- *At least 200MB of free space on the operating system's drive after installation*: The default installation is on your operating system's drive, typically C:\, needs to maintain about 200–300MB of free space on that drive in order to keep your operating system happy. Although, you can install the Visual Studio and the Express Editions on any drive, the installation process installs around 500MB of files on your system drive. Consequently, ensure that about 800MB of space is available for Visual Studio on your system drive at the start of the installation, regardless of the Visual Studio or the Express Edition's location.

Note You can choose to install only VB .NET Express or C# Express, but we recommend both. The first one you install should take less then an 1 hour depending on your Internet connection, but the next one will take about a quarter of that time. If you are using the Express Editions, you will also need to download and install Visual Web Developer Express for our chapters on web programming. You can download all of the Express Editions from the Microsoft website at http://msdn.microsoft.com/vstudio.

We recommend that your computer meet the following *optional* configuration:

- *Internet Information Server (IIS) version 5.0*: Since the 2005 web development tools include their own web server, this one will only be of use if you are familiar with IIS and want to deploy an ASP.NET or Web Service to a production server or you want to check out some of the configuration screens we show in this book. IIS version 5 comes with both Windows 2000 and Windows XP Professional. However, it is installed by default on Windows 2000, but not with Windows XP Professional. To check if it is installed on your computer, or to install it if you already know it is not, you can open the Add Or Remove Programs applet in the Control Panel and select the Add Or Remove Programs icon when it launches. From there you would select the Add/Remove Windows Components button on the left side of the screen. If it is there, you are done. If it is not, select Internet Information Services (IIS) from the Components list and then use the onscreen instructions to complete the installation. Please note that IIS 6.0, which comes with Windows Server 2003, will have different administration screens than we show in the book; however, if you are familiar with this version, it should not pose an issue.

- *Microsoft Office 2000, XP, or 2003*: You will still be able to work with the Access database files used in the exercises even without Office installed. It just gives you more options as you study. A free evaluation version of Office is available for download at www.microsoft.com/office/trial/default.mspx.

- *Microsoft SQL Server 7.0, 2000, or 2005*: We tried to use Microsoft Access in most cases, since it is simple to use and most readers will have it installed along with Microsoft Office. Still, you may want to try out some of the code we included for SQL Server as well. A free evaluation version of SQL Server is available for download at http://microsoft.com/sql/default.asp. A smaller version, called SQL Server Express, comes with the Visual Studio installation. SQL Server Express is the only version of SQL Server 2005 that will work with Visual Basic 2005 Express Edition and Visual C# 2005 Express Edition. If you did not specify SQL Server Express when you installed your Express Edition, you can install it by using Add Or Remove Programs icon in the Control Panel.

FrontPage Extensions Issues

Visual Studio lets you upload your ASP.NET project to a live Web Server. This is done using FrontPage extensions. Although originally used only for Microsoft's FrontPage program, they are now used in a number of products to command a remote IIS Web Server to upload files and set configurations on those files. If these extensions are not installed or not correctly configured, you will not be able to use the automated deployment options that come with Visual Studio. We show you how to manually deploy your web application in this book, but if you would like more information on how to get the FrontPage extensions working, check out the "How To Configure FrontPage Server Extensions in Internet Information Services" article at http://support.microsoft.com/kb/298158/EN-US/.

Unsupported Operating Systems

The following operating systems are not supported. If you have any one of these, you will have to find another computer to work from or upgrade the OS to one of those listed earlier:

- Microsoft Windows 95/98/ME

- Microsoft Windows NT 4.0

- Windows Server 2003, Enterprise Edition for Itanium-based systems

---

■Note These are the most common operating systems you should know about, but there are a few more as well. For a more detailed list, check out `http://msdn.microsoft.com/vstudio/support/readme/default.aspx`.

Setup Instructions

After your computer's hardware is set up according to the manufacturer's instructions, we have found it best if your software is installed in this order:

1. Operating system

2. IIS (optional)

3. SQL 2000 or SQL 2005 (optional)

4. Visual Studio

5. SQL Express Edition

We tested this book using only the default settings for these installs so that most readers would not have problems installing and using this software. If you do have problems, you can try Microsoft's support site for help at `http://support.microsoft.com`. Common issues include the following:

- *Not uninstalling Beta software*: We have more on this issue later in this appendix.

- *Not having the latest service packs installed*: The setup programs will tell you about this and you will have to cancel the installation until you install the service packs.

- *Not rebooting between installs*: We have found that there are less installation issues if you reboot your computer after installing any one piece of software. This includes the service packs as well.

- *Moving back and forth between the installation screens*: Many people click optional installation buttons to see what is listed there and then go back to the original screen without making any choices. While this should not be an issue, we have noticed that this will sometimes corrupt an installation. We recommend that if you want to check out the optional screens, then you should cancel the install when you are done. Then you should start over and proceed through the installation without going back to previous screens when possible.

Uninstalling Visual Studio or Express Beta Editions

Some versions of Visual Studio are not compatible with others and must be uninstalled first. The uninstall programs in the pre-release versions of SQL Server 2005, Visual Studio 2005, or the .NET Framework 2.0 will not always remove all of the files or Registry entries. So, it is best if you install Visual Studio 2005 on a computer that was not used with the Beta software. Still, we uninstalled and reinstalled several times while writing this book and saw very few problems.

One thing we did note was that the pre-release versions *must be removed in the correct order BEFORE you begin installing the release version*. You can find this information on the Microsoft support site at http://msdn.microsoft.com/vstudio/express/support/uninstall, but you will note the website also says that this process is "not officially supported." Still, we also went through the process several times and it all seemed to work just fine.

Here is a general outline of how to uninstall, but please look at the website for complete details:

1. Use the Control Panel's Add/Remove Programs.

2. Remove any SQL Server 2005 products before you remove the .NET Framework.

3. Then either run the Auto-Uninstall tool or follow the manual uninstall instructions, both of which can be found on the website.

4. Now, install the version of Visual Studio you wish to use.

As mentioned, Microsoft has an Auto-Uninstall tool that uninstalls *all* pre-release Visual Studio 2005 products, including Visual Studio Express Editions, Visual Studio Team System, Visual Studio Professional, and Visual Studio Standard. However, note that SQL 2005 is not uninstalled by this tool and must be removed first.

Not uninstalling Beta software in a particular order may cause the uninstall or the new install to fail. If this happens, you may have to reinstall the software and begin the removal process all over again. This could add a couple of hours to your installations so it's pretty important to get it right. If Microsoft's website has moved the address listed previously, or you just want to make sure you have the latest information, search Microsoft's website with the keywords **Visual Studio Uninstall** instead.

Choosing Between Visual Studio 2005 or Express Editions

You can choose to use either Visual Studio 2005 or the Express Editions for this book. There are a few exercises that you will not be able to do in this book with the Express Editions, but this should not impact you too much. While you can install both on the same operating system and compare the differences, you should probably choose one over the other. To help with that decision, here are some things to consider:

- Express is an inexpensive option and has about 90 percent of the features you need for both this book and simple testware.

- The most expensive version, Visual Studio 2005 Team System, has advanced options that allow you to try all of the examples in this book.

- Visual Studio 2005 will cost you well over a $100, while Express is less than $100. In fact, at this time, Express is free until November 2006.

- The system requirements are roughly the same.

- Both Express and Visual Studio 2005 take about 2 hours to install. In general, Express's installation is a bit shorter and easier than Visual Studio 2005.

- There are no licensing restrictions for applications built using either Visual Studio 2005 or the Express Edition.

- Express Edition includes documentation targeted to help the beginning programmers.

- The Express Edition's user interface has fewer features, which simplifies the learning process of beginning programmers.

- The installation of the Express Edition is very easy, but requires an Internet connection.

- Express takes less room on the hard drive. Each Express Edition you need (C#, VB .NET, and Web Developer) are broken into 30–70MB downloadable sections. However, if you install the optional components, like the MSDN Express Library and SQL Server 2005, then the install can increase total download size to approximately 400MB.

Note Although, many of the samples and exercises will still work with Visual Studio 2002 and 2003, this book was written and tested with Visual Studio 2005 and Visual Studio Express Editions. If you are already using an earlier edition, you may want to download and run the Express Editions. As of the time of this writing, we have confirmed that Visual Studio 2005 and Visual Studio Express Editions install side-by-side with Visual Studio .NET 2003.

The Exercise Files

You can get the exercise files that go with this book free of charge from the Apress website at www.apress.com/book/download.html. The files are in a compressed downloadable file that includes the exercise solutions for each chapter.

When you get to the website, you will see a list for books. You will need to locate this book within that list and click the Submit button. That will take you to another web page that will have a link called Download Source Code File. You can click this link to download the file to your local computer.

Once you have downloaded the files, you will need to unzip them onto your hard drive. We have created a self-extracting file for you that will place them at C:\TGNet by default. Each exercise is listed by chapter and language within this folder.

If you have a problem downloading, please see the Apress support site for more information at `http://support.apress.com`.

Technical Support

We have made every effort to ensure the accuracy of this book and the contents of the downloadable files. If you have comments, questions, or ideas regarding this book or the exercise files, please send them to Apress using any of the methods in the next section.

Business Address

Apress L.P.
2560 Ninth Street, Suite 219
Berkeley, CA 94710
Business Hours: 9AM–5PM Pacific Standard Time
Phone: (510) 549-5930
Fax: (510) 549-5939
E-mail: support@apress.com

APPENDIX B

■ ■ ■

VB .NET and C#
Quick Reference

When we started this book, we needed to estimate the level of programming skills for a typical reader and then make sure to write as closely to that level as possible. This was difficult because these skill levels vary from tester to tester, company to company, and region to region. In the end, we decided that we did not want the first hundred pages to be about basic programming, but rather about testing and building testware. So, we wrote this book for readers that have some basic skill with either VB .NET or C#.

Rest assured that to be successful you do not have to be an expert programmer in either language, but having basic skills in at least one of them will help you get the most out of this book.

Since we know that some of our readers many never have programmed or, at most, would only have experience in another non-.NET language, we have included the syntax and basic use of typical statements in VB .NET and C# in this section. If you have lightly programmed in at least one other language, we are sure that you will find this appendix a useful place to start.

Please note that this appendix is not intended to be a complete introduction on either language. However, if you are a reader that has never programmed before, we hope that this section will help you get started programming and become a convenient reference afterward.

■Note Unless noted otherwise, the screenshots in this appendix are from the VB .NET or C# Express Editions.

Setting Up to Test the Samples

We chose to create all the code samples here using Console applications. These are the types of applications that run from the command prompt (or "DOS window" if you prefer). When you create one of these applications in Visual Studio .NET, you are given a "project" with a default code file in it. A project in Visual Studio is a way to organize one or more code files, and the default file is a convenient place for you to add the code from the following examples.

You may want to start this appendix by creating one of these Console application projects before you begin reading the rest of this section. That way, the following code samples can be typed and tested as you go. While you find out more on how to create Console applications in Chapter 7, here is an overview of the process.

To create a Console application, follow these steps:

1. Open Visual Studio and choose File ➤ New ➤ Project from the menu.

2. Choose a Console application template when the New Project dialog window appears (see Figure B-1).

Figure B-1. *Starting a Console project*

3. Find the Main() method when the Code window appears. Unless otherwise noted, inside of the Main() method is where you will type out all of your example code. Note that the code looks different in either VB .NET or C#, and we have added some extra comments to help you identify where your code should go in our examples (see Figures B-2 and B-3). The commented part is the text that comes after the ' or the // symbol.

```
1 Module Module1
2
3   Sub Main() '<-- START HERE
4     '... type your example code inside
5   End Sub
6
7 End Module
```

Figure B-2. *Finding the Main() method in VB .NET*

```
 1 □ using System;
 2    using System.Collections.Generic;
 3 └ using System.Text;
 4
 5 □ namespace ConsoleApplication1
 6    {
 7 □   class Program
 8      {
 9 □     static void Main(string[] args)//<-- START HERE
10        {
11          //...type your example code inside
12 ┤      }
13 ┤    }
14 └ }
```

Figure B-3. *Finding the Main() method in C#*

4. Later, when you type your code into the Main() method, you can press Ctrl+F5 to start your program and see the results. A black and white command-prompt window will appear and display your results. You will review the results and then close this window by pressing any key on the keyboard. After the window closes, the program will stop so that you can change your code and test it again.

In Figure B-4, we are using the Console.WriteLine() method to print out a message to the command prompt. When you run this program using Ctrl+F5, you will see this message and the program will pause until you press a key.

Note If you do not use the control key, the program will run but it will also immediately close the command window, leaving you to wonder if the program ran at all. So, always use both keys.

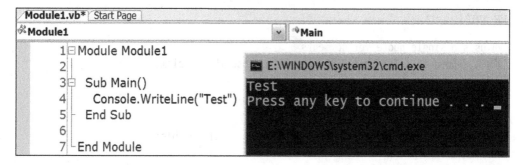

Figure B-4. *Running your program using Ctrl+F5*

Programming Basics

On a very general basis, you can consider programs to break down into two distinct categories: *data* and *operations* on that data. Data is the information you want to work with, such as a person's name and phone number. Operations are the things you want to do with the data, such as printing out the data or adding two numbers together. Of course, a program may also have other things as well, like *comments*, *namespaces*, or *directives*, but the data and operations are the core of the program. As for the others, comments provide additional information to humans; namespaces provide an easy way to organize your code into named groups; while directives provide additional information to the computer, but are not directly part of the program.

To create your program, you need to add statements to a code file. A *statement* is one instruction to the computer. Each of these statements will be made up of one or more keywords or symbols (sometimes called *tokens*). Since these can be more than one token per statement, you also need a way to indicate to the computer that you are done with a statement. In VB .NET, you do this by pressing the Enter key to add a carriage return, while in C# you use a semicolon (;) at the end of the statement.

VB .NET

```
x = 4 'This is one statement
y = 5 'This is another
```

C#

```
x = 4; //This is one statement
y = 5; //This is another
```

Comments

In the previous code, we used comments to identify the purpose of a statement. Commenting code is useful for notes like these, but also for when you want to see if disabling a particular set of statements solves a problem. Any code that follows a comment will not be processed. So, if you *comment out* a section of code and the problem disappears, then you know that the error is related to that set of statements. The comment only affects code on one line unless you use a block comment. However, block comments are only available in C#.

VB .NET

```
'VB uses a single quote for comments
'x = 5 <-Note to self: this line seemed to cause the problem
```

C#

```
//C# uses two slashes for comments.
//x = 5 <-Note to self: this line seemed to cause the problem
```

or

```
/*
C# uses a slash-star and star-slash pair for a block comment.
Note to self: Both these statements are commented out for testing
x = 5;
y = 10;
*/
```

Methods

Professional developers have found that it is good practice to organize your statements into groups. In .NET, statements are often grouped into *methods*—also know as *functions* or *subprocedures*. After you create a method, you can run its group of statements by *calling* the method. To indicate the end of the method, VB .NET uses words while C# uses the closing brace symbol (}). You will find more on this subject later in the "More on Methods" section of this appendix.

VB .NET

```
Shared Sub DemoMethod()
  Console.WriteLine("This is a VB .NET statement")
  Console.WriteLine("This is a another statement")
End Sub

Call DemoMethod 'Calling the method runs both statements
```

C#

```
static void DemoMethod()
{
  Console.WriteLine("This is a C# statement");
  Console.WriteLine("This is a another statement");
}

DemoMethod(); //Calling the method runs both statements
```

Organizing Code into Classes and Namespaces

Methods themselves are grouped together as well, but this time into *classes* or *structures* (or *modules* if you are using VB .NET). These also will be grouped together, but this time into *namespaces*. In general, you can figure that a namespace will contain one or more classes, a class will contain one or more methods, and a method will contain one or more statements.

VB .NET

```
Namespace

   Class (or Structure or Module)

      Method (Typed out as a Function or Sub)
         Statement
         Statement
      End Method

   End Class
End Namespace
```

C#

```
namespace
{
   class (or struct)
   {
      method
      {
        Statement;
        Statement;
      }
   }
}
```

Shared and Static

In many examples, we will use the keyword Shared in front of a VB .NET method and static in front of a C# method. You do not need to know all of the rules and reasons for this, but you will at least want to know what it means when you see it. Both Shared and static do roughly the same thing—i.e., they allow you to call a method directly from a class or structure. Without these keywords, you must first make an object from the class and call the method through the object. You will find out more about objects and classes in Chapter 6, but here is some code that shows the different syntax for calling methods both ways:

VB .NET

```
Class myClass1
   Public Sub StandardMethod()
     'Code to do something
   End Sub
   Public Shared Sub MySharedMethod()
     'Code to do something
   End Sub
End Class
```

```
'This method is called in-directly using an object
Dim MyObject1 = New MyClass1 'Create a new Object
MyObject1.StandardMethod() 'Call through the object
'This method is called directly from the class
MyClass1.MySharedMethod 'Call directly, no Object needed
```

C#
```
class MyClass1
{
  public void StandardMethod()
  {   //Code to do something
  }
  public static void MySharedMethod()
  {   //Code to do something
  }
}


  //This method is called in-directly using an object
  MyClass1 MyObject1 = new MyClass1(); //Create a new Object
  MyObject1.StandardMethod(); //Call through the object

  //This method is called directly from the class
  MyClass1.MySharedMethod(); //Call directly, no Object needed
```

METHODS IN MODULES VS. CLASSES

Instead of a class, Microsoft chose to use a code module in the VB .NET version of the Console application. Modules do not require the use of the Shared keyword. This is because the Shared keyword is implied in a VB .NET module. C# does not have code modules, so you will see that a class is made for you instead of a module when you first create your project. This means that you have to add the keyword static to your C# examples, while most VB .NET examples will not need this. In summary:

- A module in VB .NET is similar to a class in that it can hold data and methods, but it is designed to be simpler. One of the differences is that you do not need to type the Shared keyword. In fact, you will get an error if you do.

- Shared means that you can use the method directly from the memory location of the class, structure, or module. C# uses the word static to indicate this same command, making Shared and static equivalent.

- Without using either Shared or static, you could not call the method directly. Instead, you would first have to create a new space in the computer's memory that would act as a copy of the class or structure, and then call the method indirectly. These *copies* are called objects, and we discuss both objects and methods more throughout this book.

- If you test the VB .NET code samples using a class and not a module, make sure you add the Shared keyword.

The Main() Method

As mentioned at the beginning of this appendix, the Main() method is where you will want to put the code to test the following examples. This is because Microsoft designed .NET applications to run this method as soon as a program is started. Within the Main() method, any code you type in will be processed one line after the other. If you call another method from the Main() method, it will jump to that method, run the statements inside of the called method, and return to the Main() method when it is done. Here is an example that outlines the order in which your statements will be processed, numbered first to last:

VB .NET

```
Sub DemoMethod() '#3
  Console.WriteLine("This is a statement") '#4
  'The Program jumps back to #2 after next line
End Sub


Public Sub Main()'#1
  DemoMethod();  '#2 This statement calls the method above
  Console.WriteLine("This is another statement") '#5
End Sub
```

C#

```
static void DemoMethod() // #3
{
  Console.WriteLine("This is a statement"); // #4
  // The Program jumps back to #2 after next line
}


static void Main()// #1
{
DemoMethod(); // #2 This statement calls the method above
Console.WriteLine("This is another statement"); //  #5
}
```

Both of these examples will print out the following:

```
This is a statement
This is another statement
```

Namespaces

Programmers use namespaces for much the same reason you use folders and subfolders on your hard drive. Consider what a disorganized mess your files would be if you did not use folders on your hard drives—if, instead, you put all of your files in the root directory of C:\. It's true that if you only had a few files it might not be too bad; but once you ended up with hundreds of files, you would have a real mess.

When you install Microsoft's .NET Framework as part of Visual Studio, you are really installing thousands of classes, structures, and enumerations. These classes, structures, and enumerations are collectively known as *types*. Microsoft makes working with all these types much easier by using namespaces to categorize them into groups. For example, there is the System.Data namespace for classes that work with database code, and System.IO for classes that work input and output to text files.

Both C# and VB .NET use a dot notation for listing the full path to namespaces, classes, or methods. This is also similar to how you find a file on a hard drive, but there you use a slash (e.g., C:\MyFolder\MyFile) instead of a dot (e.g., MyNamespace.MyClass.MyMethod).

For example, the first part of a full name for a class or method includes the namespace name, while the last part of the full name is the class or method name itself. Each is separated by dots, as shown here:

VB .NET

```
Namespace MyCompanysCode

'The full name of this class is MyCompanysCode.Employees
Class Employees

  'The full name of this method is MyCompanysCode.Employees.Test()
  Shared Function Test() as string
     'you would put statements here
  End function
 End Class
End Namespace
```

C#

```
namespace MyCompanysCode
{
  //The full name of this class is MyCompanysCode.Employees
  class Employees
  {
  //The full name of this method is MyCompanysCode.Employees.Test()
  static string Test()
  {
    //you would put statements here
  }
 }
}
```

Continuing with the analogy of files on a hard drive, if you are already in a folder that has the file you want, you can call the file without using the full path to the file. (See Figure B-5.)

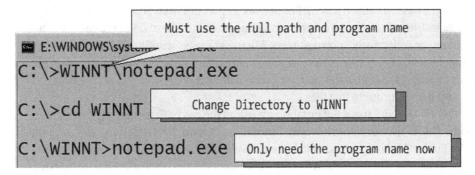

Figure B-5. *Namespaces are similar to folders.*

Referring to a class or method follows the same rules used to refer to a file in a folder. If you are trying to reference code that is in the same namespace, you do not need to use the full path. You can even provide .NET hints about which namespace to automatically consider when trying to find a class or method. This is done by using a directive keyword: Imports in VB .NET and using in C#.

VB .NET

```
Namespace MyCompanysCode
  Class Employees
    Shared Sub TestMethod() As String
     'add code here
    End Sub

    Shared Sub TestMethod2() As String
      'This calls the Method using the full path
      MyCompanysCode.Employees.TestMethod()

      'But this also works since they are both in the same path
      TestMethod()
      Return "test2"
    End Sub
  End Class
End Namespace
```

C#

```
namespace MyCompanysCode
{
  class Employees
  {
    static void TestMethod()
    {
      //add code here
    }
```

```
  static void TestMethod2()
  {
    //This calls the Method using the full path
    MyCompanysCode.Employees.TestMethod();

    //But this also works since they are both in the same path
    TestMethod();
  }
 }
}
```

Directives

Directives are used to tell the computer additional information about the program. These can be things like indicating which namespace to automatically look in when finding VB .NET or C# commands, or something like identifying *regions* of code. The #Region directive affects how Visual Studio displays the code file when you are editing it, but it does not affect the actual program at all. In essence, it allows Visual Studio to expand and collapse a section of code while you are programming. For example, when you use Visual Studio to create a Windows application, you will often see the following code along with a – or + symbol to the left of this code (as you do in Figure B-2).

VB .NET

```
'Tells the computer to automatically search in the System Namespace
Imports System

'Tells Visual Studio to allow a click on the -/+ to
'collapse/expand a section of code
#Region "Windows Form Designer generated code"
```

C#

```
//Tells the computer to automatically search in the System Namespace
using System;

//Tells Visual Studio to allow a click on the -/+ to
//collapse/expand a section of code
#region "Windows Form Designer generated code"
```

Holding Data

Of course, it is a rare program that does not use any data. Your programs data will exist in one of two states: stored or in memory. Programs store their data in a variety of ways: in a file, in the Registry, or in some type of database. In the end though, these are really just different types of files on some kind of drive. Although data is stored this way, computers do not process the data until it has been loaded into memory. All data will be read or modified while in memory, even with simple applications like Notepad. When the program has completed using the data, it can save back the data to a hard drive, or some other removable media, before shutting down.

It should be noted that not all data you use in a program must be saved. Often you will just ask the user to supply you with temporary values as they are using your program. After the user provides this data, it is your choice to save it somewhere or to just let it evaporate as the program closes. The Windows calculator is an example of this kind of program.

When you are loading data into memory, either from stored data or from the collected user data, you need to tell the computer what kind of data is being loaded. This does two things: it allows the computer to reserve enough memory space to hold the data you are going to load, and it allows the computer to restrict certain types of data from that space. For example, if you create a space in memory for an integer, then .NET will tell the computer to set aside 4 bytes of memory and only allow whole numbers within that memory space. If you later try to add character data to that space, the computer will report an error.

Declaring Constants

Many programmers will place a further restriction on their program's data—one that stops it from being changed while the program is running. These read-only data values are referred to as *constants*. The initial value of a constant must be set on the same line of code where you create the constant. Once your code is saved in either an .exe or .dll file, the value will always be the same each time the code is loaded into memory. It is a common programming convention to name your constants using all uppercase letters, making them easy to spot:

VB .NET

```
Const PI as Double = 3.14
```

C#

```
const double PI = 3.14;
```

Declaring Variables

If the programmer wants to allow changes to a value, they can create a variable instead. A *variable* allows both reading and writing of the data. Unlike constants, variables store data that can be set with an initial value and then be changed while the program is running:

VB .NET

```
Dim x as Int32 = 5 'x starts off with the value of 5
x = 10 'x now hold the value of 10
```

C#

```
Int32 x = 5; //x starts off with the value of 5
x = 10; //x now hold the value of 10
```

Again, this is different from constants, which store data that can be set with an initial value but *cannot* be changed while the program is running:

VB .NET

```
Const Y As Int32 = 5
Y = 10 'This causes an Error!
```

C#

```
const Int32 Y = 5;
Y = 10; //This causes an Error!
```

ASSIGNMENTS ALWAYS GO RIGHT TO LEFT

Both VB .NET and C# use the = symbol to assign values and references to a variable or constant. One thing that every programmer needs to know is that items on the left of the = symbol always receive that which is on the right. It may seem so simple if you have some programming experience; but when we are teaching, we see many students become confused by this simple statement. It is our guess that the reason for this is because when we were children we always saw our teachers write out equations as follows:

```
4 + 5 = 9
```

It was not until later that a teacher might write the same equation like this:

```
9 = 4 + 5
```

By the time we saw the second example, we had seen the first example for years. Perhaps this is why some people struggle with the fact that programming code like the following will always write out the value of x as 10 and that y will never be 5:

```
x = 5
y = 10
x = y 'the variable x will now be set to the value of y
Console.WriteLine(x)
```

Choosing Types

Both variables and constants are declared by choosing a name and deciding on the type of data you want to store. Computers do not really deal in subtle distinctions when it comes to data, but humans do. We see a number and think that it is very different from a name. We see a picture and think that it is different from collections of numbers. However, computers don't care. Even pictures are just all ones and zeros to a computer.

Still, it is important to force a computer to see these distinctions sometimes. That way, you can receive an error message from the computer when a program tries to set incompatible values to your variables or constants. To make a computer understand the distinction between numbers, names, dates, etc., you must formally tell the computer the difference. In .NET this is done by defining *types*.

These data types are a description of data. In other words, a type defines that one memory location will allow only numbers while another can only hold characters. Tables B-1 and B-2 list some of the common predefined types built into .NET.

Table B-1. *Data with Characters*

Type	Description	VB .NET	C#
char	A single unicode character	`Dim x as Char = "h"`	`char x = 'h';`
string	A set of unicode characters	`Dim x as String = "Test"`	`string x = "Test";`

Table B-2. *Data with Whole Numbers (Integers)*

Type	Description	VB .NET	C#
byte	Whole numbers up to 8 bytes long	`Dim x as byte = 5`	`byte x = 5;`
short or Int16	Whole numbers up to 16 bytes long	`Dim x as Int32 = 5`	`short x = 5;`
int or Int32	Whole numbers up to 32 bytes long	`Dim x as Integer = 5`	`int x = 5;`
long or Int64	Whole numbers up to 64 bytes long	`Dim x as int64 = 5`	`long x = 5;`
UInt32	Whole numbers up to 32 bytes long	`Dim x as UInt32 = 5`	`UInt32 x = 5;`

Note that the last example in Table B-2 is an unsigned version of an `Int32`. This means that no negative sign is allowed when you set the value. The unsigned integers allow numbers twice as big as the signed ones, since the computer does not have to reserve bits for any numbers lower than zero. The unsigned versions of a type are easy to spot since they have a `U` in front of them.

You have three basic choices when you want to store data that includes a decimal point: `Single`, `Double`, and `Decimal` (see Table B-3). The size of each determines how many numbers you can place after the decimal point. Since your computer will actually hold the data in a binary form of 1's and 0's, the conversion to this format can cause the number to be rounded either up or down. If you are storing something that needs to be very accurate, such as monetary values, then choosing the `Decimal` is likely your best choice.

Table B-3. *Data with Numbers That Can Include Decimal Values*

Type	Description	VB .NET	C#
Single	Up to 7 digits long	`Dim x as Single = 1.23F`	`Single x = 1.23F;`
Double	Up to 16 digits long	`Dim x as Double = 1.23`	`Double x = 1.23D;`
Decimal	Up to 29 digits long	`Dim x as Decimal = 1.23D`	`Decimal x = 1.23M;`

You may notice that there is not a lot of difference in the values being assigned to these different data types. Since Singles, Doubles, and Decimals can all hold values with a decimal point, you can help the computer understand what data type you mean by adding a character to the end of the number:

- F is used for Single or Floating point values. A Single can also be called a Float.

- D in C# is used for Double values. This is the default in VB .NET, so no letter is needed.

- D is used in VB .NET and M is used in C# for Decimal values.

There are also many specialized data types included with .NET; three of the more common ones are the Boolean, Date, and Object data types (see Table B-4).

Table B-4. *Data That Is Not Characters or Numbers*

Type	Description	VB .NET	C#
Boolean	Values are either true or false.	Dim x As Boolean= true	bool x = true;
Date	Holds dates and times.	Dim x as DateTime = "1/1/2001"	DateTime x = DateTime.Parse("1/1/2001");
Object	Can be used to reference all other data types	Dim x as Object	object x;

Note Object, in this case, refers to a build in Type made by Microsoft. Programmers also use the term Object to indicate an in-memory instance of a class's code. You will find more on this meaning of the term Object later in the "More on Objects" section of this appendix.

As you can see, Microsoft has created many built-in types for your convenience. Having a set of predefined types makes programs, even when written by many different people, more consistent. This, in turn, makes it easier for one programmer to see someone else's code and know how a type of data was intended to be used.

Reference Types and Value Types

In .NET, types are divided into two categories: *reference types* and *value types*. These names identify how .NET stores and refers to the data through the variables and constants.

To help you understand the difference, consider the kind of things a computer must track to allow you to use a variable or constant. The computer would need the name, data type, and address in memory where the actual values are stored. It may be useful to think of what the computer stores as a table of values, as shown in Table B-5.

Table B-5. *Picturing How Metadata is Recorded for a Variable*

Name	Type	Address of Data
x	Int32	stack(42)
y	string	heap(address = #123)

In Table B-5, we have recorded information about two variables, x and y. The types are record as Int32 for x and string for y. One obvious difference is that one will hold numbers and one will hold characters, but another is that Microsoft chose to make Int32 a value type while they made string a reference type. Without going into a lot of technical details, here are a few things you should know:

- For value types, the program itself is responsible for managing the memory where the data is stored. This area of memory is known as the *stack* of memory that the program is running in. Value types store the value of their data directly with the program's stack. In Table B-5, we indicate that x is holding the value of 42.

- For reference types, the .NET engine, or Framework, is responsible for managing the memory where the data is stored. Microsoft's .NET Framework uses a special space of reserved memory known as the .NET *heap*. Reference types are stored in memory and managed by .NET, not by the program itself. When your program refers to a variable or constant that uses a reference type, .NET will retrieve the data from the managed heap. Since the actual data is stored in the .NET managed heap, all your program needs to store is some reference to the address within the heap. Technically, .NET uses an advanced numbering system for addressing, but we simplified our example by showing y as holding an address of #123 in Table B-5 and not a true memory address. Although we just made this number up, this still gives you a good idea of how the system works.

- All of the .NET programs will share the managed heap. This means that if you have two programs running on the computer, both will store the reference type data on the .NET heap (see Figure B-6).

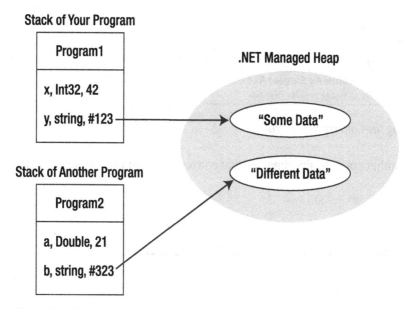

Figure B-6. *Value types and reference types are stored differently.*

Data Conversions

There are times when a program needs to transfer one type of data to a memory location of another type of data. When this happens, your program may need to convert that data from one type to the other; either implicitly or explicitly. Both VB .NET and C# allow you perform these conversions in a number of ways:

- Using the Convert class
- Using built-in methods
- Using the C# cast operator
- Using the VB .NET CType()
- Implicitly converting for you

The Convert Class

Microsoft created the Convert class for the purpose of changing one data type into another. This class contains a number of methods that you can call directly. These methods all work similarly: you select the method with the name of the data type you want to convert to and then place the variable you want converted within the parentheses. For example, if for some reason you have a variable that is using data type Single and you want to convert it to a Double data type, your code might look like the code shown in Figure B-7. In that example, you may notice that the ToolTip message indicates that there are a total of 18 different versions of this method. Each of these versions is designed to convert a different data type to a Double.

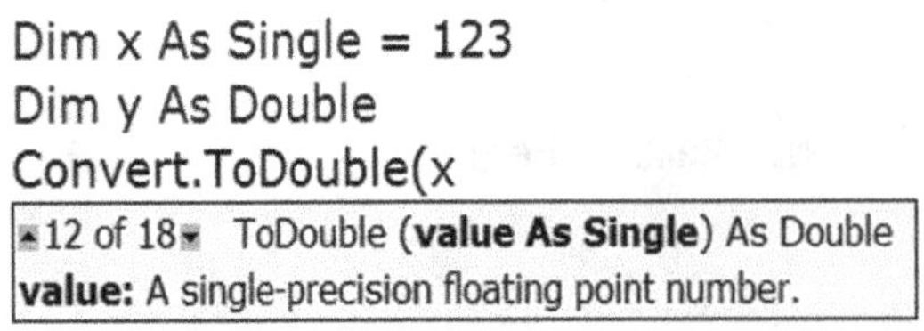

```
Dim x As Single = 123
Dim y As Double
Convert.ToDouble(x
```

```
▲12 of 18▼  ToDouble (value As Single) As Double
value: A single-precision floating point number.
```

Figure B-7. *Using the Convert class methods*

Here is another example, this time one that converts from an Int32 to an Int16 data type:

VB .NET

```
Dim x As Int32 = 5
Dim y As Int16
y = Convert.ToInt16(x) 'explicitly changes Int32 to int16
```

C#

```
Int32 x = 5;
Int16 y;
y = Convert.ToInt16(x); //explicitly changes Int32 to int16
```

Built-In Conversion Methods

In addition to the Convert class, Microsoft added some conversion methods as part of the data types themselves. There are only a few of these, but the ToString() method is one that you will come across quite often. As the name implies, the purpose of this method is to return a string value for the data being held in the variable. For example, you can use the ToString() method to convert an integer variable to a string representation of that number.

VB .NET

```
Dim x As Int32 = 123
Dim y As String
y = x.ToString() 'y now holds 123 as a string of characters
```

C#

```
int x = 123;
string y;
y = x.ToString(); //y now holds 123 as a string of characters
```

Although this example works much as you would expect it to, you should be aware that the ToString() method does not work the same way with all data types. What is returned is dependent on which data type you are using. This is because each of these data types is really just a class or a structure with a ToString() method included inside. This method is part of the code in each data type itself, and not all of the data types were written the same way or by the same person. With some data types, all that is returned is a string with the name of the type you are trying to convert, which is not all that useful. When that happens, you will need to use another way to convert it. Of course, that other way could be the Convert class methods or, but if you are programming in C#, you can also try using the cast operator. However, if you are using VB .NET you should know that it does not have the cast option.

The C# Cast Operator

The C# *cast operator* as another way to do type conversions. You can think of operators as methods that use a symbol instead of a name. In this case, the symbol you use is (), with the data type you want to convert to indicated in the middle. You will see the cast operator used frequently in the C# examples of many books. Like the ToString() method, the cast operator is also part of the data types themselves. Using cast will not always work the same, depending on the type you are trying to convert to. Once again, if the type you are using does not convert the data in the manner you want, you must use another choice.

To create a cast, you place the parentheses before the type you want to convert and the type you want to convert to within the parentheses.

C#

```
double x = 123.4;
int y;
y = (int)x; //cast double to int. Note that the .4 will be lost
Console.WriteLine(y.ToString()); //Displays 123
```

The VB .NET CType()

Although VB .NET does not allow you to use the () symbols for casting, it does provide the use of the CType() command for these conversions. You will see the CType() command used in many VB .NET code examples, but most of these will be in using the "short-cut version" and not the standard version of the method. These short-cut versions include the following VB .NET conversion functions: CBool(), CByte(), CChar(), CDate(), CDec(), CDbl(), CInt(), CLng(), CObj(), CShort(), CSng(), and CStr(). C# does not have this option, so if that is your language of choice, you an ignore this.

VB .NET
```
Dim x As Double = 123.4
Dim y As Integer
Dim z As Integer

y = CType(x, Integer) 'Casts a Double to Integer.

'Will display 123, since the .4 was rounded down.
Console.WriteLine(y.ToString())

'This short-cut version calls CType as shown above.
z = CInt(x)
Console.WriteLine(y.ToString()) 'Displays 123
```

Implicit Conversions

Implicit conversions happen automatically when you assign a value from one variable to another variable. If the conversion is considered "safe," then the conversion is allowed. This will happen without you having to add any additional code. Both VB .NET and C# allow these, but C# is much stricter as to what is considered "safe."

The comments in the previous code example indicate that the .4 is rounded during the conversion, thereby causing the program to lose some of its data. If this was your intention, then there is no problem. The computer figures that since you are explicitly using a conversion method, then you must know what you are doing. However, if the conversion was done without your explicit approval, then it could end up being a nasty bug within your program. Neither VB .NET nor C# considers data loss to be safe, so neither would allow an implicit conversion in this case. If this is what you really wanted to do, you would have to force the conversion using one of the conversion options we just mentioned.

Still, since not all conversion will result in loss of data, it's not strictly necessary to use explicit conversion all of the time. Sometimes you will just let the system convert data as needed. For example, the following code does not need an explicit conversion because it will not lose any data when it is implicitly converted. In this example, the value will be considered 123.0 after the conversion, which is fundamentally the same as 123:

VB .NET

```
Dim x As Int32 = 123
Dim y As Double
y = x 'implicitly changes integer data to double data
```

C#

```
int x = 123;
Double y;
y = x; //implicitly changes integer data to double data
```

Working with Groups of Data

Sometimes it is useful to hold a list of values together under one name. Both C# and VB .NET have a number of ways to do this. They include enumerations, structures, classes, and arrays. Although there is a lot to know about each of these, in general, an enumeration holds a set of constants, a structure or class can hold sets of both variables and/or constants, and an array is a set of objects made from these enumerations, structures, or classes.

Enumerations

Enumerations, or *enums* as they are sometimes called, are used to create a list of named constants. For example, say that you have a list of products your company sells and each product has a quality rating of Good, Better, or Best; you could create an enum that would list only those three ratings. In your program, you could then use the enum to restrict your code from using any description other than one of those three. In Figure B-8, you can see that when the variable called q1 is created from the enum quality, your code will only be able to set a value that is one of the listed values.

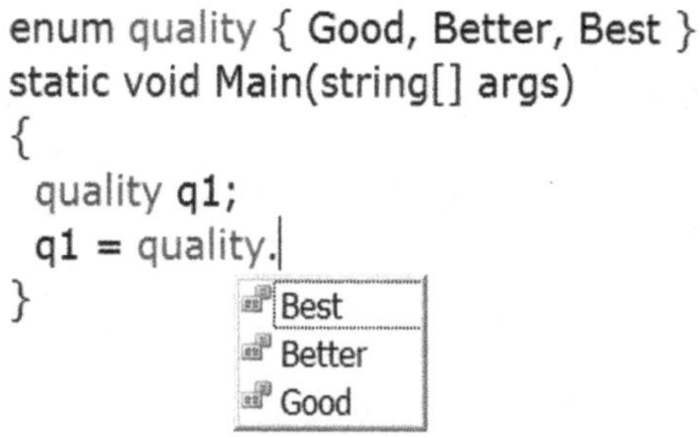

```
enum quality { Good, Better, Best }
static void Main(string[] args)
{
  quality q1;
  q1 = quality.|
}               Best
                Better
                Good
```

Figure B-8. *Using an enumeration*

Values in enumerations will have numbers as well as names. Having numbers associated to names is typical of many systems that store data. For example, when you try to find data from inside a database, you can ask for either a customer's ID number or his name, since there is a direct correlation between the two. Enums are not as sophisticated as a database, but they can hold integer values that match to a named value. In fact, if you do not tell .NET what number to associate with a name, .NET will set one for you, starting at zero. If you want to use a different set of numbers, you can declare a number for each item as long as it's some type of integer:

VB .NET

```
Enum quality
  Good
  Better
  Best
End Enum

Enum size
  Sm = 10
  Med = 15
  Lg = 20
End Enum

Sub Main(ByVal args As String())
  Dim q1 As quality
  q1 = quality.Good
  Console.WriteLine(q1.ToString)'Shows Good
  Console.WriteLine(Convert.ToInt32(q1)) 'Shows 0
  Dim s1 As size
  s1 = size.Med
  Console.WriteLine(s1.ToString) 'Shows Med
  Console.WriteLine(Convert.ToInt32(s1)) 'Shows 15
End Sub
```

C#

```
enum quality { Good, Better, Best }
enum size { Sm = 10, Med = 15, Lg = 20 }
static void Main(string[] args)
{
  quality q1;
  q1 = quality.Good;
  Console.WriteLine(q1.ToString()); //Shows Good
  Console.WriteLine(Convert.ToInt32(q1)); //Shows 0

  size s1;
  s1 = size.Med;
  Console.WriteLine(s1.ToString()); //Shows Med
  Console.WriteLine(Convert.ToInt32(s1)); //Shows 15
}
```

Structures

Enumerations can only hold a named set of integers, but you can work with more complex data by creating a *structure*. Structures can include most types of data. They can even include both data and methods; but let's focus on the data aspect for now.

To create a structure, you start by typing out all of the data members that you want to use. Remember that unlike an Enumeration, you can choose from any of the .NET data types, not just integers. For example, if you wanted to store information about an employee, you might create a structure with an employee's ID and name as data members. Then you would choose the appropriate data type for each member, such as Integer/int for the ID and String/string for the name:

VB .NET

```
Structure Employee
 Public EmpID As Integer
 Public Name As String
End Structure
```

C#

```
struct Employee
{
 public int EmpID;
 public string FirstName;
}
```

Whenever you used a variable made from the employee structure, you would have access to both pieces of data.

Using a structure allows your program to restrict what you can store in a variable to a predefined set of values. To understand why this is a good thing, consider what a company's records would look like if they handed new employees a blank sheet of paper and asked them to write out any personal information the company should know. Some people would write a little and some would write a lot, but it would not likely be very consistent. For this reason, companies give new employees a form to fill out. You can consider structures as being the same as one of those forms—in that when you design the structure, you are really designing the basic form of your data. Like the paper form, you do not put the actual data you want to store into the structure until later, after the structure is designed.

To use your structure, you would create a variable with its data type set to the name of your structure. Enough memory space will be set aside to store all the individual data from your data members and you will have the advantage of being able to refer to the entire set of data members by one name, such as Emp1 and Emp2.

In the following code example, we are using a variable called Emp1, which is made from the Employee type. Emp1 uses the Employee type as its template to create a new space in memory designed to hold the data outlined in the Employee structure. This space in memory is referred to as an *object*. The way to read the line Dim Emp1 As Employee or Employee Emp1; is "Create an object called Emp1 from the structure called Employee."

VB .NET

```
Shared Sub Main(ByVal args As String())
 'Storing Data
 Dim Emp1 As Employee 'Creates a space in memory based on the Employee struct
 Emp1.EmpID = 100
 Emp1.FirstName = "Bob Smith"

 'Reading Data
 Dim EmpData As String
 EmpData = Emp1.EmpID.ToString() + " , "
 EmpData = EmpData + Emp1.Name
 Console.WriteLine(EmpData) 'Shows 100 , Bob Smith
End Sub
```

C#

```
static void Main(string[] args)
{
  //Storing Data
  Employee Emp1; //Creates a space in memory based on the Employee struct
  Emp1.EmpID = 100;
  Emp1.FirstName = "Bob Smith";

  //Reading Data
  string EmpData;
  EmpData = Emp1.EmpID.ToString() + " , ";
  EmpData = EmpData + Emp1.Name;
  Console.WriteLine(EmpData); //Shows 100 , Bob Smith
}
```

Classes

Classes and structures are similar to each other. So much so that many beginners have a hard time deciding when to use one over the other. A full discussion is beyond the scope of this book, but here are some facts you should know:

1. In a structure, it is an error to directly set a initial value at the same time as declaring a variable. This is not the case with a class:

VB .NET

```
Class demo1
 Public z As Integer = 4 'This is ok in a Class!
End Class

Structure demo2
 Public z As Integer = 4 'This gives an error in a Structure!
End Structure
```

C#

```
class demo1
{
   public int z = 4; //This is ok in a Class!
}

struct demo2
{
   public int z = 4; //This gives an error in a Structure!
}
```

2. When you call the new variable from a class, it will be allocated on the .NET managed heap. However, a variable from a structure is created on that individual program's memory stack. Microsoft decided that classes would be reference types and structures would be value types. This allows a developer to fine tune how they would like to load the data into memory without having to use some arcane memory management code. Be aware that choosing one over the other will affect the ways the variables behave. For example, consider the following code:

Note This next example is shown with a class and structure inside of a VB .NET module and a C# class. This makes demo1 and demo2 nested types, since they are nested inside of Module1 and Program. Going forward, whenever you see a structure or class shown next to the Main() method, consider it one of these nested types. If ever you get confused about how to create the examples, just use this example as a guide.

VB .NET

```vbnet
Module Module1

Class demo1
  Public number As Integer
End Class

Structure demo2
  Public number As Integer
End Structure

  Sub Main()
    Dim x As demo1 = New demo1
    Dim y As demo1
    y = x   'Both y and x point to the same memory location
    x.number = 5
    Console.WriteLine(x.number) ' Shows 5
    Console.WriteLine(y.number) ' Shows 5


    Dim a As demo2 = New demo2
    Dim b As demo2
    b = a   'b and a point to different memory locations
    a.number = 5
    Console.WriteLine(a.number) ' Shows 5
    Console.WriteLine(b.number) ' Shows a default value of 0
  End Sub

End Module
```

C#

```csharp
namespace ConsoleApplication1
{
  class Program
  {

    class demo1
    {
      public int number;
    }

    struct demo2
    {
      public int number;
    }
```

```
static void Main()
{
  demo1 x = new demo1();
  demo1 y;
  y = x; // Both y and x now point to the same memory location
  x.number = 5;
  Console.WriteLine(x.number); // Shows 5
  Console.WriteLine(y.number); // Shows 5

  demo2 a = new demo2();
  demo2 b;
  b = a; // b and a still point to different memory locations
  a.number = 5;
  Console.WriteLine(a.number); // Shows 5
  Console.WriteLine(b.number); // Shows a default value of 0
}//end of Main

}//end of class Program

}//end of namespace ConsoleApplication1
```

As the comments indicate, when a variable made from a class is assigned to another variable made from the same class, that variable will reference the same memory location. Any changes to the data referenced in one will affect the other. With a structure, this is different. Each variable is a distinct copy of the data and each has its own memory location. A change to one location does not affect the other.

Understanding this is important because Microsoft's .NET code uses both classes and structures for their data types. Two examples are an integer, which was created as a structure, and a TextReader, which is made from a class. A TextReader, which is a class that allows you to read text out of a file, is much more complex than an integer—and that highlights a general pattern you will find in .NET. For the most part, structures are used whenever Microsoft needed a type that would be used mostly for data and simple tasks. If Microsoft had more complex data and tasks, then they unusually used a class instead. You also may find this a useful pattern to imitate when choosing which one to use in your programs.

■**Note** Although Microsoft chose to use a class for their *String* data type, it does not always act like a class should. In fact, they changed the way it works so that is acts more like a structure instead. This may sound odd, but it seems like a good choice on Microsoft's part, since it makes string variables behave as you would naturally expect them to. Still, when you find out later that they are a reference type behaving like a value type, it might cause you to doubt your understanding of the concepts. Don't worry, there are very few exceptions like this one.

Arrays

An *array* is a way of grouping one or more pieces of data. With arrays, you organize your data into list of values. You can refer to these values later by the variable's name along with a number to indicate the item in the list you want. The numbers, or *indexes* as they are called, are created for you by .NET and they always start at zero. So, the first item in the list, perhaps we should call it the "zeroth" item, can be accessed by using the number 0 and not 1:

VB .NET

```
Dim MyDemoArray() As String = {"One", "Two"}
Console.WriteLine(MyDemoArray(0)) 'Shows One
```

C#

```
string[]MyDemoArray = {"One", "Two"};
Console.WriteLine(MyDemoArray[0]); //Shows One
```

Many programmers use arrays to group together a set of structure or class objects and reference them collectively by one variable. For example, let's say that you had a list of employee data you wanted to refer to in your program. You could create an object for each individual employee's data, create a variable called MyEmployees as an array, then assign the individual employees to that one variable.

Here are some general facts you should know about arrays:

- An array contains a list of variables or constants. The data contained in an array is also called the elements of the array.

- Each element can be individually referred to by using its array name and a number.

- The number you use to tell the computer which item from the group you want is known as an *index* or *subscript* of the array.

- In both VB .NET and C#, arrays are always *zero-indexed*, meaning that the array index numbers start at zero. There is no option that lets you change this in .NET.

- Arrays in VB .NET are similar to the ones in C#; however, one important difference is that in VB .NET you use parentheses (()) after the variables name to indicate that you want that variable to be an array, while in C# you use square brackets ([]) instead. Also, C# places these after the data type, while VB .NET uses them after the variable name.

VB .NET

```
Structure Employee
 Public EmpID As Integer
 Public Name As String
End Structure

Sub Main(ByVal args As String())
 Dim Emp1 As Employee
 Emp1.EmpID = 100
 Emp1.Name = "Bob Smith"
```

```
Dim Emp2 As Employee
Emp2.EmpID = 100
Emp2.Name = "Sue Jones"

'Now make an Array by using () after the variable name
Dim MyEmployees() As Employee = {Emp1, Emp2}

'Refer to the Zeroth employee by using the () symbols again
Console.WriteLine(MyEmployees(0).Name) 'Shows Bob Smith
End Sub
```

C#

```
struct Employee
{
 public int EmpID;
 public string FirstName;
}

static void Main()
{
 Employee Emp1;
 Emp1.EmpID = 100;
 Emp1.Name = "Bob Smith";

 Employee Emp2;
 Emp2.EmpID = 100;
 Emp2.Name = "Sue Jones";

 //Now make an array by using the [] symbols after the data type
 Employee[] MyEmployees = {Emp1, Emp2};

 //Refer to the Zeroth employee by using the [] symbols again
 Console.WriteLine(MyEmployees[0].Name); //Shows Bob Smith
}
```

Arrays in .NET have a number of built-in properties and methods that you will find useful in your programs. One example is the ability to tell how many elements are in the array using the Length property. This will report an integer number zero or greater. If you have created an array but have not assigned any values to it yet, the number would be zero.

```
Console.WriteLine(MyEmployees.Length) 'Shows 2
```

Assign Values to an Array

One way to assign a set of values to the array, and the one we have used so far, is to use an *initializer list*. You create this by typing out a set the initial values for your array and enclosing those values in curly braces ({}). You place a set of values on the right-hand side of the assignment operator at the time you declare your array. However, you will get an error if you try to assign values this way after the array has been created.

The following are some examples showing different ways to initialize an array. Note that you can either assign a list of values or you can set the number of values allowed and then assign them later. The first example uses an initializer list, just as before:

VB .NET

```
'The short version
Dim numbers As Integer() = {1, 2, 3, 4, 5}
Dim names As String() = {"Bob", "Sue", "Tim"}
'The long version
Dim numbers As Integer() = New Integer(4) {1, 2, 3, 4, 5}
Dim names As String() = New String(2) {"Bob", "Sue", "Tim"}
```

C#

```
//The short version
int[] numbers = { 1, 2, 3, 4, 5 };
string[] names = { "Bob", "Sue", "Tim" };

//The long version
int[] numbers = new int[5] {1, 2, 3, 4, 5};
string[] names = new string[3] {"Bob", "Sue", "Tim"};
```

In both of these examples, we used an initializer list to add elements at the same time we created the variables; but in the long version of the VB .NET code, the number inside the parentheses is a 4, while in the C# version, it is a 5. This is because the 4 in the VB .NET version indicates the highest index number allowed: 0 to 4. The 5 in the C# version indicates the amount of values it will accept.

Another common way to add data to an array is by telling the computer how many elements there will be and then setting the values later. For example, let's say that you want to create an array of integers; you would tell the computer what type to use and how many integers to expect later. Note that this syntax replaces using the initializer list, so you would not see both being used on the one line:

VB .NET

```
Dim MyDemoArray() As String = {"One", "Two"} 'Ok
Dim MyDemoArray2(1) As String 'Still Ok, but has not set any values yet.
Dim MyDemoArray3(1) as String = {"One", "Two"} 'NOT Ok, will cause an error
```

C#

```
string[]MyDemoArray = {"One", "Two"}; // Ok
string[2]MyDemoArray; //Still Ok, but has not set any values yet.
string[2]MyDemoArray = {"One", "Two"}; //NOT Ok, will cause an error
```

Again, notice that the index value in this example is different in the VB .NET and C# versions of the code. Remember that in VB .NET, you need to tell the computer the highest index number to allow; if the program goes beyond that index number, then an error will be thrown. Since C# is different, you stipulate the number of elements you want to hold, not the highest index number.

In the next code example, we show how to set the individual values after the array has been created. Notice that we use the same index number for each language.

VB .NET

```
Dim numbers(2) As Integer 'numbers is a 3-element array (0,1,2)
numbers(0) = 5
numbers(1) = 10
numbers(2) = 15
numbers(3) = 20 'cause an error because it is outside the index range
```

C#

```
int[] numbers = new int[2];  // numbers is a 2-element array (0,1)
numbers[0] = 5;
numbers[1] = 10;
numbers[2] = 15; //cause an error because it is outside the index range
numbers[3] = 20; //cause an error because it is outside the index range
```

The VB .NET version of this code worked until it got to the index of 3, while the C# had an error after 1. Since the C# index number is set at [2], many people expect the index of 2 will work. This type of bug is so common that it has its own name—it's known as an "off by one" error.

Copying Array Data to Another Array

Microsoft programmed in several methods you can use to copy data form one array to another. One of them is the CopyTo() method. This method copies all the elements of the current array to another array starting at the specified destination array index:

VB .NET

```
Numbers.CopyTo(SomeNumbers,1) 'skip over (0) and start at (1)
```

C#

```
Numbers.CopyTo(SomeNumbers,1); //skip over [0] and start at [1]
```

Changing the Size of an Array

In C#, an array's length cannot change once it is made and still keep its data. In reality, VB .NET works the same way, but that language has a command called ReDim with a Preserve option that allows you to keep the existing values. Behind the scenes, VB .NET is really making a new array, copying the old array's data to the new one, then reusing the variable name to point to the new copy. Since there is no ReDim or Preserve command in C#, you have to do this yourself. It sounds like more work than it really is; you just create a new copy of the array using the CopyTo() method and then set the original variable to point to the new array's memory location.

VB .NET

```
Dim numbers As Integer() = {10, 20} 'Now the array has two elements
Console.WriteLine(numbers(0)) 'Shows 10

'Create a copy and preserve the data (will use the same name)
ReDim Preserve numbers(2) 'Now it has 3 elements (0)=10,(1)=20,(2)=0
Console.WriteLine(numbers(0)) 'Still Shows 10

'Change the size of the array
ReDim numbers(2) 'without using Preserve, the data is lost.

'This time it shows 0, since .NET resets integers to zero for you
Console.WriteLine(numbers(0))
```

C#

```
int[] numbers = {10, 20}; //Now the array has two elements
Console.WriteLine(numbers[0]); //Shows 10

//Create a copy and preserve the data (must use a different name)
int[] MyCopy = new int[3];
numbers.CopyTo(MyCopy, 0); //[0]=10,[1]=20,[2]=0
Console.WriteLine(MyCopy[0]); //Still Shows 10

//Now, point the numbers array to the same memory
//location as the MyCopy array to complete the resizing.
numbers = MyCopy;

//Changing the size of the array w/o using the CopyTo() method.
numbers = new int[3];  // now it has three elements, but its data is gone

//Shows 0, since .NET resets integer to zero for you
Console.WriteLine(numbers[0]);
```

Using a For-Each Loop with an Array

Both VB .NET and C# provide a simple, clean way to loop through all of the elements of an array called the For-Each/foreach loop. For example, the following code creates an array called numbers, accesses each element, and prints the contents to the screen. The statements inside of the loop will continue to run again and again until it runs out of elements to access.

VB .NET

```
Dim numbers As Integer() = {5, 10, 15}

For Each i As Integer In numbers //start of loop
 Console.WriteLine(i) 'i contains a copy the data
Next //end of loop
```

C#

```
int[] numbers = { 5, 10, 15};

foreach (int i in numbers) //start of loop
{
  Console.WriteLine(i); //i contains a copy of the data
}// end of loop
```

The Array.Copy() Method

Much like the CopyTo() method, this method copies a section of one array to another array. It has more options than the CopyTo() method. In this one, you can specify which element to start the copy from, where to place the copied elements, and how may elements you want to copy. It will even convert most types of data for you as needed.

The syntax it a bit tricky at first, but becomes easy once you know what the parameters do. Microsoft created four different version of this, but let's look at the meaning of this one version: Array.Copy(Array, Int32, Array, Int32, Int32).

- Parameter 1 is the array that contains the data you want to copy; let's call it the Source-Array.

- Parameter 2 is the index in the Source-Array where you want to begin copying data.

- Parameter 3 is the Destination-Array, the array that will receive the copied data.

- Parameter 4 is the index that you want to start at when pasting your data to the Destination-Array.

- Parameter 5 is the number of elements you want to copy over from the Source-Array.

So, you would read Array.Copy(Numbers, 1, SomeNumbers, 0, 2); as the following:

- Copy the data from Numbers to SomeNumbers.

- Start the copy at index 1.

- Place the copied data starting at the "zeroth" index of the SomeNumbers array.

- Only copy 2 of the elements.

VB .NET

```
Dim Numbers As Integer() = {5, 10, 15, 20}
Dim SixNumbers(5) As Integer '//integers set to zero

Array.Copy(Numbers, 1, SixNumbers, 0, 2)
For Each i As Integer In SixNumbers
  Console.WriteLine(i) 'Shows 10 15 0 0 0 0
Next
```

```vb
    Console.WriteLine("-- CopyTo() Demo --")
    Numbers.CopyTo(SixNumbers, 1) ' Skip over [0] and start at [1]
    For Each i As Integer In SixNumbers
      Console.WriteLine(i) ' Shows 10 5 10 15 20 0
      'Note: The first 10 comes from the earlier copy
    Next

    Console.WriteLine("-- Clone() Demo --")
    SixNumbers = CType(Numbers.Clone, Integer())
    For Each i As Integer In SixNumbers
      Console.WriteLine(i) 'Shows 5 10 15 20
    Next
```

C#

```csharp
  int[] Numbers = { 5, 10, 15, 20};
  int[] SixNumbers = new int[6]; //Integers set to zero

  Array.Copy(Numbers, 1, SixNumbers, 0, 2);
  foreach (int i in SixNumbers)
  {
    Console.WriteLine(i); //Shows 10 15 0 0 0 0
  }

Console.WriteLine("-- CopyTo() Demo --");
  Numbers.CopyTo(SixNumbers,1); //Skip over [0] and start at [1]
  foreach (int i in SixNumbers)
  {
    Console.WriteLine(i); //Shows 10 5 10 15 20 0
    //Note: The first 10 comes from the earlier copy
  }

Console.WriteLine("-- Clone() Demo --");
SixNumbers = (int[])Numbers.Clone();
foreach (int i in SixNumbers)
 {
    Console.WriteLine(i); //Shows 5 10 15 20
 }
```

The Array.Clone() Method

In the previous example, we used the Clone() method. This method also creates a copy of one array and places it into another array. Be a bit careful with this one since if you were previously holding data in the second array, it will be overwritten. In fact, even the number of elements will be redefined.

Note For more advanced programmers, you may like to know that `Array.Clone()` creates a "shallow copy" of the array. A *shallow copy* of an array copies the elements of value types or reference types differently. If you are using a reference type, it just copies the reference pointing to the object and does not make a true copy of the original objects. The reference in the new array will point to the same objects that the reference in the original array does. Since both the elements are pointing to the same memory location, changing the data in one array will affect the other array as well. This is not an issue when you are using a value type because it creates a true copy of the data.

Using Multidimensional Arrays

Arrays in both languages can be organized into subsets, called *dimensions* or sometimes *ranks*. Dimensions can be thought of as a way of grouping one or more sets into an outer set.

An array with only one list of values one is called a *single-dimensional* array, and an array that contains subsets of lists is called a *multidimensional* array. How you refer to a multidimensional array is determined by its layers of sets. Arrays can be two-dimensional, three-dimensional, four-dimensional, and so on, with the increase of each number being a new outer set. For example, if your array is a set that has subsets inside of it, you would call that a two-dimensional array (see Figure B-9).

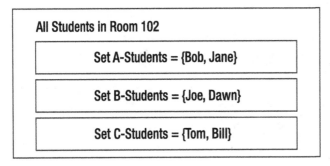

Figure B-9. *Using subsets to organize data*

If we were to create an array using the data in Figure B-9, we would have a two-dimensional array, since there are two layers of organization. The first layer is the list of students that received a particular grade. There are three of these sets and each is a one-dimensional array. The second layer of organization is all the students in Room 102. This would be represented as the second dimension (or rank) of the array. These dimensions are numbered starting at zero, so the inner set of arrays are dimension 0 while that outer set is dimension 1. In this example, each of the zeroth dimension arrays contains two elements (one for each name), while there are three elements in the first dimension array (one for each of the set of students).

One classic example of a two-dimensional array is a spreadsheet. A spreadsheet is a collection of columns and rows. Columns hold individual values while rows are a grouping of columns. Values in one column of a spreadsheet represent a list of individual values. Here is a list of values that represent a one-dimensional list of customer names:

```
Joe Smith
Jim Allen
```

This list could be easily stored in a one-dimensional array with this code:

VB .NET

```
Dim Customers() As String = {"Joe Smith", "Jim Allen"}
```

C#

```
string[] Customers = { "Joe Smith", "Jim Allen" };
```

Now consider adding more information about the customers, such as the country they live in:

```
Joe Smith, US
Jim Allen, US
```

This data would now need to be stored in a two-dimensional array, using the following code:

VB .NET

```
Dim Customers(,) As String = _
{ {"Joe Smith", "US"}, {"Jim Allen", "US"} }
```

C#

```
string[,] Customers =
{ {"Joe Smith", "US"}, {"Jim Allen", "US"} };
```

Note that each set of names and countries are like a row of data in a spreadsheet. This analogy might be easier to see if you write out the code like this:

C#

```
string[,] Customers =
{ //Start of outer set, a set of rows
{"Joe Smith", "US"}, //one row of data,  i.e., a set of columns
{"Jim Allen", "US"}, // second row of data
}; //end of the outer set
```

You access the data from this two-dimensional array by indicating which elements from each dimension you want. For example, to print the name of "Joe Smith" you need to access the zeroth element of dimension 0 and the zeroth element of dimension 1:

VB .NET

```
Console.WriteLine(Customers(0, 0)) 'Row zero Column zero is "Joe Smith"
Console.WriteLine(Customers(1, 0)) 'Row one Column zero is "Jim Allen"
```

C#

```
Console.WriteLine(Customers[0, 0]); //Row zero Column zero is "Joe Smith"
Console.WriteLine(Customers[1, 0]); //Row one Column zero is "Jim Allen"
```

Like the number of elements in an array, the number of an array's dimensions cannot change once it has been created. At least it cannot be changed and still keep its data. After an array is made, the dimensions and length of an array must stay the same for the entire lifetime of the array or you will lose the data you put into it.

Multidimensional arrays can include three, four, five, or more dimensions, but usually they will only have two. Perhaps this is because humans get confused when reading code using more than two dimensions. In fact, it is not uncommon for even two dimensions to be difficult for new programmers to grasp. If you find them confusing, rest assured that you are not alone, many people do.

Still, a table of values, as in our spreadsheet example, is an undoubtedly useful way to store data. When you find yourself needing to store data like this, you may want to know about a somewhat easier way to do this. This easier way is done by using a single-dimensional array that holds a set of structures. Here is an alternative example using a structure and the same data we just used. Although both will do the job, many people find this one easier to read:

VB .NET

```
Structure Customers
   Public Name As String
   Public Country As String
End Structure

Sub Main()
 Dim c1 As Customer
 c1.Name = "Joe Smith"
 c1.Country = "US"

 Dim c2 As Customer
 c2.Name = "Jim Allen"
 c2.Country = "US"

 Dim USCustomers As Customer() = {c1, c2} 'Contains a list of Customers objects
End Sub
```

C#

```
struct Customer
{
 public string Name;
 public string Country;
}

static void Main()
{
   Customer c1;
   c1.Name = "Joe Smith";
   c1.Country = "US";
```

```
  Customer c2;
  c2.Name = "Jim Allen";
  c2.Country = "US";

  Customer[] USCustomers = { c1, c2 };//Contains a list of Customers objects
}
```

Now that you have seen both single and multidimensional arrays, you may want to know that VB .NET and C# actually support three types of arrays: single-dimensional arrays, multidimensional arrays (rectangular arrays), and array-of-arrays (jagged arrays). Although jagged arrays are an advance concept, we have included it here for completeness. The following examples compare how to declare the three different kinds of arrays:

VB .NET, To Declare Single-Dimensional Arrays

```
Dim numbers As Integer()
```

C#, To Declare Single-Dimensional Arrays

```
int[] numbers;
```

VB .NET, To Declare Multidimensional Arrays

```
Dim Customers As String(,)
```

C#, To Declare Multidimensional Arrays

```
string[,] Customers;
```

VB .NET, To Declare Array-of-Arrays (Jagged Arrays)

```
Dim Departments()() As String
```

C#, To Declare Array-of-Arrays (Jagged Arrays)

```
string[][] Departments;
```

To understand the Array-of-Arrays example, consider this list of employees and their departments:

```
Programmers: Hal Olson and Dan Duncan
Testers: Joe Hunter
```

Notice that this is really two lists: one for the departments and one for the employees in the departments. This could be represented by creating two interrelated arrays: one for the programmer employees and one for the tester employees. In code, it would look like this:

VB .NET

```
Dim Deptarments As String()() = _
    New String()() {New String() {"Programmers", "Hal Olson", "Dan Duncan"}, _
                    New String() {"Testers", "Joe Hunter"}}
```

C#

```
string[][] Deptarments =
 new string[][]{new string[]{"Programmers", "Hal Olson", "Dan Duncan"},
           new string[]{"Testers", "Joe Hunter"} };
```

This code works almost like the two-dimensional array, but there is a subtle difference. If you look closely, you will see that the number of elements in the two-dimensional arrays will always be the same for each set. However, in the Array-of-Arrays, the number of elements can be different for each array, giving it a "jagged" appearance. Here are both examples side-by-side so you can compare them:

VB .NET

```
'Two-dimensional array
Dim Customers(,) As String = _
{{"Joe Smith", "US"}, {"Jim Allen", "US"}, {"Tim Thompson", "CA"}}
Console.WriteLine(Customers(1, 0)) 'Shows Jim Allen


'Jagged Array
Dim Deptarments As String()() = _
New String()() {New String() {"Programmers", "Hal Olson", "Dan Duncan"}, _
           New String() {"Testers", "Joe Hunter"}}
Console.WriteLine(Deptarments(1)(0)) 'Shows Testers
```

C#

```
string[,] Customers =
{
{"Joe Smith", "US"},
{"Jim Allen", "US"},
{"Tim Thompson", "CA"}
};
Console.WriteLine(Customers[1,0]);//shows Jim Allen

string[][] Deptarments =
 new string[][]{new string[]{"Programmers", "Hal Olson", "Dan Duncan"},
           new string[]{"Testers", "Joe Hunter"} };
Console.WriteLine(Deptarments[1][0]);//Shows Testers
```

Again, when you consider how confusing multidimensional are, jagged arrays can be even more so. Our recommendation is to use only single-dimensional arrays along with structures whenever possible. Besides, many of the built-in array methods will only work with single-dimensional arrays: such Array.Copy(), Array.Clone(), and Array.CopyTo(). For that matter, even the For-Each loop is only set up to process single-dimensional arrays. Microsoft apparently followed the same advice when they created .NET, because they use the single-dimensional array and structure pattern in many places.

Collections

Collections include a number of classes that act like one-dimensional arrays, but have built-in methods that make it easy to add, remove, and organize the elements in the collection. Although there are many different ones, and they each have their own unique aspects, they are all considered collections.

One common example of a collection is the ArrayList class. Like an array, this stores its elements, referred to as *items* now instead of *elements*, using a zero-based subscript. For instance, let's say you have an ArrayList consisting of three names, "Bob", "Sue", and "Tim". You would refer to the "Sue" item using a subscript of 1:

VB .NET

```
Dim MyArrayList as ArrayList  = New Arraylist
MyArrayList.add("Bob")
MyArrayList.add("Sue")
MyArrayList.add("Tim")
```

C#

```
ArrayList MyArrayList = new Arraylist();
MyArrayList.add("Bob");
MyArrayList.add("Sue");
MyArrayList.add("Tim");
```

What really sets a collection apart from an array is the ease of use. For example, note that you did not have to tell the ArrayList what size you wanted. ArrayList just expanded as needed. You also don't have to tell the ArrayList what data type you are holding. Once again, it will automatically adjust to your program's needs. There are some more subtle distinctions between arrays and ArrayList as well—such as using, the Count property to find out how many items there are in the collection instead of the Length property, as you do with an array.

VB .NET

```
Console.WriteLine(MyArrayList.Count)
```

C#

```
Console.WriteLine(MyArrayList.Count);
```

One popular feature of the ArrayList class is the Sort() method. With this, you can sort the elements of the ArrayList, in ascending order, just by calling Sort(). You can also reverse the sort with the Reverse() method if you want. Notice in the following code that you still access the items in the ArrayList using a subscript just as you do with arrays:

VB .NET

```
Dim MyArrayList As System.Collections.ArrayList = New System.Collections.ArrayList

MyArrayList.Add("Sue")
MyArrayList.Add("Bob")
MyArrayList.Add("Tim")
Console.WriteLine(MyArrayList(0)) ' Shows Sue

MyArrayList.Sort() 'a-z
Console.WriteLine(MyArrayList(0)) ' Show Bob

MyArrayList.Reverse() 'z-a
Console.WriteLine(MyArrayList(0)) ' Shows Tim
```

C#

```
System.Collections.ArrayList MyArrayList = new System.Collections.ArrayList();

MyArrayList.Add("Sue");
MyArrayList.Add("Bob");
MyArrayList.Add("Tim");
Console.WriteLine(MyArrayList[0]); //Shows Sue

MyArrayList.Sort(); //a-z
Console.WriteLine(MyArrayList[0]); //Shows Bob

MyArrayList.Reverse();//z-a
Console.WriteLine(MyArrayList[0]); //Shows Tim
```

More on Objects

We have mentioned objects a number of times so far, and even give a couple of brief descriptions of what they are. Since many of our examples in the book will use objects, this section will outline some of the basic concepts you need to know about them.

Objects are created by using an enumeration, class, or structure as a template. All three of these are considered types, and an object can be thought of as a copy of code from a particular type. For example, when you create a string variable you are really creating an object based on Microsoft's string data type. A more technical way to put this is that your string variable points to an object instance of the string type.

When a program starts, it reads the program files, usually .exe or .dll files, and loads into memory any of the types found inside. When objects are created from the loaded types, both the object instances and the types will be held in memory while the program is running. Each will be in a separate memory space; any changes to the data in the object will not affect the type. When the program shuts down, the types are still defined in the code inside your files, but the objects are removed from memory.

■**Note** It is important to remember that although the code in your classes exists within an .exe or .dll file, the objects made from these classes exist only while your program is running. Once the program stops, the data that was in the object instance will be lost. You can save this data by sending it to a text file or storing it in a database. We will show you several ways to save your object's data within this book.

Once an object instance is made, you can use them much like you would use a copy or a paper form. To understand this analogy, consider having three order forms used to order office supplies. In real life, each of the order forms would look the same and you would assume that someone photocopied them from an original. You would also consider each of the three forms as being a unique instance of the original template. When you filled out all three forms, you would consider the line items in each of the forms as belonging to the form it was a part of. Any changes to one form would not affect the other. (See Figure B-10.)

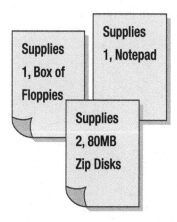

Figure B-10. *Objects are like individual copies of a template.*

Since an object can be thought of as an individual copy of a type, any changes to the data in one object will not affect the other. Working with a copy and not the actual template makes sense with computer programs for the same reason it does with paper forms; you can create a template that defines what a form looks like, and have a consistent representation of data.

Imagine the chaos if you allowed employees to turn in any scrap of paper instead of the various forms your company uses. Although humans are adaptable and would likely be able to process even unorganized scrapes of paper, computer must be told exactly what to do. So, it seems only natural that when Microsoft's programmers sat down to create .NET, they chose to organize their code into types and allowed the creation of object instances from these types as needed.

The syntax for creating any object is quite easy. You need to provide a name, a type, and use the new keyword to start setting some initial values in your new object (see Figure B-11). Using the new keyword to create an object is only required when the type is a class. With enumerations and structures the new is implied, but the process that new initiates is still performed behind the scenes.

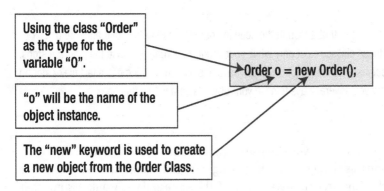

Figure B-11. *Making an object*

In many chapters of this book, you will be creating your own custom types using enumeration, classes, or structures, so you will get lots of practice. Still, let's take a quick look at an example using the order form analogy. This example creates a new class called Order which has an ArrayList inside of it. It also show the creation of a new instance of the Order class:

VB .NET

```
Imports System
Imports System.Collections

Class Order 'This is the Order Type
  Public LineItems As ArrayList = New ArrayList
End Class

Class Program
  Shared Sub Main()
    Dim o As Order = New Order 'This makes an Order object
    o.LineItems.Add("1, Box of Floppies")
    o.LineItems.Add("2, 80MB Zip Disks")
    o.LineItems.Add("1, Notepad")

    Console.WriteLine(o.LineItems(2)) 'Shows 1, Notepad
  End Sub
End Class
```

C#

```
using System;
using System.Collections;

class Order //This is the Order Type
{
```

```
  public ArrayList LineItems = new ArrayList();
}

class Program
{
  static void Main()
  {
    Order o = new Order(); //This makes an Order object
    o.LineItems.Add("1, Box of Floppies");
    o.LineItems.Add("2, 80MB Zip Disks");
    o.LineItems.Add("1, Notepad");

    Console.WriteLine(o.LineItems[2]); //Shows 1, Notepad
  }
}
```

Working with String

The String/string class is one that you will work with all of the time. This class is designed to hold an array of character data. Since character data is so common in a program, Microsoft has included a number of features in the String/string class that you should know about.

String Can Act Like an Array

You can read an individual character from a string using the same syntax we used on arrays:

VB .NET

```
Dim name As String = "bob"
Dim letter As Char = name.Chars(0)
Console.WriteLine(letter) ' Shows b
```

C#

```
string name = "bob";
char  letter = (char)name[0];
Console.WriteLine(letter); // Shows b
```

Strings Cannot Be Changed Once Their Data Is Set

Although you can read an individual character from a string, you cannot change it the same way:

VB .NET

```
Dim name As String = "bob"
name(0) = "B" 'This will cause an error
```

C#

```
string name = "bob";
name[0] = "B"; //This will cause an error
```

You can change the value of the whole string, or at least .NET makes it seem that you can. Setting a new value to the whole string really just creates a new string object in memory and then resets the variable to point to the new object; much like the process we saw with arrays. This process of copying can slow programs down, but since most of the programs that testers write are small, it may not be an issue for you.

VB .NET

```
Dim name As String = "bob" ' Makes a new String object and has name point to it
Console.WriteLine(name(0)) ' Shows b
name = "Bob" ' Makes a different String object and has name point to the new one
Console.WriteLine(name(0)) ' Shows B
```

C#

```
string name = "bob"; //Makes a new string object and has name point to it
Console.WriteLine(name[0]); // Shows b
name = "Bob";//Makes a different string object and has name point to the new one
Console.WriteLine(name[0]); // Shows B
```

Adding Two Strings Together

You can add two strings together, technically called *concatenation*, by using the + symbol. Since the + symbol is also used to add two numbers together, the VB .NET language includes a special symbol just for strings. This symbol, the &, is used when you want VB .NET to be certain that your intent is to concatenate two numbers together and not add them:

VB .NET

```
Console.WriteLine("Test" & "String") 'Shows TestString
Console.WriteLine("Test" + "String") 'Shows TestString
Console.WriteLine(4 & 5) 'Shows 45
Console.WriteLine(4 + 5) 'Shows 9
```

C#

```
Console.WriteLine("Test" + "String"); //Shows TestString
Console.WriteLine("4" + "5"); //Shows 45
Console.WriteLine(4 + 5); //Shows 9
```

Strings Can Use Special Characters (Escape Sequences)

Escape sequences are special characters that allow you to store characters in your string that would normally be interpreted by your program as a command. They can also provide additional formatting instructions:

VB .NET

```
'Add a Tab
Console.WriteLine("Test" & vbTab & "String") 'Shows Test      String
'Add a \
Console.WriteLine("Test\String") 'Shows Test\String
'Add a Single Quote using two ' and not a single "
Console.WriteLine("''Test String''") 'Shows 'Test String'
'Add a Double Quote using two "
Console.WriteLine("""Test String""") ' Shows "Test String"
'Add a Carriage Return
Console.WriteLine("Test" & vbCrLf & "String") 'Shows Test and String on two lines
```

C#

```
//Add a Tab
Console.WriteLine("Test\tString"); //Shows Test       String
//Add a \
Console.WriteLine("Test\\String"); //Shows Test\String
//Add a Single Quote without an escape
Console.WriteLine("'Test String'"); //Shows 'Test String'
//Add a Single Quote
Console.WriteLine("\'Test String\'"); //AlsoShows 'Test String'
//Add a Double Quote
Console.WriteLine("\"Test String\""); //Shows "Test String"
//Add a Carriage Return (Does not work well with the WriteLine() method)
Console.WriteLine("Test \r String"); //Shows only      String
//Add a New Line (Does work well with the WriteLine() method)
Console.WriteLine("Test \n String"); //Shows Test and String on two lines
```

C# Can Use String Literals by Adding the @ Symbol

If you have a string with a lot of characters that need escaping, or you want C# to print out a string exactly as you typed it, you can use the @ symbol to have the string be considered a literal value. However, this option is only available in C#:

C#

```
//The @ symbol indicates a string literal, no escape sequence is requried for the \
string message = @"Would you like to open File c:\MyFile.exe";

// works as before but this time a escape sequence is required for the \
string message = "Would you like to open File c:\\MyFile.exe";
```

■**Note** One last thing . . . We want to remind you again that although strings are a reference type, they often act like value types. We will point this out in some of the examples in the next section.

Programming Statements

In addition to data, your programs will also have operations to perform. These operations take the form of one or more statements. A *statement* is a command for the computer to do something. These statements are usually grouped together into methods. As the code inside of a method begins to run, all the statements execute in the same order that they were typed.

Both C# and VB .NET have a number of predefined statements for performing common operations. Except where noted, these examples must be grouped inside of a method, like the Main() method, in order to be considered legal syntax.

Conditional Statements

Conditional statements allow you to run zero or more statements based on a condition. Perhaps the most common of these is the if statement. It appears in almost every computer language you will come across. The general syntax of an if statement looks like this:

```
if (condition1 == true)
  {
  // statements executed only if condition1 is true.
  if (condition2 == true) // this is a nested if statement.
    {
    //statements executed only if condition2 is true as well as condition1 one.
    }
  }
else
  {
  statements; // executed only if condition1 is NOT true.
  }
```

Simple If Statement

VB .NET

```
Dim x As Integer = 5
If x = 5 Then
 Console.WriteLine("it is true")
End If
```

C#

```
int x = 5;
if (x == 5)
{
Console.WriteLine("it is true");
}
```

If with Else Statement

VB .NET

```
Dim x As Integer = 5
If x = 5 Then
 Console.WriteLine("it is true")
Else
 Console.WriteLine("it is false")
End If
```

C#

```
int x = 5;
if (x==5)
{
Console.WriteLine("it is true");
}
else
{
Console.WriteLine("it is false");
}
```

If with Else-If and Else Statement

VB .NET

```
Dim x As Integer = 5
If x = 5 Then
 Console.WriteLine("it is five")
ElseIf x = 10 Then
   Console.WriteLine("it is 10")
 Else
   Console.WriteLine("it is neither")
 End If
End If
```

C#

```
int x = 5;
if (x==5)
{
Console.WriteLine("it is five");
}
else if (x == 10)
{
Console.WriteLine("it is 10");
}
```

```
else
{
Console.WriteLine("it is neither");
}
```

Select-Case Statement (VB .NET Only)

A Select-Case statement is much like an If with Else statement, it is just easier to organize when you have a lot of choices. The general pattern for this statement looks like this:

```
Select Case  ExpressionToEvaluate
     Case ExpressionThatMatches
          statements
     Case Else
          statements to run if no match was found
End Select
```

■**Note** The ExpressionToEvaluate part of this statement must resolve into one of the standard data types: Boolean, Byte, Char, Date, Double, Decimal, Integer, Long, Object, SByte, Short, Single, String, UInteger, ULong, and UShort.

Simple Select-Case Statement

VB .NET

```
'Using numbers
Select Case 5 + 5
  Case 10
    Console.WriteLine("It was 10")
  Case 20
    Console.WriteLine("It was 20")
End Select

'Using strings
Select Case "Yes"
  Case "Yes"
    Console.WriteLine("It was Yes")
  Case "No"
    Console.WriteLine("It was No")
End Select
```

Select-Case with Else Statement

VB .NET

```
Select Case 5 + 7
   Case 10
     Console.WriteLine("It was 10")
   Case 20
     Console.WriteLine("It was 20")
   Case Else
     Console.WriteLine("It was somthing else")
   End Select
```

Using a Ranged Expression

Another nice feature about the Select-Case statement is that you can use a ranged expression. In the following example, notice that you can define a range of values by either making a comma-separated list or indicating a range using the word To. Also, notice that when there are two matches, only the first one will ever be evaluated. Once a match is found for the original expression, the program jumps down to the End Select clause and exits the statement:

VB .NET

```
'Using numbers
Dim number As Integer = 8
Select Case number
  Case 1 To 5
    Console.WriteLine("Between 1 and 5, inclusive")
  Case 6, 7, 8
    Console.WriteLine("Between 6 and 8, inclusive")
  Case 8 'This line will never be evaluated
    Console.WriteLine("Between 6 and 8, inclusive")
  Case Else
    Console.WriteLine("Not between 1 and 8, inclusive")
End Select

'Using a date
Dim d1 As Date = #1/1/2006# 'Dates use the # sign much like strings use "
Select Case d1
  Case #1/1/2006#
    Console.WriteLine("It's a new year!")
  Case #1/2/2006# To #12/31/2006#
    Console.WriteLine("Same old Same old")
End Select
```

Switch-Case Statement (C# Only)

In C#, you use the switch-case statement to do much the same thing as VB .NET's Select-Case statement. The switch-case statement works on a number or a string, using one over the other determines switch-case's governing data type. Once the governing type is set, the same data type must be used throughout that particular switch-case statement.

Note The expression must resolve into one of the standard data types: a Boolean, some type of number (Byte, Date, Double, Decimal, Integer, Long, SByte, Short, Single, UInteger, ULong, and UShort), or some type of character data (char or string). The C# switch-case is not as flexible as the VB .NET Select-Case when it comes to dates, so you might just want to use an If-Else instead.

To understand the way a switch statement is executed, we have outlined the process as follows:

1. The switch expression is evaluated and converted to the governing type.

2. If one of the constants specified in a case label in the same switch statement is equal to the value of the switch expression, control is transferred to the statements following the matched case label. If there is more than one matching case statement, the last one wins.

3. If none of the constants specified in case labels in the same switch statement is equal to the value of the switch expression, and if a default label is present, then control is transferred to the statements following the default label.

4. If none of the constants specified in case labels statements is equal to the value of the switch expression, and if *no* default label is present, then control is transferred to the end point of the switch statement.

5. If the end point of the statement list of a switch section is reachable, a compile-time error occurs. This is known as the *"no fall-through"* rule.

C#

```
//Using numbers
int x = 10;
switch (x)
{
  case 10:
    Console.WriteLine("It was 10");
    break;
  case 20:
    Console.WriteLine("It was 20");
    break;
}
```

```
//Using strings
string y = "Yes";
switch (y)
{
  case "Yes":
    Console.WriteLine("It was Yes");
    break;
  case "No":
    Console.WriteLine("It was No");
    break;
}
```

The previous examples are valid because the break statement exits the switch statement whenever a match of found. However, consider the next example without the break statements:

C#

```
//Using strings
switch ("Yes")
{
  case "Yes":
    Console.WriteLine("It was Yes");
  case "No":
    Console.WriteLine("It was No");
} //Control should NEVER get here.
```

This example results in a compile-time error. Execution of a switch section is not permitted to "fall through." This is unlike C and C++, where this behavior is allowed. The *no fall-through* rule prevents bugs that commonly occur in C and C++ when the break statements are omitted. VB .NET handles this by automatically breaking out of the Select-Case statement after each match, but this is not automatic in C#.

This may seem odd at first, but it does allow you to list multiple values to match. This is needed because C# does not include the ranged expressions you saw in the VB .NET examples:

C#

```
switch (20 + 1)
{
  case 10:
    Console.WriteLine("It was 10");
    break;
  case 20:
  case 21:
    Console.WriteLine("It was either 20 or 21");
    break;
  default:
    Console.WriteLine("It was some other number");
    break;
} //Control should NEVER get here.
```

In this example, if a match is found for 20, it will "fall through" to the next case clause. This is legal as long as it runs into a break statement before it reaches the end brace of the switch statement. When it falls to case 21:, it is still considered a match because case 20: was empty. You can use this to specify a range of values much like Select-Case in VB .NET. If none of the cases match, you can use a default to process a default command.

Iteration and Jump Statements

Of course, like other languages, both VB .NET and C# support loops and jumps. Loops allow you to repeat one or more statements based on a condition. Jumps allow you to force your program to jump over one or more lines of code to another line.

The For-Each Loop

You looked at the For-Each/foreach loop already in the "Arrays" section. This loop was designed specifically to work with arrays and collections.

VB .NET

```
Dim numbers As Integer() = {5, 10, 15}

For Each i As Integer In numbers
 Console.WriteLine(i)
Next
```

C#

```
int[] numbers = {5, 10, 15};

foreach (int i in numbers)
{
  Console.WriteLine(i);
}
```

Some advanced topics you should know about loops are the following:

- Although other loops allow you to change data while the loop is running, in C#, the foreach loop is read only. In other words, you cannot change the values of your variable from within the loop. VB .NET does not have this restriction.

- With loops that allow you to change the data, reference types and value types react differently when you make changes within a loop.

VB .NET

```
Class Customers
   Public Name As String
End Class
```

```vb
Sub Main(ByVal args As String())
  'Integers are value types, so you get a copy of the value
  Dim numbers As Integer() = {5, 10, 15}
  For Each i As Integer In numbers
    Console.WriteLine(i)
    i = 20 ' i is only a copy of the original integer's data
  Next
  Console.WriteLine(numbers(0)) 'Still shows 5

  'Even though Strings are Reference types, you still get a copy of the value
  Dim Names As String() = {"Bob", "Sue", "Tim"}
  For Each s As String In Names
    Console.WriteLine(s)
    s = "Joe" 's is only a copy of the original string's data
  Next
  Console.WriteLine(Names(0)) 'Still shows Bob

  'Normal Reference Types, like the Customers Class we made earlier,
  ' act as a true reference.
  Dim c1 As New Customers
  c1.Name = "Bob"
  Dim c2 As New Customers
  c2.Name = "Sue"
  Dim arrCust() As Customers = {c1, c2}

  For Each c As Customers In arrCust
    Console.WriteLine(c.Name)
    c.Name = "Joe" 'c points to the same memory as each array element
  Next
  Console.WriteLine(c1.Name) 'Now shows Joe
  Console.WriteLine(c2.Name) 'Now shows Joe
End Sub
```

C# (foreach is Read Only)

```csharp
int[] numbers = {5, 10, 15};
foreach (int i in numbers) {
 Console.WriteLine(i);
 i = 20; // This is NOT allowed!
}
Console.WriteLine(numbers(0));
```

The For Loop (C# Only)

While you cannot modify data within a C# foreach loop, you are able to if you use the standard for loop in C#. To understand this loop, let's examine the code that comes after the for keyword (see Figure B-12).

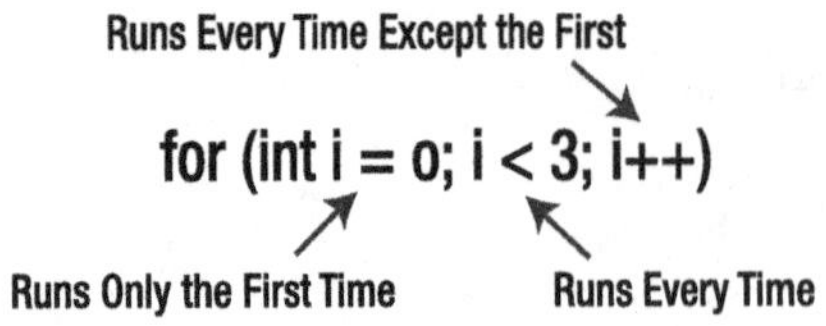

Runs Every Time Except the First

for (int i = 0; i < 3; i++)

Runs Only the First Time   Runs Every Time

Figure B-12. *The for loop*

- The first section sets the initial value of the counter variable. It only runs the first time through the loop; so the counter, in this example i, is only set to 0 once.

- The second section checks if the counter variable is more than the limit value. The limit value is what you use to tell the computer how many times you will to run the loop. In this example, once the value of i is more than the value of 3, the loop will stop.

- The third section takes the current value and adds 1 to it. The ++ symbol in C# can be used to add 1 to a variable holding a number. Although this symbol is used here in a for loop, you can use it other places as well. The ++ symbol only works in C#, not in VB .NET.

C#

```
int[] numbers = {5, 10, 15}; //Elements [0], [1], and [2]
for (int i = 0; i < 3; i++)
{
  Console.WriteLine(numbers[i]); //shows 5 then 10 then 15
  numbers[i] = 22; // You can change values in a for loop.
}
Console.Write(numbers[0]); //now shows 22
```

The For-Next Loop (VB .NET Only)

VB .NET does not have an exact match for the C# For loop, but its For-Next loop comes close. The way this loop works is as follows:

1. After the For keyword, you place a counter variable.

2. The counter variable will automatically be set to the starting value you put before the To keyword. The number after the To keyword indicates the stopping number, which controls the number of times you want the statements to run.

3. After the statements inside the loop run, the Next keyword will automatically add 1 to the counter. You can control how the counter increments by adding the Step keyword to the loop's definition.

VB .NET

```
Dim numbers As Integer() = {5, 10, 15} ' Elements (0),(1), and (2)
Dim i As Integer
For i = 0 To 2
Console.WriteLine(numbers(i)) 'Shows 5 then 10 then 15
Next i
```

```
Dim numbers As Integer() = {5, 10, 15} ' Elements (0),(1), and (2)
Dim i As Integer
For i = 0 To 2 Step 2
Console.WriteLine(numbers(i)) 'Shows 5 then 15
Next i
```

The While Loop

This loop runs a set of statements while a specified expression evaluates as true. In this example, as soon as i is no longer less then 3, the loop will stop:

VB .NET

```
Dim numbers As Integer() = {5, 10, 15}
Dim i As Integer = 0
While i < 3
  Console.WriteLine(numbers(i)) 'Shows 5 then 10 then 15
  i = i + 1
End While
```

C#

```
int[] numbers = {5, 10, 15};
int i = 0;
while (i < 3)
{
  Console.WriteLine(numbers[i]); //Shows 5 then 10 then 15
  i++;
}
```

The Do-While Loop

Like the While loop, this loop also executes one or more statements repeatedly until a specified expression evaluates to true. Once it is no longer true that i is less than 3, then the loop will end. The difference between the Do-While loop and the standard While loop is that your statements will always run at least once, even if the expression is false the first time through.

VB .NET

```
Dim numbers As Integer() = {5, 10, 15}
Dim i As Integer = 0
Do
  Console.WriteLine(numbers(i)) 'Shows 5 then 10 then 15
  i = i + 1
Loop While i < 3
```

C#

```csharp
int[] numbers = {5, 10, 15};
int i = 0;
do
{
  Console.WriteLine(numbers[i]); //Shows 5 then 10 then 15
  i++;
} while (i < 3);
```

In VB .NET, you can also put the While right after the Do keyword, but this makes the Do-While loop react like the standard While loop:

VB .NET (Only)

```vbnet
Dim numbers As Integer() = {5, 10, 15}
Dim i As Integer = 0
Do While (i < 3)
  Console.WriteLine(numbers(i)) 'Shows 5 then 10 then 15
  i = i + 1
Loop
```

The Do-Until Loop (VB .NET Only)

This loop is like the Do-While loop yet again. It also executes one or more statements repeatedly, but this time it only does so until the specified expression evaluates to true. Once it is no longer false that i is greater than 2, then the loop will end. As with the While keyword, the Until keyword can be placed at the beginning or at the end of the loop. If placed at the end, the statements will always run at least once.

VB .NET

```vbnet
Dim numbers As Integer() = {5, 10, 15}
Dim i As Integer = 0
Do Until (i < 2) 'Use 2 this time or you will be out of the index range
  Console.WriteLine(numbers(i)) 'Shows 5 then 10 then 15
  i = i + 1
Loop

Dim numbers As Integer() = {5, 10, 15}
Dim i As Integer = 0
Do
  Console.WriteLine(numbers(i)) 'Shows 5 then 10 then 15
  i = i + 1
Loop Until (i > 2) 'Use two this time or you will be out of the index range
```

The GoTo Jump Statement

The GoTo statement allows you to repeat statements like a loop, or to skip over one or more statements and move to a later part of the program. While it was used extensively in the 1980s, it is now considered a poor choice for looping.

The way this statement works it to jump from a GoTo statement with that label's name to the matching "label" in your program. The label can appear either before or after the GoTo statement. If it appears before, GoTo acts much like a loop. If it appears after, GoTo acts much like a call to a method. It is recommended that you use either a standard loop or a method instead of GoTo, but we are showing it here for completeness.

VB .NET

```vbnet
Dim numbers As Integer() = {5, 10, 15} ' Elements (0),(1), and (2)
Dim i As Integer
MyGotoLable1: 'Note that you need a colon here
Console.WriteLine(numbers(i)) 'Shows 5 then 15
  i = i + 1
  If (i < 3) Then
   GoTo MyGotoLable1
  End If
```

C#

```csharp
int[] numbers = {5, 10, 15}; // Elements [0],[1], and [2]
int i = 0;
MyGotoLabel1: //Note that you need a colon here
Console.WriteLine(numbers[i]); //Shows 5 then 10 then 15
i++;

if (i < 3)
{
  goto MyGotoLabel1;
}
```

The Continue Jump Statement

You can use this statement if you want to restart a loop without executing the remaining statements in that loop:

VB .NET

```vbnet
Dim numbers As Integer() = {5, 10, 15}
Dim i As Integer = 0
While i < 3
  If numbers(i) = 10 Then
    i = i + 1
    Continue While 'Go back to the beginning of the while loop
  End If
```

```
      Console.WriteLine(numbers(i)) 'Shows 5 then 15
      i = i + 1
End While
```

C#

```
int[] numbers = { 5, 10, 15 };
int i = 0;
while (i < 3)
{
  if (numbers[i] == 10)
  {
    i++;
    continue; //Go back the the beginning of the while loop
  }
  Console.WriteLine(numbers[i]); //Shows 5 then 15
  i++;
}
```

The Break or Exit Jump Statements

You can use these statements if you want to end the loop before it would normally finish. In VB .NET, you use the word Exit, while in C#, you use the word break, but they both do the same thing:

VB .NET

```
Dim numbers As Integer() = {5, 10, 15}
Dim i As Integer = 0
While i < 3
   If numbers(i) = 10 Then
     i = i + 1
     Exit While    'Go back to the end of the While loop
   End If

   Console.WriteLine(numbers(i)) 'Shows 5 then 15
   i = i + 1
End While
```

C#

```
int[] numbers = { 5, 10, 15 };
int i = 0;
while (i < 3)
{
  if (numbers[i] == 10)
  {
    i++;
    break; //Go back the the end of the while loop
  }
```

```
  Console.WriteLine(numbers[i]); //Shows 5
  i++;
}
```

The Return Jump Statement

You can use this statement if you want to exit a loop, but you should be aware that it will also exit out of the entire method and not just the loop. In fact, exiting out of a method is its most common use. As it leaves the method, you can also return a value back to the line of code that originally called the method. Here is an example:

VB .NET

```
Sub Main()
  Dim StatusCode As Integer
  StatusCode = MyTestMethod() 'Jump to MyTestMethod
  Console.WriteLine(StatusCode) 'Shows -1
End Sub

Function MyTestMethod() As Integer
  ' ... Process some lines of code
  Return -1  'Return a value and Jump back to the method call in Main()
End Function
```

C#

```
static void Main()
{
  int StatusCode;
  StatusCode = MyTestMethod(); //Jump to MyTestMethod
  Console.WriteLine(StatusCode); //Shows -1
} //end of Main method

static int MyTestMethod()
{
 // ... process some lines of code
  return -1 ; //Return a value and Jump back to the method call in Main()
}//End of MyTestMethod
```

The Scope of Variables Inside Loops

VB .NET and C# support variable declarations in classes or structures, methods, conditional statements, and in loops. Since both conditionals and loops are considered *statement blocks*, when you create a variable inside of these, that variable is considered a *block scope* variable. This means that the variable is available only within that loop or conditional statement. If you are unaware of this, it can be easy to write statements with "out of scope" variables. Here is an example of what that would look like:

VB .NET

```
Dim numbers As Integer() = {5, 10, 15}
Dim i As Integer = 0
While i < 3
  Console.WriteLine(numbers(i)) 'Show 5 then 10 then 15
  i = i + 1
  Dim InsideVariable As Integer
End While
InsideVariable = 13 'Error due to being out of scope
```

C#

```
int[] numbers = {5, 10, 15};
int i = 0;
while (i < 3)
{
  Console.WriteLine(numbers[i]); //Show 5 then 10 then 15
  i++;
  int InsideVariable;
}// End of loop
InsideVariable = 13; //Error due to being out of scope
```

Operations

Operations are a set of one or more commands you would like the computer to perform. In VB .NET and C#, operations come in two basic forms: *methods* and *operators*. Operators are small pre-made methods that use symbols instead of the standard method syntax. While most operators are made up of one symbol, some operators are made up of two or even three symbols. Also, operators in one language may be different in the other; for example, VB .NET = operator is the same as C# == operator.

Although you could create methods that do the same things as operators, most people prefer to use operators. This is because the symbols look and act like the mathematical statements we learned as children, and thus are often easier for people to read. For example, while you could create a method that would take in two numbers, add them together, and return the results like so:

```
x = MyCustomClass.Add(5, 5)
```

most people would find the following code more intuitive:

```
x = 5 + 5
```

Still, either one would fundamentally perform the same operation, so you could choose to implement your code by using either one.

Operators

If it's been awhile since your last math class, you may not remember what is meant by the phrase, "Operators work with operands." That being the case, let's start with a refresher on these two common terms:

- The *operator* is the symbol that indicates the action or operation to perform.

- The *operands* are the items that you wish to perform the action against.

Some operators require only one operand (known as *unary* operators), while some require two (known as *binary* operators), and others need three operands (known as *ternary* operators). Figure B-13 shows an equation with two operators (= and +) and three operands (X, 5, 4). The 5+4 is an expression that evaluates to nine. The + operator has a higher order of precedence and therefore runs before the = operator. Once the + operator is finished, the value of 9 is assigned to the variable X using the *assignment* operator, which is the = symbol. Remember that in computer programming, the value of the operand on the right side of the assignment operator (=) will always be assigned to the operand on the left.

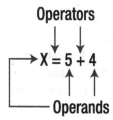

Figure B-13. *Operators and operands*

VB .NET and C# include a number of different operators. The following examples demonstrate some of the commonly used ones. We have listed them in their order of precedence from highest to lowest.

The Dot Operator

The . operator is used to *"drill down"* through namespaces, classes, or structures to locate variables and methods (as well as other things like events).

VB .NET and C#

```
MyNamespace.MyClass.x
MyNameSpace.MyClass.MyMethod()
```

The Parentheses Operator

The ( ) operator is used for conversions (C# only), array indexes (VB .NET only), and grouping expressions to set the order of precedence:

C#

```
x = (int)y;
```

VB .NET

```
x = MyArrayData(0)
```

VB .NET and C#

```
x = (4 * (2 + 2))
```

The Bracket Operator

The [ ] operator is used for array indexes in C#:

C#

```
x = MyArrayData[0]
```

The Pre and Post Increment Operators (C# Only)

The pre (++) and post (--) operators are used only in C#. These operators will either increase a number by one or decrease a number by one, respectively. You can place the symbols either before or after a variable, but where they are placed determines when they will run. For instance, if the ++ symbols are after the variable, *post-increment*, the increase does not happen until after all the other operations on that line of code are processed. If the ++ symbols are before the variable, *pre-increment*, then the increase happens before all the other operations on that line of code are processed.

C#

```
int x;
x = 1; //Set value and test
Console.WriteLine(x++); //Shows 1 still

x = 1; //reset and test again
Console.WriteLine(++x); //Shows 2 now

x = 1;//reset and test again
Console.WriteLine(x--); //Shows 1 still

x = 1; //reset and test again
Console.WriteLine(--x); //Shows 0 now
```

The Negation Operator (C# Only)

The ! operator negates the expression. In other words, if the operand was true, it will now be false:

C#

```csharp
int x = 1;
if (!(x == 1)) //It starts as true, but then is changed to false
 {
  Console.WriteLine("It is true");
 }
else
 {
  Console.WriteLine("It is false"); // This is what will print out
 }
```

The Multiplicative Operators

The * operator multiplies operands and returns the results (known as a *product*):

VB .NET

```vbnet
Dim x As Integer = 20
Dim y As Integer = 10
Console.WriteLine(x * y) 'Shows 200
```

C#

```csharp
int x = 20;
int y = 10;
Console.WriteLine(x * y); //Shows 200
```

The / operator divides the operands and returns the results (known as a *quotient*):

VB .NET

```vbnet
Dim x As Integer = 20
Dim y As Integer = 10
Console.WriteLine(x/y) 'Shows 2
```

C#

```csharp
int x = 20;
int y = 10;
Console.WriteLine(x/y); //Shows 2
```

The % operator in C# and the mod operator in VB .NET are known as the Modulo operators. They divide the operands and return any remainder (known as the *Modulus*):

VB .NET

```vbnet
Dim x As Integer = 21
Dim y As Integer = 10
Console.WriteLine(x mod y) 'Shows 1
```

C#

```
int x = 21;
int y = 10;
Console.WriteLine(x % y); //Shows 1
```

The Additive Operators

The + and - operators work as you would expect—they add and subtract:

VB .NET

```
Dim x As Integer = 20
Dim y As Integer = 10
Console.WriteLine(x + y) 'Shows 30
Dim a As Integer = 20
Dim b As Integer = 10
Console.WriteLine(a - b) 'Shows 10
```

C#

```
int x = 20;
int y = 10;
Console.WriteLine(x + y); //Shows 30
int a = 20;
int b = 10;
Console.WriteLine(a - b); //Shows 10
```

The Concatenation Operators

Microsoft changed the way the + operator works when the operands are both strings. This allows you to add two strings together, otherwise know as a *concatenation*. In VB .NET, you can also use the & operator for concatenations. (Note: The & operator has a different meaning in C#.) You might choose to use this if one of the operators is a number and one is a string. This tells VB .NET to implicitly convert the number to a string before it concatenates the values. In C#, you have to manually convert the number first or you will get an error.

VB .NET

```
Dim x As string = "Bob"
Dim y As string = "Smith"
Console.WriteLine(x + y) 'Shows BobSmith
Dim x As string = "Sue"
Dim y As string = "Jones"
Console.WriteLine(x & y) 'Shows SueJones
```

C#

```
string x = "Bob";
string y = "Smith";
Console.WriteLine(x + y); //Shows BobSmith
```

Note Both VB .NET (version 2.0) and C# allow you to change the behavior of some of the pre-made symbols, as Microsoft did for the string's + operators. This is called *operator overloading*. However, although you should be aware that this can happen, that topic is beyond to scope of this book.

The Relational Operators

The <, >, <=, and >= are collectively known as the *relational operators*. They allow you to compare one operand in relation to another (see Table B-6).

Table B-6. *The Relational Operators*

VB .NET	C#	Meaning
=	==	Equals
not	!=	Not equal
<	<	Less than
>	>	Greater than
<=	<=	Less than or equal to
>=	>=	Greater or equal to

VB .NET

```
Dim x As Integer = 20
Dim y As Integer = 10
Console.WriteLine(x > y) 'Shows True
```

C#

```
int x = 20;
int y = 10;
Console.WriteLine(x > y); //Shows True
```

More on the Equality Operators

The = operator in VB .NET or the == operator in C# are known as the *equality operators*. They allow you to ask the program if it is true that both operands are equal. Here is a list of common facts you should know:

- If the operands are two value-type variables, then a comparison is made against the variable's data. If both value-type variables hold the same value, then they are considered the same.

- If the operands are two reference-type variables, then the comparison is made on the variable's memory address and not the values. If both reference-type variables are pointing to the same address in memory, then they are considered the same.

- If you are comparing two objects of a custom class, like the demo1 class we show next, you cannot use the = operator in VB .NET to compare them. Use the Is operator instead.

- If the operands are both strings, then the = or == operators will act as they would for value types. In other words, they will compare their values, not their memory locations. This is because Microsoft changed the behavior of the operator to make it more intuitive.

- The != operator negates the equity in C#, but will not work in VB .NET. In that language, you use the keyword not instead.

VB .NET

```
Class demo1
  Public number As Integer
End Class


Sub Main()

  'Using a built-in value type
  Dim a As Integer = 5
  Dim b As Integer
  b = a  'a and b point to different memory locations but now have the same value
  Console.WriteLine(a = b) ' Shows True

  b = 1 'Change the value and test again
  Console.WriteLine(a = b) ' Shows False

  'Using a custom reference type
  Dim x As demo1 = New demo1
  Dim y As demo1
  y = x  'Both y and x point to the same memory location
  Console.WriteLine(x Is y) ' Shows True, VB .NET cannot use the = operator here.

  'Using the built-in reference type of string
  Dim s1 As String = "A"
  Dim s2 As String
  s2 = s1  'Although String are reference types s1 and s2
  'point to different memory locations, now with the same value
  Console.WriteLine(s1 = s2) ' Shows True

  s2 = "B" 'Change the value and test again
  Console.WriteLine(s1 = s2) ' Shows Flase
```

```
  'Test the not keyword
  Console.WriteLine(not(s1 = s2)) 'Now shows True

End Sub
```

C#

```csharp
class demo1
{
  public int number;
}

static void Main()
{
  // Using a built-in value type
  int a = 5;
  int b;
  b = a; //a and b point to different memory locations but now have the same value
  Console.WriteLine(a == b); //Shows True

  b = 1; //Change the value and test again
  Console.WriteLine(a == b); //Show False

  // Using a custom reference type
  demo1 x = new demo1();
  demo1 y;
  y = x; //Both y and x point to the same memory location
  Console.WriteLine(x == y); //Show True

  // Using the built-in reference type of string
  string s1 = "A";
  string s2;
  s2 = s1; //Although String are reference types s1 and s2
  //point to different memory locations, now with the same value
  Console.WriteLine(s1 == s2); //Shows True

  s2 = "B";//Change the value and test again
  Console.WriteLine(s1 == s2); //Shows False

  //Test the != operator
  Console.WriteLine(s1 != s2); //Now shows True

}//End of Main
```

The Logical Operators

Both VB .NET and C# use the standard logical operators that have been used in computer programming for decades: *And, inclusive Or,* and *exclusive Or.* These act like the previous comparison operators, but are specifically made for the Boolean values of True and False. Their purpose is to allow you to compare two operands and come to a conclusion about the overall expression based on the following "True tables" (see Tables B-7 through B-10).

Table B-7. *The And (VB .NET) and & (C#) Operators*

Operand 1	Operand 2	Conclusion
true	true	true
true	false	false
false	true	false
false	false	false

VB .NET

```
Dim a As Boolean = True
Dim b As Boolean = False
If a And b Then
 Console.WriteLine("True")
Else
 Console.WriteLine("False") 'Show False
End If
```

C#

```
bool a = true;
bool b = false ;
if (a & b)
 { Console.WriteLine("True");}
else
 { Console.WriteLine("False");} //Shows False
```

Notice that with the And operator, only one operand has to evaluate to False before the conclusion is False. Both VB .NET and C# have a "short-circuit" version of the And/& logical operator. This short-circuit version will not compare the second operand if the computer already knows that the first operand is False. This saves the computer time and can make your program run a bit faster.

Table B-8. *The AndAlso (VB .NET) and && (C#) "Short-Circuit" Operators*

Operand 1	Operand 2	Conclusion
true	true	true
true	false	false
false	true	false
false	false	false

VB .NET

```
Dim a As Boolean = True
Dim b As Boolean = False
If a AndAlso b Then
 Console.WriteLine("True")
Else
 Console.WriteLine("False") 'Show False faster
End If
```

C#

```
bool a = true;
bool b = false ;
if (a && b)
 { Console.WriteLine("True");}
else
 { Console.WriteLine("False");} //Shows False faster
```

The inclusive Or operator evaluates to true as long as one of the operands it true.

Table B-9. *The Or (VB .NET) and | (C#) Operators*

Operand 1	Operand 2	Conclusion
true	true	true
true	false	true
false	true	true
false	false	false

VB .NET

```
Dim a As Boolean = True
Dim b As Boolean = False
If a Or b Then
 Console.WriteLine("True")
Else
 Console.WriteLine("False") 'Show True
End If
```

C#

```
bool a = true;
bool b = false ;
if (a | b)
 { Console.WriteLine("True");}
else
 { Console.WriteLine("False");} //Shows True
```

Once again, notice that the Or operator only needs one operand to evaluate to True before the conclusion is True. Both VB .NET and C# also have a "short-circuit" version of the Or/| logical operator. They work by not comparing the second operand if the computer already knows that the first operand is True. This, again, saves the computer time and can make your program run a bit faster.

Table B-10. *The OrElse (VB .NET) and || (C#) "Short-Circuit" Operators*

Operand 1	Operand 2	Conclusion
true	true	true
true	false	true
false	true	true
false	false	false

The Substitution Parameter Operator

You can use substitution parameters to *conditionally* change the contents of a string like this:

```
Console.WriteLine("result is {0}", Method1() | Method2());
```

Both VB .NET and C# allow you to use the {} operator to un-*conditionally* change a string value as well. When the program encounters this operator, it will replace each substitution parameter with the values listed after the comma. For example, if you typed in this command:

```
Console.WriteLine("This is a {0} {1}", "test", "message");
```

the Console application would print out "This is a test message". The string "test" would be substituted for the {0}, while "message" would be substituted for the {1}. This takes place because of the order that the strings "test" and "message" are defined in the comma-separated list after the string.

By creating two methods, one that returns true and one the returns false, you can create some test code and see an example of the short-circuit operators in action:

VB .NET

```
Function Method1() As Boolean
  Console.WriteLine("Method1 called")
  Return True
End Function

Function Method2() As Boolean
  Console.WriteLine("Method2 called")
  Return False
End Function

Public Sub Main()
```

```vbnet
'Both Method1 and Method2 will be called
Console.WriteLine("Regular OR result is {0}", Method1() Or Method2())

'Only Method1 will be called since it returns True
Console.WriteLine("Short-circuit OR result is {0}", Method1() OrElse Method2())

End Sub
```

C#

```csharp
static bool Method1()
{
 Console.WriteLine("Method1 called");
 return true;
} //End of Method1

static bool Method2()
{
  Console.WriteLine("Method2 called");
  return false;
}//End of Method2

public static void Main()
{
 //Both Method1 and Method2 will be called
 Console.WriteLine("Regular OR result is {0}", Method1() | Method2());

 //Only Method1 will be called since it returns true
 Console.WriteLine("Short-circuit OR result is {0}", Method1() || Method2());
} //End of Main
```

The Ternary Operator

C# has another operator that works similar to the substitution parameter we just demonstrated. This operator is called the *ternary* operator. It can be thought of as a simplified If-Else statement. Its name reflects the fact that it needs three operands. The symbols ? and : are the ones used for this operator.

VB .NET does not have an operator exactly like this one, but it does have a method that works almost the same, called IIf(). Although the VB .NET version is not really an operator, as we have mentioned before, operators are really just symbols used instead of a method's name, so we have included IIf() as the VB .NET version of the ternary operator:

VB .NET

```vbnet
Dim testData As String = "yes"
Dim answer As String
answer = IIf(testData = "yes", "Then it is true", "Then it is false")
Console.WriteLine(answer) 'Shows Then it is true
```

C#

```
string testData = "yes";
string answer;
answer = (testData == "yes")? "Then it is true" : "Then it is false";
Console.WriteLine(answer); //Shows then it is true
```

More on Methods

As mentioned before, methods are a way to group one or more statements within classes or structures. One reason you use methods is to organize statements based on the actions they will perform. Another reason is they dictate the order that statements will run. When a method is called, each statement within is evaluated in a sequential order. While you will see many practical examples in this book, here are some basic facts that you should know for now.

Methods Can Return Values

If you want a value returned, you use the keyword Function in VB .NET and then indicate the type of data you want to return. In C#, you just need to indicate the type of data you want to return. Methods like these can be used as an expression. Although you cannot see it happen since the code is running in memory, after your program calls the method, the code used to call that method is replaced with the returned value. That being the case, you can use these returned values to set other variables.

VB .NET

```
Sub Main()
  Dim x As String = MethodA()'This calls the method and becomes "test"
  Console.WriteLine(x)
End Sub

Function MethodA() As String
  Return "test"
End Function
```

C#

```
static void Main()
{
  string x =  MethodA();//This calls the method and becomes "test"
  Console.WriteLine(x);
}

static string MethodA()
{
  return "test";
}
```

Note One thing that confuses beginning programmers is that you can call MethodA( ) from the Main( ) method even though it's listed afterward. This is because all of the code in a class or structure is loaded into memory before any of it starts to run. So, the sequence of the methods inside of a class or structure is not important. However, don't forget that the order of the statements *inside* of a method is important since these always run first to last.

Some Methods Do Not Return Values

When you create a method, you can also choose not to return a value after the method is called. If you do not wish to return a value, you indicate this by using the keyword Sub in VB .NET or the keyword void in C#. You cannot use a method that does not return a value as an expression.

VB .NET

```
Sub Main()
   MethodA() 'This calls the method
End Sub

Sub MethodA()
   Console.WriteLine("test")
End Sub
```

C#

```
static void Main()
{
  MethodA(); //This calls the method
}

static void MethodA()
{
  Console.WriteLine("test");
}
```

Methods Can Include Parameters

If you would like to give a method some values to process, you can create a list of one or more *parameters* for your method. Each parameter is like a variable that will be used only by that method. In fact, they follow the same rules we discussed earlier regarding variables. Such as, you must give them a name and specify their data types. To create a parameter, you place a comma-separated list within the parentheses after the method's name:

VB .NET

```
Sub Main()
  'Pass the "test" and "this" arguments to parameters p1 and p2 for processing
  MethodA("test", "this")
End Sub
```

```vb
Sub MethodA(ByVal p1 As String, ByVal p2 As String)
  Console.WriteLine(p1 & " " & p2) 'Shows Test This
End Sub
```

C#

```csharp
static void Main()
{
  //Pass the "test" and "this" arguments to parameters p1 and p2 for processing
  MethodA("test", "this");
}
static void MethodA(string p1, string p2)
{
  Console.WriteLine(p1 + " " + p2); //Shows test this
}
```

Note The terms *parameters* and *arguments* are often interchanged in normal conversation. For the sake of clarity, we will use the formal definition of an *argument* as being the actual value passed into the method's *parameter*.

Value and Reference Types Affect Parameters

Parameters that are reference types and parameters that are value types behave differently. If a parameter is a value type, then the parameter will receive a copy of the argument's data. If the parameter is a reference type, then the parameter will receive a reference to the same memory location as the argument. A change to a parameter's data using a value type does not affect the argument's data. This is because both argument and parameter are using two distinct memory locations. Changes to the parameter of a reference type will affect the argument. This is because both argument and parameter are using the same memory location.

VB .NET

```vb
Module Module1
  Class demo1 'Classes are reference types
     Public number As Integer
  End Class

  Structure demo2 'Structures are values types
     Public number As Integer
  End Structure

  Sub Main()
    Dim x As New demo1 'Reference type
    Dim y As demo2 'Value type
```

```vb
        'Set some starting values
        x.number = 1
        y.number = 1

        'Pass arguments x and y to parameters p1 and p2
        MethodA(x, y)

        Console.WriteLine(x.number) 'Now shows 10
        Console.WriteLine(y.number) 'Still shows 1

    End Sub

    Sub MethodA(ByVal p1 As demo1, ByVal p2 As demo2)
        'p1 is a reference to the same memory location as x
        'so changes to p1 affect x
        p1.number = 10

        'p2 is a copy of the same value as y
        'so changes to p2 do NOT affect y
        p2.number = 10
    End Sub
End Module
```

C#

```csharp
class Program
{
    class demo1 //Classes are reference types
    {
        public int number;
    }
    struct demo2 //Structures are value types
    {
        public int number;
    }

    static void Main()
    {
        demo1 x = new demo1(); // Reference type
        demo2 y; // value type

        //Set some starting values
        x.number = 1;
        y.number = 1;

        //Pass arguments x and y to parameters p1 and p2
        MethodA(x, y);
```

```
      Console.WriteLine(x.number);//Now shows 10
      Console.WriteLine(y.number);//Still shows 1
  }

  static void MethodA(demo1 p1, demo2 p2)
  {
    //p1 is a referance to the same memory location as x
    //so changes to p1 affect x
    p1.number = 10;

    //p2 is a copy of the same value as y
    //so changes to p2 do NOT affect y
    p2.number = 10;
  }
}//End of class Program
```

You Can Change the Way Value Type Parameters Behave

You can force a value type parameter, such as an integer, to behave as if it were a reference type. You do this by including the ByRef keyword in VB .NET and the ref keyword in C#:

VB .NET

```
 Sub Main()
    Dim x As Integer = 1
    'Pass argument x to parameters p1
    MethodA(x)
    Console.WriteLine(x) 'Now shows 10
  End Sub

  Sub MethodA(ByRef p1 As Integer)
    'p1 is a reference to the same memory location as x
    'so chages to p1 affect x
    p1 = 10
  End Sub
```

C#

```
static void Main()
{
  int x = 1;
  //Pass argument x to parameters p1
  MethodC(ref x);
  Console.WriteLine(x);//shows 10
}
```

```csharp
static void MethodC(ref int p1)
{
  //p1 is a reference to the same memory location as x
  //so chages to p1 affect x
  p1 = 10;
}
```

String Parameters Behave Like Value Types

Even though they are officially reference types, string parameters act like value type parameters. In other words, you can control their behavior using the ByVal, ByRef, and ref keywords:

VB .NET

```vbnet
Sub Main()
  Dim x As String = "A"
  Dim y As String = "B"
  MethodA(x, y)
  Console.WriteLine(x) 'Now shows A-1
  Console.WriteLine(y) 'Still shows B
End Sub

Sub MethodA(ByRef p1 As String, ByVal p2 As String)
  p1 = "A-1"
  p2 = "B-1"
End Sub
```

C#

```csharp
static void Main()
{
  string x = "A";
  string y = "B";
  //Pass argument x to parameters p1
  MethodC(ref x,  y);
  Console.WriteLine(x);//Now shows A-1
  Console.WriteLine(y);//Still shows B
}

static void MethodC(ref string p1, string p2 )
{
  p1 = "A-1";
  p2 = "B-1";
}
```

VB .NET Has Optional Parameters

If you are coding in VB .NET, you can use *optional parameters*. These are just like the standard parameters, but they include a default value. If you do not pass in an argument to the parameter, then the default value will be used. Optional parameters must be listed after any parameter without a default value:

VB .NET

```
Sub Main()
    MethodA("Bob Jones")'Shows Hello Bob Smith
    MethodA("Bob Jones", "Mr.")'Shows Hello Mr. Bob Smith
End Sub

Sub MethodA(ByVal name As String, Optional ByVal prefix As String = "")
    Console.WriteLine("Hello, " & prefix & " " & name)
End Sub
```

Using Multiple Versions of a Method

Optional parameters are an older way of making methods perform in multiple ways. Both C# and VB .NET can use a new way, which is just to create two methods with the same name but different parameters. When the method is called, .NET will automatically use the number and data types of the arguments to determine which version of the method to call:

VB .NET

```
  Sub Main()
    MethodA("Bob Jones")'Shows Hello Bob Smith
    MethodA("Bob Jones", "Mr.")'Shows Hello Mr. Bob Smith
  End Sub

  Sub MethodA(ByVal name As String)
    Console.WriteLine("Hello, " & " " & name)
  End Sub
  Sub MethodA(ByVal name As String, ByVal prefix As String)
    Console.WriteLine("Hello, " & prefix & " " & name)
  End Sub
```

C#

```
static void Main()
{
  MethodA("Bob Jones");//Shows Hello Bob Smith
  MethodA("Bob Jones", "Mr.");//Shows Hello Mr. Bob Smith
}
```

```
static void MethodA(string name)
{
  Console.WriteLine("Hello, " + " " + name);
}

static void MethodA(string name, string prefix)
{
  Console.WriteLine("Hello, " + prefix + " " + name);
}
```

Using Properties

Properties are a special type of method. They are used to access and modify variables in a structure or class. Instead of passing arguments to a property, you use the assignment operator, as in MyProperty = 5.

With property procedures, you can add code to control the way your program sets a variable's value. This code can also control the way a program gets a variable's values. While we cover property procedures in Chapter 6, here is a quick look at what one of these looks like:

VB .NET

```
'This variable is private and must be accessed or
'modified with the property Quantity
Private intQuantity As Integer

Public Property Quantity () As Integer
  'This part of the property procedure runs when code asks to read Quantity
  Get
    Return intQuantity
  End Get

  'This part of the property procedure run when code asks to change Quantity
  Set (ByVal Value As Integer)
    If Value < 0 Then ' This is an example of some validation code.
      intQuantity = 0 'Sets the all negative numbers to zero
    Else
      intQuantity = Value
    End If
  End Set
End Property

Sub Main()
  Quantity = 5 'Sets the value of Quantity
  Console.WriteLine(Quantity) 'Reads the value of Quantity

  Quantity = -5 'Try to set the value of Quantity to a negitive number
  Console.WriteLine(Quantity) 'Reads Quantity and shows 0
End Sub
```

C#

```csharp
static private int intQuantity;

static public int Quantity
{
  //This part of the property procedure runs when code asks to read Quantity
  get
  {
    return intQuantity;
  }
  //This part of the property procedure runs when code asks to change Quantity
  set
  {
    if (value < 0) // This is an example of some validation code.
      {intQuantity = 0;} //Sets the all negative numbers to zero
    else
      {intQuantity = value;}
  }
}//End of property

static void Main()
{
  Quantity = 5; //Sets the value of Quantity
  Console.WriteLine(Quantity); //Reads the value of Quantity

  Quantity = -5; //Try to set the value of Quantity to a negitive number
  Console.WriteLine(Quantity); //Reads Quantity and shows 0
}
```

Summary

Well, that should get you started with enough programming to make your way though this book. As you read through the book, you will find scores of other examples to advance your understanding about VB .NET and C#. Afterward, we hope that you will find this appendix a useful reference.

■ ■ ■

Resources and References

This appendix contains a bibliography of references that we have used in the writing of this book, which is also a list of resources for you to get more information on the myriad of topics we have touched upon in this text—things like ADO, SQL, ASP, and so on.

Testing Books

Dustin, Elfriede, Jeff Rashka, and John Paul. *Automated Software Testing: Introduction, Management, and Performance*. Addison-Wesley Professional, 1999.

Dustin, Elfriede. *Effective Software Testing: 50 Specific Ways to Improve Your Testing.* |Addison-Wesley Professional, 2002.

Kaner, Cem. *Testing Computer Software*, 2nd ed. John Wiley & Sons, 1999.

Kit, Edward. *Software Testing in the Real World: Improving the Process*. Addison-Wesley Professional, 1995.

Myers, Glenford, et al. *The Art of Software Testing*, 2nd ed. John Wiley & Sons, 2004.

Sweeney, Mary Romero. *Visual Basic for Testers*. Apress, 2001.

Whittaker, James, and Herbert Thompson. *How to Break Software Security*. Addison Wesley, 2003.

.NET Books (VB .NET and C#)

Appleman, Dan. *Regular Expressions with .NET*. Dan Appleman (PDF download at Amazon.com), 2002.

Appleman, Dan. *Tracing and Logging with .Net*. Dan Appleman (PDF download at Amazon.com), 2002.

Appleman, Dan. *Visual Basic .NET or C#, Which to Choose? (VS2005 edition)*. Dan Appleman (PDF download at Amazon.com), 2004.

Bradley, Julia Case, and Anita C. Millspaugh. *Programming in Visual Basic .NET*. McGraw-Hill Technology Education, 2004.

Guckenheimer, Sam. *Software Engineering with Microsoft Visual Studio Team System*. Addison-Wesley Professional, 2006.

Huddleston, James, et al. *Beginning C# Databases: From Novice to Professional*. Apress, 2004.

Hundhausen, Richard. *Working with Microsoft Visual Studio 2005 Team System.* Microsoft Press, 2005.

Malik, Sahil. *Pro ADO.NET 2.0.* Apress, 2005.

Wright, Peter. *Beginning Visual C# 2005 Express Edition.* Apress, 2006.

Journals/Periodicals

The Journal of Software Testing Professionals. International Institute for Software Testing. Published quarterly. Golden Valley, MN. (www.testinginstitute.com)

Software Testing and Quality Engineering (STQE) Magazine. Software Quality Engineering. Published bi-monthly. Orange Park, FL. (www.sqe.com/stqemagazine.asp)

Recommended Testing Websites

Applied Testing and Technology (ApTest): www.aptest.com/resources.html

This is a commercial website, but you don't have to be ApTest's client to take advantage of the resources and information they provide on their Resources page. It's a wonderful service and a good place to start for finding tools.

International Institute of Software Testing (IIST): www.iist.org

This organization provides training and consultation on testing topics including the most recognized certification program, nationally. The website contains the BugFree Zone, which has forums and information on testing. Mary Romero Sweeney also happens to be on the faculty and the board of IIST.

Microsoft Team Edition for Software Testers Forum: http://forums.microsoft.com/msdn/showforum.aspx?forumid=19&siteid=1

These forums are used by Microsoft to determine the features to put into the tool, so they're a good way to get your input about what you want to see in future releases. They are also, of course, a good forum for understanding and using the tool.

Microsoft Webcasts: www.microsoft.com/webcasts

Microsoft webcasts give detailed demonstrations of the products by senior team members.

QA Forums: www.qaforums.com

This is the best one-stop shop for information on software testing. There are forums for all types of testing and links to just about everything you'll ever want to know regarding testing.

Quality Tree Software, Inc.: Elisabeth Hendricksen at www.qualitytree.com

Excellent articles on automated testing. Check out Elisabeth's Publications ➤ Articles and Automation Advice links. We especially like "Build It or Buy It" and "Bang for the Buck." Required reading for all test professionals.

Other Recommended Websites

Developer Fusion: www.developerfusion.co.uk

Developer Fusion is a web-based developer community in the UK. This site has many pages of VB .NET and C# tutorials and source code. They also have a VB .NET to C# converter page that makes it very easy to translate one language to another.

Microsoft Developer's Network: http://msdn.microsoft.com and the library at http://msdn.microsoft.com/library/

The MSDN and its associated library is one of the first places to go for information on any Microsoft product. The library has essentially all of the Help files you will need regardless of what you have installed.

nUnit Home page: www.nunit.org

nUnit is mentioned in Chapter 11. It's the original unit-testing framework for all .NET languages. It's open source and many developers and testers have used it for years. Much of its functionality has been incorporated into the new Team Test software in the Team Edition of Visual Studio. However, those of you not using Team Test can make excellent use of nUnit. You'll find a tutorial on the web page and lots of help getting started.

Whatis.com: www.whatis.com

This site will not only help you get definitions of basic computer terms, but it also contains links to the appropriate websites for these terms.

World Wide Web Consortium: www.w3.org

If you do any web testing or web development, you should visit here on a regular basis. This site contains the standards for all things web-related, including HTML and XML. There are tools for testing websites, many of them free.

To compare products, Microsoft provides a Product Line Overview web page at http://msdn.microsoft.com/vstudio/products/compare/default.aspx.

Recommended Database Design and SQL Resources

Hernandez, Michael J. *Database Design for Mere Mortals: A Hands-On Guide to Relational Database Design*. 2nd ed. Addison-Wesley Professional, 2003.

Hernandez, Michael J., and John L. Viescas. *SQL Queries for Mere Mortals: A Hands-On Guide to Data Manipulation in SQL*. Addison-Wesley Professional, 2000.

The Hernandez books are clearly written and easily understood yet they don't talk down to you. These are popular with our college-level students in software testing.

SQL Course: www.sqlcourse.com

This website is an excellent way to get up to speed with free training on SQL and database topics. It has nothing to do with testing, but it will give you a good start to understanding the underlying concepts of databases and the SQL language. It also has great links to database forums and newsletters for all kinds of database management systems.

LazyDBA: www.lazydba.com

This website can save you a lot of money because it has many reference books online for almost all major database systems. It's also searchable so that you can find what you're looking for quickly. It's free, but you do need to sign up to become a member.

Vieira, Robert. *Professional SQL Server 2000 Programming (Programmer to Programmer)*. Wrox Press, Wiley Publishing Inc., 2000.

This book will help you learn SQL Server 2000 basics. It's a good core reference.

Resources on Additional Topics of Interest

Weisfeld, Matt. *The Object-Oriented Thought Process*. 2nd Ed. Sams Publishing, 2003.

This book will give you an excellent background in understanding all of the terminology and the intent of the object-oriented world. It's really a very important, yet underutilized, book!

Index

F

Printed in the United States
By Bookmasters